Financial Accounting: The Main Ideas

To Carolyn,

who rarely bothers with financial statements.

Ginger and Pickles retired into
the back parlour.
They did accounts. They added up
sums and sums, and sums.

Beatrix Potter

Financial Accounting: The Main Ideas

Arthur L. Thomas

McMaster University

Wadsworth Publishing Company, Inc.
Belmont, California

ISBN-0-534-00093-2
L. C. Cat. Card No. 72-182068
Printed in the United States of America

1 2 3 4 5 6 7 8 9 10—76 75 74 73 72

Preface

This book is designed for a one-term course in financial accounting. It emphasizes the fundamentals of accounting procedure and theory in order to help students attain full comprehension of these basics, rather than mere memorization of accounting practices. It differs from existing texts in three main ways.

Topic coverage. Much more space is devoted to fundamentals than is customary in other texts. Students must master certain topics in order to read and interpret financial statements knowledgeably; I have chosen to explore these essential topics in depth, rather than to discuss a broader variety of topics superficially. These key topics include two kinds usually avoided in elementary texts: (1) controversial theoretical issues, such as problems of asset valuation and revenue recognition, and (2) vital mechanicals that are all too often dismissed as pedestrian or obvious. In addition, of course, the standard elementary topics receive full discussion. A summary of this book's coverage is given on pages 12–14.

Organization. As you will see from this summary, an attempt has been made to start from scratch and completely re-think the methods and order of presenting fundamentals, so that students will readily grasp their underlying logic. For this reason also, theory permeates the entire text; at each step, students are given the reasoning behind the rule or practice that is being discussed.

Reinforcement and assignment materials. An exceptional amount of reinforcement materials, including numerous problems accompanied by detailed solutions, has been provided to give the student constant feedback on whether or not he really comprehends the material. (This is the main reason for this book's exceptional length.) Much of this reinforcement material is designated as optional, for the student to use if he needs it. In this way, some of the flexibility of the more sophisticated programmed texts is gained, yet a conventional format is retained. Additional exercises at varying levels of difficulty have been developed for specific assignment by the instructor; some of these stress drill, others analysis or theory. They are intended to allow for differing abilities and flexibility in topic coverage. A more detailed discussion of unusual features of this book, directed to the student, will be found on pages 7–12. Additional topics (bank reconciliations and adjusting and closing worksheets, for example), reinforcement material, and a practice set complete with working papers are included in a supplement to this text.

Acknowledgements

This book has been class tested over a period of four years at the University of Oregon, the University of New Mexico, and McMaster University. I am deeply indebted to the students who used these preliminary editions for the care with which they criticized successive drafts, their willingness to make constructive suggestions, and their patience.

Many academic reviewers have also offered valuable criticism and suggestions during this book's evolution. These include Albert Abramson (Los Angeles City College), Jacob G. Birnberg (University of Pittsburgh), Carl J. Fisher (Foothill College), John C. Burton (Columbia University), David Green, Jr. (University of Chicago), Melvin N. Greenball (Ohio State University), Earl Littrell, III (University of Pittsburgh), Walter S. Maus (Foothill College), Robert S. Maust (West Virginia University), Herbert E. Miller (Arthur Andersen & Co.), Curtis H. Stanley (Ohio State University), Howard F. Stettler (University of Kansas), John A. Tracy (University of Colorado), and Lawrence Williams (American River Junior College).

I am especially grateful to Edwin H. Caplan (University of New Mexico), Elwyn L. Christensen (Fresno State College), Donald H. Drury (McMaster University), John G. Helmkamp (Arizona State University), William Huizingh (Arizona State University), Donald J. Johnston (McMaster University), and the co-author of the supplement to this book, Sanjoy Basu, for detailed reviews and suggestions that led to major changes in organization and content. While none of the reviewers should be held responsible for the final product, I hope that each will be gratified to discover that I followed his advice much more often than I rejected it. More generally, I would like to thank my colleagues at the University of Oregon and McMaster University for listening to dilemmas as the book developed, offering useful ideas, and generally providing an intellectual environment that encouraged experimentation. Similarly, the administrations of both universities were generous in providing time and technical assistance.

Special thanks are due Mrs. Delia Craik for help in reproducing successive manuscripts, often under onerous deadlines, and to the following former students for checking my arithemetic: Peter J. Aust, Bernhard Graf, Christopher B. Harrison, John G. Heersink, Swaroop H. Rangam, Lefter Samoglou, Alfred E. Shoemaker, Surinder K. Singh, and Sooi-Kuang Song.

This book also owes a great deal to its Wadsworth editors: H. Hadley Bland, who got the project rolling, William H. Hicks, who saw it through its many revisions, Violet M. Boyd, who provided initial editing, and Bruce Caldwell, who helped bring it to completion. I am particularly grateful for the assistance of this book's Coordinating Production Editor, Ellen Bell—*Lo que Puede un Sastre!*

Finally, this book could not have been completed without the patience and support of my wife, Mary, and my children, Robin, Susan, and Stephen.

Arthur L. Thomas

Contents

A Foreword to the Student

I want to begin this book with a general description of its contents and with some suggestions concerning how to study financial accounting. Some of you already know what financial accounting is, but a rough definition (to be explained in detail later) may be useful to others. *Financial accounting* is a system whereby economic information about business firms is gathered and made available to individuals who have invested money in these firms. When someone invests money in a business (or considers doing so), he is interested in such things as what the firm owns, what its debts are, how the firm's resources are being used, and how profitable the business is. Financial accounting attempts to answer these and a variety of other investor questions through formal reports called *financial statements.*

These formal financial statements often comprise part of larger (and otherwise less formal) documents prepared for investors at regular intervals. If the firm prepares such documents once a year, they are called *annual reports*; if prepared every three months they are called *quarterly reports,* and so on. Besides financial statements, such reports often include general discussions of business conditions, information about new products or services offered by the firm, photographs of company activities, and other matters deemed to be of interest to investors.

Several financial statements are illustrated on pages 80–85. Most of this book deals with showing how financial statements are constructed and what their strengths and limitations are.

Troublesome Characteristics of Financial Accounting

On first impression, financial statements may seem strange and complicated. Financial accounting has acquired the reputation of being a "difficult" subject. Yet it is not. The subject matter of accounting is no harder than that of most other university courses (and is easier than some). The trouble is that accounting is different. Most of you have never taken a course quite like financial accounting. Study techniques that work well enough in your other courses may backfire in this one. We should spend time right now considering some of the things that make accounting different from most of your other courses—and we should talk about how to use this book.

Some of you won't need this help. Some students take to accounting very naturally and seem to learn it without strain or effort.[1] You may be fortunate in this way, but most students aren't. The information that follows assumes that you are typical in your first responses to accounting and that you need a little guidance.

Let's look at some of the characteristics of financial accounting that can lead beginning students into difficulties. This kind of overview requires a number of assertions about accounting that just can't be backed up at this time. Most of what follows will be discussed in greater detail later on in this book. But, for the present, you'll have to take some assertions on faith. Here are some of the troublesome characteristics of financial accounting—and some suggestions of ways to keep them from giving you trouble.

Abstraction

Accounting is an attempt to reflect economic phenomena by figures. This makes accounting a slightly abstract, intangible subject. Contrast, say, chemistry. The intellectual underpinnings of chemistry are also abstract. But the beginning chemistry student is dealing with physical objects. The things he handles in the laboratory are obviously real: they can be poured from one container to another; they change color; many of them have odors. The chemistry student has no reason to doubt that he is dealing with something quite genuine.

The student in a basic literature course is one step removed from this kind of reality. All he actually has before him are pages of type. But what he reads usually *refers* to things that are quite concrete: people, for example. However abstract the underlying ideas may be, the immediate referent of most literature is reassuringly tangible.

Financial accounting is at least two steps removed from physical reality. First, essentially all that the accounting student sees are sets of labeled and organized numbers. This is abstract enough in itself. But to what do these numbers refer? They refer to things that are almost as abstract as the numbers: rights, obligations, and— especially—economic phenomena. These intangible matters are tremendously important, but they aren't physical. Most of us feel much easier with physical objects than with abstractions; this can lead you into pitfalls:

1. Some students automatically underrate accounting just because it *is* abstract. The student is particularly likely to do this if he is taking accounting as a required course—something to get out of the way, rather than something he really wants to study. Perhaps the only remedy for this is to be open-minded—to recognize that while a bias in favor of the concrete is perfectly natural, it *is* a bias.

---

[1] On the other hand, some students who seem to be learning the material very easily have had accounting before—in high school. Don't be discouraged by such people.

Other students become a little frightened by the lack of something tangible to hold on to. Abstraction breeds anxiety. Because accounting is different from your other courses, you may tend to worry about it unproductively. You may underrate yourself and feel that you cannot possibly grasp the subject or keep up with the others. If you do feel this way at any point, be assured that this is also a common reaction and that it should pass. Most students have to make an adjustment to accounting. Typically, this takes from two to six weeks. During the adjustment period, matters (which later will seem perfectly clear) just don't seem to hang together very well. You may feel overwhelmed by the number of things you must learn.

Once again, you may be a fortunate exception to all this. But if not, remember that you're not unique in having trouble shifting over to thinking in accounting terms—and that your troubles are not apt to persist long. Most of these suggestions are designed to ease you through this transition period. The main thing is not to get nervous.

2. Some students misunderstand parts of accounting because they try to make things tangible that are not. For example, the first major accounting idea introduced in Chapter One is the concept of an *asset*. The accountant's notion of asset is almost entirely abstract—he views the asset mainly as a set of rights. If the student forgets this, much of what the accountant does with the figures he shows for assets will seem peculiar. For instance, the accountant will show a smaller figure each year for a machine, even though the machine itself may be "as good as new"—and as big as new, for that matter. We'll see that this is because the accountant isn't directly concerned with the physical machine at all. Instead, the accountant is concerned with something very abstract: the company's rights to the machine's expected services. If you fight this, if you try to make the notion of asset less abstract than it really is, you often will end up misunderstanding what the accountant is saying about machines and other assets.

Compactness

The particular methods of abstraction used by the financial accountant let him say things in a much more compact, efficient way than ordinary English would allow. This may tempt you to read accounting reports too fast.

Mathematics presents a similar problem, one that is already familiar to you. The mathematician has also developed compact, efficient ways of saying things. Consider the following equation:

$$Y = 7X^2 - 3X + 4.$$

To put this in ordinary English, we'd have to say something like:

Whenever you want to know what figure should be associated with Y, you must first find out what figure is associated with X. Take this X-figure and multiply it by itself. Then multiply the result by seven. Set this second result aside for a moment and multiply the original X-figure by three. Subtract this latter product from the figure that you set aside. Now add four to the result. The final figure is the one that should be associated with Y.

Importance of reading carefully

Obviously, the equation is a much more efficient way to state the information. But a danger accompanies the efficiency: the danger of reading the equation too rapidly. Everything in the equation is vital. Nothing can be overlooked. In ordinary English, many words are not essential ("the," for instance), and there's much repetition. You don't always have to read ordinary English closely. In contrast, mathematics must be read very closely, character by character.

Financial accounting reports are not as compactly written as mathematics, but they are much more compactly written than ordinary English. *This means that you must read these reports—and this book—much more slowly and carefully than you read the materials for most of your other courses.* If you don't, you are apt to miss a small, vital point (like the 2 in the equation) and be confused. An important reason why accounting often seems unusually hard, is that beginning students try to read the text and the problems at too fast a pace. It may work well in other courses, but it is inappropriate to accounting.

Also, because accounting *is* compact and efficient, it is sometimes easy to convince yourself that you understand what you have studied when, actually, you have overlooked a small, vital part. This is why so much emphasis is put on doing homework, on checking your understanding.

Simplification

The final thing that troubles beginning students is closely related to financial accounting's abstractness and compactness. The economic facts about any business are tremendously detailed and complicated. To report them intelligibly, the accountant has to organize and simplify them. And any method of doing this is bound to be a bit arbitrary.

We will see later that financial accounting tries to tell investors in an enterprise what has happened to the company over a period of time and what shape the company is in at a given time. Without simplifying, this would be an impossible job. It would be impractical to report the innumerable activities of a fair-sized company over a time period of, for example, a year. Even a single day's activities are so complex that it would be impractical to report all of them. A big part of the financial accountant's job is to organize, to select the relatively small amount of information that is significant enough to merit reporting, and then to present this information in a clear, efficient way.

Models

In other words, the accountant's report is a simplified descriptive model of the company's status and history. There's nothing mysterious about descriptive models. They're attempts to describe, by drawing out the most significant characteristics, things that are just too complex to reconstruct in their totality. Whether or not the model "works" depends on the purpose that it is to serve. For instance, here is a model of the state of Oregon.

The X marks the city of Eugene, Oregon, where much of this book was written. If you want to show someone that Eugene is in the western part of the state, the model works. But it doesn't show how to drive to Eugene. For that, you need a road map. The road map is also a model. It works beautifully for some purposes,

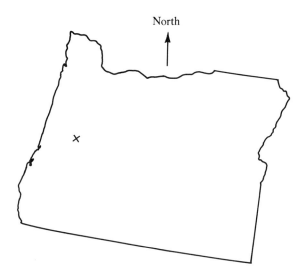

but not at showing how the country looks. For this you'd want a topographical map, a painting, a photograph, a prose description, or a poem—each of which is another descriptive model.[2] In turn, none of these models may tell as much as you might want to know about climate, industry, or voting habits. To report on these you'd need other descriptive models, perhaps special maps. All models have their limits.

Distortion

All descriptive models distort. This is obvious with the sketch map; however, a road map distorts, too. Roads are three-dimensional—they go up and down with the land—yet the map is a flat surface. The colored lines used to represent roads are proportionately much wider on the map than the roads are on the land. In true proportion, the lines would be almost invisible. Labeling and symbolizing also induce certain minor distortions. The Oregon road map has the word "Eugene" written below an irregular yellow polygon representing this city. Yet Eugene itself is not colored yellow. And there are no enormous letters lying on the hills south of town.

Similarly, financial accounting simplifies when it describes the economic history and status of a business. Financial accounting necessarily leaves things out, it distorts. But all we really should ask of the financial accountant is that his report hold distortion to a minimum and be as reliable as possible, while at the same time providing his readers with the kinds of information they need in order to make decisions regarding

---

[2] Notice that the photograph and the painting are two-dimensional models, whereas reality has depth. And even the clearest photograph leaves out a lot of detail. The notion of language as a model troubles some students; yet the intent of a good prose description is to represent something by discussing those of its characteristics that are the most significant. Much the same is true of poetry, though what is "significant" may differ.

the firm. Unfortunately, as we shall see, these two goals of reliability and relevance sometimes are in conflict: information that is relevant to reader decisions may be unreliable, while reliable information may be irrelevant.

Difficulties of this sort cause the common observation that accounting is an art, not a science. Over many centuries, mostly by trial and error, financial accountants have developed a descriptive model that works fairly well. It does not work perfectly. It *does* distort; it *is* arbitrary in places; there still is a great deal of argument in accounting circles about ways in which the model might be improved. But it works well enough that readers of accounting reports have found them useful, and businessmen have been willing to spend large sums to have such reports prepared.

The need for memory

Because the accounting model simplifies and is arbitrary in places, there are some things about it that you will just have to memorize. To repeat the earlier example, once you have learned what the financial accountant means by an asset, the general way in which he reports on assets should make sense to you. But the notion itself is something you just have to memorize. It works in the sense that it leads to a useful model; but it still has to be memorized. Similarly, automobile designers have found that it works for the driver to do certain things with his hands and other things with his feet. The tasks are probably logically divided, but the logic is not explicit and the novice driver pretty much has to memorize what to do.

Driving offers another valuable example. Some things in driving are pure convention, but everyone must memorize and respect them. Driving on the right side of the road is such a convention. It would be perfectly possible for everyone to drive on the left side, and the British do just that. The important thing is that all drivers follow the same rule, whatever it may be. There are similar conventions in accounting. These also have to be memorized.

Despite all this, the amount of memory work required in financial accounting is small. Most of the time you should be able to appreciate why the accountant does what he does, why his model is set up the way it is. If you are to understand accounting, you must pay as much attention to the "whys" as to the "whats." Memory usually fades after a little time has passed. But when you see the reason for something, when you really comprehend it, you will probably remember it. This book will try to indicate clearly those things that you must memorize. Make sure that you do memorize these. But whenever possible, try to substitute understanding for memorizing.

Additional simplifications in this book

Financial accounting thus is an abstract, compact, simplified descriptive model of certain kinds of economic phenomena. This book is an elementary text, designed to provide you with solid background knowledge of financial accounting, whether or not you plan to specialize in accounting. In particular, it is designed to train you to read actual financial accounting reports with full comprehension of the matters they discuss. But in an elementary text only the basics of financial accounting should be discussed—those minimum concepts and techniques needed for an intelligent understanding of these reports. More specialized topics must be omitted.

Some of the omitted topics (such as accounting for pension plans and other forms of employee compensation) are inherently complex. Other omitted topics are simple enough but require considerable space to discuss their details adequately. Examples of the latter, omitted because they are time-consuming and unnecessary for an understanding of actual financial accounting reports, are the reports prepared for economic and political entities other than corporations: governments, universities, and charities, for example. We will look at the financial accounting reports of only one kind of entity: the business operated to make a profit. There are several kinds of profit-seeking businesses: the single-owner enterprise, the partnership, the corporation. Apart from a short discussion in Chapter Five, we will study corporation accounting only.

Some corporations have very complicated arrangements whereby different classes of owners have different sorts of rights. With one exception, we will study only the simpler kinds of corporations. If you understand financial accounting for simple corporations, you will have learned the main features of accounting for any kind of economic entity. Specialized features of accounting for other kinds of entities can be learned in more advanced courses.

Differences Between This and Other Accounting Texts

This book is the result of a comprehensive attempt to rethink elementary financial accounting from the ground up, and to reorganize the ways in which this subject is explained. As I indicated earlier, my goal in this reconstitution has been to help the student comprehend the basics of financial accounting, instead of merely memorizing its traditional rules.

Inevitably, this book differs from other elementary accounting texts in several ways. Students who are familiar with these other texts may find these differences surprising. Accordingly, it is worthwhile to explain what these differences are before going any further.

Bookkeeping mechanics

The information presented in financial accounting reports is drawn from various detailed accounting records. These records often are referred to as the firm's *books*; their preparation and maintenance constitute *bookkeeping*. Although there is nothing conceptually difficult about bookkeeping, it often requires an enormous amount of work. Accountants have developed complicated bookkeeping techniques in order to perform the work efficiently.

If you decide to specialize in accounting, you eventually should learn these fine points of bookkeeping. But this understanding is unnecessary for comprehension of the financial accounting reports themselves; instead, all that you need is a clear grasp of the general principles that underlie all detailed bookkeeping techniques.

Certain specialized bookkeeping procedures are illustrated by the practice set that has been designed to accompany this text. Your instructor may choose to assign a version of the practice set, or he may prefer to delay study of these matters until an advanced course. In any event, this book places less emphasis on the mechanics of bookkeeping than do most elementary accounting texts. Instead, a very simple record-ing system is illustrated—one detailed enough to show you how to generate the information that appears in financial accounting reports, yet compatible with both traditional and computerized bookkeeping practices. One side effect of using this simplified recording system is avoiding much of the "busy work" usually associated with the study of accounting.

Integrated discussion

Another side effect is that it becomes feasible to discuss the entire economic activity of a firm without getting tangled up in a maze of detail. Most financial accounting texts are divided into individual chapters describing each of the main kinds of assets and obligations of the firm. In contrast to the fragmented approach, this book provides an integrated discussion of all aspects of the firm; you can see the relationship of each asset, obligation, record, and report to the firm's total economic activity. This is the way economic activity is perceived from within the firm itself: as a unified whole or "totality."

Many of the illustrations and problems in later chapters are based upon the actual financial accounting reports of real companies, and they describe the total activities of these firms during specific periods of time. Some of these illustrations may seem lengthy, not because they require complicated bookkeeping, but because these illustrations and problems are *complete*.

Order of topic presentation

For you to attain full comprehension of all basic financial accounting practices, much more time must be spent covering fundamentals than in other texts. Moreover, all topics should be presented in a strictly logical order, moving from simple ideas to complex ones. For example, you will learn later on that a major financial accounting report, the *income statement,* describes the firm's profits. Yet in the next several chapters profits are mentioned only in passing, and, except for a brief overview at the beginning of Chapter Two, the income statement is not discussed as such until Chapter Eight. The information that is reported on income statements is important, but its background is very complicated. Before you can fully comprehend the significance of the income statement, you must understand the underlying concepts and rules and the simpler ideas from which they in turn have been developed. (For the same reason, when learning a foreign language, you should be well grounded in its grammar and vocabulary and begin to deal with the language on its own terms before you try to read the best literature written in that tongue. Similarly, income statements involve a com-plex use of accounting concepts and rules, and their study is best delayed until you are familiar with the basics.)

Most financial accounting texts introduce the main accounting concepts and reports in the first few chapters, regardless of how complicated they may be, then return to them in later chapters as the material is studied in more detail. In contrast, this book introduces concepts and reports one at a time, as they are needed to clarify the matters under discussion. One result of this is to delay the introduction of many useful accounting terms until late in the discussion. For now you need not worry about *debit, credit, expense, revenue, income, valuation account,* etc.

Students who have been exposed to other accounting texts (either through another course or through conversations with others who already have studied accounting) may find this approach disconcerting. It may seem that you are progressing much more slowly than others have during the first six weeks or so, and you may worry about falling behind or being insufficiently prepared for later courses. These worries are natural but unnecessary. This book has been used as a text at several universities, on graduate and undergraduate levels, over a total period of several years. By the time you have completed it, you will have covered all materials needed for subsequent courses and contained in other texts, and you will also have studied important topics that are not discussed (or are discussed only superficially) in other texts.[3]

The apparent slowness of presentation is a direct result of not introducing all concepts and reports at the outset, and of concentrating on fundamentals. This orderly way of organizing the book makes it possible to present material in an efficient, rapid manner later on. Material on accounting theory, which ordinarily is regarded as "too difficult" for an elementary book, yet which is vital to your understanding of the significance of financial accounting reports, is also presented logically. Accordingly, by the time you have finished this book you actually should have learned *more* than you would have from other texts, and you should understand it better.

Reinforcement material

This book is a thick one, mainly because it contains an exceptionally large amount of reinforcement material—extra material intended to help you make sure that you really comprehend the points that are being discussed. All descriptions of accounting procedures are backed up with detailed illustrations and by problems for you to solve. The solutions are given in step-by-step fashion in the text itself. Finally, there are a large number of other problems (whose solutions are not printed in the text) for your instructor to assign if he wishes. My goal has been to make all discussions of accounting procedures as close to self-teaching as possible.

The difficulty here (and presumably one reason why other texts do not provide similar reinforcement materials) is that different students grasp financial accounting concepts at different rates of speed. If you happen to be one of those fortunate students who learn accounting readily, you may find some of the detail in the illustrations and problem solutions excessive and a bit low-level. You also may find it unnecessary to study or solve all of these reinforcement materials. Throughout the text I have tried to indicate those illustrations and reinforcement problems which may be omitted

---

[3] If you have had previous practical experience in accounting, you may encounter an additional difficulty at first: in the early chapters of this book you will be asked to do things differently. For instance, in recording a sale you will be asked to credit Stockholders' Equity instead of Sales. Most experienced students find that after their initial surprise has worn off, the methods used in this book deepen their understanding of the techniques they have previously employed. But there *is* a short-run problem of adjusting oneself to what at first seem to be new rules. This problem will be particularly severe if you previously memorized ordinary accounting practices without fully understanding them; unfortunately, you may have been trained to do just that.

or skimmed by students who experience no difficulties with the topics under discussion. Extra help is available for students who need it, those who do not can save time.

Some of the reinforcement material, however, is *not* designated as optional. All students should make use of the latter material. It is very important that you repeatedly test your comprehension of successive topics in accounting as you go along, rather than waiting until just before formal examinations. The discussion in this book is cumulative in the sense that each concept builds upon those concepts which have been introduced earlier. If you try to read one chapter before you have mastered previous chapters, you can become badly confused. For a clear understanding it is vital that you solve the reinforcement problems in the text, compare your answers with the "official" ones, make sure that you understand the correct procedures if your solutions went wrong, ask questions in class if you can't straighten things out by re-reading the text, and *do not fall behind*.

Discussion of accounting theory

Full comprehension of financial accounting reports requires a discussion of some controversial matters. Currently there is a great deal of intellectual ferment going on in financial accounting. In many instances there is active disagreement over the rules accountants should follow in preparing reports. In other cases, numerous conflicting rules are available with no clear-cut, conclusively defensible way of deciding which rule to follow. Beginning students naturally prefer certainty and want to be told the "right" way to do things, but often there is no completely right way.

Most elementary accounting texts sidestep this problem by giving standard conventional explanations of why actual accounting procedures are followed, without questioning the logic of these explanations and only rarely questioning the logic of the procedures themselves. They describe the conventional alternative accounting practices that are allowed in preparing reports, but they are apparently not concerned that *all* practices are allowed, despite the conflicting results that they yield. In contrast, this book will examine the major issues in financial accounting theory, explaining the matters at issue from a unifying perspective.

Accounting theory is concerned with why accountants choose a particular model of economic activity in reporting on firms, the kinds of information their reports can give you, and the limitations of these reports. Accounting theory also deals with several major controversies among accountants over the rules that should be followed in financial accounting reports.

With one major exception, my own views on accounting theory are conservative. Most of my explanations will lead to conclusions that are compatible with accepted contemporary accounting practices. But occasionally the explanations and justifications that I give for certain practices will be far from conventional. Most accountants would agree with my descriptions of *what* financial accountants do, but many (perhaps including your instructor) will disagree with parts of my explanations of *why* they do it.

Such disagreements are a price of trying to achieve comprehension instead of mere memorization of accounting practices. They could, of course, be avoided either by omitting explanations of accounting rules or giving vague, plausible-sounding explanations that don't really get down to the issues.[4] Your study of accounting will be less open-and-shut than it might otherwise be because controversial matters are discussed, but perhaps it also will be livelier. In any event, discussion of controversial matters will provide insights that should be helpful to you in later courses, or as a member of management or an investor.

How to Use This Book

Here are some suggestions on how to use this book.

1. Read slowly and carefully. Make sure that you understand the illustrations in all their detail. A good way to insure this is to come back to the illustration later on, remind yourself of its basic data, then see if you can reconstruct it without referring to the text.

Avoid going on to the next chapter until you understand the one before it. Don't be reluctant to ask questions in class. If something puzzles you, it probably puzzles several other students, too. If you hesitate to ask for fear of seeming foolish, the matter may never get cleared up.

Keep as up-to-date in your assignments as possible. Because accounting is different from your other subjects, you have to make an adjustment to it. Usually you can't manage this adjustment by last-minute cramming. Learning the language and learning the way accountants think takes persistent day-by-day practice.

Earlier, some similarities between studying accounting and studying mathematics were mentioned. Here is another important similarity. As was mentioned in the previous section, most accounting students find that the course becomes very hard to comprehend if they fall behind in their work. The materials discussed in any one chapter build upon the foundation of the materials covered in all the previous chapters. If you don't keep up, you're apt to get lost.

2. Practice is the key. To learn accounting you must do problems—both to make you apply ideas that you have learned in a general way, and to help you discover what you still need to learn. Each chapter in this book has a set of problems and discussion questions for your instructor to assign. But as was mentioned earlier, each chapter has something more: one or more sets of sample problems with solutions for use in checking your understanding as you go along. Some of these reinforcement problems are located at the ends of chapters, some in the middle. In general, they are located wherever other students have found a review of the text most helpful. These sample problems are one of the most important parts of this book. If you do them carefully as you read the text, you will be constantly reinforcing what you have learned, as well as making sure that you understand what you have read. If you don't do the sample problems (or if you do them in a half-hearted way), you will have thrown away that chance. Working the sample problems is no guarantee of success, but it will improve the odds.

---

[4] Of course, occasionally I do the same things myself when the matters at stake are not important enough to justify the space required for a full discussion. But I try to face all really significant issues.

3. After you have done the sample problems, pay at least as much attention to the structure, form, and efficiency of your solution as to whether or not you have the "right answer." The "official" solutions are carefully designed to illustrate a logical and well-organized approach. This doesn't mean that there aren't other, equally logical ways of setting up the solution. Usually there are several such ways. But you should compare your solution with the printed one to see whether yours is clear and well-organized. If you get into the habit of setting up your solutions in a logical way, you'll be able to transfer what you learn from this course to new situations. Just finding the right answer won't help.

This is the chief reason for doing the sample problems by yourself. Remember, your goal is to be able to transfer your knowledge of accounting from the classroom to real-life situations. Actual circumstances will almost never duplicate the examples you have seen in this text or in class. You need to develop the kind of understanding that will carry over to new situations. The illustrations and sample problems in this book are designed to help you develop good general approaches to any accounting situation you happen to meet. Learning these approaches so well that they become second-nature to you requires doing your own work, making your own mistakes, and comparing what you've done with the suggested approach in the solution.

I emphasize this because in many of your other courses you can learn the subject more passively, sometimes just by sitting back and letting it sink in. In financial accounting, however, you are trying to do more than simply learn a particular set of facts or relationships. You are trying to develop your intellectual muscles, your analytical ability. You are trying to increase your capacity to approach problems intelligently. To do this you can't be passive. You have to take part.

The Plan of This Book

This is a good point at which to outline the course of our discussion. To begin, this book is divided into four main parts.

Part I is a discussion of certain fundamental concepts used in financial accounting. These are not the only concepts that could have been chosen; the ideas underlying financial accounting are closely interrelated, and we could have begun with others. The great advantage of the ones used here is that they are very simple, yet they suffice to explain most of what the financial accountant does.

Chapters One and Two are a discussion of the most basic ideas of financial accounting (for our purposes):

1. The ways financial accounting data are used.

2. The accountant's concept of an *asset*—a notion similar, but not identical, to the notion of asset used in ordinary life.

3. The ways in which the accountant classifies different kinds of assets and the distinctions that he makes among them.

4. The ways in which the accountant associates dollar amounts with assets.

Chapter Two gives some examples of actual financial accounting reports and provides an introduction to amortization and the current/noncurrent distinction.

Chapter Three is a discussion of an accounting concept complementary to the notion of an asset—an *equity*. An equity is most easily described as a company's obligation to a creditor or to its owners. Chapter Three also discusses one of several financial reports prepared by accountants to provide economic information about the company to outsiders—the *balance sheet*. A balance sheet is merely an organized list of the company's assets and equities at a given point in time, together with the dollar amounts associated with these assets and equities.

Part II explains how the accountant is able to use information about assets and equities to record any kind of economic activity experienced by the company. Those readers who already have some familiarity with accounting will be aware that accountants ordinarily employ additional concepts besides the asset and equity concepts in recording economic activity. For example, they use concepts of *revenues, expenses,* and *income*. These additional concepts are convenient ones, and will be introduced in Part III. It will aid your understanding of accounting, however, if first you become convinced that these additional concepts are not essential to accounting—at least not until the accountant wishes to summarize and report economic activity to outsiders. As far as *recording* economic activity goes, only assets and equities are needed.

Chapter Four demonstrates how economic activity might be directly recorded on successive balance sheets. While theoretically feasible, this approach turns out to be very cumbersome. Therefore, a separate data-accumulation device (called a *ledger account*) is prepared for each asset and equity. The purpose of such ledger accounts is simply to allow the accountant to indicate the effects of each economic event on the individual assets and equities affected without disturbing what has already been recorded for the remaining assets and equities. Chapter Four also discusses the natures of the measurements made in financial accounting, pointing out that some of these are simple counts or observations of market prices, while others are more complicated and less reliable.

This ledger device files economic information by individual assets and individual equities. But it also is convenient to maintain another record, one in which the same information is filed by the individual kind of economic event.

Chapter Five discusses the device used to accomplish this: the *journal entry*. Essentially, a journal entry is just a highly compressed description of a particular economic occurrence. Finally, the chapter discusses a few refinements in the method for recording owner investment in a company.

In *Part III,* the orientation of the discussion changes. Instead of being concerned with recording economic activity, the stress shifts to summarizing economic events and reporting them to outsiders. The related reports are designed to help answer various questions that an investor in a company might have about what has happened to the company and what it has been doing.

Chapter Six is an introduction to such reports. It discusses a report summarizing a company's inflows and outflows of *cash*. Such a cash report contains most of the features of more complicated reports while remaining easy to understand at first glance. Chapter Six also continues a discussion that began with the comments on measurement in Chapter Four. Accountants wish to measure the contributions that individual inputs make to a firm's outputs. But such measurements usually are ambiguous. Unexpectedly, it turns out in Chapters Eight and Thirteen that this ambiguity places important limits on the significance of accounting's profit calculations.

Chapter Seven examines a report called a *funds statement*. Funds statements focus their attention on major, semi-permanent, or permanent commitments made by the company as it purchases land, buildings, and equipment. Funds statements are also concerned with reporting changes in long-term investments in the company. Finally, funds statements reflect changes in the company's general *liquidity*—its capacity to raise the financial wherewithal to seize unexpected opportunities or to respond to emergencies.

Chapter Eight examines a report called an *income statement*. Income statements focus on a matter of great concern to investors—the company's profits. Also included in Chapter Eight is a detailed look at the rules governing when the accountant will report that a profit has occurred, and certain controversies that have arisen concerning these rules.

Chapter Nine examines some of the relationships between funds statements and income statements and discusses certain confusions that arise from these relationships. An Appendix to Chapter Nine also discusses the use of ratios to analyze certain other relationships between and within financial statements in order to determine the significance of reported data.

Through Part III, the discussion of financial accounting is deliberately kept simple. Details of actual accounting techniques are held to a minimum; various alternative practices followed by accountants are not discussed. While there has been considerable discussion of accounting theory, certain theoretical issues relating to the cost and valuation of assets have been postponed. This simplification occurs because it is not necessary to understand these complications in order to grasp the essence of what the accountant's recording and reporting involves. But if the reader is to comprehend actual accounting practice, he must be introduced to various refinements and complications. This is what *Part IV* attempts to do.

Chapter Ten in Part IV is concerned with refinements in recording, it is a discussion of the specialized ledger accounts used to accumulate data about particular kinds of economic events as they affect individual assets and equities. These specialized accounts are called *nominal* and *valuation* accounts. Chapter Ten concludes by examining the details of a company's record-keeping procedures over an entire year.

All assets and equities may be divided into two broad groups: the *monetary* items, which are cash, rights to receive cash, and obligations to pay cash; and *nonmonetary* items, which include such things as inventories, buildings, and equipment. Chapter Eleven examines two problems in reporting upon monetary items: (1) some debt inevitably turns out to be uncollectible, and (2) the proceeds received from issuing debt often differ from the amount that will be owed at the due date. The accountant's response to the latter problem requires us to examine the fundamentals of compound interest calculations.

Some of the most difficult problems in accounting arise with nonmonetary assets. Chapter Twelve deals with problems of determining what such assets cost, particularly manufactured inventories. Chapter Thirteen discusses various conflicting ways in which these costs are written off as the related assets eventually yield their services to the company.

Part I

One

The Background of
Financial Accounting

What Financial Accounting Does

Financial accounting is a method of obtaining, analyzing, organizing, and communicating information. It is a way of gathering and reporting certain kinds of news. We are all familiar with many such systems for gathering and reporting information. A magazine for hobbyists is such a system—a stamp collectors' journal is a good example. When you stop and think about it, a thermometer is another system for gathering and giving news, though it's a very simple one.

Any such system is designed to collect and report particular kinds of information and nothing else. The stamp magazine tries to give thorough coverage of important developments concerning stamps, but it contains little general news. A thermometer is limited to giving information about temperature. Financial accounting is also a specialized system. It gathers and reports economic information. In particular, it gathers and reports economic information relating to individual enterprises that are in business to make a profit.[1]

Ways in which financial accounting specializes

Financial accounting could have specialized in some different directions. There are all kinds of economic information that could be gathered and reported. One could discuss the national economy as a whole, or certain industries as a whole. Financial

---

[1] For simplicity, call these enterprises "profit-making" businesses even though some of them fail in their attempt to make profits.

17

accounting does neither. Instead, it concerns itself solely with economic information about *individual* companies, considered in isolation from the rest of the economy and the rest of their industries. There are many kinds of individual economic entities: cities, universities, and charities, as well as profit-making businesses. We shall restrict our attention to the last of these—profit-making businesses.

Financial accounting is even more restricted. Various kinds of economic information could be gathered and reported about the individual profit-making business. Some of this information would be of primary interest to the *management* of the company, the individuals responsible for the day-to-day conduct of the business. For instance, the management might want to know whether a department was operating efficiently, whether a product should continue to be made, whether a new machine was worth buying, or how much money the company needed to borrow on short-term loans to meet cash requirements over the next few months. Other kinds of economic information might be developed to meet the special needs of tax collectors or governmental regulatory agencies.

Financial accounting is designed for investors

But financial accounting is not directly concerned with such information. True, financial accounting does gather and report news that management, tax collectors, and regulatory agencies find useful. But that is not its primary objective. *The main purpose of financial accounting is to develop and communicate information about the company that will be useful to investors.*

Kinds of investors: stockholders

Let's specify who these investors are. As was indicated on page 7, this book confines itself to one particular kind of profit-making business, the corporation. We need a rough definition of a corporation at this point—one that will be explained in more detail later in this chapter. A *corporation* is an artificial legal entity that, under the law, has nearly the same rights as a private individual and is regarded as being separate and distinct from its owners and management. This entity is created by a grant of authority from a state government (or, occasionally, from the federal government). There is no set limit to the life of a corporation, and since ownership rights in corporations are easily transferred from one investor to another, it is entirely possible for the life of a corporation to extend beyond the lifetimes of its original owners. As a distinct legal entity, the corporation can sue and be sued; moreover, it has its own debts and usually its owners cannot be held responsible if the corporation is unable to pay these debts.

Also, as a distinct legal entity the corporation has its individual financial accounting reports, which are entirely separate from any that may be prepared about the status and activity of its owners. Later on we shall see that this preparation of separate accounting reports for the corporation is a sufficiently important feature of accounting that it has been given a special name: the *entity rule.*

The corporation allows a number of owners (often strangers to one another) to pool their economic resources and create a larger and more powerful economic entity than any one part-owner might be able to create alone. The individual part-owner of a corporation is called a *stockholder*. At the time a corporation begins its life, the stockholder invests his money in the corporation in exchange for a proportionate interest in the business. His rights are evidenced by shares of stock. The number of shares (and thereby the proportionate size of his investment) depends on the amount he has invested compared with the amounts invested by other stockholders.

Suppose that a particular company decided to issue 10,000 shares of stock, and that stockholders decided to invest $1,000,000. This works out to $100 a share. A stockholder who invested $2,000 would get twenty shares of stock, representing a 20/10,000 (or 1/500th) proportionate ownership interest in the company. A stockholder who invested $25,000 would get 250 shares, or a 1/40th proportionate interest.

What are the rights that the stockholder acquires by his investment? The list that follows is only partial.[2] He is entitled to a proportionate vote in the conduct of the affairs of the company, a proportionate share in any distributions of the company's profits, and a proportionate share in the proceeds, should the business ever be sold. A distribution of profits is called a *dividend*. Most dividends are in the form of cash payments, though occasionally some other valuable asset—such as shares in the capital stock of another company—is distributed instead.

The stockholder therefore gets rights to vote and rights to receive dividends. Based on the first example, the stockholder with twenty shares would have 1/500th of the total voting power in the company and would be entitled to 1/500th of any dividend distribution made to company stockholders. These rights are *transferable*. If the stockholder becomes dissatisfied with his investment, he has the right to sell his shares of stock to someone else.

When a stockholder does sell his shares of stock to someone else, the corporation itself is unaffected. It goes on, regardless of who its particular stockholders (or other investors) are at any given time. Because of this, a corporation potentially has an indefinite life. If it is economically successful, there is no reason why a corporation cannot continue forever, outliving all of its original investors.

Subsequent stockholder investments

So far we have dealt only with investments made by stockholders at the beginning of a corporation's life. In these cases the stockholder pays his money to the corporation itself, receiving shares of stock in return. But once the corporation is in being, a new stockholder may buy his shares of stock *from another stockholder* instead of from the corporation. In that case the amount paid for the shares is something for the buyer and seller to determine between themselves, and the amount the new stockholder invests need not be proportionate to the amount invested by other stockholders. For example, if the corporation has gotten off to a successful start, the market price of its shares may rise above the price at which the shares were issued—a new investor would have to pay the higher price.

---

[2] For simplicity, the discussion here and in the next several chapters assumes that only one kind of stock is issued by corporations. The kind of stock discussed here is the most common (in fact it often is designated *common stock*), and it is issued by all corporations. But some corporations issue additional kinds of stock offering investors different sets of rights; these are discussed in Chapter Five.

Delegation of stockholder powers

Two special features of corporations should be discussed. Often the stockholders do not run the business themselves. They invest their money in the company but leave its detailed operation to a hired management. This is accomplished in the following way. Each year stockholders attend an annual meeting and elect individuals to represent their interests. These individuals are called *directors*; as a group they are called the *board of directors*. In turn, the board of directors appoints the *management*, consisting of the various company officers (president, vice-presidents, treasurer, and so forth) who are in charge of the actual detailed running of the company. Thereafter, the board of directors usually confines itself to a general supervision of management.

This means that while the individual stockholder has the right to vote in company affairs, he delegates most of this right to the board of directors, which, in turn, delegates most of its powers to management. (Of course, none of this prevents the individual stockholder from being elected a director or being appointed a part of management.) Obviously, the stockholder needs to know whether he has delegated wisely and whether management is doing a good job as a steward of the resources given it. Indeed, financial accounting evolved from individuals who were entrusted with the resources of others and had the responsibility of explaining how they had handled the resources; in traditional language this was called "giving an accounting." Although modern financial accounting serves additional purposes, *stewardship accounting* remains one of its major functions.

A formal diagram of these relationships

A simplified version of the foregoing relationships is shown in the diagram on page 21. Arrows represent the delegation of authority from the owners of the corporation to its employees. This particular company has a simple form of organization with only six principal officers:

President	The chief executive officer who assumes general responsibility for the firm as a whole.
Vice-President— Finance	The officer who assumes primary responsibility for the firm's financial, resource obtaining, and accounting activities.
Vice-President— Manufacturing	The officer who assumes primary responsibility for the firm's manufacturing activities.
Vice President— Marketing	The officer who assumes primary responsibility for the firm's selling, advertising, and other promotional activities.
Treasurer	The officer responsible for making sure that the firm has the financial resources necessary to conduct its activities. In this firm the Treasurer is a subordinate of the Vice President— Finance, although other organizational arrangements are possible.
Controller	The chief accounting officer, sometimes called a *comptroller*. Once again, the exact organizational relationships between the Controller, Treasurer, and Vice President—Finance will vary from firm to firm; sometimes these offices are combined.

Illustration 1-1

Relationships of Stockholders, Directors, and Management

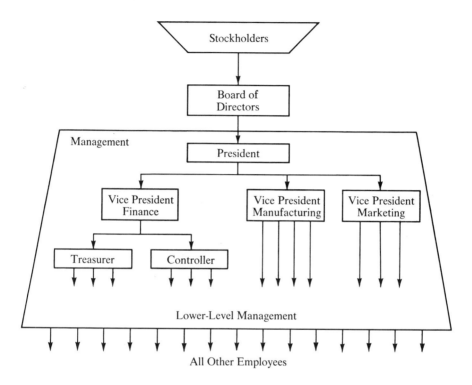

Each of these principal officers in turn directs the activities of various subordinates, who may have subordinates of their own.

Illustration 1-1 is really an idealized picture of the relationships of stockholders, directors, and management—an ideal closely corresponding to the democratic ideal whereby voters elect representatives who, in turn, supervise the detailed operations of government. In practice, stockholders rarely attempt to intervene in the affairs of the firm, and various informal relationships between individuals within the company tend to complicate the actual flows of authority. Finally, it should be noted that ordinarily the president and at least a few other principal officers of the firm are also members of the board of directors, complicating matters still further.

Kinds of investors: creditors

The stockholder is not the only investor in his company. Anyone who has lent money to the company, or has given it goods or services without being paid immediately, has a temporary investment in the company, even though he is not an *owner*. Firms, individuals, and other parties to whom the company owes money (or, less often, goods or services) are called *creditors*. Every creditor is an investor in the company until his debt is settled. Some creditors invest money for long periods of time and may receive interest on their investments. If the creditor's investment is for more than one year, we will refer to him as a *long-term creditor*. Other creditors are just suppliers of merchandise, supplies, or services, who expect to be paid in the near future. If the creditor's investment is for one year or less, we will refer to him as a *short-term creditor*.[3] Both long-term and short-term creditors need information about how secure their investments are.

Limited liability

Creditor needs are particularly great because of a second special feature of corporations. Suppose that you and I were to organize our own business—not a corporation. Suppose that this business were unsuccessful, ran out of money, and were unable to pay its debts. Any creditors of this unincorporated business could then turn to us, the owners, for their money. Under present laws, one of the distinctive features of corporations is that unsatisfied creditors cannot do this. They cannot collect what is owed them from the corporation's owners. If the corporation cannot pay its debts, the creditor must accept the loss himself. He cannot collect from the stock-holder.

This is called *limited liability*. The corporation's limited liability gives it a great advantage over other kinds of business in attracting ownership investments. In fact, limited liability has been so attractive to owner investors that most of the economically significant business in this country is conducted by corporations. (That is another reason why this book confines itself to corporation accounting.) A corporation may, of course, be a perfectly good credit risk. Nevertheless, limited liability creates a particularly strong reason for creditors to seek information about a company's economic condition.

Information needs of investors

Thus there are two groups of investors: stockholders and creditors. Stockholders need to know how the company is doing so that they can judge whether or not management is effectively carrying out the responsibilities delegated to it. If a stock-holder is dissatisfied, he may want to help elect a board of directors who will hire new management. But if the stockholder feels that the other stockholders are not equally dissatisfied and that efforts to elect a new board of directors would be fruitless, he may wish to sell his shares of stock to someone else. (With large corporations, selling is usually the simplest thing for the stockholder to do.) In addition to present stock-holders, potential stockholders need information about how management is performing and about the general economic condition of the company.

Long-term creditors can also transfer their rights to others, and they need much the same kind of information as do stockholders. The short-term creditor is typically

---

[3] This use of one-year periods to distinguish *short-term* from *long-term* is very typical in accounting. Those readers who are familiar with economics should notice that the accountant's *short-term* is a good deal longer than the economist's *short-run*. (For those of you who are *not* familiar with economics, the short-run is the brief period during which an economic system is unable to react to a change.)

a regular supplier who is repeatedly extending credit to the company for short periods. He needs to know whether anything is happening to the company's economic condition that should make him stop granting credit.

Just what kinds of information do present and potential stockholders and creditors need? First of all, they need to know about the company's present financial condition. How big is it? How much cash does it have? How much is owed to it? What does it own, in addition to cash and debts from others? How much does it owe creditors? How much money have owners invested in it? Does it seem able to pay its bills as they come due?

All of this comprises information about the company at a single point in time. Investors also need to know what has been happening to the company—say, over the previous year. How profitable has the company been? Have profits been increasing or decreasing? If they've been increasing and the company has been getting bigger, have profits been getting bigger at the same rate or a greater rate, or has the additional growth been progressively less profitable? How has the company been financing its activities? What has management been doing with the investment entrusted to it? Where's all the money going? How much does the company pay out to stockholders in dividends (see page 19)? Are the company's profits adequate to cover the interest charges on all its long-term debts with a good safety factor besides?

These are the kinds of questions financial accounting tries to answer. Information about the company's present condition is given in a report called a *balance sheet*. Information about what has happened to the company is given in reports called *funds statements* and *income statements*. You do not need to understand these reports until later in this book. But if you are curious as to where we are heading in the discussion that occupies the next few chapters, examples of a balance sheet, an income statement, and a funds statement are given on pages 80–81 and 83–84. The information contained in these statements is at least part of what stockholders and creditors need to know. Financial accounting is mainly a report to these investors.

Later on in this book you will begin to discover that financial accounting can't always do an entirely satisfactory job of answering all of these investor questions. In fact, one of the most interesting parts of studying accounting is seeing why financial accounting cannot give perfect answers, and in what ways it is limited. But the questions given above are of the sort that financial accounting tries to answer.

Resource-allocation versus institutional uses of financial accounting

At this point, an important distinction should be made. The uses of financial accounting described in the previous subsection are related to *resource-allocation* decisions that must be made by investors. Stockholders must periodically decide which companies they wish to own stock in, and this may involve transfers of their resources from investment in one company to investment in another. Creditors must make similar resource-allocation decisions about the firms they will lend money to.

But there is a large class of uses of financial accounting information that relates only indirectly to these economic decisions of investors—various laws and other institutions of society require that financial accounting reports be prepared, and many aspects of these reports are strictly specified. Here are some examples:

1. Corporations are regulated by the states in which they do business. Under existing laws, a corporation can be created only by permission of a state government. This is not true of other forms of business; if, for instance, a man wishes to open a store (acting as a private individual in doing so), he may have to meet various requirements set by local authorities, but he need not obtain the approval of any authorities higher than the municipal or county level. However, if he wishes the limited-liability protection that the corporate form of business provides (see page 22), he must seek the permission of his state government. The permission is evidenced by a legal document called a *corporate charter*. States use their right to grant or withhold corporate charters as authority for imposing various requirements upon corporations; some of these pertain to the firm's financial accounting records and reports.

2. Those corporations that are large enough to have their shares bought and sold on a nation-wide basis are required under federal law to comply with certain financial accounting requirements of the Securities and Exchange Commission.

3. The courts impose various requirements and restrictions on financial accounting as do various regulatory bodies.

These might appropriately be called *institutional* uses of financial accounting. Another subtle institutional constraint on financial accounting may be the most important of all. Financial accounting as we know it acquired most of its important characteristics by the end of the nineteenth century. After a final period of experimentation in the 1920s, the details of present-day financial accounting practice were settled by the 1930s. Therefore, most things in financial accounting have been done in the same ways for more than a generation—sometimes for more than three generations. When practices have persisted unchanged for this long, people begin to presume that the practices have been proved effective and therefore they should *continue* unchanged. Besides, everyone is used to them. All of this leads many people in business and government to expect that financial accountants should continue to prepare the kinds of records and reports that we will examine in this book.

Information not given by financial accounting

There are certain kinds of information that investors would be delighted to receive, but that financial accounting does not try to provide. If we consider why this is so, we will begin to understand one major limitation of financial accounting.

Here are some questions that investors would like to have answered: What's going to happen to the company next year? Will the company continue to be as profitable as it is now? Will profits increase? Is the company apt to run out of money next year? How much would be received if the company were sold as a going business to a larger company? How much would be received if the company became insolvent and had to be sold at auction?

The importance of reliability

The accountant could probably give estimated answers to at least some of these questions. But most accountants feel that such estimates would be terribly unreliable— so unreliable that they would be worthless, even harmful. There is much controversy in accounting right now about the *degree* of reliability needed for information to be given to investors. But it is generally agreed that investors should be able to depend on what they read in their financial accounting reports.

The issue here is essentially one of the quality of information to be given to investors. Similar problems of information quality arise whenever an individual is trying to decide upon *any* major purchase. For example, if you are considering buying a new car, you naturally want maximum information in order to compare makes, options, and so forth. Yet certain information—such as the claims made by automobile salesmen—may not be sufficiently reliable to be useful in your decision process. Highly unreliable information may even lead you into making a poor decision. You must strike some kind of balance between your need for as much information as possible and your need for information that is reliable.

Similarly, some kind of balance must be struck between the needs of investors for as much information as possible and their need for information that is reliable. As we shall see later in this book, the initial responsibility for the correct balance lies with the accountant. Much of the information about the firm's economic position and activities first passes through the hands of the accountant, and it is his job to make sure that this information satisfies minimum standards of quality. In practice, accountants traditionally attempt to achieve this balance by insisting that, to the extent possible, information in accounting reports be *objective*. It should be the sort of information that could be independently verified by some outside observer. This usually means information that can be verified by *documentary evidence*: contracts, old bills, cancelled checks, and the like. (We will see more clearly why this is so when we discuss the public accounting profession.) In fact, financial accounting has traditionally *confined the reports largely to matters of historical fact*. This tips things heavily in the direction of "reliable" information about the past and present, as opposed to speculative information about the future.[4]

This does not mean that accounting reports can be perfectly objective or reliable. As we saw earlier, accounting reports are *models* of a company's economic position and activity. They are representations of the economic facts about a company, and any representation distorts. The accountant simply tries to hold this distortion to a minimum—to provide information that is the most objective and reliable that he can obtain.

An example of investor use of financial accounting

Yet the question remains whether, in his search for objectivity, the accountant may be unintentionally providing information that is not so useful as it could be. The American Accounting Association's 1966–68 Committee on External Reporting provided an excellent illustration of this problem.[5] Let us suppose that a stockholder

---

[4] The origins of contemporary financial accounting in stewardship accounting may also help explain this preference for historical data. The steward was expected to report what *had* happened in the past to the resources he managed, not upon what might happen in the future. Whether stewardship responsibilities really can be adequately reflected by a purely historical report is something to be considered later.

[5] "An Evaluation of External Reporting Practices—A Report of the 1966–68 Committee on External Reporting," *The Accounting Review,* Supplement to Vol. XLIV (1969), pages 79–123.

is trying to decide whether or not to sell his shares of a particular stock. One thing he may try to estimate is the future cash dividends that he will receive if he continues to own this stock—for, as we already have seen, the right to receive dividends is one of the main rights that the stockholder receives in exchange for his investment.

If the stockholder is to predict the firm's future dividend policy, he must in turn predict what will happen to the various things that *affect* dividend policy. The Committee on External Reporting listed the following things as matters that could be expected to affect future cash dividend policy, and that the stockholder might want to predict (the list has been paraphrased to avoid technical language):

1. The future effects on cash of the company's dealings in the products and services it sells to customers.

2. The future effects on cash of certain routine activities not directly connected with the company's regular products and services, such as sales of used equipment, investments made in other companies and sales of these investments, proceeds from renting property not currently used by the firm, educational and charitable contributions made by the firm, and so on.

3. The future effects on cash of changes in the levels of investments made by stockholders and creditors.

4. The future effects on cash of purchases of new land, buildings, equipment, and other things needed by the firm in order to conduct its planned activities.

5. The future effects on cash of payments that must be made to investors other than stockholders.

6. The future effects on cash of chance (since the investor is making predictions, his estimates are inherently statistical ones—they must allow for uncertainty).

7. The firm's future policy on the sizes of minimum cash balances. Just as any individual should try to maintain a certain minimum amount of cash for emergencies, so firms should maintain minimum cash balances. The size of the minimum will vary with different firms and with the preferences of different managements. Company policies here will affect how much cash is available for future dividends.

8. Management's future attitude toward the payment of dividends. For example, some firms try to pay very regular dividends to their stockholders, even when doing so places a strain on the firm's cash position; at an opposite pole, other firms tend to pay dividends only when there is "nothing better" to do with the cash.

Of course, each of these eight things the stockholder might want to predict is in turn affected by a variety of other detailed matters that the stockholder must also try to predict—but we need not worry about these details here, since what has been said is sufficient to support the point that is made in the next subsection.

All of these estimates relate to the future

This point is simple: all of the stockholder's predictions relate to the future, not to the past. Yet, as was indicated previously, present financial accounting practice insists on reporting information about the past, and this is done because only past information is considered sufficiently reliable. Now past information often can be very useful in predicting the future. As an example, if a particular company has been paying a cash dividend of $2.00 a share to its stockholders for the last ten years, it probably will continue to do so; information about the past dividend policy may be the most important single thing that the investor needs to know. But the investor's problem still is one of predicting the future—and, as we will see later on in this book, sometimes information about the past is not the most useful kind for prediction purposes. For example, if the firm intends to sell land that it has held since the 1930s, information concerning its current market value will be much more useful in predicting the future effect of this sale on cash than will information about the price at which the company purchased the land. In fact, the past purchase price is largely irrelevant for the purpose of predicting future dividends. But the past price, not the current market value, appears on accounting reports. We will look at this problem in more detail later on; some major controversies in financial accounting theory arise here.

Summary

To repeat, financial accountants try to maintain the reliability of their reports by restricting them as much as possible to objectively documented history. Investors have generally accepted the accountant's decision to prepare historical reports rather than estimates of the future. Investors use these historical reports in making their *own* estimates. Later on you will begin to realize that this is an important decision—one crucial to understanding what the financial accountant is doing and the limits to what he can achieve.

The entity rule

One further restriction on financial accounting reports is implicit in the foregoing discussion, but it should be emphasized at this point. Financial accounting reports are descriptions of the economic condition and economic activities of individual businesses; they are not reports on the condition and activities of their *investors*. An individual may own shares of stock in several different firms. Each of these firms will have its own financial accounting records and will issue its own financial accounting reports. In addition, the individual may have his own personal accounting records. All of these are kept separate and are treated as unrelated.

This is often called the *entity rule*. An accounting *entity* is any individual, group of individuals, business, or nonprofit organization for which separate, self-contained accounting records are maintained. The *entity rule* in financial accounting specifies that the accounting records and reports of different entities are kept separate from and independent of the records and reports of other entities. In particular, the entity rule specifies that the records and reports of corporations shall be independent of the records and reports of their owners. The implications of this rule will become clearer by Chapter Three.

Definition of financial accounting

All of this can be summarized in the following rough definition of financial accounting:[6]

---

[6] It would be convenient, if it were possible, to provide a brief yet precise definition of *financial accounting* at this point in our discussion. Unfortunately, once you attempt to refine a description of financial accounting much beyond the very general one given here, it becomes necessary to discuss matters that turn out to be very complicated. Accordingly, we

Financial accounting is a system for gathering certain objective information about the economic condition and history of individual profit-making enterprises, and for summarizing and reporting that information to investors.

A good deal of this book will be devoted to examining exactly what is meant by "certain objective information" in this definition.

Users of financial reports

Two final things need to be said here. First, there is an important sense in which the accountant's primary responsibility is to the stockholders rather than to the creditors. His reports are reports to the stockholders, telling them what management has done with the investment entrusted to it, and providing information that the stockholder may utilize to predict the future prospects of his investment. But while there may be some differences in the information needs of stockholders and creditors, there seems little conflict between their needs. Therefore, it is possible to speak, as we do here, of reporting to both kinds of investors at once.

More importantly, nothing said here is meant to imply that financial accounting reports are restricted to investors. Many other groups use these reports, too. Management needs to know the company's condition and the results of its own actions. Also, management is vitally interested in any communication made to outsiders by the firm, because these affect the ease with which the firm's future needs for additional investment may be satisfied; financial accounting reports are one of the firm's most important communications to outsiders. Tax collectors, regulatory bodies, unions, economists, and other social scientists—all are interested in what has happened to the company, and they may make use of the financial reports. But investor needs still come first in financial accounting.

You, as a potential member of management, need to understand financial accounting even if you intend to specialize in some other aspect of business activity. Much of the economic information that will guide your business decisions will come to you from your firm's financial accounting system or will be indirectly affected by financial accounting rules.

Also, it is likely that you will eventually become affluent enough to invest in the shares of other firms; financial accounting reports will be a major aid in your investment decisions. Finally, whether or not you intend to specialize in accounting, many of the decisions that will be made by others in your firm will be heavily influenced by financial accounting, and you should understand what motivates these decisions.

Other Kinds of Accounting

Investor needs come first in financial accounting, but there are other kinds of accounting as well. For instance, there is a whole separate branch of accounting

---

will have to settle for what philosophers call an "ostensive" definition: defining financial accounting through a series of *examples* of what the financial accountant does and what the natures of his reports are. This ostensive definition of financial accounting will be conducted throughout much of this book.

devoted to helping the company meet the needs of the taxing authorities. Tax accounting has its own rules and techniques, which serve to help the company report to tax collectors. But, with only a few exceptions, *tax accounting is irrelevant to financial accounting.*

Students are apt to be confused by this for at least three reasons. First, most of the ordinary layman's contact with accounting is with tax accounting; people generally think that all accounting is similar to tax accounting, and that all accountants are tax experts. Second, tax regulations do have important effects upon decisions made by firms, and these decisions are subsequently reflected in financial accounting reports. Finally, many aspects of tax accounting grew out of financial accounting, and much of the language is similar; because of this it is necessary to understand financial accounting in order to understand tax accounting; but the reverse is not true. In fact, an understanding of tax accounting is apt to confuse your understanding of financial accounting.

Most large firms do their financial accounting independently from their tax accounting. In fact, rules that are appropriate for tax purposes often are inappropriate for financial accounting. This is partly because many features of tax law were developed to satisfy social and economic goals not directly related to the purposes of financial accounting. The resulting tax rules sometimes conflict with good financial accounting practice. But, with a few exceptions, there is nothing to prevent a company from keeping one set of records for its investors and another for tax purposes. *Accordingly, tax matters will be almost entirely ignored in this book.*

Governmental and nonprofit accounting

Governmental bodies and nonprofit organizations have developed various accounting systems to meet their own specialized needs. Some of these, such as the accounting systems of the federal government and of certain large cities, have become quite elaborate. Although there is much overlap between financial accounting and the principles and techniques used in reporting for governments and nonprofit organizations, the latter have developed special rules that make them different from financial accounting. This makes governmental and nonprofit accounting an interesting area of study for the advanced student who wants to see how accountants adapt their reports to differing circumstances. But these special reports can be ignored in an elementary book, as can the curious kinds of accounting required in certain regulated industries such as railroading.

Managerial accounting

There is one other major kind of accounting: *managerial accounting.* As the name suggests, managerial accounting is designed to meet the information needs of operating management. Management must be deeply concerned with cost and efficiency. A major part of managerial accounting, called *cost accounting,* has been developed to answer such questions as: Is there any waste in our operations? If so, what is causing it? Is there any way we could make at a lower cost the things we are now producing?

Cost accounting leads into accounting techniques that are intended to answer such additional questions as: Which of our departments (or foremen) are doing the best job? Which of our products should we be stressing? What cost constraints are there on the prices we can charge our customers? To which customers should we be devoting the most selling effort?

Such questions are also related to another branch of managerial accounting, which is concerned with planning. For example, *budgeting* involves making sure that the company's future needs for such things as cash, inventories, buildings, equipment, and the like will be met. In general, managerial accounting can be almost anything developed (by the accountant and from numerical records) to meet the control and planning needs of management. At its fringes, managerial accounting blends into the work performed by the company's engineers, statisticians, economists, and other specialists.

This book will not concern itself with managerial accounting, though from time to time we'll make use of the information that managerial accountants typically develop. For instance, when we discuss accounting for manufacturers, we will need figures to represent inventories. Ordinarily, these figures are worked up by the company's cost accountants. Instead of studying cost accounting, we'll just assume that the cost accountant knows his job, accept his figures as correct, and go on with our financial accounting.

This example of inventories reflects something worth emphasizing. Although financial and managerial accounting are addressed to different groups of readers, the interests and goals of these groups overlap; there are corresponding overlaps in the information reported by these two accounting systems as well as tendencies for each accounting system to provide some of the data inputs employed by the other system. The costs of inventories are of interest both to investors and management; inventory costs are an output of managerial accounting and a data input to financial accounting. As another example, estimates of future needs for cash and inventories of materials and supplies are in part determined by considering present quantities of these goods. Maintenance of at least some of the basic quantities data is the responsibility of the financial accounting system; in this case, financial accounting provides inputs to managerial accounting. The underlying data-collection techniques of both managerial and financial accounting are very similar (discussed on pages 224–227); so are the basic data collected (discussed in part in Chapter Twelve). But the two systems differ widely in what is *done* with the data.

Some of the things that concern investors were mentioned earlier. Management is also concerned with many of the same matters. In fact, management is interested not only in the total profitability of the firm as a whole, but also the profitability of different *parts* of the firm. For instance, the manager of a supermarket may be interested in the comparative profitabilities of the produce department and the meat department.

Finally, management is interested in any financial accounting information that is reported to investors simply because such reports are official public statements from the firm and they often have significant effects on public attitudes toward the firm. Similarly, financial accounting is employed to satisfy certain legal and regulatory obligations, which are also of considerable interest to management. Therefore, even though this text does not discuss managerial accounting *per se,* the matters that are discussed are extremely important to management.

Applicability of this book to other kinds of accounting

Although this book restricts itself to financial accounting for corporations, much of what we will discuss is pertinent to other kinds of accounting because financial accounting for corporations has influenced and has been influenced by several other kinds of accounting. Here are some examples:

1. Almost everything in this book is applicable to unincorporated businesses. The only differences are that unincorporated businesses record the investments made by owners differently than do corporations, and financial accounting by corporations tends to be slightly more elaborate than the financial accounting of unincorporated businesses. This will be discussed in more detail in Chapter Five.

2. Although tax accounting and financial accounting differ in their purposes, many of their features are similar.

3. To the extent that governments and other nonprofit institutions perform activities similar to those of profit-making businesses, their accounting systems parallel those of corporations in many ways. For example, the financial accounting system employed by a municipal- or state-owned utility often will be similar to the system employed by an equivalent privately-owned utility.

Summary

Four different kinds of accounting have been distinguished in this discussion:

Financial accounting: a system for gathering certain objective information about the economic condition and history of individual profit-making enterprises, and for summarizing and reporting that information. Financial accounting reports are directed primarily to investors, though they also are of significance to management and other readers, such as economists, union officials, and members of the general public.

Managerial accounting: a similar system for gathering, summarizing, and reporting economic information that is of particular interest to management—including information that the firm believes it would be dangerous to have its competitors learn, which therefore would not be included in reports designed to be read by the general public. Management accounting reports are prepared solely for management and the information in them does not need to be quite so reliable as the information in financial accounting reports.

Tax accounting: a system for gathering, summarizing, and reporting economic information about a firm in compliance with the requirements imposed by taxing authorities. There are enough similarities between tax accounting and financial accounting to make knowledge of the latter essential to a full understanding of the former. But the reverse is not true; an understanding of tax accounting does not help in understanding financial accounting. Accordingly, the two kinds of accounting are best regarded as entirely separate things when financial accounting is being discussed. Tax accounting reports are prepared solely for use by taxing authorities.

Governmental (and other non-profit) accounting: systems for gathering, summarizing, and reporting economic information about governmental (and other non-profit) entities. The information is relevant to decisions made by individuals and groups who have the responsibility of supervising and controlling the activities of these entities. Since many of them are tax-supported, governmental accounting reports are often at least partly addressed to the general public. While there are similarities between financial and governmental accounting, a knowledge of governmental accounting is not helpful to understanding financial accounting. Governmental accounting is therefore not discussed in this book.

Kinds of Accountants

Our discussion of the different kinds of accounting leads naturally to a discussion of different kinds of *accountants*. Like most professional men, accountants tend to specialize. Some accountants are primarily concerned with keeping financial records, others with cost accounting, planning and budgeting, or other aspects of managerial accounting. Governmental and nonprofit entities have their own accountants specializing in their particular problems. Other accountants become experts in taxation.

Bookkeepers and clerks

In addition, most companies (and other economic entities) hire various bookkeepers, clerks, office machine operators, file girls, and others to support and do detail work for the accountant. These people are indispensable. They often call themselves accountants.

It is hard to draw a dividing line between the accountant and the bookkeepers and other individuals who assist him. One indication may be that the accountant should have enough training and experience to develop new accounting practices for the company to use in coping with new circumstances. This definition would categorize the bookkeepers and other clerical workers as technicians who follow the systems designed by the accountant, rather than as innovators. However you define it, the point remains that most people in an accounting department spend most of their time just following instructions. When this book refers to "accountants," it is talking about the people who give the instructions.

Public accountants

Surprisingly enough, the accounting profession in this country is most deeply influenced by a group we haven't even discussed yet: the public accountants. A *public accountant* is an independent professional accountant whose job is to examine and comment upon the financial accounting reports prepared by a given company. This work is called *auditing*. To repeat, the public accountant is an *independent* accountant, and *he does not work as an employee of the company he audits*.

Being independent is tremendously important to the public accountant. His examination of and comments on financial accounting reports must be accepted by the general business community—otherwise there is little point to them. For his comments to be accepted, it must be clear that the public accountant is being entirely impartial; he must avoid anything that might suggest a conflict of interest or other source of bias in his reports.

Accordingly, public accountants scrupulously avoid investing in the firms that they audit, participating in their management, or doing anything else they believe might be interpreted as threatening their independence. (Sometimes a fine line must be walked in these matters; for example, it is part of the public accountant's job to *advise* management in certain business matters, yet he must be careful not to go one step too far and inadvertently become one of the group that makes basic decisions for the firm. If he were to do the latter he would thereafter be commenting upon the results of his own work when he audited the firm's financial accounting reports—a conflict of interest.)

The company has the right to decide whether or not to obtain the public account-ant's services. Most large firms (and many smaller firms) are required to be audited; but such firms have the right to decide *which* public accountant they will hire, to select one whom they expect will perform a satisfactory audit, etc. But, once the company hires him, the public accountant has the sole responsibility for deciding how he shall perform his work. (Much the same is true with doctors; the doctor is an independent professional man who assumes the sole responsibility for determining how to treat you. Of course, you may go to the doctor of your choice.) Public accountants are often referred to as *auditors*. This is proper language, but we will see that some auditors are not public accountants, because they are the employees of the firms that obtain their services.

What the public accountant does—and doesn't do

When we discussed financial accounting, we stressed the importance of reliability. The public accountant's main job is to further the reliability of financial accounting reports by subjecting the information they contain to independent testing. Financial accounting reports are prepared by the company's own financial accountants from the company's own records. The public accountant examines these financial reports and the underlying records in an attempt to determine whether the reported information is sufficiently complete, supported by evidence, and prepared according to good accounting practices. As part of this investigation, the public accountant also makes extensive tests designed to detect possible theft or fraud by the company's employees. But his main job is not theft detection. Instead, it is to make sure that the financial reports given investors meet certain minimum standards of evidence and propriety— and that the company has not changed its reporting system significantly since its previous reports. If he can say this, the public accountant usually renders a formal opinion on these financial reports, saying in effect:

> "I have examined the financial reports of this company, following standard, well-established techniques for performing this kind of examination.
>
> "Given what is generally regarded as acceptable accounting practice, in my opinion the financial reports do a proper job of presenting the company's present situation and the results of its activities during the period under consideration. Moreover, the accounting methods employed are consistent with those used in the company's previous reports."[7]

---

[7] Of course, like other professional men, public accountants prefer to use more technical language than this. On the next page is the public accountant's evaluation accompanying the 1970 financial reports of the company that published this book. Note that despite the formal language, this opinion says exactly those things that appear in the above paraphrase.

Notice that the public accountant does not say that the financial reports are *true*. He says that he has performed a standard investigation, and that he has not uncovered anything that looks improper when compared with what is ordinarily considered good accounting practice. (Of course he *also* says that he has found evidence that supports the matters disclosed in the financial reports.) The public accountant *is* saying that the reports meet minimum standards. From the standpoint of anyone concerned with the reliability of the reports, this is saying a lot.

On those relatively rare occasions where the public accountant cannot render his usual opinion that the reports meet minimum standards, investors are often thoroughly disturbed, and management's reputation may suffer severely. Since the public accountant has a good deal of say in deciding what minimum standards shall be, public accountants as a group have become very influential in financial accounting.

Who determines accounting standards?

The public accountant does not completely dominate decisions on what constitutes acceptable accounting practice. While he has the power to render an unfavorable opinion on the financial reports, the company has the power to discharge him and hire another public accountant if he seems too unreasonable. The result is that financial accounting standards have developed over the years by what amounts to negotiation. Often these standards represent compromises between the wishes of the public accountants and their client companies. This problem is examined in more detail in later chapters. Two things are particularly worth noting about these compromise rules.

1. Public accountants have succeeded in getting companies to agree that anything appearing in the audited financial reports should be capable of being examined and verified by public accountants. This seems natural enough. But it is one big reason why financial accounting leans so heavily towards historical information (see page 25). It is impossible to verify anything that has yet to occur. Conclusive evidence exists only about the past and the present. When companies agree to restrict financial reports to audited information, they agree in effect to hold estimates to a minimum, especially estimates about the future.

Those companies that want to tell investors things that the public accountant

---

ACCOUNTANTS' OPINION

TO SHAREHOLDERS AND BOARD OF DIRECTORS OF WADSWORTH PUBLISHING COMPANY, INC.:

We have examined the consolidated balance sheets of Wadsworth Publishing Company, Inc. and subsidiaries as of December 31, 1970 and 1969 and the related statements of consolidated income and retained earnings and consolidated sources and applications of funds for the years then ended. Our examination was made in accordance with generally accepted auditing standards, and accordingly included such tests of the accounting records and such other auditing procedures as we considered necessary in the circumstances.

In our opinion, the accompanying consolidated financial statements present fairly the financial position of Wadsworth Publishing Company, Inc. and subsidiaries at December 31, 1970 and 1969 and the results of their operations and the sources and applications of their funds for the years then ended, in conformity with generally accepted accounting principles applied on a consistent basis.

San Francisco, February 26, 1971   HASKINS & SELLS

cannot verify use some form of supplementary disclosure. Such a supplementary disclosure does not form part of the financial accounting reports. Its reliability is not attested to by the public accountant. Often this kind of unaudited supplementary information is contained in a letter, which accompanies the financial accounting report, from the president of the company to the stockholders.

2. On the other hand, the business community has persuaded the public accounting profession to allow a good deal of latitude in "acceptable" accounting practice. One reason companies desire this kind of elbowroom is that accounting needs to be flexible enough to reflect the differing circumstances of individual companies. No one system of accounting is expected to be equally appropriate for all companies. In addition, often there will be no conclusive way to choose among different accounting practices, which result in differing figures in the accounting reports. This problem (which will be discussed in Chapters Six, Eight, and Thirteen) arises whenever individuals who are affected by these reports have conflicting purposes that lead them to prefer conflicting figures.

In the first part of this book, for simplicity, we will act as though accountants and companies had agreed on uniform ways to report things. Later we must face facts. In many important instances, accounting rules allow a company considerable latitude in its financial accounting practices.

Certified Public Accountants

The most important group of public accountants is that of the certified public accountants, or CPAs. The title of CPA is given to a public accountant by the particular state in which he works. There is a good deal of difference in what different states require, but some generalizations can be made.

States are increasingly requiring all prospective CPAs to have college degrees with formal training in accounting and business subjects. Usually they require the prospective CPA to put in a period of apprenticeship with a firm of CPAs: two years is a usual period. Regardless of the state he lives in, every prospective CPA must pass a comprehensive, nation-wide examination in accounting and related matters. In addition, some states require the prospective CPA to take specific, state-wide examinations. The nation-wide examination is usually referred to as *the* CPA exam. It is offered every May and November, takes $2\frac{1}{2}$ days, and is quite demanding.

Other kinds of auditors

Most states allow other public accountants to practice even if they have not met some of the requirements for the CPA. These auditors are often simply called *public accountants*. Frequently, the only restriction on their activities is that they cannot call themselves certified public accountants. CPAs receive a title—and usually a license—from their state. This provides a formal recognition of their competence that public accountants do not receive. Because of this, CPAs are more respected and influential than other public accountants.

Finally, in contrast to public accountants, there is another group of auditors with which you should be familiar—*internal auditors*. Public accountants are independent auditors who come in from the outside to examine the firm's records. Internal auditors are employees of the firms that they audit, and they are not independent. Instead of investigating the fairness and consistency of the firm's financial accounting reports and their conformity with accepted accounting rules, the main duties of internal auditors involve investigation into the various operations of the company in order to determine (1) whether the individual departments (or other subdivisions) of the firm are adhering to the policies that have been set by management, (2) whether the systems for providing accounting information to management and outsiders are working effectively and efficiently, and (3) whether management's system of control for safeguarding the firm's resources and preventing fraud is working effectively and efficiently. In performing these duties, internal auditors examine the firm's records. But internal auditors do *not* express a formal opinion to the public concerning the financial accounting reports prepared by the company.

The work performed by internal auditors is known, simply enough, as *internal auditing*. Many internal auditors are former public accountants.

Other work done by CPAs

Many public accountants eventually decide to go to work for a single company, often a former client. Accountants who now specialize in managerial or governmental accounting, tax work, general financial accounting, or internal auditing are often former public accountants who are still CPAs. Other CPAs (this author, for example) go into teaching. Another reason why CPAs have great influence over accounting is that CPAs occupy many of the highest positions in the field of accounting. For that matter, more and more CPAs are rising to high positions in general company management. Increasingly, company officers and even company presidents are being drawn from the ranks of CPAs.

The CPAs themselves have expanded their own services to cover a number of things other than auditing: tax advice, development and installation of data-processing systems, and various kinds of management-consulting work. Nowadays the large CPA firm is likely to hire mathematicians, engineers, and a variety of other specialists to help the auditor provide management some of these extra, nonauditing services.

Accounting organizations and publications

The several kinds of accountants have formed several different national organizations, each of which does research and each of which tries to further the professional development of its members. A few of the more important organizations are discussed below.

The CPAs have formed the American Institute of Certified Public Accountants and numerous state CPA societies. The AICPA, as it is usually abbreviated, sponsors research into major accounting and auditing problems and has published many useful studies. The AICPA also publishes *The Journal of Accountancy,* a monthly magazine directed mainly to CPAs. An agency of the AICPA called the *Accounting Principles Board* expresses influential opinions on matters relating to good financial accounting practice. These opinions are authoritative enough that CPAs are required to indicate within their reports when a company's practices violate the Accounting Principles Board recommendations. In future years the Accounting Principles Board may become increasingly important in setting financial accounting standards. So far it has acted cautiously. We will discuss several authoritative opinions of the Accounting Principles Board in later chapters.

The university teachers of accounting have formed the American Accounting Association. The AAA sponsors research and publishes a quarterly journal, *The Accounting Review*. This group is more concerned with theory and the general long-run development of accounting than with the details of day-to-day practice. Although accounting teachers have less direct influence on the profession than do CPAs, teaching has attracted some outstanding accountants, and some accounting teachers have played a great role in the development of the profession. Individual universities publish occasional books and monographs on accounting theory. Two important theoretical journals, *Journal of Accounting Research* and *Abacus*, are published entirely under university sponsorship.

Managerial accountants have formed the National Association of Accountants, which publishes *Management Accounting* and many individual research studies. There are also flourishing organizations of tax accountants, internal auditors, government accountants, and CPAs specializing in management-consulting work. Each specialization within accounting has developed its own organization and its own publications. Those named here only begin to tell the story.

Why Study Financial Accounting?

The need for financial accounting information
Most readers of this book are not going to end up becoming accountants of any kind. Why, then, study financial accounting—except that you may be required to by your school? Naturally, no author would dare ask a question like this unless he has some fairly persuasive answers. Some of these answers should already be clear to you. Financial accounting provides one of the main sources of economic information about individual companies, and the only major source that has been tested for reliability by an independent outside investigator. If you are going to invest in a company—or even if you are considering becoming an employee of such a company—you need this information.

Anyone concerned with the social sciences needs to understand accounting: the sociologist, the economist, the student of commerce, the behavioral scientist. Financial accounting reports offer one of the major sources of economic information used in the social sciences.

Finally, should you ever become part of a company's management yourself, you will have accountants working for you and with you. In dealing with specialists, it is always important to know enough about their specialty so that you can talk with them in an intelligent way and get the maximum use from them. If you don't understand what they are doing, there's always the danger of ending up at the mercy of your experts.

The need for training
To use financial accounting reports effectively, *you must understand them*. This takes study. We have seen that there are at least two things about financial accounting reports that make them difficult for the untrained reader to understand.

1. There are limits to the information that is allowed to appear in these reports. We will see later on that this sometimes makes the accountant *seem* to be discussing things that actually he is not talking about at all.

2. There are many instances in which financial reports can be prepared in any one of several acceptable ways. The reader of these reports needs to know the range of choice and the results of any one choice.

There are many other barriers to understanding financial accounting reports that we will discuss as we go along. As an investor, manager, or social scientist, studying accounting is the way you learn to handle a great body of valuable information that you would otherwise be confused by and have trouble employing. You study accounting so that you can intelligently use a powerful tool: financial accounting reports. You don't have to become an accountant to do this. But you do have to learn quite a lot about accountants and what they are trying to accomplish.

Intellectual reasons

Learning to understand financial accounting reports is not the only reason for studying accounting. You can study accounting in much the same spirit as you might study history, music, chemistry, or any other academic subject. Accounting is part of your intellectual environment. It is a complicated and interesting part of human behavior. To some of us, parts of accounting are strangely beautiful. Though accounting has its roots in practicality, you can get interested in it for all sorts of impractical, intellectual reasons.

But there may be an even deeper reason for studying financial accounting. We live in an economic system characterized by enormous accumulations of power centered in large individual corporations. Many American corporations possess greater economic power than some of the members of the United Nations. Any society must develop ways both to control power and to make its exercise acceptable to the public as a whole. One major way this is done in the United States is by publicity. Much public control over large corporations comes about because these companies are required to operate out in the open where people can see what they are doing. Much of the public's acceptance of these vast concentrations of power comes from a feeling that the large corporations have to operate in a sort of goldfish bowl. Publicity has succeeded in the past in keeping corporate behavior fairly close to the public interest.

Financial accounting plays a major part in this publicity. It is the main source of independently tested economic information concerning powerful corporations available to the public. Whatever its limitations, financial accounting is part of the cement that holds our society together. As an educated person, you should be familiar with it.

A Fundamental Concept: The Asset

One of the most fundamental notions in financial accounting is that of an *asset*. We'll spend a lot of time with assets before going on to anything else. A number of important ideas can be introduced this way without unnecessary complication. Later on we can use these ideas to discuss more difficult matters.

The ordinary meaning of "asset"

As you study accounting, you'll find that many of the concepts used by accountants resemble concepts in day-to-day life, without being quite the same. This can confuse you unless you're aware of the differences between what the accountant means by a particular word and what you and I might mean by that word in ordinary conversation. "Asset" is a good example.

"Good health is one's greatest *asset*."

"Poor Sally, her only *asset* is her personality."

"You're an *asset* to the company, Parker; I don't know what we'd do without you!"

In each of these sentences, the word "asset" conveys a general flavor of something good or useful, something from which one can benefit. Also, either the asset or its services can be possessed. The asset belongs to the entity it benefits or, in the case of Parker, the entity has the right to receive its services.

The financial accountant's notion of asset fits within this broad description, but is a great deal narrower. In fact, none of the three examples given satisfies the accountant's idea of asset. Health, Sally's personality, Parker's services—not one of these is an accounting asset.

The economist's notion of a "good"

I pointed out earlier that financial accounting involves the gathering, analyzing, and reporting of economic information. Economists have a concept that is similar to the ordinary idea of asset—a concept that helps bridge the gap between ordinary speech and the accountant's specialized meaning. Economists speak of *goods*.

In its most general sense, a "good" is *anything* wanted or desired by someone, or capable of satisfying someone's wants. Bread is a good; so is air. Many people like cats, so cats are goods. Sunny weather is a good; so are honesty, a mother's sacrifices, the United Nations, an understanding of financial accounting, a view of distant mountains, and a shrimp pizza. People want all these things.

The economist usually narrows this notion of goods by restricting his discussion to *economic goods*. Economic goods are goods that are bought and sold in a market—goods that command a *price*. To command a price, they must be *scarce*—any good that is freely available to everyone is not an economic good. Air, sunlight, and the commoner sorts of cats are examples of goods that are not economic goods.

The accountant's notion of an "asset"

The financial accountant's notion of an "asset" narrows the theoretical concept of an economic good down several stages, making it something that can be used for practical purposes and that the accountant believes is consistent with the needs of his readers. The following definition applies in most cases, though, as we shall see, there are exceptions:

An *asset* is an economic good reported by the financial accountant. To be reported it must offer future economic benefits to the firm under consideration and have the following additional characteristics. It must be either:

1. A *monetary asset*: cash or a legally enforceable right to receive a specific amount of cash at a specific date, or
2. A *nonmonetary asset*: a good (not a monetary asset) for which each of the following can be determined
   (a) the historical purchase price incurred by the firm to acquire the good,
   (b) the benefits provided the firm by the good (as distinguished from those benefits provided by other goods),
   (c) the total of such benefits that the good will provide to the firm, and
   (d) the total of such benefits that have been received by the firm up to any given date
   —and for which any estimates required can be made in a manner the accountant regards as sufficiently reliable (allowing greater latitude in cases where information about the good is considered essential for investor uses or is required by law, custom, etc.).

This is a very complicated definition; unfortunately, it takes something this complicated to reflect actual accounting practice. In the next few pages I will explain what is involved in this definition and some of the reasons why accountants employ it.[8] Our previous discussion has pointed out the following characteristics of financial accounting:

1. It is designed to report on specific individual firms (or other individual economic entities).

2. It is concerned with reporting economic information to investors, who use this information to make predictions about the future activities and characteristics of the firm.

3. On the one hand, financial accountants wish to report whatever information investors appear to need; but, on the other hand, financial accountants want to provide information that is as objective and reliable as possible.

These characteristics serve as constraints that determine how the financial accountant adapts both the meaning of an economic good and the ordinary broad meaning of an asset to fit what he perceives to be the purposes of his readers. An asset is an economic good that the accountant has decided to report to investors; often the decision to report a good is designated the accountant's "recognizing" the good as an asset, and one speaks of this as *asset recognition*. An economic good will be recognized as an asset if it possesses the necessary characteristics.

First, and most important of all, it must offer future economic benefits to the firm. We have seen that a "good" is anything that is desired by someone. Since financial accounting is concerned with reporting economic information, these goods should be ones desired for economic reasons—desired because they offer economic

---

[8] Readers who have previous familiarity with accounting may at first find this definition of an asset strange; however, by the end of the following discussion they should agree that this definition corresponds well to actual practice. I anticipate that my discussion of the reasons behind this definition may prove to be a bit more controversial. If the reader is troubled by anything that I say, I hope he will reserve judgment until he has read the more detailed discussions of these matters in Chapters Six, Eight, and Thirteen. In any event, though, the following description of accounting practice is conventional, even if the explanations given are somewhat unorthodox.

benefits. Since financial accounting is designed to report on individual firms, these goods should be ones whose economic benefits will be received by the specific firm for which the financial accounting report is being prepared. Since investors use financial accounting reports to make predictions, these goods should be ones which offer *future* economic benefits to the firm.

In addition to being goods, assets are *economic* goods—ones that are bought and sold in some kind of market.[9] This means that there must be a market price for any good reported as an asset. Conceivably, the accountant might report assets in terms of their weights, temperatures, acquisition dates, or other characteristics. But since his report is concerned with economic information it is natural for him to report these economic goods at their market prices. Unfortunately, any individual economic good may have several different market prices; the accountant must choose one to report.

Monetary versus nonmonetary assets

The market price reported depends in part on the good involved. A distinction—which turns out to be very important—must be made between *monetary* and *nonmonetary* goods.

A *monetary* good, as the name suggests, is either money (cash) or a right to receive cash, such as a debt owed the firm by some individual or some other business. Since financial accountants want to report reliable, economically significant information, a right to receive cash must be clear-cut before it is recognized as an asset. Usually it must be a legally enforceable right to receive a specific amount of cash at a specific time.

The market price chosen to represent a monetary asset is either its amount (in the case of cash itself), the magnitude of the right to receive cash (that is, the amount of cash owed), or that magnitude reduced by interest charges that pertain to the period between the date of the accountant's report and the date that the debt becomes due. (The latter possibility will be examined later when we discuss *accrual* of claims; for the present it may be ignored.)

Not all goods are monetary. For example, inventories, equipment, and buildings are economic goods, even though they neither are cash nor rights to receive a definite amount of cash at a definite time. Any goods that are not monetary are called, simply enough, *nonmonetary* goods.

Many different market prices might be used to represent nonmonetary goods: their historical costs to the firm, what the firm could sell them for now or in the future, and so on. Since financial accountants want to report information that is as reliable and objective as possible, they choose what they consider to be the most reliable and objective kind of market price. For the reasons indicated on pages 25 and 34, this usually will be the historical costs to the firm of the nonmonetary goods.[10] (Exceptions

---

[9] Ordinary rain water is an example of a good that is not an economic good and would not be reported as an asset; in contrast, tap water is an economic good.

[10] Later I will contend that historical costs are not always the most objective and reliable; I already have suggested that they are not necessarily the most relevant. But most accountants believe otherwise, and I am trying here to describe actual accounting practices.

to this will be discussed in a later chapter, when the accountant's rule of *conservatism* is examined, but that may also be ignored for the present.) As is emphasized in Chapter Three, an important consequence of this use of historical market prices to represent nonmonetary goods is that financial accounting does not report the current worth of these goods.

Unless the accountant can determine the historical cost of a nonmonetary good (from documentary evidence and/or by making a reliable estimate), he will be extremely reluctant to recognize the good as an asset. In fact, he will refuse to do so unless asset recognition is required for institutional purposes or he is convinced that the related information is so important for investor predictions (or other reader uses) that reporting unreliable information is preferable to reporting no information about the good at all. Gift assets provide an example of this situation; they have no historical cost to the firm, yet they are reported at estimated costs if knowledge about the related goods is deemed significant.

Ordinarily, though, if the historical cost to the firm of a good cannot be determined, the accountant will not report that good as an asset of the firm. An important consequence of this is that ordinarily a good will not be recognized as an asset unless the firm has purchased it and the amount paid or to be paid for the specific good can be distinguished from the amounts paid or to be paid for other goods that were purchased by the firm. For example, a firm's reputation among its customers may be one of its most valuable goods. Yet ordinarily either it has not paid for this good or there is no reliable way to determine what additional costs (over and above its ordinary costs of doing business) the firm has incurred to acquire a favorable reputation; therefore this good is not reported as an asset. In contrast, if one firm buys up another and pays a premium price because the other firm enjoys a fine reputation, the historical cost to the buyer firm of this *other* company's reputation is determinable, and the related good may be recognized as an asset of the buyer firm (under the technical name *goodwill*).

Reductions in historical cost figures

We have seen that for a good to be an asset it must offer economic benefits to the firm. Since financial accounting is concerned with reporting economic information to investors who use this information to make predictions about future activities and characteristics of the firm, the economic benefits that the good offers must be *future* ones. He may have a sentimental fondness for a good that provided benefits in the past, but if it does not offer future economic benefits, the accountant will not report it as an asset. If, for instance, a firm stops manufacturing a particular product, any specialized machinery used for making that product will cease to be an asset unless it has an alternative use or scrap value.

Often, the economic benefits provided by a nonmonetary good are received gradually over a period of time. For example, a firm may receive the services of a particular building over a thirty-year period. As time passes and benefits are received, the amount of *remaining* benefits to be received in the future from the nonmonetary good will decline. Since the accountant represents the good by its historical cost to the firm, he believes that it is appropriate to reflect this decline in remaining future benefits *by a proportionate reduction in the historical cost figure used to represent the good.*

For example, if the building cost $300,000, was estimated to be useful to the firm for a total of 30 years and valueless thereafter, and was at present eight years old, the accountant might reason that only 22/30ths of its original future benefits remained (30 − 8 = 22), and that it should be reported at the amount $300,000 × 22/30 = $220,000. We will pay much more attention to this kind of calculation in later chapters. Meanwhile, though, notice that if the future economic benefits to be provided by the nonmonetary asset decline with time, the accountant does at least three things:

1. He distinguishes the economic benefits to be received from that good from those that are received from all other goods used by the firm.

2. He estimates the total benefits that will be received from the good.

3. He estimates (or otherwise determines) the amount of these benefits the firm has received to date and adjusts the good's original historical market price proportionately.

In later chapters we will see that at this point arises one of the most serious dilemmas facing financial accounting theory. These three steps require the making of numerous estimates, and it is very difficult to make these estimates in a reliable way. First, estimates of the total benefits to be received from a good are inherently uncertain. Second (as will be argued later), the distinction between the economic benefits provided by one good and those provided by the firm's other goods is inherently ambiguous. As a result, if individuals disagree over how the original historical market price should be adjusted, there usually will be no conclusive way to decide who is right. Such disagreements are common, and any adjustment that is made will be subjective and arbitrary from the standpoint of anyone who might prefer a different adjustment.

The accountant might reflect his preference for reporting only objective, reliable information by refusing to adjust the historical costs of nonmonetary goods for estimated declines in future benefits—just as he refuses to report a firm's good reputation as an asset because of estimation difficulties. But whether they are right or wrong, accountants believe that such adjustments provide information that is very important to investors—so important that subjective and arbitrary information seems preferable to no information at all. Also, there are strong institutional requirements for such data.

Accordingly, to use the previous example, no matter how unreliable the $220,000 figure for the building may be, to him it is preferable to the unadjusted $300,000 historical purchase price. Use of the latter implies that there has been no decline at all in the future benefits to be received from the building; reporting the $220,000 figure at least *approximates* this decline.

As was emphasized on pages 5–6, all models distort, and the economic model of the firm provided by financial accounting is no exception to this rule. Accountants can minimize unreliability in their models, but they cannot eliminate it entirely. We have just seen a good illustration of this: not reporting something that has happened may result in even more distortion than would a subjective, arbitrary estimate. The accountant's decision in such matters depends in part on how important he thinks the information is to the investor. This opinion is based on experience—there are no simple rules here—and has evolved out of a long process of trial and error. Because financial accounting practices have their origins in empirical observation rather than in theory, it often happens that the accountant believes he knows what kinds of information investors find essential without knowing *why* this is so. In these cases, all the author of a textbook can do is to report that accountants believe that it is essential for investors to be informed about a good's declining future benefits while, in contrast, they do not believe it is essential to inform investors about that good's current market price. One can describe the accountant's behavior, but may not be able to defend it to someone who does not have the accountant's background experience.[11] In any event, considerable time will be devoted to both of these decisions in later chapters, as well as to other examples in which accountants are willing to violate their usual rules and make estimates.

Meanwhile, one final point should be made: the accountant is reluctant to recognize a nonmonetary good as an asset even if he can determine its historical cost unless he has some way to adjust that cost for estimated declining future benefits. With goods such as buildings he has developed several agreed-upon ways for doing this (which will be discussed in Chapter Thirteen). Although I will contend that these methods are little more than arbitrary conventions, they are satisfactory for institutional purposes and are accepted by accountants. With other goods, no such conventions have been developed, and accountants are reluctant to recognize them as assets. For example, a firm's research and development efforts offer future economic benefits, and the costs of these efforts may be reliably determined. But the total amount of future economic benefits involved often cannot be estimated, at least not reliably. Accordingly, any decline in these future economic benefits cannot be reliably compared with the total amount in order to adjust the costs of these goods proportionately to that decline; therefore, many accountants refuse to recognize an asset as the result of research and development activities. Other examples of this kind of situation are discussed later in this chapter.

Summary

It now is appropriate to repeat the earlier definition of an *asset*:

> An asset is an economic good reported by the financial accountant. To be reported it must offer future economic benefits to the firm under consideration and have the following additional characteristics. It must be either:
> 1. A monetary asset: cash or a legally enforceable right to receive a specific amount of cash at a specific date, or
> 2. A nonmonetary asset: a good (not a monetary asset) for which each of the following can be determined
>   (a) the historical purchase price incurred by the firm to acquire the good,
>   (b) the benefits provided the firm by the good (as distinguished from those benefits provided by other goods),

---

[11] It happens that in later chapters I will express grave reservations about these two decisions. But even if I agreed with them fully, the issues involved cannot at present be resolved by theory. This will be demonstrated later, too.

(c) the total of such benefits that the good will provide to the firm, and

(d) the total of such benefits that have been received by the firm up to any given date

—and for which any estimates required can be made in a manner the accountant regards as sufficiently reliable (allowing greater latitude in cases where information about the good is considered essential for investor uses or is required by law, custom, or for other institutional purposes).

The concept of an asset is the single most important concept in accounting. We will often refer back to the ideas and limitations embodied in this definition. Its monetary/nonmonetary distinction is one that is not often made either in elementary accounting textbooks or in actual financial accounting reports. It is made here for two reasons: it permits a simple, yet accurate description of the ways in which the accountant obtains the figures he reports for assets (he employs two rules—one for monetary assets and the other for nonmonetary assets). Also, use of this distinction allows a unified treatment of many controversies concerning the amounts reported in financial statements. Because of this, the monetary/nonmonetary distinction is one of the more fundamental ones in financial accounting.

The asset definition diagrammed

If you have had any difficulties with the accountant's definition of an asset, a diagram might be useful to you here. (If you have not had any difficulties, feel free to move on to the next subsection.) Shown below are a series of yes/no questions that embody the definition of an asset given above. Each answer leads either to a result (such as "The accountant does not recognize an asset" or "The good is reported as a monetary asset") or to another question. Answer the successive questions, following the arrow labeled with your answer, until a box is reached; at that point you learn whether the thing in question is an asset and, if it is an asset, whether it is monetary or nonmonetary.

This kind of diagram often is called a *flow chart*. A flow chart is merely a way of giving directions or other information in a highly systematic manner, as you would to a computer. As an illustration, the series of questions and answers relating to a particular good (the cumulative effects of a firm's advertising on its customers and potential customers), has been indicated with double lines. A firm knows what these campaigns cost and often knows that it will receive some future benefits from a completed campaign in addition to the benefits received during the actual campaign itself. But it does not know how great these benefits will be, there are no institutional pressures requiring recognition of an asset here, and the accountant does not believe that this kind of information is essential to his readers. Accordingly, he does not recognize an asset for this good.

Gift assets

Gift assets create a special problem for accountants; fortunately corporations only rarely receive significant gifts—the most common instance occurs when a local governmental body donates land or a building to a firm to induce it to locate in that area.

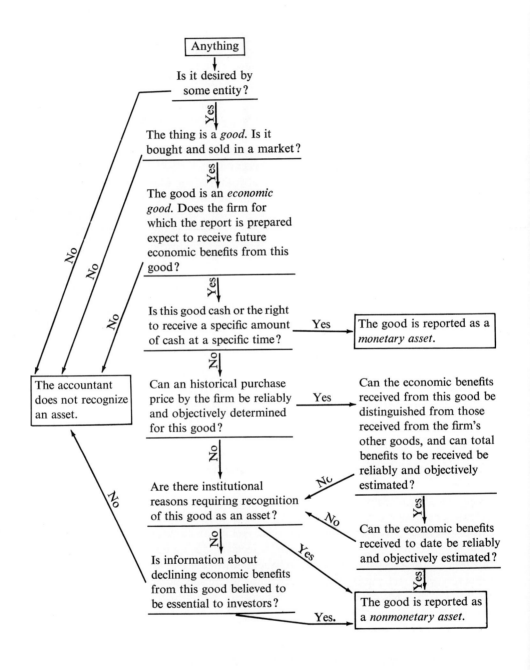

Since the firm did not incur a purchase price for the gift asset, the accountant must either ignore it in his reports or else make some estimate of what the asset would have cost if the firm *had* purchased it. Neither treatment is entirely satisfactory. Ignoring the existence of the asset results in omission of what may be significant information to investors; but estimated purchase prices are subjective and unreliable. As indicated earlier, the accountant acts to minimize distortion—and with gift assets he believes that less distortion is created by estimating a purchase price than by pretending that the asset doesn't exist.

There are other instances in which no historical purchase price is available, and the accountant feels he must make estimates. For example, sometimes a company swaps one asset for another or acquires an asset by issuing additional shares of its own capital stock. In such cases the accountant obtains his figure for the new asset in terms of either (1) some estimate of the market price of the asset acquired, or (2) some estimate of the market price of the asset (or shares of capital stock) given up.

Which possibility he chooses depends upon which alternative impresses him as the *more* objective and reliable. Of course he may consider both alternatives so unreliable that distortion would be best minimized by reporting nothing at all. (We will see examples of such situations shortly.) It is also possible that both estimates might give equally reliable-seeming results, in which case the accountant might "split the difference" by reporting their average. The important thing to recognize here is that the accountant acts to minimize unreliability, not to eliminate it. Obviously, this effort requires judgment. Many disputes in accounting theory are the result of differing opinions about how to minimize distortion in accounting reports.

Goods that don't satisfy this definition

Turn back now to the three examples on page 39 of the ways the word *asset* is used in ordinary conversation. None of these involve either cash or an enforceable right to receive a specific amount of cash at a specific time; so, they are not monetary assets. But they aren't really nonmonetary assets, either.

Consider health and personality first. Of course, these are the personal goods of individuals, and therefore do not fit our definition of assets (which is oriented to the goods of corporations). But corporations do purchase similar goods: for instance, it is common for corporations to pay for part or all of the health care of their executives and, occasionally, to pay for courses designed to improve their executives' personalities (though such courses usually employ euphemisms to describe what they are attempting to do). The costs of such programs can be determined reliably and objectively, and they often provide future economic benefits to the firm. The difficulty is that the extent of these benefits cannot be estimated reliably; additionally, there is no reliable way to calculate how these costs should be proportionately reduced as the executives age and future benefits gradually decline. Accordingly, such goods usually are not reported as assets. Certainly the original health and personality the executives brought with them to the firm would not be recognized as assets—the firm hasn't paid for these (or else any salary premiums paid for superior health and personality can't be estimated reliably).

These have been good examples of something that was emphasized earlier. The accountant tries to maximize the objectivity and reliability of his reports. He cannot escape some kind of distortion. As data become progressively more and more depend-ent on subjective estimates and interpretation, a point eventually is reached where the accountant feels that less distortion would result from ignoring a good than from trying to report a figure for it. With personality and health, almost everything is a matter of interpretation and estimate. The accountant believes that he can do a better job here by saying nothing at all.

Purchases of services

Now, consider Mr. Parker as "an asset to the company." The man himself cannot be an asset, since the firm did not incur any purchase price to acquire him. Instead, the firm purchased Mr. Parker's *services*. But this purchase of services may result in the firm's acquiring an asset; this could occur in either of two ways, both of which turn out to be important in our later discussions.

For greater clarity, though, let's begin with a case in which an asset *doesn't* result from the purchase of Mr. Parker's services. Suppose that he is a janitor. Ordinarily once his services have been rendered, they immediately expire or, at best, they expire within a day in the sense that thereafter they offer no identifiable future economic benefits to the firm. Therefore there is no asset, though Mr. Parker will keep on providing *new* services every working day.

Now, let's contrast a different case. Suppose instead that Mr. Parker is a carpenter employed by the firm, and that for the past several weeks he has been building shelves for the company. These shelves offer future economic benefits. The firm can estimate what they cost, and shelves are a kind of asset for which accountants have agreed-upon methods for reducing an historical cost in proportion to estimated declines in remaining future benefits. Accordingly, in this case the accountant would recognize an asset. But notice two things:

1. The asset that is recognized would be shelves, not Mr. Parker nor Mr. Parker's services—although part of the historical cost of these shelves would be the cost of obtaining Mr. Parker's services. Similarly, if the company were a manufacturer and Mr. Parker had helped manufacture one of the firm's products, the cost of his services would become part of the cost of the resulting inventory of manufactured product. This will be quite significant when we discuss accounting for manufacturers in Chapter Twelve.

2. If Mr. Parker had not made something—something one could point to or touch—it would be much harder for the accountant to decide whether Mr. Parker's services really did have some remaining capacity to benefit the firm and how much of these services offered future benefits. Unless the accountant has some way of deciding this, he usually prefers not to make guesses and will refuse to recognize an asset. (This is another instance where he uses judgment, and where his decision is open to dispute.)

At this point you might ask: If the accountant doesn't recognize an asset, what happens to the services? The answer is that the accountant recognizes an expense instead. The reason for this relates to his concept of the nature of income. The accountant's income concept is complicated. As pointed out in the previous chapter, any discussion of income should be deferred until we've studied the simpler notions from which it is constructed. The accountant's general income model, including what he means by expenses, is summarized at the beginning of the next chapter, but it is not discussed in detail until Chapter Eight. However, here is a brief, simplified sketch. If what follows does not seem entirely clear, don't worry; you really need not understand these matters yet, and they will be explained in detail when understanding them *is* important.

To an accountant, a *revenue* is an increase in assets resulting from a sale of whatever product or service the company is "in business" to sell. If a furniture store sells a chair for $150, cash, it has had a $150 revenue. An *expense* is a decrease in assets resulting from a revenue. If the chair cost the furniture store $80, then by giving the chair up in the sale the company had an $80 expense. (The *cost* of the chair to the company is simply whatever the company had to pay to obtain that chair in a condition suitable for it to be sold.) If a salesman were paid a 10 percent commission on the sale, this would result in another $15 expense. (The decision to treat both of these costs of sales in the same way is discussed on pages 391–394.) The difference between the total of all revenues and all expenses for a period of time is an entity's *net income* for that period.

For the present we will avoid using the terms *revenue, expense,* and *net income,* and instead speak of *profits and losses*—terms you may interpret as meaning what they mean in ordinary conversation: a firm's *profit* is the difference between the amount for which it sells its goods and services to its customers and the costs of providing these goods and services; *losses* are negative profits. As you will see later, the accountant gives somewhat special meanings to the words that he uses; it would only confuse matters if we employed this technical accounting language now.

Let's return to the earlier question: If the accountant doesn't recognize the existence of an asset, what happens to the services? Presumably the firm either receives the services or not, regardless of what the accountant does. But if the accountant doesn't recognize an asset, the *cost* of these services is charged against profits. A simplified example will illustrate this point.

Suppose that a firm is brought into being to exploit a patented industrial process. The firm charges other firms royalties for the use of this process. It has three assets: cash, royalties owed it by other firms, and the patent; it owes no debts itself. During the first year the owners do not receive any dividends. Total assets at the beginning of the year were $100,000; total assets at year end are $120,000; therefore, the firm's profits for the year totalled $20,000 ($120,000 − $100,000 = $20,000).

Suppose that one of the firm's end-of-year assets was a $4,000 debt for royalties owed it by another company and that this other company was in poor financial condition. If the accountant decided not to recognize this debt owed to the firm as an asset, total end-of-year assets would decline by $4,000 to $116,000; correspondingly, total profits for the year would decline by $4,000 to $16,000.

Notice from this that the amount of profits that a firm reports for a year depends simultaneously on at least two different things: what actually happens to the firm, and *what the accountant decides to record* as having happened. We will see that the accountant has considerable latitude in what he decides to record.

Rights to receive services

We can summarize the foregoing. Ordinarily, a firm will receive a great variety of services: telephone services, utilities services, and services of various kinds of employees, for example. All such services expire when they are received; no asset results from these goods unless something new is generated by these services—something that offers future economic benefits to the firm and satisfies the other requirements for being an asset.

This kind of situation must be carefully distinguished from one that it seems at first to resemble. We have been considering the accounting treatment given to services received by the firm. In contrast to purchasing the services themselves, the firm might instead purchase *the right to receive services.* Such a right to receive services will be an asset as long as the services are expected to be of economic benefit to the firm, the purchase price is known, and both the total amount and the receipt of services are readily determinable.

For example, suppose again that Mr. Parker is a janitor. His janitorial services themselves do not result in an asset. But if he earned $140 for a five-day week and was paid in advance, then at the beginning of each week the firm would have the right to receive a week's janitorial services from him, and this right would be a nonmonetary asset:

1. The good offers future economic benefits to the firm—although the janitorial services themselves are not an asset, they still are goods that *benefit* the firm.

2. The purchase price of this right is known: $140.

3. The total amount of benefits to be received can be determined readily: 5 days of janitorial services.

4. The total amount of benefits that have been received by any given date also can be determined readily.

Mr. Parker is earning $140 \div 5 = \$28$ per day. After one day, the firm has the right to only four more days of janitorial services and the amount at which its right to receive future services should be reported would be adjusted downward from $140 to $140 - \$28 = \$112$. At the end of the second day, the remaining right would be reported at $112 - \$28 = \$84$.[12]

All of this can be generalized. A service itself will not be an asset unless it results in something that offers future economic benefits to the firm—and in that case it is the resulting "something" that is the asset, not the service itself. But a right to receive services will be a nonmonetary asset—as long as it satisfies our other criteria.

As I will emphasize in later chapters, the accountant's concern with *any* nonmonetary asset is confined solely to its purchase price and to the economic benefits that it offers. This is a consequence of the accountant's confining himself to an economic model of the firm. For example, if the asset is a machine, the accountant, as an accountant, is not interested in its size, weight, aesthetic qualities, principles of operation, or the alloys out of which it is constructed, etc. His sole concern is its cost and the future benefits it offers. Since he has an identical attitude toward future services, we see that such a right is not merely a nonmonetary asset; it is a *typical* nonmonetary asset.

---

[12] The calculations made here correspond to the way in which such calculations are made in actual accounting practice and, hopefully, they will seem plausible to the reader at this point. In later chapters, however, I will contend that this is not necessarily the only plausible way to adjust the purchase price of the asset. For example, there is an implicit assumption in these calculations that Mr. Parker's services are of equal economic benefit during each day of the week; this assumption may not be correct. However, all such complications are saved for later chapters.

Illustrations

Before we are through, we will discuss assets in much more detail than this. Meanwhile, some illustrations are in order. Illustration 1–2 lists some goods that might be assets for a company. Illustration 1–3 lists some goods that would not be assets and indicates why they would not.

Illustration 1-2

Examples of Assets

	Monetary or Nonmonetary?
Cash	Monetary
Debts owed to the company	Monetary
Merchandise, stock in trade, things the company sells	Nonmonetary
Supplies: such as lightbulbs, accounting forms, sweeping compound, pencils, machine oil, ink	Nonmonetary
Prepaid rent	Nonmonetary*
Prepaid employee services	Nonmonetary*
Investment in bonds (long-term debt) of another company	Monetary
Land	Nonmonetary
Buildings	Nonmonetary
Machinery	Nonmonetary
Automobiles and trucks	Nonmonetary
Patents	Nonmonetary

* *The asset is a right, but it is a right to receive a kind of service, not a right to receive cash.*

Illustration 1-3

Examples of Goods That the Accountant
Would Not Recognize as Assets

Good	*Why not an asset*
The loyalty of company employees	There is no objective and reliable way to determine either how much this good cost or the extent of its future benefits.*
An efficient sales organization	Same as above.*
A specialized machine (which is in perfect operating condition) that can be used for no other purpose than manufacturing an illegal pesticide.	The machine offers no future economic benefits unless it has some kind of scrap value. (If it does have a scrap value it will be reported as an asset at that amount.)
Good luck in finding reliable suppliers	This was not purchased, so there is no purchase price and no objective way to determine any other figure to represent this good.*
A fine advertising slogan thought up by the wife of a company officer	Same as above.*
A favorable local tax climate	Same as above.*

* *In each case there are no institutional requirements for reporting the good as an asset, nor does the accountant believe that information about this good is sufficiently vital to investors to justify reporting unreliable data.*

Things that do not limit the concept of an asset

So far, our examples appear to have been of cash, claims to receive cash, and assets for which cash has been paid. Actually, though, cash payment is not necessary for accounting recognition of an asset. A *purchase* is necessary for nonmonetary assets, but that purchase need not be for cash: instead, the purchaser can buy on credit and pay later. A machine with a $5,000 purchase price is a $5,000 asset, whether the $5,000 was paid at the time of purchase or weeks (or months) afterward. (A possible exception to this is that if payment is greatly delayed, part of the total amount may be regarded as being for payment of interest.) A professional man's automobile is his asset even if he is still making payments on it.

This latter example leads to another point. Accountants often recognize a non-monetary asset in circumstances where the entity is not technically the legal owner of the good. Often a purchaser does not legally own an asset until he has paid for it; yet, as we have seen, the accountant does not consider cash payment necessary in recognizing an asset. In such cases the accountant elects to place economic substance before legal form: the most important characteristic of an asset is its provision of economic benefits to the entity; as long as the entity has an enforceable right to receive the economic benefits of a good, legal ownership is not required.

For example, in the eyes of the law, the real owner of an automobile purchased on an installment plan is often the creditor to whom the installments are being paid, rather than the person who possesses and drives the auto. The professional man making payments for his car may not be its legal owner until the last installment has been paid, but the accountant would consider the automobile the man's asset.[13]

The accountant's model of economic condition

The accountant ignores technicalities of legal ownership in these cases because they are not pertinent to his reports. As we saw on pages 4–6, the accountant tries to present a model of the firm's economic history and status. Crucial elements in this model are the economic services that the firm is entitled to receive. If the firm is receiving the economic benefits of a nonmonetary good, the accountant often believes that he can better reflect the firm's true economic condition by recognizing the good as an asset rather than by ignoring it, regardless of whether the company owns it. When legal technicalities seem to contradict economic realities, the accountant often conforms his report to his own perception of the firm's economic situation.

Pragmatism in accounting

In the example of the automobile, the logic of what the accountant does should be apparent. In other cases the accountant's logic may not be quite as evident. We saw on pages 25–27 that most users of financial statements employ them in attempts to predict future economic characteristics of the firm—the specific characteristics estimated will, of course, vary from user to user. The accountant has been pragmatic in his response to these needs. We've seen that much of the historical development of accounting was a matter of trial-and-error experimentation in providing information

---

[13] Notice that the creditor has its own asset: a claim to receive cash from the professional man. *A debt owed by one entity is usually a monetary asset to some other entity.*

that users might find valuable for one or another kind of prediction. By the beginning of the Second World War, financial accounting had crystallized into a set of rules and practices that have changed only slightly in the decades since. Most of these practices originated in trial-and-error attempts to provide useful information for reader predictions—attempts that readers seemed to approve. But the results of trial and error don't always make obvious sense, despite intensive efforts by accountants to provide theoretical explanations and justifications of their practices.

Sometimes the accountant ends up believing that he knows what to do, but not why his readers seem to find it appropriate. At present, formal research is being done by some accountants into the uses made of the information that financial accounting reports and the extent to which some traditional reporting practices are useful for purposes of prediction. (One such piece of research influences what is said in Chapters Six, Eight, and Thirteen.) But much additional research remains to be done here, and it is not always clear why certain traditional accounting practices are acceptable to accounting's readers. This is an important point to remember while you are reading later chapters. Although I will try to explain all of the accountant's practices, occasionally the best explanation is that the particular practice is one the accountant believes to "work."

This creates a problem for both teacher and student. This book will try to emphasize accounting's underlying logic. But some things in accounting aren't necessarily logical, though they are widely accepted. If you like, consider these as matters that ultimately may seem perfectly logical, but that aren't yet fully understood. Still, don't deceive yourself into expecting a fully logical explanation for everything in accounting. Even more important, *don't expect that there will be just one right answer to every question.* Trial and error often leads to finding several different approaches to a single problem—all of which may seem to satisfy the purposes for which the accountant's report has been prepared. This is one reason why companies have been able to persuade their auditors to accept a variety of different accounting practices (see pages 34–35).

Summary

Certain points raised so far are summarized here to emphasize important matters that you'll need to keep in mind. Try to avoid using this kind of summary as a substitute for thought. Treat it as a checklist. Are you confident about all the matters listed below?

1. Accounting is a way of communicating economic information, a method that has evolved over the centuries by trial and error. Although accounting is often logical, its main emphasis is usefulness in practice, particularly usefulness for prediction. Accountants often accept a number of different solutions to a problem, whether or not these solutions are mutually consistent, so long as they all seem to be accepted by accounting's users.

2. The accountant's definition of an asset reflects this. The accountant has found that it is useful to recognize two kinds of assets.

(a) *Monetary*: cash itself or a legally enforceable right to receive a specific amount of cash at a specific time.

(b) *Nonmonetary*: an object or right offering future economic benefits to the company, purchased by the company for a known price. The dollar amount of this price, which is used to represent the asset, can be reduced in some accepted way as parts of the original future benefits are determined to have been yielded.

3. Neither cash payment nor technical legal ownership is a necessary condition for recognizing the existence of a nonmonetary asset.

4. We should distinguish between the right to receive services and the services themselves. The right to receive services is often an asset. The services themselves are an asset only if they help produce some other asset. If so, the cost of these services makes up part of the historical cost of that other asset. In a sense, then, services are an asset only if they are transformed into some other asset.

5. There is an underlying tension in financial accounting. On one hand, the accountant wishes to report as much economic information as he can about companies. On the other hand, the accountant wishes his reports to be as reliable as possible, and he wants independent auditors to be able to check what he says. Since some economic information is not entirely reliable (or is hard to audit), these goals conflict. The financial accountant presently resolves this conflict by insisting that the information in his reports be objective, and often that it be supported by tangible evidence, such as bills from a supplier. This is why the accountant represents nonmonetary assets by figures related to their historical costs rather than any other kind of market price. This is also why the financial accountant often deliberately says nothing at all about certain important economic matters when he cannot develop reliable ways to associate historical market-price figures with them.

Historical Purchase
Prices and "Conservatism"

We have seen that accountants usually represent a nonmonetary asset by a figure derived from its historical purchase price. This point needs more discussion.

I will start with a personal example that will illustrate several important points. As a hobby, I build model ships—plastic ones from kits. Two years ago I spent the better part of one summer building an elaborate model clipper ship, which is on a shelf above me as I write this. It's about three feet long, fully rigged, and quite detailed. The costs of making it were about as follows:

Two kits (because I'm clumsy and apt to break things)	$21.00
Paints, wax, thread, chain, and glue	3.00
Knife blades, paint brushes, masking tape, sandpaper, steel wool, and other supplies	2.00
Total cost	$26.00

The historical purchase price of this ship model is $26. Let's temporarily ignore any problems raised by the ship model's services diminishing over time. (We'll examine these problems in the next chapter.) The accountant would report this ship at a $26 figure, its historical purchase price. Notice that this purchase price does not allow anything for my services, even though I spent several hundred hours making the model. I didn't *purchase* my services, so they don't count.[14]

When the accountant wants me to report this model at $26, he is ruling out a major alternative possibility. I could instead try to estimate what price the model would command if I tried to sell it. Suppose I estimate that I could get $90 for it. Call this $90 the model's *current value*. The current value of a nonmonetary asset is an estimated amount representing either the price one might get for it if one sold it, or the price one might have to pay to buy the asset in its present state. The current value is thus an estimated current market price for the asset.[15]

Many nonmonetary assets will have current values that differ significantly from their historical purchase prices. For instance, a company may have bought its land in the 1930s when industrial land was much cheaper than it is now. Suppose the historical purchase price of a company's land was $26,000, but now the company estimates it would cost $90,000 to buy the same property. Why not use the $90,000 current value to represent the asset rather than the $26,000 historical purchase price?

Some reasons for using historical purchase prices

The accountant gives a number of reasons for using historical purchase prices. Some of these involve technical points that will not make much sense until you have read several chapters further, but some of the reasons can be made clear now.

1. *Current values are subjective.* A current value is an estimated market price. Like many estimates, it is subjective and subject to personal bias and error. For example, I may have a much higher opinion of my model ship than it really deserves; perhaps it would not sell for more than I paid for it. Different people might have very different ideas of its worth. Similarly, different appraisers would often have different ideas of the value of a plot of land. In fact, these differences of opinion about such things as land values are what make real estate speculation possible.

In contrast, the historical purchase price of a nonmonetary asset usually is a

---

[14] This decision not to count my services rejects at least two alternative approaches to obtaining a figure to represent the ship. (1) One approach would be to try to find out how much it would have cost me to hire someone, perhaps a student who needed part-time employment, to build the ship. The amount could be included as part of the ship's cost. (2) Another approach would be for me to try to estimate how much I could have earned if I had spent the same number of hours trying to earn money, instead of spending my time with a hobby.

Both of these approaches lead to what are called *opportunity costs*—the costs of not having done something that one might have done, or the costs of pursuing some alternative that, in fact, one did not actually take. Using this language, we could say that accountants presently ignore opportunity costs in their financial reports. This is another controversial decision.

[15] Actually, there are many possible current values, depending on such things as the particular market from which the estimated price is drawn, and whether the entity is acting as a buyer or a seller. For example, the maximum price at which an individual can sell a used car to a dealer will be lower than the cost to this seller were he instead to buy an equivalent car at a used car lot. A still different price may be obtained on a trade-in. But these differences are not vital to our discussion and will be ignored here.

A few market prices are not estimates. For example: The market prices of goods (such as wheat) that are actively traded on commodity exchanges are known magnitudes at any given time, or at least are known within a very narrow range of possible error.

matter of objective, recorded fact. The firm has bills and cancelled checks to back up the amount that is reported, and often this evidence is conclusive.

2. *Current values are uncertain.* The market price of a plot of land usually fluctuates a good deal in response to economic conditions and speculation. Even if we know that the land could be sold for $90,000 now, its market price may change again before we actually sell it. (The market for model ships would be even more erratic.)

In contrast, the historical purchase price of an asset is a changeless fact. This makes it a much more stable and reliable figure than the current value for representing the asset.

3. *Current values are irrelevant.* The current value is often irrelevant to investors. The price at which I could sell my model ship is not really important because I have no intention whatever of selling it. Similarly, if the company has built its factory on the plot of land, it would not be able to sell the land without selling or moving its factory. Often this would be quite impractical, and the company would never consider selling the land. Why, then, should one be interested in what the land would sell for?

Some tentative responses

At this point it should again be emphasized that *I am describing the way in which most practicing accountants perceive historical costs.* Someone who wished instead to employ current values could reply to each of these arguments.

Historical costs are themselves often quite subjective. For example, we will see in Chapter Thirteen that when a company buys a nonmonetary asset (such as a machine) that is expected to provide services over a period of several years, the cost figure that is associated with this asset is steadily decreased each year until it disappears when the asset finally is retired. Yet this pattern of decreases usually cannot be defended conclusively against any conflicting pattern preferred by a user of this data. At the same time, there may be conclusive objective evidence of the current market value of the asset; where this is true, current market values will be *more,* not less, objective than historical costs.

To be sure, current values are sometimes irrelevant, but there are also circumstances in which the reverse is true. It all depends upon the purposes of the user of financial accounting information. We saw on pages 25–27 that many of the uses made of financial accounting require predictions of things that will happen in the future. Current values usually are far more relevant to prediction than are historical costs. If I am considering selling my model ship, I need to predict what it will sell for in the future. Its current market value is relevant to this prediction; its historical cost is not directly relevant. If I wish to decide whether or not I can afford to build another ship, the current costs of ship model kits are more relevant than the historical costs (unless kit prices haven't changed, in which case the historical cost *is* the current cost). Indeed, according to this reasoning, the certainty of historical costs is one of their most serious defects. The investor must constantly be adapting to a changing world, and something that is a changeless fact soon pertains only to the past and is irrelevant to present investor decisions.

Institutional insistence upon historical costs

On pages 23–24, attention was given to the distinction between *resource-allocation* and *institutional* uses of accounting—use of accounting in determining how one is going to spend one's money (or other assets) *versus* use of accounting to comply with record keeping and reporting requirements imposed by the law and by other institutions of society. The previous discussion indicates that there is a controversy concerning the appropriateness of the use of historical costs for resource-allocation purposes. But there is no question that historical costs are appropriate for institutional purposes. Our laws and regulatory bodies usually insist on the use of historical costs. (So does the Accounting Principles Board of the American Institute of Certified Public Accountants—that alone would be enough to ensure their continued use.) Finally, use of historical costs has a great weight of tradition supporting it; except as indicated below, there has been little use of current values in actual financial accounting since the 1930s. People expect that historical costs will be used, thus they *are* used. Underlying this tradition is a somewhat older tradition of *conservatism* in financial accounting, discussed in the next subsection. This conservatism probably came to dominate financial accounting practice as a result of the severe strains put on financial accounting by the depression of the 1930s.

Conservatism

Accountants are not completely consistent in representing nonmonetary assets by their historical purchase prices. If the asset has significantly *de*creased in value, he may represent it by its current value after all.

Suppose the janitor accidentally knocked my ship model on the floor. It's a fragile thing and probably couldn't be repaired. The accountant would urge that I no longer report the model as an asset, that I represent it by a zero figure, if you like. Industrial site land usually doesn't suffer this kind of irreversible decline in value, but other nonmonetary assets do. To use an earlier example, suppose that a company buys a specialized machine for a specific purpose, perhaps to manufacture a particular product. Suppose that this product becomes impossible to sell. When this happens, often the figure derived from the machine's historical purchase price will be much higher than the value of the future economic benefits of that machine to the company, or to anyone else. In such cases the accountant may urge that the equipment be represented by its lesser current (scrap) value.

Here is an actual example. A company had considered making certain small parts out of plastic by a process involving heat treatment. They wanted to experiment with the process without buying a lot of expensive equipment. One of their engineers suggested providing the necessary ovens by buying several electric turkey roasters. The company bought the roasters, used them for a few months, then abandoned the experiment.

Afterwards, these roasters still had a lot of service left in them; they probably could have been used for years. But the company had no further use for them and they were too stained to have any resale value. The accountants urged that they be reported at a zero figure.

Accountants ignore small differences between historical purchase price figures and current values. Accountants even ignore major differences if they are temporary (or, if, as we shall see, the assets are actively used by the firm). And accountants usually prefer historical purchase prices to current values whenever current values are the higher of the two. *But if current values are considerably lower than the figure derived from historical purchase prices, if that low current value seems permanent, and if the asset is being held for resale or retirement, accountants often will represent the asset by its current value.*

Why are accountants inconsistent in this way? The traditional answer is that doing this gives a more "conservative" report. The reasoning might run as follows. Many readers of financial reports want to know what would be the worst that could be said about the company. Creditors, for example, need to know how secure their investment will be even if things go badly for the company. But creditors have no reason to be interested in whether the company might do exceptionally well; they just want the company to do well enough for their investment to be safe. This makes creditors take a cold view of the company and its prospects. Creditors are much more interested in possible sources of trouble than in possible good fortune. A report that shows nonmonetary assets at historical purchase prices, but reduces these figures where current values are significantly lower, helps satisfy these creditor needs.

Conservatism has other virtues, too. Management tends to be optimistic; a little pessimism in the reported figures may be a good corrective to this. Accountants honestly feel that the kinds of mistakes caused by painting too dark a picture are much less serious than those caused by painting one that looks too favorable; the drastic experiences of the 1930s appeared to bear out this view. More companies have perished through excessive optimism than through excessive caution.[16]

Thus, there is a tendency in financial accounting to report a nonmonetary asset either at its current market value or at an amount based on its historical purchase price, whichever is lower. In practice, ordinarily this use of current market values extends only to those nonmonetary assets that are being held for sale or other disposal in the near future: for example, to inventories of goods that the firm is in business to sell, or to used buildings and equipment that have been retired from service. In contrast, those nonmonetary assets that are actively being used by the firm to produce goods and services ordinarily are reported only at figures based on their historical purchase prices. The logic of this is simple: since the company intends to use these assets rather than to sell them, their current market values (current selling prices) are irrelevant.[17]

This rule of ignoring the current market values of assets that are held for future use (instead of sale), even when these current market values are lower than are figures based on historical purchase prices, is obviously based upon an implicit assumption

---

[16] Finally, one may speculate that income and property tax accounting indirectly influence financial accounting in this instance. Whenever it is allowed for tax purposes, conservatism has the effect of reducing a firm's tax bill—at least in the short run. Firms that use conservative asset figures for tax purposes may also incline toward using them for financial accounting purposes, even though the two kinds of accounting are quite different.

[17] Occasionally when such an asset has experienced an especially severe decline in future utility, its cost also will be written down, even though the firm does not intend to sell or retire it. But such cases seem rare and, for brevity, will be ignored in the remainder of this book. Similarly, certain *monetary* assets may suffer a permanent decline in value and be written down prior to their maturity date; one example of this would be a debt owed to the firm by an entity that has suffered such severe financial difficulties that it is unlikely to pay the full amount owed. The accountants' techniques here involve complications discussed in Chapter Eleven.

that the company will remain in business long enough to use (rather than sell) these assets. This could well be called the "remaining-in-business" assumption. Instead, accountants call it the *going-concern assumption*; it means the same thing: it is assumed that the firm will keep its present operations going on into the future. Of course, if it should be expected that the firm will *not* continue in business, then the going-concern assumption is inappropriate and, in theory at least, nonmonetary assets should be reported at their current market values—often at the amounts they would command at auction or other emergency sale.

Summary

The accountants' basic rule for determining the amounts at which nonmonetary assets will be reported is *conservatism*. This rule is expressed in practice by requiring that nonmonetary assets be reported either at amounts based on their historical purchase prices or at their current market values, whichever is lower. This rule is modified for any nonmonetary assets that are being held for use rather than for sale or retirement; here, the *going-concern assumption* allows the accountant to regard current market values as irrelevant and to report these assets only at figures based on their historical purchase prices. The relationships among these rules might be diagrammed as follows:

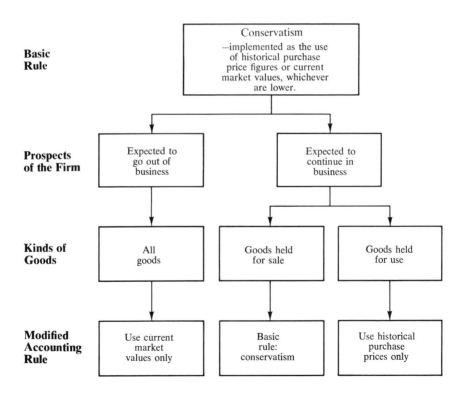

The next few chapters will ignore situations in which an asset's current market value is lower than its historical purchase price figure, or in which the company is expected shortly to go out of business.

This is done to keep the discussion simple; it allows us to say that all nonmonetary asset figures are based on historical purchase prices. We will examine conservatism again later on.

Monetary Assets

We now look in a bit more detail at these assets mentioned on page 41, which are either cash or rights to receive cash. Illustration 1-4 gives a list of such monetary assets (and related dollar amounts) for an imaginary company, Illustrative Corporation. This illustration does not show all possible kinds of monetary assets, nor is it intended to be very realistic (few companies would have the particular combination of monetary assets shown). But the illustration allows us to discuss all those matters that need to be raised at this time.

Illustration 1-4

Illustrative Corporation
Monetary Assets
December 31, 19X1

Cash	$ 47,600
5% Notes Receivable—due 4/1/X2	16,000
Accounts Receivable	180,290
Interest Receivable	2,050
6% Notes Receivable—due 2/1/X4	48,000
Investment in 4-1/2% Bonds Receivable—due 3/1/X9	30,000
	$323,940

The heading

Begin by looking at the last line of the heading, "December 31, 19X1." The notation "19X1" is used instead of "1970," "1971," or the like in order to avoid tying the discussion too closely to particular dates. Of course, in actual practice real dates are employed. A list of company assets relates to one and only one moment in time—like a photograph of its economic status at a particular instant. Why? Because as a company goes about its business, its assets are always changing. Cash is used to pay for nonmonetary assets, claims to receive cash are collected, and so forth. It is essential that any list of company assets show the related date. To be more precise, take "December 31, 19X1" to mean: "As of the end of business on December 31, 19X1," or "As of 11:59 PM on December 31, 19X1."

Cash

The figure shown for cash might represent any (or all) of three things:

1. "Petty cash"—coin and currency kept in the company's offices to pay small bills and to make minor purchases.

2. Recent collections from customers that have not yet been deposited in the bank—these could be currency or customer checks payable to the company.

3. Cash in the bank—the total of the company's checking account balances in whatever banks it deals with.

Notice that there are three main kinds of cash: coin and currency, checks payable to the company, and bank balances. Postage, IOU's, trading stamps, and the like are not considered to be cash, but are shown as separate types of assets.

Accounts receivable

Besides holding cash, Illustrative Corporation is a creditor investor in other companies (or a creditor of individual customers). As Illustration 1-4 indicates, it has five different kinds of claims to receive cash: accounts receivable, interest receivable, two kinds of notes receivable, and bonds receivable. Each of these monetary assets reflects Illustrative Corporation's rights as a creditor of some other accounting entity (or entities). We will look at these different kinds of monetary assets one by one.

Accounts receivable are ordinary trade debts owed the company by customers who buy goods or services on credit. Typically, these customers are expected to pay within a month or two and are not charged interest. For example, many university bookstores allow students to make purchases on credit; if you bought this book on credit, you thereby created an account receivable for the bookstore. Most sales by one business enterprise to another are made on credit, therefore most such sales result in the seller acquiring an account receivable. Compared with other rights to receive cash, an account receivable is evidenced in an informal way; after the seller has shipped goods to the customer (or performed services, if services were what the customer purchased), the seller just sends the buyer a bill, or *invoice*.

To summarize, an *account receivable* is an informal, usually non-interest-bearing debt owed to the firm as the result of an ordinary sale of goods or services by the firm.

Notes receivable

Sometimes the credit buyer has difficulty paying on time—perhaps he's having temporary financial problems. Sometimes, from the start, the trade debt is intended to be outstanding for a relatively long time, say, three months or more. In such cases the debt may be handled in a more formal way. The seller may ask the buyer to sign a document that, among other things, contains a promise to pay the amount owed on some particular date. If so, the asset is classified as a note receivable. Unlike an account receivable, a note receivable may also arise when one entity simply borrows money from another (without any sale of product). Banks, for example, own notes receivable from numerous borrowers. Typically, notes receivable arise in cases where the borrower is borrowing from some single creditor; in contrast, as we shall see, bonds receivable usually result from a firm's simultaneously borrowing from a number of different creditors. From an accounting standpoint, the main differences between a note receivable and an account receivable are the greater formality and (typically) longer life of the note. (There are also some important legal differences between the two, but these need not concern us here.)

The seller may also charge interest on the note—a fee for the privilege of borrowing—though this need not always be so. For simplicity, we will assume in the early parts of this book that all notes receivable are interest-bearing. We will consider other kinds of notes receivable in a later chapter.

Different kinds of notes receivable are often kept distinct from one another. In Illustration 1-4 the company has two kinds of notes receivable.

Notice the way the interest rates and the due dates are shown in the illustration. While there are several other ways of doing this, typically some method must be found to report the following main items of information about each note.

1. The amount borrowed—exclusive of interest charges. This corresponds to what we ordinarily mean when we speak of the amount of a loan. Technically, it is called the *principal* of the loan.

2. The interest rate.

3. The due date, or *maturity* date, at which time the principal and any unpaid interest charges must finally be paid by the borrower. The total life of the note may be any period decided upon by lender and borrower, but it rarely exceeds three years.

A *note receivable* is a formal (usually interest-bearing) debt owed to the firm; notes receivable usually arise from an entity's purchasing goods or services (or borrowing) from a single firm and usually have a total life of less than three years.

Interest receivable

Interest charges are a fee for the use of money over time. Unless otherwise indicated, *interest rates are always given in annual terms,* regardless of the actual duration of the note. Let us use the 6 percent note as an example. Six percent of $48,000 is $2,880. Illustrative Corporation is entitled to receive $2,880 a year for allowing one or more debtors to borrow $48,000 from it. This works out to about $240 a month (6/12 percent), or about $7.89 a day (6/365 percent). If the $48,000 were loaned for an entire year, the total fee would be $2,880. If it were loaned for only 100 days, the total fee would be only about $789 ($100 \times \$7.89 = \$789$). As a simplification, we will act as though *all months are an equal, 30-day length*; this saves a lot of arithmetic detail without doing any violence to our discussion.

Interest may be *paid* monthly, quarterly, semiannually, annually, when the principal itself is due, or according to any other system that may be worked out between the lender and the borrower. Until this fee is paid, there will be a *cash claim* related to it—a right to receive cash that will increase with time as the fee itself increases.[18] This kind of cash claim is called *interest receivable*. Observe that interest

---

[18] Another simplification is used in this discussion. There are two different ways to calculate interest: either as a constant percentage of the principal of the loan, or as a constant percentage of the *principal plus any accumulated interest receivable*.

Here is an example that illustrates the difference. Suppose that interest fees are calculated once a year, and that a lender accepts a two-year, 5 percent note the principal of which is $10,000 from a borrower. No interest is to be paid until the principal becomes due. If interest is calculated as a constant percentage of the principal, then in both years the interest fee will be $10,000 \times 5\% = \$500$. But if, instead, interest is calculated as a constant percentage of

receivable is an entirely different right to receive cash from that reflected in the note itself. Notes receivable refers only to the principal of the note. Interest receivable refers to the unpaid portion of the fee charged for borrowing that principal.

> *Interest receivable* is a right to receive an interest fee for the services of money owed to the firm by another entity; this right may be recognized even if payment of the interest is not yet due.

The following is optional—feel free to ignore it if algebra troubles you. On the other hand, use of the following formulas can speed your interest calculations. There is a simple formula for calculating interest receivable. Let:

I = the amount of interest receivable at the date under consideration
P = the principal of the related debt
r = the interest rate per year
t = the time elapsed from the beginning of the loan to the date under consideration, expressed as a fraction of a year.

If no interest has yet been paid on the loan:

$$I = Prt$$

If interest has previously been paid on the loan, it will have been paid through some particular date. In that case, let:

t' = the time elapsed from that particular date (through which interest has been
   paid) to the date under consideration, expressed as a fraction of a year.
$$I = Prt'$$

Examples

A few examples are in order. Suppose that the 5 percent note, due 4/1/X2, is a nine-month note. Then it must have been acquired about 7/1/X1. The total interest fee over its whole nine-month life would be:

(Principal) × (Interest rate) × (Fraction of whole year)
($16,000)   (5%)   (9/12)

This works out to $600. But the interest receivable on this note at 12/31/X1 is not $600. Suppose that the lender and borrower had agreed that the interest fee was to be paid only when the principal became due. No interest was owed at the outset, 7/1/X1. At maturity, $600 will be due. This $600 increase does not occur in a sudden lump. Instead, it occurs gradually with the passage of time, for interest is calculated on the basis of time elapsed. Accordingly, accountants prorate the total $600 fee and

---

the principal plus accumulated interest receivable, the fee will differ from year to year. The fee will still be $500 in Year 1; but in Year 2 it will be ($10,000 + $500) × 5% = $525.

Interest calculated the first way (on the principal only) is called *simple interest*; interest calculated the second way (on principal plus accumulated interest receivable) is called *compound interest*. Both interest methods are used in practice, and we will see in Chapter Eleven that compound interest must be used in many calculations involving debts with lives greater than one year. But for simplicity, *only simple interest will be used in the next several chapters*. Compound interest is discussed in Chapter Eleven.

report an appropriate portion of it as receivable at 12/31/X1. Such proration is given the technical name of *accrual* of the appropriate portion of the interest fee (accrual is pronounced uh-*crew*-al) and an asset which results from an accrual is called an "accrued" asset (uh-*crude*). The appropriate fee for the period 7/1/X1 through 12/31/X1 would be a fee for only six of the nine months, or:

$$\$16,000 \times 5\% \times 6/12 = \underline{\$400}$$

Interest receivable on this note at 12/31/X1 would be only $400. Similarly, on 9/30/X1 (after only three months) accrued interest receivable on this note was only $200 ($16,000 \times 5\% \times 3/12 = \$200$). On 7/1/X1 interest receivable on this note was zero ($16,000 \times 5\% \times 0/12 = \$0$). Only on the date that the principal is due will the total interest fee of $600 be owed. Interest fees—and interest receivable—are direct functions of the passage of time; accordingly, the accountant is willing to accrue them as time passes, even though *payment* of interest is not yet due. Accruals are widespread and important in accounting; they may occur whenever an entity earns a receivable over a period of time by providing a stream of services (or products) and the proportionate amount of the receivable earned to date can be estimated to the accountant's satisfaction. These conditions often are met when the firm has a service contract with another entity.

For example, suppose that a firm supplies night watchmen to other firms, billing them at an agreed monthly rate per man on the 10th of each month for services provided the previous month. At the end of each month the amount owed by each customer can be calculated and accrued as a receivable, even though payment is not due until later. Similarly, an electric utility may accrue a receivable for power consumed by its customers prior to billing these customers if it has reliable information about the amount of power consumed.

> An *accrued asset* is a receivable that has been recognized prior to the date that it is legally owed to the firm; such receivables arise when the firm's related rights are earned (by providing services or products) over a period of time, and the amount earned to date can be estimated to the accountant's satisfaction.

Now refer back to Illustration 1-4 on page 60. The total interest receivable is $2,050. We have accounted for $400 of this with the 5 percent note. Illustration 1-5 shows how the remaining $1,650 of this $2,050 was determined. But first read the discussion of the investment in bonds receivable.

Bonds receivable

Illustrative Corporation owns one more kind of debt. It has an investment in the $4\frac{1}{2}$ percent bonds of some other company. Bonds are a very formal kind of long-lived debt. (It is common for bonds to have lives of 20 years or more.) They usually pay regular interest fees every six months as well as repaying their principal at maturity. Most bonds offer some kind of special protection (if only the right to be repaid before the claims of other creditors are satisfied) to the creditors in case the company undergoes financial difficulties.

Ordinary notes usually have much shorter lives. They often originate in sales on credit and are frequently used as a way of helping the borrower meet short-term needs for cash. A company may issue ordinary notes to meet its cash requirements for its busy season, or to finance a major construction project. While ordinary notes may have lives longer than a year, the usual intent is to repay them as soon as the particular need for extra cash is over.

In contrast, bonds never originate in credit sales. More importantly, they are not used to meet short-term cash requirements. Instead, debtors issue bonds as a way to obtain an extended long-term creditor investment in their business. As we saw earlier this doesn't mean that the *individual* creditor investor has to hold his bonds receivable until their due date. The creditor can sell his rights to some other investor by a process called *negotiating* the bonds. But it does mean that both borrowers and lenders intend for the bonds to be a relatively enduring part of the investment in a company (although, as we will see in a later chapter, not as enduring as *ownership* investment). Usually, bonds are issued in order to obtain much larger amounts of money than could be obtained through issuing ordinary notes. In fact, these amounts usually are substantial enough that the bonds end up being purchased by a variety of different creditors (called *bondholders*)—in contrast to notes, which usually are issued to single creditors.

Still, the resemblances of bonds to other kinds of notes are greater than the differences. For present purposes, we can ignore the differences and simply regard bonds receivable as particularly long-lived notes receivable.

A *bond receivable* is a highly formal, long-lived, interest-bearing debt owed to the firm by another firm; bonds usually offer special protection to creditors and usually are issued to more than one creditor.

Illustration 1-5

Illustrative Corporation

Calculation of Interest Receivable at 12/31/X1

Assumptions made for this illustration:
1. The 5% notes were acquired on 7/1/X1; no interest has yet been paid on them.
2. The 6% notes were acquired on 2/1/X1; interest fees through 8/1/X1 have been paid on them.
3. The $4\frac{1}{2}$% bonds were acquired on 1/1/X0; interest fees have been paid on them through 9/1/X1.

Type of Interest-Bearing Monetary Asset	Principal Amount	×	Interest Rate	×	Fraction of Year for Which Interest Fee Is Owed	=	Interest Receivable: Amount of Interest Owed to Company on 12/31/X1
5% Notes	$16,000		5%		6/12		$ 400
6% Notes	48,000		6%		5/12		1,200
$4\frac{1}{2}$% Bonds	30,000		$4\frac{1}{2}$%		4/12		450

Total Interest Receivable 12/31/X1 . . . . $2,050

Summary

1. Monetary assets are cash and rights to receive cash. Accountants consider cash as coin and currency, checks payable to the entity, and balances in bank accounts. Rights to receive cash usually are either debts owed the entity by customers or investments in other companies.

The simplest kind of a right to receive cash is an account receivable—a short-lived, non-interest-bearing debt from a customer who bought on credit. Other, more formal cash claims include notes receivable and investments in bonds receivable; these cash claims tend to be interest-bearing, and thereby give rise to still another kind of right to receive cash: interest receivable. Illustration 1-6 summarizes the main features of these different kinds of rights to receive cash.

2. Interest fees depend on the principal amount of the debt, the interest rate, and the life of the debt. Interest *receivable* depends on the principal amount of the debt, the interest rate, and the length of time since interest fees were last received. Over the whole life of a debt, the entire interest fee will become receivable. But over any part of this life only a proportionate part of this fee will become receivable. Recognition of this proportionate part is called *accrual* of interest receivable.

Illustration 1-6

Main Features of Different Kinds of Rights to Receive Cash
(Only the most typical cases are considered.)

	Interest Bearing?	Amount Increases as a Function of the Passage of Time?	Relative Duration of Loan	Arises from Credit Sales of Goods or Services?
Accounts Receivable	Sometimes*	No	Short	Yes
Interest Receivable	No†	Yes	Short	No
Notes Receivable	Yes	No	Short to Medium	Usually
Bonds Receivable	Yes	No	Long	No

   * *Examples of interest-bearing accounts receivable include revolving charge accounts. It is rare for one business to charge another* business *interest on an account receivable.*
   † *An exception to this arises with compound interest, which involves interest being charged on interest receivable. However, as mentioned earlier, only simple interest is discussed in this section.*

Problems for Study and Self-Examination

From this point on, each main section of this book will conclude with a set of problems, followed by a set of solutions. These are intended to give you some practice in working with the ideas discussed. As suggested in the Foreword, in studying accounting it is very easy to fool yourself into thinking that you understand the material when, in fact, you have overlooked or misunderstood some small but vital point. That's why you should work problems—to test your understanding and discover where your understanding is deficient.

Every effort has been made to keep the problems short, to the point, and free of "busy work"; in addition, some problems are designated as "optional" ones—to be solved only if you believe that you need the additional review. But be sure to solve all of the other problems, and don't look ahead to the solutions until you have made a serious try for the right answer. *A good deal of what you get out of this book will depend on your ability to discipline yourself.* If you have trouble with a particular problem, do the best you can, study the solution, then go back to the problem in a couple of days and try it again.

Problem 1-1:

For each of the rights to receive cash described below, determine both the total interest fee over the life of the right and the related figure for interest receivable at 12/31/X1. The problems concern Edwards Company.

(a) A 4% note receivable was acquired on 11/1/X1, and is due on 11/1/X4. Principal amount is $6,000. All interest is due when the principal is due.

(b) A 5½% note receivable was acquired on 3/1/X1, and is due on 2/28/X2. Principal amount is $21,000. Interest has been paid through 9/1/X1.

(c) 7% bonds receivable were acquired on 10/1/X1, and are due on 9/30/X9. Principal amount is $72,000. The first payment of interest is due on 4/1/X2.

Problem 1-2:

See Problem 1-1. Suppose that on 12/31/X1, Edwards Company has total cash of $17,375 and that its customers owe it $40,250 on ordinary informal trade debts. Prepare a statement as similar as possible to Illustration 1-4 (page 60), showing Edwards Company's monetary assets at 12/31/X1. You will learn later that the order in which the different assets are listed is important. The order used in Illustration 1-3 is an acceptable one.

Problem 1-3 (Optional):

Do this problem only if you believe that you need the additional review; otherwise go on to Problem 1-4. Turn back to Illustration 1-5 (page 65). Determine what the total accrued interest receivable on these rights to receive cash was at both of the following dates: 11/1/X1 and 12/1/X1. Round the figures off to the nearest penny, if necessary.

Problem 1-4 (Brain-teaser):

If you really understand a computational technique, you should be able to apply it backwards. This problem provides an opportunity to test your comprehension of interest calculations. All notes are acquired from the original borrowers.

1. Dickinson Company owns a 6% note receivable, which it acquired on 1/1/X0. The principal amount is $7,500. Listed below are some hypothetical figures for 12/31/X2 accrued interest receivable on this note. In each case, determine when the last payment of interest was made on this note—that is, determine the date through which interest fees on this note have been paid.

(a) $ 75   (c) $ 675
(b) $450   (d) $1,350

2. Fairbanks, Inc. owns a 7% note receivable, which it acquired on 3/1/X2. At 12/31/X2, $8,400 of accrued interest receivable is owed on this note. Interest fees on this note have been paid through 8/31/X2. What is the principal amount of this note?

3. Rhodes Company owns a note receivable, which it acquired on 5/31/X1. The principal amount is $26,400. At 12/31/X2, $2,717 of accrued interest receivable is owed on this note. No interest has been paid on this note since Rhodes Company acquired it. What is the interest rate on this note?

Problem 1-5:

Which of the following describe monetary assets?

(a) The company owns a mortgage on the store building of another company.
(b) A tenant owes the company rent.
(c) The company has paid a supplier for goods which have not yet been received.
(d) The company expects that new municipal tax legislation will be passed granting it a refund on its past taxes.

Solutions

Solution 1-1:

Cash Claim	(a) Principal Amount	(b) Interest Rate	(c) Total Life of Asset	(a × b × c) Total Interest Fee	(d) Fraction of Year for Which Interest Fee is Owed	(a × b × d) Interest Receivable on 12/31/X1
4% Note	$ 6,000	4%	3 years	$ 720	2/12	$ 40
5½% Note	21,000	5½%	1 year	1,155	4/12	385
7% Bonds	72,000	7%	8 years	40,320	3/12	1,260

Total Interest Receivable $1,685

Solution 1-2:

Edwards Company
Monetary Assets
December 31, 19X1

Cash	$ 17,375
5½% Notes Receivable—due 2/28/X2	21,000
Accounts Receivable	40,250
Interest Receivable	1,685
4% Notes Receivable—due 11/1/X4	6,000
Investment in 7% Bonds Receivable—due 9/30/X9	72,000
	$158,310

Solution 1-3 (*Optional*):

Interest Receivable

Date	5% Note	6% Note	4½% Bonds	Total
11/1/X1	$266.67	$720.00	$225.00	$1,211.67
12/1/X1	333.33	960.00	337.50	1,630.83

Detailed calculation for 11/1/X1:

5% Note: $16,000 × 5% × 4/12 = $266.67
6% Note: $48,000 × 6% × 3/12 = 720.00
4½% Bonds: $30,000 × 4½% × 2/12 = 225.00

Solution 1-4 (*Brain-teaser*):
1. (a) $75 is 1% of $7,500, or 2 months' interest. Interest fees must have been paid through *10/31/X2, or 11/1/X2*.
   (b) $450 is 6% of $7,500, or 1 year's interest. Interest fees must have been paid through *12/31/X1 or 1/1/X2*.
   (c) *6/30/X1 or 7/1/X1*.
   (d) *1/1/X0*.
Notice that 6% a year is equivalent to ½% a month.

2. Interest Receivable = (Principal) × (Interest rate) × (Fraction of whole year)
          $8,400   (Unknown)   (7%)   (4/12)

$$\text{Principal} = \frac{\$8,400}{7\% \times 4/12} = \$360,000$$

3. Interest Receivable = (Principal) × (Interest rate) × (Fraction of whole year)
          $2,717   ($26,400)   (Unknown)   (19/12)

$$\text{Interest rate} = \frac{\$2,717}{\$26,400 \times 19/12} = 6\tfrac{1}{2}\%$$

Solution 1-5:
  (a) and (b) are both monetary assets.
  (c) is an asset. But since it is a right to receive goods, instead of a right to receive cash, it is a nonmonetary asset.
  (d) is not an asset. It is not a right to receive cash, though if the new tax legislation is passed, such a right might then come into being.

Assignment Problems

General Instructions for all problems

1. If the problem requires an expression of opinion, your answer should indicate the reasons supporting the position that you take.

2. If the problem requires a numerical answer, your solution should include all necessary supporting calculations (unless they are extremely simple).

3. If you need to round an answer, do so to the nearest dollar.

Problem 1-A:

On 1/1/X3, Clawson Flour Company acquired a $6,000, 3-year, 5% note receivable from Compton Stay-Fresh Products. Principal and interest on this note are both payable at maturity, 1/1/X6.

1. What is the total interest fee over the life of this note?

2. How much interest receivable should Clawson Flour Company report on a list of its assets dated 12/31/X3?

3. How much interest receivable should Clawson Flour Company report on a list of its assets dated 12/31/X5?

4. How much cash will Clawson Flour Company receive at maturity?

Problem 1-B:

As part of your training in accounting, you must become able to extend what you have learned into new situations. This problem provides an opportunity to increase your flexibility and broaden your understanding. The text provides all background information needed to solve this problem, but the circumstances described will be unfamiliar. Apply what you already have learned to this new situation.

1. Refer to Problem 1-A. On 1/1/X3, Clawson Flour Company acquired a 3-year note receivable from Compton Stay-Fresh Products. To vary what was assumed in Problem 1-A, assume that this note was *non-interest-bearing* (that is, it did not explicitly provide for any interest fee), and that it had a maturity value of $6,900 (that is, at the due date Compton Stay-Fresh Products was to pay Clawson Flour Company $6,900). In obtaining this note on 1/1/X3, Clawson Flour Company paid Compton Stay-Fresh Products only $6,000. In answering the following questions, the rule to be followed is:

> The total interest fee over the life of a note is the difference between the amount received by the borrower and the total of all amounts paid to the lender.

As before, assume simple interest.

(a) What is the total interest fee over the life of the note?

(b) At what amount should Clawson Flour Company report the note receivable on a list of its assets dated 1/1/X3? (You may assume that the amount to be reported for a non-interest-bearing note is the sum of the amount actually lent—the principal—plus any accumulated interest fee.)

(c) At what amount should Clawson Flour Company report the note receivable on a list of its assets dated 12/31/X5?

(d) At what amount should Clawson Flour Company report the note receivable on a list of its assets dated 12/31/X3?

2. On 6/30/X4, Reinecke Riparian Ltd. acquired a 9-month, non-interest-bearing note from Tujunga Corporation. The maturity value of this note was $34,101. In obtaining it, Reinecke Riparian Ltd. paid Tujunga Corporation $32,400.

(a) What is the total interest fee over the life of this note?

(b) At what amount should Reinecke Riparian Ltd. report the note receivable on a list of its assets dated 12/31/X4?

(c) Suppose that Tujecke Company obtained a 9-month, *interest-bearing* note from Reinunga, Inc.; the note will pay the principal and all interest at the maturity date. The maturity value of this note (including interest) is $34,101. In obtaining it, Tujecke Company paid Reinunga, Inc., $32,400. What is the interest rate on this note?

(d) Comment on the following assertion: "There is no such thing as a non-interest-bearing note."

Problem 1-C:

On 1/1/X3, Cameron Hyacinthine Company purchased six $1,000, 5% bonds issued by Whittier Hydraulics for a total cost of $6,000. These bonds are due on 1/1/X6, and pay accumulated interest fees every January 1st and July 1st. Cameron Hyacinthine Company intends to hold these bonds to maturity; it did not receive any interest fee on 1/1/X3, nor should it have. Assume simple interest.

1. What will be the total amount of interest fees received by Cameron Hyacinthine Company over the life of its investment in these bonds?

2. How much cash did Cameron Hyacinthine Company receive on 7/1/X3?

3. How much interest receivable should Cameron Hyacinthine Company report on a list of its assets dated 12/31/X3?

4. How much cash will Cameron Hyacinthine Company receive at maturity?

Problem 1-D:

As part of your training in accounting, you must become able to extend what you have learned into new situations. This problem provides an opportunity to increase your flexibility and broaden your understanding. The text provides all background information needed to solve this problem, but the circumstances described will be unfamiliar. Apply what you already have learned to this new situation.

In the following questions, assume simple interest, and that the company involved closes its books once a year, every December 31st, and that the total principal and interest on the note are due at maturity. (*Note:* while it may appear otherwise at first, both parts of this question *are* solvable.)

1. On 7/15/X4, a note was issued, due 5/15/X7. The principal of this note was $10,200.00; its maturity value was $11,861.75. What is the interest rate on this note?

2. A 7½%, $2,200 note is due on 10/1/X6. At 12/31/X5, the interest receivable on this note was $137.50. When was it issued? What is the total maturity value of this note (including interest)?

Problem 1-E:

In the following questions, assume simple interest, and that the company involved closes its books once a year, every December 31st, and that the total principal and interest on the note are due at maturity. (*Note:* while it may appear otherwise at first, all parts of this question *are* solvable.)

1. On 9/1/X6, a $7\frac{1}{4}\%$ note was issued. Its principal was $27,600.00; its total maturity value (including interest) was $31,101.75. When was this note due?

2. On 4/30/X2, a note was issued, due 1/31/X4. The principal of this note is $42,000, the total maturity value (including interest) is $46,593.75. What is the amount of interest receivable on 12/31/X3?

3. On 3/31/X1, a $4\frac{1}{2}\%$ note was issued, due 2/28/X5. On 12/31/X3, the interest receivable on this note was $193.05. What is the total maturity value (including interest) of this note?

Problem 1-F:

As part of your training in accounting, you must become able to extend what you have learned into new situations. This problem provides an opportunity to increase your flexibility and broaden your understanding. The text provides all background information needed to solve this problem, but the circumstances described will be unfamiliar. Apply what you already have learned to this new situation.

Hagen Corporation employs a manufacturing process that requires a near-perfect vacuum. It constructed a suitable vacuum chamber for $500,000. It then pumped all the air out, at a cost of $1,400. There is no doubt that the $500,000 expenditure resulted in an asset. But what about the $1,400? After all, the whole purpose of exhausting the air in the chamber was to leave nothing there. You may assume that the costs of maintaining this vacuum, once it is created, do not exceed $10 per week.

Problem 1-G:

Holifield Enterprises, Inc., purchased all of the capital stock (see page 19) of Montebello Manufacturing Company; the latter firm, however, is continued as a separate corporation, conducting its own business affairs.

1. Is this capital stock an asset of Holifield Enterprises, Inc.? If so, is it a monetary or a nonmonetary asset?

2. Holifield Enterprises, Inc., is the sole owner of Montebello Manufacturing Company. Are the assets of Montebello Manufacturing Company now the assets of Holifield Enterprises, Inc.?

3. Chaim I. Holifield is the principal stockholder in Holifield Enterprises, Inc.; he owns 70% of its capital stock. In addition to his investment in Holifield Enterprises, Inc., he owns a private automobile that he often uses for business purposes. Is this automobile an asset of Holifield Enterprises, Inc.? Is some fraction of it an asset of the firm?

Problem 1-H:

1. Ten years ago, A. F. Smith and Associates bought 100 shares of the capital stock of Glendale Corporation for a total price of $1,000, and 100 shares of the capital stock of Van Nuys Perfect Bakery for $20,000. Since then, Glendale Corporation

has been very successful; its stock now sells for $200 per share. Van Nuys Perfect Bakery has suffered a number of reverses; its stock now sells for $10 per share. At what amounts should A. F. Smith and Associates show its two investments if it is preparing a list of its assets now?

2. Hawkins Company manufactures a common household product. During the last ten years it has never failed to sell at least 1,000,000 units of this product to retailers, and it has always sold them for at least $30 per hundred. There is no reason to doubt that this will continue to be true for at least another five years.

The product costs $16 per hundred to manufacture. At present, the company owns 25,000 units. What amount should the company associate with these 25,000 units?

Problem 1-I:

1. At the beginning of his freshman year, Mr. Cecil R. Sisk bought a used combination color television and stereo set for $360. He estimates that it will be virtually worthless by the time that he graduates, and plans to abandon it then. Assume that he expects to receive four years' entertainment services for his $360. What amount should he associate with the machine after one year?

2. The school year lasts a total of 30 weeks; Mr. Sisk does not take the machine home with him on vacations. During the school year, he finds so many other things to do that he averages only three hours per week of television viewing and listening to stereo. What is his average cost per hour? (Ignore costs of electricity, repairs, and the like.)

3. Mr. Sisk is disturbed by the answer to question 2. He complains to a friend that this amount exceeds the hourly cost of going to the movies. His friend suggests that he could lower the average cost per hour by leaving the set on whenever he goes to class. Comment.

4. After Mr. Sisk had owned his machine for half a year, another friend offered him $315 for it. Mr. Sisk refused, but the friend said he would leave the offer open for a week. Is the machine a monetary asset?

5. Disregard question 4. After owning the machine for one year, Mr. Sisk became curious about how much it would be worth if he tried to sell it. He discovered that the most he could receive for it was $200. He doesn't *plan* to sell the set, but the information distresses him. What amount should he associate with the machine after one year?

Problem 1-J:

1. Undergraduate tuition at the University of Alabraska is $396 per quarter. The fall quarter is twelve weeks long. Mr. B. F. King, a sophomore, is paying his own way through college. He pays the full $396 at the beginning of each quarter. At the end of the seventh week of the fall quarter, what amount should he associate with his remaining rights to receive educational services?

2. Because of various vacations, the winter quarter is only ten weeks long. At the end of the fifth week of the winter quarter, what amount should Mr. King associate with his remaining rights to receive educational services?

3. Suppose that Mr. King is taking an equally heavy load in both quarters. Does anything trouble you about your answer to the first two questions? Suppose that the

spring quarter is eleven weeks long, and that Mr. King never goes to summer school; do you see any other way to answer questions 1 and 2?

4. Disregard questions 2 and 3. Suppose that, at the end of the fifth week of the fall term, Mr. King is convinced (correctly) that he will fail half of his fall term courses. Does this affect your answer to question 1? In what way?

Problem 1-K:

As part of your training in accounting, you must become able to extend what you have learned into new situations. This problem provides an opportunity to increase your flexibility and broaden your understanding. The text provides all background information needed to solve this problem, but the circumstances described will be unfamiliar. Apply what you already have learned to this new situation.

1. Fresno Supply Company made a $5,000 deposit with a manufacturer. This deposit pertained to special merchandise that Fresno Supply Company had ordered. This merchandise will have a total purchase price of $50,000. Upon receiving it, Fresno Supply Company will pay the remaining $45,000.

(a) Is the deposit an asset? If so, is it monetary or nonmonetary?

(b) Is the *merchandise* an asset? If so, is it monetary or nonmonetary?

2. Los Angeles Automatic Implement, Inc.'s contract with its union expired on 6/30/X1. The parties continued under the terms of the old contract until a new 3-year contract was signed on 6/30/X2. This contract called for raises of $680,000 per year, retroactive to 6/30/X1 (that is, the raise applies to 4 years, including the one just past). The $680,000 for the previous year is payable immediately. Does this $680,000 expenditure result in an asset?

Problem 1-L:

As part of your training in accounting, you must become able to extend what you have learned into new situations. This problem provides an opportunity to increase your flexibility and broaden your understanding. The text provides all background information needed to solve this problem, but the circumstances described will be unfamiliar. Apply what you already have learned to this new situation.

Corman Compressor Corporation purchased a tract of land in 1934 for $25,000. By 19X1, this land had become worth approximately $1,300,000. On 1/15/X2, the company sold this land to Lipscomb, Incorporated, for $1,300,000. On 7/30/X2, Corman Compressor Corporation repurchased this land from Lipscomb, Incorporated, for exactly the amount that it had received—$1,300,000. Ignore tax implications in answering the following questions.

1. In accordance with conventional accounting, at what amount should Corman Compressor Corporation have shown the land in a report dated 12/31/X1? You may assume that the sale to Lipscomb, Incorporated, was being negotiated at that date, but had not been completed.

2. Assume that Lipscomb, Incorporated, is entirely independent of Corman Compressor Corporation, and that the 1/15/X2 and 7/30/X2 sales were genuine ones, arrived at through arms-length negotiations. In accordance with conventional accounting, at what amount should Corman Compressor Corporation show the land in a report dated 12/31/X2?

3. Disregard question 2. Assume that Lipscomb, Incorporated, is entirely independent of Corman Compressor Corporation, and that the 1/15/X2 sale was a genuine one, arrived at through arms-length negotiation. Because of unexpected financial difficulties, Lipscomb, Inc., was unable to pay for the land when its purchase price became due (on 4/15/X2). After considerable additional negotiation, the two companies finally agreed to cancel the sale; to accomplish this, on 7/30/X2 Lipscomb, Incorporated, sold the land back to Corman Compressor Corporation for $1,300,000. In accordance with conventional accounting, at what amount should Corman Compressor Corporation show the land in a report dated 12/31/X2?

4. Disregard questions 2 and 3. Assume that Corman Compressor Corporation and Lipscomb, Incorporated, are owned by essentially the same group of stockholders; that Lipscomb, Incorporated, never paid Corman Compressor Corporation for the land; and that there was no evidence of any motive for the two sales except Corman Compressor Corporation's distaste for reporting the land at an amount far less than its estimated market value. In accordance with conventional accounting, at what amount should Corman Compressor Corporation show the land in a report dated 12/31/X2?

Two

A Preview,
Then Some Refinements

The Main Financial
Statements and the Accounting Cycle

As I mentioned on pages 12–14, this book involves considerable study of the fundamentals of accounting before more complicated financial statements and accounting techniques are introduced. There are many such fundamentals, and if you are to comprehend them fully, their discussion must be quite detailed. Eventually you will understand how all of these basic matters relate to the financial statements the accountant prepares, but in the meantime it may be hard to see how some matters (including those discussed in later sections of this chapter) are pertinent.

Rather than ask you to take things on faith for the next six chapters, it seems preferable to give you a quick view of what's ahead—the main financial statements and main accounting techniques.

Unless you have had previous accounting experience, you are bound to encounter a few unclear points. Don't worry—they will be explained in detail later. One final word of caution: it is impossible at this stage in our discussion to define all of the terms used below as precisely as a purist would like; regard all definitions in this section as rough ones.

Revenues

You already have been introduced to a key accounting concept—the asset. One major source of assets to the firm is the sales of products and services to its customers. While some of these sales are for cash, most large firms sell mainly *on account*—that is, the asset they receive from the customer at the time of sale is an account receivable (see page 61). Later on, of course, cash is received when the account receivable is collected.

As an example, suppose that Pella Pen Co. sells two gross (288) of ballpoint pens to the campus bookstore at Sioux Lookout State College, for $60.56, on account. At the time of sale, Pella Pen Co. has acquired a new asset, an account receivable for $60.56. When the bookstore pays what it owes, that account receivable will be exchanged for a different asset: $60.56 of cash.

The inflows of new assets at the times of a firm's sales of products or services are called that firm's *revenues,* and accountants would say that the sale to the bookstore resulted in a $60.56 revenue for Pella Pen Co. The later $60.56 cash collection would *not* result in a revenue for two reasons: (1) it occurred after the sale itself, and (2) recording of a revenue at the time of cash collection would involve double-counting it—the revenue already was recorded at the time of sale.

Expenses

The previous chapter (page 49) briefly discussed situations in which a firm acquires services, but the related goods are not treated as assets—instead, the costs of these services are charged off against profits. It also discussed, a bit indirectly, situations in which a good is recognized to be an asset and its services expire over a period of time in which these services contribute to the firm's profit-seeking activities; this latter situation is the focus of the second and third sections of this chapter.

Both of these cases may be perceived as ones of services acquired by the firm expiring as a result of efforts to obtain revenues. The total cost of the asset or other services expended to obtain revenues during a particular period of time is called the *expense* of that period, and the individual outflows and expirations are called *expenses.*

For instance, one expense resulting from Pella Pen Co.'s sales to the campus bookstore is the cost to Pella Pen Co. of the 288 pens. This kind of expense, which can easily be associated with a particular sale, is called a *product expense.* But over the course of a year, for example, Pella Pen Co. will incur a number of other asset outflows and service expirations that help cause the revenues of the year *as a whole,* but they may be impossible to associate with individual sales, except arbitrarily. These are called *period expenses.*

For instance, the firm may have made substantial advertising expenditures during the year; these benefit sales as a whole, but the effect of a particular ad on any individual sale may be unclear: thus advertising expense is a period expense. Similarly, the firm's company headquarters building offers services that are of benefit to the firm as a whole and help to further all of its revenue-seeking activities. As we saw in the previous chapter, these services are steadily expiring as the building gets older; eventually all of the services embodied in the building will be exhausted. The cost of the building services that are deemed to have expired during a particular year are called a *depreciation expense* of that year, and this depreciation expense is also a period expense.

Expenses versus costs of other assets

Of course, not all asset outflows and service expirations result in expenses. Only those that are deemed to have resulted in revenues are so categorized. Instead of a revenue, another asset may have resulted; in that case (as we saw with Mr. Parker and the shelves on pages 48–49) the cost of the expended asset or other service becomes part of the cost of the new asset.

As an example, depreciation of Pella Pen Co.'s factory machinery involves an expiration of services as a result of manufacturing pens—these depreciation costs would form part of the total cost of pens to the firm, not expenses (though when the *pens* are sold, an expense equal to their total cost—including depreciation—will be recorded).

In general, then, when an asset or a service is expended, its cost is recorded either as an expense or as part of the cost of a new asset, depending upon whether the expiration is regarded as being for the current period's revenues or for the production of an asset that will benefit the revenues of future periods.[1]

Net income

I commented in the last chapter that accountants use the technical language *net income* where laymen would speak of a firm's profits. As a rough definition, the net income of a company during a particular period (such as a year) is simply the difference between that year's revenues and expenses; the resulting amount may be either positive or negative. Net income is the difference between total inflows of new assets to the firm at the time of sale (revenues) and the asset outflows and other service expirations incurred to obtain these revenues.

Notice that there is a conceptual order to these definitions. The accountant begins by identifying the revenues of a particular period; then he determines the expenses that should be associated with these revenues. Finally, and only as a kind of residual, he determines net income by subtracting expenses from revenues.

An example

I will illustrate these definitions by an extended example, which also illustrates several other things that should be mentioned in this section. For simplicity, this example is of a very small business, which ordinarily would not be incorporated. Its accounting system, however, would be appropriate for a corporation.

Mr. Germán F. Rodríguez is a machinist with Pella Pen Co., but in his spare time he has developed his own business, Kyoto Ornamental Lawn and Garden. The latter firm had its origin five years ago when his wife, Mrs. Esperanza G. Rodríguez, expressed a heartfelt desire for a six-foot Japanese stone lantern for the garden. Mr. Rodríguez was astonished at the prices charged for such lanterns, became intrigued, and figured out how to make a concrete facsimile. A neighbor offered to buy one from him, and things went on from there.

By 19X6 Mr. Rodríguez was selling six kinds of lamps and various other garden decorations, all made of a special-formula concrete (which he had perfected) resembling granite. He also had developed a process whereby growths of lichen on concrete could be convincingly simulated for an added touch of authenticity. Sales had neared the $25,000-a-year mark, necessitating employment of two part-time helpers if Mr. Rodríguez was to continue his regular work as a machinist.

At the end of October 19X6, Mr. Rodríguez took a further step to expanding his part-time business by buying expensive plastic molding equipment and various

---

[1] For brevity, a third possibility, recording a *loss,* is not considered here.

associated tools. Although quite a gamble is involved, he intends to quit his machinist job early in 19X7 and devote full time to his own business.

As of the end of the previous year, Mr. Rodríguez's accountant prepared a financial statement called a *balance sheet* for Kyoto Ornamental Lawn and Garden. This is a summary of the firm's assets; monetary assets are reported at amounts equal to the cash or rights to receive cash involved, and nonmonetary assets are reported at their *amortized historical costs*—their purchase prices, as reduced in proportion to services already received. This balance sheet is shown in Illustration 2-1. The amount reported for prepaid insurance is the unexpired balance of a comprehensive fire, casualty, and public liability policy purchased in 19X4; one-and-a-half years of coverage remain at 12/31/X5.

The distinction made on the balance sheet between *current* and *noncurrent* items may be regarded as a technicality that will be explained later. Basically, a current asset is one that will be used up and replenished within one year; all other assets are non-current. But there are exceptions to this, such as prepaid insurance (which, as indicated above, will not be used up and replenished for a year and a half).

In addition to a list of assets, this balance sheet shows two other things: *liabilities,* or the debts owed by Kyoto Ornamental Lawn and Garden to creditors, and *stockholders' equity,* or the firm's owners' residual rights to the firm's total assets after all creditor claims against the company have been allowed for.

The liability *accounts payable* refers to the ordinary trade debts that the firm owes to its suppliers of raw materials, supplies, and such. The current/noncurrent distinction applies to liabilities, too: a current liability is a debt which will come due within one year. Notice that stockholders' equity is divided into two components: one (capital stock) reflects what stockholders regard as their permanent investment in the firm; the other (retained earnings) may be considered to represent the accumulated net income of prior years, reduced by any dividends that the firm has paid.

Illustration 2-1

Kyoto Ornamental Lawn and Garden
Balance Sheet
December 31, 19X5

Assets

Current Assets:		
Cash	$ 4,078	
Accounts Receivable	2,870	
Raw Materials Inventory	143	
Finished Goods Inventory	1,107	
Prepaid Insurance	510	$ 8,708
Noncurrent Assets:		
Concrete Mixing and Molding Equipment	$ 6,240	
Tools	873	
Truck	1,240	8,353
Total Assets		$17,061

Equities

Current Liabilities:
Accounts Payable . . . . $ 987
Taxes Payable . . . .   317 $ 1,304

Stockholders' Equity:
Capital Stock $10,000
Retained Earnings   5,757   15,757

Total Equities $17,061

Here is a complete summary of this firm's 19X6 economic activity:
1. The firm purchased $940 of raw materials on account (on credit).
2. The firm manufactured finished goods at the following costs:

Raw materials used . . . . $ 916
Cost of part-time labor (paid in cash) 1,590
Depreciation of concrete mixing and molding equipment   780
Depreciation of tools   291
Cost of insurance   125

Total cost of goods manufactured $3,702

Obviously the cost of raw materials forms part of the total cost of the finished goods that were made from these raw materials. The previous chapter's discussion of Mr. Parker and the shelves he made indicates why the cost of part-time labor is part of the total cost of finished goods. The depreciation of the concrete mixing and molding equipment and the depreciation of tools both reflect expiration of asset services as a result of manufacturing activities for the year. These manufacturing activities result in the production of finished goods; accordingly, these depreciation charges are included in the cost of finished goods. On similar grounds, to the extent that the firm's insurance relates to its manufacturing operations, as prepaid insurance expires its cost becomes part of the total cost of the firm's products.

3. The firm's sales totalled $24,655; of these sales, $883 were for cash and $23,772 were on account.
4. Accounts receivable totalling $23,522 were collected during 19X6.
5. The finished goods sold in 3 had cost the firm $3,549 to manufacture.
6. The firm had the following expenses of delivering and installing finished goods for their customers:

Cost of part-time labor (paid in cash) $1,473
Gasoline, oil, etc. (purchased on account)   882
Depreciation of truck   620
Cost of insurance   175

Total delivery and installation expense $3,150

7. The firm had the following selling expenses:

Advertising (purchased on account) $4,130
Costs of participating in a local garden show (paid in cash) 1,200

Total selling expense. $5,330

8. The firm had the following administrative and general expenses:

Cost of insurance not allocated to other activities	$ 40
Telephone (purchased on account)	73
Accounting services (purchased on account)	300
Miscellaneous (purchased on account)	84
Total administrative and general expense	$497

9. The firm's taxes expense totalled $2,176.

10. In November 19X6 the firm bought new tools for use with plastics. These were purchased on account, for $2,800. Since the firm will not be making plastic goods until 19X7, these tools were not depreciated during 19X6.

11. On 10/31/X6 the firm bought plastic molding equipment for $12,370. It paid $6,370 cash as a down payment, and issued a 10% note payable due in two years for the $6,000 balance. The first interest payment on this note is due on 4/30/X7. This equipment was not depreciated during 19X6, either.

12. Just as interest receivable was accrued in the previous chapter, so a $100 liability called *interest payable* and a related $100 interest expense were accrued for interest on the 10% note payable for the period from the issue of the note to the end of 19X6 ($6,000 × 10% × 2/12 = $100).

13. The firm does not pay Mr. Rodríguez any salary. But during the year he withdrew $4,370 to provide for unexpected family medical expenses.

14. During 19X6 the firm paid accounts payable totalling $8,887 and taxes payable totalling $2,125.

Shown below are four financial statements the firm might prepare as of December 31, 19X6. The first is used internally by the firm's management and is never included in reports submitted to investors; the other three statements are included in the firm's annual reports to stockholders. For clarity, index numbers have been used in what follows to indicate the sources of various amounts; these correspond to the index numbers 1 through 14 employed above. Such index numbers and parenthetical cross-references to other financial statements would not appear in actual financial statements.

Illustration 2-2

Kyoto Ornamental Lawn and Garden
Cost of Goods Manufactured and Sold
For the Year 19X6

Direct Materials (2)		$ 916
Direct Labor (2)		1,590
Manufacturing Overhead:		
Depreciation of Concrete Mixing and Molding Equipment (2)	$780	
Depreciation of Tools (2)	291	
Cost of Insurance (2)	125	1,196
Cost of Goods Manufactured		$3,702
Finished Goods Inventory—12/31/X5 (See Ill. 2-1)		1,107
Total		$4,809
Finished Goods Inventory—12/31/X6 (See Ill. 2-5)		1,260
Cost of Goods Sold (5)		$3,549

This statement tells management (in this case Mr. Rodríguez) the details of what it cost to manufacture the year's output of finished goods. *Direct materials* and *direct labor* are standard nomenclature for raw materials and the labor of individuals who are actually engaged in making the firm's products. All other manufacturing costs are designated as *overhead*. Notice that this statement is designed to calculate the expense *cost of goods sold* (the cost to the firm of the finished goods that it sold during the year); the information in item 5 above was calculated in this way.

Illustration 2-3

Kyoto Ornamental Lawn and Garden
Statement of Income and Retained Earnings
For the Year 19X6

Revenues:
Sales (3)		$24,655
Expenses:		
Cost of Goods Sold (See Ill. 2-2)	$3,549	
Delivery and Installation Expense (6)	3,150	
Selling Expense (7)	5,330	
Administrative and General Expense (8)	497	
Interest Expense (12)	100	
Taxes Expense (9)	2,176	14,802
Net Income		$ 9,853
Dividends (13)		4,370
Increase in Retained Earnings		$ 5,483
Retained Earnings—12/31/X5 (See Ill. 2-1)		15,757
Retained Earnings—12/31/X6 (See Ill. 2-5)		$21,240

This is the statement that reports the firm's profits for the year. Notice how the *revenue, expense,* and *net income* language that was introduced at the beginning of this section is used. Dividends are treated as a distribution of profits—a simple withdrawal by the owner—rather than as an expense of doing business.

Illustration 2-4

Kyoto Ornamental Lawn and Garden
Sources and Uses of Net Working Capital
For the Year 19X6

Sources:
Funds from Operations:		
Net Income (See Ill. 2-3)	$ 9,853	
Add: Depreciation*	1,691	$11,544
Issue of Noncurrent Notes Payable (11)		6,000
Net Sources		$17,544

continued on page 84

Uses:
Purchase of Noncurrent Assets:
Plastic Molding Equipment (11)	$12,370	
Tools (10)	2,800	$15,170

Dividends (13).		4,370
Net Uses		$19,540
Decrease in Net Working Capital		$ 1,996

Net Working Capital—12/31/X5:
Current Assets (See Ill. 2-1)	$ 8,708	
Current Liabilities (See Ill. 2-1)	1,304	$ 7,404

Net Working Capital—12/31/X6:
Current Assets (See Ill. 2-5)	$ 7,185	
Current Liabilities (See Ill. 2-5)	1,777	5,408

Decrease in Net Working Capital		$ 1,996

---

* *Depreciation of concrete mixing and molding equipment (2)*. .	$ 780
Depreciation of tools (2)	291
Depreciation of truck (6)	620
Total depreciation.	$1,691

The income and retained earnings statement summarizes the firm's profits for the year; the sources and uses of net working capital statement summarizes its *financial* activities, such as purchases of long-lived assets and issuing of long-term debt. Simultaneously, this statement reflects changes in the firm's *net working capital.* For the present you may simply regard net working capital as an index of the firm's general liquidity; arithmetically, net working capital equals the firm's current assets less its current liabilities.

The main information given by Illustration 2-4 is that the firm's net current resources decreased during the year by $1,996. This resulted from using these resources for dividends ($4,370) and purchases of new equipment and tools ($15,710); however, the effects of these uses were partly offset by issue of long-term debt ($6,000) and by a favorable effect of the firm's profit-making activities on its net current resources ($11,544). Statements of sources and uses of net working capital often are called *funds statements.*

Illustration 2-5

Kyoto Ornamental Lawn and Garden
Comparative Balance Sheets
December 31, 19X6 and 19X5

	December 31	
	19X6	*19X5*
Assets		
Current Assets:		
Cash	$ 2,468	$ 4,078
Accounts Receivable	3,120	2,870
Raw Materials Inventory.	167	143
Finished Goods Inventory	1,260	1,107
Prepaid Insurance	170	510
Total Current Assets	$ 7,185	$ 8,708

Noncurrent Assets:

Concrete Mixing and Molding Equipment.	$ 5,460	$ 6,240
Plastic Molding Equipment	12,370	–0–
Tools	3,382	873
Truck	620	1,240
Total Noncurrent Assets	$ 21,832	$ 8,353
Total Assets	$ 29,017	$ 17,061

Equities

Current Liabilities:

Accounts Payable.	$ 1,309	$ 987
Taxes Payable.	368	317
Interest Payable	100	–0–
Total Current Liabilities	$ 1,777	$ 1,304

Noncurrent Liability:

10% Note Payable—due 10/30/X8	6,000	–0–
Total Liabilities	$ 7,777	$ 1,304

Stockholders' Equity:

Capital Stock	$ 10,000	$ 10,000
Retained Earnings.	11,240	5,757
Total Stockholders' Equity.	$ 21,240	$ 15,757
Total Equities	$ 29,017	$ 17,061

This is the firm's 12/31/X6 balance sheet, cast in a form that allows ready comparison with the 12/31/X5 balance sheet (the source of its 19X5 column).

The recording process

Of course, no medium- or large-sized firm can prepare its financial statements directly from something like our items 1 through 14. Instead, an extensive detailed recording process is employed. We can get a little insight into this process by asking how the firm's 12/31/X6 figure for cash might be determined from the information given in items 1 through 14. Here is one way to do it:

Cash Receipts:

Sales (3)	$ 883	
Collections on account (4)	23,522	$ 24,405

Cash Expenditures:

Manufacturing labor (2)	$ 1,590	
Delivery and installation labor (6)	1,473	
Garden show (7)	1,200	
Plastic molding equipment (11)	6,370	
Dividends (13)	4,370	
Payment of current liabilities (14)	11,012	26,015

Decrease in Cash during 19X6 .	$ (1,610)
Cash—12/31/X5 (See Ill. 2-1)	4,078
Cash—12/31/X6 (See Ill. 2-5)	$ 2,468

Actually, the 12/31/X6 figure for cash is calculated in a manner more like the following:

Cash

√	4,078	(2)	1,590
(3)	883	(6)	1,473
(4)	23,522	(7)	1,200
		(11)	6,370
		(13)	4,370
		(14)	11,012
		√	2,468
	28,483		28,483
√	2,468		

This is called a *ledger account* (or, in the simplified form shown here, a *T-account*). This cash ledger account is just a compressed form of the previous schedule, turned on its side, with check marks (√) signifying beginning and ending balances. Of course in practice this ledger account would be much more detailed, since day-by-day information would be shown instead of the summarized information for the whole year. Without such an information-accumulation device as a ledger account, preparation of financial statements could become impossibly complicated.

For comparison, here is the simpler T-account for the firm's accounts receivable:

Accounts Receivable

√	2,870	(4)	23,522
(3)	23,772	√	3,120
	26,642		26,642
√	3,120		

Notice that the events indexed with a 4 affect both cash and accounts receivable. Ledger accounts record a firm's economic activities by the kinds of assets, liabilities, or stockholders' equity they affect. But all economic activity affects at least two different ledger accounts (for reasons that will be explained in the next two chapters), and it is helpful to have an additional way of recording activity by the kind of *event* involved. We might in this case summarize the overall effect of the collections of accounts receivable by writing:

> *Cash increased by $23,522 while Accounts Receivable decreased by $23,522.*

Instead, accountants use the following shorthand, which is called a *journal entry*:

Cash	23,522	
Accounts Receivable		23,522

During the year, many journal entries are made and much recording in ledger accounts is done. At year end, the firm's records are brought up to date, certain events are recorded that didn't need to be recorded during the year itself, financial statements are prepared, and the firm's records are made ready to receive information about next year's economic activity. (If the firm prepares quarterly or monthly financial statements, this may be done on a quarterly or monthly instead of an annual basis.) The totality of these activities over a year is called the *accounting cycle.*

Theory

Finally, if you are to understand fully the various matters mentioned in this section, it is necessary that you take a close look at the theory of financial accounting: the logical structures and reasoning processes that lie beneath the published financial statements and largely determine their significance. We shall see that there are several crucial areas of theory in financial accounting, the totality of which might be designated the *theory of financial accounting measurement.* One area is *asset valuation theory,* which concerns the amounts reported for assets on balance sheets. This is closely related to *revenue recognition theory,* which concerns the amount of revenue to be reported on the income statements of individual accounting periods. Asset valuation theory is also closely related to *amortization theory,* which concerns the ways in which the amounts reported for nonmonetary assets should be written down, and the ways expenses or other assets should be reported as these nonmonetary assets yield their services. Finally, all of these kinds of theory turn out to be closely related to the general topic of *allocation theory,* which concerns such things as the ways profits are assigned to individual periods of time or to individual assets. The relationship of allocation theory to financial accounting will be explained as we progress.

Order of topic presentation

To avoid introducing too many new concepts at once and to clarify the interrelationships of the various concepts, this book will discuss the matters mentioned in this section in a different order than we used above. Here is the order in which this section's topics are introduced (for a somewhat more detailed outline of this book including secondary topics not mentioned above, see pages 12–14):

Remainder of Chapter Two: depreciation and other amortizations; current/noncurrent distinction; elementary amortization theory.

Chapter Three: liabilities, stockholders' equity, balance sheet; asset valuation theory.

Chapter Four: ledgers; general theory of accounting measurements.

Chapter Five: journal entries; stockholder's equity.

Chapter Six: introduction to other financial statements; discussion of financial activities; allocation theory.

Chapter Seven: net working capital; statement of sources and uses of net working capital.

Chapter Eight: revenues, expenses, net income; statement of income and retained earnings; revenue recognition theory.

Chapter Nine: interrelationships of financial statements.

Chapter Ten: the accounting cycle.

Chapter Eleven: monetary assets and liabilities.

Chapter Twelve: statement of cost of goods manufactured and sold.

Chapter Thirteen: amortization of nonmonetary assets; amortization theory.

Another example

For those readers who may be interested, here are other examples of a balance sheet, a statement of sources and uses of net working capital, and a statement of income and retained earnings. The financial statements of C. M. de Céspedes Cigar Co. for the year ended December 31, 19X5, are given below. The style of presentation in these reports was deliberately chosen to deviate somewhat from the style of the Kyoto Ornamental Lawn and Garden reports (which is the style used in the bulk of this book), thus illustrating some of the variations in form that are allowed. As before, do not worry at this point about anything that you do not happen to understand in what follows.

Illustration 2-6

C. M. de Céspedes Cigar Co.
and Subsidiary Companies
Consolidated Balance Sheets

Assets

	December 31, 19X5		December 31, 19X4	
Current Assets:				
Cash		$ 4,829,134		$ 4,277,506
Marketable securities (market value $765,892)		726,670		–0–
Receivables:				
Trade accounts, less allowance of $256,164 (19X4—$261,051)	$12,568,521		$11,493,347	
Other	1,451,171	14,019,692	1,288,008	12,781,355
Inventories, principally at average cost:				
Raw materials, including tobacco in process of aging	$25,710,344		$23,065,167	
Manufactured products . . .	12,947,176		10,340,519	
Supplies	2,244,961	40,902,481	2,179,066	35,584,752
Prepaid expenses		480,225		517,387
Total current assets		$60,958,202		$53,161,000
Other Assets:				
Investment in and advances to affiliated company. . . .		$ 307,311		$ 245,636
Long-term receivables		263,200		177,100
Unamortized bond discount and other assets.		565,617		601,135
		$ 1,136,128		$ 1,023,871
Property and Equipment, at cost				
Land		$ 2,487,637		$ 2,671,891
Buildings.	$ 9,405,868		$ 9,304,429	
Equipment and machinery. . .	15,307,608		14,443,796	
Total	$24,713,476		$23,748,225	
Accumulated depreciation . . .	9,387,712	15,325,764	8,145,870	15,602,355

Unamortized cost of cigar machine licenses	2,457,191	2,792,533
	$20,270,592	$21,066,779
Total assets	$82,364,922	$75,251,650

Liabilities and Stockholders' Equity

Current Liabilities:

Accounts payable and accrued liabilities	$ 9,746,072	$10,129,055
Short-term notes payable . . .	18,841,907	9,660,000
Portion of long-term debt due within one year	1,914,532	3,255,717
Income taxes	570,205	507,482
Total current liabilities	$31,072,716	$23,552,254
Long-Term Debt	$24,262,668	$25,705,439

Stockholders' Equity:

Preferred stock, par value $100: Authorized 100,000 shares; issued 47,340 shares . .	$ 4,734,000		$ 4,734,000	
Common stock, par value $1: Authorized 5,000,000 shares; issued 1,634,282 shares including 60,121 shares in treasury (19X4—61,398 shares)	1,634,282		1,634,282	
Paid-in capital in excess of par .	1,172,123		1,172,123	
Retained earnings	22,171,131	$29,711,536	21,192,517	$28,732,922
Less: Treasury stock, at cost . .		2,681,998		2,738,965
		$27,029,538		$25,993,957
Total liabilities and stockholders' equity		$82,364,922		$75,251,650

Illustration 2-7

C. M. de Céspedes Cigar Co.
and Subsidiary Companies
Consolidated Income and Retained Earnings
For the Year Ended December 31, 19X5

Net sales and other revenues		$165,701,527
Costs and expenses:		
Cost of goods sold	$132,706,749	
Selling, administrative, and general expenses	26,178,638	
Interest expense	2,622,296	
Income taxes	1,357,631	162,865,314
Net income		$ 2,836,213
Retained earnings at beginning of year		21,192,517
		$ 24,028,730
Dividends (per share: common—$1, preferred—$6). . .		1,857,599
Retained earnings at end of year		$ 22,171,131

As before, the income and retained earnings statement is a report on the firm's profits, in this case for the year 19X5, giving a summary description of the firm's profit-seeking activities. During 19X5 the firm had an inflow of $165,701,527 of new assets, mainly from sales of its principal products (*other revenues* relate to such things as interest received on investments). Costs of providing these products to customers included $132,706,749 for the products themselves, $26,178,638 for general costs of running the business, $2,622,296 for interest, and $1,357,631 for taxes. The net profit for the year was $2,836,213, and dividends of $1,857,599 were paid to stockholders.

Illustration 2-8

C. M. de Céspedes Cigar Co.
and Subsidiary Companies
Consolidated Sources and Uses of Funds
For the Year Ended December 31, 19X5

Sources of funds:

Net income for the year		$ 2,836,213
Add items which did not require current use of funds:		
Depreciation and amortization	$1,757,042	
Other	245,721	2,002,763
Funds provided by operations		$ 4,838,976
Increase in common stock outstanding		56,967
Disposals of property and equipment		154,709
Other, net		63,691
		$ 5,114,343

Uses of funds:

Additions to property and equipment	$ 1,475,558
Dividends	1,857,599
Decrease in long-term debt	1,442,771
Investment in and advances to affiliated company	61,675
	$ 4,837,603
Increase in net working capital	$ 276,740
Net working capital: Beginning of year	29,608,746
End of year	$29,885,486

As was indicated earlier, "funds" is an alternate name for net working capital, and a funds statement is a summary of certain major changes in noncurrent assets and liabilities that were not reported on the statement of income and retained earnings—in particular, changes in the firm's long-term obligations and commitments to long-lived assets, such as its $1,442,771 repayment of long-term debt and $1,475,558 purchase of property and equipment. In addition, this statement reflects a $4,838,976 short-term effect of the firm's profit seeking activities on its current assets and liabilities, the same $1,857,599 dividend payment that is reflected on the income and retained earnings statement, and various relatively minor matters.[2]

Nonmonetary Assets
and Their Amortization

A nonmonetary asset has been defined (in a slightly abbreviated way) as:

> An object or right offering future economic benefits to a company, purchased by the company for a known price. The dollar amount of this price, which is used to represent the asset, can be reduced in some accepted way as parts of these benefits are determined to have been yielded. (See page 54.)

How the accountant views nonmonetary assets

A number of things need to be emphasized at the start. Some may be surprising; others may appear unimportant. Yet understanding what is discussed in the next few pages will be very helpful in understanding other parts of this book.

The way in which the accountant looks at nonmonetary assets is another example of his viewing things differently from the layman. When the layman thinks of a building, he visualizes a physical object: walls, roof, doors, and windows. But when the accountant speaks of the asset *Building,* his reference is to nothing of the sort. He is little concerned with the physical building itself, except as its physical characteristics may affect its purchase price or the services the building will offer. The accountant doesn't care whether the building is wood, brick, or concrete, or whether it is brown, green, or polkadot. *His primary concern is with a set of expected economic benefits: benefits from the services that the company has purchased and that the building is expected to provide in the future.* The accountant simply ignores all other properties of nonmonetary assets.

Notice again that the way in which the accountant looks at the asset *Building* parallels the way he looked at the asset *Prepaid Employee Services* in Chapter One (see pages 49–50):

1. In both cases, the accountant is primarily interested in the company's purchased right to a set of expected benefits. The accountant is essentially unconcerned with the physical building itself, or with the employee's actual appearance, habits, and personality.

2. While the right to receive services is considered an asset, the actual services themselves are not, unless they lose their identity by becoming incorporated in some

---

[2] A few readers already will be generally familiar with the kinds of financial statements that are shown here. Two bits of additional information will clarify what might at first seem to be discrepancies:

(1) Some dividends on common stock were paid prior to the firm's reissue of treasury stock; therefore the total income statement figure for dividends seems inconsistent with the number of shares of common and preferred stock that are outstanding at year end.

(2) The firm unwisely purchased land at an inflated price a few years ago. It sold the land at a loss this year and included the loss among its general expenses since it was not judged to be of sufficient magnitude to be reported as an extraordinary item.

other asset. Chapter One (pages 48–50) discussed this in reference to employee services; it is also true of buildings, for unless incorporated in some other asset: (a) building services offer no benefit past the moment they are received; or (b) the magnitude and duration of the future benefit cannot be estimated satisfactorily.

3. On the other hand, when some other asset is in part brought into being through the release of building services, the cost of building services becomes part of the historical cost of the new asset. We have seen that part of the historical cost of manufactured inventories is the cost of the services of the employees who made them. Another part of the historical cost of manufactured inventories is some (prorated) part of the cost of the building in which they were made.

The accountant thus treats all nonmonetary assets as abstract bundles of services —as service potentials (or collections of potential benefits), not as physical objects. All that really concerns the accountant is the quantity of expected benefits offered by a nonmonetary asset and its purchase price. This information is closely related to the way in which the accountant determines the figures he reports for these assets.

Allocation

Before going any further it will be helpful to introduce a technical term: allocation. An *allocation* occurs whenever a total is divided into parts. If a pizza is sliced and divided among several people, the pizza has been allocated. If you buy new shoes for cash, some of your total cash has been allocated to the purchase of shoes. If portions of the cost of a building are associated with successive years in which the building is used, that is an allocation, too.

On page 23 we saw a specialized use of the word "allocation" when "resource allocation" decisions made by investors were discussed—decisions as to how to divide money available for investment among different possible common stocks of different firms, for example. In the remainder of this book we will need to be able to speak both of allocation in its general sense of *any* kind of division into parts as well as of resource allocation *per se*.

How the accountant determines the figure used to represent the nonmonetary asset

The figure at which the accountant first reports the nonmonetary asset is its purchase price. As was indicated on page 42, at any future date, the figure associated with the nonmonetary asset is determined in the following general way (with one or two minor exceptions of the sorts discussed on pages 57–59).

1. The accountant decides on some measure or index of the quantity of economic benefits that the nonmonetary asset is expected to provide. For a building, this might be years of occupancy.

2. The accountant then estimates how many units of this kind of service the particular asset will provide over its whole life. For a building, this might be 50 years. (For simplicity, we will also assume that the estimates made by accountants are always correct; later we'll discuss what to do when the estimates are wrong.)

3. The accountant next decides how these units of service are to be associated with the purchase price. Some interesting and difficult problems can occur at this point, but we will simplify again. For the time being, assume that *each unit of service bears*

the same share of the purchase price as each other unit. For example, if our 50-year building cost $250,000, each year of service will be associated with a cost of $5,000 ($250,000 ÷ 50 = $5,000). Each unit of service is treated in the same manner as each other unit of service.

4. Finally, the accountant determines the figure at which the asset will be reported by multiplying all units of service still to be received by the allocated cost associated with each unit of service. For instance, if our building is exactly seven years old, it has 43 service years left (50 − 7 = 43). It will be reported at the figure $215,000 (43 × $5,000 = $215,000). At the end of next year, it will be shown at the figure $210,000 (42 × $5,000 = $210,000).

These figures of $215,000 and $210,000 are what the accountant is referring to when he speaks of reporting the building at its historical cost. What he is actually doing is allocating part of the historical cost of the building to the remaining future economic benefits still to be received from the building.

(As we saw in the first section of this chapter, the remainder of the building's historical cost—those parts that are *not* allocated to its future economic benefits— are treated as current period costs and either expensed or regarded as part of the costs of other assets. For example, in the previous illustration if the building is written down from $215,000 to $210,000 during the current year, the $5,000 depreciation either appears as an expense on the income statement or as a product cost on the statement of cost of goods manufactured and sold.)

Why the accountant does this

At first, this may seem an overly complicated set of things for the accountant to do. But the alternatives are all quite unsatisfactory to him:

1. He could record the purchase of the building, but immediately thereafter reduce the figure at which it was reported to zero (i.e., treat its costs the way that those of research and development often are treated, and refuse to recognize an asset—see page 45). The problem is that doing this implies that the building yields up all of its economic benefits in the first year. This violates the facts; these services will be received for the next 50 years and, as will be demonstrated in Parts II and III of this book, the accountant has strong reasons (relating mostly to income measurement) to allocate the costs of these services to the years in which they are received.

2. The accountant could report the building at its original purchase price until its year of retirement, *then* reduce the figure at which it was reported to zero (i.e., treat buildings in the same way that, we will see on page 102, he treats land). But if he did, the full $250,000 would be reported as a decline in buildings in the last year—an alternative that has all of the defects of the first approach.

3. The accountant could report the building at its current market value or at its original purchase price, whichever was lower. The main problem with this is again that (for income measurement purposes) the accountant wishes to allocate portions of the building's costs to the services that the building provides in different years, and to decrease the amount reported for the asset proportionately to the receipt of these services and the resulting decline in its future service potential. Declines in market values are rarely proportionate to declines in service potentials, because market values are affected by various things which are unrelated to the firm itself. Also, as a practical

matter, market values may be unobtainable for specialized buildings and other non-monetary assets tailor-made to the firm's specific needs.

Accordingly, the accountant follows the only remaining alternative; he gradually decreases the amount reported for the building by allocating a portion of its cost to each year in which it provides service, in an amount intended to be proportionate to the amount of these services. I will argue in Chapters Six, Eight, and Thirteen that this approach isn't really satisfactory, either; but at present accountants *believe* that it is. Moreover, this method of reporting nonmonetary assets is acceptable for nearly all legal, regulatory, and other institutional purposes.

A comparison of the treatments given nonmonetary assets and interest receivable

Notice that the figure shown for a nonmonetary asset is determined in much the same way as the figure for accrued interest receivable in Chapter One (see pages 62–63). There is one big difference: interest receivable starts out at zero, then, a uniform fee for each unit of service is added; but the unit of service still is a period of time—the period for which the money is lent. In contrast, a nonmonetary asset starts with a purchase price, then a uniform "fee" for each unit of service is subtracted.

Compare two cases. Assume that a company owns a six-year, 5 percent note receivable for $100,000, all interest due at the time the principal is due. Assume that the company also owns a building costing $30,000, with an estimated service life of six years. (To explain the building's relatively short service life, suppose that it is a temporary shelter erected over an outdoor storage area.) The figures reported for interest receivable and the building will be:

		Interest Receivable*	Building
At the Outset:		$ –0–	$30,000
At the End of Year:	1	5,000	25,000
	2	10,000	20,000
	3	15,000	15,000
	4	20,000	10,000
	5	25,000	5,000
	6	30,000	–0–

* The reader is reminded that simple interest is being assumed until Chapter Eleven. However, the same general principle illustrated here holds true with compound interest.

(Of course, the figure reported for the 5 percent note receivable will be $100,000 throughout the six years.)

Accrual, depreciation, amortization

This is a good time to introduce some technical language that we shall use often in what follows. First, to repeat what was said on pages 63–64, in accountant's jargon, what we have been doing with interest receivable is called *accrual*. Interest fees of $30,000 accrue over the six-year period for the 5 percent note receivable. *Accrual* means a kind of regular, systematic increase, or adding-on. What we have been doing with the building is called *depreciation*. Over the six-year period, the building depreciates by $30,000. *Depreciation* means a kind of regular, systematic decrease, or subtracting down.

We could also speak of "writing up" the interest receivable and of "writing down" the building: "write-up" would mean exactly the same thing as accrue; "write-down" would mean exactly the same thing as depreciate. Technically, the word "depreciation" relates only to such nonmonetary assets as buildings, equipment, and certain other items of plant. When speaking of writing down a patent or a lease, we should use the term *amortization*; the term for writing down natural resource assets such as mining properties or timberlands is *depletion*. These words have essentially the same meaning as depreciation.

General terms that can be used to describe decreases in figures reported for any nonmonetary assets are "write-down," "write-off," or "amortization." Many accountants confine "amortization" to patents and leases,[3] but it has begun to acquire a more general significance in recent usage. All of this language is conventional, but, like any other technical jargon, it may seem strange at first. You need to memorize it if you wish to discuss accounting matters clearly with others. To summarize:

1. An increase in the figure reported for an asset: write-up or accrual.
2. A decrease in the figure reported for an asset:
   (a) Any asset: write-down, write-off,[4] or amortization.
   (b) Buildings, equipment, tools: depreciation.
   (c) Patents, leases: amortization.
   (d) Mining or timber property: depletion.

Finally, I will refer to the figure at which a nonmonetary asset is reported either as its *amortized historical cost* or, for brevity, simply as its *historical cost*.[5]

Nonmonetary Assets:
Examples and Further Complications

So far, the only nonmonetary assets discussed in any detail have been buildings. We should now apply what we've learned to a representative collection of other

---

[3] The term is also used with goodwill, and discount and premium on debt—matters that will be discussed later.

[4] Some accountants prefer to restrict these first two words to buildings, equipment, and other items of plant. This book will instead use them in a broad sense, as opposite in meaning to "write-up" and applicable to any asset whatever.

[5] Of course, one might also refer to this amount as the asset's *unamortized* historical cost—that portion of its purchase price that has not yet been written off. I prefer *amortized historical cost* because it makes clear that the accountant is reporting a figure that results from taking a straightforward measurement (the historical cost), then transforming it by an amortization process (which, as we shall see later, is far from straightforward). In any event, the following three phrases usually have the same significance: *the historical cost of a nonmonetary asset, the amortized historical cost of a nonmonetary asset,* and *the unamortized historical cost of a nonmonetary asset*; whenever finer distinctions are required, they will be made.

nonmonetary assets. Illustration 2-9 lists the nonmonetary assets of Illustrative Corporation and the related dollar figures. As with certain other illustrations in this book, Illustration 2-9 is not necessarily realistic.

Illustration 2-9

Illustrative Corporation
Nonmonetary Assets
December 31, 19X1

Inventories	$200,000
Supplies	23,000
Prepaid Rent	12,000
Land	65,000
Buildings	95,000
Equipment	230,000
Patents	40,000
	$665,000

An additional difficulty with nonmonetary assets

Nonmonetary assets create more reporting problems than do monetary assets. A monetary asset is either cash itself or a right to receive a specific amount of cash; it is recorded at a figure equal to that amount of cash. The only complication in reporting monetary assets comes when it is necessary to accrue a receivable (see pages 62–64).

In contrast, *most* nonmonetary assets are reported at amounts that are the result of one kind or another of calculation. For as we saw on pages 42–44, as a nonmonetary asset's services are released to the firm, the historical cost at which it initially was reported is reduced prorata. Therefore, with most nonmonetary assets we must be concerned both with what they cost and with the extent to which parts of these costs should be written off to reflect services already received. Unavoidably we must make a number of arithmetic computations to calculate appropriate write-downs; fortunately these computations are simple.

Rather than discuss nonmonetary assets in the order in which they are listed in Illustration 2-9, it will be helpful to skip around a little.

Prepaid rent

Prepaid rent offers an excellent example of a typical nonmonetary asset. Suppose that on 5/1/X1 the company paid one year's rent of $36,000 in advance on warehouse facilities. The company thereby acquired a nonmonetary asset: a year of warehouse services. The measure of the quantity of these services is time: twelve months. A cost of $3,000 a month would be associated with these services ($36,000 ÷ 12 = $3,000). (Remember, for simplicity we assume equal-length months.) At 12/31/X1, eight months' service will have been used up, leaving four months' service. At an allocated cost of $3,000 a month, $12,000 is the figure to be associated with prepaid rent at 12/31/X1 (4 × $3,000 = $12,000). This $12,000 is the net historical cost of the asset: it represents a write-down, or an amortization of the original $36,000 expenditure.

The $36,000 rental prepayment was made to obtain twelve months of warehouse services. There were eight months of warehouse occupancy under this prepayment during the current year, and there will be four more months of occupancy next year. In effect, the accountant is *allocating* $24,000 of the original $36,000 to the first eight months and $12,000 to the four months of services that are yet to be received ($36,000 × 4/12 = $12,000). Regardless of what rental rates are at 12/31/X1, the accountant would show $12,000 as the figure for the asset. Suppose that local rental rates had doubled in the last eight months and that four months' rent would now cost $24,000. As far as the present asset is concerned, the accountant is unconcerned, although if next year's rent costs twice as much, he will certainly record next year's prepaid rent at the higher figure.

> *Prepaid rent* is a right to receive the nonmonetary services provided by properties (usually land and buildings) which themselves are the assets of other entities; this asset comes into being when the firm makes payments in advance for these non-monetary rights.

Patents

Patents work in much the same way. Loosely speaking, a patent is a legal right to keep your competitors from manufacturing something that you are manufacturing or from making it in a particular way. The useful life of a patent is set by the shorter of the following two events:

1. Expiration of the patent. The legal right is granted for only a limited number of years (17 years), after which competitors can do whatever they like.

2. Obsolescence of the product. Patents become obsolete as the market for the related product dries up. To take the standard example, a buggy whip patent probably would no longer be an asset, even if the related legal right had not yet expired. Much the same would be true of a patent on a fad item (such as hula-hoops) in which the public has lost interest.

Suppose that Illustrative Corporation's patents were all purchased exactly three years ago, at which time they were four years old and had a 13-year remaining legal life. The service life of these patents to the company would be the shorter of either 13 years or the time at which the related product would no longer be worth making. If the company expected to make the product for at least 15 years, the service life of the patents would be 13 years. If the patents originally cost Illustrative Corporation $52,000, the figure at which they would be reported after three years' ownership by the company would be $40,000, as shown in Illustration 2-9 (page 96). This figure is computed as follows:

$$\$52,000 - 3/13(\$52,000) = \$40,000$$

Notice that the $12,000 amortization of the patents ($52,000 − $40,000 = $12,000) relates to the three years in which the patents have been owned by Illustrative Corporation. It has nothing to do with the previous period of four years, during which the patents were owned by some other entity. With *any* method of write-down, the accountant is concerned only with the entity that his report is about and what has happened to that entity. (This restriction of the accountant's concern to the individual entity was discussed on pages 27 and 40.) Patent amortization allocates only that cost of the asset that was incurred by the company discussed in the financial report.

A *patent* is a right granted by the government to an entity entitling that entity to be the sole manufacturer of a product or the sole user of a process; accordingly, a patent is a nonmonetary right to receive protection for a period of years against the entity's competitors making the product or using the process.

Service life

Before going any further, we should introduce an additional concept: the *service life* of an asset. This may be defined as that period of time during which the services yielded to the firm by the asset are great enough to outweigh the costs of using that asset, and during which it is uneconomical to acquire the same services from some competing source. Most assets are retired from service long before they have reached the point of physical disintegration—usually because they have become too expensive or troublesome to maintain in good operating condition or because technology has changed. Such changes in technology can either render the services provided by the asset obsolete or introduce improved assets that do a better or cheaper job of providing these services. The service life of an asset is simply the period of time between the point at which the firm first begins to use the asset and the point at which the asset is retired. (Such asset retirement and replacement decisions usually are assisted by calculations made by managerial accountants; the financial accountants' job is to record the *consequences* of such decisions. This is another example of something mentioned on page 30: an output of one system of accounting influencing the inputs of a different accounting system.)

Buildings

The definition of *buildings* used in accounting is identical with the one used in ordinary English. Let's contrast two different possibilities for a single building.

1. Suppose the building cost $150,000 and is expected to have a 25-year service life. On 12/31/X1, the building will be eleven years old, and it is expected to be worthless at the time it is retired. (For simplicity, assume also that any value that the building has at retirement is expected to be approximately equal to the demolition costs.) Over its service life, this building should be written down from an initial figure of $150,000 to zero, at a rate of $6,000 a year ($150,000 ÷ 25 = $6,000). Part A of Illustration 2-10 shows this graphically.

The diagonal line in Illustration 2-10 shows the figure associated with the building at any point in its service life. At the outset, the building is reported at $150,000. At the end of its 25-year life, the building is reported at $0. At the end of eight years, it is reported at $102,000.

$$\$150,000 - 8/25(\$150,000) = \$102,000$$

The slope of the diagonal line is $6,000 a year, the rate at which the building is being depreciated. Over its 25-year service life, the whole $150,000 purchase price is written off by allocating $6,000 of it to each year. When the building is eleven years old, $66,000 will have been written off ($6,000 × 11 = $66,000), leaving a remaining net historical cost of $84,000 ($150,000 − $66,000 = $84,000).

Illustration 2-10

Write-down of a Building under Two Different Assumptions
(*In both cases the building is assumed to have cost $150,000 and to
have an estimated life of 25 years.*)

A. Assume a scrap value at retirement of zero.

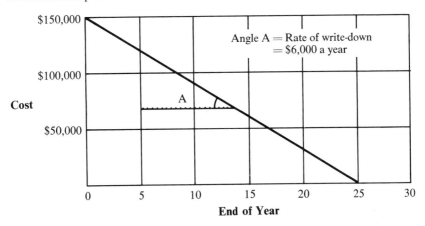

B. Assume a scrap value at retirement of $25,000.

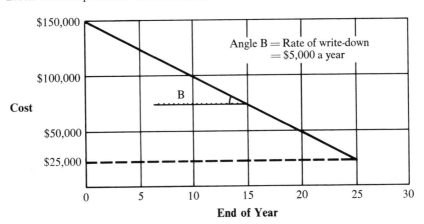

Despite a few complications, which we'll discuss later, that's about all there is to depreciation: just an attempt to write off the cost of the asset in a systematic way during the periods in which the services of that asset have been utilized. Portions of the asset's cost are associated with these services as they are received. The total amount of cost so associated is the difference between the asset's purchase price and what the asset is worth at the end of its service life.

Often the services offered by an asset are exhausted as the asset itself gradually wears out or otherwise deteriorates; for example, this would be true of many kinds of dies and cutting tools, furnace linings, and so on. But depreciation in the accounting sense need have nothing to do with "wearing out," or physical deterioration; instead, it quite possibly may result from an otherwise serviceable asset's becoming obsolete. For instance, once a new edition of a textbook has been printed, the printing plates for the old edition are virtually worthless, even if they are in perfect condition. Their service life is determined by obsolescence, not by wear and tear.

Nor has depreciation anything to do with current market values; this is one consequence of the accountant's decision to base his nonmonetary asset figures on historical purchase prices (see pages 56–59). It is quite important to be aware of this when you are considering depreciable assets that have a ready secondhand market—automobiles, for example. When you buy a new car, the amount at which you can resell it is always significantly less than the amount you paid; yet this drop in resale price has nothing to do with accounting depreciation. Suppose you buy a new car for $2,400, expecting to get 4 years', or 48 months' service from it. Ignore possible scrap values. Suppose that at the end of one month the car could be resold for $1,900. An accountant would represent the car by a figure of $2,350 ($2,400 − 1/48($2,400) = $2,350), not $1,900. As indicated earlier, the accountant is essentially unconcerned with the physical properties of the asset. The building in Illustration 2-10 may be in as good shape at the end of the first year as it was at the outset, but the figure at which it will be reported will be $6,000 less. Why? Because the building offered an estimated total of 25 years of service (costing a total of $150,000), and 1/25th of the service is now gone.

2. Let's add a complication. So far we've been writing all nonmonetary assets down to zero over their service lives. But this procedure will not always be appropriate; even after the asset has yielded all of its services, it may still have some sort of scrap value, if only as junk.

Turn to Part B of Illustration 2-10 (on page 99). The facts about the building are the same as before ($150,000 cost; 25-year life), with one difference: the company expects the building to have a $25,000 scrap value on retirement. (You might assume that the company plans to move to a new location in 25 years and expects to sell the building for $25,000 at that time.) The term *scrap value* can refer to *any* kind of residual value after the asset has yielded the services for which it was purchased. Given a scrap value of $25,000, the total cost that must be written off over the 25 years is only $125,000 ($150,000 − $25,000 = $125,000). Therefore, annual depreciation will be at a rate of only $5,000 a year ($125,000/25 = $5,000). At the end of its eleventh year, the building will be reported at $95,000.

$$\$150,000 - 11(\$5,000) = \$95,000$$

This is the figure at which the building is shown in Illustration 2-9 (page 96). Illustration 2-9 reports (among other things) an eleven-year-old building that cost $150,000 with an estimated scrap value at retirement of $25,000.

In general, the figure at which buildings or equipment will be reported can be determined from the following formula:

$$\text{Purchase Price} - \left[\frac{\text{Actual Life to Date}}{\text{Estimated Total Life}} \times \left(\text{Purchase Price} - \substack{\text{Estimated Scrap} \\ \text{Value at} \\ \text{Retirement}} \right) \right] = \substack{\text{Figure To Be} \\ \text{Reported}}$$

$$\$150,000 - [\quad 11/25 \quad \times \quad (\$150,000 - \$25,000) \quad] = \quad \underline{\$95,000}$$

(Some students are distressed by algebra, but don't let *this* kind of algebra trouble you. It is merely a way of putting a set of instructions concisely instead of at length. If you prefer, here is this formula in ordinary English:

> The rule for determining the amount at which buildings or equipment will be reported is as follows: first, subtract the asset's estimated scrap value at retirement from its purchase price; the result is the total amount to be depreciated over the asset's life. Second, determine the fraction of the asset's total life that has occurred to date and multiply this by the total amount to be depreciated; the result is the total depreciation of the asset to date. Finally, subtract the total depreciation to date from the purchase price itself; the result is the amount at which the asset should be reported.

The formula says exactly the same things as the paragraph, but it says them more simply and in a way that facilitates more rapid depreciation calculations. We will see at the end of this section that the same formula can be applied to all other non-monetary assets, too. Accordingly, you will find it worth your while to use this formula.)

Equipment

As used in accounting, the term *equipment* may refer to all kinds of machines that are assets of the firm, as well as items of furniture, bins and shelves, tools, counters, and so on. Many firms, however, use separate asset categories for individual kinds of equipment, such as *automobiles and trucks, furniture, fixtures* (shelves, lighting installations, and the like), and *tools*. But if the firm prefers, all of these may be classified simply as "equipment."

The figure for equipment in Illustration 2-9 is $230,000. For simplicity, assume that the equipment was all purchased four years ago for $332,000, at which time it had an estimated life of 12 years and an estimated scrap value on retirement of $26,000. Using our formula, the figure at which this asset should be reported on 12/31/X1 would be:

$$\$332,000 - [4/12 \times (332,000 - \$26,000)] = \underline{\$230,000}$$

The same figure could have been determined in the following way. The total cost of owning the equipment over its whole service life is the difference between its purchase price and its scrap value on retirement: $306,000 ($332,000 − $26,000 = $306,000). An equal part of this cost should be allocated to each year: $25,500 ($306,000/12 = $25,500). The asset is four years old, so the figure at which it is reported should be reduced by four years' depreciation: $102,000 (4 × $25,500 = $102,000). This gives a figure for the asset on 12/31/X1 of $230,000 ($332,000 − $102,000 = $230,000).

Land

As was the case with buildings, the definition of *land* used in accounting is identical with that used in ordinary English. Land that is used for factories, warehouses, stores, etc., is called *site land*. The accountant regards site land as one of the relatively few nonmonetary assets whose services are never used up. He takes the simplest possible view of the services provided by such land: to the accountant, site land serves mainly to support the other company assets. *The accountant does not amortize such land.*[6] He continues to show it at its purchase price. The $65,000 figure shown for land in Illustration 2-9 is nothing more or less than the purchase price of that land.

Inventories

I will refine the following definition shortly, but for now *inventories* consist of goods that a firm is holding for sale to its customers, plus raw materials to be used in manufacturing and incomplete goods that are still in the process of being manufactured. We shall make two simplifying assumptions in discussing inventories:

1. All units of the same kind of inventory have the same purchase price.
2. All inventory is sold before it deteriorates.

Later on we shall discuss how to handle the complications that result when you cannot make these assumptions, but such complications would only get in our way now.[7]

---

[6] In contrast, mineral deposits found on a tract of land are proportionately amortized as these minerals are mined. The principles of this are discussed in Chapter Thirteen, but essentially this amortization is performed as follows:

The owner of the land knows how much was paid for it. Often mining land has a *residual value*—that is, an amount (similar to a scrap value) for which the land can be sold after mining operations are completed. The owner calculates the cost of the mineral deposit to be the difference between the purchase price of the land and its estimated residual value. The total tonnage of the mineral deposit is then estimated, and the amortization of the mineral deposit during any period of time is calculated as:

$$\text{Cost of mineral deposit} \times \frac{\text{Tons mined during period}}{\text{Total tonnage}}$$

In theory, a similar amortization method might be applied to agricultural land whenever the productivity of the soil is allowed to decline.

Another reason for not amortizing site land is that often it is assumed that the firm will be able to recover the cost of the land through future sale—i.e., that the land's "scrap value" is equal to or greater than its cost.

[7] Readers who have had previous exposure to accounting may at first be surprised by one aspect of the following comments: inventories are discussed in much the same fashion as were buildings and other depreciable assets. Of course there are important differences between the two. Inventories are purchased to be sold, whereas buildings are purchased to be used. In preparing accounting reports, it is relatively easy to decide what figure should represent inventory: you just count the units on hand and multiply by their prices. It is much harder to determine the amount of building service left. This kind of consideration leads most accountants to view accounting for inventories as a very different sort of thing than accounting for buildings. Yet there are important similarities, and it is these similarities rather than the differences that are emphasized here. However, if you like, consider this an additional simplification in the discussion.

Inventories can be amortized in exactly the same way as other nonmonetary assets if two conditions (which are explained below) are met:

1. We must regard the basic asset as the purchased "lot."
2. We must regard the unit of service as the individual unit of inventory.

A retailer serves as a good example here. Retailers don't usually buy individual units of inventory; they buy their inventory in batches, or *lots*. The services provided by these inventory lots are used up as the individual units of inventory are sold. A *cost per unit* is determined for each lot purchased; this unit cost is multiplied by the number of units sold to determine how much of the total cost should be written off and how much should be carried forward as the remaining cost of the asset. Suppose that the retailer buys 100 chairs for $1,400. Following the same line of attack that he uses with buildings (but making the service unit a "chair" instead of a "year"), the accountant would allocate $14 to each individual chair ($1,400 ÷ 100 = $14). If there are only 85 chairs left when the accountant wishes to determine a figure for inventory, the accountant would report a figure of $1,190 for the remaining inventory. (Notice that scrap values do not apply to inventories.)

$$85 \times \$14 = \underline{\$1,190}$$

or

$$\$1,400 - [15/100(\$1,400)] = \underline{\$1,190}.$$

(As we saw in the first section of this chapter, the cost of the 15 chairs that were sold would be reported as an expense—a subtraction in arriving at profit—of the period during which they were sold.)

In reality, a company usually owns hundreds of different inventories, and this complicates things. But the line of attack remains the same no matter how many varieties of inventories a company owns. Suppose a company owns three different inventories—Alphas, Betas, and Gammas—and has purchased the following three lots. (These figures are very unrealistic, partly because we are dealing with so few kinds of inventories.)

		Total Cost
Alphas	10,000 units	$ 40,000
Betas	2,500 units	175,000
Gammas	48 units	48,000

The unit costs for each kind of inventory will be:

Alphas	$ 4	($40,000 ÷ 10,000 = $4)
Betas	70	($175,000 ÷ 2,500 = $70)
Gammas	1,000	($48,000 ÷ 48 = $1,000)

If the accountant wishes to report a figure for a remaining inventory of 6,000 Alphas, 2,000 Betas, and 36 Gammas, he would determine his figure as follows:

Alphas	6,000 × $ 4 =	$ 24,000
Betas	2,000 × $ 70 =	140,000
Gammas	36 × $1,000 =	36,000

Total (Shown in Illustration 2-9) $200,000

To repeat, if we regard the basic asset as the purchased lot and regard the unit of service as the individual unit of inventory, then inventories are amortized the same way as other nonmonetary assets (such as buildings). The same holds true of supplies.

Supplies

The main difference between other inventories and supplies is that other inventories are sold to the company's customers (or incorporated in things sold to customers if the seller is a manufacturer), whereas supplies are things such as paper clips, machine oil, and lightbulbs, which are not sold to customers.[8]

Imagine a company having only two kinds of supplies: Alephs and Beths. Some time ago, the company bought 3,000 Alephs for $30,000 and 5,000 Beths for $10,000. At the time of this report, supplies have been reduced to 2,000 Alephs and 1,500 Beths. The $23,000 figure for Supplies is derived as follows:

Alephs $30,000 ÷ 3,000 = $10 a unit × 2,000 units left = $20,000
Beths $10,000 ÷ 5,000 = $ 2 a unit × 1,500 units left =   3,000

Total (Shown in Illustration 2-9) $23,000

An ambiguity in ''Inventories''

Strictly speaking, the word "inventory" pertains to any collection of goods— thus we could describe a process of determining what kinds of equipment were owned by a firm as the "taking of an inventory" of this equipment; similarly, we could speak of the firm's "supplies inventory." Accountants sometimes use the word in this broader sense, but more often they mean the following: the "inventories" of a retailer consist of the merchandise that it is holding for resale; the "inventories" of a manufacturer consist of the raw materials and parts that it intends to use in manufacturing, the incomplete goods that are still being manufactured, and the finished

---

[8] Many accountants regard the cost of supplies (other than supplies used in manufacturing) as being a kind of prepayment, similar to prepaid rent—this is one of the reasons for the ambiguity discussed in the next subsection. There is nothing wrong with classifying supplies as a prepayment, but the exposition of this book becomes sharper when they are regarded as inventories. This is because the accountant does not experience any difficulty in amortizing most prepayments (prepaid rent, prepaid insurance, prepaid taxes, etc.)—he has consistent, clear-cut ways of writing prepayments down. Supplies, though, are subject to the same amortization difficulties (discussed in Chapter Thirteen) as are merchandise or raw materials inventories. Accordingly, throughout this book I will speak of supplies as though they were inventories.

goods that have been completed and are ready for sale. (We will see the details of this in Chapter Twelve.) In practice, most firms distinguish between two kinds of inventories in their reports: inventories in the narrower sense described above and, in addition, the inventories summarized under the category of "supplies." I will do likewise in the remainder of this book. Still, as indicated above, you will find it helpful to regard the two as different varieties of the same thing.

Summary

1. Given our simplifying assumptions, the figure shown for *any* nonmonetary asset can be obtained from the following formula:

$$\text{Purchase price} - \left[\frac{\text{Number of units of service received to date}}{\text{Total number of units of service expected over life}} \times \left(\text{Purchase price} - \text{Scrap value on retirement}\right)\right]$$

For inventories (including supplies) there are no scrap values, and the "unit of service" is the physical inventory or supply unit itself. This makes the computation conceptually simple. For land, the number of units of service expected can be considered unlimited, so that the figure reported for land is always the purchase price. For buildings, equipment, and leases, the unit of service is some measure of time— usually a month or a year.

Later on, some of the simplifying assumptions used here will be removed, and things will be a little more complicated. But the essence of what is going on will remain the same, even in more complicated cases.

2. The simplifying assumptions used in this discussion are:
   (a) All units of service bear the same portion of the purchase price.
   (b) Accountants' estimates are always correct.
   (c) Units of service are either lengths of time or physical units.
   (d) With inventories and supplies, the asset is the purchased lot.
   (e) Deterioration of inventories and supplies can be disregarded.

3. Underlying this discussion of nonmonetary assets are two important considerations:
   (a) The accountant views nonmonetary assets as essentially nothing more than collections of services to be received by the company.
   (b) The accountant obtains the amount reported for any nonmonetary asset from its historical purchase price.

Problems for Study and Self-Examination

Problem 2-1:

If an accountant is preparing his report as of 12/31/X3, at what figures would he show the nonmonetary assets referred to on the following page?

(a) Fire insurance was purchased on 1/1/X2 for $660. The policy covers a 3-year period.

(b) On 5/1/X3 the company paid a year's rent ($4,800) in advance for downtown office space.

(c) On 4/1/X1 the company purchased a 5-year lease of a warehouse for $30,000. Rental prices have risen in the meantime. If the company were to sign such a lease today, it would cost $40,000.

(d) On 1/1/X1 the company purchased land to use as an employee parking lot. The land cost $6,000. The company plans to use this land as a parking lot for only 5 years, after which better parking facilities will be provided for its employees.

(e) On 6/30/X0 the company purchased a patent for $26,000. The patent does not legally expire for more than 13 years; however, the company felt then (and still believes) that the patent will be valueless to it by 6/30/X8.

Problem 2-2:

Three different buildings are described below. In each case calculate the amount at which the buildings should be reported on 12/31/X4.

	Purchase Price	Total Estimated Life (Years)	Date Purchased	Estimated Scrap Value on Retirement
(a)	$84,000	12	1/1/X2	$ –0–
(b)	$84,000	12	1/1/X2	$1,080
(c)	$84,000	12	7/1/X0	$1,080

Problem 2-3:

This problem is the same as Problem 2-2, except that the assets involved are machines, not buildings.

Problem 2-4 (Brain-teaser):

If you really understand a computational technique, you should be able to apply it in reverse. This problem provides an opportunity to test your comprehension of depreciation calculations. Assume that the present date is 12/31/X3.

(a) A machine is being depreciated at a rate of $4,200 a year. It is estimated that this machine will be retired 6 years from now, and that its scrap value on retirement will be $3,900. The machine was purchased on 7/1/X1. What was its purchase price?

(b) A building is being depreciated at a rate of $17,000 a year. It is estimated that it will be retired 20 years from now, and that its scrap value will then be $8,000. This building originally cost $386,250. When was it purchased?

(c) A building is being depreciated at a rate of $8,300 a year. It is estimated that the building will be retired 15 years from now. It was purchased on 1/1/X0 for $160,000. What is its estimated scrap value on retirement?

Problem 2-5:

A company purchased the following inventory lots in 19X1. At what figure should inventory be reported on 12/31/X1?

Kind of Inventory	Quantity Purchased (in Units)	Total Cost	Quantity Left at 12/31/X1 (in Units)
Able	100	$ 300	20
Baker	200	1,400	30
Charlie	400	6,000	80

Problem 2-6:

This problem is the same as Problem 2-5, with one exception: assume that the lots are supplies, rather than inventories.

Problem 2-7 (Optional Problem):

This problem is for students who are familiar with algebra. If you aren't, don't be distressed; just go on to the next section of text.

Do this problem without referring back to the text. Imagine a nonmonetary asset (kind unspecified) whose purchase price is P and whose estimated scrap value on retirement is S. The company estimates that throughout the service life of this asset it will yield U units of service. At the point when the asset has yielded a total of V units of service (V being less than U), the accountant must determine a figure at which to report the asset. Give an algebraic expression for that figure.

Solutions

Solution 2-1:

(a) The total write-down of this asset over 3 years = $660, or $220 a year. One year is still remaining, so the figure for the asset would be $220.

(b) The rent is $4,800/12 = $400 a month. Four months are still prepaid, so the figure for the asset would be 4 × $400 = $1,600.

(c) The lease cost $30,000 for 5 years, or $6,000 a year. The accountant bases his figures for nonmonetary assets on purchase prices only. What has happened to prices since the purchase date is considered irrelevant. Two and three-fourths years have expired on this lease, leaving $2\frac{1}{4}$ years to go. Multiplying $2\frac{1}{4}$ times $6,000 gives a figure of $13,500 for the asset.

(d) Site land is always shown at its purchase price: $6,000.

(e) The patent should be written off over the shorter of either its legal life, or its period of usefulness to the company. In this case, the patent should be written off over the 8-year period of 6/30/X0 to 6/30/X8. It has already been owned for $3\frac{1}{2}$ years, so the figure for the asset would be:

$$\$26,000 - [(3\tfrac{1}{2}/8)(\$26,000)] = \$14,625.$$

Solution 2-2:

| | Asset | | |
	a	*b*	*c*
Purchase price	$84,000	$84,000	$84,000
Estimated scrap value on retirement	− -0-	− 1,080	− 1,080
Amount to write off over total service life	$84,000	$82,920	$82,920
Total service life (in years)	÷ 12	÷ 12	÷ 12
Amount to write off per year	$ 7,000	$ 6,910	$ 6,910
Years of life expired at 12/31/X4	× 3	× 3	× $4\frac{1}{2}$
Accumulated depreciation at 12/31/X4	$21,000	$20,730	$31,095
Figure to be shown for asset: purchase price less accumulated depreciation to date	$63,000	$63,270	$52,905

Solution 2-3:

Same as Solution 2-2. It does not matter whether the assets involved are machines or buildings.

Solution 2-4:

The formula developed on page 101 offers one way to answer the various parts of this problem: substitute the information given concerning these three assets for the terms in the formula. You can also get correct answers by the following, more round-about, approaches:

(a) Estimated life of machine in years (6 + 2½) 8½
Annual depreciation . . . . × $ 4,200

Total write-down over estimated life . . . . $ 35,700
Estimated scrap value on retirement . . . . + 3,900

Purchase price . . . . $ 39,600

(b) Purchase price $386,250
Estimated scrap value on retirement. . . . . − 8,000

Total write-down over estimated life $378,250
Annual depreciation . . . . ÷ 17,000

Total estimated life (in years). 22¼

Since the building has 20 years of life left, it must be 2¼ years old. It was purchased on 9/30/X1 or 10/1/X1.

(c) Total estimated life in years (15 + 4) 19
Annual depreciation . . . . × $ 8,300

Total write-down over estimated life $157,700
Purchase price 160,000

Estimated scrap value on retirement. . . . . $ 2,300

(Don't be distressed by this upside-down subtraction.)

Solution 2-5:

Kind of Inventory	Unit Cost	Units on Hand	Figure at Which Inventory Should Be Reported
Able	$ 3.00	20	$ 60
Baker	7.00	30	210
Charlie	15.00	80	1,200
			$1,470

Solution 2-6:

Same as 2-5. It does not matter whether the assets involved are inventories or supplies. The figure shown for them would be the same.

Solution 2-7:

The formula would be:

$$P - [(V/U) \times (P - S)] = \text{Figure at which to report the asset.}$$

As an example, suppose that the asset is a machine with a 10-year total estimated life; scrap value on retirement is expected to be $20,000. The machine cost $120,000 and is 3 years old. $P = \$120,000$, $V = 3$, $U = 10$, and $S = \$20,000$.

$$\$120,000 - [(3/10) \times (\$120,000 - \$20,000)] = \$120,000 - 3/10(\$100,000)$$
$$= \underline{\$90,000}$$

Current and Noncurrent Assets

We can complete our preliminary discussion of assets by introducing one more major distinction and a few related ideas. The distinction is between "current" and "noncurrent" assets.

The operating cycle

The distinction between current and noncurrent assets is closely related to another accounting concept: the *operating cycle*. To illustrate this concept, we can use the example of a business selling to other companies. Imagine that this business buys household gadgets in large lots from a variety of manufacturers, then sells them in smaller batches to grocery and variety stores. Such a company would be called a *wholesaler*. Suppose this wholesaler allows its customers to buy on credit, but that the wholesaler itself pays cash for its purchases. This is not likely to occur in actual business practice, but it allows us to defer discussing accounting for the company's own debts until the next chapter. At that time, we shall use a more realistic example.

Visualize the wholesaler's day-by-day operations as starting out with an amount of cash that it uses to buy inventories of goods for sale and a few other things needed currently, such as supplies. After holding these inventories awhile (and after using up the supplies), the company sells the inventories to its customers, obtaining accounts receivable in exchange. After still more time has passed, the customers pay their accounts and the company uses the new cash to buy new inventories and supplies, beginning the cycle again.

This sort of day-by-day chain of activities is called the *operating cycle* and is diagrammed in Illustration 2-11. Notice that the amount of accounts receivable is shown to be greater than the amount of inventories and supplies. The wholesaler must try to charge a high enough price to cover all of its costs plus make a profit.

Of course the company is simultaneously engaged in a number of different operating cycles, roughly one for each different lot of inventory that it has purchased. These cycles overlap: the company will always be buying, always be selling; it will always have some cash, some inventories and supplies, and some accounts receivable. Also, these cycles usually are of different lengths, depending on the inventory involved and the speed with which customers pay their receivables. Therefore the operating cycle of the firm as a whole is defined as the *average* period of time required to convert cash to inventory to accounts receivable then back to cash again.

Illustration 2-11

The Operating Cycle
(Greatly Simplified)

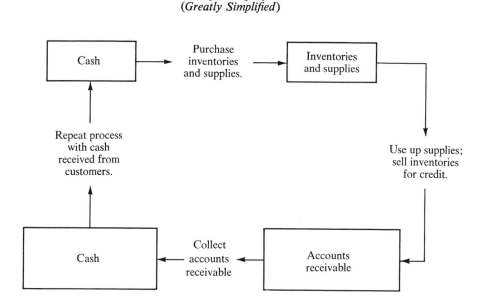

The typical operating cycle lasts less than a year, but practices vary a great deal from one company to another. Suppose the wholesaler is trying to maintain an average quantity of inventory sufficient to meet its customers' needs for one to two months. Perhaps it allows its customers from one to two months to pay for their purchases. If so, the period elapsing between the time the company invested cash in a certain lot of inventory and the time it collected cash from the sale of these inventories would be somewhere between two and four months. In such a case, the length of the operating cycle for this particular wholesaler would be from two to four months, perhaps three months on the average. A fruit stand selling perishable goods for cash might have an average operating cycle of less than a week. Few companies would have operating cycles longer than a year.

The wholesaler also owns a number of assets that are not directly reflected in the operating cycle. Presumably he owns or leases storage facilities, delivery equipment, and so forth. Cash, inventories, and supplies are used up and replaced in less than a year, but land, buildings, and equipment have much longer lives.

Definition of current and noncurrent assets

The above distinction underlies the difference between current and noncurrent assets. Basically, most current assets are ones directly involved in the operating cycle; a noncurrent asset is a long-lived asset that is not directly involved in the operating cycle. In actual practice, operating cycles become complicated and hard to identify, so the financial accountant uses the following rule of thumb to define current and noncurrent assets:

An asset will be classified as *current* if the accountant expects either that it will be used up or converted into cash within one year. All other assets will be classified as *noncurrent*; accordingly, a noncurrent asset is one that the accountant expects will *not* be used up or converted to cash within one year.

Notice that nonmonetary and monetary assets are disposed of in different ways. Nonmonetary assets are "used up"; either they are physically consumed (as in the case of merchandise and supplies) or their services are exhausted (as in the case of prepaid insurance or equipment). Monetary assets, which are rights to receive cash, are converted into cash. Of course, all current assets and most noncurrent assets are replaced with new ones so that, for example, the firm always has *some* receivables and some inventories.

This rule of thumb definition is convenient because the accountant usually prepares his major financial reports once a year. Thus a current asset will be used up and replaced before the next annual financial report is prepared.[9] Here are some examples of how this "one year" definition is consistent with the concept of current assets as operating cycle assets:

1. A company rarely maintains a cash balance adequate for more than a month or so. Instead, as the company spends its present cash balance, new cash is steadily flowing in from sales and collections of accounts receivable. Cash is a current asset.

2. If a company sells goods on credit, it rarely extends credit to its customers for more than 90 days. Accounts receivable at any date are expected to be collected well within a year's time. Accounts receivable are current assets.

3. Most companies keep considerably less than a year's quantity of inventories and supplies in stock at any one time. Inventories and supplies are current assets.

In contrast, land, buildings, equipment, and patents all usually have lives greater than one year. They are noncurrent assets. (The exception to this would occur if the company were a dealer in land, buildings, equipment, or patents. To such a dealer, these assets would be inventories and, therefore, current assets.)

Some accountants refer to current assets as *working capital*. The word "capital" here signifies "a collection of assets being put to economic use"; the word "working" seems to signify "readily available for day-by-day operating purposes."

Illustration 2-12 is based on our earlier Illustrations 1-3 (page 51) and 2-9 (page 96). Illustration 2-12 shows all the assets of Illustrative Corporation, classified according to whether they are current or noncurrent.

---

[9] In turn, this rule-of-thumb definition is extended to include certain assets that are *not* directly involved in the operating cycle—as long as they will be used up within one year. For example, if the company has set aside cash, intending to use it during the next year to buy equipment, this cash would ordinarily be classified as current even though the purchase of new equipment is not an activity that is directly involved in the operating cycle. Similarly, if the firm temporarily has more cash than it needs for operating purposes and invests the excess (perhaps in short-term notes of the federal government) so as not to leave it idle, this investment would be treated as a current asset, despite its not being directly involved in the operating cycle, as long as management's intention was to convert this investment back to cash within one year.

Despite these exceptions, the underlying *significance* of the current/noncurrent distinction lies in its general parallel to the distinction between assets that are and assets that aren't directly involved in the operating cycle.

Illustration 2-12

Illustrative Corporation
Assets
December 31, 19X1

Current Assets:

Cash	$ 47,600*	
5% Notes Receivable—due 4/1/X2	16,000*	
Accounts Receivable.	180,290*	
Interest Receivable	2,050*	
Inventories	200,000	
Supplies	23,000	
Prepaid Rent .	12,000	$480,940

Noncurrent Assets:

6% Notes Receivable—due 2/1/X5	$ 48,000*	
Investment in 4½% Bonds Receivable—due 3/1/X9 .	30,000*	
Land .	65,000	
Buildings .	95,000	
Equipment	230,000	
Patents	40,000	508,000
Total Assets .		$988,940

* Monetary asset

First of all, notice that these are the assets and related dollar amounts that we've been working with all along. Next, notice that the current-noncurrent distinction is not the same thing as the monetary-nonmonetary distinction (discussed on pages 41–42). To help clarify this, the monetary assets in Illustration 2-12 have been starred, although this would not ordinarily be done in the accountant's report. As you can see, current assets can be either monetary or nonmonetary. The same applies to noncurrent assets. Monetary assets can be either current or noncurrent. This also applies to nonmonetary assets. Consider notes receivable, for example. Whether they are current or noncurrent depends entirely upon the date the principal amount is due, not the date any interest is due. (Interest due dates affect only interest receivable.) The 5 percent notes are current because their principal is due within less than a year (3 months). The 6 percent notes are noncurrent because they are not due for over a year. Such notes would be current if the company intended to sell them in a year or less. The same is true of an investment in bonds receivable. But in this illustration it is assumed that the company intends to hold on to its 6 percent notes and 4½ percent bonds for more than a year.

Sometimes current assets are called *short-term* or *circulating* assets. Noncurrent assets may be called *long-term, fixed,* or *long-lived.* (These differences in terminology are not significant.) Sometimes noncurrent investments are separated from the other noncurrent assets, and a separate category called *Investments* is created. This book ordinarily won't bother to use an investments category, but it can be useful when an entity owns several different kinds of investments.

The order in which assets are listed in Illustration 2-12 is a conventional one which eventually you should memorize. Notice that current assets are listed before non-current assets, and that within either category monetary assets are listed first. In turn, within these groupings, the standard order is:

Current monetary: Cash, notes receivable, accounts receivable, other receivables;
Current nonmonetary: Inventories, supplies, prepayments;
Noncurrent monetary: Any order;
Noncurrent nonmonetary: Land, buildings, equipment, other.

Asset order is discussed in a bit more detail on pages 149–151, but this will suffice for the present.

Monetary/Nonmonetary and Current/Noncurrent Classifications

It is important that you recognize that the definitions introduced in the last two chapters involve classifying all assets under *both* of two classification systems. The monetary/nonmonetary classification depends upon whether or not an asset is an enforceable right to receive a fixed amount of cash (or is cash itself); as an entirely separate issue the current/noncurrent distinction depends upon whether or not an asset will be used up or converted to cash within a year. This may be diagrammed as follows:

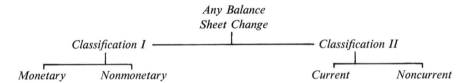

Any monetary asset will be either current or noncurrent; any nonmonetary asset will be either current or noncurrent. Similarly, any current asset will be either monetary or nonmonetary, and any noncurrent asset also will be either monetary or nonmonetary. Thus there are four possibilities, as indicated above: current monetary assets, current nonmonetary assets, noncurrent monetary assets, and noncurrent nonmonetary assets. Examples of each possibility are given in Illustration 2-12.

Problem for Study and Self-Examination

Problem 2-8:

Below are the assets of Union Springs Associates, Inc., on December 31, 19X1. Prepare a list of assets, using good form and distinguishing current from noncurrent assets. Remember that the order in which assets are listed is important. Try to make your list parallel the order used in Illustration 2-12, without referring back to that illustration.

Accounts Receivable.	$ 30,000
Buildings .	60,000
Cash .	10,000
Equipment	18,000
Interest Receivable .	600
Inventories	68,000
Land .	22,000
Marketable Securities	24,000
6% Notes Receivable.	10,000
Patents	17,300
Prepaid Rent .	14,000
Prepaid Utility Bills .	3,800
Small Tools .	6,300
Supplies .	7,000
	$291,000

Other data: $6,000 of the notes receivable are due on 12/1/X2; the rest are due on 3/1/X3. All of the accrued interest receivable shown is due on 1/1/X2, one day after the date to which your list of assets applies. The small tools have a total service life of two years; all were purchased during the summer of 19X1. The company rents warehouse space at a cost of $28,000 a year. The *marketable securities* mentioned are various kinds of investments that can easily be converted into cash. You may assume that either they mature within one year or the company intends to sell them within one year. Examples include such things as investments in federal government debt and, occasionally, investments in the common stocks of large, widely owned corporations.

Solution

Solution 2-8:

Union Springs Associates, Inc.
Assets
December 31, 19X1

Current Assets:

Cash	$10,000	
Marketable Securities	24,000	
6% Notes Receivable—due 12/1/X2	6,000	
Accounts Receivable	30,000	
Interest Receivable	600	
Inventories	68,000	
Supplies	7,000	
Prepaid Rent	14,000	
Prepaid Utility Bills	3,800	$163,400

Noncurrent Assets:

6% Notes Receivable—due 3/1/X3	$ 4,000	
Land	22,000	
Buildings	60,000	
Equipment	18,000	
Small Tools	6,300	
Patents	17,300	127,600
Total Assets		$291,000

Notice that marketable securities are an example of the partial exception to the current/noncurrent rule that was discussed in the note on page 112: marketable securities are not directly involved in the operating cycle, but they usually are owned for a year or less, and therefore are classified as current. Evidently the prepaid rent represents 6 months' rent on the warehouse space, so it is a current asset. As a rule, assume that all prepayments are current assets unless there is evidence to the contrary. It is rare for companies to pay such things as rent or utility bills more than a year in advance.

Notice that current assets are listed before noncurrent assets. The order of accounts within the current and noncurrent categories will be discussed in the next chapter.

Assignment Problems

Problem 2-A:

1. Indicate the amounts at which the following nonmonetary assets should be shown on a report dated 12/31/X6. Your answer should include your calculations.
   (a) A shed purchased on 3/31/X1 for $14,100. At that date, the shed had an estimated service life of 12 years, and an estimated scrap value upon retirement of $900.
   (b) An ore pile. The company purchased 600 tons of dry ore on 10/1/X6 for a total price of $24,300. The ore pile has been exposed to the elements, and has become wet. It weighed 300 tons on 12/31/X6, but the company estimates that 56% of the original amount of ore purchased has been used up.
   (c) Land purchased on 1/1/X2 for $18,000. The company intends to sell this land on 3/31/X7.
   (d) Equipment purchased on 12/31/X0 for $23,400. The equipment had a total estimated service life of 5 years, an estimated scrap value upon retirement of $1,400, and was sold by the company for $1,380 on 12/31/X5.
   (e) Advances to suppliers made on 11/1/X6, and totalling $1,080. The related goods will be delivered about 1/31/X7.
2. Which of the foregoing assets are current assets at 12/31/X6?

Problem 2-B:

As part of your training in accounting, you must become able to extend what you have learned into new situations. This problem provides such an opportunity to increase your flexibility and to broaden your understanding. The text provides all background information needed to solve this problem, but some of the circumstances described will be unfamiliar. Apply what you already have learned to this new situation.

Professor Craig L. Beach keeps detailed accounting records. He wishes to prepare a list of his personal assets as of 12/31/X7. At what amounts should he show the assets referred to below in conformity with generally accepted accounting rules?

1. His residence, purchased on 6/30/X2 for $24,500. Professor Beach intends to own this house for a total of ten years; he estimates that he can then resell it for $20,000, less brokerage commissions of $1,200. The house has an estimated current market value of $26,500 (before brokerage commissions, which would be $1,590 at a $26,500 selling price).
2. Prepaid property taxes. Professor Beach pays taxes on his residence every November 15th, for the fiscal year running from the previous July 1 to the next June 30. His payment for the present fiscal year was $743.40.
3. His automobile, purchased on 1/30/X5 for $2,940. Professor Beach estimates that he will trade his car in after a total of four years, and that its value at the time of trade-in will be $600.
4. Dehydrated food. On 5/30/X7, Professor Beach purchased $120 of camping food, intending to spend much of the summer camping with his family. Unseasonable rains cut the trip short after only one third of the food was consumed. The

dehydrated food tastes fine in the woods, but is not especially attractive at home. Professor Beach plans to go camping again next summer, but doubts that his family will consume more than three fourths of the remaining food on this trip. He doubts that any leftover food will keep well enough to be used a third summer. Although he is concerned over the possible waste of one sixth of his original purchase

$$\{1 - [\tfrac{1}{3} + (\tfrac{3}{4} \times \tfrac{2}{3})] = \tfrac{1}{6}\},$$

his wife says that this is better than what she *expected* would happen when he bought all that food.

Problem 2-C:

As part of your training in accounting, you must become able to extend what you have learned into new situations. This problem provides such an opportunity to increase your flexibility and to broaden your understanding. The text provides all background information needed to solve this problem, but some of the circumstances described will be unfamiliar. Apply what you already have learned to this new situation.

Shown below are the assets of Hosmer Standard Holdfasts, Inc., at December 31, 19X3. These assets are listed in alphabetical order.

Accounts Receivable.	$168,773
Advances to Suppliers	12,316
Building	340,000
Cash	103,269
Equipment	212,000
Franchise	84,000
Interest Receivable	1,825
Land	70,100
Loans to Officers and Directors	15,000
Manufactured Goods Inventories	193,308
Notes Receivable, 7%—due 5/30/X4	10,000
Notes Receivable, 7½%—due 1/30/X5.	6,000
Prepaid Insurance	3,162
Prepaid Taxes	10,574
Prepaid Travel and Per-Diem	3,407
Raw Materials Inventories	14,905
Supplies Inventories	8,703

The following information relates to the company's 19X4 activities, and to its assets at December 31, 19X4:

Several years ago the company purchased exclusive franchise rights to manufacture and distribute a particular product within the United States and Canada. This franchise had twenty years more to run at 12/31/X3; however, the company estimates that it will cease manufacturing the related product within 15 years from 12/31/X3, and that its remaining rights under the franchise will be worthless by that date.

The company's building was purchased on 6/30/X0, at which time it had an estimated service life of 25 years, and an estimated scrap value upon retirement of $17,500.

The 7% note receivable was collected when due; no new notes receivable were acquired during 19X4. During 19X4, the company sold land that had cost it $20,800, receiving $32,000. During 19X4, the company purchased $12,309 of supplies and used up supplies that had cost $13,310.

Prepaid Travel and Per-Diem is used to record advance payments made to employees to cover costs of travel made by them on the company's behalf. During 19X4, $7,301 of such advances were made; employees expended $7,210 of advances (including all of those outstanding at 12/31/X3).

All loans to officers and directors receivable at 12/31/X3 were repaid during 19X4; no new loans were granted during 19X4.

Prepaid insurance consists of a combined fire and casualty insurance policy that had 17 months to run at 12/31/X3. No new insurance was purchased during 19X4.

At 12/31/X4, the company's other assets were as follows:

Accounts Receivable	$175,321	Manufactured Goods	
Advances to Suppliers	5,200	Inventories	$191,619
Cash	97,119	Prepaid Taxes	11,220
Equipment	243,704	Raw Materials Inventories	15,203

Make up a list of assets as of December 31, 19X4; use good form and asset order. Distinguish current from noncurrent assets. Show all necessary calculations. You need not list assets with zero balances.

Problem 2-D:

In the following questions, assume that the present date is 12/31/X7. Show all calculations necessary to support your answers.

1. A building cost $285,000. It was estimated to have a total service life of 35 years, and a scrap value of $12,000 on retirement. At present, it is reported at $248,600. When was it purchased?

2. A set of special tools was purchased on 9/1/X6. It was estimated to have a total service life of 3 years, and a scrap value of $300 on retirement. At present, it is reported at $880. What did it cost?

3. A machine cost $32,300. At 12/31/X6 it was reported at $9,225; at present it is reported at $5,675. When was it purchased?

4. Equipment cost $15,000. It was purchased on 3/1/X7, and was estimated to have a total service life of 12 years. At present, it is reported at $14,125. What is its estimated scrap value on retirement?

5. A machine cost $42,800. It was purchased on 8/1/X5, and is estimated to have a $2,000 scrap value upon retirement. At present, it is reported at $37,000. What is its total estimated service life?

Problem 2-E:

In the following questions, assume that the present date is 12/31/X8. Show all calculations necessary to support your answers.

1. Equipment cost $16,900. It was purchased on 3/31/X8 and was estimated to have a total service life of 14 years. At present, it is reported at $16,000. What is its estimated scrap value upon retirement?

2. A machine cost $48,600. It was purchased on 11/30/X6, and is estimated to have a $3,000 scrap value upon retirement. At present, it is reported at $43,600. What is its total estimated service life?

3. A machine cost $547,200. At 12/31/X7 it was reported at $473,700; at present it is reported at $456,060. When was it purchased?

4. A machine cost $48,300. It was estimated to have a total service life of nine years and a scrap value of $6,000 on retirement. At present, it is reported at $11,875. When was it purchased?

5. A set of special tools was purchased on 8/1/X7. It was estimated to have a total service life of three years and a scrap value of $50 on retirement. At present, it is reported at $1,095. What did it cost?

Problem 2-F:

Chez Oona's, a ladies' dress shop, and Roush's Barber Shop both lease store space in the Martinsville Mall, a large suburban shopping center. The proprietors of these two stores, Ms. O. Roudebush and Mr. E. Ross Roush, are close personal friends who often discuss their business problems with each other. It happens that both recently bought identical sets of chairs for their establishments; these chairs are being used for the same general purpose in both businesses: to provide a place for customers (and those who accompany customers) to sit while they wait. Finally, the chairs in each establishment are receiving approximately the same amount of physical wear.

Therefore, Mr. Roush was surprised to discover that Ms. Roudebush was depreciating her chairs almost twice as rapidly as he was: she had assumed that they would have a three-year service life with a small salvage value, he was assuming a six-year service life with no salvage value. Mr. Roush remarked, "Oona, one of us has got to be wrong, and I don't think it's me. Those chairs are well built; they'll probably last longer than the six years I'm using, only I didn't want to be too optimistic."

Ms. Roudebush replied, "How many times do I have to tell you? We're in very different businesses, Ross."

Under what circumstances could both Mr. Roush and Ms. Roudebush be using what for them was the correct depreciation method—i.e., both be right? Explain your answer.

Problem 2-G:

Ignore tax implications in answering the following questions.

1. With proper maintenance, a railway's tracks and roadbed will last indefinitely. Should they be depreciated? Justify your answer.

2. Bell Insurance Agency bought a house in 19X1. The company planned to use the building for its offices for a period of five years. Local real estate prices had been steadily rising for the last ten years; the company estimated that the house could be resold at the end of five years for an amount at least as great as its cost.

The company resold the house in 19X6 for $2,000 more than its cost. In accordance with conventional accounting, should the company have depreciated this house during the period of ownership? Should it have *appreciated* it (written it *up*)? Justify your answer.

Problem 2-H:

As part of your training in accounting, you must become able to extend what you have learned into new situations. This problem provides such an opportunity to increase your flexibility and to broaden your understanding. The text provides all background information needed to solve this problem, but the circumstances described will be unfamiliar. Apply what you have already learned to this new situation.

Edward R. Park is a student at a large urban university. He spends his summers at his home, a small New England village. Each summer, he selects numerous attractively rounded stones from the bed of a nearby stream. When school begins in the fall, he hauls these stones to the apartment he shares with three roommates, and stores the rocks in cartons. During the school year, he paints and shellacs these stones. One some he paints enigmatic inscriptions (such as "TOAD" and "Is this really a rock?"); others he converts into brightly colored bugs. He paints one or two dozen stones per day, and sells them through local stores.

In the fall of 19X1, Mr. Park brought 3,000 stones to his apartment; he estimates that the haulage cost $3.00 in extra gasoline. The fall term began on September 15; no rocks were sold during September. By the end of October he had completed 800 stones and had sold 500. Paints and other materials for the month and a half cost $40. The apartment rents for $200 per month. Mr. Park pays $65; his other roommates pay $45 apiece. Mr. Park considers his payment of $20 more rent than the others pay a result of the extra space he needs for rock storage. The school year lasts nine months.

If Mr. Park were to prepare a financial report as of 10/31/X1, at what amount should he report the 2,500 rocks on hand at that date? Show all calculations necessary to support your answer; indicate any assumptions that you needed to make in order to answer this question. (*Hint:* there may be more than one "right" way to handle the $20-per-month excess rent.)

Problem 2-I:

Different kinds of businesses have different kinds of operating cycles. Contrast the operating cycles of the following four kinds of businesses—consider the types of assets involved in the operating cycle and the length of the operating cycle. If you are unfamiliar with the kinds of business involved, make plausible guesses and state your assumptions.

1. A bank.
2. A grocery store.
3. A furniture store.
4. A company that owns and manages several apartment houses.

Problem 2-J:

The text indicates that most businesses have an operating cycle of one year or less, and that accordingly the accountant uses a one-year test to determine whether an asset is current or noncurrent. List two kinds of business that you would expect to have operating cycles longer than one year. Indicate why you would expect this. What do you anticipate the definition of current assets would be for such businesses? Explain your reasoning.

Problem 2-K:

What follows is the history of a tract of land in an industrial area of the Midwest. Toward the end of the nineteenth century, the tract was purchased by the Roybal family from a land company. It was farmed by the Roybal family until 1934, at which time it passed out of cultivation because of declining productivity and the general economic difficulties of that period.

A moderate-sized clay deposit lay beneath part of this tract. In 1938, Wilson Ceramics Corporation purchased the property; from 1938 through 1952, Wilson Ceramics Corporation mined clay from it. By 1952 the clay was exhausted and the tract was left idle again. About half of it now consisted of a very large hole, in which water collected.

In 19X0, the tract was acquired by Friendly Sanitary Service, a commercial refuse collector. Friendly Sanitary Service had been experiencing increasing difficulty in finding suitable locations for dumping. During the years 19X0 through 19X4 it dumped refuse in the hole, employing a sanitary land-fill technique approved by the state. By 19X4, the hole was filled, and dumping ceased.

Meanwhile, the suburbs of a neighboring city had been growing vigorously. In 19X6 the tract was acquired by Fairview Country Estates, a firm of real estate developers. Fairview Country Estates subdivided the tract and built inexpensive houses upon it. The last lot was sold in 19X9.

Describe the accounting treatments that each owner should have given to this tract. Exact dollar amounts have been omitted from this problem, since numerical calculations are not needed. But you may assume that this land was nearly valueless to the Roybal family in 1934, to Wilson Ceramics Corporation in 1952, and to Friendly Sanitary Service in 19X4, except for resale. Assume that in each case the likelihood of resale seemed low. You may also assume that during periods in which the land lay idle, its owners still paid property taxes on it. Justify your answers.

Problem 2-L:

As part of your training in accounting, you must become able to extend what you have learned into new situations. This problem provides such an opportunity to increase your flexibility and to broaden your understanding. The text provides all background information needed to solve this problem, but the circumstances described will be unfamiliar. Apply what you have already learned to this new situation.

On 1/1/X4, Brown-Beverly Corp. purchased the entire assets of Hills' Marine Equipment Company from its founder, who wished to retire. The following were among the assets acquired. It is estimated that each will have a zero scrap value at the end of its service life.

1. Landscaping and plantings around the Hills' Marine Equipment Company factory: the original landscaping work had been done in 19X2. During the purchase negotiations, the parties agreed that this asset was worth $25,000. Brown-Beverly Corp. estimates that a complete relandscaping will be necessary within 25 years after 1/1/X4.

2. A long-term lease on rented warehouse facilities: Hills' Marine Equipment Company had obtained this lease at an unusually favorable price. During the purchase

negotiations, the parties agreed that this asset was worth $120,000. The lease had six years left to run as of 1/1/X4.

3. Goodwill: Hills' Marine Equipment Company sold mostly to commercial fishermen. Over the years it had built up a large number of regular customers for its products. Since Brown-Beverly Corp. was going to continue most of Hills' Marine Equipment Company's business practices, it was expected that the majority of these customers would continue doing business with the new management. Brown-Beverly Corp. paid an additional $40,000 for the Hills' Marine Equipment Company assets over what it otherwise would have paid, in recognition of Hills' Marine Equipment Company's favorable relations with its customers. However, it estimates that such goodwill will last no more than ten years.

Answer the following questions:

1. Determine the amount at which each of these assets should be reported by Brown-Beverly Corp. as of 12/31/X8.

2. Examining the records of Brown-Beverly Corp. as of 12/31/X8, its president is troubled. He comments as follows to the company's chief accountant:

"Hey, do you know that you're showing the landscaping, the warehouse lease, and the goodwill all at the same figure. Yeah, the marine goodwill. Aw, come on; don't start telling me about generally accepted accounting principles again. I'm sure you *are* doing what other accountants do here. But you've still lumped a lot of different things together under the same numbers.

"Look, I don't mind calling landscaping an asset; if I ever got worried and wanted to know whether we've still got landscaping, I can stand up and look out the window. Or go outside and kick a bush. But these other things are different. With the lease, I suppose I *could* go to the safe and look at the contract. But what the heck; a lease is really just a set of rights, and I'd have to be a lawyer to figure out exactly what those rights *are*. And with this goodwill, I haven't got *anything* to look at, unless I want to throw a party for all the customers we got from old Bud Hills. Yet you accountants want to report all three of these things at the same figure!"

Write a clear, concise memo to the president to help clarify the issues he has raised.

3. There is something else in this situation that *should* trouble the president and the chief accountant. Based on whatever you know about business, what else do you believe might be questioned in the accounting figures? In answering this question, suppose that the Brown-Beverly Corp. scrap value and service life estimates are correct (though of course these are subject to error in actual practice). *Hint:* notice that a single purchase price was paid for all the Hills' Marine Equipment Company assets that were acquired.

Three

A Complementary Concept: The Equity

Kinds of Equities

Assets are rights—rights to receive cash and rights to receive services. We must now look at the other side of the coin—equities. Equities are a corporation's obligations. As demonstrated in Chapter One (pages 18–22), a corporation has obligations to two different kinds of investors:

1. *Creditors* are individuals or companies that have lent money to the corporation or have given it goods or services without being paid immediately. Different creditors invest in corporations for different periods of time, but all debts to creditors must eventually be repaid by the firm.

As shown in the last chapter, the creditor-investor regards these debts as assets. The debts of any one entity are always the assets of one or more other entities. From the standpoint of the company that owes the debts, however, they are not assets at all. Quite the opposite: they are obligations to pay out assets, usually cash. The technical term for such an obligation is a *liability*.

2. *Stockholders* are the owners of the corporation. Stockholders' investments entitle them to a number of rights, and the corporation has a corresponding number of obligations. The corporation must give the stockholder his proportionate vote and his proportionate share in any distribution of profits. Should the company ever sell all its assets and go out of business, the stockholder is entitled to his share of the proceeds after all liabilities have been paid.

This is not to say that the company is ever obliged to sell out and repay stockholders their investments. In the eyes of the law, the corporation is considered to be an entity distinct from the stockholders, with an indefinite life (background to this was discussed on pages 18 and 27). Most corporations *intend* to go on indefinitely, without ever returning stockholder investments. Therefore, the corporation is not considered to be in debt to its owners and *the corporation's obligations to its stock-holders are not liabilities.*

Now, this doesn't mean that the corporation's obligations to its stockholders aren't perfectly respectable obligations. It just means that they are a different kind of obligation from a liability.[1] The company's obligations to stockholders are often called its *net worth,* but this term is beginning to be considered a bit old fashioned; usually, therefore, I will refer instead to a company's *stockholders' equity,* which means the same thing.

In summary, a corporation has two kinds of obligations:

1. Liabilities—debts owed to creditors.
2. Stockholders' equity—obligations to owners.

Instead of "obligations," the accountant uses the technical term *equity. An "equity" is an obligation to an investor. If the obligation is to a creditor, the equity is called a "liability." If the obligation is to an owner, the obligation is called "stock-holders' equity."*[2]

In practice you will find language used more loosely. Published annual reports often refer to all equities as liabilities, even though the company is in debt only to its creditor-investors. This is fairly harmless so long as you are aware of what is really meant, but since it is misleading to call stockholders' equity a liability, this book will use more exact language. Some writers (particularly economists and financial analysts) restrict the term "equity" to stockholders' equity; for example, they would contrast investments in equities (capital stock) with investments in a firm's debt. The definitions that are used here reflect what the major accounting organizations regard as good terminology.

Examples of equities

Illustration 3-1 shows the equities of Illustrative Corporation; these obligations match the assets shown in Illustration 2-12 (page 113). Notice that the same current-noncurrent distinction is made with liabilities as with assets (see page 111). A current liability is one for which payment is due within one year. A noncurrent liability is one whose principal is due more than a year from the date of the report.

Notes and accounts payable

Notes payable and accounts payable are the exact analogs of the notes receivable and accounts receivable discussed on pages 61–62. An account receivable is a right to receive cash from a customer who buys on ordinary credit terms; it is a seller's asset. An *account payable* is a non-interest-bearing, informal obligation to pay for

---

[1] It is perfectly possible, however, that a stockholder-investor may also be a creditor-investor. For instance, one of the company's suppliers might own shares of its stock. In such cases, the corporation treats the two obligations separately, ignoring that they are obligations to the same entity.

[2] As indicated earlier, the discussion in this book is confined to corporations. However, businesses that are not corporations use similar language for their equities: obligations to creditors are still called *liabilities,* obligations to owners are called *owners' equity* or some similar term.

something purchased on ordinary credit terms; it is the buyer's liability. A note receivable is another kind of right to receive cash, one that is evidenced in a more formal way and that may be interest-bearing; this right is an asset of the seller or the lender of money. The same right is also an obligation of the buyer or borrower, who views it as a *note payable*. (Similarly, the bonds receivable discussed on pages 64–65 must be reflected on some other firms' records as *bonds payable*, a liability.)

Illustration 3-1

Illustrative Corporation
Equities
December 31, 19X1

Current Liabilities:

5¼% Notes Payable—due 2/1/X2	$ 12,000	
Accounts Payable	145,100	
Advances from Customers	19,800	
Wages Payable	58,400	
Interest Payable	2,255	
Taxes Payable	26,100	
Miscellaneous Accrued Payables	3,705	$267,360

Noncurrent Liabilities:

4% Mortgage Notes Payable	129,000

Total Liabilities.	$396,360
Stockholders' Equity	592,580
Total Equities	$988,940

Imagine the following highly simplified situation. Suppose that Lender, Inc., has $1,000 cash and no other assets, while Borrower, Inc., has $125 cash and no other assets. Assume that the only equities are stockholders' equities. We could prepare the following reports for these two companies:

Lender, Inc.		*Borrower, Inc.*	
Assets		*Assets*	
Cash	$1,000	Cash	$125
Equities		*Equities*	
Stockholders' Equity	$1,000	Stockholders' Equity	$125

Now, assume that Lender, Inc., loans Borrower, Inc., $300, receiving a 6 percent note in exchange. If we were to prepare reports immediately afterward (before any interest fee has accrued), we would have the following:

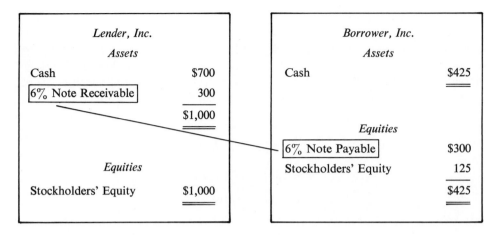

Usually, any monetary asset is a liability on some other entity's records.[3] This is another way to define monetary assets (compare the definition on page 41). Notice that the related liability is also monetary: the monetary asset is a right to receive cash; the related liability is an obligation to pay cash.

Advances from customers

Most liabilities are monetary, but a few are exceptions. *Advances from customers* is a nonmonetary liability. It arises from a customer's making an advance payment for goods or services to be delivered. Such advance payments can occur in a number of ways. Perhaps the customer has made a special order for the company to manufacture nonstandard goods. The seller may wish the customer to make an advance deposit to ensure that the customer will not change his mind, cancel the order at the last minute, and leave the seller stuck with inventories that would be hard to sell elsewhere.[4] The seller may require payment to accompany an order, as do mail-order houses of their cash customers. If so, there will be a short delay between the time cash is received and the time goods are shipped. During this brief period an obligation exists to send goods to the customer. Notice that this is an obligation to send goods, not cash. This is why *advances from customers* is a nonmonetary liability, rather than a monetary one (see the monetary/nonmonetary distinction on page 41). Other examples of customer advances would be tickets sold by railways and buses before the trip is actually taken, meal tickets sold by restaurants, and the like.

> *Advances from customers:* a liability that reflects the firm's obligations to its customers to provide them with products or services for which these customers have already paid.

---

[3] Even cash is a liability—of a bank or of the government. However, there are a few exceptions to this. If the lender and borrower prepare financial statements as of different dates, one party may accrue a receivable or payable that will not appear on the other party's records; such accruals are discussed on pages 64 and 129–130.

[4] In such cases, the manufacturer might be able to sue the defaulting customer, but lawsuits are inconvenient. The whole problem is avoided by demanding a large enough advance deposit.

Wages payable, taxes payable

Wages payable is simply a liability for cash owed to employees for their services. Perhaps Illustrative Corporation's employees are paid early each month for their services of the previous month. If so, the $58,400 liability for wages payable at 12/31/X1 would be the December, 19X1 wages earned by employees in 19X1, but not paid until January, 19X2.

Taxes payable is a liability for amounts owed to city, state, and federal taxing authorities. The amount of taxes paid is usually subject to review by the taxing authority concerned. Often disputes occur and the exact amount owed may not be decided for some time after the financial report is prepared. Thus the figure for taxes payable is often an estimated rather than an exact figure. As was mentioned on page 24, accountants are reluctant to make estimates, but the alternative would be to show no liability at all for taxes. Once again the question arises: which would cause greater distortion—showing a figure that may be a bit higher or lower than the amount eventually paid, or showing a figure of zero and not reporting the liability at all? As we saw on page 52, the accountant tries to present a model of the firm's economic status that will be of maximum usefulness to his readers. In the past, accountants have determined what will be "useful" by trial-and-error experimentation, selecting those accounting practices that their readers seem to approve. Such experimentation has indicated that reports of tax estimates, though inexact, reflect the firm's economic status more usefully than does showing no amount at all for estimated taxes payable. (The accountant is similarly motivated in determining figures for buildings and equipment. As you will see later, his depreciation estimates are inexact, but he feels that less distortion is caused by estimating depreciation than by reporting unadjusted purchase prices for these assets, or not reporting them at all.)

Miscellaneous accrued payables

The figure for *miscellaneous accrued payables* is also at least partly estimated. Often a company has received services for which it has not yet been billed at the end of the year. For example, the company may receive a telephone bill on the 15th of each month. If so, the company has an obligation to pay for services for the last half of December, even though payment will not be due until next year. Not knowing the exact amount of the bill, the company must estimate. In addition to these estimated liabilities, the account *miscellaneous accrued payables* could include a variety of other minor liabilities—especially accrued liabilities on uncompleted contracts.

Accrued liabilities also arise in connection with other utilities. In general, whenever a company is receiving goods or services for which bills are submitted at intervals, an accrued liability may exist at the end of the year. Notice two things here:

1. The word "accrued" is used in the same sense here as when accruing a receivable (see page 64): an *accrued liability* is a liability that is recognized prior to the date that it is legally owed its creditor. Such liabilities arise when the firm's related obligations are incurred over a period of time and the proportionate amount of obligation incurred to date can be estimated to the accountant's satisfaction.

2. Accordingly, an accrued liability may be reported by the accountant even though there is not yet any legal claim against the firm. This is particularly apt to happen with liabilities for contractual services, such as telephone services. The company

may not be legally responsible for its telephone bill until the 15th of the next month, but the company has been receiving telephone services on credit, and the extent and eventual cost of these services can be determined. Therefore the proportionate amount incurred through December 31 can be reliably calculated. Accordingly, the firm reports an accrued liability as of December 31, instead of waiting for the technicality of its being billed. Similarly, if salaried employees are paid once per month for their services received during the previous month, on December 31 a liability for unpaid salaries would be accrued even though payment will not be due for ten days, since the related services have been received. Similar accruals may be made when a contract is for delivery of products instead of services. For instance, if one firm has contracted with another to purchase 15,000 units of a product, payment to be made upon delivery of the final unit, the buyer will report an accrued liability for one third of the total cost after the first 5,000 units have been delivered (15,000 × $\frac{1}{3}$ = 5,000).

The word "accrual" applies to all such cases in which the company recognizes an asset or liability at some point before it is technically a legal claim. Interest receivable is a good example. Illustrative Corporation cannot legally collect any of its $2,050 of interest receivable on December 31, 19X1. (See Illustration 2-12 on page 113.) It has to wait until the interest fee comes due. But this interest fee is a fee for the use of money over a period of time. Part of that time has passed during 19X1 without payment having been made. On 12/31/X1 the company accrues the related part of the eventual interest fee and shows it as an asset—a right eventually to receive cash. Similarly, the company accrues the December, 19X1, part of its eventual fee for telephone services and shows it as a liability.

Accruals of this sort run all through accounting. Why does the accountant accrue the asset or the liability, instead of waiting until the related fee is finally due? For the same reason that the accountant recognizes an automobile being purchased on installments as the purchaser's asset, even though the creditor-seller may be the automobile's legal owner. The accountant believes that he can better represent the actual economic situation of the company by accruing than by waiting until the entire right or obligation is legally receivable or payable. He accrues a liability when the firm has received services (or, occasionally, products) from another entity, yet payment for these services is not due until later; failure to accrue the liability would involve ignoring this receipt of services. Similarly, he accrues a receivable when the firm has provided a service (or, occasionally, products) to another entity, yet payment is not due until later.

> *Accrual:* recognition of a receivable or a liability prior to the date upon which it is a legal debt of the entity that owes it.

By accruing assets and liabilities, the accountant obtains better representation of the company's economic condition than if he delayed recognition to the legal due date of the claim. Miscellaneous accrued payables consist of various minor liabilities of this kind.

Mortgage notes payable, interest payable

Mortgage notes payable are a particular kind of long-term notes payable: besides being interest-bearing, they are secured by some of the company's noncurrent assets.

With most liabilities, if the company becomes unable to pay all of its debts, the creditors must parcel out among themselves whatever money the company can raise and share losses. The creditors are on an equal footing with each other. With a secured debt such as a mortgage, however, the creditor is able to insist that its claims be satisfied through the particular noncurrent asset involved (perhaps by selling the company's land and buildings in this case and using the proceeds to repay the secured debt before any of these proceeds are used to satisfy other creditors).

While these distinctions are important, they do not affect the accounting for any but insolvent companies. If the company is able to pay its debts, secured notes are reported in the same way as other kinds of notes.

Interest payable is accrued in exactly the same way as is interest receivable (see pages 62–64). Assume for Illustration 3-1 that the $5\frac{1}{4}$ percent notes payable were issued by the company on 11/1/X1 and that no interest has been paid on them. The last payment of interest on the 4 percent Mortgage Notes Payable was on 7/31/X1. The calculation for interest payable then would be:

$5\frac{1}{4}\%$ Notes Payable: $\$12,000 \times 5\frac{1}{4}\% \times 2/12 = \$\ \ 105$
4% Mortgage Notes Payable: $\$129,000 \times 4\% \times 5/12 = \ \ 2,150$

Interest Payable—12/31/X1 $\$2,255$

Dividends payable

Illustration 3-1 omits one common liability: dividends payable. This liability is created when a corporation's board of directors *declares a dividend*—that is, promises to pay a dividend to its stockholders at a later date. Usually, stockholders are not creditors. But when a dividend is declared, it becomes a debt of the corporation to its stockholders—a liability for the amount of that dividend. The board of directors has the right to decide whether or not to declare dividends. If it does declare a dividend, a liability comes into being; if it does not declare a dividend, there is no liability. We will see many examples of dividends payable in later chapters.

Stockholders' equity

We have discussed Illustrative Corporation's creditor equities. The remaining equities represent the investment made by stockholders. This investment has two principal parts. First, at one time or another, stockholders must have made a direct, explicit investment in the company. Although the original stockholders may sell their shares to new stockholders, this investment itself is intended to be permanent—the corporation is not expected to repay it. The stockholders may have made only one such permanent investment—when the original stockholders brought the company into being. (Of course, stockholders may since have purchased additional shares of capital stock directly from the company.)

But the stockholders' rights don't end there. As indicated on page 19, as owners, stockholders are entitled to any profits that the company makes. (They also have to absorb any losses—something we'll worry about later.) This is part of the "residual" right of the stockholders—the right to anything "left over" after all the company's liabilities have been settled. If the company is profitable, stockholders may receive dividends—distributions of what is "left over" or, at least, distributions of cash in an amount related to the amount of profits. The amount of dividends will not necessarily be as great as the amount of profits. In this case, the stockholders' investment will be increased by the amount of undistributed profits.

As was mentioned in Chapter Two (page 80), these undistributed profits usually are called the firm's *retained earnings,* to distinguish them from its permanent stockholders' investment:

Stockholders' equity = Permanent investment + Retained earnings

For simplicity, until Chapter Five I will use the single term *stockholders' equity* to refer to both components of owners' investment, but you should recognize that this comprises both a permanent and a residual element.

An example may help here. Go back to the simplified example of Lender, Inc., and Borrower, Inc., on page 127. Consider just Lender, Inc. Suppose that Lender, Inc., was created by its stockholders just before it made its $300 loan. Then a report on Lender, Inc., right after the loan might look like this:

Lender, Inc.

Assets

Cash	$ 700
6% Note Receivable	300
Total Assets	$1,000

Equities

Stockholders' Equity	$1,000
Total Equities	$1,000

Suppose that another report were prepared after one year, and that neither the note nor any interest had been paid. During the year, $18 of interest would have accrued ($300 × 6% = $18). Lender, Inc., would have an $18 profit. Assuming no dividends have been paid to Lender, Inc., stockholders, the stockholders' investment will have increased by the amount of the undistributed profits—from $1,000 to $1,018:

Lender, Inc.

Assets

Cash	$ 700
6% Note Receivable	300
Interest Receivable	18
Total Assets	$1,018

Equities

Stockholders' Equity	$1,018
Total Equities	$1,018

This example is greatly simplified. It involves no liabilities, and no distinction is made between current and noncurrent assets. Yet it illustrates the nature of the stockholders' residual equity. Stockholders have a residual right to all company assets not claimed by creditors. If the company is profitable (and dividend payments are not made to stockholders) the residual rights of stockholders increase because the company's assets are increasing faster than its liabilities.[5] The $1,018 amount of stockholders' equity now includes this increase, which is the difference between the original explicit investment of stockholders and the total of their present rights after the company has made profits.[6] The permanent investment still equals $1,000, but now there are also $18 of retained earnings, for a total owners' equity of $1,018.

Stockholders' equity: the residual right of the owners of a corporation to their firm's assets, after allowance has been made for the total rights of creditors.

Another interpretation of equities

It may be helpful to look at equities from a slightly different point of view from the one used so far. Up to now, we have been considering assets as rights, and equities as obligations of the firm (and, correspondingly, equities as the rights of different kinds of investors in the firm). This is correct. But another interpretation of equities is also correct: *equities are sources of assets.*

Illustration 2-12 (page 113) shows that Illustrative Corporation's assets total $988,940. These assets had to come from somewhere. Now look at Illustration 3-1 again. Total liabilities are $396,360, so $396,360 of the assets came from investments by creditors. But all parts of the corporation's asset total must have a source, for a corporation is just a creation of its investors. The remaining $592,580 ($988,940 − $396,360 = $592,580) also has to have a source. Since the stockholders have the ultimate rights to any assets not claimed by the creditors, the whole $592,580 must belong to the stockholders.

We could carry this a step further and say that assets and equities are merely different aspects of the same general thing. Illustration 2-12, which shows Illustrative

---

[5] A company will also be profitable if both its assets and liabilities decrease, but its liabilities decrease more rapidly; of course this kind of thing cannot go on indefinitely. Algebraically, the basic relationship here is a very simple one (though feel free to ignore what follows if algebra troubles you). Let:

$$A = \text{total assets}$$
$$L = \text{total liabilities}$$
$$S = \text{stockholders' equity}$$

Since stockholders' equity is a residual right to all company assets not claimed by creditors, $S = A - L$.

[6] As mentioned on page 49, the word "profit" is being used here in the ordinary, man-in-the-street sense. In the chapter on revenue and expense, the more exact language that the accountant uses for such matters will be introduced. At that point, we will stop talking of "profit" and begin talking of "income." Meanwhile, the less exact language suffices for the present, and allows us to avoid certain unnecessary complications. To reiterate, interpret the word "profit" in its ordinary, layman's sense—as an improvement in economic situation resulting from the company's buying and selling, performing services, or doing whatever else it does to "make money." A firm's *profit* is the difference between the amount for which it sells its goods and services to its customers and the costs of providing these goods and services; *losses* are negative profits.

Corporation's assets, takes the $988,940 total of all assets and subdivides it to show the kinds of assets—the detailed rights to cash and services that make up total assets. Illustration 3-1, which shows Illustrative Corporation's equities, takes the same total and subdivides it to show these same rights classified by source. (In somewhat the same way, you might classify the 52 cards in a deck either by number or by suit.)

Under this interpretation, the asset list (2-12) subdivides the total rights of the company by asking: what, in detail, are these rights to? The equity list (3-1) takes the same total rights, but asks: from where, in detail, did these rights come? In answering the latter question, *the accountant assigns any part of the total not invested by creditors to the stockholders* (as the residual source of assets).

Assets equal equities

Whichever interpretation we use, it should be evident that total assets must equal total equities. The corporation is an entity created by its investors. The corporation's rights must equal its obligations; it cannot have any rights of its own, rights not accompanied by obligations. Alternately, every right must have its source in some investor. The total of all assets must be the same figure as the total of all sources of assets. This is reflected in Illustrations 2-12 and 3-1, both of which come to totals of $988,940.

Assets must equal equities, because any part of the asset total that does not have its source in the investments of creditors is always assigned to the residual source (the stockholders). Assets equal equities because there is a residual equity that serves to take up the difference between assets and liabilities.

An analogy might help here. Consider the contents of a refrigerator. You could classify them by such categories as meat, dairy products, vegetables, and beverages, and you could then associate purchase prices with these categories. From this classified list, you could obtain a total cost of all items in the refrigerator.

But you could also classify the contents in another way by asking, "Who will eat these things?" You might need to assign certain things that no one wants to eat (such as stale cheese) to some sort of "residual consumer"—perhaps the dog. You could then come up with a list of refrigerator contents classified by consumers, and associate purchase prices with *this* list, too. Obviously the resulting total purchase prices would have to be the same, whichever classification method you used, for both methods would be classifying the same contents.

Similarly, suppose that you classify the total cost of a company's rights according to the kinds of rights involved; the result would be a list of the company's assets. Next, classify the total cost of the company's rights in terms of the *sources* of these rights; the result would be a list of the company's equities. Both lists, however, are merely different ways of dividing up the same original cost total. The asset total must equal the equity total because each is the same total cost, seen from a different vantage point.

Purchases and sales of stock between stockholders

It should be repeated that, as pointed out on page 19, although stockholders' equity is affected by profits and by the investments made by stockholders, it is not affected by purchases and sales of stock *between* stockholders. For example, suppose that in Illustration 3-1 the stockholders' equity of Illustrative Corporation is represented by 10,000 shares of capital stock, and that a stockholder sold 10 shares of stock to another investor for a total of $600. The buyer would record a $600 decrease in cash, and a corresponding $600 increase in his investments. The seller would record a $600 increase in cash, a decrease in his investments for an amount equal to what he had paid for the 10 shares when he acquired them, and either a profit or a loss (unless he had paid exactly $600 himself). From the standpoint of Illustrative Corporation, nothing would have happened. There still would be 10,000 shares of capital stock outstanding, even though 10 of them now are in the hands of a different owner. Illustrative Corporation would neither have received nor paid out cash. The company would be affected only if it had issued or reacquired shares of its capital stock.

All of this is a consequence of the accountant's treating the company as a distinct accounting entity, as something separate from its investors. This treatment is discussed in the next subsection.

The entity rule

In the eyes of the law, a corporation is considered to be an entity distinct from its stockholders, with an indefinite life. This was stressed on pages 18–19; in all subsequent discussion of business enterprises, a distinction has carefully been made between the company itself and the various individuals and other enterprises concerned with it: owners, creditors, employees, customers. For example, the company's balance sheet is not the balance sheet of its owners; they have their own balance sheets listing their assets, liabilities, and residual equity. As was indicated on page 27, this distinction is important enough that accounting theorists have given it a special name: the *entity assumption* or the *entity rule*.

In effect, an entity was defined earlier as any center of economic activity that recipients of accounting reports find convenient to distinguish from other centers of economic activity.[7] As an example of how the entity rule works, imagine John Doe as a vice president of A. Company, a stockholder (owner) of B. Company, a bondholder (creditor) of C. Company, and a customer of D. Company. There are at least five entities involved here, five distinct centers of economic activity—the four companies and John Doe himself. Separate accounting reports would be prepared for each entity.

But John Doe is engaged in more than one kind of economic activity: he is both a consumer and an investor. If he finds it convenient to keep two separate sets of accounting records (one for each role), he is, in effect, treating himself as two entities. The entity rule simply reflects the accountant's willingness to subdivide economic activity into small enough categories to keep different kinds of activities from overlapping and becoming confused. A. Company, B. Company, and John Doe the investor—each has its own balance sheet showing individual assets and liabilities. The bonds, for instance, are an asset (bonds receivable) on John Doe's investor balance sheet, but a liability (bonds payable) on C. Company's balance sheet, and are not reflected at all on D. Company's balance sheet. Each entity also has its own residual

---

[7] This definition is deliberately a bit vague. Basically, an entity is whatever people receiving accounting reports wish it to be. It is customary to distinguish centers of economic activity from each other if they are owned by different owners, to distinguish between business enterprises and individuals, and so forth. But as the example to follow indicates, even finer distinctions can be made.

equity. With C. Company, the residual equity would be that company's stockholders' equity. With John Doe, the residual equity on his consumer balance sheet would be what would be called, in ordinary language, his "net worth"—his total assets less his total liabilities (see page 126). In general, the entity rule allows the accountant to prepare separate financial statements for any distinct center of economic activity— each set of statements with its individual assets, liabilities, and residual equity.

Summary

1. Equities are obligations of the company to its investors. Because all assets of a corporation are either contributed by investors or attributed to the residual ownership rights of stockholders, equities can also be regarded as sources of assets.
2. The two different kinds of investors result in two different kinds of equities:
   (a) *Liabilities* are debts owed to creditor-investors. Liabilities can be either current or noncurrent, depending on whether or not they will be paid within a year or less. Liabilities can be either monetary or nonmonetary, depending on whether or not they are to be settled in cash. Any liability represents a claim against the company and is mirrored by an asset on some creditor's list of assets.
   (b) *Stockholders' equity* is the ownership investment of the company's stockholders. It may be conceived of as reflecting two things: the permanent investment of the stockholders, and the profits of the company since it was founded (less any distributions of these profits that have been made to stockholders as dividends), or its *retained earnings*:

Stockholders' equity = Permanent investment + Retained earnings

3. These relationships may be diagrammed as opposite. As the diagram indicates, the classification of the total investment in the firm into various economic rights is identical to its classification into various assets. Similarly, the classification of the total investment in the firm into different kinds of obligations is identical to classifying it into different sources of total assets. Finally, total assets equal total equities under either system of classification—for a firm's rights must equal its obligations, and no portion of its total assets can lack a source. This may be expressed in any of the following ways:

Assets = Equities
Assets = Liabilities plus Stockholders' Equity
Stockholders' Equity = Assets − Liabilities

Problems for Study and Self-Examination

Problem 3-1:

Answer the following questions.

(a) Anniston Corporation has assets of $785,000 and a total stockholders' equity of $430,000. How much does the company owe creditors?

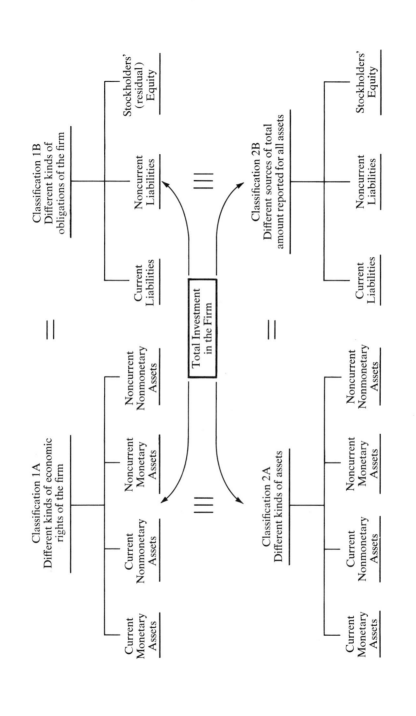

(b) Selden Co. owns rights to receive cash totalling $103,600 and nonmonetary assets totalling $170,300. It owes $94,500 to creditors and has a stockholders' equity of $188,200. How much cash does the company own?

Problem 3-2:

Greensboro Company has the following interest-bearing liabilities on 12/31/X1:

(a) $64,000 of $5\frac{1}{4}\%$ Notes Payable—due 3/15/X2. The company issued these notes on 8/15/X1, and has paid interest fees on them through 11/15/X1.

(b) $300,000 of $6\frac{1}{2}\%$ Bonds Payable—due 5/1/X9. Interest on these bonds is payable every May first and November first.

What is the company's accrued interest payable on 12/31/X1?

Problem 3-3:

Turn back to Problem 2-8, the solution to which is on page 116. Suppose that on 12/31/X1, Union Springs Associates, Inc., owes $72,000 of ordinary trade debts to its suppliers, $17,600 to its employees, and $21,160 to various taxing authorities. The company also owes $60,000 on 5% notes payable due 9/1/X3. The company issued these notes on 9/1/X1 and has not yet paid any interest on them.

Prepare a list of equities for Union Springs Associates, Inc., using good form and distinguishing between current and noncurrent liabilities, and between the different kinds of equities.

Solutions

Solution 3-1:

(a) Since Assets = Liabilities + Stockholders' Equity, and since the amount of liabilities is the amount owed creditors, we know that:

$$\$785,000 = \text{Liabilities} + \$430,000$$
$$\text{Liabilities} = \$785,000 - \$430,000$$
$$\text{Liabilities} = \underline{\$355,000} = \text{Amount owed creditors}$$

(b) Total equities:

Liabilities	$ 94,500	
Stockholders' equity	188,200	$282,700
Total assets (other than cash):		
Rights to receive cash . . .	$103,600	
Nonmonetary assets	170,300	273,900
Cash owned		$ 8,800

Because assets equal equities, this demonstrates that if we know the figures for all assets and equities except one asset or one equity, we always can determine the figure for the remaining asset or equity. Later, you will see that this gives you a useful way to check your work.

Solution 3-2:

No interest has been paid on the $5\frac{1}{4}\%$ notes payable for the last $1\frac{1}{2}$ months; $1\frac{1}{2}$ months equals 3/24ths of a year. No interest has been paid on the $6\frac{1}{2}\%$ bonds payable for the last 2 months. Interest payable would be calculated as follows:

$$5\tfrac{1}{4}\% \text{ Notes payable: } \$64,000 \times 5\tfrac{1}{4}\% \times 3/24 = \$ 420$$
$$6\tfrac{1}{2}\% \text{ Bonds payable: } \$300,000 \times 6\tfrac{1}{2}\% \times 2/12 = 3,250$$

Interest Payable—12/31/X1. . . . . $3,670

Solution 3-3:

Union Springs Associates, Inc.
Equities
December 31, 19X1

Current Liabilities:		
Accounts Payable	$72,000	
Interest Payable	1,000	
Wages Payable	17,600	
Taxes Payable	21,160	$111,760
Noncurrent Liabilities:		
5% Notes Payable—due 9/1/X3.		60,000
Total Liabilities		$171,760
Stockholders' Equity		119,240
Total Equities		$291,000

The figure for Stockholders' Equity is determined by subtracting the total of all other equities from the total of all assets (see note 5, page 133). Interest payable is calculated as follows: $60,000 \times 5\% \times 4/12 = \$1,000$.

The Balance Sheet

We can now consider the first of the major financial accounting reports: the *balance sheet*. As Chapter One indicated, one of the things the financial accountant wants to report to investors is the company's present economic situation. This depends on the company's economic rights and its economic obligations. In order to report on these, the accountant must report on the company's assets and equities at a particular point in time. To prepare such a report for Illustrative Corporation as of 12/31/X1, the list of the company's assets is combined with the list of its equities for that date. The resulting report is called the balance sheet of Illustrative Corporation for December 31, 19X1, and is shown as Illustration 3-2. Satisfy yourself that Illustration 3-2 is just a combination of Illustration 2-12 (page 113) and Illustration 3-1 (page 127).

Up to this point, we have been speaking of assets and equities and the figures used to represent them. It will simplify exposition if we begin to use the accountant's technical language and speak of *accounts* when referring in a general way to assets or equities. Instead of saying "the figure used to represent the account," we can use another technical term and speak of the account's *balance*. (Later you will see why it is natural to use the word "balance.") In Illustration 3-2, the cash account has a balance of $47,600; the taxes payable account has a balance of $26,100; and so on. Another way, then, to describe a balance sheet is to say that it is a list of asset and equity accounts and their balances, organized in a formal way. Why is this report called a balance sheet? Because it lists balances and possibly also because assets balance, or equal, equities.

Investors use balance sheets to obtain information about the company. As was pointed out on page 24, here are some of the things that investors need to know about a company's current financial conditions:

> How big is it? How much cash does it have? How much is owed it? What does it own besides cash and debts from others? How much does it owe creditors? How much money have owners invested in it? Does it seem able to pay its bills as they come due?

All of these questions, except perhaps the last, can be easily answered from an inspection of the balance sheet. The last question—"Does it seem able to pay its bills?" —can be partially answered by analyzing the balance sheet. Readers of financial statements often put considerable effort into analyzing them to obtain information not immediately apparent from simple inspection. There is a common (though somewhat superficial) way in which the balance sheet is analyzed to obtain clues about the

Illustration 3-2

Illustrative Corporation
Balance Sheet
December 31, 19X1

Assets

Current Assets:

Cash	$ 47,600	
5% Notes Receivable—due 4/1/X2	16,000	
Accounts Receivable	180,290	
Interest Receivable	2,050	
Inventories	200,000	
Supplies	23,000	
Prepaid Rent	12,000	$480,940

Noncurrent Assets:

6% Notes Receivable—due 2/1/X5	$ 48,000	
Investment in 4½% Bonds Receivable— due 3/1/X9	30,000	
Land	65,000	
Buildings	95,000	
Equipment	230,000	
Patents	40,000	508,000

Total Assets	$988,940

Equities

Current Liabilities:

5¼% Notes Payable—due 2/1/X2	$ 12,000	
Accounts Payable	145,100	
Advances from Customers	19,800	
Wages Payable	58,400	
Interest Payable	2,255	
Taxes Payable	26,100	
Miscellaneous Accrued Payables	3,705	$267,360

Noncurrent Liabilities:

4% Mortgage Notes Payable	129,000
Total Liabilities	$396,360
Stockholders' Equity	592,580

Total Equities	$988,940

company's debt-paying ability. This analysis is not complicated, and it provides a good example of other analytical techniques. We will examine it here.

Net working capital

Refer back to Chapter Two and the operating cycle (pages 110–111). In Illustration 2-11 (page 111), it was assumed for simplicity that the company paid cash for its inventories and supplies. Illustration 3-3 makes the more realistic assumption that the company buys inventories, supplies, and services on credit, while paying cash for other nonmonetary current assets. Even so, Illustration 3-3 is simplified; it leaves out notes and interest payable and receivable, as well as advances from customers and to suppliers. But it nonetheless is detailed enough to show something that is important in the firm's day-by-day operations. Illustration 3-3 indicates that, on the average, current liabilities ordinarily are paid from the proceeds of sales (sales that, among other things, use up the current assets and services that were purchased on credit).

Assume that the company is able to sell its product at prices high enough to cover its current costs of operating. By the end of the operating cycle, the cash col-

Illustration 3-3

The Operating Cycle
(Still Somewhat Simplified)

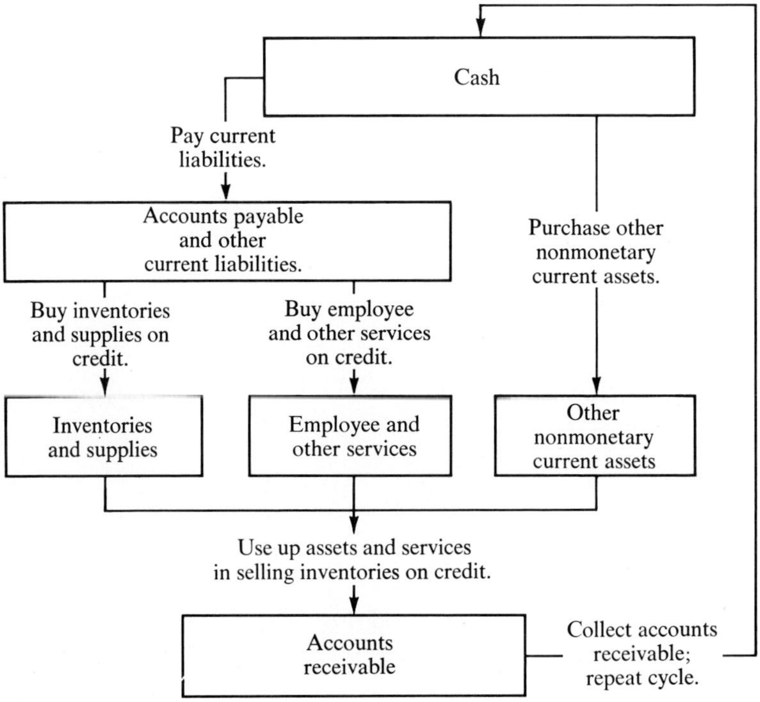

lected will be equal to (or greater than) the cost of the current assets given up in making the sale; therefore, there will be enough cash to pay current liabilities. Although things never work out perfectly, current operations usually do generate cash for paying current liabilities, and the amount of current assets does provide some indication of how much cash will become available to pay current liabilities. Current liabilities often don't have to be paid immediately; in many industries the customer is allowed 30 days or so, and may settle his bill even later by paying a small penalty. Therefore the relationship between current assets and current liabilities offers a crude test of whether the company will be able to pay its current debts as they come due (assuming that it can make use of ordinary ways to delay payment if necessary).

This relationship between current assets and current liabilities is ordinarily expressed in two ways:

1. You can compare current assets and current liabilities by a ratio.[8] This is called the *current ratio* and is calculated as follows (the figures are from Illustration 3-2):

$$\text{current ratio} = \frac{\text{current assets}}{\text{current liabilities}} = \frac{\$480,940}{\$267,360} = \text{about 1.8 to 1}$$

The amount of current assets is used as an indication of whether there will be enough cash from operations to pay current bills. Presumably there should be a safety factor just in case some inventories can't be sold or some customers pay especially late. A popular (though overly simplified) rule of thumb is that the current ratio should be about 2 to 1. If this is so, Illustrative Corporation may be running some risk, though more information would be needed before becoming really concerned. For example, you would need to know the typical current ratio in this industry; that is, how much risk similar companies take. You would also want to know the trend of Illustrative Corporation's current ratio—whether it has been rising or falling over the last few reports.

2. You can just subtract current liabilities from current assets. The resulting figure is called the company's *net working capital*. The word "net" is used here to distinguish this concept from "working capital," which, as was indicated on page 112, is an alternate name for current assets alone. Using the figures in Illustration 3-2, net working capital is calculated as follows:

$$\text{Net working capital} = \text{current assets} - \text{current liabilities} = \$480,940 - \$267,360 = \$213,580.$$

The amount of a company's net working capital is the amount of "flexible" assets available to management in the short run. Once a company has purchased non-current assets, such as buildings or equipment, the funds employed usually are

---

[8] A ratio is simply a number obtained by dividing one number by another. For example, if John Doe is 60 inches tall and weighs 180 pounds, the ratio of his weight to his height is $180/60 = 3$ pounds per inch. In Illustration 3-2, the ratio of stockholders' equity to total assets is $592,580/988,940 = 0.598$.

effectively committed to these assets for the duration of their lengthy lives. Ordinarily, it is impractical to sell present buildings and equipment. Not only would this interrupt operations, but it would usually involve serious losses.

Most companies are in a much more flexible position with their current assets. Bills must be paid when they come due, but so long as this is done, companies are fairly free to change the kinds of inventories they hold and to decide how much credit is to be extended to individual customers. Assuming that operations generate more than enough cash to pay for current assets and services, the extra cash is available for other purposes such as buying new noncurrent assets or paying long-term debts. In general, the larger the figure for net working capital, the more power the company has to seize new opportunities and react quickly to changes in its environment. The amount of net working capital serves as an index of the company's flexibility, as well as of its ability to pay current debts. Notice that the amount of current assets alone is not a good index of flexibility. If a company had a million dollars of current assets but also had a million dollars of current liabilities, flexibility would be low.[9]

Since it is an important element in the construction of a major financial accounting report—the funds statement—later chapters will pay considerable attention to the notion of net working capital. Some companies prepare their balance sheets to emphasize it. Illustration 3-4 rearranges the balance sheet of Illustration 3-2 (p. 141) to emphasize the amount of net working capital.

Illustration 3-4

Illustrative Corporation
Balance Sheet
December 31, 19X1

Current Assets:

Cash	$ 47,600	
5% Notes Receivable—due 4/1/X2	16,000	
Accounts Receivable.	180,290	
Interest Receivable	2,050	
Inventories	200,000	
Supplies	23,000	
Prepaid Rent	12,000	$480,940

Current Liabilities:

5¼% Notes Payable—due 2/1/X2	$ 12,000	
Accounts Payable	145,100	
Advances from Customers	19,800	
Wages Payable	58,400	
Interest Payable	2,255	
Taxes Payable	26,100	
Miscellaneous Accrued Payables	3,705	267,360

Net Working Capital	$213,580

[9] It is also true that the whole concept of net working capital is only a rough approximation of flexibility or debt-paying ability. For instance, Illustrative Corporation's noncurrent 6 percent notes receivable probably could be negotiated (sold) to raise cash were cash really needed. Yet, by convention, these notes are not usually included in net working capital. This is not to criticize the concept of net working capital, but just to suggest that, like most concepts, it has its limitations.

Noncurrent Assets:

6% Notes Receivable—due 2/1/X5	$ 48,000
Investment in 4½% Bonds Receivable—due 3/1/X9	30,000
Land	65,000
Buildings	95,000
Equipment	230,000
Patents	40,000
	$508,000

Noncurrent Liabilities:

4% Mortgage Notes Payable	129,000	379,000
Stockholders' Equity		$592,580

Two more comments should be made about Illustration 3-4. First, it happens that in Illustration 3-2, assets are shown to the left of equities in a horizontal arrangement. In Illustration 3-4, the arrangement is vertical. Either horizontal or vertical arrangements are acceptable. You will find when you do your homework that a vertical balance sheet usually fits on an 8½″ by 11″ page better than does a horizontal one. For this reason, all solutions for problems in this book will use vertical balance sheets.

Second, notice that more than one kind of balance sheet is acceptable. (The next section will discuss certain technical rules of balance sheet construction.) Whether or not you use the net working capital form of the balance sheet is mostly a matter of personal choice. The form of balance sheet that lists all assets and then all equities is still the most commonly used in practice and will be employed in most homework solutions.

Does the balance sheet report position?

Does the balance sheet really report a company's economic position? Does it really tell investors the company's present condition?

The balance sheet is a combined list of assets and equities. The amounts reported for liabilities and monetary assets reflect very closely the company's cash, rights to receive cash, and the creditor claims against the company. As far as *these* assets and equities go, the balance sheet does a satisfactory job of reporting the company's economic condition.

But, as you have seen, the balances for nonmonetary assets represent the historical costs of services purchased in the past—historical costs that have been adjusted to reflect partial receipt of these services. The accountant uses a technical term here: *book value*. A depreciable asset's book value equals its original cost less all depreciation amortization to date. At least three things make the resulting book values of depreciable assets and the other nonmonetary asset balances poor reflections of the company's current position:

1. Many valuable nonmonetary goods that are owned by firms are not recognized as assets, either because there is no objective and reliable way to associate a purchase price with them or because there is no objective and reliable way to amortize these costs as the services are yielded. This problem was discussed on pages 42 and 45. For instance, an efficient management or an effective sales force may be of great economic

significance to a firm, yet it would not be recognized as an asset on the firm's balance sheet.

2. When nonmonetary goods are recognized as assets, their costs are amortized on the balance sheet to reflect the decline in the future economic benefits that they offer to the firm. The resulting book values often are arbitrary. For instance, it will be contended in Chapter Thirteen that when an individual or group of individuals selects a particular method of depreciating a building, their choice usually cannot be conclusively defended against any other method (proposed by some other individual) if all parties are attempting to maximize their own economic interests and these interests conflict.

3. As was pointed out on pages 54–57, the historical cost figures themselves are not entirely satisfactory figures with which to represent nonmonetary assets, simply because they *are* historical. The company's economic condition is something that exists in the present, not in the past, and past prices may not be altogether relevant. For example, presume that a firm bought land in 1948 for $10,000, which it uses as an employee parking lot. Since 1948, the price of comparable plots has risen substantially. Perhaps the firm could now sell this land for $80,000. Which is a better reflection of economic condition: reporting the land at its historical cost of $10,000 or at an estimated current market value of $80,000?

There is no clear-cut answer to this question; it all depends upon what you want to do with the information. For most legal, regulatory, and other institutional purposes, historical costs are the only acceptable ones. (Recall, though, the conservatism rule—whereby goods held for sale, retired assets, and so on can be represented at current market values when these are lower than historical costs.) But we have previously seen that, for resource-allocation decisions involving prediction of the future, it is plausible to expect estimated current market values often to be more relevant than historical costs.

A serious problem of choice arises here if the estimates of current market values are unreliable, as they are for some nonmonetary assets—highly specialized machinery, for example, may not *have* a current market value. In general, the resource-allocator is sometimes faced with the problem we have discussed before: whether to use a reliable but rather irrelevant piece of information, or a relevant but unreliable one; there may be situations in which a suitable reflection of economic condition simply cannot be found.

In any event, it should be clear that the sense in which the accountant reports economic condition is a specialized one. We saw on page 93 that depreciation has nothing whatever to do with current market values; this conclusion can be generalized: *the position of a company, as reported by the accountant, has little to do with what an investor might pay for the company, the market value of its shares of stock, or any other estimation of current worth.* Instead, the balance sheet reports the amount of monetary assets, the amount of liabilities, and the historical costs less amortization of nonmonetary assets. In other words, the balance sheet reports cash, claims, and the remainders of past purchase prices.

Because the stockholders' equity is treated as the residual equity, any errors in the nonmonetary asset balances will be reflected by corresponding errors in the stockholders' equity balances. An example demonstrates this: suppose that the balance sheet for a company is summarized as follows:

Assets		*Equities*	
Monetary Assets	$120,000	Liabilities	$100,000
Nonmonetary Assets . . .	180,000	Stockholders' Equity . . .	200,000
Total Assets	$300,000	Total Equities	$300,000

Imagine that, because of an error, nonmonetary assets are instead reported at $150,000. Equities must equal assets. There would be no reason to change the amounts reported for liabilities and monetary assets, since the appropriate amounts for these are easy to determine and are unaffected by the figures reported for nonmonetary assets. Therefore, stockholders' equity—the residual equity—would have to be adjusted and thus would be shown incorrectly too. (Compare this reasoning with the discussion of the residual nature of stockholders' equity on pages 18–19.) The erroneous balance sheet is summarized as follows:

Assets		*Equities*	
Monetary Assets	$120,000	Liabilities	$100,000
Nonmonetary Assets . . .	150,000	Stockholders' Equity . . .	170,000
Total Assets	$270,000	Total Equities	$270,000

In the light of this, does the balance sheet report position? Yes, but only if we understand position to mean the amount of monetary assets and liabilities, together with written-down historical costs of nonmonetary assets and a balancing figure for stockholders' equity. Some accountants prefer to call the balance sheet by the name *position statement*. This is a perfectly good name so long as you are aware of the sense in which the word "position" is being used.

Book value per share

It is fairly common for those who discuss the financial statements of a firm to calculate a figure called the firm's *book value per share*. You will recall from page 19 that the stockholders' equity of a corporation is evidenced by shares of stock held by the firm's stockholders. Book value per share is calculated as follows:

$$\text{Book value per share} = \frac{\text{Stockholders' equity[10]}}{\text{Number of shares of stock outstanding}}$$

Since stockholders' equity is the difference between total assets and total liabilities, *book value per share* signifies:

$$\frac{\left(\begin{array}{c}\text{The net amount of}\\\text{monetary assets}\\\text{less total liabilities}\end{array}\right) + \left(\begin{array}{c}\text{The amortized historical}\\\text{costs of nonmonetary}\\\text{assets}\end{array}\right)}{\left(\begin{array}{c}\text{The number of shares}\\\text{of stock outstanding}\end{array}\right)}$$

---

[10] As elsewhere in this book, it is assumed here that the firm in question has issued only one kind of stock. Chapter Five discusses exceptions to this assumption. Where a firm has issued more than one kind of stock, the calculation of book values per share can become relatively complicated—these complications are best saved for an advanced course.

The significance of the resulting numeral will be no greater than the significance of the amounts reported for the amortized historical costs of nonmonetary assets, and, in any case, this numeral is too much a mixture of unlike things to be especially meaningful.

In contrast, the *market price per share* of a firm's stock (essentially equivalent to the price per share that investors are willing to pay for the firm's capital stock) can be very significant, particularly to someone who is considering buying or selling the related shares.

Basic accounting rules summarized

Some major accounting rules have been discussed in the previous two chapters. Present financial accounting practice has been greatly influenced by these rules. If you understand them, you understand a great deal about what the accountant does in his reports. These rules include the following:

1. The accountant gives specialized definitions to assets and equities (see pages 39, 125–126, 131–133). *Assets* are economic goods offering future benefits to the company and are either:

   (a) Cash or claims to receive cash.
   (b) Nonmonetary goods with which a dollar figure can be associated, according to certain minimum standards of objectivity and reliability.

Equities are simultaneously:

   (a) Company obligations to its investors.
   (b) Sources of assets.

2. *Conservatism* (see pages 57–59) insists that the amount reported for non-monetary assets be either the current market value or the amortized historical cost, whichever is lower. The *going-concern rule* (see pages 58–59) modifies this by specifying that:

   (a) If the firm is expected soon to go out of business, all nonmonetary assets should be reported at their current market values; often these equal whatever these assets would command at auction or other emergency sale.
   (b) Otherwise, retired assets and assets held for sale should be reported at the lower of current market values or amortized historical costs, while all other nonmonetary assets should be reported at their amortized historical costs; this latter rule often is referred to as the *historical-cost rule*.[11]

---

[11] Many accountants claim that the basic rule here is one of objectivity, not conservatism —that financial accounting should employ objectively verifiable data, instead of subjective estimates. They argue, in particular, that historical costs are employed because these provide the requisite objective data (this reasoning was summarized on page 55). There is no harm in looking at things in this way, but there are at least two reasons for believing that this position is oversimplified as a description of actual accounting practice:

1. Accountants are willing to make subjective estimates in their determination of profits and amortized historical costs (Chapters Six, Eight, and Thirteen attempt to demonstrate this). The implication is that conservatism is more fundamental than objectivity.

2. It is common knowledge that often the current market value of a manufactured inventory can be determined with less subjectivity than can that asset's historical cost. The reasons for this have to do with the complexity of the cost-accumulation process discussed in Chapter Twelve and the subjectivity of cost allocations, mentioned above. Yet, once again, accountants follow the rule of conservatism and report historical costs for manufactured inventories (except when these are higher than current market values).

3. *The matching rule* is closely associated with the historical-cost rule. Whenever it is proper to assume a going concern, the historical purchase prices of nonmonetary assets should be allocated to the activities or periods of time benefited by these assets, as they are on pages 91–102. Depreciation is an excellent example of such an allocation. When a company buys a machine, it acquires an asset that will offer services for a number of years. Eventually, though, these services will be used up, and the magnitude reported for the machine must be reduced to zero or a scrap value. The accountant *could* amortize the machine entirely in the year of purchase or entirely in the year of retirement. But the accountant believes that either of these approaches would be misleading: the machine offers services in all the years it is owned, so all years should bear a share of its cost. Accordingly, the accountant allocates some of the cost of the machine to each service year; that is, he "matches" part of the cost with the results of each year's activities, on the grounds that the machine's services helped generate these results. (We saw on pages 49 and 78–79 that when such a cost is allocated to an individual year it forms part of either the firm's expenses for that year or its cost of goods manufactured; in either case, this cost of the services provided by the machine in an individual year is a consideration in determining the firm's profits.)

The costs of insurance policies are also allocated according to the matching rule. A company buying a three-year fire insurance policy would allocate one-third of its cost to the first year, and so on. In general, any procedure whereby the acquisition price of a nonmonetary asset is amortized involves some kind of "matching" allocation.

Notice that two kinds of "matching" are being performed when nonmonetary assets are amortized. First, the historical cost of the asset (less any estimated scrap value) is allocated pro-rata to its estimated services—to the total economic benefits it is expected to provide to the firm. Then, the resulting costs of these services are in turn allocated to the periods in which the services are received. When the accountant speaks of "matching," ordinarily he does not bother to distinguish between these two allocations; but both exist, even though they may be performed simultaneously.

4. *The entity rule* (see pages 135–136) allows (and encourages) the accountant to prepare separate sets of reports for distinct centers of economic activity, each with its own assets, liabilities, and residual equity. One implication of this rule is that business enterprises are considered separate from their owners, their creditors, and their management.

5. The practice of *accrual* allows the accountant to recognize receivables and liabilities resulting from the provision of services (and, occasionally, products) before these claims are legal obligations of the entity which has received the service (or product).

Each of these rules represents judgments—decisions made by the accountant. Some of these rules (especially those relating to the amounts reported for nonmonetary assets) are open to debate and will be debated in later parts of this book. Nonetheless, these rules lie at the heart of the work of the financial accountant.

Balance Sheet
Punctuation and Grammar

Balance sheet punctuation

Turn back to Illustration 3-2 (page 141). Notice the way in which pairs of columns are used to obtain subtotals for total current assets, total noncurrent assets, total liabilities, and so on. This is not the only way to show subtotals, but it is a good one. Notice where the dollar signs and the single and double lines fall. All of this is the accounting equivalent of punctuation. As in punctuation, there are different acceptable ways of doing things—for instance, this sentence uses a "dash" or "bar" where it might have used a semicolon. But it is important to follow some reasonably standard practices in the use of indentations, lines, and dollar signs when preparing financial statements.

After all, accounting reports are a kind of technical writing, and you want to avoid puzzling or jolting your reader. Nonstandard punctuation brings your reader up short and makes him waste time trying to figure out what you're saying. Even though accounting punctuation may seem arbitrary, respect it. This book uses a consistent system of accounting punctuation in its problems and examples. Learn this system as you read the text and do your homework. Various other systems, such as the ones illustrated on pages 88 and 155, also are possible. But the system that is illustrated here is unobtrusive and acceptable to trained readers, which makes it suitable for our purposes at this stage.

Accounting grammar

In addition to punctuation, accounting reports require the use of a sort of grammar. All the illustrations in this book list accounts in the standard order shown in Illustration 3-2 (page 141). This style is by no means the only acceptable one, but it is a conventional order that readers of balance sheets find familiar and unobtrusive. The following rules have been used:

1. Assets are listed either above equities or to the left of equities.

2. Current assets are listed before noncurrent assets. Current liabilities are listed before noncurrent liabilities. Liabilities are listed before stockholders' equity.

3. Within the current assets, cash is always shown first. After cash come the current monetary assets. Although there is much variation in actual practice, current monetary assets are often shown in the following order: short-term investments (such as temporary investments in government securities), notes receivable, accounts receivable, interest receivable, and various minor receivables. Next come the non-monetary current assets, usually in the following order: inventory, supplies, and prepayments. If there is more than one prepayment, the order in which prepayments are shown is unimportant.

4. Within the noncurrent assets, land, buildings, and equipment may be placed in a separate category called "plant and equipment" with other noncurrent assets categorized as "other assets," or (less often) a separate category called "investments" may be used for long-term investments. If all noncurrent assets are listed together, usually long-term investments are listed first (in any order), followed by land, buildings, equipment, and patents (in that order).

5. Within the current liabilities, notes payable to banks usually are distinguished from other notes payable and are listed first; next, other notes payable and accounts payable are reported. There seems to be a preference for listing current notes payable before accounts payable, but no hard-and-fast generalizations can be made here. In any event, after notes and accounts payable, there are no rules for order within the current liabilities; do whatever satisfies you.

6. There is no set order within the noncurrent liabilities.

It is important to memorize an acceptable order of accounts for the same reason that it is important that a foreign student memorize an acceptable order of words in an English sentence. Consider the following sentence:

Few accountants eat snails.

Word order is very important if you are going to communicate exactly what you mean. With a different word order, you might get:

Accountants eat few snails.

That doesn't mean quite the same thing; nor does:

Accountants few eat snails.

A reader can figure this last sentence out with some effort, but only by wasting his time. The order of account titles in accounting reports is almost as important as the order of words in English. The main difference is that mistakes in account-title order will rarely distort your meaning completely.[12] But poor account-title order will make needless work for your reader and make you appear awkward. Since the order used in this book is an acceptable one, the best thing to do is to memorize it.

Summary

1. A balance sheet (or "position statement") is a list of a company's asset and equity accounts, together with their balances at a particular point in time. This list is prepared in one of several standard orders.

2. Balance sheets are used by investors to answer a number of questions about the company's current economic condition. Some of these questions can be answered by simple inspection of the balance sheet. Others require additional analysis.

3. The sense in which the balance sheet reports current economic condition is a special one, relating to the accountant's use of historical costs for his nonmonetary asset balances. Essentially, the balance sheet reports:

(a) The amount of monetary assets owned.

(b) The amount of debts owed creditors.

(c) The original purchase prices of nonmonetary assets, as reduced by depreciation, amortization, or other appropriate kinds of writedown.

(d) A "balancing" figure for stockholders' equity sufficient to make total assets equal total equities; this figure is affected by any limitations of the other items reported on the balance sheet. Because stockholders' equity is a residual equity, this balancing figure also reflects the firm's obligations to its stockholders.

---

[12] Complete distortion *can* happen in English. Consider the following: Few snails eat accountants.

Consolidated Balance Sheets

When you look at actual balance sheets, you will discover that many are titled *consolidated* balance sheets. For our purposes these may be treated in exactly the same ways as any other balance sheets. Nevertheless, a brief explanation is desirable.

It is common for large firms to acquire some or all of the capital stock of other companies, then to allow the acquired companies to operate as separate corporations. In such cases it is customary to speak of the purchaser company as a *parent* and the purchased corporations as *subsidiaries*. Firms acquire subsidiaries to assure themselves continuous supplies of raw materials, to diversify into new activities, and for various other reasons.

Since the parent and subsidiary companies remain separate corporations and are considered (in the eyes of the law at least) to be separate entities, each prepares its own individual financial statements. In many cases, though, the parent owns enough of the subsidiary's capital stock that it can elect its candidates to the subsidiary's board of directors (see pages 20–21) and thereby dictate the subsidiary's actions. In such cases, there is an important sense in which a *single* economic entity is present, even though it takes the form of two separate corporations. Accountants reflect this by preparing a combined set of financial statements for the two corporations. Such combined statements are called *consolidated* financial statements.

Preparation of consolidated financial statements leads to fascinating technical and theoretical problems, the details of which are studied in advanced courses. But the general principles of consolidations can easily be understood if certain simplifications are made, as in the following example.

Example of consolidated balance sheet

Assume in what follows that three zeros have been omitted from the data. On January 1, 19X1, Parent Company acquired all of the capital stock of Subsidiary Company for a total price of $8,720. Illustration 3-5 shows the summarized balance sheet of Subsidiary Company at the time of purchase, while Illustration 3-6 shows the summarized balance sheets of both firms at 12/31/X1.

Illustration 3-5

Subsidiary Company
Balance Sheet
December 31, 19X0

Assets

Current Assets:		
Cash	$1,720	
Receivables	2,620	
Inventories	3,760	
Other current assets	470	$ 8,570
Noncurrent Assets		9,280
Total Assets		$17,850

Equities

Liabilities	$ 9,130
Stockholders' Equity	8,720
Total Equities	$17,850

Illustration 3-6

Parent Company and Subsidiary Company
Balance Sheets
December 31, 19X1

Assets

	Parent Co.	Sub-sidiary Co.	Simple Totals
Current Assets:			
Cash	$ 2,300	$ 1,830	$ 4,130
Receivables.	16,300	2,860	19,160
Inventories	24,000	3,870	27,870
Other current assets	900	520	1,420
Total Current Assets	$43,500	$ 9,080	$ 52,580
Noncurrent Assets:			
Investment in Subsidiary Co.	$ 8,720	$ –0–	$ 8,720
Other noncurrent assets	32,700	9,390	42,090
Total Noncurrent Assets	$41,420	$ 9,390	$ 50,810
Total Assets	$84,920	$18,470	$103,390

Equities

Liabilities	$31,900	$ 8,950	$ 40,850
Stockholders' Equity	53,020	9,520	62,540
Total Equities	$84,920	$18,470	$103,390

Elimination of intercompany investment

Notice that a Simple Totals column has been provided in Illustration 3-6. This column merely gives the arithmetic sum of the amounts on the financial statements of the two firms. Assume that a combined report on both companies is to be prepared. Does this Simple Totals column provide the figures that should be reported?

Obviously it does not, for one of the assets in the Simple Totals column is the $8,720 investment of Parent Company in Subsidiary Company. Illustration 4-5 indicates that the $8,720 worth of rights acquired by this investment correspond exactly to the amount of Subsidiary Company's stockholders' equity at the time the rights were acquired. Both the $8,720 of Parent Company rights and the corresponding $8,720 of Subsidiary Company obligations are still reflected a year later in the individual 12/31/X1 balance sheets. From the standpoints of the separate companies, these are genuine rights and obligations. But if you regard the two firms as a single economic entity, these rights and obligations simply cancel out; it is meaningless to speak of an economic entity's rights from itself and obligations to itself.

As a parallel example, suppose that a man lends his watch to his wife. He has a right to receive the watch back from her; she has an obligation to return his watch. But if he were to prepare a balance sheet for his family as a whole, the right and obligation cancel out, and it would be meaningless to report a receivable and a liability for the combined entity. Similarly, when preparing a combined balance sheet for the Parent Company–Subsidiary Company entity, the accountant would never report the $8,720 investment by Parent Company and the related $8,720 of Subsidiary Company's stockholders' equity. Instead, the simple totals would be corrected by eliminating both.

Elimination of intercompany debt

By the same logic, any intercompany debt between the two parties should be eliminated, since the related receivables and payables simply cancel out when one reports on the combined entity. Suppose that Parent Company had purchased $1,200 of its inventories from Subsidiary Company, and that these goods had not yet been paid for; then there is a $1,200 intercompany debt. Subsidiary Company's $1,200 receivable should be eliminated; so should Parent Company's $1,200 liability. After all four eliminations have been made, the following balance sheet could be prepared from the revised simple totals:

Assets

Current Assets:

Cash (unchanged)	$ 4,130	
Receivables ($19,160 − $1,200)	17,960	
Inventories (unchanged)	27,870	
Other current assets (unchanged).	1,420	$51,380

Noncurrent Assets:

Investment in Subsidiary Company ($8,720 − $8,720)	$ –0–	
Other noncurrent assets (unchanged).	42,090	42,090
Total Assets		$93,470

Equities

Liabilities ($40,850 − $1,200)	$39,650
Stockholders' Equity ($62,540 − $8,720)	53,820
Total Equities	$93,470

Actually, this is not yet the consolidated balance sheet (which is why it was not given a heading). Certain additional eliminations usually must be made; an example of these will be mentioned in a later chapter when consolidated income statements are discussed. But the kinds of eliminations made above are typical and provide good illustrations of what is involved in preparing consolidated balance sheets.

To repeat—as far as the matters discussed in this text are concerned, you may treat consolidated balance sheets in the same ways that you would the balance sheets of individual firms. Accordingly, little reference to this topic will be made in subsequent chapters.

What follow are the balance sheets of Wadsworth Publishing Company, Inc., (the publisher of this book) for December 31, 1970 and 1969. This financial statement has been slightly simplified to remove some technical matters; but nothing that is important to you at this stage in your studies has been omitted. Several features of these balance sheets are worthy of comment:

1. They are *consolidated* balance sheets of the firm and its subsidiaries.

2. The company uses a different way to obtain subtotals than the one used in this book, and there are other minor differences in form. The company also follows the common practice of calling equities "liabilities." Assets that we have called prepayments are here called "prepaid expenses."

3. Advances to authors are a special kind of advances to suppliers, made to authors who are writing books for the company. Book writing takes time, so such assets are apt to be noncurrent. Here the company has done something a little unusual (though quite acceptable) by making up a whole separate category for these assets and certain other noncurrent assets (perhaps prepayment of some kind, for the term "deferred charges" is a fairly broad one). Amounts owed authors are called "accrued royalties."

4. Buildings and equipment are reported at their full original historical cost, and depreciation-to-date is subtracted. We have been showing plant balances *net* of accumulated depreciation. Wadsworth Publishing Company, Inc., follows the standard practice of showing plant at its gross original purchase price, then reducing this purchase price to the kind of net figure that we have been reporting.

If nothing else, the following balance sheet should give you a sense of the variety of presentation allowed in accounting.

Wadsworth Publishing Company, Inc. and Subsidiaries
Consolidated Balance Sheet,
December 31, 1970 and 1969

Assets

	1970	1969
Current Assets:		
Cash	$ 256,047	$ 234,228
Accounts receivable	3,036,603	2,482,959
Inventories:		
Finished goods	2,130,033	1,591,105
Raw materials and work in process	570,560	664,863
Prepaid expenses	80,833	58,863
Total Current Assets	6,074,076	5,032,018
Property, Plant, and Equipment		
Land and land improvements	968,963	968,613
Building	412,549	411,860
Equipment	192,303	159,888
Construction in progress	172,667	–0–
Total	1,746,482	1,540,361
Less accumulated depreciation	197,544	161,395

continued on page 156

Property, Plant, and Equipment—net	1,548,938	1,378,966
Advances to Authors and Other Deferred Charges	408,026	331,833
Total Assets	$8,031,040	$6,742,817

Liabilities

Current Liabilities:		
Notes payable—current portion	$ 963,089	$ 449,278
Accounts payable	415,888	550,616
Accrued royalties	911,246	790,664
Taxes on income	221,286	387,512
Other current liabilities	298,135	320,349
Total Current Liabilities	2,809,644	2,498,419
Long-Term Notes Payable	254,967	258,056
Stockholders' Equity	4,966,429	3,986,342
Total Liabilities	$8,031,040	$6,742,817

Problems For Study
and Self-Examination

Problem 3-4:

The following are the balance sheet accounts of Buchanan Products at 12/31/X1, arbitrarily listed in alphabetical order. Prepare a balance sheet, using the form that employs two dollar columns and lists assets first, followed by equities.

The company is owed $14,410 by its insurance company in settlement of a claim for wind damage that resulted from a storm on 3/12/X1. It expects the claim to be paid within three months. "Commissions payable" represent estimated amounts owed to salesmen for December, 19X1. "Customer deposits on uncompleted goods" are advances from customers. "Equipment purchase contracts" is a liability that arose when the company bought $100,000 of equipment on 12/1/X1. The first payment of principal (of $25,000) is due on 3/1/X3. The balance for the stockholders' equity account is deliberately omitted. Try to solve this problem without referring back to the text.

Accounts Payable	$121,650
Accounts Receivable.	178,300
Automobiles and Trucks	65,310
Bonds Payable: $6\frac{1}{4}\%$—due 9/1/X8.	300,000
Buildings	212,300
Cash	47,340
Commissions Payable	4,070
Customer Deposits on Uncompleted Goods	24,300
Due from Insurance Company	14,410
Equipment Purchase Contracts.	100,000
Interest Payable	9,070
Interest Receivable	580
Inventories	205,790

Investment in Short-Term Government Securities	25,000
Land	75,000
Manufacturing Equipment	309,850
Notes Payable: 6%—due 1/15/X2	32,000
Notes Receivable: 5½%—due 9/1/X2	18,000
Other Current Payables	2,130
Other Prepayments	3,700
Patents	104,300
Prepaid Insurance	2,060
Stockholders' Equity	?
State and Federal Taxes Payable	35,680
Supplies	6,320
Tools and Dies	88,970
Wages and Salaries Payable	19,100

Problem 3-5:

Use the solution to Problem 3-4 in answering this question. Does Buchanan Products seem able to pay its bills as they come due? Justify your answer.

Problem 3-6:

Refer again to Problem 3-4. Suppose the accountant made a clerical error in calculating depreciation when determining the balance in the buildings account, and that the figure for buildings should have been $213,650. What other account (or accounts) would be affected by this error? How? What correction would be necessary on Buchanan Product's 12/31/X1 balance sheet? (Ignore tax effects in answering this question.)

Solutions

Solution 3-4:

Buchanan Products
Balance Sheet
December 31, 19X1

Assets

Current Assets:

Cash	$ 47,340	
Investment in Short-Term Government Securities	25,000	
Notes Receivable: 5½%—due 9/1/X2	18,000	
Accounts Receivable	178,300	
Due from Insurance Company	14,410	
Interest Receivable	580	
Inventories	205,790	
Supplies	6,320	
Prepaid Insurance	2,060	
Other Prepayments	3,700	$ 501,500

Noncurrent Assets:

Land	$ 75,000	
Buildings	212,300	
Manufacturing Equipment	309,850	
Automobiles and Trucks	65,310	
Tools and Dies	88,970	
Patents	104,300	$ 855,730

Total Assets		$1,357,230

Equities

Current Liabilities:

Notes Payable: 6%—due 1/15/X2	$ 32,000	
Accounts Payable	121,650	
Wages and Salaries Payable	19,100	
Customer Deposits on Uncompleted Goods	24,300	
Interest Payable	9,070	
State and Federal Taxes Payable	35,680	
Commissions Payable	4,070	
Other Current Payables	2,130	$ 248,000

Noncurrent Liabilities:

Bonds Payable: 6¼%—due 9/1/X8	$300,000	
Equipment Purchase Contracts	100,000	$ 400,000

Total Liabilities		$ 648,000
Stockholders' Equity		709,230

Total Equities		$1,357,230

If an account is titled "prepaid" or "receivable," it is an asset; if it is titled "payable," it is a liability. On the other hand, not all receivables and payables are so titled; for instance, "due from insurance company" is a receivable, and "equipment purchase contracts" is a liability.

The order given to receivables in the solution is an acceptable one, but the following would also be proper (as would several other possibilities): accounts receivable, notes receivable, interest receivable, due from insurance company. Similarly, the three different kinds of equipment could have been listed in some different order. The order used lists them by diminishing service life expectancy: manufacturing equipment usually lasts longer than automobiles and trucks, which in turn usually last longer than tools and dies. This is a standard order, but accountants aren't rigid about this. Almost any order within the current liabilities would be proper, although notes and accounts payable are typically shown first.

Notice the use of dollar signs and the device of extending totals from left columns, which are called *short columns*, to right columns, which are called *long columns*. Observe the way in which account titles are indented, and how totals are indicated.

The amount reported for stockholders' equity is, of course, the one that makes total equities exactly equal total assets.

Solution 3-5:

Buchanan Products seems able to pay current bills as they come due. The current ratio for Buchanan Products at 12/31/X1 would be:

$$\frac{\text{current assets}}{\text{current liabilities}} = \frac{\$501,500}{\$248,000}, \text{ or about 2 to 1.}$$

This suggests that, over its operating cycle, the company will generate enough cash to pay its current liabilities, with a 100% safety margin. Other tests of the company's ability to pay its bills might include a comparison of those assets easily converted into cash with current liabilities. One way to do this would be to compare current monetary assets (cash, short-term investments, and receivables) with current liabilities. A one to one ratio should be sufficient here. The figures would be:

$$\frac{\text{current monetary assets}}{\text{current liabilities}} = \frac{\$283,630}{\$248,000}, \text{ or about 1.14 to 1.}$$

This ratio is often called the *quick ratio*. Still another ratio, perhaps even more significant in determining short-run debt-paying ability, would involve estimating how much cash could be raised if you disposed of all monetary assets (current and noncurrent) in a hurry. This amount is compared with the total current liabilities.

Solution 3-6:

The only other account affected would be stockholders' equity.[13] There would be no reason to change the figures for other assets; cash and rights to receive cash would be unaffected by the accountant's mistake, as would the purchase prices and write-downs of the other nonmonetary assets. The amounts owed creditors would not be affected by this error.

Since assets must equal equities, however, the understatement of buildings must have been reflected somewhere. By elimination, the only possibility is the residual

---

[13] Of course, several *totals* are changed, as demonstrated in the solution to follow. But total assets, total noncurrent assets, and so on are not themselves accounts, a point that will be made clear in the next chapter.

equity, or stockholders' equity, which functions in a balancing role. Since buildings were understated by $1,350 ($213,650 − $212,300 = $1,350), stockholders' equity must also have been understated by $1,350. The corrected figure for stockholders' equity would be $710,580 ($709,230 + $1,350 = $710,580). The changes to be made in Buchanan Products' balance sheet can be summarized as follows:

	Before Correction	*After Correction*
Buildings	$ 212,300	$ 213,650
Total Noncurrent Assets	855,730	857,080
Total Assets	1,357,230	1,358,580
Stockholders' Equity	709,230	710,580
Total Equities	1,357,230	1,358,580

Assignment Problems

Problem 3-A:

The 12/31/X3 balance sheet of Arizona Rocker Corporation is shown below, with X's substituted for amounts.

Arizona Rocker Corporation
Balance Sheet
12/31/X3

Assets

Current Assets:
Cash . . . . $XXX
Accounts Receivable XXX
Inventories XXX
Prepayments . . . . XXX $XXX

Noncurrent Assets:
Land . . . . $XXX
Buildings XXX
Equipment XXX   XXX

Total Assets . . . . $XXX

Equities

Current Liabilities:
Accounts Payable . . . . $XXX
Other Current Liabilities . . . . XXX $XXX

Noncurrent Liabilities:
Bonds Payable   XXX

Total Liabilities . . . . $XXX
Stockholders' Equity   XXX

Total Equities . . . . $XXX

1. (a) If total assets are $10,000,000 and total liabilities are $4,000,000, how much is stockholders' equity?
   (b) If total assets are $7,000,000, stockholders' equity is $5,000,000, and current liabilities total $800,000, how much is bonds payable?
   (c) If stockholders' equity is $10,000,000, total liabilities are $3,000,000, current assets total $5,500,000, buildings are $2,000,000, and equipment is $4,400,000, how much is land?

2. State the general rule illustrated by the three previous examples. What will always be true of the balance sheet?

3. Express this rule in algebraic form, using the accounts of Arizona Rocker Corporation as an example.

Problem 3-B:

The following information pertains to St. Onge Pharmaceutical Company's

12/31/X4 balance sheet. The last three digits have been omitted from all figures; you should do likewise in your answers.

The company has borrowed under a series of 7.2% notes payable. Each note is for $5,500. Notes are due on each May 1st, from 5/1/X5 through 5/1/X9. Interest on outstanding notes is payable once a year, each May 1st.

The company's other long-term debt totals $12,000, and is at $7\frac{1}{2}\%$ interest. Half of this debt was incurred on 1/1/X4, the other half on 9/1/X4. Interest is payable on this debt once per year, too, but no payments had yet been made at 12/31/X4.

The company reflects all land, buildings, and equipment in a single asset account called "property, plant and equipment." This asset was recorded at $111,332 on 12/31/X4. The only other noncurrent asset, investments, was recorded at $19,085 on 12/31/X4.

The company's remaining assets and equities at 12/31/X4 are as shown below. "Deferred charges" is a title employed by the company for the asset that we have been calling "prepayments." The amount of taxes payable is deliberately omitted—you are to calculate it.

Accounts Payable and Accrued Payables .	$ 44,798
Cash . . .	31,536
Deferred Charges	5,779
Inventories . .	65,993
Marketable Securities	8,041
Receivables . . .	67,355
Stockholders' Equity	212,178
Taxes Payable	?

1. Prepare a balance sheet for this company as of 12/31/X4, using the vertical style that employs two dollar columns; use good form.

2. Suppose that the company's accountant had made a clerical error in determining the amount of inventories on hand at the end of the year, and that inventories costing $1,200 had been overlooked. The company had paid for these inventories. Once this was learned, what corrections would be necessary on the company's 12/31/X4 balance sheet? (Ignore tax effects in answering this question.)

Problem 3-C:

All data in the following problem have been rounded to the nearest million dollars. You may do likewise in your answer. Ratios should be rounded to two significant digits.

Hartford Manufacturing Company acquired all of its present land and buildings on 6/30/X0, when it moved to a new locale to obtain a favorable property tax climate and what it regarded as a better quality workforce. The land cost $32, and the buildings $211.5. The company estimates that the buildings will have a total service life of 30 years, and a scrap value of $1.5 upon retirement. The company neither bought nor sold land and buildings between 6/30/X0 and 12/31/X8. At 12/31/X8, the company had the following other assets:

Accounts and Notes Receivable. $258
Cash 80
Inventories 336
Machinery and Equipment 646
Marketable Securities. 296
Prepayments 18

The company employs a single account called "payables" for accounts payable, interest payable, and all other current liabilities except taxes payable and dividends payable. On 12/31/X7, the amount of taxes payable was $121. During 19X8, $352 of taxes were charged against the company by federal, state, and local authorities; during 19X8, the company paid $348 of taxes. On 12/31/X8, the balances of other liabilities were:

Dividends Payable . . . . $ 56
5% Convertible Debentures 50
Other Noncurrent Liabilities. 39
Payables 240

The 5% convertible debentures are a kind of bonds payable. They are due nineteen years from 12/31/X8.

1. Prepare a balance sheet for Hartford Manufacturing Company, as of 12/31/X8. Employ the vertical style of balance sheet that shows two dollar columns; use good form.

2. Calculate the company's net working capital and its current ratio, as of 12/31/X8.

3. Turn to Problem 3-E (page 164). Calculate the net working capital and current ratio of Tunney Bayou Enterprises, as of 12/31/X8.

4. Which of these two companies seems better able to pay its bills as they come due? Defend your answer. What else would you like to know before answering this question?

Problem 3-D:

As part of your training in accounting, you must become able to extend the concepts and techniques you have learned into situations that require different methods of analysis. This problem provides an opportunity to increase your flexibility and broaden your understanding. The background needed to solve this problem has been provided by the text, but the particular method of analysis required may at first seem unusual. Apply what you already have learned to this new situation.

Show all calculations necessary to support your answers.

1. Mobile Cincture Company requires advance deposits on special orders. During 19X2, $23,000 of such advances were received. Shipments were completed on special orders for which $24,250 in advances had been received (some of the advances had been made in 19X1). At 12/31/X2, the company correctly reported a liability of $4,200 for advances from customers. What was the company's liability at 12/31/X1?

2. Birmingham Avenue Corporation pays its employees every two weeks for work done during the previous two weeks. The company correctly reported $23,400

of wages and salaries payable on 12/31/X1, and $24,170 of wages and salaries payable on 12/31/X2. During 19X2, the company's employees earned a total of $625,000. How much in total were they paid during 19X2?

3. Refer back to part 2. Suppose that $150 of salaries owed to a newly hired secretary in the company's administrative offices had been overlooked. The wages and salaries payable liability would be understated by $150 at 12/31/X2. What else (if anything) would be understated (or overstated)? Ignore taxes and payroll withholdings in answering this question.

Problem 3-E:

The 12/31/X8 balance sheet of Tunney Bayou Enterprises is shown below. Answer the following questions and defend your answers.

1. The mortgage payable is secured by the company's land and buildings, all of which were acquired in 19X1. Suppose that an error had been made in recording the cost of the land, and that the land had really cost $66,000. Assume that all other assets and the mortgage are recorded correctly. Which (if any) equities would be affected by this error?

2. After studying this balance sheet, John V. Rogers, a stockholder of Tunney Bayou Enterprises commented: "As far as I can figure out, the bank has a $300,000 claim on the land and buildings under the mortgage, and the other creditors have rights to all of the cash and $274,000 of the other current assets. So, we stockholders own about $196,000 of land and buildings, $917,000 of equipment, and $508,000 of receivables, inventories, and prepayments. Looks like all the stockholders get is the right to bits and scraps after everyone else has been taken care of." Comment on Mr. Rogers' observations.

Tunney Bayou Enterprises
Balance Sheet
12/31/X8

Assets

Current Assets:		
Cash	$220,000	
Accounts Receivable	340,000	
Inventories	405,000	
Prepayments.	37,000	$1,002,000
Noncurrent Assets:		
Land	$ 60,000	
Buildings.	436,000	
Equipment	917,000	1,413,000
Total Assets		$2,415,000

Equities

Current Liabilities:		
Accounts Payable	$212,000	
Taxes Payable	53,000	
Other Current Liabilities	229,000	$ 494,000

Noncurrent Liabilities:
Mortgage Payable   300,000

Total Liabilities . . . . $ 794,000
Stockholders' Equity   1,621,000

Total Equities $2,415,000

3. Mr. Rogers continues: "Another thing; how can you show that $1,621,000 figure for stockholders? I own one percent of the company. If I wanted to sell out, I could get about $25,000 for my stock, not just $16,210. If we sold the company as a whole to some big outfit, we could get at least $2,500,000 for it. On the other hand, if we ran out of cash, went insolvent, and had to be sold at a sheriff's auction, shoot! —there wouldn't be enough left for the creditors, much less anything left over for stockholders!

"And, of course, if we keep on doing well, and *don't* sell out to another company, and *don't* go broke, the company's going to keep the stockholders' money anyway. Why should we want all our money back if we've got a good thing going? Seems to me like whatever the stockholders get from the company, the one thing you can be sure of is that it won't be $1,621,000."

Comment on Mr. Rogers' observations.

Problem 3-F:

As part of your training in accounting, you must become able to extend what you have learned into new situations. This problem provides such an opportunity to increase your flexibility and broaden your understanding. The text provides all background information needed to solve this problem, but the circumstances described will be unfamiliar. Apply what you already have learned to this new situation.

Upon graduation from college you obtain a position as a junior accountant with the public accounting firm of Denton, Hamilton, Harvey & Newcastle. One of your first clients, Bray-Huntington, Inc., is a small manufacturing company that closes its books once a year, every December 31st. The company's records indicate that, as of the year-end presently under review (12/31/X6), the firm's current assets were just slightly more than double its current liabilities, a circumstance that is a source of some pride to management.

Upon investigation, you determine the following additional information, none of which is reflected in the firm's assets or equities as of 12/31/X6:

1. The firm is billed on the 10th of every month for long-distance telephone calls made during the previous month. Such a bill was received on 1/13/X7; it covers December 19X6 calls totalling $108 and January 19X7 calls totalling $43. You discuss this bill with the firm's chief accountant, Mr. Lee Ralph Culver, who argues that it should not be reported as a liability as of 12/31/X6 since payment was not due then and nothing was even *billed* until the middle of January.

2. The firm has not recorded any liability for the audit you are helping to conduct. The contract for this audit was signed in the fall of 19X6. Work on this year's audit began on January 1, 19X7, but of course the firm's records and financial accounting reports for the year ended December 31, 19X6 are to be examined.

3. On December 15, 19X6, the company entered into a firm purchase commitment with Evansville Manufacturing Company, whereby the latter will supply Bray-Hamilton, Inc., with 3,000 units of a particular component part per month for eight months, beginning on January 15, 19X7. The total cost of the 24,000 component parts to be delivered is $12,000; payment is to be made at a rate of $1,500 on the 15th of each month, also beginning on January 15, 19X7. Bray-Hamilton, Inc., is legally bound to honor this contract and intends to fulfill its terms.

Which, if any, of these situations gives rise to a liability that should be reported on Bray-Hamilton, Inc.'s 12/31/X6 balance sheet? In at least one of these situations you would need additional information to answer this question; specify what information would be required and how it would affect your answer.

Problem 3-G:

As part of your training in accounting, you must become able to extend what you have learned into new situations. This problem provides an opportunity to increase your flexibility and broaden your understanding. The text provides all background information needed to solve this problem, but the circumstances described will be unfamiliar. Apply what you already have learned to this new situation.

1. A tea ball is a small perforated metal ball designed to hold tea leaves. The hot water in the teapot or cup circulates through the ball, and the flavor from the leaves is released. But the tea doesn't end up with a lot of soggy leaves in it.

One evening, Mr. Wayne N. Daddario, President of Million-Dollar Idea Products was sitting in his kitchen, watching his wife make beef stew. To his astonishment, he saw her place a tea ball in the stew.

"Darling," he asked, "are you feeling all right?"

"Of course. Oh, you mean the tea ball. That's for the cloves."

"Cloves?"

"The recipe. It says to use cloves. But you're supposed to pull them out afterwards—I think they taste funny if you eat them. Anyway, they're hard to find in all that stew. So I put them in the tea ball. The flavor's the same as always. And when everything's cooked enough, I just pull out the tea ball, with no hunting around. It works with bay leaf and garlic, too."

"Honey, that's a million-dollar idea!"

Shortly thereafter, Million-Dollar Idea Products added a line of perforated metal balls specially designed to hold seasoning, seasoning bags that resembled tea bags, and perforated stirring spoons designed to hold seasoning. The company was very successful. On 2/4/X4, the entire company was sold to Alabama-Alaska Corporation, a giant food chain. It was clear from the negotiations that the price paid for Million-Dollar Idea Products included about $1,000,000 for rights to the basic idea that had occurred to Mrs. Daddario.

At what amount was this basic idea reported on Million-Dollar Idea Product's 12/31/X3 balance sheet? You may assume that depreciation and other forms of amortization are inappropriate here. Explain your answer, and comment on its significance.

2. Professor Frank E. Aspinall, an American citizen, has accepted a three-year teaching appointment at a Canadian university. Since he plans to remain in Canada

for more than twelve months, he is required to apply for permanent admission to Canada. While the red tape is not elaborate, it does require his completing a four-page form. One of the questions on this form is:

9. If I were moving to Canada, I would: (a) take with me the following assets:	CASH (money)	PENSION (transferable)	OTHER (specify)	TOTAL VALUE

In answering this, Professor Aspinall is perplexed by one thing. He owns 100 shares of the capital stock of Opelika Corporation. He paid $20 per share for this stock several years ago. Its present market value is $140 per share. Professor Aspinall is unsure at what amount he should report this stock.

What advice would you give? Explain your answer. Would your advice differ if instead Professor Aspinall was applying for a bank loan, and the bank requested a personal balance sheet from him? Defend your answer.

Problem 3-H:

As part of your training in accounting, you must become able to extend what you have learned into new situations. This problem provides an opportunity to increase your flexibility and broaden your understanding. The text provides all background information needed to solve this problem, but the circumstances described will be unfamiliar. Apply what you already have learned to this new situation.

In each of the following situations, you first should determine what the *question* is. Identify the principal accounting issue or issues involved, ignoring minor ones. Then make whatever comments you believe are appropriate, defending the position that you take. Ignore taxes.

1. Pueblo Minerals owns two mines, both of which yield approximately the same grade of the same kind of ore for the same extraction costs per ton. The Arkansas Traveler mine was purchased in 1933 for $5,000,000. It was estimated to contain a total of 50,000,000 tons of usable ore, of which 46,000,000 tons had been mined by 12/31/X2. The California Prophecy mine was purchased in 1965 for $40,000,000. It was estimated to contain a total of 10,000,000 tons of usable ore, of which 6,000,000 had been mined by 12/31/X2. During 19X2, the company extracted 2,000,000 tons of ore from the Arkansas Traveler mine, and 500,000 tons from the California Prophecy mine. The executive vice-president of the company explained that a larger proportion of ore from the Arkansas Traveler mine had been extracted, as part of the company's efforts to keep costs down. He went on to say that it was obvious, though, that costs could not be kept down this way much longer.

2. Early in January, 19X3, the company decided to substantially reduce its activities relating to this particular type of ore. Another company offered it $20,000,000 for either mine. There was considerable debate within the company concerning which mine to sell. Part of this discussion related to effects the sale would have on the company's 1/31/X3 balance sheet.

3. On 1/28/X3, the company sold the Arkansas Traveler mine for $20,000,000. The company prepares financial statements every January 31st. In May of 19X3, Mr.

Lionel H. Evans, a former stockholder of Pueblo Minerals, sued the company. Mr. Evans had purchased 1,000 shares of Pueblo Minerals in 1928, and had sold these shares on 1/15/X3. The market price of Pueblo Minerals stock rose sharply immediately after its 1/31/X3 financial statements were published.

Problem 3-I:

As part of your training in accounting, you must become able to extend what you have learned into new situations. This problem provides an opportunity to increase your flexibility and broaden your understanding. The text provides all background information needed to solve this problem, but the circumstances described will be unfamiliar. Apply what you have already learned to this new situation.

Throughout most of the previous year, Van Deerlin Piston Company's current assets totalled approximately $2,000,000, and its current liabilities totalled approximately $1,200,000. However, during the month of June, 19X4, the company made an extra effort to collect its accounts receivable. It also allowed its inventories to fall to levels lower than those of the rest of the year. At the end of the month it paid a great number of accounts payable, resulting in a 6/30/X4 cash balance that was lower than it had been for a year, despite the company's unusually high cash collections from customers. On 6/30/X4, the company's current assets totalled $1,600,000 and its current liabilities totalled $800,000.

In early July, 19X4, the company purchased equipment costing $300,000; the equipment manufacturer accepted the company's 9-month note payable for the purchase price. The company has badly needed this equipment since late May, 19X4; it could have purchased this equipment at any time.

Evaluate the accounting significance of the company's behavior. What is this firm really trying to accomplish? Defend your answer.

Problem 3-J:

As part of your training in accounting, you must become able to extend what you have learned into new situations. This problem provides such an opportunity to increase your flexibility and to broaden your understanding. The text provides all background information needed to solve this problem, but the circumstances described will be unfamiliar. Apply what you already have learned to this new situation.

1. The text gives the following examples of the liability "advances from customers": advance payments for the manufacture of special goods, cash payments to mail order houses, tickets sold by railways and buses, and meal tickets sold by restaurants. Give five examples of other kinds of advances from customers (or of similar nonmonetary liabilities). Make these examples as different as possible from the foregoing and from each other.

2. St. Bernard Mills manufactures cloth. Some of this cloth is shipped to Hong Kong, where another firm, K. Y. Tsu, Ltd., makes it into men's suits. Some of these suits are then returned to St. Bernard Mills, which sells them under its Gotham Suburban Squire label. About 70 percent of the shipments to K. Y. Tsu, Ltd. are made in the summer or winter; the other 30 percent are made in the spring or fall. Suits are returned about three months after each shipment of cloth. The two companies make cash payments to each other only when the net indebtedness of one to the other

exceeds $50,000. Despite a large volume of shipments both ways, this has not happened in over four years; in effect, K. Y. Tsu, Ltd. is paying for its cloth in suits.

St. Bernard Mills employs an account titled "Tsu, Ltd." What is the nature of this account? Explain your answer.

3. Among other matters, Problem 2-K (page 122) discussed the activities of a commercial refuse collector. Refuse is clearly nonmonetary. But should the refuse collector regard it as an asset, a liability, or *what*? Justify your answer.

Problem 3-K:

As part of your training in accounting, you must become able to extend what you have learned into new situations. This problem provides such an opportunity to increase your flexibility and to broaden your understanding. The text provides all background information needed to solve this problem, but the circumstances described will be unfamiliar. Apply what you already have learned to this new situation.

1. Craig Dyal is a graduate student in Business Education. He is receiving financial support from the Santa Ana Foundation. This support is in the form of a $5,000 forgiveable loan. The loan is non-interest bearing and does not require cash repayment. Instead, $1,000 of its principal will be forgiven for each consecutive year of teaching done by Mr. Dyal after he graduates. Does Mr. Dyal have a liability? Defend your answer.

2. Professor Hanna W. Utt has received a $5,000 advance on future royalties from Fullerton Publishing Company, as part of a contract whereby she will write an introductory business statistics textbook. At present, all that she has completed is an outline of the book and a few sample chapters. The project is a huge one, and Professor Utt is unsure whether she will be able to complete it. In fact, she is so unsure that at first she was reluctant to accept an advance. But a colleague remarked to her, "Don't be foolish, my dear. Who ever heard of a publisher suing a textbook author for an advance? They'd be cutting their own throats if they did!"

Does Professor Utt have a liability? Defend your answer. In answering this question you may wish to distinguish between several different possibilities. For instance, if the book is a success, the advance will be deducted from Professor Utt's future royalties; if the *publisher* cancels the project (perhaps because of changing market conditions), the author ordinarily would be allowed to keep her advance.

3. Dynamics of San Diego, Inc. printed a brochure in which it contrasted one of its products with a competing product manufactured by Wilson Turbine, Inc. The comparisons made were emphatic, and Wilson Turbine, Inc., is suing for $10,000,000. The following comment was made by the Dynamics of San Diego, Inc., lawyer:

"Nobody can say you weren't warned. You bet your sweet life they have a case. If they carry it all the way, they've got a 50/50 chance to collect maybe half of what they're asking. On the other hand, they might settle out of court for only a million or two. We might want to aim for that. It's to their advantage to settle out of court—you can't tell what a jury will do with something like this. If it came to trial, you *might* just get away scot-free."

Does Dynamics of San Diego, Inc., have a liability? For how much? Defend your answer.

Problem 3-L:

As part of your training in accounting, you must become able to extend what you have learned into new situations. This problem provides an opportunity to increase your flexibility and broaden your understanding. The text provides all background information needed to solve this problem, but the circumstances described will be unfamiliar. Apply what you have already learned to this new situation.

1. The President of Brown-Beverly Corp. has become interested in the accrued liabilities reported on the company's 12/31/XI balance sheet. After some checking back in the accounting records, he remarks to the chief accountant: "Correct me if I'm wrong, but most of these accrued liabilities fall into three groups. There's interest that isn't due yet, but that's been building up. There are services that haven't been billed yet, but we've received the services—the estimated phone and electricity bills, for instance. Finally, there are things we've got to pay, whether we get any service or not—like taxes. OK, I suppose; but why stop there?

"Look, next April or May we're going to get a bill from the auditors, sure as tulips come up in the spring. I can tell you almost exactly how much it will be, too. Why not start accruing *it* now? Same thing with charities: I can tell you almost to the dollar how much every cause in town is going to ask for next year. Why not start recognizing some of that now, too—instead of pretending they won't be coming after us?"

Comment on the President's suggestion. Be concise, but defend your comments.

2. Brown-Beverly Corp. has retail outlets in more than 200 different locations. The company rents the store buildings, but owns their contents. Three years ago, the company cancelled all of its fire insurance on store merchandise, furniture and fixtures, equipment, etc. This decision resulted from calculations indicating that no probable combination of fire losses would be sufficiently great to embarrass the company financially, and that expected total fire losses were significantly less than the cost of carrying fire insurance.

The company has not had a major store fire since this policy was adopted. The President has another suggestion for the chief accountant: "You know, we're due for a fire one of these days. Shouldn't we be accruing some kind of liability?"

Comment on the President's suggestion. Be concise, but defend your comments.

Problem 3-M:

As part of your training in accounting, you must become able to extend what you have learned into new situations. This problem provides an opportunity to increase your flexibility and broaden your understanding. The text provides all background information needed to solve this problem, but the circumstances described will be unfamiliar. Apply what you already have learned to this new situation.

1. In 19X1, Colorado Metals, Ltd., invested $150,000 to found another company, Denver Exploration Company. Colorado Metals, Ltd., maintains one-hundred percent ownership of Denver Exploration Company.

Mr. Byron G. McVicker owns 50% of the capital stock of Colorado Metals, Ltd. He paid $200,000 for these shares in 19X3. Mr. McVicker also holds an 8% note receivable for $18,000 from Denver Exploration Company. This note was issued on 6/1/X7; principal and total interest are due on 3/1/X8. On 11/15/X7, Mr. McVicker borrowed $10,000 from Colorado Metals, Ltd., on an 8% note, principal and interest of which are both due on 3/1/X8.

Insofar as possible, list all assets and liabilities of Colorado Metals, Ltd., Denver Exploration Company, and Mr. McVicker as of 12/31/X7, and indicate the amounts at which they should be reported. Mr. McVicker has prided himself for years on never owing money to anyone; he does not believe that he owes any money at 12/31/X7.

2. Assume that on 12/31/X7 the residual equities of the three entities were as follows:

Stockholders' Equity—Colorado Metals, Ltd.	$510,000
Stockholders' Equity—Denver Exploration Company	150,000
Net Worth—Byron G. McVicker	500,000

On 1/2/X8, Denver Exploration Company discovered an ore deposit that was estimated to be worth $1,000,000. Denver Exploration Company intends to develop this deposit before selling it. Shortly thereafter, Mr. McVicker remarked to a friend that on 1/2/X8 he suddenly became worth twice as much as he had been the day before. Comment on Mr. McVicker's observation. Ignore taxes. Defend your comments. What exactly did happen to the assets and equities of the three entities on 1/2/X8?

3. Assume instead that Denver Exploration Company decided *not* to develop the deposit itself, and that on 1/9/X8 Denver Exploration Company sold the ore deposit to Wheat Ridge Refining Corporation for $1,000,000. What, if anything, happened to the assets and equities of the three entities on 1/9/X8? Defend your answer.

Problem 3-N:

As part of your training in accounting, you must become able to extend what you have learned into new situations. This problem provides an opportunity to increase your flexibility and broaden your understanding. The text provides all background information needed to solve this problem, but the circumstances described will be unfamiliar. Apply what you already have learned to this new situation.

Installation of factory equipment is often a complicated and expensive process. At the end of its service life, most equipment must then be disinstalled, because it takes up valuable space. Disinstallation may be expensive, too: the costs of removal may exceed the equipment's scrap value. Sometimes a situation like this can be predicted at the time of acquisition—the buyer *knows* that costs of removing the equipment will exceed its scrap value.

1. Riverside Institute is engaged in classified research. A substantial part of its laboratory facilities is permeated by lethal radiation. Experiments are conducted at a distance, using TV and robot equipment. On 1/1/X1, the company installed equipment having a total cost of $200,000 in a newly-built laboratory (which had not yet become uninhabitable). This equipment has an estimated service life of 10 years. It is expected that its removal and disposal costs upon retirement will total $50,000, with no scrap value (the equipment will have to be buried in an abandoned lead mine). What should the annual depreciation charge on this equipment be? Defend your answer.

If you answered $25,000, go on to part 2. If you answered anything other than $25,000, go on to part 3.

2. But at depreciation of $25,000 per year, by the end of the ninth year the equipment will be reported at a $25,000 *minus* value: $200,000 − ($25,000 × 9) = − $25,000. How can you justify this? The equipment isn't an equity—the $25,000 doesn't reflect ownership, nor is it a liability to anyone. And the idea of a "negative" asset doesn't make much sense, does it? Comment. If you've changed your answer to part 1, go on to part 3.

3. Suppose that another company purchased a machine for $250,000, that the estimated service life of this machine was 10 years, and that its estimated scrap value and retirement costs exactly cancel each other out. Presumably, you would want to depreciate this machine at a rate of $25,000 per year:

$$\frac{(\$250,000 - \$0)}{10} = \$25,000.$$

Presumably also, your answer would not change if it happened that the machine was paid for in five installments of $50,000 apiece. If it *would* change, explain why.

Would your answer change if the machine were paid for in one installment of $200,000 at the time of purchase, and another installment of $50,000 at the time of retirement? If it *would* change, explain why.

But this latter cost pattern is identical to that of the Riverside Institute equipment. Are you now willing to change your answer to part 1 and charge $25,000 a year depreciation on the Riverside Institute equipment? If not, explain why. If you are willing, go on to part 2.

Problem 3-O:

As part of your training in accounting, you must become able to extend what you have learned into new situations. This problem provides an opportunity to increase your flexibility and broaden your understanding. The text provides all background information needed to solve this problem, but the circumstances described will be unfamiliar. Apply what you already have learned to this new situation. Show all calculations necessary to support your answers.

1. Palisade Standard Corporation guarantees to service its products for three years after the date of sale. Sales occur evenly throughout the year. Service costs are approximately the same during each year of the three-year period, and total about $60 per unit of product. The company began its policy of service guarantees on 1/1/X6. It sold 10,000 units of product in 19X6, and 12,000 units in 19X7. Approximately what amount would you expect to see reported as the company's liability for service guarantees on 12/31/X6? How much on 12/31/X7?

2. Palisade Standard Corporation is in an industry characterized by high employee turnover; the average employee remains with the company for only three years. The company spends a good deal for employee recruitment. Since 1/1/X6, the company has made a practice of amortizing recruitment costs over a three-year period, instead of writing them off entirely in the year of incurrence. For this purpose, it accumulates recruitment costs in an account called "deferred cost of employee services." Recruitment costs occur evenly throughout the year. 19X6 recruitment costs totalled

$600,000; 19X7 recruitment costs totalled $720,000. What amount would be reported for the asset deferred cost of employee services at 12/31/X6? How much at 12/31/X7?

Recreational Problem:

Professor H. P. Arkham was a great teacher. Over his long career, he carefully studied the difficulties that students had in understanding certain accounting rules. Finally, just before he retired, he formulated what has since become known as Arkham's Accounting Rule.

Arkham's Accounting Rule explains all accounting rules that are not self-explanatory; naturally, it does not explain any accounting rules that *are* self-explanatory. Is Arkham's Accounting Rule self-explanatory? Defend your answer.

Part II

Recording Economic Activity

Four

Recording Balance Sheet Changes: Ledgers

So far this book has concentrated on reports about an entity's economic condition as of a particular point in time. Now we will consider how the accountant records and reports *changes* in an entity's condition. There are many different kinds of changes that can occur in balance sheet accounts and several different ways of considering and classifying these changes. It is a good idea, at the outset, to get a quick, general impression of the nature of the more common balance sheet changes.

A Note to the Student

By this point in the course you will have discovered that the study of financial accounting makes substantial demands on your time; meanwhile your other courses are making their own demands. There is a natural temptation (especially if the course has been going well so far) to slack off a bit in your study of accounting—perhaps by merely reading instead of actually solving the Problems for Study and Self-Examination, or by telling yourself that you will get around to solving the problems as soon as you have a bit more time at your disposal.

Accordingly, this is a good time to repeat a warning that was given at the beginning of this book. Financial accounting is a subject in which the material cumulates: each point builds upon previous material and, in turn, forms the foundation for further discussion. It is very important not to fall behind. If you do, it will be difficult for you to understand what is said in class. The concepts that are being introduced each take time to be absorbed and understood; once you have fallen behind, it's hard to catch up again.

One way of falling behind and not knowing it is to believe that you understand the material before you have tested your understanding. It is extremely important that you keep current with the Problems for Study and Self-Examination. As long as you remain up to date with these, any important deficiencies in your understanding of basic concepts will be revealed, and you can either correct these deficiencies yourself or ask help from your instructor before they interfere with your understanding of subsequent material.

In general, the material in the next two chapters is vital for understanding the rest of this book; don't fall behind.

Balance Sheet Changes

To discuss balance sheet changes, we need some sort of classification system. This book will use two different ways of classifying any individual balance sheet change: (1) as a transaction or an internal change, and (2) as an operating or a financial change.

Transactions and internal changes

One convenient way to classify changes in balance sheet accounts is to divide them into transactions and internal changes.

1. *Transactions* always involve other entities; in this sense, they are external changes. A transaction is any change in an entity's assets or equities that is accompanied by a related change in the assets or equities of some other entity.[1] Here are two examples of transactions:

    (a) A store buys cash registers from a manufacturer on credit. The store's assets have changed, for it now owns cash registers it didn't own before. Its liabilities have also changed, for it now owes a new account payable. There is a related change in the manufacturer's assets: the manufacturer now has fewer cash registers, but a new account receivable.

    (b) Interest charges accrue on a loan. The borrower's interest payable liability has changed by an increase. The lender's asset interest receivable has also changed by an increase.

Other examples of transactions include collection of an account receivable, purchase of employee services, issue of additional capital stock, and advances made by a customer to a supplier.

Transactions may be further subdivided into complete and incomplete transactions, which are respectively called *exchanges* and *accruals*. An *exchange,* as the word suggests, is a purchase, sale, or swap that takes place in some kind of market. The purchase of cash registers is an exchange: the store gives a promise to pay cash in exchange for the equipment. A purchase of employee services is an exchange: the company exchanges

---

[1] For purposes of this definition, it makes no difference whether or not the other entity actually gets around to recording this change—that is, the nature of a change that is recorded by one entity does not depend upon the accounting practices of some other entity.

cash (or a promise to pay cash) for the employee services. The trade of one parcel of land for another is an exchange, even though no cash or claim to receive cash is involved.

As shown on pages 130–131, an *accrual* is a way of giving partial recognition to an exchange before that exchange is completed. For example, suppose that on 9/1/X1 a borrower issues a 6%, $1,000 note payable, principal and interest both due on 8/31/X2. The borrowing itself is a complete exchange. Over the entire one-year life of the note, there will be an additional exchange: one year's use of $1,000 is being exchanged for a $60 interest fee.[2]

Assume that the borrower and lender want to prepare financial statements as of 12/31/X1. At this point, neither the $60 fee nor any part of the $60 would be legally due. It would not be due until 8/31/X2. Yet the borrower would accrue a $20 interest payable liability ($1,000 × 6% × 4/12 = $20), and the lender would accrue a $20 interest receivable asset as of 12/31/X1.

2. *Internal changes* involve only the entity itself and, indirectly, its stockholders (in their role as residual equity holders). Here is an example of an internal change. Suppose that a store suffers a small fire in which some uninsured merchandise is destroyed. The store's assets have decreased. Because all profits and losses are borne by the stockholders, the related loss reduces the stockholders' residual equity.[3] But no other entity's assets or equities have changed. We will define any such one-entity change as internal.

Another example of internal change would be the store's depreciation of its cash registers. The balance in its equipment account will decrease when the cash registers are depreciated. Except for the effect of this decrease on the store's residual equity, there is no related change in the assets or equities of any other entity. The depreciation of an asset involves a genuine change in the entity's asset account, but it is a private, or internal, change.

Alternate language

In discussing balance sheet changes, many accountants use language slightly different from the language employed here. They describe *all* balance sheet changes as transactions; what I have called "transactions" they call "external transactions"; what I have called "internal changes" they call "internal transactions." In addition, some accountants would be willing to speak of accruing certain internal changes, such as depreciation.

Such alternate language is entirely acceptable. In this book, however, these words will consistently be used in the senses defined in the previous subsection. There are

---

[2] Notice that accountants use the word *accrual* in several related senses:
1. Any kind of regular, systematic increase or adding on.
2. An incomplete transaction that is given partial recognition:
   (a) The proration of a contractual fee to the periods during which it is earned, even though this fee may not yet be legally due;
   (b) Recognition of a receivable or a liability prior to the date upon which it is a legal debt of the entity that owes it.

[3] This point will be discussed at length later in this chapter. If it's not entirely clear now, don't worry. The tax effects of internal changes are ignored in this whole discussion; this book is not much concerned with tax accounting for the reasons given in Chapter One.

two reasons for this. First, these definitions dovetail well with the distinctions between primary and secondary measurements made toward the end of this chapter. Second, in ordinary usage the word "transaction" implies something that has occurred, been accomplished, actually *happened*. It will be argued in Chapter Thirteen that for the majority of internal changes it is not at all clear what *has* happened to the firm (except that the accountant has recorded a change); if this is true, calling internal changes "internal transactions" is potentially misleading.

Operating and financial changes

There is another way of classifying balance sheet changes that becomes very important in Chapter Six, where it will be discussed in greater detail. Firms exist to deal in particular products and services. For example, a shoe store exists primarily to sell shoes. Most of the firm's day-by-day balance sheet changes will relate directly to dealing in these products and services; these are designated *operating* changes (compare the discussion of the firm's *operating cycle* on pages 110–111). However, a few balance sheet changes involve activities not directly related to dealings in the firm's main products and services. For example, the shoe store might decide to redecorate, and sell its old customer chairs to a secondhand dealer. This would not be a sale of the store's regular products or services, since shoe stores are rarely in the used-furniture business. Such balance sheet changes are designated *nonoperating* changes.

An alternate name for nonoperating changes is *financial* changes. We will use both terms in what follows, but the latter term can be slightly confusing at first. The kind of accounting discussed in this book is *financial* accounting; most of the accounting reports that are discussed in it are called *financial* statements; yet financial accounting and financial statements record and report both financial and operating changes. What is happening here is that the word "financial" is being used in two different senses:

> "Financial," when referring to financial statements or financial accounting means directed first and foremost to outside investors, instead of primarily to the firm's internal management. When referring to financial changes, "financial" means "not operating."

Summary

An introductory overview of balance sheet changes demonstrates that any balance sheet change can be classified in two different ways:

1. As either a transaction or an internal change.
2. As either an operating or nonoperating change.

Illustration 4-1 is a glossary of these terms.

Illustration 4-1

Glossary of Balance Sheet Changes

Transaction: Any change in an entity's assets or equities that is accompanied by a related change in the assets or equities of some other entity.

Exchange: A complete transaction—a purchase or sale that takes place in some kind of market.

Accrual: An incomplete transaction that is given partial recognition by the accountant.

Internal change: Any balance sheet change that is not a transaction, and that therefore involves only the entity and its owners (in their role as residual equity holders).

Operating change: Any balance sheet change directly related to an entity's dealings in its main products and services.

Financial change: Any balance sheet change that is not an operating change.

Notice that these definitions involve classifying all balance sheet changes under *both* of two classification systems. This may be diagrammed as follows:

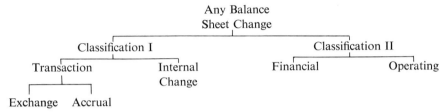

Any financial change will also be either a transaction or an internal change; any operating change will also be either a transaction or an internal change. Any internal change will also be either a financial or an operating change. Any transaction will also be either a financial or an operating change; *in addition,* any transaction will also be either an exchange or an accrual. Any exchange will also be a transaction (and will also be either a financial or an operating change), and so on.

Examples:

Here are a few examples of how balance sheet changes are classified under the distinctions discussed above. Modden's Mod Ties, Inc., is a retailer of men's neckwear. The following are a few of its balance sheet changes for the month of April, 19X7:

1. The firm sold several thousand neckties for cash. These were transactions because they affected the assets of outsiders; they were exchanges because they were complete transactions; they were operating changes because they related directly to the firm's dealings in its principal product.

2. The firm paid several accounts payable for amounts owed by it to necktie suppliers. These changes were also transactions, exchanges, and operating changes for the same reasons as in the previous example.

3. Before preparing its April 30, 19X7, balance sheet, the firm recorded accrued interest payable on a note payable owed to its bank; principal and interest on this note are not due until June 30, 19X7. (This is an example of the kind of change, mentioned on page 87, that often firms do not bother to record until the end of an accounting period.) This is a transaction, since an external party's assets should reflect a related change; it is an accrual, since the transaction is not yet complete. Accountants disagree whether such interest accruals are operating or nonoperating—strictly speaking, the answer might depend upon whether the purpose of the borrowing was to support the entity's dealings in its main products and services. Most accountants would treat all interest accruals as operating; we shall do likewise in this book.

4. The firm sold an old cash register on account. This would be a transaction and an exchange. It would be nonoperating, since the firm is in the necktie business, rather than in the used-office-equipment business.

5. For some time the firm has owed a noninterest-bearing note payable to Mr. Roman W. Moddenescu, a brother of one of the firm's principal stockholders; during April, Mr. Moddenescu agreed to accept shares of common stock issued for this purpose by the firm in exchange for his loan. This unusual transaction involves an exchange of one equity for another, and is nonoperating.

6. The firm declared a cash dividend on its common stock, to be paid in May. This is a transaction, since stockholders acquire an asset (dividends receivable) and the firm a liability (dividends payable) as soon as a dividend is declared. It is an exchange, since the entire amount of the dividend will be recorded. It is nonoperating, since it has nothing directly to do with the sale of neckties. When this dividend is paid, that change also will be a nonoperating transaction involving an exchange.

7. Before preparing its April 30, 19X7, balance sheet, the firm recorded depreciation on its cabinets, counters and racks. (This is another example of a change that often is not recorded until the end of an accounting period.) This is an internal change, since no external party's assets or equities are affected (other than those of stockholders). It is an operating change, since this depreciation reflects the services provided by these racks, cabinets and counters in the sale of the firm's main products.

Other examples of transactions and internal changes, and of operating and nonoperating changes, are given in the next section.

Simple, Two-Account
Balance Sheet Changes

All balance sheet changes involve at least two accounts. Since assets must equal equities (for the reasons given on pages 134–135), any change in an asset must be accompanied by an offsetting change in another asset or equity. Similarly, any change in an equity must be accompanied by an offsetting change in another equity or asset. What is an "offsetting" change? Assets must remain equal to equities, so when an asset increases, either another asset must decrease or an equity must increase. If an asset decreases, either another asset increases, or an equity decreases. There is simply no way for a balance sheet change to occur without affecting at least two accounts Here are some examples:

1. *Increase in an asset, decrease in an asset* (operating transaction, exchange). A $117 account receivable is collected. Increase Cash by $117; decrease Accounts Receivable by $117.

2. *Increase in an asset, increase in an equity* (operating transaction, exchange). A store purchases merchandise on credit; the merchandise costs $823. Increase Merchandise Inventory by $823; increase Accounts Payable by $823.

3. *Decrease in an equity, decrease in an asset* (operating transaction, exchange). A $425 account payable is paid. Decrease Accounts Payable by $425; decrease Cash by $425.

4. *Decrease in an equity, increase in an equity* (nonoperating transaction, exchange).[4] A company owes an ordinary trade creditor $311, but is in temporary financial difficulties. It persuades its creditor to accept a three-month, interest-bearing note for $311, instead of cash. Decrease Accounts Payable by $311; increase Notes Payable by $311.

Of course, a balance sheet change can affect more than two accounts. For example:

5. *Increase in an asset, decrease in an asset, increase in an equity* (nonoperating transaction, exchange).[5] A company buys land costing $17,750. It makes a down payment of $3,750 and issues an interest-bearing note for the remainder ($14,000) of the purchase price. Increase Land by $17,750; decrease Cash by $3,750; increase Notes Payable by $14,000.

Call a balance sheet change that affects only two accounts a *simple change*; call a balance sheet change that affects three or more accounts a *compound change*. It will simplify our discussion to regard all compound changes as composed of two or more simple changes, and then deal with simple changes only.[6] In this case, the compound change (5) would be broken down into the following two simple changes:

(a) Increase in an asset, decrease in an asset. A company bought land. It paid $3,750, cash. Increase Land by $3,750; decrease Cash by $3,750.

(b) Increase in an asset, increase in an equity. The rest of the purchase price of the land (see 5) was paid by issuing an interest-bearing note for $14,000. Increase Land by $14,000; increase Notes Payable by $14,000.

These two simple transactions have the same total effect as the one compound transaction (Land + $17,750; Cash − $3,750; Notes Payable + $14,000); simple changes are easier to deal with than compound ones. Here is another example of a compound change and the related simple changes:

6. *Increase in an asset, decrease in an asset, increase in an equity* (operating transaction, exchange). A company sells merchandise for cash, but at a price higher than the goods originally cost: assume that merchandise costing $120 is sold for $150. To keep things simple, assume that there are no other costs. There would be a $150 increase in cash and a $120 decrease in merchandise inventory, or a net increase in assets of $30. This net increase in assets must be accompanied by a $30 increase in equities (since no other assets have increased or decreased). No liability is affected by this change, but:

Total Equities = Liabilities + Stockholders' Equity

By elimination, the equity affected must be the residual equity or stockholders' equity. (The basic reasons were given in Chapter Three, pages 131–133.) Even though this result is arrived at by elimination, it makes good sense, for a $30 profit was made

---

[4] Some accountants would view all short-term loans as directly related to sale of a firm's principal products or services; they would regard this transaction as operating.

[5] This would be an operating transaction if the firm were a dealer in land.

[6] If you have had previous exposure to accounting you will know that, in practice, compound changes usually are not broken into simple changes. They are broken into simple changes in this book so as to make it possible in Chapters Six through Eight to provide a concise set of rules for constructing cash, funds, and income statements. Once this is accomplished, compound changes are used again in later chapters.

on the sale and stockholders' equity is supposed to reflect profits. Thus the compound change as a whole is: increase Cash by $150; decrease Merchandise Inventory by $120; increase Stockholders' Equity by $30.

There are at least two ways we could break this compound change up into simple changes.[7] Before going any further, be sure you understand that either set of simple changes is the equivalent of the original compound change (Cash + $150; Merchandise Inventory − $120; Stockholders' Equity + $30).

Merchandise Inventory + $30	Cash + $150
Stockholders' Equity + $30	Stockholders' Equity + $150
Cash + $150	Stockholders' Equity − $120
Merchandise Inventory − $150	Merchandise Inventory − $120

Earlier I emphasized that, in learning accounting, it usually is possible to understand the reasons for accounting practices instead of merely memorizing these practices. An exception may be necessary here, though it is only a temporary one. The accountants' rule for breaking up a compound change involving stockholders' equity depends upon whether this change is operating or nonoperating:

Operating change: Break up all compound changes in such a way that Stockholders' Equity appears in as many simple changes as possible.

Nonoperating change: Break up all compound changes in such a way that Stockholders' Equity appears in no more than one simple change.

The reasons for this rule are discussed in Chapter Eight (pages 402–406). At this point you do not yet have the background to understand them fully, but a rough explanation can be given. The effect of this rule is to maximize the amount of detail recorded concerning operating changes in stockholders' equity, and to minimize the amount of detail recorded concerning nonoperating changes in stockholders' equity. We've already seen that a firm's profits are reflected in changes in its stockholders' equity. We will see in Chapter Eight that these changes are summarized in a report called an *income statement*. In this profits report, a great deal of space usually is given to details of profits from operating activities, whereas the details of nonoperating profits and losses are omitted. One reason for reporting profits this way is that information about profits from operations is more useful for prediction of the future than is information about nonoperating profits and losses; accordingly, it is worth the readers' while to give them more detail about the former.

Change 6 is an operating change. The right-hand treatment shown above provides the maximum detail about stockholders' equity: it indicates a change in stockholders' equity for both simple changes. The left-hand treatment nets these changes into a

---

[7] A third possibility would be:

Cash + $120
Merchandise Inventory − $120
Cash + $30
Stockholders' Equity + $30

The significant feature in how a compound change is broken up is the number of simple changes in which Stockholders' Equity appears. In this respect, this possibility is identical with the left-hand treatment; the latter is used in this book because it is more consistent with later discussions of what the accountant does at the time of sale.

single $30 change. Following the previous rule, change 6 is broken up as follows:

    (a) *Increase in an asset, increase in an equity.* The company made a $150 cash sale of merchandise. Increase Cash by $150; increase Stockholders' Equity by $150.

    (b) *Decrease in an equity, decrease in an asset.* The merchandise that was sold in change 6 cost the company $120. Decrease Stockholders' Equity by $120; decrease Merchandise Inventory by $120.

These simple changes reflect an overall $30 increase in stockholders' equity; they *also* show that this $30 is the *net* result of receiving and giving up assets.[8]

Since assets = liabilities + stockholders' equity, we could summarize all of the previous balance sheet changes in a slightly different way:

Simple Change	Assets	=	Liabilities	+	Stockholders' Equity
1	+ $117, − $117				
2	+ $823		+ $823		
3	− $425		− $425		
4			+ $311, − $311		
5a	+ $3,750				
	− $3,750				
5b	+ $14,000		+ $14,000		
6a	+ $150				+ $150
6b	− $120				− $120

Summary and Examples of Exchanges, Accruals, and Internal Changes

Exchanges: An exchange is a complete transaction, involving a two-way transfer or swap between the entity and an external party. An exchange affects the assets and/or equities of *both* of these entities, whether or not both entities actually record it. There are four main kinds of exchanges:

    1. *Exchanges of one asset for another.* Examples include sales for cash and on credit, collections of accounts receivable, and purchases for cash.

    2. *Exchanges involving simultaneous increases in assets and equities.* Examples include issues of capital stock for cash, purchases made on credit, issues of long-term debt for cash, and receipts of advances from customers.

    3. *Exchanges involving simultaneous decreases in assets and equities.* Examples include payments of liabilities for cash, satisfaction of responsibilities to customers who have made advance payments (by delivery of related goods), and payments of dividends.

    4. *Exchanges of one equity for another.* Examples include settlements of accounts payable by issuing a note payable, and declarations of dividends to be paid at a later

---

[8] Had change 6 been a nonoperating change (perhaps the sale of a used office machine instead of merchandise) under our rule it would have been given the left-hand treatment. The compound change would be: increase Cash by $150, decrease Office Equipment by $120, increase Stockholders' Equity by $30. This would be broken into the following simple changes: Increase Office Equipment by $30, increase Stockholders' Equity by $30; increase Cash by $150, decrease Office Equipment by $150.

date (thereby cancelling a portion of stockholders' equity in exchange for creation of a dividends payable liability).

Accruals: An accrual is identical to an exchange except that it is an *incomplete* transaction. As with an exchange, an accrual affects the assets or equities both of the firm under consideration and of some external party (whether or not both parties actually record these effects). There are two main kinds of accruals:

1. *Accruals of assets.* These are accumulations of rights to receive cash, resulting from the gradual provision of services to another entity over a period of time. Examples include accruals of rent receivable (for provision of the services of property) and accruals of interest receivable (for provision of the services of money).

2. *Accruals of liabilities.* These are accumulations of obligations to pay cash, resulting from the gradual receipt of services from another entity over a period of time. Examples include accruals of rent payable and interest payable.

Internal Changes: An internal change is any balance sheet change that is *not* a transaction—a change involving only the firm under consideration and its stockholders in their capacity as residual equity holders. (Notice that when dividends are declared, stockholders become *creditors* for the amount of the dividend; thus a dividend declaration is a transaction, not an internal change.) There are three main kinds of internal changes:

1. *Writedowns of the costs of assets to reflect the uses of their services in the creation of other assets.* Examples include the using up of raw materials, supplies, and other assets in the manufacture of a firm's products (these products are recorded as being inventories, but are kept distinct from raw materials or supplies inventories—the details of this are given in Chapter Twelve).

2. *Writedowns of the costs of assets to reflect the uses of their services, where these uses do not result in the creation of other assets.* Examples include the using up of merchandise when it is sold by a store (or of finished goods sold by a manufacturer), and the depreciation of office equipment (or of any other depreciable asset that is not used in manufacturing some other asset).

3. *Writeups or writedowns in response to changes in market values.* Examples include writedowns of assets to a lower market value under "conservative" accounting practices; later we shall see that these examples also include the adjustment of the depreciated historical cost of a depreciable asset to a higher or lower market value at the time it is sold as a used asset.

Usually, information about accruals and internal changes is needed only for preparation of financial statements. Often, therefore, these changes are recorded only when such statements are to be prepared, at the ends of accounting periods.

Recording Changes on
Successive Balance Sheets

Most of the foregoing probably seems a bit abstract. To make things more tangible, this section will give an extended example of the balance sheet changes of an imaginary company, Nadir Caves Souvenir Shoppe.

Nadir Caves Souvenir Shoppe sells curios (bearing little stickers saying "Souvenir of Bottomless Nadir Caves"). The company has no noncurrent assets. Instead, it rents its store building and equipment from the owners of the caves, paying rent of $200 a day during the tourist season. This rental fee covers all costs except those of the curios themselves and certain supplies. For simplicity, this example ignores salaries, taxes, and the like. The company was founded on May 1, 19X1. Naturally, before it was founded, it had no assets, no equities, and, therefore, no balance sheet. The following are the company's balance sheet changes for the first week of May, 19X1. In each case, after the change has been described, the related new balance sheet is shown so that you can see what has happened to assets and equities. Some of these changes are *summary* changes; for instance, all sales of curios are shown as a single transaction, even though sales occurred over several days. This is done primarily for the sake of brevity, and since summary changes are being used, dates will not be shown for the related balance sheets. In fact, *headings* will be omitted for all but the first and last balance sheets. This example is such a simple one that assets and equities will not be labeled as "current assets," "current liabilities," etc.

1. (+Assets, +Equities) Stockholders invest $10,000, cash. Increase Cash by $10,000; increase Stockholders' Equity by $10,000.

Nadir Caves Souvenir Shoppe
Balance Sheet
May 1, 19X1

Assets

Cash	$10,000

Equities

Stockholder's Equity	$10,000

2. (+Assets, −Assets) The company pays one month's rent ($6,000) in advance. Increase Prepaid Rent by $6,000; decrease Cash by $6,000. (Notice that equities are unaffected by this kind of transaction. Do you see why?)

Assets

Cash	$ 4,000
Prepaid Rent	6,000
	$10,000

Equities

Stockholders' Equity	$10,000

3. (+Assets, −Assets) The company purchases $3,000 of curios for cash. Increase Merchandise Inventory by $3,000; decrease Cash by $3,000.

Assets

Cash	$ 1,000
Merchandise Inventory	3,000
Prepaid Rent	6,000
	$10,000

Equities

Stockholders' Equity	$10,000

4. (+Assets, +Equities) The company buys an additional $6,500 of curios on credit. (This is often described as buying *on account*). Increase Merchandise Inventory by $6,500; increase Accounts Payable by $6,500.

Assets

Cash	$ 1,000
Merchandise Inventory	9,500
Prepaid Rent	6,000
	$16,500

Equities

Accounts Payable	$ 6,500
Stockholders' Equity	10,000
	$16,500

The total investment in the company has increased as a result of this transaction. Creditors have joined with stockholders in furnishing assets to the company. The investment of creditors makes the "size" of the company increase, even though the amount of the stockholders' investment remains the same.

5. (+Assets, +Equities) The company buys $800 of supplies on account. Increase Supplies by $800; increase Accounts Payable by $800.

Assets

Cash	$ 1,000
Merchandise Inventory	9,500
Supplies	800
Prepaid Rent	6,000
	$17,300

Equities

Accounts Payable	$ 7,300
Stockholders' Equity	10,000
	$17,300

6. (+Assets, +Equities) Curios are sold for $3,950, cash. Increase Cash by $3,950; increase Stockholders' Equity by $3,950.

Assets

Cash	$ 4,950
Merchandise Inventory	9,500
Supplies	800
Prepaid Rent	6,000
	$21,250

Equities

Accounts Payable	$ 7,300
Stockholders' Equity	13,950
	$21,250

7. (−Assets, −Equities) The curios sold in change 6 had cost the company $1,900. Decrease Merchandise Inventory by $1,900; decrease Stockholders' Equity by $1,900.

Assets

Cash	$ 4,950
Merchandise Inventory	7,600
Supplies	800
Prepaid Rent	6,000
	$19,350

Equities

Accounts Payable	$ 7,300
Stockholders' Equity	12,050
	$19,350

Compare this balance sheet with the one shown after change 5. As a result of sales, total assets have increased by a net of $2,050 (from $17,300 to $19,350). Every asset must have a source; every right must have some matching responsibility. Clearly this $2,050 of additional assets does not involve any additional responsibility to creditors, so the equity that is increased must be stockholders' equity. (For review of this point, see pages 131–134.)

Once again, even though reached by elimination, this conclusion makes sense: the $2,050 represents the profit made on these sales. (The $2,050 is not the whole story about the profit on these sales, as you will see when considering the changes discussed in the next subsection, but it is part of what goes into determining profits.) Stockholders' equity is the account that should reflect profits.

8. (−Equities, −Assets) The company pays $4,200 of its accounts payable. Decrease Accounts Payable by $4,200; decrease Cash by $4,200.

Assets

Cash	$ 750
Merchandise Inventory	7,600
Supplies	800
Prepaid Rent	6,000
	$15,150

Equities

Accounts Payable	$ 3,100
Stockholders' Equity	12,050
	$15,150

Examples of internal changes

Suppose that a week has passed since Nadir Caves Souvenir Shoppe was founded and the company prepaid its rent. At this point (May 7, 19X1), the company wishes to report its economic condition. The previous balance sheet does not report the company's situation as well as it might for two reasons:

1. Seven days of prepaid rent have expired; yet the previous balance sheet shows prepaid rent at its full original purchase price.

2. Presumably some supplies were used up during the week; however, the previous balance sheet does not reflect this.

Neither of these matters involves exchanges with outsiders. Even though purchased supplies as well as the rented building and equipment were used in making sales to customers, the customers did not actually buy any supplies or any prepaid rent. The customers bought only curios. For this reason, any writedown of the figures for prepaid rent and supplies will be internal changes (defined on page 178), and often the accountant does not bother to record these internal changes until he needs figures that adequately reflect economic condition. This saves unnecessary effort.

Using prepaid rent as an example, the accountant *could* write down $200 of rent every day. For that matter, if the store were open ten hours a day, the accountant could write prepaid rent down by $20 an hour, or even $33\frac{1}{3}$¢ a minute. But until he prepares a formal balance sheet for investors, there is really no need to do all this recording. Once the accountant decides to prepare a formal report, he must then catch up and adjust his figures for prepaid rent and supplies to reflect partial receipts of the services acquired when these assets were purchased.

9. (−Equities, −Assets) Write down prepaid rent to reflect the passage of seven days since rent services for 30 days were purchased. A total of $6,000 was paid for 30 days, at the rate of $200 a day. Prepaid rent should be written down by $1,400 ($200 × 7 = $1,400). Decrease Prepaid Rent by $1,400; decrease Stockholders' Equity by $1,400.

Assets

Cash	$ 750
Merchandise Inventory	7,600
Supplies	800
Prepaid Rent	4,600
	$13,750

Equities

Accounts Payable . . . . $ 3,100
Stockholders' Equity 10,650

$13,750

Let's review again the logic of accompanying the $1,400 decrease in prepaid rent with a $1,400 decrease in stockholders' equity, rather than in some other account. Total assets have decreased by $1,400. (They decreased over the entire seven days, of course, but this is now being recognized in a single summary adjustment, just as the whole week's sales were recognized in a single summary transaction.) This decrease in total assets does not affect any liabilities, for it has nothing to do with creditors. Since it has to affect *some* equity, the only remaining possibility is stockholders' equity, the residual (or balancing) equity. But take note that it is *reasonable* to reduce stockholders' equity. Prepaid rent was used up over the week as the company made sales to its customers. These sales were possible in part because there was a store building, shelves, and various equipment to display the goods and attract customers. *The $1,400 decrease in prepaid rent was just as much a cost of making those sales as was the $1,900 decrease in merchandise inventory.* The company could not have made any sales without curios, nor could the company have made many sales without a store.

When determining the profit from company sales, you cannot simply compare the cost of the merchandise sold ($1,900) with the cash received ($3,950), and treat the entire difference ($2,050) as profit. Merchandise is only one of *three* assets that Nadir Caves Souvenir Shoppe used in obtaining the $3,950 cash. The company used merchandise, prepaid rent, and supplies.

Stockholders' equity is the account that should reflect the profit from the sale of curios. It should reflect everything that goes into determining profit. The decrease in prepaid rent is one of those things, so it is natural to match the decrease in prepaid rent with an equal decrease in stockholders' equity. Notice finally that the decrease in prepaid rent and the decrease in stockholders' equity are quite different things. The $1,400 decrease in prepaid rent reflects a decrease in an asset resulting from the passage of time (a decrease that the accountant finally recognizes when he prepares his formal financial report to investors). This decrease in assets must be accompanied by a corresponding decrease in sources of assets, which is what the decrease in stockholders' equity represents. Alternately, the decrease in stockholders' equity represents a decrease in the company's obligations to a particular class of investors—stockholders. This decrease is accompanied by a corresponding decrease in the company's economic rights—its rights to the services provided by rented property. Either of these interpretations is correct. Under either interpretation, the decreases in prepaid rent and in stockholders' equity reflect two different things.

10. (−Equity, −Asset) At the end of the first week, a count is made of remaining supplies in the Nadir Caves Souvenir Shoppe. Supplies costing $683 are still on hand. The other $117 worth of supplies ($800 − $683 = $117) was used up in operations during the week. Decrease Supplies by $117; decrease Stockholders' Equity by $117.

Assets

Cash	$ 750
Merchandise Inventory	7,600
Supplies	683
Prepaid Rent	4,600
	$13,633

Equities

Accounts Payable	$ 3,100
Stockholders' Equity	10,533
	$13,633

Stockholders' equity is decreased here for exactly the same reason that it was decreased in change 9.

The company's sales activities as a whole

We now can tell the whole story about the company's sales activities for the week. Nadir Caves Souvenir Shoppe received $3,950 in cash from its customers. To make these sales, it used $1,900 worth of merchandise, $1,400 worth of prepaid rent, and $117 worth of supplies—a total of $3,417. The net increase in assets is therefore $533 ($3,950 − $3,417 = $533). As we saw on pages 49 and 79, a firm's *profit* is the difference between the amount for which it sells its goods and services to its customers and the costs of providing these goods and services. This net increase of $533 is reflected, as a profit, in the residual equity account, stockholders' equity. Stockholder's equity is increased for sales, but it must also be decreased for all assets used up in obtaining these sales. Why was stockholders' equity decreased when decreases in prepaid rent and supplies were recognized? Because not to do so *would have been to act as though only $1,900 of old assets had been given up to obtain the $3,950 new cash.*

The company's balance sheet changes for the week are summarized in Illustration 4-3. Illustration 4-2 is the company's formal balance sheet at the end of the week.

Illustration 4–2

Nadir Caves Souvenir Shoppe
Balance Sheet
May 7, 19X1

Assets

Current Assets:	
Cash	$ 750
Merchandise Inventory	7,600
Supplies	683
Prepaid Rent	4,600
Total Assets	$13,633

Equities

Current Liabilities:	
Accounts Payable	$ 3,100
Stockholders' Equity	10,533
Total Equities	$13,633

Illustration 4-3

Nadir Caves Souvenir Shoppe
Summary of Balance Sheet Changes
For the Week Ended May 7, 19X1

	Change Number	Assets				Equities	
		Cash	Merchandise Inventory	Supplies	Prepaid Rent	Accounts Payable	Stockholders' Equity
1. Stockholders made a permanent investment of $10,000.	1	+ $10,000					+ $10,000
2. Creditors made a temporary investment of $7,300, of which $4,200 was later repaid.	4		+ $6,500			+ $6,500	
	5			+ $800		+ 800	
	8	− 4,200				− 4,200	
3. Other assets were purchased.	2	− 6,000			+ $6,000		
	3	− 3,000	+ 3,000				
4. Cash was received from customers and assets were used to make the related sales.	6	+ 3,950					+ 3,950
	7		− 1,900				− 1,900
	9				− 1,400		− 1,400
	10			− 117			− 117
Net change during the week. (The result equals the amount reported on the 5/7/X1 Balance Sheet, since this is the first week of the entity's life.)		+ $ 750	+ $7,600	+ $683	+ $4,600	+ $3,100	+ $10,533
			+ $13,633			+ $13,633	

Problems for Study and Self-Examination

Problem 4-1:

Below is a narrative summary of the balance sheet changes for the first three days of the life of Martin Company. This problem is not intended to be realistic.

A. Classify these balance sheet changes according to whether each is a transaction (exchange or accrual) or an internal change. (See if you can do this without referring back to the text.)

B. Prepare informal balance sheets as of the ends of each of the first two days, and a formal balance sheet suitable for reporting to investors as of the end of the third day. (Notice that you are asked to prepare only three balance sheets, not fourteen!)

C. Explain and justify the amount that you report for stockholders' equity as of 3/3/X1.

Compare your solution of this problem with the "official" one before going on.

Martin Company
Narrative Summary of Balance Sheet Changes
For the Period March 1–3, 19X1

March 1, 19X1:
1. The company was brought into being by stockholders investing $64,000, cash.
2. The company purchased land for $5,000, cash.
3. The company purchased buildings for $15,000, cash.
4. The company purchased equipment for $19,000, cash.

March 2, 19X1:
5. The company purchased $18,000 worth of merchandise for cash.
6. The company purchased $30,000 worth of merchandise on account.
7. The company purchased $4,000 worth of supplies on account.

March 3, 19X1:
8. The company made cash sales totalling $1,800.
9. The company made credit sales totalling $2,220.
10. The merchandise sold in 8 and 9 cost the company $3,200.
11. The company's accountant estimates that $100 worth of supplies was used up in activities related to selling this merchandise.
12. The company's accountant estimates that $30 worth of building service potential was used up in activities related to selling this merchandise.
13. The company's accountant estimates that $50 worth of equipment service potential was used up in activities related to selling this merchandise.
14. Employee salaries were $410, all paid in cash.

Problem 4-2 (Optional Problem):

If you had any serious difficulty with the previous problem, you should solve this problem, too; otherwise, feel free to move on to page 200 after skimming this problem (its figures are used in subsequent problems). Turn back to Illustration 4-2. The following is a narrative summary of the balance sheet changes of Nadir Caves Souvenir Shoppe for the week ending May 14, 19X1. Prepare a formal balance sheet as of May 14, 19X1. (*Note:* prepare just one balance sheet.)

Nadir Caves Souvenir Shoppe
Narrative Summary of Balance Sheet Changes
For the Week May 8–14, 19X1

1. The company bought $270 worth of curios for cash.
2. The company bought $1,475 worth of curios on account.
3. The company bought $79 worth of supplies on account.
4. The company paid a $300 cash dividend to its stockholders (a distribution of profits to its owners).
5. The company made cash sales of $4,460.
6. The curios sold in change 5 cost the company $2,103.
7. Supplies that cost $121 were consumed in operations.
8. One week's prepaid rent, costing $1,400, expired in operations.
9. The company paid accounts payable of $2,760.

Solutions

Solution 4-1(A):

Description of Change	Classification
1. Stockholder investment	Transaction: exchange
2. Purchase of land	Transaction: exchange
3. Purchase of buildings	Transaction: exchange
4. Purchase of equipment	Transaction: exchange
5. Purchase of merchandise	Transaction: exchange
6. Purchase of merchandise	Transaction: exchange
7. Purchase of supplies	Transaction: exchange
8. Cash sales	Transaction: exchange
9. Credit sales	Transaction: exchange
10. Cost of merchandise sold	Internal change*
11. Cost of supplies used	Internal change
12. Building depreciation	Internal change
13. Equipment depreciation	Internal change
14. Cost of salaries	Transaction: exchange

* The customer reflects the sale by a change in his balance sheet (involving an increase in the asset account for the amount of the selling price, and an equal decrease in cash or increase in accounts payable). But the customer does not make any entry reflecting the cost to Martin Company of the merchandise sold. Since this is the private concern of Martin Company, the write-off of merchandise is an internal change.

Solution 4-1(B):

Explanation

3/1/X1

Assets

Cash	$25,000	($64,000 − $5,000 − $15,000 − $19,000)
Land	5,000	
Buildings.	15,000	
Equipment	19,000	
	$64,000	

Equities

Stockholders' Equity	$64,000

Explanation

3/2/X1

Assets

Cash	$ 7,000	($25,000 − $18,000)
Merchandise Inventory . . .	48,000	($30,000 + $18,000)
Supplies	4,000	
Land	5,000	
Buildings.	15,000	
Equipment	19,000	
	$98,000	

Equities

Accounts Payable	$34,000	($30,000 + $4,000)
Stockholders' Equity . . .	64,000	
	$98,000	

Martin Company
Balance Sheet
March 3, 19X1

Explanation

Assets

Current Assets:			
Cash	$ 8,390		($7,000 + $1,800 − $410)
Accounts Receivable.	2,220		
Merchandise			
Inventory . . .	44,800		($48,000 − $3,200)
Supplies . . .	3,900	$59,310	($4,000 − $100)
Noncurrent Assets:			
Land	$ 5,000		(Unchanged)
Buildings	14,970		($15,000 − $30)
Equipment . . .	18,950	38,920	($19,000 − $50)
Total Assets		$98,230	

Equities

Current Liabilities:		
Accounts Payable	$34,000	(Unchanged)
Stockholders' Equity	64,230	
Total Equities	$98,230	

Solution 4-1(C):

Increase in assets related to sales:		
Increase in cash	$1,800	
Increase in accounts receivable	2,220	$4,020
Decrease in assets related to sales:		
Decrease in cash (payment of salaries)	$ 410	
Decrease in merchandise inventory	3,200	
Decrease in supplies	100	
Decrease in buildings	30	
Decrease in equipment	50	$3,790
Net increase in assets		$ 230

The $230 net increase in assets occurred without creating any matching liability. For assets to continue to equal equities, Stockholders' Equity must increase by $230. This is appropriate, since there was a $230 profit on these sales, and stockholders' equity should reflect profits.

Notice that the payment of salaries results in a decrease in net assets and, therefore, a smaller increase in stockholders' equity than if there had been no cost for employee services.

Solution 4-2:

An explanation of this balance sheet appears on the following page.

Nadir Caves Souvenir Shoppe
Balance Sheet
May 14, 19X1

Assets

Current Assets:	
Cash	$ 1,880
Merchandise Inventory	7,242
Supplies	641
Prepaid Rent	3,200
Total Assets	$12,963

Equities

Current Liabilities:	
Accounts Payable	$ 1,894
Stockholders' Equity	11,069
Total Equities	$12,963

Nadir Caves Souvenir Shoppe
Summary of Balance Sheet Changes
For the Week Ended May 14, 19X1

	Change number	Assets				Equities	
		Cash	Merchandise Inventory	Supplies	Prepaid Rent	Accounts Payable	Stockholders' Equity
1. Purchase of curios and supplies	1	−$ 270	+$ 270				
	2		+ 1,475			+$1,475	
	3			+$ 79		+ 79	
2. Payments of dividends to stockholders*	4	− 300					−$ 300
3. Sales and related costs	5	+ 4,460					+ 4,460
	6		− 2,103				− 2,103
	7			− 121			− 121
	8				−$1,400		− 1,400
4. Payment of accounts payable	9	− 2,760				− 2,760	
Net changes for the week		+$1,130	−$ 358	−$ 42	−$1,400	−$1,206	+$ 536
Balances—May 7, 19X1		750	7,600	683	4,600	3,100	10,533
Balances—May 14, 19X1		$1,880	$7,242	$641	$3,200	$1,894	$11,069
		$12,963					$12,963

* Recall that stockholders' equity is supposed to reflect amounts explicitly invested by the firm's stockholders, plus the company's profits since it was founded, less the amount of dividends that have been distributed to stockholders. Alternately, one could argue that the distribution of $300 of cash reduces total assets by $300 without affecting liabilities. By elimination, stockholders' equity is the only account remaining for the dividend to reduce.

Recording Changes in Ledger Accounts

By preparing a new balance sheet, accountants could record balance sheet changes each time a transaction or internal change was recognized, but doing so would involve a tremendous amount of work. A company of reasonable size will have thousands of transactions in a single month. Even if the accountant were to summarize these before preparing successive balance sheets, a great deal of work would be required. Instead, accountants have developed more efficient ways of recording things.[9]

One way of doing this is to record information about balance sheet changes in *ledger accounts*. Ledger accounts are devices that allow the accountant to record all of the changes in any given balance sheet account in a single place. Each balance sheet account is given a separate piece of paper, which is divided vertically down the middle and labeled at the top to indicate which account is involved. Here is a ledger account for cash, with no information in it:

Cash

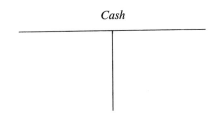

Though in actual practice each ledger account has a page to itself, there is no need to provide this much space here (nor should you in your homework). Instead, this book will represent each ledger account by a " T."[10] Such a ledger account is prepared for each asset and each equity. Increases in the asset or equity are shown on one side of the vertical line, decreases on the other. (This allows the accountant to leave out plus and minus signs, which are a bit of a nuisance.)

Conventions for asset increases and decreases

The accountant must decide *which* side of the ledger account will show increases and which side will show decreases. There is no way to settle this except by arbitrarily

---

[9] The most efficient and modern way—recording balance sheet changes directly on electronic computers— is not discussed in this book. Computers are being used more and more for accounting purposes; yet, with minor exceptions, what the computer does with balance sheet change information closely parallels what is done in the hand-operated system described in this book. It is much easier to see what is going on if we use a noncomputerized system for studying the ways accounting information is recorded and processed.

[10] Those of you who have had high school bookkeeping or who have seen actual commercial ledger systems in operation will be aware of additional simplifications here. The ledger accounts used in this chapter leave out a lot of incidental information ordinarily included in ledger systems. The details of this incidental information vary tremendously from one company to the next, which is one reason for leaving them out. The main reason, however, is that although these complications are important in the processing of information by the company's accounting department, they have no significance for the final financial accounting reports—and it is the final reports with which we are concerned. Ledger accounts of the simplified kind used here are often called "skeleton" ledger accounts, or *T-accounts*. The T-account language will be used occasionally in what follows.

making a rule (and then memorizing it). The problem is similar to that of deciding which side of the road automobiles should drive on. In this country we drive on the right; in Britain they drive on the left. Both systems work perfectly well so long as everyone is consistent. Similarly, as long as the accountant always shows increases and decreases the same way, it makes no difference which way he uses. Here is the convention that has been chosen by American accountants:

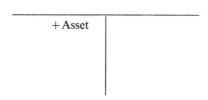

Increases in assets are shown on the left sides of ledger accounts. This is arbitrary. You have to memorize it. But once you have memorized it, the rest of the rules relating to increases and decreases follow in a logical way. If increases in assets are shown on the left sides of ledger accounts, decreases in assets should be shown on the *right* sides of ledger accounts:

```
_____|_____
      + Asset          |      − Asset
                       |
                       |
                       |
                       |
```

Using this convention, here is the ledger account for Nadir Caves Souvenir Shoppe's cash account for the period May 1 through May 7, 1968. Numbers in parentheses refer to change numbers in the original example (pages 187–190).

Cash

	(Increase)		(Decrease)
(1)	10,000	(2)	6,000
(6)	3,950	(3)	3,000
		(8)	4,200

In change 1, cash was increased by stockholders investing $10,000 in the company. This $10,000 investment is shown on the left. In changes 2 and 3, cash was decreased as $6,000 was spent for prepaid rent and $3,000 for merchandise. These changes are shown on the right. Changes 4 and 5 did not affect cash. In change 6, $3,950 was received from customers; this increase is shown on the left. In change 8, $4,200 of cash was paid to creditors; this decrease is shown on the right. Changes 7, 9, and 10 did not affect cash. Notice how the information contained in this ledger account duplicates information contained in the cash column of Illustration 4-3 (page 193). The ledger account is just another way of grouping and summarizing information.

Balancing asset accounts

Although the preceding ledger account records changes in cash, it does not give a *balance*. When the accountant wishes to prepare a balance sheet, he needs a single figure to represent cash (such as the bottom figure in the cash column of Illustration 4-3). This figure can be obtained very easily: just subtract the total of the right-hand side of the ledger account from the total of the left-hand side. Here is how a balance can be obtained for cash on 5/7/X1:

Cash

(1)	10,000	(2)	6,000
(6)	3,950	(3)	3,000
		(8)	4,200
	13,950		
	13,200	←——— 13,200	
√	750		

The check mark (√) indicates that the figure of $750 is a balance rather than a change. (Accountants often use a slightly different method for obtaining balances, but this method is simple and will do for now.) Observe something very important: not only are increases in assets shown on the left, but *asset balances are shown on the left*. This is logical, since before an asset can *have* a balance, its increases must be greater than its decreases.

Conventions for equity increases and decreases

Assets equal equities; therefore, an increase in an asset must be accompanied either by a decrease in another asset or an increase in an equity. Thus asset decreases and equity increases serve the same balancing function in accounting. This implies that asset decreases and equity increases should be treated in the same way in ledger accounts, which in turn implies that *equity increases should be shown on the right* and equity decreases on the left.

+ Asset	− Asset
− Equity	+ Equity

By putting equity increases on the opposite side from asset increases, all balance sheet changes automatically balance (and so does the balance sheet itself, as long as you keep asset balances on the left side and equity balances on the right side). Here again are the four basic kinds of changes:

left side	right side
1. Increase Asset	Decrease Asset
2. Increase Asset	Increase Equity
3. Decrease Equity	Increase Equity
4. Decrease Equity	Decrease Asset

Change 1, as converted into ledger accounts, shows how balance sheet changes become symmetrical when increases in assets and equities are placed on opposite sides.

Cash		Stockholders' Equity
(1) 10,000		(1) 10,000

Here is another example of an equity ledger account, showing accounts payable for May 1 through May 7, 19X1:

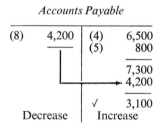

Accounts Payable

In changes 4 and 5, accounts payable increased by $6,500 and $800 when merchandise and supplies were purchased on credit. These increases are shown on the right side. In change 8, accounts payable were decreased by a cash payment of $4,200. This decrease in the equity is shown on the left side. The balance ($3,100) in Accounts Payable after change 8 is, of course, on the right-hand side: there wouldn't be a balance if increases in accounts payable hadn't exceeded decreases. Normally, all assets will have a left-hand-side balance and all equities will have a right-hand-side balance.

Frequency of balancing ledger accounts

Ordinarily, ledger accounts are not balanced except when a company needs to know the balance in one or more accounts. Different accounts are balanced with different frequency. Usually Cash is balanced at least daily, since the company needs to know just how much cash it has. Other accounts may be balanced only monthly or quarterly.

Once a new balance has been inserted in a ledger account, additional changes are added to or subtracted from it, and the earlier information used in arriving at that new balance is not counted in again. For instance, in the Accounts Payable ledger account, once the $3,100 balance has been inserted, the $7,300 and $4,200 figures are thereafter disregarded.

Ledger accounts for Nadir Caves Souvenir Shoppe

1. Here are the ledger accounts for Nadir Caves Souvenir Shoppe after change 1, in which stockholders invested $10,000, cash:

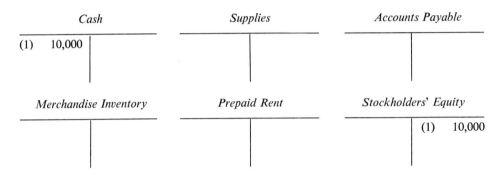

Cash	Supplies	Accounts Payable
(1) 10,000		

Merchandise Inventory	Prepaid Rent	Stockholders' Equity
		(1) 10,000

The ledger accounts below show how balance sheet changes would be recorded through the rest of the company's first week. In each case, the transaction or internal change is indicated, followed by the resulting change in the ledger accounts. The accounts are not balanced until after the last change.

2. The company paid $6,000 for one month's rent.

Cash	Supplies	Accounts Payable
(1) 10,000	(2) 6,000		

Merchandise Inventory	Prepaid Rent	Stockholders' Equity
	(2) 6,000	(1) 10,000

3. The company paid $3,000 for merchandise.

Cash	Supplies	Accounts Payable
(1) 10,000	(2) 6,000		
	(3) 3,000		

Merchandise Inventory	*Prepaid Rent*	*Stockholders' Equity*
(3) 3,000	(2) 6,000	(1) 10,000

4. The company bought $6,500 of merchandise on account.

Cash	*Supplies*	*Accounts Payable*
(1) 10,000 | (2) 6,000 | (3) 3,000		(4) 6,500

Merchandise Inventory	*Prepaid Rent*	*Stockholders' Equity*
(3) 3,000 (4) 6,500	(2) 6,000	(1) 10,000

5. The company bought $800 of supplies on account.

Cash	*Supplies*	*Accounts Payable*
(1) 10,000 | (2) 6,000 | (3) 3,000	(5) 800	(4) 6,500 (5) 800

Merchandise Inventory	*Prepaid Rent*	*Stockholders' Equity*
(3) 3,000 (4) 6,500	(2) 6,000	(1) 10,000

Notice that the total of the left-side amounts equals the total of the right-side amounts:

Left	=	*Right*
$10,000		$ 6,000
3,000		3,000
6,500		10,000
800		6,500
6,000		800
$26,300	=	$26,300

The remaining changes are recorded as shown below.

6. Curios were sold for $3,950, cash.
7. These curios cost the company $1,900.
8. The company paid $4,200 of its accounts payable.
9. Seven days' prepaid rent ($1,400) have expired.
10. Supplies costing $117 have been used.

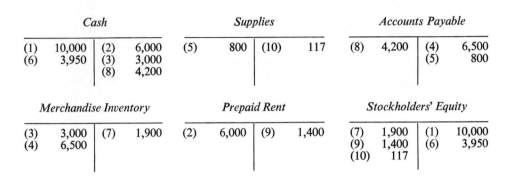

The ledger accounts are then balanced.

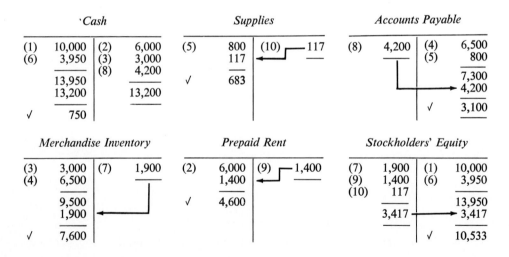

The resulting balances are the same as those appearing on the company's 5/7/X1 balance sheet (see Illustration 4-3, page 193).

The effects of a sale of merchandise

A sale of merchandise involves a compound change in which usually either cash or accounts receivable increases, merchandise inventory decreases, and stockholders' equity increases. The way in which this compound change is broken up into simple changes is discussed on pages 183–184. Notice that when a sale of merchandise is recorded as simple changes, at least two things happen: there is an inflow of assets (in this case $3,950 of cash) accompanied by a corresponding increase in stockholder's equity, and there is an outflow of merchandise (in this case $1,900 of curios) accompanied by a corresponding decrease in stockholders' equity. Any sale of merchandise will have these effects if it is recorded in simple changes and recorded completely.

Sometimes, though, the recording of the outflow of merchandise is delayed until the end of the time period covered by the financial statements. For example, if Nadir Caves Souvenir Shoppe prepares financial statements once a month, it might wait until the end of the month to record the outflow of merchandise. It could determine merchandise outflow at the month's end from the ledger account Merchandise: the firm would know the cost of merchandise (if any) that it owned at the beginning of the month and the cost of merchandise purchased during the month. By counting what was on hand, it could learn the cost of merchandise owned at the end of the month; then the cost of merchandise sold during the month could be calculated as follows:

$$\begin{matrix} \text{Beginning} \\ \text{Inventory} \end{matrix} + \begin{matrix} \text{Purchases} \\ \text{for Month} \end{matrix} - \begin{matrix} \text{Ending} \\ \text{Inventory} \end{matrix} = \begin{matrix} \text{Cost of} \\ \text{Merchandise Sold} \end{matrix}$$

If the firm keeps its records this way, it will record an increase in cash and an increase in stockholders' equity at the time that a sale is made. But the second part of the changes resulting from the sale will not be recorded until the end of the accounting period, when it will form part of the total outflow of merchandise that is recorded then.

These two ways of recording the outflow of merchandise are designated the *perpetual* and the *periodic* inventory methods, respectively. Under either method, the inflow of assets and corresponding increase in stockholders' equity will be recorded at the time of sale. Under the *perpetual inventory method,* the outflow of merchandise and corresponding decrease in stockholders' equity will also be recorded at the time of sale; under the *periodic inventory method,* these decreases will not be recorded until the end of the accounting period, at which time they will be recorded in total, together with merchandise outflows from all other sales.

The distinction between the perpetual and periodic inventory methods is not usually crucial in this book, because we will be discussing the firm's balance sheet changes in summary form and will view them as of the end of the accounting period. But this distinction does make an important difference in the firm's day-by-day recording process.

Problems for Study and Self-Examination

Problem 4-3:

It is an old cliche to say, "We're running this business like a peanut stand." Tee-Wheet Redhots, Inc., *is* a peanut stand.[11] The company's position at the end of business on 8/7/X1 was as follows:

---

[11] Admittedly, few businesses of this nature or size would be incorporated or keep detailed accounting records.

Tee-Wheet Redhots, Inc.
Balance Sheet
August 7, 19X1

Assets

Current Assets:
Cash	$3.00	
Nuts	4.00	
Oil	0.50	
Fuel	1.00	$ 8.50

Noncurrent Assets:
Stand.	10.00

Total Assets	$18.50

Equities

Current Liabilities:
Accounts Payable	$ 2.50
Stockholders' Equity	16.00

Total Equities	$18.50

The following events occurred on 8/8/X1. The company sold nuts that had cost $3.50 for $8.50, cash. The company used up $1.00 worth of oil and $2.00 worth of fuel in roasting the nuts. (Nuts are roasted only at the time of sale.) The company estimated that the stand had a remaining service life of 50 days at the beginning of business on 8/8/X1, and that it would have no scrap value upon retirement.

The company spent $4.25 for nuts, 85¢ for oil, and $2.10 for fuel, paying cash for the nuts and purchasing the oil and fuel on credit. The company paid accounts payable of $2.50. The company paid cash dividends totalling 75¢. (For this simplified illustration, the stand is treated as a noncurrent asset, even though it has only a 50-day remaining life.)

Record the company's 8/7/X1 balance sheet in ledger accounts. Record all 8/8/X1 balance sheet changes (as simple, two-account changes). Prepare a balance sheet as of the close of business on 8/8/X1. Compare your solution to this problem with the "official" one before going on.

Problem 4-4 (Optional):

Do this problem only if you believe that you need the additional review; otherwise feel free to move on to Problem 4-5. Turn back to Problem 4-1 (page 194). Record the information in Martin Company's Narrative Summary of Balance Sheet Changes in ledger form. Use only one set of ledger accounts. Determine balances on 3/3/X1 and compare your results with Martin Company's 3/3/X1 balance sheet (page 197).

Solutions

Solution 4-3:

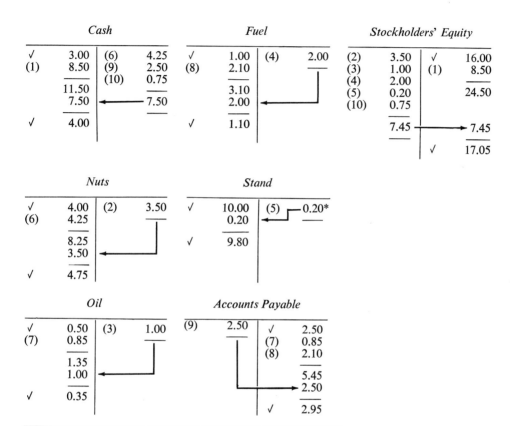

	Cash				Fuel				Stockholders' Equity		

Cash

√	3.00	(6)	4.25
(1)	8.50	(9)	2.50
		(10)	0.75
	11.50		
	7.50		7.50
√	4.00		

Fuel

√	1.00	(4)	2.00
(8)	2.10		
	3.10		
	2.00		
√	1.10		

Stockholders' Equity

(2)	3.50	√	16.00
(3)	1.00	(1)	8.50
(4)	2.00		
(5)	0.20		24.50
(10)	0.75		
	7.45		7.45
		√	17.05

Nuts

√	4.00	(2)	3.50
(6)	4.25		
	8.25		
	3.50		
√	4.75		

Stand

√	10.00	(5)	0.20*
	0.20		
√	9.80		

Oil

√	0.50	(3)	1.00
(7)	0.85		
	1.35		
	1.00		
√	0.35		

Accounts Payable

(9)	2.50	√	2.50
		(7)	0.85
		(8)	2.10
			5.45
			2.50
		√	2.95

* *Depreciation of the stand is 1/50 of the amount reported for the stand at the start of the day.*

Tee-Wheet Redhots, Inc.
Balance Sheet
August 8, 19X1

Assets

Current Assets:

Cash	$4.00	
Nuts	4.75	
Oil	0.35	
Fuel	1.10	$10.20

Noncurrent Assets:

Stand		9.80

Total Assets		$20.00

Equities

Current Liabilities:

Accounts Payable	$ 2.95
Stockholders' Equity	17.05

Total Equities	$20.00

Solution 4-4:

Cash			
(1)	64,000	(2)	5,000
(8)	1,800	(3)	15,000
		(4)	19,000
	65,800	(5)	18,000
		(14)	410
	57,410		57,410
✓	8,390		

Accounts Receivable	
(9) ✓ 2,220	

Merchandise Inventory			
(5)	18,000	(10)	3,200
(6)	30,000		
	48,000		
	3,200		
✓	44,800		

Supplies			
(7)	4,000	(11)	100
	100		
✓	3,900		

Land	
(2) ✓ 5,000	

Building			
(3)	15,000	(12)	30
	30		
✓	14,970		

Equipment			
(4)	19,000	(13)	50
	50		
✓	18,950		

Accounts Payable			
		(6)	30,000
		(7)	4,000
		✓	34,000

Stockholders' Equity			
(10)	3,200	(1)	64,000
(11)	100	(8)	1,800
(12)	30	(9)	2,220
(13)	50		
(14)	410		68,020
	3,790		3,790
		✓	64,230

An Additional Example (Optional)

    If you had any serious difficulties with the previous two problems, you may wish to use the following additional example of ledger recording for further review. Otherwise, feel free to move on to Problem 4-5.

Problem 4-2 gave the balance sheet changes for the second week of Nadir Caves Souvenir Shoppe's life. These are repeated below, and the information is recorded in the same ledger accounts as those previously shown. The second-week ledger accounts begin with their first-week ending balances. For instance, the Cash ledger account will start off with a balance of $750.

Nadir Caves Souvenir Shoppe
Narrative Summary of Balance Sheet Changes
For the Week May 8–14, 19X1

1. The company bought $270 of curios for cash.
2. The company bought $1,475 of curios on account.
3. The company bought $79 of supplies on account.
4. The company paid a $300 cash dividend to its stockholders.
5. The company made cash sales of $4,460.
6. The curios sold in Change (5) cost the company $2,103.
7. Supplies costing $121 were consumed in operations.
8. One week's prepaid rent ($1,400) expired in operations.
9. The company paid accounts payable of $2,760.

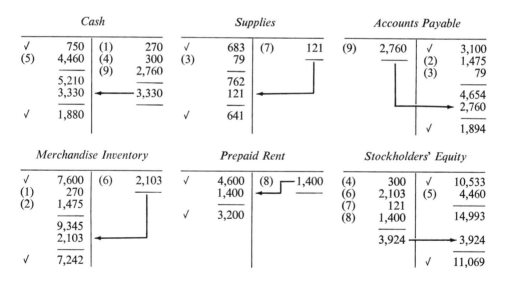

The ending balances shown in the accounts are the same figures that appear in the company's 5/14/XI balance sheet (see the solution to Problem 4-2, page 198).

Problem for Study and Self-Examination

Problem 4-5 (Brain-teaser):

As part of your training in accounting, you must become able to extend the concepts and techniques you have learned into situations that require different methods of analysis. This problem provides opportunity to increase your flexibility and broaden your understanding. The background needed to solve this problem has been provided by the text, but the particular method of analysis required may at first seem unusual. Apply what you already have learned to this new situation.

Udall Stores prepares financial statements once a year on December 31. On that day, the company takes a physical count of inventories and supplies on hand. It then determines how much merchandise and supplies have been consumed in operations by comparing the total cost of the beginning inventory plus all purchases made during the year with the cost of the goods on hand at the end of the year (that is, it uses the periodic inventory method discussed on page 207). As an example, suppose the company had $3,600 worth of supplies on hand at 1/1/X1. (This information came from last year's December 31 physical count.) The company knew from its ledger account, Supplies, that it had purchased $21,900 of supplies during the year. Its 12/31/X1 physical count indicated that there were $2,400 worth of supplies on hand at 12/31/X1, so the company must have used up $23,100 of supplies during the year:

$$\text{(Beginning Balance)} + \text{(Purchases)} = \text{(Ending Balance)} + \text{(Amount Used)}$$
$$\$3,600 \quad + \quad \$21,900 \quad = \quad \$2,400 \quad + \quad X$$

$$\text{Amount used} = X = \$3,600 + \$21,900 - \$2,400 = \underline{\$23,100}.$$

Shown below are some errors made by the company's accountant in 19X1. These errors are unrelated to each other. Dollar figures have deliberately been omitted since they are unnecessary. For each error, indicate the effect of that error (if any) on each of the following, as of 12/31/X1. The effects of the first error have already been indicated.

> Current Assets
> Noncurrent Assets
> Total Assets
> Current Liabilities
> Net Working Capital
> Noncurrent Liabilities
> Total Liabilities
> Stockholders' Equity
> Total Equities

A. Merchandise was purchased on account from a supplier in late December, 19X1. Even though the goods had been delivered by 12/31/X1, they had not yet been unloaded. Neither the merchandise nor the related account payable was recorded until early 19X2.

Answer: Both merchandise inventory and accounts payable are understated. Therefore, current assets and total assets are understated; current liabilities, total liabilities, and total equities are also understated. Net working capital (current assets minus current liabilities) is affected in ways that offset each other: an understatement minus an equal understatement cancels out, so there's no net effect on net working capital. Nothing else is affected.

B. Udall Stores forgot to record a sale on account that was made on 12/28/X1. The related merchandise was delivered to the customer on the day of the sale.

C. During October, 19X1, the company issued a $6\frac{1}{4}\%$ note payable whose principal and interest will be due on 3/15/X2. Udall Stores recorded the issue of the note correctly, but forgot to accrue interest at 12/31/X1.

D. During November, 19X1, Udall Stores bought a 3-year fire insurance policy for cash. The purchase of this policy was recorded correctly, but the company did not write off any of the cost of this policy at 12/31/X1 (or at any other time during 19X1).

E. The company bought a storage building in April, 19X1; the purchase was recorded correctly. In calculating depreciation, however, the building's total service life was underestimated.

F. The company purchased some merchandise on account in November, 19X1, recording the purchase correctly. In early December (before the goods had been paid for), this merchandise was returned as defective. The company never paid the related account payable, but it neglected to record the return of merchandise.

Solution

Solution 4-5:

   B. Since the related merchandise has been delivered to the customer, it would not have been counted during the 12/31/X1 physical count of merchandise. Therefore, the 12/31/X1 physical count correctly reflected that the company no longer owned this merchandise. The only error is in not recording the sale itself. Accounts receivable is understated and so is Stockholders' Equity. Thus current assets, total assets, Stockholders' Equity, total equities, and net working capital are all understated. Nothing else is affected.

   C. Interest Payable is understated; Stockholders' Equity is overstated. (Some account in addition to Interest Payable must be misstated, or assets would no longer equal equities. Stockholders' Equity is the other account involved because no asset or other liability is affected.) Current liabilities and total liabilities are, therefore, understated. Stockholders' Equity and net working capital are overstated: net working capital equals current assets minus current liabilities; an understatement of current liabilities results in an overstatement of net working capital. The effects on total equities offset each other; thus there is no net effect on total equities. Nothing else is affected.

   D. Prepaid Insurance and Stockholders' Equity are overstated. See the summary below for the other effects of this error.

   E. The amount of depreciation for any year will be determined as follows:

$$\frac{\left[\left(\begin{matrix}\text{Purchase} \\ \text{Price}\end{matrix}\right) - \left(\begin{matrix}\text{Estimated Scrap} \\ \text{Value on Retirement}\end{matrix}\right)\right] \times \left(\begin{matrix}\text{Fraction of} \\ \text{Year Owned}\end{matrix}\right)}{\text{(Estimated Service Life in Years)}}$$

   If the service life is underestimated, the amount of depreciation will be too high. Depreciation is reflected by reducing Stockholders' Equity, so Stockholders' Equity has been overreduced and is understated. Buildings have been overdepreciated and are also understated. See the summary below for the other effects of this error.

   F. This is tricky. First of all, Accounts Payable is obviously overstated. Merchandise Inventory is not overstated: under the company's system, the physical count on 12/31/X1 correctly reflected that the company no longer owned the merchandise. Yet some other account must be misstated or assets would no longer equal equities. By elimination, this account must be stockholders' equity. This makes sense as demonstrated by the following equation:

(Beginning Balance) + (Purchases) = (Ending Balance) + (Amount Used)
   Correct   *Overstated*   *Correct*   *?*

Merchandise purchases have been overstated. Since the beginning and ending balances are correct, the amount used must be overstated. Stockholders' Equity is reduced to reflect the amount of merchandise (or supplies) consumed in operations. Since the amount of merchandise consumed is overstated, Stockholders' Equity has been overreduced. Therefore, Stockholders' Equity is understated. The upshot of all this is that Accounts Payable is overstated and Stockholders' Equity is understated. See the following summary for the other effects of this error.

Summary:

In the following, "+" means overstated; "−" means understated; and "0" means not affected.

	Error					
	A	*B*	*C*	*D*	*E*	*F*
Current Assets	−	−	0	+	0	0
Noncurrent Assets	0	0	0	0	−	0
Total Assets	−	−	0	+	−	0
Current Liabilities	−	0	−	0	0	+
Net Working Capital	0	−	+	+	0	−
Noncurrent Liabilities	0	0	0	0	0	0
Total Liabilities	−	0	−	0	0	+
Stockholders' Equity	0	−	+	+	−	−
Total Equities	−	−	0	+	−	0

Typical Changes within Ledger Accounts

Comprehension of the following section is fairly important to your ability to analyze accounting information and record balance sheet changes. Both here and when reading subsequent discussions of financial accounting recording techniques, you should pay particular attention to two things. First, you need to develop a good intuitive sense of which balance sheet changes are reflected in which accounts; if you lack this, you will waste time later on. This section is intended to help you begin to develop this understanding.

Second, you should be aware that most actively used balance sheet accounts go through the following process during each accounting period. At the beginning of the period the account has a balance (which summarizes the related effects of the economic activities of all prior periods). During the period various transactions and/or internal changes increase that balance while various other changes decrease that balance. Whatever remains at the end of the period is both the ending balance for the current period and the beginning balance for the next period.

Beginning balance + Increases − Decreases = Ending balance

What follows indicates typical *causes* of such increases and decreases.

Most ledger accounts are fairly limited in the kinds of balance sheet changes they reflect, and you can easily learn what to expect from them. For example, a prepaid insurance account will show beginning and ending balances, purchases of insurance policies (on the left side), and writedowns of expired insurance (on the right side).

It's rare that a prepaid insurance account will show anything else. If you were to see the following example, you could be fairly sure in advance what every figure represented.

Prepaid Insurance

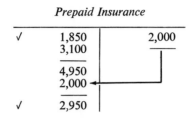

The $1,850 and the $2,950 are, of course, beginning and ending balances. Since the $3,100 is on the left, or asset increase side, it probably represents purchases of insurance policies that, in total, cost $3,100. Similarly, the $2,000 probably represents the expiration of $2,000 worth of insurance during the year. Admittedly, this isn't quite certain: some of the $2,000 could represent cancellation of a policy rather than insurance expiration. Still these explanations are highly likely ones. In uncomplicated situations, you could expect a prepaid insurance account to reflect the following:

Prepaid Insurance

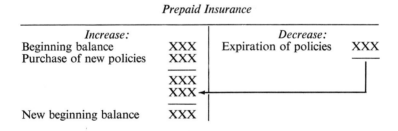

Similarly, in uncomplicated situations, you could expect a wages payable account to reflect the following:

Wages Payable

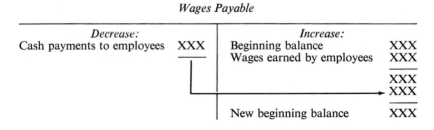

This assumes that all wages are first recorded as a liability before they are paid. Of course, there may be hundreds of cash payments to employees within an accounting period. But all cash payments will be reflected on the left-hand side of the wages payable ledger account, and all unpaid wages will be reflected on the right-hand side.

Shown below are the typical balance sheet changes that you see in more common balance sheet accounts. Each kind of change is shown on the side of the account where it would be reflected. To save space, *beginning and ending balances have been omitted.*

Illustration 4-4

*Typical Changes in
Commonly Used Balance
Sheet Accounts*

Cash

Increase:	*Decrease:*
Cash sales	Purchases of assets
Collections of accounts receivable	Payments of salaries and other costs of
Other collections	current operations
Proceeds from issue of capital stock	Payments of liabilities
Proceeds from issue of notes, bonds, mortgages, etc.	Payments of dividends
Proceeds from sales of used buildings, equipment, furniture, and fixtures	

Accounts Receivable

Increase:	*Decrease:*
Sales on account	Cash collections
	Writeoffs of uncollectible customer accounts

Merchandise Inventory

Increase:	*Decrease:*
Purchases of merchandise	Merchandise sold

Supplies

Increase:	*Decrease:*
Purchases	Supplies used

Prepayments *(Prepaid Rent, Prepaid Insurance, etc.)*

Increase:	*Decrease:*
Purchases	Writedowns

Land

Increase:	*Decrease:*
Purchases	Sales

Buildings, Equipment, Furniture, and Fixtures

Increase:	*Decrease:*
Purchases	Depreciation
	Sales of used assets

Patents

Increase:	*Decrease:*
Purchases	Amortization

Accounts Payable

Decrease:	*Increase:*
Cash payments	Credit purchases

Interest Payable

Decrease:	*Increase:*
Cash payments	Interest fees

Wages Payable

Decrease:	*Increase:*
Cash payments	Wages earned by employees

Dividends Payable

Decrease:	*Increase:*
Cash payments	Dividends declared

Taxes Payable

Decrease:	*Increase:*
Cash payments	Tax charges

Notes Payable, Mortgages Payable, Bonds Payable, etc.

Decrease:	*Increase:*
Cash payments	Notes, mortgages, bonds, etc. issued

Stockholders' Equity

Decrease:	*Increase:*
Merchandise consumed in operations	Cash sales
Supplies consumed in operations	Sales on account
Wages and salaries earned	Capital stock issued
Taxes	
Interest fees	
Depreciation and amortization	
Writedowns of prepayments	
Writedowns of uncollectible accounts receivable	
Dividends declared	

Problem for Study and Self-Examination

Problem 4-6 (*Brain-Teaser*):

As part of your training in accounting, you must become able to extend the concepts and techniques which you have learned into situations which require different methods of analysis. This problem provides such an opportunity to increase your flexibility and to broaden your understanding. The background needed to solve this problem has been provided by the text, but the particular method of analysis required may at first seem unusual. Apply what you already have learned to this new situation.

Shown below are the comparative consolidated balance sheets of Tucson Enterprises as of 12/31/X1 and 1/7/X2, followed by a partial summary of the company's balance sheet changes for the week ending 1/7/X2. For brevity, three zeros have been omitted from these figures. Several of the company's summary balance sheet changes have not been listed; part of your job will be to determine what changes have been left out. (The significance of "consolidated" financial statements was discussed on page 152.) No unusual balance sheet changes occurred during the week; instead all changes were of the normal kinds discussed in this chapter.

Tucson Enterprises and Subsidiaries
Consolidated Balance Sheets
12/31/X1 and 1/7/X2

Assets	*12/31/X1*		*1/7/X2*	
Current Assets:				
Cash	$17,500		$ 9,700	
Accounts Receivable	30,200		27,700	
Merchandise Inventory	54,700		53,600	
Supplies	4,400		4,200	
Prepaid Rent	15,000	$121,800	14,400	$109,600
Noncurrent Assets:				
Equipment		186,900		188,500
Total Assets		$308,700		$298,100

continued on page 220

Equities

Current Liabilities:				
Accounts Payable	$42,600		$49,100	
Wages Payable.	20,800		4,900	
Dividends Payable	3,000	$ 66,400	–0–	$ 54,000
Stockholders' Equity		242,300		244,100
Total Equities		$308,700		$298,100

Other summary data for the week ended 1/7/X2:

1. The company sold merchandise that had cost $48,300 for $57,600. Of these sales, $38,200 were on account; the rest were for cash.
2. During the week, $600 worth of prepaid rent expired.
3. Depreciation of equipment for the week totalled $300.
4. The company purchased supplies costing $1,500 on account; no other supplies were purchased.
5. The company paid $44,100 of accounts payable and $20,800 of wages payable. Employee wages are paid once a month, on the first working day of each month; wages are always recorded as a liability before they are paid.
6. No dividends were declared during the week.
7. No merchandise was returned to suppliers.

Answer each of the following questions. In doing so, avoid making any complicated assumptions. No unusual balance sheet changes occurred during the week, and the company's accountant made no errors. The answers to the questions are implicit in the data that you already have been given. As a convenience, the first question has already been solved, using a variety of different ways to get the correct answer.

A. How much in wages did employees earn during the week?

Answer: Some students look for too complicated an answer here. The beginning balance of wages payable was $20,800. The ending balance was $4,900, despite the fact that $20,800 of wages were paid during the week. Therefore, balance sheet changes must have occurred during the week that increased wages payable by $4,900. Since employee wages are always recorded as liabilities before being paid (and since wages payable is the appropriate liability account), employee wages must have totalled $4,900.

This could all be expressed by using the wages payable ledger account. We know the following from the data provided:

Wages Payable

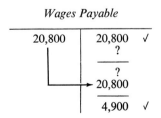

Adding backward, we successively arrive at the following:

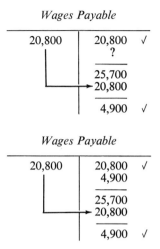

Wages Payable

20,800	20,800 ✓
	?
	25,700
	20,800
	4,900 ✓

Wages Payable

20,800	20,800 ✓
	4,900
	25,700
	20,800
	4,900 ✓

The resulting figure is the same $4,900 increase for the week previously calculated. Given the data, and knowing that there are no errors or unusual changes, this $4,900 must reflect the earnings of employees for the week.

Here is a third way to reach the same result:

Ending balance of wages payable	$ 4,900
Payments made during the week	20,800
	25,700
Beginning balance of wages payable	20,800
Wages earned during the week	$ 4,900

Any one of these three approaches "works." In answering the following questions, use whatever line of attack suits you best. Personally, I solve most problems of this kind by using ledger accounts; however, when you are trying to explain the steps in your reasoning to someone else, successive ledger accounts use up too much space. Consequently, most of the explanations in this book use schedules similar to the one immediately above. If one of these schedules does not make sense to you, try it in ledger form to see if it is clearer. Individuals hold widely differing opinions as to which kind of approach is the most efficient. The main thing is to answer the questions in a systematic way, whatever approach you use.

Question A was answered in terms of the effects of employee earnings upon wages payable. Stockholders' equity was also affected by these earnings, but stockholders' equity is affected by so many changes that it is a confusing account with which to work. In answering questions of this kind, it often pays to focus your attention on the account least affected by other changes.

B. How much in dividends did the company pay during the week?
C. How much of accounts receivable did the company collect during the week? (Assume that no accounts receivable were uncollectible.)
D. How much in supplies did the company use during the week?
E. How much merchandise was purchased during the week?
F. How much equipment was purchased during the week?

Solution

Solution 4-6:

The following solution is quite detailed, for the sake of providing maximum help to students who are having difficulties; if you don't need this much help, feel free to skim some of these details.

B. <u>$3,000</u>. Dividends payable decreased from $3,000 at 12/31/X1 to $0 at 1/7/X2. Since no dividends were declared, $3,000 of dividends must have been paid.

C. <u>$40,700</u>. Accounts receivable decreased from $30,200 to $27,700 during the week, despite sales on account of $38,200. There must have been decreases in accounts receivable totalling $40,700 during the week ($30,200 + $38,200 − $27,700 = $40,700). This decrease will result either from cash being collected or from accounts receivable becoming worthless when customers are unable to pay. Since all customers were able to pay their accounts, the $40,700 must represent cash collections.

D. <u>$1,700</u>. The balance of supplies decreased $200 during the week (from $4,400 to $4,200), despite the purchase of $1,500 worth of supplies. Evidently $1,700 worth of supplies were used during the week ($1,500 + $200 = $1,700). Here is the same solution using the supplies ledger account. We know the following:

Supplies

√	4,400		?
	1,500		
	5,900		
	?		
√	4,200		

The missing figure represents the cost of supplies used during the week:

$$\$5,900 - \underline{\$1,700} = \$4,200$$

E. <u>$47,200</u>. We know the following:

Merchandise Inventory

√	54,700	48,300
	?	
	?	
	48,300	
√	53,600	

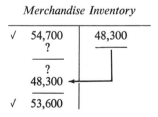

Adding backward, we get:

Merchandise Inventory

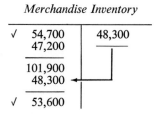

Since no merchandise was returned to suppliers, merchandise purchases must have totalled $47,200. Alternately, you could reason that, despite selling merchandise that had cost the company $48,300, the merchandise inventory account decreased by only $1,100 during the week ($54,700 − $53,600 = $1,100). Therefore, $47,200 of merchandise must have been purchased ($48,200 − $1,100 = $47,200).

F. $1,900. Equipment increased by $1,600 during the week ($188,500 − $186,900 = $1,600), despite depreciation of $300. A total of $1,900 worth of equipment must have been purchased ($1,600 + $300 = $1,900).

Equipment

√	186,900	300
	?	
	?	
	300	
√	188,500	

Measurement in Financial Accounting[12]

In the sciences, the word "measurement" is used in a very general sense: measurement occurs whenever numerals are assigned to phenomena (objects, events, traits) on the basis of observation and according to rules. Under this definition, financial accounting is a way of measuring the economic phenomena of individual accounting entities. It is good review at this point to consider exactly what financial accounting measures.

At bottom, financial accounting's measurements are nothing more complicated than *counts, estimates,* and *observations of market prices.* We may see this by examining the measurements that underlie each item that appears on a balance sheet.

Cash. Inflows and outflows are counted; as a byproduct of this, balances of cash at individual points in time are obtained. Periodically, these balances are verified—either by counting or by requesting confirmation from banks of the balances of cash in banks; but the basic measurement procedure remains one of counting inflows and outflows.

[12] The following discussion is based in part on "Report of the Committee on Foundations of Accounting Measurement," *The Accounting Review,* Supplement to Vol. XLVI (1971) pages 1–48.

Other monetary assets (for example, accounts receivable, long-term notes receivable, and the other assets discussed on pages 61–66). Inflows and outflows are counted. The quantities of these assets are expressed in terms of equivalent amounts of cash (therefore, if one wished to be very precise, he could say that inflows and outflows of quantities of these assets are counted, then these quantities are converted into dollar values by multiplying them by equivalent amounts of cash). Once again, as a byproduct, balances of these assets are obtained, and these balances are periodically verified by counts and by requesting confirmations from borrowers.

In the cases of certain contractual receivables, such as interest receivable, the measurement procedure for inflows (discussed on pages 61–64, 129–130, 178–179) is less direct than this. The total amount of interest receivable over the entire life of the related debt is calculated (by counting the principal amount of the debt, observing the interest rate and the total life of the debt, then multiplying). Next, the amount of time that has passed since the inception of the debt is observed, then the total amount of interest is allocated so that the amount reported for interest receivable equals:

$$\left(\frac{\text{Time passed since inception}}{\text{Total life}}\right) \times (\text{Total interest})^{13}$$

Of course, any receipt of interest (or other contractual payments) already will have been reflected in recorded outflows of these assets, so that the balances remaining in these accounts after the allocation has been performed will be the accrued receivables at the particular point in time involved.

Monetary liabilities (for example, accounts payable, bonds payable, and the other liabilities discussed on pages 126–131). The same measurement procedures are followed as for *other monetary assets.*

Nonmonetary assets (for example, merchandise inventory, buildings, and the other assets discussed on pages 97–103): Inflows of physical quantities are counted: these are converted by multiplying them by market prices with which they are, according to the accountant's observation, associated. Under the rule of conservatism (discussed on pages 57–59), these market prices usually are the historical costs of these assets. (The market price may be the current market value, however, if the assets are intended only for sale and the current market value is less than historical cost).

As the discussion on page 92 first indicated, accountants are primarily interested in nonmonetary assets as sources of expected future economic benefits. As a nonmonetary asset yields up its services, the accountant records this just as he would a physical outflow of the asset. But something less straightforward than counting quantities and observing market prices is involved in these outflow measurements:

1. The accountant first must identify the services of the particular asset, as distinct from those provided by the other inputs to the firm.

2. He must *estimate* the total quantity of these services; simple counting is not possible here since these services will occur in the future, and one cannot count what does not yet exist.

---

[13] The reader is reminded that simple interest is assumed in this book until Chapter Eleven; at that point compound interest and several other matters that are ignored here are discussed.

3. He then allocates to these estimated services the dollar magnitude that was recorded for the asset at the time of its inflow (less any estimated scrap value at retirement).

4. Thereafter, in each successive period he estimates the amount of services that were received from the asset during that period.

5. Then, by a further allocation, he reduces the dollar magnitude recorded for the asset in proportion to the ratio of estimated services during the period to estimated total services.[14]

You can see that this outflow measurement technique, which I have been calling *allocation of the nonmonetary asset's purchase price* (or, sometimes, *matching*), is far less direct than the *inflow* measurement technique for nonmonetary assets, discussed earlier. Once again, as a byproduct, balances of these assets are obtained; these balances are periodically verified by counts, rechecking observations made of market prices, rechecking allocations, and so on.

Nonmonetary liabilities (for example, advances from customers, discussed on page 129). The same measurement procedures are followed as for nonmonetary assets.

Stockholders' equity (discussed on pages 131–133). An inflow is recorded when stockholders invest; an outflow is recorded when stockholders disinvest (when dividends are declared). No independent measurements are made for these inflows and outflows—the amounts recorded are identical with those recorded for the related assets and liabilities.

An inflow is recorded when assets are received from customers in exchange for sales of goods and services; an outflow is recorded when an outflow of assets or increase in liabilities is recorded related to such sales. Once again, no independent measurements are made of these inflows and outflows of stockholders' equity; the amounts recorded are identical with those recorded for the related asset and liability inflows and outflows. As a byproduct of all this, balances of stockholders' equity are obtained.

Primary versus secondary measurements

As the previous discussion indicates, many of the measurements made in financial accounting are very direct and straightforward: counts of cash, monetary assets and liabilities, physical quantities of nonmonetary assets, and observations of market prices. Call these *simple,* or *primary* measurements. Other measurements—especially those relating to amortization of nonmonetary assets—are not nearly as straightforward as these primary measurements. Of course, in practice these amortizations are performed only in rough, approximate ways. Still, they all depend upon making estimates of the total services to be provided by the nonmonetary asset (as distinct from those provided by other inputs) and the services provided by the asset to date. Chapters Six, Eight, and Thirteen will argue that the concept of the "services provided by an individual asset" is seriously ambiguous whenever different assets work together in close conjunction as parts of a complicated system.

All successful firms are worth more than the sum of their parts in the sense that their assets provide more services when they are working in combination with each

---

[14] The detailed arguments for applying this description to inventories and to depreciable assets simultaneously are incorporated in Chapter Thirteen.

other than they would if used separately. For instance, machines protected by buildings produce more product than would empty buildings and machines exposed to the weather. Call this phenomenon *interaction:*

> *Interaction* occurs whenever the services provided by a combination of two or more inputs to the firm differ from the services that would be obtained by using these inputs separately.

In Chapters Six, Eight, and Thirteen, I will argue that when assets interact it becomes impossible for anyone who is amortizing a nonmonetary asset to defend conclusively his estimates of the asset's services against a contrary estimate offered by another interested party with conflicting goals. Instead, any such estimates will be arbitrary (subject to manipulation) and therefore unsatisfactory to the other party. In turn, this means that the amortization methods (which are based on these service estimates) will be equally arbitrary. In essence, the problem of determining the services provided by one nonmonetary asset of a large number of interacting inputs to the firm is similar to that of determining the services provided by an individual gear in a watch, or of determining exactly how much of one's pleasure in eating a complicated dish (say, a pizza) was the result of an individual ingredient.

In any event, the point to emphasize here is that the measurements involved in the amortizations of nonmonetary assets are much more difficult, much less clear-cut, than primary measurements such as counts of physical quantities. For nonmonetary assets, each of these allocations begins with the total purchase price of the asset, derived from primary measurements of physical quantities and prices. This total primary measurement then is divided up in proportion to estimates of the asset's services. Since this procedure is performed upon primary measurements, call it a *secondary* measurement. Most "internal changes" (depreciation, patent amortization, expiration of prepayments, etc.) are allocations; all accruals involve allocations; all of these would be classified as secondary measurements. Accountants make various other kinds of secondary measurements that we have not yet discussed; they are examined later in this book.

The distinction between primary and secondary measurements is important for a reason that will become evident as you read later chapters in this book: *most of the difficult unsolved problems in financial accounting relate to secondary measurements and, in particular, to allocations.* The counts and observations of prices constituting primary measurements are simple enough that they can be routinely made in as precise a fashion as management desires (or, at least, as precisely as management can afford—accounting costs money). Any serious problems that the accountant might once have had in making primary measurements have long since been mastered. But difficulties related to secondary measurements remain a great headache to accountants; they are the source of most of the limitations to be found in published financial statements.

Assignment Problems

Problem 4-A:

General background: most of the illustrations in this book concern business enterprises that are intended to earn profits. Yet, certain kinds of nonprofit enterprises maintain their accounting records in almost the same ways as do conventional business firms.

This problem discusses one such enterprise: a cooperative nursery school. It was chosen because its activities are quite simple—so simple that it is feasible to provide a nearly complete description of those activities.

Salaries are the primary cost of running a nursery school; at least two teachers (or one teacher and two nonprofessional assistants) are usually required for a class of twenty children. A cooperative nursery school holds down costs (and thereby reduces tuition charges) by having the children's mothers serve in rotation as assistant teachers. Custodial costs are minimized or eliminated by the mothers, who do the necessary cleanup and minor repairs. Most cooperative nursery schools achieve further cost savings by arranging to use public or church facilities and by persuading the children's fathers to build equipment and perform major repairs and cleanup.

In the example that follows, there is only one difference between the way the school records are kept and the way records would be kept by a corporation: since the school is not a corporation, its residual equity is not called "stockholders' equity." Instead, its residual equity is called "general reserve." The account General Reserve functions in exactly the same way for this entity as the account Stockholders' Equity would function for a corporation.

Data: Community Co-op Nursery School was founded fifteen years ago. It meets five mornings a week, using the Sunday-school rooms of the local nondenominational Community Church. The church provides these facilities free, as a public service.

The school prepares financial statements once a year, every June 30th. The school's 6/30/X3 balance sheet is shown below, followed by a summary of its activities for the fiscal year ended 6/30/X4. The mother who served as treasurer for the fiscal year ended 6/30/X3 knew little accounting, and the form of the 6/30/X3 balance sheet is unusual; its figures, however, are correct.

BALANCE SHEET—6/30/X3
COMMUNITY CO-OP NURSERY SCHOOL

Equipment	$ 973
Cash	74
Tuition Receivable	36
Supplies	15
Refreshments	2

[EQUALS]

General Reserve	$1,100

1. The school conducts a three-day program on Mondays, Wednesdays, and Fridays, and a two-day program on Tuesdays and Thursdays. Tuition is $11.00 per month for children in the three-day program, and $7.50 per month for children in the two-day program. All tuition is recorded in the account Tuition Receivable at the time that it is billed. The school operates a total of nine months each year. During the entire period of operations for the fiscal year ended 6/30/X4, there were 20 children in the three-day program and 20 children in the two-day program.

2. The mother who had served as treasurer during the fiscal year ended 6/30/X3 had been reluctant to press for collection of tuition. Despite the eventual efforts of other school officers, $36 of tuition was still owed the school at the start of the current year. The new treasurer not only collected this past-due tuition, but made certain that all tuition for the current year was collected by 6/30/X4.

3. The teacher receives a salary of $300 per month for nine months. This salary is recorded as a liability before being paid.

4. Supplies consist mostly of art materials (paper, paste, paint, crayons, clay, etc.). During the year, the school bought supplies costing $63; these were purchased on account.

5. During the year, the school bought refreshments (cookies, juice, etc.) costing $118; these were purchased for cash.

6. The school pays $2 per child to a local insurance agency for comprehensive insurance coverage. This payment is made at the beginning of each school year.

7. $2,700 of salaries were paid to the teacher during the year.

8. During the year, it was necessary to repair certain equipment. Welding and other repairs to tricycles and wagons were done at a local repair shop; the repair shop billed the school $33 for these services.

9. Repairs to plumbing were required after a child's misguided efforts to clean a hamster cage. The plumber billed the school $10 for his services.

10. Remaining repair and painting costs were for materials only. These totalled $28 and were paid in cash.

11. $101 of accounts payable were paid during the year. The remaining accounts payable resulted from June, 19X4, purchases of supplies. These were not billed until July, 19X4.

12. Supplies costing $67 were used up during the year.

13. Refreshments costing $117 were consumed during the year.

14. The $80 of insurance expired during the year.

15. During the year, the children were taken on several trips (to a local museum, a bakery, and a nearby turkey farm). The mothers provided the transportation; other costs of these trips totalled $23, paid in cash.

16. Depreciation of equipment totalled $176 for the year.

17. Most of the new equipment acquired by the school during the year was built by fathers of the children. The school paid for all materials. New equipment acquired during the year cost a total of $202, paid in cash.

The new treasurer desires that her records and reports follow good business accounting practices. Prepare all necessary ledger accounts, inserting beginning balances where appropriate. Record all summary balance sheet changes for the fiscal year ended 6/30/X4. Determine and record ending balances in all accounts as of

6/30/X4. Prepare a balance sheet as of 6/30/X4 (using a better form than was employed at 6/30/X3).

Suppose that the new treasurer had been unable to collect $15 of tuition that had been owed on 6/30/X3, and that it was decided that the receivable was worthless. What effect would this have on the school's records and reports?

Problem 4-B:

In the following narrative, names and amounts have been disguised; but, otherwise, events are related in the way that they actually happened. A few years ago, I subscribed to a mail order *World of History* book series distributed by World International Books, Ltd., a subsidiary of a large publishing company. Volumes cost $4.45 apiece, plus 50¢ apiece for postage and handling, and were mailed to my home. The series plan involved these books being sent out at the rate of one volume every two months. After receiving five this way, I wrote World International Books, Ltd., to ask whether I could buy the remainder of the series in a single purchase. They replied that I could, and that postage and handling charges were waived on prepaid orders. On August 9, 19X8 I ordered 14 *World of History* books and 21 books from another series called *World of Nature,* a total of 35 books. I enclosed my check for $35 \times \$4.45 = \$155.75$, requesting that the books be sent to my office, since I was going on vacation. Thereafter, the following events occurred:

September, 19X8: 19 *World of Nature* books arrived at my office. A *World of History* book, "The World of Genghis Khan," arrived at my home, bearing a bill for $4.95; this was a book that I had paid for on August 9th.

September 30, 19X8: I wrote to Mr. Clyde Floyd, the company's series manager, explaining the situation. I never received a reply.

November 5, 19X8: I wrote to Mr. Floyd again, enclosing a copy of my previous letter. I never received a reply.

November, 19X8: A *World of History* book, "The World of Attila the Hun," arrived at my home, bearing a bill for $4.95; this was a book that I had paid for on August 9th.

November 26, 19X8: I wrote to the parent company at their home office (copy to Mr. Floyd) explaining the situation, and asking that they help me straighten things out.

December, 19X8: I received a postcard from Mr. Floyd, saying that he was sorry that I had cancelled my subscription, and requesting payment for "The World of Genghis Khan." I received one *World of Nature* book, without bill, at my office.

January, 19X9: I received an *URGENT—OPEN AT ONCE* letter requesting immediate payment for "The World of Genghis Khan" and "The World of Attila the Hun."

January 12, 19X9: Upon the advice of a colleague, I wrote a letter to the president of the parent company at his home (his address was determined from a directory of corporate directors).

February 13, 19X9: I received a letter from World International Books, Ltd., containing a refund check ($13.35) for three books that were temporarily out of print, and concluding with the following paragraph:

> Our sincere apologies for any inconvenience or concern this has caused you. We know that when you do receive the volumes you will find they were well worth waiting for.

February, 19X9: I received the remaining 10 books.

Assume that I kept very detailed accounting records. I recorded purchases of postage stamps, stationery, etc., in an account called "office supplies." About 7¢ of supplies were used in writing and mailing a letter (for simplicity assume that any one letter cost 7¢, no matter how thick it was). I paid all bills by check, and checks cost me 10¢ apiece.

Set up the following ledger accounts: cash, advances to suppliers, office supplies, personal library, accounts payable, and net worth (the latter being a residual equity account). Do not concern yourself with beginning balances—you may assume that they were adequate to cover all balance sheet changes. In theory, the cost of checks and other office supplies consumed in acquiring books should be treated as part of the cost of the books themselves. In practice, this is rarely done; instead, as office supplies are consumed both the office supplies and the net worth accounts are reduced. Record the following in the ledger accounts:

1. The receipt of the first five *World of History* books. (You may record a single summary change for all five books.)

2. Payment for the first five *World of History* books. (You may record a single summary payment.)

3. The 8/9/X8 order. (You may assume that this required two letters and one check.)

4. The September receipt of 19 *World of Nature* books.

5. The September receipt of "The World of Genghis Khan." (It is considered to be bad accounting practice to offset a liability against an asset, even when both are from the same firm.)

6. The events of the period 9/30/X8 through 11/5/X8.

7. The receipt of "The World of Attila the Hun" in November.

8. The remaining events of the period ending January 31, 19X9.

9. The receipt of the 2/13/X9 letter from World International Books, Ltd.

10. The February receipt of the remaining ten books.

If any aspects of your recording are debatable, defend what you did.

Problem 4-C:

The following problem requires that you record some, but not all, of the balance sheet changes of Putnam Pharmaceutical Corporation for the year ended 12/31/X5. The company's comparative balance sheet for 12/31/X4 and 12/31/X5 is given on page 233. This balance sheet has been designed to incorporate certain accounts and reporting practices that were not discussed in the text; where necessary, these variations are discussed in the notes to the balance sheet.

Here is a partial list of the company's balance sheet changes for the year ended 12/31/X5. All changes described pertain to 19X5 only unless explicitly stated otherwise. Do not concern yourself with the remaining changes. Instead, you may assume that they have been (or will be) correctly recorded. Similarly, do not worry if there appear to be insufficient amounts in certain accounts to allow certain changes to occur—such apparent impossibilities arise only because various other balance sheet changes have been omitted to save you time. Also, the last three zeros have been omitted from all figures; you should do likewise.

1. All sales are on account and result in either notes receivable or accounts receivable. Ordinary sales totalled $502,524.

2. The company also sold buildings on account, for a price of $5,120.

3. These buildings had a book value (acquisition price less accumulated depreciation) of $5,523 at the time they were sold.

4. The company also sold retired machinery and equipment for a total price of $3,243.

5. This machinery and equipment had a book value of $3,985 at the time it was sold.

6. The company earns interest on some of its investments and royalties on some of its patents. As interest and royalties are earned, the related receivables are reflected in notes and accounts receivable. Interest and royalties totalled $4,870.

7. The only other balance sheet changes affecting notes and accounts receivable were collections of cash. You are to calculate the amount collected.

8. Depreciation of buildings totalled $2,185.

9. Land and buildings costing a total of $5,042 were purchased on account; under the firm's accounting system, the liability affected is accounts payable.

10. In addition, land and buildings costing $1,823 were purchased overseas, in exchange for long-term notes payable.

11. Depreciation of machinery and equipment totalled $5,464.

12. Machinery and equipment costing $8,211 were purchased on account.

13. The only other balance sheet change affecting machinery and equipment was the purchase of machinery and equipment overseas in exchange for long-term notes payable. You are to calculate the amount purchased.

Prepare all ledger accounts necessary to record these balance sheet changes. Do not prepare any other ledger accounts. Insert opening balances, if any. Record all balance sheet changes for the year in the ledgers, using good form and appropriate index numbers. Obtain the ending ledger balances for notes and accounts receivable, land and buildings, notes payable—foreign, and machinery and equipment; compare these ending balances with the figures reported on the balance sheet.

Problem 4-D:

The following problem requires that you record some, but not all, of the balance sheet changes of Putnam Pharmaceutical Corporation for the year ended 12/31/X5. The company's comparative balance sheet for 12/31/X4 and 12/31/X5 is given on the next page. This balance sheet has been designed to incorporate certain accounts and reporting practices that were not discussed in the text; where necessary, these variations are discussed in the notes to the balance sheet.

Here is a partial list of the company's balance sheet changes for the year ended 12/31/X5. All changes described pertain to 19X5 only unless explicitly stated otherwise. Do not concern yourself with the remaining changes. Instead, you may assume that they have been (or will be) correctly recorded. Similarly, do not worry if there appear to be insufficient amounts in certain accounts to allow certain changes to occur—such apparent impossibilities arise only because various other balance sheet changes have been omitted to save you time. Also, the last three zeros have been omitted from all figures; you should do likewise.

Putnam Pharmaceutical Corporation
Financial Position
(In Thousands)

	12/31/X5		12/31/X4	
Current Assets				
Cash	$14,565		$12,481	
Time deposits—interest bearing	35,579		19,684	
Marketable securities	8,534		5,872	
Notes and accounts receivable	73,622		70,445	
Inventories	93,762		93,559	
Prepaid expenses and other current assets	8,712	$234,774	5,959	$208,000
Current Liabilities				
Notes payable to banks	$ 5,828		$32,665	
Current portion of long-term debt	525		1,747	
Accounts payable, trade	18,414		14,222	
Other payables and accrued expenses	34,374		29,846	
United States and foreign income taxes	26,516	85,657	19,685	98,165
Working capital		$149,117		$109,835
Investments and Deposits		3,690		3,160
Land and Buildings		61,265		62,108
Machinery and Equipment		54,014		53,490
Goodwill and Unamortized Cost of Patents		13,503		13,406
		$281,589		$241,999
Long-Term Debt				
$4\frac{1}{4}\%$ debentures	$10,000		$10,000	
$4\frac{1}{2}\%$ debentures	15,000		–0–	
$4\frac{1}{4}\%$ sinking fund notes	6,475		7,000	
Notes payable—foreign	3,585	35,060	–0–	17,000
Net assets represented by stockholders' equity		$246,529		$224,999
Stockholders' Equity		$246,529		$224,999

Notes to balance sheet:

"Prepaid expenses" are another name for what the text calls "prepayments" or "prepaid services."

The company has made deposits with airlines and certain suppliers. These deposits are intended to be of a relatively permanent nature, and therefore are classified as noncurrent. The company chooses to combine these deposits and its incidental investments in other companies into a single account, Investments and Deposits.

Debentures are a kind of bonds payable. Some corporate bonds are secured by a mortgage or other legal claim upon specific noncurrent assets of the company. In contrast, a debenture is a corporate bond that is unsecured by mortgage or any other specific claim to assets, but is secured by the general credit of the company.

The company's $4\frac{1}{4}\%$ sinking fund notes have various maturity dates. Each year a new group of these notes becomes due. At the end of each year, the company transfers the amount that must be paid next year (which thus has become a current liability) from the noncurrent liability "$4\frac{1}{4}\%$ sinking fund notes" to the current liability "current portion of long-term debt."

1. The company made cash payments of $8,079 for prepaid services (be sure to read the related note to the company's comparative balance sheet).

2. The company acquired $5,354 of other current assets on ordinary trade accounts payable.

3. Prepaid services and other current assets totalling $8,603 expired as a result of the company's selling and administrative activities.

4. $2,077 of prepaid services and other current assets were used in the manufacture of inventories.

5. Raw materials used in manufacturing inventories cost a total of $106,510; these raw materials were purchased on ordinary trade accounts payable.

6. The remaining costs of manufacturing inventories consisted of salaries and a variety of general factory expenses. These costs totalled $107,314; their incurrence resulted in the creation of various liabilities, all of which were reflected in the account Other Payables and Accrued Expenses.

7. The company sold inventories that had cost it $199,664. (It sold them for a considerably higher amount, but you need not record this.)

8. The only other kind of balance sheet change affecting inventories was that various manufactured inventories were used for marketing purposes—mostly as free samples for physicians and surgeons. You are to determine the amount of inventories used for marketing purposes.

9. Interest costs totalled $2,923; the related liability is reflected in Other Payables and Accrued Expenses.

10. The company's selling and administrative activities resulted in $166,721 of costs. No asset resulted from incurrence of these costs, but they did give rise to $166,721 of various liabilities reflected in Other Payables and Accrued Expenses. These costs are in addition to those recorded in change 3.

11. $294,112 of other payables and accrued expenses were paid.

12. The only other balance sheet change affecting other payables and accrued expenses was the declaration of dividends. You are to determine the amount of dividends declared.

Prepare all ledger accounts necessary to record these balance sheet changes. Do not prepare any other ledger accounts. Insert opening balances, if any. Record all balance sheet changes for the. year in the ledgers, using good form and appropriate index numbers. Obtain the ending ledger balances for inventories, prepaid expenses and other current assets, and other payables and accrued expenses; compare these ending balances with the figures reported on the balance sheet.

Problem 4-E:

The following problem requires that you record some, but not all, of the balance sheet changes of Putnam Pharmaceutical Corporation for the year ended 12/31/X5. The company's comparative balance sheet for 12/31/X4 and 12/31/X5 is given on the previous page. This balance sheet has been designed to incorporate certain accounts and reporting practices that were not discussed in the text: where necessary, these variations are discussed in the notes to the balance sheet.

Here is a partial list of the company's balance sheet changes for the year ended 12/31/X5. All changes described pertain to 19X5 only unless explicitly stated otherwise. Do not concern yourself with the remaining changes. Instead, you may assume that they have been (or will be) correctly recorded. Similarly, do not worry if there appear to be insufficient amounts in certain accounts to allow certain changes to occur—such apparent impossibilities arise only because various other balance sheet changes have been omitted to save you time. Also, the last three zeros have been omitted from all figures; you should do likewise.

1. $4\frac{1}{2}\%$ debentures were issued for $15,000, cash.
2. Capital stock was issued for $894, cash.
3. See the notes to the company's comparative balance sheet, as they pertain to the account Current Portion of Long-Term Debt; $525 of $4\frac{1}{4}\%$ sinking fund notes will be due in 19X6.
4. Current portions of long-term debt totalling $1,747 were paid.
5. Interest-bearing time deposits totalling $34,632 were made.
6. Interest totalling $1,382 accrued on time deposits. No separate receivable is used to reflect this interest; instead, it is simply added to the balance of time deposits—interest-bearing.
7. Time deposits were reduced by the withdrawal of cash. You are to determine how much cash was withdrawn.
8. Notes payable totalling $5,828 were issued to banks.
9. Notes payable to banks were repaid. You are to determine how much of these notes payable were repaid.
10. Patents costing $3,050 were purchased for cash.
11. The only other balance sheet change affecting goodwill and unamortized cost of patents was their amortization. You are to determine the amount of this amortization.

Prepare all ledger accounts necessary to record these balance sheet changes. Do not prepare any other ledger accounts. Insert opening balances, if any. Record all balance sheet changes for the year in the ledgers, using good form and appropriate index numbers. Obtain the ending ledger balances for $4\frac{1}{2}\%$ debentures, $4\frac{1}{4}\%$ sinking fund notes, current portion of long-term debt, time deposits—interest-bearing, notes payable to banks, and goodwill and unamortized cost of patents; compare these ending balances with the figures reported on the balance sheet.

Problem 4-F:

This problem consists of a series of questions about Putnam Pharmaceutical Corporation. This company's comparative balance sheet as of 12/31/X4 and 12/31/X5 appears on page 233; you will need to refer to it in what follows.

Each of the following questions is independent of the others unless explicitly stated otherwise. In each case, you may assume that you have been given all of the information necessary to answer the question—that is, you may assume that any balance sheet changes that you have not been told about will have no effect on your answers. No unusual balance sheet changes occurred during the year; instead, all changes were of the normal kinds discussed in this chapter and in the notes to the firm's balance sheet. Time deposits are the firm's only interest-bearing investments.

Answer the following questions. Show your calculations. These calculations may be in either schedule or ledger-account form—see Problem 4-6 (Tucson Enterprises, pages 219–224) for examples of possible lines of attack to use in solving this problem.

1. The company purchased marketable securities costing $9,405 during 19X5. What was the cost to it of the marketable securities that it *sold* during 19X5?

2. The following question refers to deposits *other* than interest-bearing time deposits. Assume that no investments were sold nor deposits withdrawn during 19X5. What was the total of investments purchased and deposits made by the company during 19X5?

3. Interest-bearing time deposits increase as cash is deposited or interest is earned. $1,382 of interest was earned during 19X5, and deposits and withdrawals to interest-bearing time deposits occurred evenly throughout the year. What was the approximate interest rate on these time deposits?

4. No $4\frac{1}{4}\%$ debentures were issued during the year; how many were retired? (Assume that each debenture is for $1,000.)

5. Assume that all income taxes are recorded as a liability before being paid, and that 19X5 payments of income taxes totalled $32,332. How much were the company's income taxes for 19X5? (You may assume that the company's tax estimates were correct.)

6. See question 5. How much of 19X5 payments of income taxes were for taxes of a year (or years) other than 19X5?

7. See question 5. How much of 19X5 income taxes were paid or will be paid in some year (or years) other than 19X5?

8. See question 5. How much of 19X5 income taxes were paid during 19X5?

9. What was the company's current ratio at the beginning of 19X5? At the end of 19X5?

10. Looking at the comparative balance sheets as a whole, what were the major changes between 12/31/X4 and 12/31/X5? What might be plausible explanations of these changes? (You will not be able to answer this question conclusively, but be as specific as you can.)

Problem 4-G:

See Problem 4-C. Classify its balance sheet changes according to whether they are exchanges, accruals, or internal changes, and whether they are operating or financial changes.

Problem 4-H:

See Problem 4-E. Classify its balance sheet changes according to whether they are exchanges, accruals, or internal changes, and whether they are operating or financial changes.

Problem 4-I:

Shown below (in comparative form) are a series of balance sheets of Mesa Company. They were prepared at successive dates during the first few weeks of the company's life. Balance sheet A resulted from stockholders investing $15,000 cash, land worth $10,000, and a building worth $40,000. What happened between balance sheets A and B? B and C? C and D? D and E? Be specific in your answers. If more than one answer seems possible, choose the most likely one.

Assets	A	B	C	D	E
Cash	$15,000	$15,000	$ 6,000	$ 7,000	$ 5,000
Accounts Receivable	-0-	-0-	-0-	5,600	1,600
Merchandise Inventory	-0-	-0-	17,000	11,200	11,200
Land	10,000	10,000	10,000	10,000	10,000
Building	40,000	40,000	40,000	39,800	39,800
Equipment	-0-	12,000	12,000	11,700	11,700
Total Assets	$65,000	$77,000	$85,000	$85,300	$79,300

Equities					
Accounts Payable	$ -0-	$ -0-	$ 8,000	$ 8,000	$ 2,000
Interest Payable	-0-	-0-	-0-	20	20
Notes Payable	-0-	12,000	12,000	12,000	12,000
Stockholders' Equity	65,000	65,000	65,000	65,280	65,280
Total Equities	$65,000	$77,000	$85,000	$85,300	$79,300

Problem 4-J:

This problem consists of a series of questions about the activities of 'Tricia-Sue Foods. The company's comparative balance sheet as of 12/31/X7 and 12/31/X6 is shown below. The last three zeros have been omitted from all figures; you should do likewise in your answers. This balance sheet has been designed to incorporate certain accounts and reporting practices that were not discussed in the text; where necessary, these variations are discussed in the notes to the balance sheet.

Each of the following questions is independent of the others, unless stated otherwise. In each case you may assume that there were no unusual balance sheet changes of which you have not been told. Unless told otherwise, assume that all changes were of the normal kinds discussed in this chapter and in the notes to the firm's balance sheet.

Answer the following questions. Show your calculations. These calculations may be in either schedule or ledger-account form—See Problem 4-6 (Tucson Enterprises, pages 219-224) for examples of possible approaches to solving this problem. It is possible that some of the following questions cannot be answered, given the data provided. If so, simply indicate that data are insufficient.

1. Assuming that no investments were sold during the year, what was the cost of investments purchased during 19X7?

2. Presuppose that all sales on account are eventually collected within one year. What were total cash collections during 19X7 resulting from sales made in years other than 19X7?

3. Land costing $807 was purchased during 19X7; what was the cost to the company of land sold during 19X7?

4. How much were total payments of accounts payable and accrued expenses during 19X7?

5. Assume that depreciation of buildings totalled $1,773 during 19X7, and that buildings with a book value (acquisition price less accumulated depreciation) of $704 were sold during 19X7. What was the total cost of buildings purchased by the company during 19X7?

6. What was the *minimum* amount of bank loans that should have been repaid during 19X7?

'Tricia-Sue Foods
Balance Sheet
(000 omitted)
December 31, 19X7 and 19X6

	December 31	
ASSETS	19X7	19X6

CURRENT ASSETS:

Cash and Marketable Securities	$ 7,232	$ 14,860
Accounts Receivable.	57,406	49,338
Inventories	118,530	96,581
Prepaid Expenses	2,871	2,748
TOTAL CURRENT ASSETS	$186,039	$163,527
INVESTMENTS	11,892	7,705

PROPERTY, PLANT, AND EQUIPMENT:

Land	4,090	3,368
Buildings	31,665	24,771
Machinery and Equipment	106,365	80,576
DEFERRED CHARGES AND OTHER ASSETS	1,396	–0–
GOODWILL	35,300	13,091
	$376,747	$293,038

LIABILITIES and STOCKHOLDERS' EQUITY

CURRENT LIABILITIES:

Bank Loans	$ 33,722	$ 25,902
Current Maturities—Long-Term Debt	4,893	1,575
Accounts Payable and Accrued Expenses	54,593	51,891
United States and Foreign Taxes on Income	6,319	7,761
TOTAL CURRENT LIABILITIES	$ 99,527	$ 87,129
LONG-TERM DEBT.	83,791	24,515
RESERVES.	21,080	19,086
STOCKHOLDERS' EQUITY	172,349	162,308
	$376,747	$293,038

Notes:

"Deferred charges" are similar to what the text calls noncurrent "prepayments."

At the end of each year, those portions of long-term debt that will become due in the next year are subtracted from "long-term debt," and reclassified as current liabilities, reflected in the account Current Maturities—Long-Term Debt.

"Accrued expenses" are another name for what the text calls "accrued liabilities."

In this particular report, the account "reserves" reflects miscellaneous noncurrent liabilities.

7. Assume that the company paid a total of $9,403 of income taxes during 19X7; how much income taxes were charged against the company for 19X7? In answering this question you may assume that the firm's tax estimates are correct.

8. What seem to have been the major financial changes experienced by the company during the year? What might be a plausible explanation of these changes? (You will not be able to answer this question conclusively, but be as specific as you can.)

Problem 4-K:

This problem consists of a series of questions about 'Tricia-Sue Foods. One possible approach to its solution would parallel that used for Problem 4-5 (pages 211–213, 214–215). The company's comparative balance sheet as of 12/31/X7 and 12/31/X6 is shown in Problem 4-J. The last three zeros have been omitted from all figures; you should do likewise in your answers. This balance sheet has been designed to incorporate certain accounts and reporting practices that were not discussed in the text; where necessary, these variations are discussed in the notes to the balance sheet.

The company takes a physical count of inventories on hand every December 31st. It then determines how much of the inventories has been consumed in operations by comparing the total cost of the beginning inventory plus all purchases made during the year with the cost of inventories on hand at the end of the year. When this firm buys a depreciable asset partway through the year, depreciation is charged pro rata; for example, if such an asset was purchased on March 31st, three quarters of a year's depreciation would be charged during the first calendar year.

Shown below are some errors made by the company's accountant in 19X6 and 19X7. Unless indicated otherwise, these errors were unrelated to each other. For each error, indicate the effects of that error (if any) on the balance sheet figures for 12/31/X6 and 12/31/X7. If there was no effect, answer *none*.

1. The 12/31/X6 balance of accounts receivable overlooked a $245 sale made on 12/30/X6. The related goods were shipped on 12/31/X6, but the sale itself was not recorded until 1/2/X7; the account was paid on 2/3/X7.

2. Due to a clerical error in adding up the total cost of inventories on hand at 12/31/X7, these inventories were overstated by $33.

3. Inventories costing $1,239 purchased on account had been received by the company at 12/31/X6. Through an error, the purchase was not recorded until 1/3/X7, and the goods themselves were not included in the company's 12/31/X6 inventory.

4. During 19X8, $5,893 of long-term debt will become due; a clerical error was made in recording this at 12/31/X7.

5. A purchase of machinery on 6/30/X7 failed to charge $980 of freight and installation charges to the cost of the machinery. Instead, this cost was charged against stockholders' equity. The machinery is estimated to have a seven-year service life, with a scrap value of $350 upon retirement.

6. A building was acquired on 6/30/X6, for a total cost of $8,320. It was estimated that it would have a 30-year service life and a scrap value upon retirement of $220. Actually the correct estimate would have been a 25-year service life and a scrap value of $320.

7. Machinery was acquired on 3/31/X6, for a total cost of $425. It was estimated that it would have an eight-year service life and a scrap value upon retirement of $25. Actually, the correct estimate would have been a service life of seven and a half years and a scrap value upon retirement of $50.

Problem 4-L:

Five ledger accounts are described below. In each case you should indicate the kinds of information that the account is likely to reflect, and on which side each item of information is reflected. Use the form employed on pages 217–219 for your answer.

You may ignore beginning and ending balances and unusual balance sheet changes.

From the balance sheet of an oil company:

Serial Notes $4\frac{1}{8}\%$ (a noncurrent liability maturing in annual installments)

Marketing Properties and Equipment

Reserve for Employee Benefit Plans (a liability for pensions, health insurance, life insurance, and savings plans)

From the balance sheet of an insurance company:

Canadian Government, Provincial, and Municipal Bonds

Balance of Policyholder Dividends Due in the Following Year (a current liability)

Problem 4-M:

Five ledger accounts are described below. In each case you should indicate the kinds of information that the account is likely to reflect, and on which side each item of information is reflected. Use the form employed on pages 217–219 for your answer. You may ignore beginning and ending balances and unusual balance sheet changes.

From the balance sheet of a utility company:

Debt Maturities Due Within One Year (a current liability)

Customers' Advances for Construction (a liability)

Gas Stored Underground (an asset)

Franchises (an asset)

From the balance sheet of a bank:

Savings Deposits (a liability)

Five

Recording
Balance Sheet Changes:
Journals—and Other Devices

Recording Individual Changes in Journals

Although ledger accounts are an efficient way to record and summarize balance sheet changes, they have a major limitation. Ledger accounts "file" information on balance sheet changes *by the accounts affected.* Given a set of indexed ledger accounts, it is fairly easy to see what has happened to any one account. If the ledger accounts are balanced and a balance sheet prepared, it is also easy to see the overall changes in all accounts from one balance sheet date to the next. But, as we saw in the last chapter, any balance sheet change must involve at least *two* accounts; it is difficult to find out what all the individual changes are if ledger accounts are all you have to work with. To be sure, you can eventually uncover the individual changes; for instance, consider the following Nadir Caves Souvenir Shoppe ledger accounts for the week ended 5/14/X1 (see page 211).

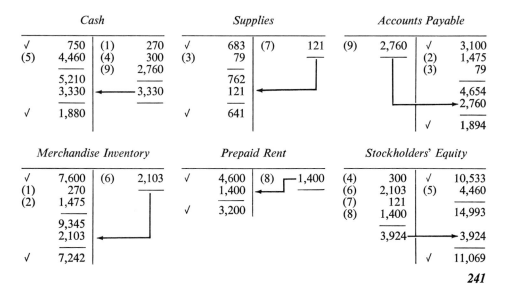

Even if you aren't told what the underlying changes are in these ledger accounts, you can figure them out. For example, find the two changes indexed for Change 3, and you can deduce that $79 worth of supplies has been purchased on account.

$$\begin{array}{ll} \text{Supplies} & +\$79 \\ \text{Accounts Payable} & +\$79 \end{array}$$

Find the two changes indexed for Change 7, and you can deduce that $121 worth of supplies have been used in operations, and so forth.

$$\begin{array}{ll} \text{Stockholders' Equity} & -\$121 \\ \text{Supplies} & -\$121 \end{array}$$

But this is an awkward way to obtain information. Most companies have many more accounts and changes than the firms in these simplified illustrations. Each ledger account is kept on one or more separate pages; thus in an *actual* situation, it is impractical to try to learn about all aspects of individual changes by reading ledger accounts. Another way of recording individual balance sheet changes is needed.

There are a number of possible ways to record all aspects of individual balance sheet changes. Illustration 4-3 (page 193) shows one way, different forms of which are widely used in practice. In Illustration 4-3, columns are provided for each account and the change information is entered in these columns, with a separate line for each individual change. This illustration is a form of *columnar journal*. Actual columnar journals have more columns than this and often are broken up into a number of interrelated subjournals.

Another way to record changes is by listing them in narrative style—just as I have been doing so far in this book. Take Change 3 of Nadir Caves Souvenir Shoppe, for the week ended 5/14/X1 as an example.

3. The company bought $79 of supplies on account.

This is a bit more wordy than necessary. All that you need to record is the following information:

$$\begin{array}{lll} 3. & \text{Supplies} & +\$79 \\ & \text{Accounts Payable} & +\$79 \end{array}$$

Now, remember the rule for increases and decreases:

Increase asset	Decrease asset
Decrease equity	Increase equity

Employing this convention, you can avoid the use of plus and minus signs by using the style below:

$$\begin{array}{lll} 3. & \text{Supplies} \quad \$79 \quad | & \text{Accounts Payable} \quad \$79 \end{array}$$

There is no need to say that supplies increased; just put supplies on the left, where asset increases belong. You don't have to say that accounts payable increased; just put accounts payable on the right, where equity increases belong.

Journal entries

You will recall that when balance sheets were first discussed in Chapter Three, it was pointed out that you could show assets either to the left of equities or above equities. It makes no difference. The accountant actually records balance sheet changes in both these ways. *He records asset increases and equity decreases above and slightly to the left of asset decreases and equity increases.* Here is the general way that Change 3 would be recorded. This method of recording is called a *journal entry*:

3. Supplies   79
      Accounts Payable   79

Observe how the left-right distinction is preserved by indentation. This distinction exactly parallels the way the transaction is recorded in the two ledger accounts. For example, the $79 increase in accounts payable appears on the right-hand side of the entry; this is consistent with the way this increase is recorded in the accounts payable ledger account. Here's how the 5/8/X1–5/14/X1 changes would be recorded in journal form:

1. The company bought $270 of curios for cash.
    1. Merchandise Inventory   270
       Cash   270

2. The company bought $1,475 of curios on account.
    2. Merchandise Inventory   1,475
       Accounts Payable   1,475

3. The company bought $79 of supplies on account.
    3. Supplies   79
       Accounts Payable   79

4. The company paid a $300 cash dividend to its stockholders.
    4. Stockholders' Equity   300
       Cash   300

5. The company made cash sales of $4,460.
    5. Cash   4,460
       Stockholders' Equity   4,460

6. The curios sold in Change 5 cost the company $2,103.
    6. Stockholders' Equity   2,103
       Merchandise Inventory   2,103

7. Supplies that cost $121 were consumed in operations.
    7. Stockholders' Equity   121
       Supplies   121

8. One week's prepaid rent ($1,400) expired in operations.
    8. Stockholders' Equity   1,400
       Prepaid Rent   1,400

9. The company paid accounts payable of $2,760.
    9. Accounts Payable   2,760
       Cash   2,760

Notice again how in each of these journal entries any individual balance sheet change is accompanied by the related change in some other account. Ledger accounts are a compact way to record balance sheet changes *by the accounts affected.* Journal entries are a compact way of recording the same changes *by the varieties of changes that have occurred*—that is, by kind of transaction or internal change. By using both methods of recording, the accountant cross-files accounting information, thereby making his records easier to use. (This is analogous to the way a library card index is cross-filed by author and subject.)

Order and timing of recording changes

In actual practice, balance sheet changes are usually recorded first in journal entry form. The journal entries are maintained in a record book simply called the *journal*. The journal provides a compact narrative diary of company events. Indeed, the word "*journal*" is related to the French word for "day," and originally it meant a kind of daybook or diary. The process of recording information in the journal is called *entering* the information. Because information is first recorded in the journal, it actually does enter the accounting records there.

Later, information is transferred from the journal to the ledger accounts (maintained in another record book called the *ledger*) by a process technically known as *posting*. Keep in mind that *posting is essentially the process of reclassifying economic information from a kind-of-event filing system to a kind-of-account filing system.* Often, it is most convenient to do this reclassifying in batches rather than by posting to the ledger immediately after each entry is made in the journal. In fact, if you use the kind of columnar journal illustrated in Illustration 4-3 (page 193), posting may be done only once a month. (This is an example of something that was mentioned on page 85—the tendency of accountants to delay recording data for which there is no immediate need.)

Typical Journal Entries

On pages 217–219 we saw the effects on common ledger accounts of some typical balance sheet changes. Below is a parallel set of typical journal entries. Since these are specimen journal entries, all dollar amounts are symbolized by the letters "XXX."

Illustration 5-1

Typical Journal Entries

Purpose of Journal Entries	*Journal Entry*	
To record cash sales	Cash 　　Stockholders' Equity	XXX 　　XXX
To record sales on account	Accounts Receivable 　　Stockholders' Equity	XXX 　　XXX

To record the collection of accounts receivable	Cash Accounts Receivable	XXX	XXX

To record collections of notes and interest receivable	Cash
	   Notes Receivable
	Cash
	   Interest Receivable
		XXX
		
		XXX
			
			XXX
			
			XXX

To record the issue of capital stock	Cash Stockholders' Equity	XXX	XXX

To record the issue of various noncurrent debts	Cash
	   Notes Payable
	Cash
	   Bonds Payable
	Cash
	   Mortgage Payable
		XXX
		
		XXX
		
		XXX
			
			XXX
			
			XXX
			
			XXX

To record purchases of various assets	Merchandise Inventory
	   Cash
	Supplies
	   Cash
	Prepaid Rent
	   Cash
		XXX
		
		XXX
		
		XXX
			
			XXX
			
			XXX
			
			XXX

To record payment of cash for various costs of operations, such as wages, utilities, delivery costs, etc. (if not first reflected by a liability)	Stockholders' Equity Cash	XXX	XXX

To record payment of various liabilities	Accounts Payable
	   Cash
	Interest Payable
	   Cash
	Notes Payable
	   Cash
	Bonds Payable
	   Cash
		XXX
		
		XXX
		
		XXX
		
		XXX
			
			XXX
			
			XXX
			
			XXX
			
			XXX

To write down accounts receivable to reflect customer accounts estimated (or proved) to be uncollectible	Stockholders' Equity Accounts Receivable	XXX	XXX

To record purchases of various assets on account	Merchandise Inventory
	   Accounts Payable
	Supplies
	   Accounts Payable
	Equipment
	   Accounts Payable
	Land
	   Accounts Payable
		XXX
		
		XXX
		
		XXX
		
		XXX
			
			XXX
			
			XXX
			
			XXX
			
			XXX

To record return of unsatisfactory merchandise to suppliers	Accounts Payable Merchandise Inventory	XXX	XXX
To record the cost to the company of merchandise given up in sales	Stockholders' Equity Merchandise Inventory	XXX	XXX
To record the cost to the company of supplies used in operations	Stockholders' Equity Supplies	XXX	XXX

To record writedowns of prepaid assets	Stockholders' Equity
	  Prepaid Rent
	Stockholders' Equity
	  Prepaid Insurance
		XXX
		
		XXX
		
			XXX
			
			XXX

To record a sale of land at a loss*	Stockholders' Equity
	  Land
	Cash
	  Land
		XXX
		
		XXX
		
			XXX
			
			XXX

To record a sale of land at a gain*	Land
	  Stockholders' Equity
	Cash
	  Land
		XXX
		
		XXX
		
			XXX
			
			XXX

To record depreciation of noncurrent assets	Stockholders' Equity
	  Buildings
	Stockholders' Equity
	  Equipment
	Stockholders' Equity
	  Furniture and Fixtures
		XXX
		
		XXX
		
		XXX
		
			XXX
			
			XXX
			
			XXX

To record amortization of patents	Stockholders' Equity Patents	XXX 	 XXX
To record earning of wages by employees	Stockholders' Equity Wages Payable	XXX 	 XXX
To record interest fees	Stockholders' Equity Interest Payable	XXX 	 XXX
To record taxes	Stockholders' Equity Taxes Payable	XXX 	 XXX
To record the declaration of dividends (to be paid later)	Stockholders' Equity Dividends Payable	XXX 	 XXX
To record the declaration and immediate payment of dividends	Stockholders' Equity Cash	XXX 	 XXX

See the next subsection for a discussion of these entries.

Simple journal entries for operating and nonoperating sales

On pages 184 and 185, a rule was given for the recording of operating and non-operating balance sheet changes involving stockholders' equity:

Operating change: Break up all compound changes in such a way that stockholders' equity appears in as many simple changes as possible.

Nonoperating change: Break up all compound changes in such a way that stockholders' equity appears in no more than one simple change.

The journal entries in Illustration 5-1 are consistent with this rule. Here are two additional examples:

Case A: Risidore Corporation is a manufacturer. It sells land, which had cost it $17,000, for $30,000 cash. Since Risidore Corporation is not a dealer in land, this is a nonoperating transaction (see page 180). It would be recorded as follows in simple journal entries:

Land	13,000	
Stockholders' Equity		13,000
Cash	30,000	
Land		30,000

Case B: Harold J. Enskaitis Realty, Inc., is a real estate firm. It sells land, which had cost it $17,000, for $30,000 cash. For this company the sale is an operating one, since land is one of the things this company is in business to sell. Accordingly, the sale would be recorded as follows in simple journal entries:

Cash	30,000	
Stockholders' Equity		30,000
Stockholders' Equity	17,000	
Land		17,000

Once again, satisfy yourself that these two sets of entries have the same total effect, and that both may be summarized by the following compound entry:

Cash	30,000	
Land		17,000
Stockholders' Equity		13,000

It is important that you remember this rule for breaking up compound operating and nonoperating entries into simple journal entries, for this rule will be actively used in preparing the cash, funds, and income statements that are discussed in the next three chapters.

Journal entries with appended explanations

In practice it is common for journal entries to be accompanied by an appended explanation of their purpose—similar to what was done in Illustration 5-1, except that the explanation ordinarily is written below the entry instead of beside it. As an example, if land were to be purchased in exchange for a $20,000, 8% note payable, the entry might be:

Land	20,000	
Notes Payable—8%		20,000
—To record purchase of land.		

If you are interested, examples of this kind of recording may be found in the data of the following problems: 5-P, page 289; 6-I, page 331; 7-G, page 379; 7-H, page 382; and 7-K, page 386.

Usually, though, this text employs a simplified form of journal entry that omits these appended explanations; such simplified entries sometimes are described as "skeleton" journal entries. (Similarly, this text leaves out other kinds of incidental and memorandum information sometimes appended to journal entries, as well as complications of coded notation used to relate entries to underlying documents in the firm's files.) The reasons for these simplifications parallel the reasons given on pages 200–201 for using skeleton ledger accounts.

Problems for Study and Self-Examination

Problem 5-1:

Turn back to Problem 4-3 (pages 207–208). Record the August 8, 19X1, balance sheet changes of Tee-Wheet Redhots, Inc., in journal entries. Compare your solution to this problem to the "official" one before going on.

Problem 5-2—(Optional):

Do this problem only if you believe that you need the additional review; otherwise feel free to move on to Problem 5-3.

Turn back to Problem 4-1 (page 358). Record the Martin Company balance sheet changes in journal entries.

Problem 5-3—(Brain-teaser):

As part of your training in accounting, you must become able to extend the concepts and techniques you have learned into situations that require different methods of analysis. This problem provides such an opportunity to increase your flexibility and broaden your understanding. The background needed to solve this problem has been provided by the text, but the particular method of analysis required may at first seem unusual. Apply what you already have learned to this new situation.

Shown below are the comparative balance sheets of Senner Home Repairs, Inc., at 12/31/X1 and 12/31/X2, followed by some (but not all) of the company's summary journal entries for 19X2. You may assume that each entry given is a complete summary of its particular kind of 19X2 balance sheet changes. For example, Entry 1 is a complete summary of the company's 19X2 cash sales (though not a complete summary of all of its sales, for some were made on account). No unusual balance sheet changes occurred during 19X2; instead, all changes were of the normal kinds discussed in this and the previous chapter. The company's accountant made no errors. Determine all of the other summary journal entries made by Senner Home Repairs, Inc., during 19X2. Explain your answers.

Illustration 5-2

Senner Home Repairs, Inc.
Comparative Balance Sheets
12/31/X1 and 12/31/X2

Assets

	12/31/X1	12/31/X2
Current Assets:		
Cash	$ 3,500	$ 5,300
Accounts Receivable	6,800	4,500(1)
Supplies	11,200	9,800
Prepaid Insurance	900	500
Prepaid Taxes	1,300	1,400
Total Current Assets	$23,700	$21,500

Noncurrent Assets:

Land	$ 5,000	$ 5,000
Building	24,900	23,500
Equipment	36,300	39,900
Total Noncurrent Assets	$66,200	$68,400
Total Assets	$89,900	$89,900

Equities

Current Liabilities:

Accounts Payable	$ 5,900	$ 7,500
Wages Payable	1,200	1,400(2)
6% Note Payable—due 9/1/X2	10,000	–0–(3)
Interest Payable	300	–0–(3)
Total Current Liabilities	$17,400	$ 8,900
Noncurrent Liabilities:		
Mortgage Payable	15,000	14,700(3)
Total Liabilities	$32,400	$23,600
Stockholders' Equity	57,500	66,300
Total Equities	$89,900	$89,900

Notes:

1. Accounts Receivable represents amounts owed by customers for completed repair work. There were no partially completed repair jobs at either 12/31/X1 or 12/31/X2.

2. All employee wages are recorded as a liability before being paid.

3. All interest payable relates to the 6% note payable. Interest on the mortgage payable is paid on the last day of each month and is never recorded as a liability.

Purpose of Journal Entry	*Journal Entry*		
To record cash sales	1. Cash Stockholders' Equity	35,400	35,400
To record collection of accounts receivable	2. Cash Accounts Receivable	112,600	112,600
To record earning of wages by employees	3. Stockholders' Equity Wages Payable	71,000	71,000
To record purchase of supplies	4. Supplies Accounts Payable	43,800	43,800
To record depreciation of equipment	5. Stockholders' Equity Equipment	10,300	10,300
To record partial payment of mortgage principal	6. Mortgage Payable Cash	300	300
To record payment of interest on mortgage payable	7. Stockholders' Equity Cash	900	900
To record 19X2 taxes; $1,300 of these taxes had been prepaid in 19X1; the remaining $6,000 were paid in 19X2.	8. Stockholders' Equity Prepaid Taxes 9. Stockholders' Equity Cash	1,300 6,000	 1,300 6,000
To record payment of accounts payable	10. Accounts Payable Cash	56,100	56,100

Other data: The 6% note payable was paid (together with interest from 7/1/X1) on 9/1/X2.

No supplies were purchased for cash during 19X2.

All equipment purchased during 19X2 was purchased on account.

There were no purchases of buildings or insurance during 19X2. A cancellation of an insurance policy occurs when the insured exchanges his rights to insurance for a partial refund; such cancellations are rare. There were no sales of building nor cancellations of insurance during 19X2.

An appropriate line of attack for solving problems such as this is one similar to that used in Problem 4-6 (page 219). Prepare T-accounts for this firm and post all information given in the problem, including beginning and end balances, then reconstruct the missing elements in the T-accounts. In doing this you will find that typically the cash, accounts payable, and stockholders' equity accounts contain too many missing elements for this procedure to work with them, but it is efficient with other accounts.

Solutions

Solution 5-1:

1. Cash	8.50		6. Nuts	4.25	
Stockholders' Equity		8.50	Cash		4.25
2. Stockholders' Equity	3.50		7. Oil	0.85	
Nuts		3.50	Accounts Payable		0.85
3. Stockholders' Equity	1.00		8. Fuel	2.10	
Oil		1.00	Accounts Payable		2.10
4. Stockholders' Equity	2.00		9. Accounts Payable	2.50	
Fuel		2.00	Cash		2.50
5. Stockholders' Equity	0.20		10. Stockholders' Equity	0.75	
Stand		0.20	Cash		0.75

Solution 5-2:

1. Cash	64,000		8. Cash	1,800	
Stockholders' Equity		64,000	Stockholders' Equity		1,800
2. Land	5,000		9. Accounts Receivable	2,220	
Cash		5,000	Stockholders' Equity		2,220
3. Buildings	15,000		10. Stockholders' Equity	3,200	
Cash		15,000	Merchandise Inventory		3,200
4. Equipment	19,000		11. Stockholders' Equity	100	
Cash		19,000	Supplies		100
5. Merchandise			12. Stockholders' Equity	30	
Inventory	18,000		Buildings		30
Cash		18,000	13. Stockholders' Equity	50	
6. Merchandise			Equipment		50
Inventory	30,000		14. Stockholders' Equity	410	
Accounts Payable		30,000	Cash		410
7. Supplies	4,000				
Accounts Payable		4,000			

Solution 5-3:

The following solution is quite detailed in order to provide maximum help for students who are having difficulties; if you don't need this much help, feel free to skim some of the details.

11. Accounts receivable declined only $2,300 during 19X2 ($6,800 − $4,500 = $2,300), despite cash collections of accounts receivable totalling $112,600 (see Entry 2). Therefore, sales on account must have totalled $110,300 ($112,600 − $2,300 = $110,300).

Accounts Receivable	110,300	
Stockholders' Equity		110,300

(The 19X2 ledger accounts for this company are shown on the last page of this solution as a convenience to those students who solved this problem by direct use of ledger accounts.)

12. Wages payable increased by only $200 during 19X2 ($1,400 − $1,200 = $200), despite that employee wages for 19X2 totalled $71,000 (see Entry 3). Consequently, cash payments to employees must have totalled $70,800 ($71,000 − $200 = $70,800).

Wages Payable	70,800	
Cash		70,800

13. Supplies decreased by $1,400 during 19X2 ($11,200 − $9,800 = $1,400), despite purchases totalling $43,800 (see Entry 4). So $45,200 of supplies must have been used during the year ($43,800 + $1,400 = $45,200).

Stockholders' Equity	45,200	
Supplies		45,200

14. Equipment increased by $3,600 during 19X2 ($39,900 − $36,300 = $3,600), in spite of depreciation of equipment totalling $10,300 (see Entry 5). As a result, $13,900 of equipment must have been purchased during the year ($10,300 + $3,600 = $13,900).

Equipment	13,900	
Accounts Payable		13,900

15. Buildings decreased by $1,400 during the year ($24,900 − $23,500 = $1,400). Since there were no purchases or sales of buildings during 19X2, building depreciation must have totalled $1,400.

Stockholders' Equity	1,400	
Building		1,400

16. Prepaid insurance decreased by $400 during 19X2 ($900 − $500 = $400). There were no purchases or cancellations of insurance during the year, so prepaid insurance must have been written down a total of $400.

Stockholders' Equity	400	
Prepaid Insurance		400

The following were paid on 9/1/X2: (a) the $10,000 note payable, (b) the six months' interest that was payable at 12/31/X1 ($10,000 × 6% × 6/12 = $300), (c) an additional $400 interest for the eight months that the note was outstanding in 19X2 ($10,000 × 6% × 8/12 = $400).

17. Stockholders' Equity	400		To record the 19X2 interest fee
Interest Payable		400	
18. Interest Payable	700		To record payment of the 19X1 and
Cash		700	19X2 interest ($300 + $400 = $700)
19. 6% Note Payable	10,000		To record payment of the 6% Note
Cash		10,000	Payable

20. All taxes prepaid at 12/31/X1 were written down during 19X2 (see Entry 8). Yet $1,400 of taxes were prepaid at 12/31/X2. Accordingly, $1,400 of taxes must have been prepaid in 19X2.

Prepaid Taxes	1,400	
Cash		1,400

As you will see from the company's 19X2 ledger, the twenty journal entries given are sufficient to record all of the company's 19X2 balance sheet changes.

Illustration 5-3

Senner Home Repairs, Inc.
Ledger
For the Year 19X2

Cash			
√	3,500	(6)	300
(1)	35,400	(7)	900
(2)	112,600	(9)	6,000
		(10)	56,100
	151,500	(12)	70,800
		(18)	700
		(19)	10,000
		(20)	1,400
	146,200	◄—	146,200
√	5,300		

Accounts Receivable			
√	6,800	(2)	112,600
(11)	110,300		
	117,100		
	112,600		
√	4,500		

Supplies			
√	11,200	(13)	45,200
(4)	43,800		
	55,000		
	45,200		
√	9,800		

Prepaid Insurance			
√	900	(16)	400
	400		
√	500		

Prepaid Taxes			
√	1,300	(8)	1,300
(20)	1,400		
	2,700		
	1,300		
√	1,400		

Land			
√	5,000		

Building			
√	24,900	(15)	1,400
	1,400		
√	23,500		

Equipment			
√	36,300	(5)	10,300
(14)	13,900		
	50,200		
	10,300		
√	39,900		

Accounts Payable			
(10)	56,100	√	5,900
		(4)	43,800
		(14)	13,900
			63,600
			56,100
		√	7,500

Wages Payable			
(12)	70,800	√	1,200
		(3)	71,000
			72,200
			70,800
		√	1,400

6% Note Payable—due 9/1/X2			
(19)	10,000	√	10,000

Interest Payable			
(18)	700	√	300
		(17)	400
	700		700

Mortgage Payable			
(6)	300	√	15,000
			300
		√	14,700

Stockholders' Equity			
(3)	71,000	√	57,500
(5)	10,300	(1)	35,400
(7)	900	(11)	110,300
(8)	1,300		
(9)	6,000		203,200
(13)	45,200		
(15)	1,400		
(16)	400		
(17)	400		
	136,900	—►	136,900
		√	66,300

A special note: a few coincidental figures were deliberately used in this problem, partly because coincidental figures do appear from time to time in actual accounting work:

12/31/X2 Prepaid Taxes = Building depreciation
$$= 12/31/X2 \text{ Wages Payable} = \$1,400$$

19X2 Write-off of Prepaid Insurance
$$= 19X2 \text{ Interest Payable on the } 6\% \text{ Note Payable} = \$ \ 400$$

19X2 Payment of Mortgage Payable = 12/31/X1 Interest Payable = $ 300

No significance should be attached to these duplications of figures; they are unrelated to each other.

Ledger Technicalities

A few technical aspects of ledgers should be mentioned before we go any further.

Ruling
Reconsider the Senner Home Repairs, Inc. supplies account, as given on page 253, and the way in which its ending balance is obtained:

Supplies

√	11,200	(13)	45,200
(4)	43,800		
	55,000		
	45,200		
√	9,800		

This informal method of obtaining end-of-period balances works well, but it is not the only way accountants obtain end-of-period balances. Accountants often use a more formal process called *ruling*, which not only looks neater but makes ledger accounts more useful as analytical tools.

Ruling is a method of obtaining the end-of-period balance by inserting in the ledger account a figure just large enough to make the left and right sides equal. Here's how it's done:

Supplies

√	11,200	(13)	45,200
(4)	43,800	√	9,800
	55,000		55,000
√	9,800		

At first glance, this method may seem a little peculiar; however, it is quite workable once you get used to it. The supplies account has a balance because left and right sides aren't equal. The new figure, which is just large enough to make them balance, must *be* the balance. The left side totals $55,000 and the right side totals $45,200. Thus it takes $9,800 to make the two sides equal, and $9,800 is the new end-of-period balance in the supplies account. This $9,800 is shown (with a √ to indicate that it is a balance) on the right side. The two sides are then added, giving proof of the clerical accuracy of what the accountant has done. Double lines are drawn (to indicate that the $55,000 figures are summary totals of the information recorded above them) and the new $9,800 balance is recorded on the appropriate left side below the double lines, where it serves as the beginning balance for the next period. All this can be generalized:

Any Asset

√	Beginning balance	XXX	Reductions during period	XXXX
	Additions during period	XXXX	√ Ending balance	XX*
		XXXX		XXXX
√	New beginning balance	XX*		

Same figure.

Initially, use of this ruling technique will appear cumbersome to many students (and a bit old-fashioned or unfamiliar to some instructors). But there is an advantage to becoming familiar with ruling.

The ruled ledger account is *self-balancing*: its left and right sides are made to equal each other by inserting the ending balance on the lesser side. As will be demonstrated later, this self-balancing quality of the ruled ledger account allows you to use it as a convenient analytical tool. Suppose that you know all items that should appear on one side of a ruled ledger account and all but one of the items that should appear on the other side. Since the two sides must come to the same total, simple subtraction allows the amount of the missing item to be determined. Examples of this, including problem material, are given later in this chapter.

Inputs and outputs

The only tricky thing about ruling is the way in which the ending balance is first inserted on the "wrong" side to make left and right totals agree. Yet even this can be intuitively justified by considering the ledger account in terms of its inputs and outputs. For any given period, the inputs to a ledger account must be its beginning balance plus any additions to the account that occur during the period. The outputs of the ledger account must be any reductions plus the ending balance, which in effect is transferred to the next accounting period (where it becomes an input of that period). The result is as follows:

Any Asset

	Inputs			Outputs	
√	Beginning balance—1	XXX		Reductions—period 1	XXXX
	Additions—period 1	XXXX	√	Ending balance—1	XX*
		XXXX			XXXX
√	New beginning balance—2	XX*		Reductions—period 2	XXXXX
	Additions—period 2	XXXXX	√	New ending balance—2	XXX†
		XXXXX			XXXXX
√	Beginning balance—3	XXX†			

* *Same figure.*
† *Same figure.*

Ruling equity accounts

Equity accounts are ruled the same way as asset accounts, except, of course, that balances go on the opposite sides. Here is Senner Home Repairs, Inc.'s wages payable account:

Wages Payable

(12)	70,800	√		1,200
√	1,400	(3)		71,000
	72,200			72,200
		√		1,400

In general, here is the ruling for any equity account:

Any Equity

	Outputs			Inputs	
	Reductions—period 1	XXXX	√	Beginning balance—1	XX
√	Ending balance—1	XX*		Additions—period 1	XXXX
		XXXX			XXXX
			√	Beginning balance—2	XX*

**Same figure.*

This points out another equality in accounting. Not only do assets equal equities and left sides equal right sides, but outputs equal inputs.

Other examples of ruling

If there has been little activity in an account during a period, its ruling will prob-ably be more simple than the examples given so far. If no change has taken place in the account, no ruling need be done at all:

Land

√	5,000	

If there has been just one change that reduced the account balance to zero, the only ruling required is the drawing of double lines.

6% Note Payable—due 9/1/X2

(19)	10,000	√	10,000

Here are five other examples of correct ruling:

Accounts Receivable				*Building*			
√	6,800	(2)	112,600	√	24,900	(15)	1,400
(11)	110,300	√	4,500			√	23,500
	117,100		117,100	√	24,900		24,900
√	4,500			√	23,500		

Accounts Payable				*Mortgage Payable*			
(10)	56,100	√	5,900	(6)	300	√	15,000
		(4)	43,800	√	14,700		
√	7,500	(14)	13,900		15,000		15,000
	63,600		63,600				
		√	7,500			√	14,700

Interest Payable			
(18)	700	√	300
		(17)	400
	700		700

Debits and credits

Up until now we've been talking of "left" and "right" sides. This is perfectly correct, but accountants use different terms. When the accountant speaks of recording something on the left side of an account (increase asset or decrease equity) he *debits* the account. When the accountant speaks of recording something on the right side of an account (decrease asset or increase equity), he *credits* the account. For example, the Senner Home Repairs, Inc. accounts receivable account above had a $110,300 debit from Change 11 and a $112,600 credit from Change 2. The accounts payable account had a $56,100 debit from Change 10 and a $43,800 credit from Change 4.

In accounting jargon, "debit" and "credit" simply mean "left" and "right." Don't get the accountant's use of "credit" confused with the way the word is used in ordinary English ("Sam, you're a credit to your profession!"): remember, "credit" just means right side. And don't make the common error of associating a credit with an increase in an asset. Actually, credits are connected with decreases in assets and increases in equities. Don't get "debit" mixed up with "debt": "debit" just means left side.

Since left sides must equal right sides, debits must always equal credits. This is true of journal entries as well as ledger accounts. For instance:

	Debit	Credit
18. Interest Payable	700	
Cash		700

Interest payable is debited for $700; cash is credited for $700; total debits equal total credits.

Summary

All of this can be summarized as follows:

Left Debit	Right Credit
Asset increase	Asset decrease
Equity decrease	Equity increase
Asset input	Asset output
Equity output	Equity input

$$\text{Assets} = \text{Equities}$$
$$\text{Left} = \text{Right}$$
$$\text{Inputs} = \text{Outputs}$$
$$\text{Debits} = \text{Credits}$$

"Debit" and "credit" are often abbreviated. The standard abbreviations are "Dr." and "Cr.," respectively.

Ownership Account Details

Throughout the previous chapters, an important distinction has been made between two different kinds of equities:

1. Liabilities: the rights of creditors, arising from debts owed to them by the company.

2. Owners' equity: the residual rights of the owners of the company to whatever is left after the rights of creditors have been satisfied.

Now a further distinction will be made between different kinds of owners' equities.

In a corporation, the owners are stockholders; therefore, the account stockholders' equity has been used to reflect owners' equity. For some purposes, such a single account for owners' equity is sufficient, but many companies use more than one account to reflect ownership. There is nothing mysterious about this; a similar thing is done with liabilities. It is possible to group all of the current liabilities of Senner Home Repairs, Inc., in a single account called "current liabilities." In a very simple company, this might be all that is needed; but in more complicated companies, useful information is provided by dividing the details of current liabilities into four different accounts. Similarly, *accountants believe it useful to divide the details of owners' equity into two or more accounts,* among which are accounts called "capital stock" and "retained earnings." These will be defined in the material to follow.

Single proprietorships

Many small businesses are one-man companies operated by their owners (or owners and their wives). The technical name for such a firm is a *single proprietorship.* It is common for a single proprietor to employ a single owner's equity account, often merely using his own name for this purpose. As an example, suppose that Senner Home Repairs, Inc., is a single proprietorship owned by Charles Roy Senner. The stockholders' equity account would not be used. Instead, the account title might simply be "C. R. Senner."

Often more detail than this is reported. The following simplified example gives a summary of all the 19X1 balance sheet changes of Sisk Shop that affected its owner's equity.

1. On 1/3/X1, O. N. Sisk founded the company by investing $80,000 cash.
2. 19X1 sales totalled $122,000, all for cash.
3. During 19X1, $88,000 of merchandise and $15,000 of prepaid rent were used up in operations.
4. During 19X1, Mr. Sisk withdrew a total of $9,000 for his personal use.

The appropriate journal entries for this single proprietorship might be:

1. Cash	80,000	
O. N. Sisk		80,000
2. Cash	122,000	
O. N. Sisk		122,000
3. O. N. Sisk	88,000	
Merchandise Inventory		88,000
O. N. Sisk	15,000	
Prepaid Rent		15,000
4. O. N. Sisk	9,000	
Cash		9,000

If the entries are made this way, they exactly parallel those that have been made for corporations. The only difference is that there is a single proprietor instead of a group of stockholders. Therefore, the ownership account is O. N. Sisk instead of stockholders' equity. Here is this owner's equity account at 12/31/X1:

O. N. Sisk

(3)	88,000	(1)	80,000
(3)	15,000	(2)	122,000
(4)	9,000		
√	90,000		
	202,000		202,000
		√	90,000

Capital and retained earnings accounts

There were two main things that affected the owner's equity of Sisk Shop during 19X1: (1) Mr. Sisk's initial investment of $80,000, and (2) operations that generated a net profit of $19,000 (122,000 − 88,000 − 15,000 = 19,000). These, together with withdrawals totalling $9,000, resulted in a net 19X1 increase in ownership of $10,000 (90,000 − 80,000 = 10,000 = 19,000 − 9,000). This increase in owners' equity is usually called a *retention of earnings*—a keeping of profits in the business instead of withdrawing them. Strictly speaking, such language is imprecise: profits are neither withdrawn nor retained; what is withdrawn or retained is cash. Nonetheless, the $10,000 would ordinarily be called *retained earnings*.

Mr. Sisk's initial investment of $80,000 is a very different kind of ownership change than the others. It will usually represent an amount that he intends to be a permanent investment in the company, a minimum needed to keep the company operating at its expected level of activity. In contrast, he may feel free to withdraw cash equal to the total retained earnings whenever he so chooses. If the proprietor makes this kind of distinction, he may wish to *divide* owner's equity to reflect these two different elements. He may wish to employ:

1. An account to reflect his permanent investment ($80,000).
2. An account to reflect all accumulated profits ($10,000).

A typical name for the permanent investment account would be O. N. Sisk—Capital; a typical name for the accumulated profits account would be O. N. Sisk—Retained Earnings. Since there is only one proprietor, there would be no confusion if O. N. Sisk were omitted and the accounts were called Capital and Retained Earnings.

Example of capital and retained earnings in a single proprietorship

Here are the previous journal entries for Sisk Shop. This time, details of the main changes in owner's equity are indicated:

1. Cash	80,000	
O. N. Sisk—Capital		80,000
2. Cash	122,000	
O. N. Sisk—Retained Earnings		122,000
3. O. N. Sisk—Retained Earnings	88,000	
Merchandise Inventory		88,000
O. N. Sisk—Retained Earnings	15,000	
Prepaid Rent		15,000
4. O. N. Sisk—Retained Earnings	9,000	
Cash		9,000

And here are the same journal entries in more simple terms:

1.	Cash	80,000	
	Capital		80,000
2.	Cash	122,000	
	Retained Earnings		122,000
3.	Retained Earnings	88,000	
	Merchandise Inventory		88,000
	Retained Earnings	15,000	
	Prepaid Rent		15,000
4.	Retained Earnings	9,000	
	Cash		9,000

Below are the 12/31/X1 ledger accounts, using the abbreviated account titles:

Capital	*Retained Earnings*

	(1) √ 80,000		

(3)	88,000	(2)	122,000
(3)	15,000		
(4)	9,000		
√	10,000		
	122,000		122,000
		√	10,000

Be aware that these two accounts contain, in total, exactly the same information as did the single account O. N. Sisk. All that has happened is that the total information has now been sorted into two different containers. On Sisk Shop's 12/31/X1 balance sheet, the owner's equity would appear as follows:

Total Liabilities.			$ XXX
Owner's Equity:			
Capital		$80,000	
Retained Earnings		10,000	90,000
Total Equities			$ XXX

Partnerships

A *partnership* is a business jointly owned by two or more individuals who share its profits and losses (and who have not gone through the legal steps to form a corporation). The details of partnership accounting can become very complicated, but there is only one essential difference on the balance sheet between partnership and single proprietorship accounting: there will most likely be individual accounts for the capital and retained earnings of each partner. Accordingly, if there are three partners, there may be three capital accounts and three retained earnings accounts, each one identified by the name of the appropriate partner.

Corporations

Differences between corporations and other forms of business enterprise were discussed on pages 18–20. The key point to remember is that the corporation has limited liability—its owners (the stockholders) ordinarily cannot be sued for the company's debts. For this reason, it is important for the protection of creditors that the initial investment of the owners be maintained as nearly intact as possible; this initial investment serves as a "cushion" to ensure sufficient funds to repay creditors even if the company should experience financial difficulties (as does any subsequent investment by the owners that is intended to be permanent). Usually there are legal restrictions on a corporation's paying dividends in excess of accumulated profits.[1]

One consequence of this is that corporation accountants always distinguish between capital and retained earnings, if only to make sure that such legal restrictions are satisfied. The capital account is usually called either Capital Stock or Common Stock. This book will use the former name. The accumulated profits account is called Retained Earnings. At one time, the alternate name "Earned Surplus" was widely employed. But this name suggests (often incorrectly) that an amount equal to total retained earnings is no longer needed by the company and might best be distributed as dividends. (Actually, most companies find it necessary to reinvest at least part of their profits in expansion or improvement, leaving only a portion of profits to be reflected in dividends.) Accordingly, the name "Earned Surplus" no longer appears on most balance sheets.

Example of capital stock and retained earnings in a corporation

Assume the same facts as in the previous example, except that Sisk Shop is a corporation. The appropriate journal entries would be as follows:

1. Cash	80,000		3. Retained Earnings	88,000	
Capital Stock		80,000	Merchandise		
2. Cash	122,000		Inventory		88,000
Retained Earnings		122,000	Retained Earnings	15,000	
			Prepaid Rent		15,000
			4. Retained Earnings	9,000	
			Cash		9,000

The *only difference* between these entries and those made in earlier chapters is that the accounts capital stock and retained earnings have been used instead of the account stockholders' equity. In this example, the retained earnings account has been used more often then the capital stock account, which is almost always the case because events affect profits much more frequently than permanent investments by the owners. This suggests a handy rule of thumb: *if a balance sheet change affects stockholders' equity, always use the retained earnings account unless a permanent investment by the stockholders is involved.* (The next section outlines the main exceptions

---

[1] At this point I am deliberately skirting some complicated legal issues. Under the laws of many states, there are *restrictions* on payments of dividends in excess of accumulated profits, but such dividends are far from being altogether prohibited. This, though, leads into matters that would require far too much space to discuss adequately. For simplicity, I will assume that none of the firms discussed elsewhere in this book pay dividends in excess of accumulated profits. This is the usual practice, anyway, except for firms that are in the process of going out of business.

to this rule, but these exceptions will thereafter be ignored in this book; you may rely on this rule of thumb in all subsequent chapters.)

At 12/31/X1, the related ledger accounts would look as follows:

Capital Stock			*Retained Earnings*	
	(1) √ 80,000	(3) 88,000	(2) 122,000	
		(3) 15,000		
		(4) 9,000		
		√ 10,000		
		122,000	122,000	
			√ 10,000	

Notice how these entries and the ledger accounts exactly parallel those for the single proprietorship. On the 12/31/X1 balance sheet, stockholders' equity would be reported as follows:

Total Liabilities.		$ XXX
Stockholders' Equity:		
Capital Stock.	$80,000	
Retained Earnings	10,000	90,000
Total Equities		$ XXX

The remainder of this book will confine itself to a discussion of corporation accounting rather than single proprietorship accounting. All corporations divide stockholders' equity into at least two parts: capital stock and retained earnings, and we shall henceforth do the same.

Problem for Study and Self-Examination

Problem 5-4:

Turn back to Problem 4-1 (page 194). Record the Martin Company balance sheet changes in journal entries, using the accounts Capital Stock and Retained Earnings. Prepare ledger accounts for these two accounts for March 1-3, 19X1.

Solution

Solution 5-4:

If a balance sheet change affects stockholders' equity, always use the retained earnings account, unless a permanent investment by the stockholders is involved.

1. Cash	64,000		8. Cash		1,800	
Capital Stock		64,000	Retained Earnings			1,800
2. Land	5,000		9. Accounts Receivable		2,220	
Cash		5,000	Retained Earnings			2,220
3. Buildings	15,000		10. Retained Earnings		3,200	
Cash		15,000	Merchandise Inventory			3,200
4. Equipment	19,000		11. Retained Earnings		100	
Cash		19,000	Supplies			100
5. Merchandise Inventory	18,000		12. Retained Earnings		30	
Cash		18,000	Buildings			30
6. Merchandise Inventory	30,000		13. Retained Earnings		50	
Accounts Payable		30,000	Equipment			50
7. Supplies	4,000		14. Retained Earnings		410	
Accounts Payable		4,000	Cash			410

Capital Stock			Retained Services			
	(1) √	64,000	(10)	3,200	(8)	1,800
			(11)	100	(9)	2,220
			(12)	30		
			(13)	50		
			(14)	410		
			√	230		
				4,020		4,020
					√	230

Stockholders' Equity:
Further Complications

Unfortunately, because of legal requirements, many corporations divide things even further. During the early days of the corporation in America, firms often associated a dollar amount with each share of stock. This was called the stock's *par value,* originally representing the intended issue price per share. Gradually the original significance disappeared, partly because the par-value device was abused. For example, the practice developed of selling stock at supposedly "bargain" prices, lower than par value—a meaningless bargain, as the following example demonstrates:

Case A: The initial stockholders' equity is represented by 20,000 shares of $50-par capital stock, sold at $50 per share.

Case B: The initial stockholders' equity is represented by 20,000 shares of $100-par capital stock, sold at the "bargain" price of $50 per share.

In both cases, stockholders have invested a total of $1,000,000. In both cases, an individual stockholder who has invested $10,000 owns 1/100th of the company, and the size of the total company is the same in both cases. The only difference is that, in Case B, a fictitious figure has been associated with the shares.

"Bargains" similar to Case B proved popular (much as they still do in fictitious "cents off" promotions in grocery stores). These abuses, together with such things as attempts to avoid state taxes on par values, eventually rendered the whole par-value concept meaningless, at least from the standpoint of investors. The same fate befell the similar notion of a stock as having no par value, but having instead a *stated value,* set by the board of directors and serving much the same purpose as a par value.

Meanwhile the capital stock of most firms ended up having a par value or (less frequently) a stated value associated with it, and various state legislatures passed corporation codes requiring balance sheet disclosure of this value. These laws are still on the books; it is quite possible that a firm will issue capital stock at a price other than its par or stated value, then have to comply with such disclosure requirements. In Chapter One (pages 23–27) a distinction was made between resource-allocation and institutional uses of accounting. Par and stated values are good examples of data that have institutional significance, even though they are useless for resource-allocation purposes.[2]

Firms rarely issue their capital stock at prices less than their par or stated values—there are legal reasons why doing so threatens the limited liability protection that stockholders usually enjoy; in some cases there is a tax disadvantage, too. But firms often issue their shares at prices greater than the par or stated values. If Sisk Shop issued 1,000 shares of capital stock for the same $80,000 shown in previous examples, but with a par value of only $50 per share, it would be necessary under many state laws to record the capital stock at its total par value (1,000 × $50 = $50,000):

Cash	50,000	
Capital Stock		50,000

The remaining $30,000 (80,000 − 50,000 = 30,000) would have to be recorded as a special kind of stockholders' equity. It is common for the term "premium on capital stock" to be used if there is an excess over par, and for "discount on capital stock" to be used in rare cases where the issue price is less than par value:

Cash	30,000	
Premium on Capital Stock		30,000

Acceptable alternate titles for premium on capital stock include "capital stock—premium," "capital stock—amount received in excess of par," "paid-in capital in

---

[2] The precise legal significance of par and stated values, together with legal limitations placed on these values, seems to vary slightly from state to state. The issues involved here are too complicated and specialized for their discussion to be appropriate in an elementary text. The same is true of several other issues mentioned in this section, including the sales of capital stock at prices less than par or stated value and the payments of dividends in excess of accumulated profits.

excess of par," "capital in excess of par," or "capital stock—amount received in excess of stated value," etc. The titles "capital in excess of par" (or stated value) and "capital surplus" seem to be the most common. Although it is often encountered, the alternate title "capital surplus" is really a misnomer, since it incorrectly implies that the amount so labeled represents some kind of unneeded excess. Actually, any amount invested by stockholders above par or stated value usually is intended by them to be part of the permanent ownership investment in the firm. Nonetheless, the term "capital surplus" is still fairly widely used.

An acceptable presentation of the premium account on the balance sheet would be as follows:

Total Liabilities.		$ XXX
Stockholders' Equity:		
Capital Stock—at Par	$50,000	
Capital Stock—Premium	30,000	
Retained Earnings	10,000	90,000
Total Equities		$ XXX

Any discount would be *subtracted* from the par value, instead of added to it. For instance, if Sisk Shop capital stock had a stated value of $100 per share, the stockholder's equity section would appear somewhat as follows:

Total Liabilities		$ XXX
Stockholders' Equity:		
Capital Stock—at Stated Value	$100,000	
Discount on Capital Stock	(20,000)	
Retained Earnings.	10,000	90,000
Total Equities		$ XXX

Here, just as in all previous cases, the total owners' equity is $90,000 and the total permanent investment is $80,000. But the stated value happens to be greater than the total permanent investment, so a subtraction is required to arrive at the true amount received upon issue of the shares.

From the standpoint of the investor, par values and stated values are both without significance. Whenever possible, the reader should just mentally add together the amounts for capital stock and any related premium (or subtract the rare discount) to obtain the true figure for the permanent investment of stockholders. Unfortunately as you will see in Problem 5-5, this is not always possible.

More complications

1. Besides par or stated values, most companies are required to report the total number of shares they are authorized to issue under their official corporate charter (the document issued by a governmental body authorizing the company's existence as a corporation—see page 18). There is often considerable related technical legal language, which tends to intimidate the inexperienced reader, in the stockholders' equity section of a published balance sheet.

2. A number of other specialized capital stock and retained earnings accounts are sometimes used. The possibilities are too complicated to discuss thoroughly in a text of this scope; however, a few brief examples should be given:

(a) Many companies issue more than one kind of capital stock. Differences in capital stock almost always involve differences in stockholder rights. As shown on page 19, the ordinary common stockholder is entitled to a proportionate vote in the conduct of the company's affairs (though this usually amounts to little more than a right to vote in the election of the board of directors); he is also entitled to a proportionate share in any dividend distributions and a proportionate share in the proceeds, should the company be sold.

Some companies issue two kinds of common stock: one having all these rights and the other having all rights except the right to vote. One reason for issuing nonvoting common stock is that it allows individuals who control a company to raise additional permanent capital without sharing (and perhaps losing) their control.

A very important type of nonvoting stock is called *preferred stock*. The investors in preferred stock are guaranteed that before any other group of stockholders receive dividends, they will receive a minimum dividend. Also, should the company be sold, the preferred stockholders are entitled to recover their initial investment (or some other prearranged amount) before the common stockholders share in the proceeds; the amount to which preferred stockholders are entitled is called the *liquidation value* of the preferred stock. In exchange for this security, preferred stockholders usually give up their right to vote and accept a limitation on the amount of dividends they will be entitled to receive in any one year (therefore, the minimum dividend also usually becomes the maximum dividend). To illustrate, a $50-par, 6 percent preferred stock would usually be nonvoting and limited to total dividends of $3 per share per year ($50 \times 6\% = \$3$). However, different kinds of preferred stock have been invented, and it is risky to generalize. Corporations have been known to issue as many as six kinds of preferred stock (as well as two kinds of common stock), each of which had different rights.

Many kinds of preferred stock are *cumulative*. As we have seen in earlier chapters, a corporation's board of directors is under no obligation to declare dividends in any year if, in its judgment, doing so would be unwise. Thus it would be possible for preferred stockholders to receive no dividends at all during one or more years. When the company begins to pay dividends again, the preferred stockholders will receive dividends before the common stockholders do. But without special agreement, they would receive dividends for only the current period. A *cumulative preferred stock* gives the preferred stockholder the right to receive all omitted dividends (formally known as *dividends in arrears*) before common stockholders receive any dividends. For example, suppose that the firm that issued the $50-par, 6 percent preferred stock paid no dividends at all for three years. If the preferred stock were cumulative, dividends in arrears of $3 \times 3 = \$9$ per share plus the current dividend would have to be paid on each preferred share before common stockholders would be allowed to receive any dividends; if the preferred stock were not cumulative, only the current dividend would have to be paid on preferred stock.

Some authors regard preferred stock as being half-way between common stock and bonds payable, and certainly a regular, limited preferred dividend resembles interest on a bond. Nevertheless, preferred stock and common stock both constitute what stockholders intend as a permanent investment, and are classified as kinds of capital stock. (In subsequent chapters, you may interpret the account Capital Stock as reflecting the total of all common stock, preferred stock, and any premiums or discounts upon either.)

(b) Many companies subdivide their retained earnings. Consider the Sisk Shop's 12/31/X1 retained earnings of $10,000. It may be that the entire $10,000 reflects cash that could be paid out in dividends without harming the company's operations. More likely, though, management had good reasons for paying only $9,000 of dividends, even though 19X1 profits totalled $19,000. Possibly the company must keep expanding if it is to remain efficient, and perhaps at least $8,000 is needed for expansion. If so, management may wish to tell stockholders that only $2,000 of total retained earnings reflect possible future dividends. One way to do this is to divide retained earnings into two accounts: "free" retained earnings of $2,000, and "reserved" retained earnings of $8,000. To do this, it is necessary to make the following journal entry. (Notice that decreases in retained earnings are shown on the left, just as they are with any equity.)

Retained Earnings	8,000	
Reserve for Expansion		8,000

If you prefer, you can use the slightly more cumbersome titles "retained earnings—unappropriated" and "retained earnings—reserve for expansion."

Retained Earnings				*Reserve for Expansion*	
(3)	88,000	(2)	122,000		(5) √ 8,000
(3)	15,000				
(4)	9,000				
(5)	8,000				
√	2,000				
	122,000		122,000		
		√	2,000		

The 12/31/X1 stockholders' equity section of Sisk Shop would appear essentially as follows (assuming that shares without a par value were issued):

Total Liabilities.		$ XXX
Stockholders' Equity:		
Capital Stock.	$80,000	
Retained Earnings—Unappropriated	2,000	
Retained Earnings—Reserved for Expansion.	8,000	90,000
Total Equities		$ XXX

or, more simply:

Total Liabilities.		$ XXX
Stockholders' Equity:		
Capital Stock.	$80,000	
Retained Earnings	2,000	
Reserve for Expansion	8,000	90,000
Total Equities		$ XXX

The $8,000 appropriation of retained earnings does not result in a change in any of Sisk Shop's assets or liabilities, nor for that matter does it suggest that specific assets have been set aside exclusively for expansion. When the reserve for expansion is no longer required (once the expansion has been completed), it is merely transferred back to retained earnings by the following journal entry:

> Reserve for Expansion   8,000
> 　　Retained Earnings　　　　　8,000

An almost limitless variety of such reserves may be employed. What makes things more confusing is that the word "reserve" is sometimes used in other senses on balance sheets—to describe certain kinds of liabilities, for example.

(c) For various reasons that are too complicated to discuss here, some corporations occasionally repurchase shares of their own stock in the stock market. Such shares are called *treasury stock*. Were the firm to purchase shares of another company, it would acquire an asset because it would obtain future benefits and rights from that company. But when it repurchases its own shares, the corporation does not acquire an asset, for it is pointless to say that a company has rights from itself and obligations to itself! Instead, the purchase should be treated for what it is: merely a cancellation of some of the company's obligations to its stockholders and a partial reduction in the size of the company's owners' equity. If Sisk Shop repurchased five shares of its own stock at $100 per share, the simplest way to reflect the resulting contraction in stockholders' equity would be as follows. (Notice that "treasury stock" is reported at cost and subtracted from total stockholders' equity.)

> Treasury Stock   500
> 　　Cash　　　　　　　500

Total Liabilities.		$ XXX
Stockholders' Equity:		
Capital Stock.	$80,000	
Retained Earnings	10,000	
Total	$90,000	
Less: Treasury Stock	500	89,500
Total Equities		$ XXX

The laws of certain states require that retained earnings be reserved in an amount equal to the cost of treasury stock held by the company. The goal once again is to protect creditors from the company's contracting stockholders' equity below the original permanent investment. Were Sisk Shop incorporated in a state having such laws, its stockholders' equity section might appear as follows:

Total Liabilities.		$ XXX
Stockholders' Equity:		
Capital Stock.	$80,000	
Retained Earnings	9,500	
Reserve for Treasury Stock.	500	
Total	90,000	
Less: Treasury Stock	500	89,500
Total Equities		$ XXX

The cost of treasury stock is not deducted from stockholders' equity twice. Instead, it is deducted once, and the retained earnings account is subdivided. This subdivision of retained earnings is another example of something that has institutional significance, even though it may lack resource-allocation significance.

Stock splits

Often the management of a corporation is keenly interested in maintaining as healthy a market as possible for the firm's stock. Shares of stock become progressively less marketable after their price increases beyond a certain point. One reason for this is that there are economies to buying shares in hundred-share blocks. If a stock is selling for, say, $300 a share, purchase of a hundred-share block requires an investment beyond the capacity of many investors.

The way to handle this problem is simple: the firm whose stock seems overpriced on the stock market simply issues *additional shares* pro rata to all of its stockholders. For example, suppose that Price-Rensselaer Corporation's stockholders' equity is composed as follows:

Capital Stock (20,000 shares, $50 par)	$1,000,000
Capital in Excess of Par	2,200,000
Retained Earnings .	3,242,000
Total .	$6,442,000

and that the firm's stock is selling for $420 per share. Upon receiving the approval of its stockholders, the firm could issue each stockholder three additional shares for each share he owns, resulting in four times as many outstanding shares. Each individual stockholder would retain the same relative rights that he had had before—the status of his investment would be unchanged, even though he'd have a greater number of shares in evidence of it. But the market price per share could be expected to drop to about $420 ÷ 4, or $105 per share. Since shares are more saleable at lower prices, and since the market usually responds favorably to this kind of action, the market price might end up being a bit higher than $105 per share. Thus the issue of additional shares would have slightly improved each stockholder's market position.

Such a pro rata issue of additional shares to all stockholders is called a *stock split*; the one described above is called a "four-for-one split." Price-Rensselaer Corporation would not need to make any journal entry to record this split, though ordinarily it would simultaneously reduce the par value of its shares proportionately, to $12.50 ($50.00 ÷ 4) per share. If it did, its stockholders' equity section would become:

Capital Stock (80,000 shares, $12.50 par)	$1,000,000
Capital in Excess of Par	2,200,000
Retained Earnings	3,242,000
Total	$6,442,000

Notice that this stock split affected only the number of shares outstanding and their par value. It did not affect retained earnings, nor did it change the *historical cost* to the stockholders of their shares (even if it served to improve the total current market value of their shares).

Stock dividends

But one kind of stock split *is* recorded as affecting the firm's retained earnings. Many firms make a practice of conducting very small stock splits, sometimes on an annual basis. For instance, a firm might split its shares 101 for 100, giving each stockholder who held 100 shares one share more.[3] Often after a very small stock split like this, the market price per share will not decrease and the total market value of any investor's holdings will have increased by 101/100. Because of this increase, such small stock splits can benefit stockholders (at least in the short run) in almost the same way that a cash dividend would. Consequently such small stock splits are called *stock dividends*. Firms often issue stock dividends when internal needs for cash prevent payment of cash dividends.

Example

Mr. Melvin Halleck is an investor who owns 500 shares of Price-Rensselaer Corporation common stock. The market price of this stock is $108 per share. On 6/30/X3 the firm declares a one percent stock dividend (splitting its stock 101 for 100), and Mr. Halleck receives five additional shares. If the market price remained constant at $108, Mr. Halleck could sell these five additional shares for about $108 × 5 = $540 and still have an investment with the same total market value ($54,000) as before the stock split. Although his proportionate rights with respect to other stockholders will have declined slightly, he may consider the result of the stock split as satisfactory as

---

[3] Problems of fractional shares resulting from holdings that are not in even 100-share lots are, for brevity, ignored in this discussion. So are dividend distributions of the shares of other firms.

a \$540 cash dividend. He would speak of this split as a "1% stock dividend." Similarly, a 105 for 100 stock split would be called a "5% stock dividend."

Recording of stock dividends

Even though they really are stock splits, stock dividends are recorded by the firm as though they were dividends—in fact, firms are required to do so by the Accounting Principles Board (see pages 36–37). This requirement is a bit controversial, but the reasoning behind it seems to be that, since investors believe that these small splits are dividends and since the firm encourages that belief, they should be recorded as dividends. Otherwise the firm would be free to *seem* to pay large dividends without incurring any accounting consequences whatever since, as we have seen, no journal entry at all is required in response to a stock split.[4]

The amount at which the stock dividend is recorded should not be less than the market price of the additional shares issued. If Price-Rensselaer Corporation recorded its 1% stock dividend at \$108 per share, it would make the following entry:

Retained Earnings (800 shares @ \$108)	86,400	
Capital Stock (800 shares @ 12.50, par)		10,000
Capital in Excess of Par		76,400

In an advanced course you would study stock dividends and other kinds of stock splits in much greater detail than this. Here, it will suffice that you know what these things are, and that you are aware of the true economic significance of stock splits.

Stock dividends and cash dividends contrasted

This economic significance is best emphasized by contrasting a stock split with a cash dividend. A cash dividend results in a decrease in the firm's total assets and a corresponding decrease in the total investment of owners. In exchange, each owner receives a new asset: cash. In contrast, after a stock split, the total assets of the firm remain the same (except for whatever expenditure was necessary to print the new certificates).[5] Accordingly, there is no decrease in the total investment of owners, and all the investors receive is some new evidence of their previous ownership rights. A stock split is not a dividend, *and this is as much true of a so-called stock dividend as it is of any other kind of stock split,* even though the firm is required to record a stock dividend as though it were a true dividend.

A few words of reassurance

By now, many readers may have begun to suspect that accounting for stockholders' equity can be fairly complicated. Such suspicions are correct, although accounting

---

[4]A skeptic might reply that the informed reader of financial statements does not believe that stock dividends really are dividends, and that the effect of this rule is to lend official authority to the folly of uninformed investors.

[5] To be sure, in the previous journal entry the stock dividend was recorded by reducing retained earnings. But a corresponding increase was recorded in the two other stockholders' equity accounts, so that total stockholders' equity was unaffected by the stock dividend.

and finance majors usually have little difficulty mastering these complications.[6] But from the standpoint of an investor, these complications are usually irrelevant. Don't be intimidated by the complicated legal language in some stockholders' equity sections. For that matter, don't allow yourself to be frightened by any of the stockholders' equity complications. With the possible exception of the distinction between preferred and common stock, for resource-allocation purposes investors dealing with published balance sheets usually need be concerned only with changes in total stockholders' equity and why the changes occurred. Almost always, these changes can be understood without understanding the precise details of the complications discussed in this section. These details are of considerable legal significance, and they are important to accountants for institutional reasons, but the average investor should not be overawed by them.

A major purpose of this book is to equip you with what you need in order to read financial statements knowledgeably. For this, all you need to know of these complications is the basic background information in this section; further details are better relegated to an advanced course. Accordingly, except in the following problems, the remainder of this book will employ only two stockholders' equity accounts: Capital Stock and Retained Earnings.

Problems for Study and Self-Examination

Problem 5-5:
The stockholders' equity section of King Products, Inc., is shown in Illustration 5-4. (This illustration is based on some actual examples from published balance sheets.) Explain as best you can the significance of each figure and each account.

Illustration 5-4

King Products, Inc.
Stockholders' Equity
12/31/X1

$2 Cumulative Preferred Stock, par value $1 per share—authorized 1,500,000 shares, issued 1,200,000 shares (preference in involuntary liquidation $60 per share—$72,000,000)	$ 1,200,000
Common Stock, no-par, stated value $1 per share—authorized 25,000,000 shares, issued 16,000,000 shares	16,000,000
Capital Surplus	125,300,000
Reserve for Contingencies	20,000,000
Reserve for Self-Insurance	5,200,000
Reserve for Treasury Stock	4,300,000
Retained Earnings	122,000,000
Total	$294,000,000
Less: Cost of Common Stock Held in the Treasury (500,000 shares)	4,300,000
Total Stockholders' Equity	$289,700,000

---

[6] In fact, some people—the author included—find much the same pleasure in solving really involved stockholders' equity situations as other people find in solving crossword puzzles or chess problems.

Problem 5-6:

On 1/1/X7 Mr. Casmir Brademas owned 100 shares of the common stock of South Bend Resonator, Inc., for which he had paid $8,190 in 19X3. As of 1/1/X7 the firm's stockholders' equity consisted of the following:

Capital Stock, 50,000 shares issued and outstanding at a stated value of $15 per share	$ 750,000
Capital in Excess of Stated Value	2,225,000
Retained Earnings	3,247,316
Total	$6,222,316

A. On 3/31/X7 the firm conducted a three-for-one stock split, by giving each stockholder two additional shares of common stock for each share that they had previously owned. Simultaneously, the firm reduced the stated value of its stock to $5 per share. Prior to this stock split, the market price of the firm's shares had been $228; after the stock split it was $76 per share.

    1. The firm used the ledger account "Capital Stock—$15 Stated Value" prior to 3/31/X7; what entry should it have made as of 3/31/X7?

    2. What effect did this stock split have on Mr. Brademas' investment?

    3. Were Mr. Brademas to sell one share of stock for $76 on 4/1/X7, what journal entry should he make to record this sale?

B. Through profitable operations, the firm's retained earnings had increased to $3,423,991 by 6/30/X7. On 7/1/X7 the firm declared and paid a cash dividend of 80¢ per share.

    1. What entry should the firm have made as of 7/1/X7?

    2. How should the firm's stockholders' equity be reported immediately after this cash dividend?

    3. What effect did this cash dividend have on Mr. Brademas' investment?

C. Through profitable operations, the firm's retained earnings had increased to $3,456,702 by 9/30/X7. On 10/1/X7 the firm declared and distributed a 5% stock dividend—that is, it gave the stockholders five additional shares for each hundred shares that they had previously owned. The market price of the firm's stock, both before and after this stock dividend, was $76 per share.

    1. What entry should the firm make as of 10/1/X7?

    2. How should the firm's stockholders' equity be reported immediately after this stock dividend?

    3. What effect did this stock dividend have on Mr. Brademas' investment?

    4. Were Mr. Brademas to sell one share of stock for $76 on 10/2/X7, what journal entry should he make to record this transaction?

Solutions

Solution 5-5:

The company has two kinds of capital stock:

1. One kind of capital stock is a preferred stock with a nominal par value of $1 per share. Investors in this stock are entitled to a regular annual dividend (limited to $2 per share) before common stockholders may receive any dividends. Should the company go bankrupt, preferred stockholders would be entitled to $60 per share of the proceeds that resulted from dissolving the company—if that much were left after the claims of creditors had been satisfied. Such disclosure of liquidation values is recommended by the Accounting Principle Board in all cases where liquidation values differ significantly from par or stated values. Presumably, the preferred stockholders lack a vote in the election of the board of directors.

2. The other kind of capital stock is a common stock with no par value, but a nominal stated value of $1 per share that corresponds to a par value. As long as annual preferred dividends of $2 per share are paid, the amount of dividends that may be paid to common stockholders is restrained only by the remaining amount of retained earnings, whatever assets are available for payment of dividends, and whatever additional restraints the board of directors wishes to impose. Were the company to be liquidated, common stockholders would receive anything left over after the claims of creditors and preferred stockholders had been satisfied. The common stockholders presumably have a right to vote in the election of the board of directors.

Legal information has been provided concerning the number of shares of each kind of capital stock authorized to be issued under the company's corporate charter and the number of shares actually issued (including treasury shares). The total issue price of all preferred and common shares outstanding, including the treasury shares, is:

Preferred Stock	$ 1,200,000
Common Stock	16,000,000
"Capital Surplus"	125,300,000
Total	$142,500,000

The relatively enormous figure for capital surplus represents the difference between the total actual investment of stockholders and the artificial par-value and stated-value amounts. "Capital surplus" is a misleading title, but it is still occasionally used.

There is no way to tell from this stockholders' equity section exactly how much was invested by common stockholders and how much by preferred stockholders. (This situation is not uncommon.) All you know for sure is that the combined preferred–common investment totalled $142,500,000. Since the preferred stock has a value in liquidation of $60 per share, it may be that the preferred stockholders invested approximately $72,000,000 (1,200,000 shares at $60 = $72,000,000), and the common stockholders approximately $70,500,000 (142,500,000 − 72,000,000 = 70,500,000). But there is no way here to be sure.

The information concerning treasury stock reveals that the company repurchased 500,000 shares of its own common stock, thereby limiting the shares of common stock actually outstanding to 16,000,000 − 500,000 = 15,500,000, and the actual total investment of stockholders to $142,500,000 − $4,300,000 = $138,200,000. Under state law, an amount of retained earnings equal to the purchase price of this treasury stock must be specifically designated as not reflecting possible dividends—a relatively unimportant matter in this case, since total retained earnings are:

Unappropriated	$122,000,000
Reserve for Contingencies	20,000,000
Reserve for Self-Insurance	5,200,000
Reserve for Treasury Stock.	4,300,000
Total Retained Earnings	$151,500,000

Management is asserting that it would be prudent to restrict possible dividends by an additional $20,000,000 because of the general uncertainty of the future. (This is all that "reserve for contingencies" usually means, despite its formidable-sounding title.) Management is also indicating that it has decided not to carry full insurance coverage, and anticipates that a further $5,200,000 restriction should be placed on possible dividends to be sure that funds are available to cover possible future uninsured losses.[7] The $122,000,000 of retained earnings reflects amounts available for possible dividends; however, few companies pay as many dividends as the retained earnings account would suggest. Most firms reinvest a large part of their profits, making the company's past dividend policy a far better guide to future dividends.

In the remainder of this book, a stockholders' equity section, such as that in Illustration 5-6, will be simplified to the following:

Stockholders' Equity:

Capital Stock	$138,200,000
Retained Earnings.	151,500,000
Total	$289,700,000

Solution 5-6:

A1. Presumably the firm would wish to change its account title for capital stock to reflect the new stated value. While such formality would not really be necessary, this could be accomplished by the following journal entry:

Capital Stock—$15 Stated Value	750,000	
Capital Stock—$5 Stated Value		750,000

A2. The only effect of the stock split on Mr. Brademas' investment was to triple the number of shares he owned and, possibly, to make these shares more marketable.

---

[7] Of course, reserving retained earnings does not itself assure that funds will be available; all that such reserving does is to make sure that unavailability of funds will not result from excessive payment of dividends. The only way to assure availability of funds is to actually set them aside in the form of cash or short-term investments.

His total rights in the firm remain unchanged and the historical cost of his total investment remains unchanged at $8,190. The historical cost to him of an individual share was $8,190 ÷ 100 = $81.90; now it is $8,190 ÷ 300 = $27.30.

A3. If Mr. Brademas were to sell one share for $76.00, his entry should be:

Cash	76.00	
Investment in South Bend Resonator, Inc.*		27.30
Retained Earnings		48.70

(* Or some similar account title.)

B1. The cash dividend paid by the firm was applicable to 50,000 × 3 = 150,000 shares; 80¢ × 150,000 = $120,000. The firm should have made the following entry to record the cash dividend:

Retained Earnings	120,000	
Cash		120,000

B2. Immediately after this cash dividend the firm's stockholders' equity would consist of the following:

Capital Stock, 150,000 shares issued and outstanding at a stated value of $5 per share	$ 750,000
Capital in Excess of Stated Value	2,225,000
Retained Earnings ($3,423,991 − $120,000).	3,303,991
Total	$6,278,991

B3. The cash dividend would have no effect on the cost of Mr. Brademas' investment nor on the number of shares he owned. It would reduce the total assets of the firm and, thereby, decrease the total ownership interest of all stockholders, Mr. Brademas included. It might affect the market value of Mr. Brademas' investment, but there is no way to determine the nature of that effect from the problem data.

C1. The firm should record the stock dividend at the market price of the related shares: 150,000 shares × 5% = 7,500 shares × $76 = $570,000.

Retained Earnings	570,000	
Capital Stock—$5 Stated Value (7,500 × $5)		37,500
Capital in Excess of Stated Value		532,500

C2. Immediately after this stock dividend the firm's stockholders' equity would consist of the following:

Capital Stock, 157,500 shares issued and outstanding at a stated value of $5 per share ($750,000 + $37,500)	$ 787,500
Capital in Excess of Stated Value ($2,225,000 + $532,500)	2,757,500
Retained Earnings ($3,456,702 − $570,000).	2,886,702
Total	$6,431,702

C3. The historical cost of Mr. Brademas' investment was unaffected by the stock dividend. He now has 315 shares instead of 300, for a historical cost per share of $8,190 ÷ 315 = $26.00 instead of the previous $27.30 per share. The total ownership interest of all stockholders was unaffected by the stock dividend (except for any costs of printing and mailing the additional certificates); similarly, Mr. Brademas' proportionate ownership interest was unaffected. The current market value of Mr. Brademas' investment has increased by 15 shares × $76 = $1,140.

C4. If Mr. Brademas were to sell one share for $76 on 10/2/X7 he should make the following entry:

Cash	76.00	
Investment in South Bend Resonator, Inc.		26.00
Retained Earnings (or whatever other ownership account he uses)		50.00

Assignment Problems

Problem 5-K and 5-M are from the Canadian version of this book and were written by its co-author, Mr. Sanjoy Basu.

Problem 5-A:

Refer to Problem 4-A (pages 228–229). Record the balance sheet changes described in this problem in simple journal entries. Use good form and suitable indexing. You may assume that the company employs a single residual equity account called "general reserve."

Problem 5-B:

Illustration 4-2 (page 192) is an example of a columnar journal. In an actual columnar journal, however, the column at the left of Illustration 4-2 would be omitted as unnecessary, and only simple column totals would be shown at the bottom. Prepare a columnar journal similar to Illustration 4-2 for Community Co-op Nursery School. The data for this entity are in Problem 4-A (pages 228–229). Use the following columns in your journal: Change Number, Cash, Tuition Receivable, Supplies, Refreshments, Prepaid Insurance, Equipment, Accounts Payable, Salaries Payable, and General Reserve. Record all of the company's balance sheet changes for the fiscal year ended 6/30/X4 in this journal, then total all columns.

Problem 5-C:

Refer to Problem 4-B (pages 230–231). Record the balance sheet changes decribed in this problem in simple journal entries. Use good form and suitable indexing.

Problem 5-D:

Refer to Problem 4-C (pages 231–232). Record the balance sheet changes described in this problem in simple journal entries. Use good form, suitable indexing, and the accounts capital stock and retained earnings where appropriate. You may assume that the company's stockholders' equity section of the balance sheet appeared as follows on 12/31/X5 and 12/31/X4:

	12/31/X5		12/31/X4	
Stockholders' Equity:				
Capital stock	$ 79,047		$ 78,153	
Retained earnings	167,482	$246,529	146,846	$224,999

Problem 5-E:

Refer to Problem 4-D (pages 232–233). Record the balance sheet changes described in this problem in simple journal entries. Use good form, suitable indexing, and the accounts capital stock and retained earnings where appropriate. You may assume that the company's stockholders' equity section of the balance sheet appeared as follows on 12/31/X5 and 12/31/X4:

	12/31/X5		12/31/X4	
Stockholders' Equity:				
Capital stock	$ 79,047		$ 78,153	
Retained earnings	167,482	$246,529	146,846	$224,999

Problem 5-F:

Refer to Problem 4-E (pages 234–235). Record the balance sheet changes described in this problem in simple journal entries. Use good form, suitable indexing, and the accounts capital stock and retained earnings where appropriate. You may assume that the company's stockholders' equity section of the balance sheet appeared as follows on 12/31/X5 and 12/31/X4:

	12/31/X5		12/31/X4	
Stockholders' Equity:				
Capital stock	$ 79,047		$ 78,153	
Retained earnings	167,482	$246,529	146,846	$224,999

Problem 5-G:

The following problem requires your recording some, but not all, of the balance sheet changes of Trans Eastern Rhode Island Airlines for the year ended 12/31/X9. The last three zeros have been omitted from all figures; you should do likewise in your answers. The company's comparative balance sheet for 12/31/X8 and 12/31/X9 is given below. This balance sheet has been designed to incorporate certain accounts and reporting practices that were not discussed in the text; where necessary, these variations are discussed in the notes to the balance sheet.

Trans Eastern Rhode Island Airlines
Statements of Financial Position
(In Thousands)
For the Years Ended December 31

Assets	19X9		19X8	
Current Assets:				
Cash	$ 4,315		$ 3,672	
Temporary investments	–0–		17,381	
Receivables.	10,886		10,087	
Parts inventory	4,389		3,682	
Maintenance and operating supplies . . .	805		756	
Prepayments	697	$ 21,092	629	$ 36,207
Noncurrent Assets:				
Flight equipment	$80,598		$47,879	
Advances on flight equipment purchase contracts	10,696		11,970	
Other property and equipment	12,187		9,975	
Investments and miscellaneous	1,195	104,676	569	70,393
		$125,768		$106,600

Liabilities and Stockholders' Equity				
Current Liabilities:				
Debentures maturing within one year . . .	$ 754		$ 749	
Accounts payable and accrued liabilities . .	13,193		11,142	
Customer deposits under Air Travel Plan . .	631		628	
Advance sale of tickets for transportation . .	2,444		2,051	
Accrued Federal income taxes	928		727	
Accrued interest on long-term debt . . .	759	$ 18,709	551	$ 15,848

Long-term Debt:

Debentures payable	$23,269		$24,023	
Notes payable	33,000		20,000	
Other long-term debt	2,064	58,333	1,848	45,871

Stockholders' Equity:

Common stock	$26,056		$25,997	
Retained earnings	22,670	48,726	18,884	44,881
		$125,768		$106,600

Notes:

When new aircraft are purchased, there is usually more than a year's delay between placement of the order and receipt of the aircraft by the company. Accordingly, the advances made by the company to the aircraft manufacturer are treated as noncurrent assets.

Debentures are a kind of bonds payable. Some bonds are secured with a claim upon specific assets owned by the company—usually land and buildings. In contrast, a debenture is secured only by the general credit of the firm. The company has issued debentures with varying maturity dates. At the end of each year it follows the practice of reclassifying debentures due within the next year as a current liability, by making a journal entry of the form:

Debentures Payable	XXX	
Debentures Maturing Within One Year		XXX

Both "customer deposits under air travel plan" and "advance sale of tickets for transportation" may be regarded as kinds of advances from customers. The former represent security deposits made by customers who wish to purchase tickets on account.

Here is a partial list of the company's balance sheet changes for the year ended 12/31/X9. All changes described pertain to 19X9 only, unless stated otherwise. Do not concern yourself with any changes that are not described below. Instead, you may assume that they have been (or will be) correctly recorded. Similarly, do not worry if there appear to be insufficient amounts in certain accounts to allow certain changes to occur—such apparent impossibilities arise only because various other balance sheet changes have been omitted to save you time.

1. The company made $6,046 of advances on flight equipment purchase contracts.

2 and 3. The company acquired $39,500 of new flight equipment. $7,320 of this amount had been prepaid under advances on flight equipment purchase contracts; the remainder was purchased on account. Make two simple journal entries to record these balance sheet changes.

4 and 5. Old flight equipment with a book value of $203 was sold on account, for $186. Make two simple journal entries to record these balance sheet changes.

6. The only other balance sheet change affecting flight equipment was its depreciation. You are to determine the amount of depreciation.

7. The company's purchases of flight equipment placed a heavy strain on its cash position. Accordingly, it issued $15,000 of notes payable for cash.

8. The only other change affecting notes payable was that certain notes issued in prior years became due in 19X9. The company paid these notes; you are to determine how much was paid.

9. In addition to notes payable, certain other noncurrent liabilities, designated by the company as Other Long-Term Debt, were issued. This was the only balance sheet change affecting this account. You are to determine the correct entry to make.

10. The company purchased $24,103 of temporary investments.

11. Interest earned on temporary investments totalled $1,037; the company always records a receivable for interest before it is collected.

12. The receivables in 11 were collected.

13. The only other change affecting temporary investments was that certain temporary investments were sold for an amount equal to what the company had paid for them. You are to determine the correct entry to make.

Prepare the following ledger accounts: temporary investments, flight equipment, advances on flight equipment purchase contracts, notes payable, and other long-term debt. Do not prepare any other ledger accounts. Insert the 12/31/X8 balances of these accounts, if any. Make appropriate journal entries for the balance sheet changes described above, using good form and suitable index numbers. Use the accounts common stock and retained earnings, where appropriate.

Post all journal entries affecting the five accounts listed above to these accounts. Do not concern yourself with the effect of these journal entries on other accounts. Rule and balance the five accounts, and compare the ending balances with those on the company's 12/31/X9 balance sheet.

Problem 5-H:

The following problem requires that you record some, but not all, of the balance sheet changes of Trans Eastern Rhode Island Airlines for the year ended 12/31/X9. The last three zeros have been omitted from all figures; you should do likewise in your answers. The company's comparative balance sheet for 12/31/X8 and 12/31/X9 is given in Problem 5-G. This balance sheet has been designed to incorporate certain accounts and reporting practices that were not discussed in the text; where necessary, these variations are discussed in the notes to the balance sheet.

Here is a partial list of the company's balance sheet changes for the year ended 12/31/X9. All changes described pertain to 19X9 only, unless stated otherwise. Do not concern yourself with any changes that are not described below. Instead, you may assume that they have been (or will be) correctly recorded. Similarly, do not worry if there appear to be insufficient amounts in certain accounts to allow certain changes to occur—such apparent impossibilities arise only because various other balance sheet changes have been omitted to save you time.

1. Parts costing $13,695 were purchased on account.

2. Parts costing $3,217 were utilized in flight and ground operations. No new assets resulted from using these parts.

3. The only other change affecting parts inventory was the utilization of parts in maintenance activities. No new assets resulted from using these parts. You are to determine the appropriate entry to make.

4. The company made advance sales of tickets for $43,832, cash. A liability was recognized at the time of sale.

5. The company made other advance sales of tickets on account for $14,707. A liability was recognized at the time of sale.

6 and 7. The company's remaining sales of tickets were made at (or just before) the time of the related flights, and no liability was recognized on these sales. $307 of such sales were for cash; an additional $23,802 were on account.

8. The only other change affecting the account advance sales of tickets for transportation was the discharge of some of this liability by honoring tickets purchased in advance. You are to determine the appropriate journal entry to make.

9 and 10. $749 of debentures matured during 19X9; $754 will mature next year. You are to make the two necessary journal entries.

11. Prepayments costing $454 expired during the year, without any new asset resulting.

12. The only other change affecting prepayments was their acquisition. You are to make the appropriate journal entry.

13. The only change affecting common stock was the issue of stock for cash. You are to determine the appropriate journal entry to make.

Prepare the following ledger accounts: parts inventory, prepayments, debentures maturing within one year, advance sale of tickets for transportation, debentures payable, and common stock. Do not prepare any other ledger accounts. Insert the 12/31/X8 balances of these accounts, if any. Make appropriate journal entries for the balance sheet changes described above, using good form and suitable index numbers. Employ the accounts common stock and retained earnings, where appropriate.

Post all journal entries affecting the six accounts listed above to these accounts. Do not concern yourself with the effect of these journal entries on other accounts. Rule and balance the six accounts, and compare the ending balances with those on the company's 12/31/X9 balance sheet.

Problem 5-I:

This problem consists of a series of questions about Trans Eastern Rhode Island Airlines. The company's comparative balance sheet as of 12/31/X9 and 12/31/X8 is shown in Problem 5-G; you will need to refer to it in what follows. The last three zeros have been omitted from all figures; you should do likewise in your answers. This balance sheet has been designed to incorporate certain accounts and reporting practices that were not discussed in the text; where necessary, these variations are discussed in the notes to the balance sheet.

Each of the following questions is independent of the others, unless stated otherwise. In each case you may assume that you have been given all the information necessary to answer the question—that is, you may assume that any balance sheet changes that you have not been told about have no effect on your answers. No unusual balance changes occurred during the year; instead, all changes were of the normal varieties discussed in this and the previous chapter, and in the notes to the firm's balance sheet. One possible solution technique for this problem is illustrated in Problem 4-6 and its solution (pages 219–223).

Answer the following questions. Show your calculations. These calculations may be in either schedule or ledger-account form—see Problem 4-6.

1. Assume that no sales of other property and equipment were made during 19X9, and that other property and equipment costing $2,708 was purchased during the year. How much was depreciation of other property and equipment for 19X9?

2. Assume that there were no sales of investments and miscellaneous noncurrent assets during 19X9. By how much did purchases of investments and miscellaneous noncurrent assets exceed the amortization of these assets in 19X9?

3. Dividends totalling $1,336 were declared during 19X9; how much were paid? (You may assume that all dividends are recorded as a liability before being paid, and that this liability is not one of those included in the account Accounts Payable and Accrued Liabilities.)

4. Interest charges totalling $2,325 were paid on long-term debt during 19X9. All interest is recorded as a liability before being paid. What was the total cost of interest on long-term debt during 19X9?

5. Assume that long-term debt was issued and retired evenly throughout 19X9; that is, assume that long-term debt increased smoothly during the year from $45,871 to $58,333. What was the approximate average interest rate on the company's long-term debt during 19X9? Round your answer to two significant digits.

6. See 5 above. Assume instead that long-term debt was issued and retired evenly throughout 19X9, except that $13,000 of notes payable were issued on 12/31/X9. What was the approximate average interest rate on the company's long-term debt during 19X9? Round your answer to two significant digits.

7. Same as 6, except that the $13,000 of notes payable were issued on 1/1/X9.

8. Assume that federal income taxes for 19X9 totalled $4,507. How much income taxes did the company pay during 19X9? Assume that the firm's tax estimates are correct.

9. See 8 above. How much of the payments of income taxes made by the company during 19X9 were of 19X9 taxes (taxes upon the company's 19X9 activities)? Assume that the firm's tax estimates are correct.

10. What were the major financial changes experienced by this company during 19X9? Ignore minor changes in your answer. What would be a plausible explanation of these changes? (You will not be able to give a conclusive answer to this question, but be as precise as possible.)

Problem 5-J:
    The stockholders' equity section of Marcola Edison Corporation's 12/31/X4 balance sheet is shown below. This stockholders' equity section, like many other examples in this book, is modeled after one appearing in an actual annual report. Its reporting practices and account order differ from those illustrated in the text. Three zeros have been omitted from the figures; you should do likewise in your answer.

CAPITAL:

COMMON STOCK, par value $10 per share; authorized, issued and outstanding: 5,220 shares	$52,200	
PREMIUM ON COMMON STOCK	38,252	
RETAINED EARNINGS	43,352	$133,804
CUMULATIVE PREFERRED STOCK, par value and value in liquidation $100 per share; authorized, issued and outstanding:		
4.80% Series—125 shares	$12,500	
5.00% Series—175 shares	$17,500	
DISCOUNT ON PREFERRED STOCK	(712)	29,288
TOTAL		$163,092

Shown below is a summary of all the company's 19X5 balance sheet changes that affected stockholders' equity:

1. As a result of the company's providing electric power and certain other services to its customers, retained earnings increased by $17,416 during the year. Rather than recording these balance sheet changes in detail, record the effect upon retained earnings by an entry crediting retained earnings and debiting Various Accounts.

2. The company employs a single liability account called Dividends Declared for dividends on both common and preferred stock. At 12/31/X4 this account had a balance of $2,610. Dividends totalling $600 were declared on the company's 4.80% Series preferred stock ($12,500 × 4.80% = $600).

3. The appropriate amount of dividends were declared on the company's 5.00% Series preferred stock. You are to calculate the amount declared.

4. Dividends totalling $10,962 were declared on common stock.

5. Dividends totalling $11,915 were paid, including all dividends owed at 12/31/X4.

6. On 12/27/X5 the company issued additional common stock with a par value of $8,100 for $14,581, cash.

7. On 12/27/X5 the company issued a new series of 6.37% cumulative preferred stock with a par value of $15,000 ($100 per share) for $15,826, cash. The value in liquidation of this stock is also $100 per share.

Prepare the ledger account for dividends declared; prepare ledger accounts for all stockholders' equity accounts; do not prepare any other ledger accounts. Record the foregoing balance sheet changes in journal entries. Do not concern yourself with the effect of these journal entries on any ledger accounts other than the dividends declared and the stockholders' equity accounts.

Post these journal entries to the dividends declared and stockholders' equity ledger accounts; rule and balance these ledger accounts. Prepare the stockholders' equity section of the company's 12/31/X5 balance sheet. Use good form throughout, but follow the reporting practices employed by the company.

Problem 5-K:

The shareholder's equity section of Shellac Industries, Ltd.'s December 31, 19X6, balance sheet appeared as follows:

Shareholders' Equity:
Capital Stock:
  5% Cumulative Preferred Shares of par value $100 per share, redeemable
      at par—Authorized 100,000 shares, issued 50,000 shares . . . . $ 5,000,000
  Common Shares of no-par value—
      Authorized 1,000,000 shares, issued 800,000 shares 14,275,000
Contributed Surplus:
  Premium on preferred shares 250,000
Retained Earnings:
  Reserve for Construction. 3,000,000
  Unappropriated 18,125,000

                                     $40,650,000

Below is a summary of all Shellac Industries, Ltd.'s 19X7 balance sheet changes that affected shareholders' equity:

1. Early in the year, the company issued 10,000 preferred shares for cash at $100.50 per share.

2. Early in the year, the company acquired land with a market value of $2,375,000 by issuing 40,000 common shares.

3. The company completed its construction activities. The balance in the reserve for construction account was restored to retained earnings.

4. As a result of the company's providing products and services to its customers, retained earnings increased by $3,517,300 during the year. Rather than recording these balance sheet changes in detail, record the effect upon retained earnings by an entry crediting retained earnings and debiting Various Accounts.

5. The company declared an appropriate amount of dividends on all preferred shares outstanding at December 31, 19X7. In addition, a $2 per share dividend was declared on all common shares outstanding at December 31, 19X7. You are to calculate these amounts.

Prepare ledger accounts for all shareholders' equity accounts; do not prepare any other ledger accounts. Insert beginning balances, if any, in these ledger accounts. Record the foregoing balance sheet changes in journal entries. Do not concern yourself with the effect of these journal entries on any ledger accounts other than the shareholders' equity accounts.

Post these journal entries to the shareholders' equity ledger accounts; rule and balance these ledger accounts. Prepare the shareholders' equity section of the company's December 31, 19X7 balance sheet. Use good form and suitable indexing throughout.

Problem 5-L:

As part of your training in accounting, you must become able to extend what you have learned into new situations. This problem provides an opportunity to increase your flexibility and broaden your understanding. The text provides all background information needed to solve this problem, but the circumstances described will be unfamiliar. Apply what you already have learned to this new situation.

The stockholders' equity section of Giaimo Corporation's 12/31/X6 balance sheet appeared as follows. Three zeros have been omitted from the figures; you should do likewise in your answers.

Stockholders' Equity:

Capital Stock—Par	$ 63,426
Capital Stock—Amount Received in Excess of Par	107,211
Retained Earnings	214,603
Reserve for Contingencies	50,000
Total	$435,240

Below is a summary of all Giaimo Corporation's 19X7 balance sheet changes that affected stockholders' equity:

1. Early in the year, the company issued capital stock with a par value of $1,037 for $7,259, cash.

2. Early in the year, the company acquired land with a market value of $2,380 by issuing capital stock with a par value of $340.

3. The company decided that it did not need a contingency reserve. The balance in the reserve for contingencies account was restored to retained earnings.

4. During the year, the company instituted an employee stock purchase plan. Under the terms of this agreement, the company purchases shares of its own stock in the market, then resells these shares to its employees. The company purchased stock with a par value of $117 for $831. The law of the state in which this company resides requires that retained earnings be reserved in an amount equal to the cost of treasury stock held by the company.

5. During the year, employees purchased stock with a par value of $89 for $641.

6. As a result of the company's providing products and services to its customers, retained earnings increased by $65,301 during the year. Rather than recording these balance sheet changes in detail, record the effect upon retained earnings by an entry crediting retained earnings and debiting Various Accounts.

7. The company declared dividends totalling $26,120 for the year.

Prepare ledger accounts for all stockholders' equity accounts; do not prepare any other ledger accounts. Insert beginning balances, if any, in these ledger accounts. Record the foregoing balance sheet changes in journal entries. Do not concern yourself with the effect of these journal entries on any ledger accounts other than the stockholders' equity accounts.

Post these journal entries to the stockholders' equity ledger accounts; rule and balance these ledger accounts. Prepare the stockholders' equity section of the company's 12/31/X7 balance sheet. Use good form and suitable indexing throughout.

Problem 5-M:

The shareholders' equity section of Mackenzie Corporation Ltd.'s December 31, 19X4, balance sheet is shown below. Three zeros have been omitted from the figures; you should do likewise in your answer.

Shareholders' Equity:
Capital Stock
    4% Cumulative first preference shares, par value $25 each, redeemable at
      $26.25 each; authorized and issued: 100,000 shares . . . . $ 2,500
    Cumulative second preference shares issuable in series, par value $20 each,
      redeemable at par authorized and issued:
        4.80% Series—625,000 shares 12,500
        5.00% Series—875,000 shares 17,500
    Class A common shares, no par value; authorized 4,000,000 shares, issued
      2,400,000 shares 27,125
    Class B common shares, par value $10 each; authorized and issued 100,000
      shares 1,000
Contributed Surplus
    Premium on preference shares 1,620
    Premium on common shares 1,200
Retained Earnings 21,630
                                     $85,075

Notes:

Holders of Class B common shares are entitled, on a share-for-share basis, to four times any amount paid or distributed by way of dividend or other distribution to the holders of Class A common shares.

Shown below is a summary of all the company's 19X5 balance sheet changes that affected shareholders' equity:

1. On January 2, 19X5, the company issued 100,000 Class A common shares for $5,100 cash.

2. As a result of the company's providing products and services to its customers, retained earnings increased by $9,416 during the year. Rather than recording these balance sheet changes in detail, record the effect upon retained earnings by an entry crediting retained earnings and debiting Various Accounts.

3. The company employs a single liability account called Dividends Declared for dividends on both common and preference shares. At December 31, 19X4, this account had a balance of $2,610. Dividends totalling $600 were declared on the company's 4.80% series, second-preference shares ($12,500 × 4.80% = $600).

4. The appropriate amounts of dividends were declared on the company's 4% first-preference shares and on its 5% series, second-preference shares. You are to calculate the amounts declared.

5. Dividends totalling $400 were declared on Class B common shares and the appropriate amount of dividends were declared on the company's Class A common shares. You are to calculate the amount declared on Class A common shares.

6. On December 31, 19X5 the company issued a new series of 6.37% cumulative second-preference shares with a total par value of $15,000 ($20 per share) for $15,826 cash. These preference shares are redeemable at par.

7. Dividends totalling $4,270 were paid, including all dividends owed at December 31, 19X4.

Prepare the ledger account for dividends declared; prepare ledger accounts for all shareholders' equity accounts; do not prepare any other ledger accounts. Record the foregoing balance sheet changes in journal entries. Do not concern yourself with the effect of these journal entries on any ledger accounts other than the dividends declared and shareholders' equity accounts.

Post these journal entries to the dividends declared and shareholders' equity ledger accounts; rule and balance these ledger accounts. Prepare the shareholders' equity section of the company's December 31, 19X5 balance sheet. Use good form throughout, but follow the reporting practices employed by the company.

Problem 5-N:

On 7/1/X3, Ms. Gale V. Adair owned 500 shares of Noblesville Tire and 200 shares of Honour Products. The following table summarizes information concerning these two investments as of 7/1/X3:

	Noblesville Tire	Honour Products
Stockholders' Equity:		
Capital Stock	$ 100,000	$ 500,000
Premium on Capital Stock	3,200,000	100,000
Retained Earnings	2,700,000	900,000
Total	$6,000,000	$1,500,000
Number of shares issued and outstanding	100,000	10,000
Par value per share	$ 1.00	$ 50.00
Market value per share	$ 90.00	$225.00

As of 7/2/X3, Noblesville Tire declared a cash dividend of $1.80 per share, payable on 8/1/X3, and Honour Products declared a 2% stock dividend, to be issued on 8/1/X3. The market price per share of Noblesville Tire rose to $92.00 during July 19X3, then fell back to $90.00 immediately after the 8/1/X3 dividend. The market price of Honour Products remained at $225 throughout July and early August, 19X3.

1. What journal entry should Noblesville Tire have made to record declaration of its cash dividend?

2. Make a single journal entry to reflect Honour Products' declaration and issue of its stock dividend as it should be recorded on the firm's books.

3. Show how Honour Products' stockholders' equity section should appear immediately after the stock dividend was issued. You may assume that through profitable operations the firm's retained earnings had increased to $908,000 by 7/31/X3.

4. What were the effects of these two dividends on Ms. Adair's investments?

Problem 5-O:

Illustration 4-3 (page 193) is an example of a columnar journal. In an actual columnar journal, however, the column at the left of Illustration 4-3 would be omitted as unnecessary, and only simple column totals would be shown at the bottom. In addition, Illustration 4-3 is simplified; ordinarily, there would be two columns instead of one for each account—one column would record all debits to the account, the other all credits.

Turn to text Problem 4-3 (Tee-Wheet Redhots, Inc., pages 207–208). Prepare a columnar journal using the form given on page 290. Also, prepare the company's ledger and insert the ledger balances as of the beginning of 8/8/X1. You may assume that the beginning balance in capital stock was $10.00. Record all of the company's balance sheet changes for 8/8/X1 in the columnar journal. Total the columns. Post column totals to the ledger. Rule and balance the ledger, then compare your ending balances with those in Solution 4-3 (page 209).

Problem 5-P:

The comparative balance sheets of Simplified Textiles, Inc., at 12/31/X5 and 12/31/X6, appear on page 291, followed by some (but not all) of the company's summary journal entries for 19X6. You may assume that each entry given is a complete summary of its particular 19X6 balance sheet change. For example, Entry 1 is a complete summary of all payments of accounts payable made by the company during 19X6. No unusual balance sheet changes occurred during 19X6; all changes were of the normal kinds discussed in this and the previous chapter. The company's accountant made no errors. You may assume that all needed information has been given you. Determine all of the other summary journal entries for Simplified Textiles, Inc., for 19X6. Defend your answers. (One possible line of attack in solving this problem would begin by organizing its data into T-accounts.)

Change Number	Cash		Nuts		Oil		Fuel		Stand		Accounts Payable		Capital Stock		Retained Earnings	
	Debit	Credit	Debit	Credit	Debit	Credit	Debit	Credit	Debit	Credit	Debit	Credit	Debit	Credit	Debit	Credit

Simplified Textiles, Inc.
Balance Sheet
(In Thousands)
December 31, 19X5 and 19X6

	12/31/X6		12/31/X5	
ASSETS				
Current assets:				
Cash	$ 4,354		$ 4,686	
Receivables	23,013		20,211	
Inventories	44,017		37,708	
Miscellaneous	794	$ 72,178	845	$ 63,450
Noncurrent assets:				
Investments	$ 852		$ 852	
Land and improvements	2,694		2,406	
Buildings	26,504		22,113	
Machinery and equipment. . . .	58,924	88,974	49,767	75,138
Total		$161,152		$138,588
LIABILITIES AND STOCKHOLDERS' EQUITY				
Current liabilities:				
Notes payable	$ 16,261		$ 8,197	
Accounts payable	3,640		3,739	
Accrued liabilities	2,804	$ 22,705	2,472	$ 14,408
Noncurrent liabilities		17,500		–0–
Stockholders' equity:				
Common stock	$ 5,081		$ 4,381	
Retained earnings	115,866	120,947	119,799	124,180
Total		$161,152		$138,588

Other data: all sales were made on account.

There were no sales of investments, land and improvements, or machinery and equipment.

There were no retirements of noncurrent liabilities or common stock.

Miscellaneous current assets, land, land improvements, buildings, machinery and equipment are purchased on account (accounts payable).

1. Accounts Payable   70,560
   Cash   70,560
   —To record payment of accounts payable.
2. Receivables   100
   Buildings   80
   Retained Earnings   20
   —To record sale of old buildings at an amount in excess of their book value.
3. Buildings   5,434
   Accounts Payable   5,434
   —To record purchase of buildings.
4. Retained Earnings   2,848
   Cash   2,848
   —To record declaration and payment of dividends.

5. Receivables   589
    Retained Earnings   589
    —To record accrual of interest on investments.
6. Machinery and Equipment   14,614
    Accounts Payable   14,614
    —To record purchase of machinery and equipment.
7. Cash   128,130
    Receivables   128,130
    —To record collections of accounts receivable.
8. Retained Earnings   50
    Land and Improvements   50
    —To record amortization of land improvements.
9. Inventories   119,971
    Accounts Payable   49,555
    Accrued Liabilities   70,416
    —To record cost of inventories acquired during the year.
10. Retained Earnings   571
    Miscellaneous Current
        Assets   571
    —To record cost of miscellaneous current assets consumed in operations.
11. Cash   17,116
    Notes Payable   17,116
    —To record issue of notes payable.
12. Retained Earnings   11,234
    Cash   685
    Accrued Liabilities   10,549
    —To record miscellaneous costs of operations.

Problem 5-Q:

Refer to the balance sheet of Trans Eastern Rhode Island Airlines, in Problem 5-G. The company has issued debentures (a kind of bonds payable) with varying maturity dates. At the end of each year, it follows the common practice of reclassifying debentures due within the next year as a current liability, by making a journal entry of the form:

Debentures Payable   XXX
    Debentures Maturing Within One Year   XXX

It could be argued that the company is being inconsistent here: if it is treating its long-term debt in this way, it should be doing something similar with its noncurrent assets. What is the nature of this possible inconsistency? What accounting treatment do you recommend? Defend your answer.

Part III

Reporting Economic Activity

Six

Cash Statements

The heart of this book lies in the next several chapters. Up to now, the only financial accounting report that we have studied has been the balance sheet. A balance sheet is static; it refers to the company's monetary position and to the amortized costs of its nonmonetary assets at a particular point in time. Parties who are interested in the firm's economic affairs wish also to receive information about the firm's *activities*. Such economic activity is reflected in changes in balance sheet accounts, and accountants have developed several reports that summarize balance sheet changes. We will examine three of these in succession: the cash, funds, and income statements; you already have seen examples of the latter two on pages 83–84 and 89–90.

You will recall that the goal of this book is that you understand what the accountant does, not merely memorize facts. Most students find it hard to understand these three reports fully until they have actually prepared several of them. This is why it will be especially important that you continue to make a serious effort to solve the Problems for Study and Self-Examination, even though you have probably reached a point in the term when your other courses are making heavy demands on your time. Complete comprehension of a practical technique comes only after you have *practiced* it. The next several chapters build upon each other in a step-by-step fashion. It is important that you test your comprehension of each step before going on to the next. Earlier warnings about the dangers involved in falling behind are even more pertinent here.

As a minimum, you should solve all of the required Problems for Study and Self-Examination; if you experience any difficulties with these, you also should solve the indicated optional problems. If you still are experiencing difficulties, you should seek help from your instructor. On the other hand, if you do *not* experience difficulties with the material, don't let this serve as an excuse to fall behind while you direct your attention to the demands of other courses. Once you fall behind in accounting, it can be surprisingly difficult to catch up again.

Operating and Financial Changes

Before beginning our discussion of cash, funds, and income statements, it is important to repeat and amplify a distinction that was made on page 180 between two kinds of balance sheet changes, operating and financial. Firms exist to deal in particular products and services. A railroad provides and sells transportation; a sewing machine company manufactures and sells sewing machines. Of course, a large, diversified company may deal in many products or services, but any company will have some set of things that it is "in business" to sell. Most of a company's day-by-day activities revolve around providing and selling these products and services. Chapter Three showed how these activities relate to the company's operating cycle (pages 140–144). If the company is a wholesaler, its operating cycle might resemble the one shown in Illustration 3-3 (page 142). Operating-cycle activities are often called the company's *current operations.*

Operating-cycle changes involve only current assets and current liabilities; however, they occur in an environment of services provided by the entity's non-current nonmonetary assets—its buildings, equipment, and the like. These non-current nonmonetary asset services help the company sell those things that it is in business to sell. For instance, few customers would buy from a store that did not have counters, display racks, or some kind of furniture or fixtures. Depreciation charges and other noncurrent asset write-offs reflect the services that noncurrent nonmonetary assets provide during a particular year.

Define a company's operating activities or *operations* as the activities involved in its providing and selling the products and services in which it deals. Define an *operating change* to be either (1) an operating-cycle change, or (2) a *write-off of a noncurrent, nonmonetary asset* (such as those discussed on pages 95–104), intended to reflect the services provided by this asset to a particular year's operations.

Operating changes include sales, purchases of employee services, depreciation of store equipment, and amortization of patents that protect the goods manufactured by a manufacturer. For convenience, this book will treat taxes as operating changes. The question of what classification to give interest charges is slightly controversial because interest charges occupy a borderline position among the firm's expenditures. Perceived in one way, interest fees are a distribution of profits to a particular class of investors—the creditors. Perceived another way, they are an ordinary cost of doing business, and no more a distribution of profits than is the payment of salaries to employees. Under the first interpretation, interest charges would be classified as nonoperating; under the second, they are operating expenditures. The latter interpretation is more widely held than the former, and I shall adopt it in this book; hereafter, interest charges will be treated as ordinary operating costs of doing business. Similarly, the earning and receipt of interest from other entities in which the firm has invested will also be treated as operating. All balance sheet changes that are not operating will be called *financial changes*.[1] There are three main kinds of financial changes:

1. *Purchases and sales of noncurrent assets.* Writedowns of noncurrent, non-monetary assets have, by definition, been perceived as operating changes whenever the writedown is intended to reflect services provided to operations. Nevertheless, *purchases* of these assets do not involve an operating change, because we have defined operating changes as related to a company's operations for one particular year. In contrast, when a company purchases a noncurrent, nonmonetary asset, it is acquiring a source of services which will be provided to operations for several years. This makes such a change too long-range to be an operating change. Sales of noncurrent, non-monetary assets are nonoperating because the firm is not in business to sell these kinds of assets, nor does the sale provide any service to operations; by selling the assets, the firm insures that they no longer can provide services to operations. For an example, a store may eventually want to sell its old cash registers and acquire new ones; this will not be an operating transaction unless the store is a second-hand equipment store. A company's acquisitions and collections of noncurrent monetary assets (such as long-term notes receivable or bonds receivable) are also nonoperating transactions unless the company is a bank, finance company, or some other money-lending enterprise.

It should, however, be repeated that *depreciation* of noncurrent assets (or amortization of patents or other writeoffs reflecting services provided by noncurrent assets to current operations) is regarded as an operating change.

2. *Issue and retirement of noncurrent equities.* When a company obtains cash or other assets in exchange for its own debt or capital stock, accountants speak of the company having "issued" the related equity. When the debt is repaid or the capital stock reacquired, accountants speak of "retiring" the equity. Issue and retirement of noncurrent equities are nonoperating changes because they involve increases in creditor or owner investments rather than the sale of products or services.

Changes in stockholders' equity, resulting from a company's dealing in its particular products or services, however, are classified as operating changes. All such changes reflect either an operating-cycle change in current assets and liabilities, or the amortization of a noncurrent, nonmonetary asset (where this amortization reflects the services provided by that asset to a particular year's operations).

3. *Dividends.* The declaration or payment of a dividend has nothing directly to do with the provision or sale of a product or service. A dividend is simply a distribution to owners, usually a distribution of cash.

Although payments or declarations of dividends are nonoperating transactions, many *receipts* of dividends are operating. If a firm owns the common stock of other companies, this often is because of reasons directly related to the owner firm's primary business activities: the other company may be a major source of supply, or may be a major distributor of the firm's products. For simplicity, this book will treat receipts of dividends as operating transactions, though in actual practice companies may treat them as either operating or nonoperating.

---

[1] The two senses in which the word "financial" is used in accounting were discussed on page 180.

A glossary of the terms introduced in this section is given in Illustration 6-1; Illustration 6-2 provides some additional examples.

Illustration 6-1

Glossary of Balance Sheet Changes

Operations: An entity's activities directly relating to providing and selling those products and services that it is in business to provide and sell.

Operating-cycle Activities: Changes in an entity's current assets or current liabilities resulting from operations.

Current Operations: Same as operating-cycle activities.

Operating Activity: Either an operating-cycle activity or a writedown of a noncurrent, nonmonetary asset to reflect the provision of services by that asset to current-period operations.* (Such activities are reflected in operating changes in stockholders' equity.)

Financial Activity: Any balance sheet change that is not an operating activity.

   Noncurrent Asset Activity: A financial activity involving an increase or a decrease in a noncurrent asset.

   Noncurrent Equity Activity: A financial activity involving an increase or a decrease either in a noncurrent liability or in stockholders' equity.

   Dividend: A financial activity involving a distribution of profits to an entity's owners.

---

*Notice that operating-cycle activities and operating activities are the same kinds of activities, differing only in the time dimension involved. Operating-cycle activities concern a short-run aspect of operations; this is why they are often called current operations.

Illustration 6-2

Classification of Various Balance Sheet Changes

Description of Change	*Classification*
1. Stockholders invest cash in a business.	Financial activity: noncurrent equity activity
2. A company prepays a month's rent.	Operating activity
3. A store purchases merchandise on credit.	Operating activity
4. Part of this merchandise is sold for cash.	Operating activity
5. Some of the accounts payable from 3 are paid.	Operating activity
6. Some of the prepaid rent from 2 expires.	Operating activity

7. A company issues a two-year interest-bearing note payable.	Financial activity: noncurrent equity activity
8. No interest fee is due until next year, but interest charges for the present year are recorded.	Operating activity (see page 297)
9. Equipment is purchased.	Financial activity: noncurrent asset activity
10. The equipment in 9 is depreciated.	Operating activity
11. A cash dividend is paid to stockholders.	Financial activity: dividend
12. A cash dividend is received on one of the firm's investments.	Operating activity (see page 297)
13. A liability is recorded for unpaid employee wages earned this year but not payable until next year.	Operating activity

Problem for Study and Self-Examination

Problem 6-1:

The following are some, but not all, of the balance sheet changes of Instance, Inc., during the year ended December 31, 19X2. Classify these changes as to whether each is an operating or a financial change; if the latter, indicate which kind of a financial change it is. You may assume that Instance, Inc., is a large retailer owning several stores:

(a) The firm sold used store equipment to a secondhand dealer.
(b) The firm sold merchandise to its customers.
(c) The firm has estimated and recorded its liability for 19X2 taxes.
(d) Interest payable accrued on the firm's noncurrent liabilities.
(e) Dividends were declared by the firm's board of directors.
(f) The firm issued additional capital stock (for cash).
(g) The firm repurchased and retired some of its outstanding bonds payable.
(h) The firm collected accounts receivable from customers.
(i) The firm paid accounts payable to suppliers.
(j) The firm paid taxes payable.
(k) The firm paid dividends payable.
(l) The firm purchased delivery equipment.
(m) The firm purchased land.
(n) Depreciation charges on delivery equipment were recorded.
(o) The firm received a dividend on a temporary investment in the capital stock of Inuit Industries, Inc.

Solution

Solution 6-1:

Description of Change	Classification
(a) Sale of used equipment	Financial: noncurrent asset
(b) Sale of merchandise	Operating
(c) Estimate of tax liability	Operating
(d) Accrual of interest payable	Operating
(e) Declaration of dividend	Financial: dividend
(f) Issue of capital stock	Financial: noncurrent equity
(g) Retirement of bonds payable	Financial: noncurrent equity
(h) Collection of accounts receivable . . .	Operating
(i) Payment of accounts payable	Operating
(j) Payment of taxes payable	Operating
(k) Payment of dividends payable	Financial: dividend
(l) Purchase of delivery equipment	Financial: noncurrent asset
(m) Purchase of land	Financial: noncurrent asset
(n) Depreciation of delivery equipment . .	Operating (see page 297)
(o) Receipt of dividend	Operating (see page 297)

Change Reports

We have seen that the balance sheet is limited to reporting information about conditions at a single point in time. We will now begin to examine the kinds of reports the accountant has developed through trial and error to provide investors with information about the firm's activities, its *changes*. What characteristics should such change reports have?

Selectivity in reporting changes

The investor needs an organized report devoted to the particular matters that concern him. If he is interested in what has been happening to the company's land, buildings, and equipment, he needs a report about changes in noncurrent, nonmonetary assets. If someone needed to know what has been happening to the company's cash, he'd need a report of changes in cash. Matters that do not relate to noncurrent, nonmonetary assets on the one hand, or to cash on the other, should be held to a minimum in such reports. Similarly, as we saw on pages 82–84, accountants have developed specialized change reports about financial activities (funds statements), operating activities (income statements), and manufacturing activities (statements of cost of goods manufactured and sold).

Each kind of change report tries to answer some (not all) sorts of possible questions. The cash statement tries to summarize and organize data about changes in cash; it is not concerned with noncash assets except as their changes affect cash.

The report of financial changes is not primarily concerned with operating activities (though, as you will see, mechanical considerations make it necessary for the main financial report to mention certain operating changes). The operating report is not concerned with financial activities. Each report specializes for the same reason that this book specializes and does not try to teach Greek, biophysics, and architecture at the same time it tries to teach accounting.

Organization of change reports

Besides being selective, a change report must be *organized*. One common way (though not the only way) to organize change reports is by distinguishing between financial and operating activities. If a report, such as a cash statement, contains both operating and financial activities, you can organize it by grouping all operating activities in one part of the report and all financial activities in another part. Sub-groupings are useful, too; financial activities can be subdivided into *noncurrent assets* activities, *noncurrent equity* activities, and *dividends,* and the financial activity section of a change report can be similarly subdivided, as will be illustrated in what follows.

Preparation of Cash Statements

We'll begin our discussion of change reports with the cash statement, or *statement of sources and uses of cash.* Cash statements are widely prepared and are very simple. One main purpose of a report on changes in cash is to aid the company's management.[2] A statement of changes in cash would also be of interest to investors: cash is a scarce asset and an important one; a report on how the company acquires and spends cash could provide insight into the company's general activities and sometimes indicate problems the company is facing. But cash statements are rarely provided for investors, since similar information is provided by funds statements and the latter are more popular. Still, one form of cash statement (designed to incorporate all financial changes by a technique described in Chapter Nine) is an acceptable substitute for the funds statement under current APB rules. And cash statements are an excellent introduction to change statements: they exhibit all of the important characteristics of change statements yet are easy to understand at first glance. The form of cash statement used in this chapter parallels forms appropriate to other change statements.

The logical first step in constructing a statement of changes in cash is to turn to the company's cash ledger account. Here, for example, is the cash ledger account of Gadsden Co. The account has been ruled and balanced, but the new balance has not yet been carried down.

---

[2] Cash statements are particularly useful in cash planning. Management needs to know what the company spent cash for last year in order to plan what cash needs will be during the next year. Similarly, a knowledge of this year's sources of cash is necessary in estimating where next year's cash will come from.

Cash

✓	2,000	(6)	700
(2)	5,000	(7)	42,180
(5)	44,100	(8)	1,100
		(9)	2,000
		✓	5,120
	51,100		51,100

This ledger account provides a summary of the company's 19X2 cash changes; obviously, this summary would be more informative if the reasons for these changes were indicated:

Cash

✓	Beginning balance	2,000	(6)	Payment of dividends	700
(2)	Cash sales	5,000	(7)	Payment of accounts payable	42,180
(5)	Collections of accounts		(8)	Payment of other payables	1,100
	receivable	44,100	(9)	Purchase of equipment	2,000
			✓	Ending balance	5,120
		51,100			51,100

Excepting beginning and ending balances, debits to Cash represent sources of cash, and credits to Cash represent uses of cash. This can be shown by rearranging the cash ledger account, putting credits below debits instead of to the right of them (index numbers are omitted in what follows):

Gadsden Co.
Sources and Uses of Cash
For the Year 19X2

Sources:

Cash Sales		$ 5,000
Collections of Accounts Receivable		44,100
		$49,100

Uses:

Payment of Dividends	$ 700	
Payment of Accounts Payable	42,180	
Payment of Other Payables	1,100	
Purchase of Equipment	2,000	45,980
Increase in Cash for the Year		$ 3,120
Balance of Cash—12/31/X1		2,000
Balance of Cash—12/31/X2		$ 5,120

This statement can be further organized by using the operating activities and financial activities distinctions:

Illustration 6-3

Gadsden Co.
Sources and Uses of Cash
For the Year 19X2

Sources:
Operating Activities:

Cash Sales		$ 5,000
Collections of Accounts Receivable		44,100
Total Sources		$49,100

Uses:
Operating Activities:

Payment of Accounts Payable	$42,180	
Payment of Other Payables	1,100	$43,280

Noncurrent Asset Activities:

Purchase of Equipment		2,000
Dividends		700
Total Uses		$45,980
Increase in Cash for the Year		$ 3,120
Balance of Cash—12/31/X1		2,000
Balance of Cash—12/31/X2		$ 5,120

There is one more thing that might be done to organize this cash statement. Operating activities make up a very important part of a year's cash changes. All operating activities are closely related to one another: all involve providing and selling whatever the company is in business to provide and sell and are directly aimed at making a profit for the company. It is somewhat artificial to separate them—to report some operating changes among the sources, others among the uses. For this reason, *all operating changes will be grouped together.* In the case of Gadsden Co., operating sources ($49,100) exceed operating uses ($43,280), resulting in a net source of cash from operations of $5,820 ($49,100–$43,280 = $5,820):

Illustration 6-4

Gadsden Co.
Sources and Uses of Cash
For the Year 19X2

Sources:
Operations:
Receipts:

Cash Sales	$ 5,000	
Collections of Accounts Receivable	44,100	$49,100

Expenditures:

Payments of Accounts Payable.	$42,180	
Payments of Other Payables	1,100	43,280
Net Effect of Operations on Cash		$ 5,820

continued on page 304

Uses:
Purchases of Noncurrent Assets:

Purchase of Equipment	$ 2,000	
Dividends	700	2,700
Increase in Cash for the Year		$ 3,120

Notice that there is no change of substance between Illustration 6-4 and Illustration 6-3. All operating activities have simply been grouped together, with a little incidental relabeling in the process. Instead of showing the $43,280 of expenditures as uses, they are shown as negative sources in order to get a figure for the net effect of operating activities on cash. Illustration 6-4 is but one of several forms that a cash statement might take. There are a number of other quite acceptable ways to design a cash statement, but this form will be followed in this book. Parallel forms will be used for other financial statements introduced in the next two chapters.[3] Therefore, it is important to understand how information is grouped under the cash statement's several headings.

How to prepare a cash statement

The following is a summary of the steps followed in preparing this cash statement.[4] In subsequent chapters, you will discover that all change reports can be constructed in much the same way, so this summary will serve as an introduction to the preparation of funds and income statements.

1. *Put the entity's journal entries in summary form* to avoid needless repetition within the report.[5] *Journal entries should be expressed as simple (two-line) entries.*

2. *Select all journal entries relevant to this report; ignore the rest.* For a cash statement, segregate all journal entries affecting cash. The most efficient way to do this is to make use of the cash ledger account, since all journal entries affecting cash are reflected here.

3. *Prepare separate lists of sources and uses.* Changes that increase the balance of an account are *sources* of that account (or group of accounts). Changes that decrease the balance of an account are *uses.* Make sure that all changes selected in Step 2 are reflected on one of these two lists.

---

[3] There are some important additional reasons why all operating changes are grouped together on these other financial statements. The first of these reports, the funds statement, is primarily a report of financial changes; the few operating changes that are reflected on it are segregated from the rest of the report and often are summarized into a single net figure. The second of these reports, the income statement, segregates operating from nonoperating changes, in part because the former are more useful than the latter for purposes of prediction. Both of these points are discussed in later chapters.

[4] Students who have had previous exposure to accounting may be aware that the statement preparation techniques described below are somewhat more elaborate than those ordinarily used in practice. Detailed step-by-step rules are given in what follows in order to develop your understanding of what a cash statement actually summarizes. Once you have become familiar with this statement, you can save time in its preparation by utilizing a shortcut method similar to statement preparation techniques actually used in practice. This shortcut method is illustrated on pages 314–315.

[5] For example, there should be an entry summarizing all purchases of merchandise for cash, another entry summarizing all purchases of merchandise on account, and so forth.

4. *Subdivide both lists into operating, noncurrent asset, noncurrent equity, and dividend activities.* Calculate subtotals.

5. *Combine all operating activities on one list.* If operating sources exceed operating uses, subtract operating uses from operating sources to obtain a net operating source. Do the opposite if operating uses exceed operating sources.

6. *Prepare suitable headings. Show the net increase or decrease in the balance of the ledger account (or group of accounts) at the bottom of the statement.*

Illustration 6-5

Summary of Steps in Preparing a Change Report

1. Put the entity's journal entries in simple, summary form.
2. Select all journal entries relevant to this report; ignore the rest.
3. Prepare separate lists of sources and uses.
4. Subdivide both lists into operating, noncurrent asset, noncurrent equity, and dividend activities.
5. Combine all operating activities on one list.
6. Prepare suitable headings and footings.

An additional example of cash statement construction is given on pages 315–317. If you have had any serious difficulty in understanding the foregoing, you may wish to study this example before working the following review problems. If not, feel free to move onto Problem 6-2.

Problem for Study and Self-Examination

Problem 6-2:

Illustration 6-6 shows the balance sheet of Instance, Inc., at December 31, 19X1. Illustration 6-7 gives a narrative summary of the company's 19X2 balance sheet changes. To save space, four zeros have been omitted from each of the figures.

Prepare the company's 12/31/X2 balance sheet. Use good form.
Prepare the company's 19X2 cash statement. Use good form.

If there is anything in this problem that puzzles you, review relevant parts of the text and read the optional example on pages 315–317; otherwise, you may become seriously confused. Compare your solution to this problem with the "official" one before going on.

Illustration 6-6

Instance, Inc.
Balance Sheet
December 31, 19X1

Assets

Current Assets:

Cash	$ 100	
Accounts Receivable	368	
Merchandise Inventory	570	
Supplies	37	$1,075

continued on page 306

Noncurrent Assets:

Land	$ 140	
Buildings	260	
Store Equipment	720	
Delivery Equipment	170	1,290
Total Assets		$2,365

Equities

Current Liabilities:

Accounts Payable	$ 676	
Taxes Payable	112	
Interest Payable	16	
Dividends Payable	20	$ 824

Noncurrent Liabilities:

Bonds Payable.	$ 392	
Long-Term Notes Payable	100	492
Total Liabilities		$1,316

Stockholders' Equity:

Capital Stock	$1,000	
Retained Earnings.	49	1,049
Total Equities		$2,365

Illustration 6-7

Instance, Inc.
Narrative Summary of Balance Sheet Changes
For the Year 19X2

1. The company purchased $3,960 of merchandise; all merchandise is purchased on account.
2. Sales for the year totalled $6,200; all were on account.
3. The company's 12/31/X2 physical count of merchandise on hand revealed that the company owned merchandise that had cost $460.
4. Salaries of $1,125 were paid in cash.
5. The company purchased $44 of supplies; all supplies are purchased on account.
6. The company's 12/31/X2 physical count of supplies on hand revealed that the company owned supplies that had cost $24.
7. Utility services costing $180 were purchased on account.
8. Consulting services were purchased for $153, cash; these services were entirely expended during the year.
9. Depreciation of buildings was $18.
10. Depreciation of store equipment was $144.
11. Depreciation of delivery equipment was $91.
12a. The company sold old store equipment for $42, cash.
12b. The cost (less accumulated depreciation) of the old store equipment sold was $36.
13a. The company sold an old building for $30, cash.
13b. The cost (less accumulated depreciation) of the old building sold was $48.
14. The company estimated that its liability for 19X2 taxes would be $207.
15. Interest payable of $23 accrued on the company's noncurrent liabilities.
16. The company's board of directors declared dividends of $135.

17. The company issued additional capital stock for $153, cash.
18. The company bought back and retired $21 of its bonds payable.
19. The company collected accounts receivable of $6,210.
20. The company paid $4,452 of accounts payable.
21. The company paid $216 of taxes payable.
22. The company paid $24 of interest payable.
23. The company paid $115 of dividends payable.
24. The company purchased $65 of delivery equipment on account.
25. The company purchased $200 of store equipment for cash.
26. The company purchased $23 of land on account.

Changes (12a), (12b), (13a), and (13b) are given the same index numbers because they are simple changes that, when combined, form single compound transactions.

Solution

Solution 6-2:

The following solution is quite detailed, for the sake of providing maximum help to students who are having difficulties; if you don't need this much help, feel free to skim some of these details.

Step 1. Express the entity's journal entries in simple summary form.

1.	Merchandise Inventory	3,960	
	Accounts Payable		3,960
2.	Accounts Receivable	6,200	
	Retained Earnings		6,200
3.	Retained Earnings	4,070	
	Merchandise Inventory		4,070

Beginning balance	$ 570
Purchases (1)	3,960
	$4,530
Ending balance	460
Cost of merchandise sold	$4,070

4.	Retained Earnings	1,125	
	Cash		1,125

This entry has the effect of making the cash ledger account negative, but these are all summary entries. So long as the balance in Cash is positive after all summary entries have been posted, there is nothing wrong.

5.	Supplies	44	
	Accounts Payable		44
6.	Retained Earnings	57	
	Supplies		57

Beginning balance	$37
Purchases (5)	44
	$81
Ending balance	24
Cost of supplies used	$57

7.	Retained Earnings	180	
	Accounts Payable		180
8.	Retained Earnings	153	
	Cash		153
9.	Retained Earnings	18	
	Buildings		18
10.	Retained Earnings	144	
	Store Equipment		144
11.	Retained Earnings	91	
	Delivery Equipment		91
12a.	Cash	42	
	Store Equipment		42
12b.	Store Equipment	6	
	Retained Earnings		6

This is a nonoperating sale. Pages 182–186 discussed the accounting treatment given to such sales of old noncurrent assets. The net effect of entries 12a and 12b is to increase Cash by the $42 of cash received, decrease Store Equipment by the $36 book value (cost less accumulated depreciation) of the equipment sold ($42 − $6 = $36), and increase Retained Earnings by $6 (the gain on the sale).

13a.	Cash	30	
	Buildings		30
13b.	Retained Earnings	18	
	Buildings		18

This is another nonoperating sale of old assets. The two entries serve a similar purpose to entries 12a and 12b, except that there is a loss rather than a gain on this sale.

14.	Retained Earnings	207	
	Taxes Payable		207
15.	Retained Earnings	23	
	Interest Payable		23
16.	Retained Earnings	135	
	Dividends Payable		135
17.	Cash	153	
	Capital Stock		153

If a balance sheet change affects stockholders' equity, always use the retained earnings account, unless a permanent investment by stockholders is involved. Entry 17 records such a permanent investment by stockholders.

18.	Bonds Payable	21	
	Cash		21
19.	Cash	6,210	
	Accounts Receivable		6,210
20.	Accounts Payable	4,452	
	Cash		4,452
21.	Taxes Payable	216	
	Cash		216
22.	Interest Payable	24	
	Cash		24
23.	Dividends Payable	115	
	Cash		115
24.	Delivery Equipment	65	
	Accounts Payable		65
25.	Store Equipment	200	
	Cash		200
26.	Land	23	
	Accounts Payable		23

Instance, Inc.
Ledger
For the Year 19X2

Cash

√	100	(4)	1,125
(12a)	42	(8)	153
(13a)	30	(18)	21
(17)	153	(20)	4,452
(19)	6,210	(21)	216
		(22)	24
		(23)	115
		(25)	200
		√	229
	6,535		6,535
√	229		

Accounts Receivable

√	368	(19)	6,210
(2)	6,200	√	358
	6,568		6,568
√	358		

Merchandise

√	570	(3)	4,070
(1)	3,960	√	460
	4,530		4,530
	460		

Supplies

√	37	(6)	57
(5)	44	√	24
	81		81
√	24		

Land

√	140	√	163
(26)	23		
	163		163
√	163		

Buildings

√	260	(9)	18
		(13a)	30
		(13b)	18
		√	194
	260		260
√	194		

Store Equipment

√	720	(10)	144
(12b)	6	(12a)	42
(25)	200	√	740
	926		926
√	740		

Delivery Equipment

√	170	(11)	91
(24)	65	√	144
	235		235
√	144		

Accounts Payable

(20)	4,452	√	676
		(1)	3,960
		(5)	44
		(7)	180
		(24)	65
√	496	(26)	23
	4,948		4,948
		√	496

Taxes Payable

(21)	216	√	112
√	103	(14)	207
	319		319
		√	103

Interest Payable

(22)	24	√	16
√	15	(15)	23
	39		39
		√	15

Dividends Payable

(23)	115	√	20
√	40	(16)	135
	155		155
		√	40

Bonds Payable

(18)	21	√	392
√	371		
	392		392
		√	371

Long-Term Notes Payable

		√	100

Capital Stock

		√	1,000
√	1,153	(17)	153
	1,153		1,153
		√	1,153

Retained Earnings

(3)	4,070	√	49
(4)	1,125	(2)	6,200
(6)	57	(12b)	6
(7)	180		
(8)	153		
(9)	18		
(10)	144		
(11)	91		
(13b)	18		
(14)	207		
(15)	23		
(16)	135		
√	34		
	6,255		6,255
		√	34

Step 2. Select all journal entries relevant to this report.

4.	Retained Earnings	1,125		19.	Cash	6,210	
	Cash		1,125		Accounts Receivable		6,210
8.	Retained Earnings	153		20.	Accounts Payable	4,452	
	Cash		153		Cash		4,452
12a.	Cash	42		21.	Taxes Payable	216	
	Store Equipment		42		Cash		216
13a.	Cash	30		22.	Interest Payable	24	
	Buildings		30		Cash		24
17.	Cash	153		23.	Dividends Payable	115	
	Capital Stock		153		Cash		115
18.	Bonds Payable	21		25.	Store Equipment	200	
	Cash		21		Cash		200

Step 3. Prepare separate lists of sources and uses. (See Illustration 6-7 for the details of some of these balance sheet changes.)

Sources		Uses	
12a. Proceeds from Sale of Store Equipment	$ 42	4. Payment of Salaries	$1,125
		8. Purchase of Consulting Services	153
13a. Proceeds from Sale of Building	30	18. Retirement of Bonds Payable	21
		20. Payment of Accounts Payable	4,452
17. Issue of Capital Stock	153	21. Payment of Taxes Payable	216
19. Collection of Accounts Receivable	6,210	22. Payment of Interest Payable	24
		23. Payment of Dividends Payable	115
		25. Purchase of Store Equipment	200

Step 4. Subdivide both lists into operating, noncurrent asset, noncurrent equity, and dividend activities.

Sources		Uses	
Operating:		Operating:	
Collection of Accounts Receivable	$6,210	Payment of Salaries	$1,125
		Purchase of Consulting Services	153
		Payment of Accounts Payable[6]	4,452
Noncurrent Asset:		Payment of Taxes Payable	216
Proceeds from Sale of Store Equipment	$ 42	Payment of Interest Payable	24
Proceeds from Sale of Building	30		$5,970
	$ 72	Noncurrent Asset:	
		Purchase of Store Equipment	$ 200
Noncurrent Equity:		Noncurrent Equity:	
Issue of Capital Stock	$ 153	Retirement of Bonds Payable	$ 21
		Dividends:	
		Payment of Dividends Payable	$ 115

[6] Since $65 of delivery equipment and $23 of land were purchased on account (see Changes (24) and (26)), it could be argued that $65 + $23 = $88 of the payment of accounts payable should be treated as a noncurrent asset activity, rather than as an operating activity; for simplicity, however, the $88 is treated as an operating activity.

Step 5. Combine all operating activities on one list.

Sources

Operating:		
Collection of Accounts Receivable		$6,210
Payment of Salaries	$1,125	
Purchase of Consulting Services	153	
Payment of Accounts Payable	4,452	
Payment of Taxes Payable	216	
Payment of Interest Payable	24	5,970
		$ 240
Noncurrent Asset:		
Proceeds from Sale of Store Equipment		$ 42
Proceeds from Sale of Building		30
		$ 72
Noncurrent Equity:		
Issue of Capital Stock		$ 153

Uses

Noncurrent Asset:		
Purchase of Store Equipment		$ 200
Noncurrent Equity:		
Retirement of Bonds Payable		$ 21
Dividend:		
Payment of Dividends Payable		$ 115

Notice again that under the system we are using, all operating activities are combined on one list; financial activities are not combined in a single list. The reason for this is that all operating activities are essentially different aspects of a single activity—the attempt to make profits. Although profit considerations also underlie financial activities, financial activities are more diverse in nature. This is reflected by not combining financial activities.

Step 6. Prepare suitable headings and footings.

Instance, Inc.
Sources and Uses of Cash
For the Year 19X2

Sources

Operations:		
Receipts:		
Collection of Accounts Receivable		$6,210
Expenditures:		
Payment of Salaries	$1,125	
Purchase of Consulting Services	153	
Payment of Suppliers	4,452	
Payment of Taxes	216	
Payment of Interest	24	5,970
Net Effect of Operations on Cash		$ 240

Proceeds from Sale of Noncurrent Assets:
Store Equipment . . . . $ 42
Building 30   72
Proceeds from Issue of Noncurrent Equities:
Capital Stock Issued 153

Net Sources . . . . $ 465

Uses

Purchase of Noncurrent Assets:
Store Equipment Purchased . . . . $ 200
Retirement of Noncurrent Equities:
Bonds Payable Retired 21
Dividends 115

Net Uses . . . . $ 336

Increase in Cash for the Year . . . . $ 129

Cash—12/31/X2 . . . . $ 229
Cash—12/31/X1 100

Increase in Cash for the Year . . . . $ 129

Illustration 6-8

Instance, Inc.
Balance Sheet
December 31, 19X2

Assets

Current Assets:
Cash . . . . $ 229
Accounts Receivable 358
Merchandise Inventory 460
Supplies 24 $1,071

Noncurrent Assets:
Land . . . . $ 163
Buildings 194
Store Equipment 740
Delivery Equipment 144   1,241

Total Assets $2,312

Equities

Current Liabilities:
Accounts Payable . . . . $ 496
Taxes Payable 103
Interest Payable 15
Dividends Payable . . . . 40 $ 654

Noncurrent Liabilities:
Bonds Payable . . . . $ 371
Long-Term Notes Payable 100   471

Total Liabilities $1,125

continued on page 314

Stockholders' Equity:

Capital Stock	$1,153	
Retained Earnings	34	1,187
Total Equities		$2,312

A possible shortcut

This text's method for preparing cash statements is quite reliable, but it is also quite elaborate. Most students no longer need to use this detailed a method once they have gone beyond the initial learning stages. If you believe that you understand the preparation of cash statements, the following shortcut will save you time.

Begin by putting the firm's journal entries in simple summary form. Label all operating changes that affect cash *R* for receipt or *E* for expenditure. Label all non-operating changes affecting cash *S* for source or *U* for use of cash. Ignore all remaining (unlabeled) changes. Move directly from this labeled set of simple summary journal entries to the construction of the cash statement itself. This is illustrated below for the summary simple journal entries of Instance, Inc.; the firm's cash statement is on pages 312–313.

Illustration 6-9

Instance, Inc.
Shortcut Method for Preparing Cash Statement
For the Year 19X2

1. Merchandise Inv. 3,960		11. Retained Earnings 91	
Accounts Payable	3,960	Delivery Equipment	91
2. Accounts Receivable 6,200		12. Cash 42	
Retained Earnings	6,200	Store Equipment	42 ^{S}
3. Retained Earnings 4,070		13. Store Equipment 6	
Merchandise Inv.	4,070	Retained Earnings	6
4. Retained Earnings 1,125		14. Cash 30	
Cash	1,125 ^{E}	Buildings	30 ^{S}
5. Supplies 44		15. Retained Earnings 18	
Accounts Payable	44	Buildings	18
6. Retained Earnings 57		16. Retained Earnings 207	
Supplies	57	Taxes Payable	207
7. Retained Earnings 180		17. Retained Earnings 23	
Accounts Payable	180	Interest Payable	23
8. Retained Earnings 153		18. Retained Earnings 135	
Cash	153 ^{E}	Dividends Payable	135
9. Retained Earnings 18		19. Cash 153	
Buildings	18	Capital Stock	153 ^{S}
10. Retained Earnings 144		20. Bonds Payable 21	
Store Equipment	144	Cash	21 ^{U}

21. Cash	6,210			25. Dividends Payable	115	
Accounts Receivable		6,210	R	Cash		115 U
22. Accounts Payable	4,452			26. Delivery Equipment	65	
Cash		4,452	E	Accounts Payable		65
23. Taxes Payable	216			27. Store Equipment	200	
Cash		216	E	Cash		200 U
24. Interest Payable	24			28. Land	23	
Cash		24	E	Accounts Payable		23

An Additional Example (Optional)

If you had any serious difficulties with the previous problem, you may wish to use the following additional example of cash statement construction for further review. Otherwise, feel free to move on to page 318.

The Martin Company data from Problem 4-1 are summarized below:

Illustration 6-10

Martin Company
Narrative Summary of Balance Sheet Changes
March 1–3, 19X1

1. Stockholders invest cash of $64,000.
2. Land is purchased for $5,000, cash.
3. Buildings are purchased for $15,000, cash.
4. Equipment is purchased for $19,000, cash.
5. Merchandise is purchased for $18,000, cash.
6. Merchandise costing $30,000 is purchased on account.
7. Supplies costing $4,000 are purchased on account.
8. The company makes cash sales totalling $1,800.
9. The company makes credit sales totalling $2,220.
10. The merchandise that was sold cost the company $3,200.
11. Supplies costing $100 were used in operations.
12. Building depreciation was $30.
13. Equipment depreciation was $50.
14. Salaries of $410 were paid.

Although the shortcut method could be used in solving this problem, the more detailed method will be employed instead, for the benefit of those readers who are experiencing difficulties.

Step 1. Put the entity's journal entries in simple summary form:

1. Cash	64,000		3. Buildings	15,000	
Capital Stock		64,000	Cash		15,000
2. Land	5,000		4. Equipment	19,000	
Cash		5,000	Cash		19,000

5. Merchandise Inventory	18,000		10. Retained Earnings	3,200	
Cash		18,000	Merchandise Inventory		3,200
6. Merchandise Inventory	30,000		11. Retained Earnings	100	
Accounts Payable		30,000	Supplies		100
7. Supplies	4,000		12. Retained Earnings	30	
Accounts Payable		4,000	Buildings		30
8. Cash	1,800		13. Retained Earnings	50	
Retained Earnings		1,800	Equipment		50
9. Accounts Receivable	2,220		14. Retained Earnings	410	
Retained Earnings		2,220	Cash		410

Step 2. Select all journal entries relevant to this report; ignore the rest. (In this case the rule is very simple: choose all entries that affect cash; reject all entries that don't affect cash.)

1. Cash	64,000		5. Merchandise Inventory	18,000	
Capital Stock		64,000	Cash		18,000
2. Land	5,000		8. Cash	1,800	
Cash		5,000	Retained Earnings		1,800
3. Buildings	15,000		14. Retained Earnings	410	
Cash		15,000	Cash		410
4. Equipment	19,000				
Cash		19,000			

Step 3. Prepare separate lists of sources and uses.

Sources		*Uses*	
1. Issue of Capital Stock	$64,000	2. Purchase of Land	$ 5,000
8. Cash Sales	1,800	3. Purchase of Buildings	15,000
		4. Purchase of Equipment	19,000
		5. Purchase of Merchandise	18,000
		14. Payment of Salaries	410

Step 4. Subdivide both lists into operating, noncurrent asset, noncurrent equity, and dividend activities. (The purchase of merchandise and the payment of salaries are both operating-cycle activities and, thereby, operating activities.)

Sources		*Uses*	
Operating		Operating	
Cash Sales	$ 1,800	Purchase of Merchandise	$18,000
		Payment of Salaries	410
Noncurrent Equity			$18,410
Issue of Capital Stock	$64,000		
		Noncurrent Asset	
		Purchase of Land	$ 5,000
		Purchase of Buildings	15,000
		Purchase of Equipment	19,000
			$39,000

Step 5. Combine all operating activities on one list. (Notice that the net effect of operations during the three-day period was to decrease cash.)

Sources		Uses	
Noncurrent Equity		Operating	
Issue of Capital Stock	$64,000	Purchase of Merchandise	$18,000
		Payment of Salaries	410
			18,410
		Less: Cash Sales	1,800
			$16,610
		Noncurrent Asset	
		Purchase of Land	$ 5,000
		Purchase of Buildings	15,000
		Purchase of Equipment	19,000
			$39,000

Step 6. Prepare suitable headings and footings:

Illustration 6-11

Martin Company
Sources and Uses of Cash
March 1–3, 19X1

Sources:
Proceeds from Issue of Noncurrent Equities:
Issue of Capital Stock		$64,000

Uses:
Operations:
Expenditures:
Purchase of Merchandise	$18,000	
Payment of Salaries	410	$18,410

Receipts:
Cash Sales		1,800
Net Effect of Operations on Cash		$16,610

Purchases of Noncurrent Assets:
Land	$ 5,000	
Buildings	15,000	
Equipment	19,000	39,000
Net Uses		$55,610
Increase in Cash for the Period		$ 8,390

Because Martin Company has been in business only a short time and needs to stock up on merchandise, the operations of the first three days have actually decreased cash. Accordingly, operations should be reported as a net *use* of cash. Ordinarily, a company's cash balance will be increased by its operations, and operations will be reported as a net *source* of cash. In the Martin Company example, the order of presentation under the operations heading is the opposite of what it would have been had operations been a net source of cash.

Determining the Contributions
to Cash of Individual Inputs

On pages 226–227 I contended that it is ordinarily impossible for someone estimating the services to be provided by an individual nonmonetary asset to defend his estimate conclusively against a conflicting estimate prepared by someone with different goals or interests. If the difficulty stopped there, the matter would be only of intellectual interest. But, as was also indicated, this inability to defend one's estimate of the asset's economic effects means that the amortization of nonmonetary assets is usually unavoidably arbitrary—something that creates very serious difficulties in financial accounting. Another frequent consequence of indefensible estimates is that measurements of profit are arbitrary, which creates even more difficulties for accountants.

It will be demonstrated in Chapter Thirteen that financial accounting ultimately recognizes only two kinds of economic effects from assets: effects on cash and effects on profits (and even these two effects can be reconciled). Since this chapter is concerned with cash, it is appropriate to discuss cash effects here. However, the full import of this discussion will not be evident until later.

For the sake of illustration, recall that four zeros have been omitted from the Instance, Inc., figures in the previous section. The company's net increase in cash for 19X2 was $1,290,000. Suppose that in 19X1 the company had experienced a $210,000 *decrease* in cash. It would seem natural to say that the firm's 19X2 activities resulted in a $1,500,000 more favorable effect on its cash balance than had its 19X1 activities ($1,290,000 + $210,000 = $1,500,000). Assuming that an increased cash balance was desirable, it would seem natural to congratulate management for the success of its 19X2 efforts.

Although these things seem natural, is the comparison really meaningful and are the congratulations really appropriate? It will be argued in what follows that, except under rare circumstances, there really is no way to tell but odds are that the answer should be "No." Usually, attempts to associate cash inflows and outflows with individual inputs to the firm or with the activities of particular periods of time lead to severe ambiguities, and these ambiguities cannot be resolved unless all parties to the accountant's report have entirely consistent goals. Such an absence of conflict is rare in the business world; in the presence of conflicting goals, any such allocation will be arbitrary.[7]

---

[7] The discussion in this section is based upon technical arguments that I have developed elsewhere; see *The Allocation Problem in Financial Accounting Theory* (Evanston, Illinois: American Accounting Association, 1969) and "Useful Arbitrary Allocations (With a Comment on the Neutrality of Financial Accounting Reports)," *The Accounting Review* XLVI (July, 1971) pages 472–479.

It should be emphasized that these conclusions are controversial, and that I may be wrong—many would not agree that the problems facing accountants are as severe as depicted here. Ordinarily, authors should avoid including highly controversial materials in textbooks. But these seem to have withstood initial criticism and, if correct, cast a clear light on the causes of several widely recognized limitations of contemporary financial accounting.

In any case, these limitations of financial accounting (which will be discussed here and in subsequent chapters of this book) are acknowledged by many, if not most, accountants. Controversy arises only over the severity of these limitations and the explanations of them that I will offer.

Interaction

The basic reason for this arbitrariness of allocations is that any firm's inputs interact with each other and, consequently, so do its activities, whether these activities occur in the same time period or in different periods. Recall the discussion of interaction in Chapter Four (pages 226–227). *Interaction* occurs whenever the services provided by a combination of two or more inputs to the firm differ from the services that would be obtained by using these inputs separately. Here are some commonplace examples of interaction:

1. The combination of man and a hammer can drive more nails during a given period of time than could the man if he had no hammer plus the hammer with no one to swing it.

2. The combination of an automobile with a distributor will travel farther during a given period of time than the total distance that would be traveled by an automobile without a distributor and a distributor that was not being moved by the rest of the automobile.

3. A cake tastes different than do its individual ingredients when consumed separately.

4. An especially demanding course may affect the grades that you get in your other courses.

Separate effects and interaction effects

It is convenient to distinguish between (1) the *separate effects* on output that individual inputs would have were they operating in isolation from each other, (2) the *total output,* and (3) *interaction effects* on output (which in total would be the difference between total output and the total separate effects of the individual inputs). Here is an example: two teaching assistants are grading an examination; for efficiency, each has "specialized" in grading half the examination. Working together their output is twelve papers per hour. Working separately, one teaching assistant could grade three papers per hour; the other's output would be five per hour. In this example, the *total output* is twelve papers per hour, the *separate effects* of the teaching assistants total eight papers per hour, and the *interaction effect* (here, an index of the efficiency of working together) is four papers per hour ($12 - 3 - 5 = 4$).

Sometimes there are *no* separate effects (as in the automobile/distributor example) and the total output equals the total interaction effects. Even more often, the interaction effects make up the greater part of the total output (as in the man/hammer example)—this is the most common situation in industry. Sometimes some of the separate effects are actually *negative,* even though total output is positive (as in the cake ingredient example—by themselves, some inputs to a cake such as raw flour or raw eggs taste unpleasant to many people).

The implications for allocations

As was said at the beginning of this section, ultimately the accounting significance of an input's contribution to output boils down to the effects of that input on cash or on profits. Often accountants wish to determine the contributions to output made by individual inputs. We already have seen a major example of this on pages 225–226: nonmonetary assets usually are amortized in terms of the pattern of their estimated contributions to cash and profits.

As another example, if Instance, Inc., is organized into several divisions, management might like to know the extent to which each division's activities contributed to the $1,290,000 increase in cash. Or management might want to know the different effects on cash of two successive advertising campaigns that promoted a single product. In all of these cases, the accountant is attempting to make allocations (assignments—see page 92) of cash or profits. In the first example, total cash or profits must be allocated to individual assets, so that it can be determined how much each asset has "contributed"; in the second case, the allocation is to divisions; in the third case, the allocation is to different advertising campaigns.

Limitations on the significance of these allocations

Unfortunately, the significance of these allocations often will be quite limited. This can be demonstrated by using two of our earlier examples.

1. *The distributor example.* Most large firms decentralize their decision-making by organizing themselves into a number of divisions and departments. Suppose that distributors are manufactured by one subdivision of the automobile firm, transmissions by another, and so on. Let us also suppose that the firm as a whole is considering evaluating the importance of each subdivision, so as to decide such things as which subdivisions will receive especially favorable consideration for requests for additional equipment, and which subdivision managers will receive the largest bonuses.

There are various ways in which the firm might go about deciding which subdivision is the most important to the firm as a whole. But one way that usually will *not* work is to ask which subdivision makes parts which provide the greatest contribution to the running of the completed automobile. *Some* kind of calculation could be made, but it would be indefensible against the challenge of anyone who wished to make a different calculation.

The reason for this is easily seen: without a distributor, the car will not run and therefore has no output. If you started with an automobile that was complete except for the distributor, and then you added the distributor, the result would be to obtain the entire output of the car. It would then seem plausible to allocate the car's entire output to the distributor. But of course the car will not run without a transmission, either. It would be equally plausible to allocate the car's entire output to the subdivision that manufactures transmissions—or to any other subdivision that manufactures an essential part. Of course, there are other possibilities here, too. You might split the total output evenly among all subdivisions that produce essential parts, and allocate it in proportion to the *number* of essential parts made by each subdivision, or to the costs of manufacturing such essential components, or to the market prices of these components (as spare parts), and so on. One of these possibilities may seem preferable to the others, but it can be demonstrated that each method can be successfully challenged by other alternative allocation approaches.[8] None can be sustained against the others; since none can be conclusively defended, the choice of

---

[8] This is demonstrated in detail in the book mentioned at the beginning of this section. Allocation according to the marginal contributions to output made by the components, or according to equivalent allocation techniques derived from linear programming or mathematical programming, leads to the same problems as those that characterize the less sophisticated techniques described here.

any one allocation method is unavoidably arbitrary. For brevity, in what follows I shall merely say that all *allocations* are arbitrary.

The various subdivision managers would be understandably concerned about this arbitrariness. Each manager of a subdivision that produces one or more essential parts could better his position by having the entire output allocated to his subdivision (the one exception would be the limiting case, ignored hereafter, of the allocation already being made entirely to one subdivision; here, all but one manager could improve his position). Each manager would end up in much the same position as that of, say, the student who is convinced that his instructor could have given him any of several different grades in a course, but arbitrarily assigned a low grade—and the manager would have firmer evidence to back up his belief than the student usually has.

This, of course, is one reason why, in practice, firms rarely try to determine the relative importance of their subdivisions by estimating the contributions made by components to final products. It is foolish to employ an allocation system that yields indefensible, arbitrary results.

An important distinction should be made, though. This arbitrariness *arises* from interaction of parts manufactured by the individual subdivisions in producing the final output. But arbitrariness *matters* here because the interests of the individual subdivision managers conflict. As we shall see from the next example, if the interests of affected parties are *not* in conflict, a satisfactory allocation may be obtainable, even though input interaction makes that allocation arbitrary.

2. *The teaching assistant example.* In the previous example, the inputs had no separate effects: if the distributor or the transmission is separated from the rest of the automobile, the car simply won't run; the total output is entirely an interaction effect. But even when separate effects exist, there will be limitations on the significance of allocations as long as the interaction effects are substantial.

Consider again the example of the teaching assistants; call them "Slow" and "Fast." Suppose that they were being paid 50¢ per graded examination paper. Since their total output is 12 papers per hour, they are earning a total of $12 \times 50¢ = \$6.00$ per hour. How should this $6.00 be allocated between them? There are various possibilities. The simplest would be a 50/50 split—$3.00 apiece. Another allocation method would be to Slow's advantage: if he were to leave, total output would decline from 12 papers per hour to the 5 papers per hour that Fast could grade alone. On that reasoning, 7 papers $(12 - 5)$ per hour result from Slow's presence; he should receive $7 \times 50¢ = \$3.50$ per hour, with $\$6.00 - \$3.50 = \$2.50$ per hour going to Fast.

Of course, Fast could counter with his *own* suggestion: his leaving would reduce total output from 12 to 3 papers per hour; 9 papers per hour result from his presence, so he should be paid $4.50 ($9 \times 50¢$) per hour, leaving only $1.50 per hour for Slow. Other possibilities would be to attribute each grader's separate effects to him and split the interaction effect 50/50, to split the entire $6.00 in proportion to the relative separate effects, and so on. Any such allocation is arbitrary, for none can be conclusively defended against the others. And as long as the two graders regard their interests as being opposed, any allocation method is going to be unsatisfactory to one of them.

Yet in practice, a mutually satisfactory allocation scheme often would be worked out. Though the strictly financial interests of the two graders may be opposed, they have other interests in common. We are all social beings and, as such, we have desires to get along with each other. People who work together day after day, as teaching assistants do, usually discover common goals that can best be served by cooperation. Ruthless furthering of one's strictly financial interests will jeopardize these other important interests.

For that matter, it may actually be to each grader's *financial* advantage that the other earn enough to make him willing to team up for future jobs (including jobs on which Slow may be relatively more efficient). Finally, there are pervasive egalitarian institutional pressures encouraging 50/50 splits—society seems to believe that people who are in the same general circumstances should be willing to share equally.

Because of these various considerations, the two graders may be able to decide on a division that seems fair to both of them—perhaps a 50/50 split. If so, they will have reached a mutually satisfactory allocation despite its arbitrariness. They may even perceive this allocation as being nonarbitrary, though to a disinterested observer it would be no better justified than would be other, conflicting, allocations.

In general, individuals who are affected by an allocation may be able to develop mutually satisfactory allocation methods even when inputs interact to produce output as long as they have common goals that override any conflicting interests. But notice that to a third interested party who does *not* share these common goals, the resulting allocation may still seem unsatisfactory. Suppose, for example, that Fast is married, his wife is having trouble raising several children on a teaching assistant's limited earnings, and she doesn't like Slow. Not only is a 50/50 split arbitrary, but from her standpoint it would probably be vexatious also.

Generalization to financial accounting reports

Unfortunately, the latter sort of situation seems to be typical in financial accounting practice. Most accounting allocations are made to inputs (or groups of inputs) that interact with each other, thus most accounting allocations are arbitrary. A great variety of individuals are affected by financial statements, and their financial interests are in conflict—often in sharp conflict. Although the affected individuals share *some* goals in common, this is not usually sufficient to override their conflicting interests— perhaps because no sense of community or close personal ties can be formed among so many individuals with opposed goals.

Thus, if inputs interact, financial accounting's arbitrary allocations are bound to be unsatisfactory to a large percentage of the individuals affected by the allocations. Even when they are satisfactory to a few people, the indefensibility of these allocations negates their usefulness for resource-allocation purposes. Accordingly, we must recognize that *most financial accounting allocations are of severely limited significance.*

Allocation to groups of inputs

For the same reason that allocation to individual inputs is arbitrary, so is allocation to groups of inputs (such as divisions of the firm) if these groups of inputs interact substantially in producing the output that is being allocated. Similarly, allocation to the activities of two or more different years is arbitrary if these activities interact substantially in producing the output. (Indeed, the activities of a particular year may be regarded as nothing other than a particular group of inputs, selected, in this case, by the time during which they were received.) Consider again the example of the two successive advertising campaigns employed to promote the same product. Such campaigns interact—partly because of the cumulative effects of repetition, but also because what is communicated in one campaign affects the audiences' response to the next campaign. Accordingly, the effect on sales that is observed after the second campaign is a mixture of the separate effects of both campaigns, their interactions, and for that matter, the separate effects and interactions of the earlier activities of the firm—all so thoroughly intertwined that the individual components cannot be separated out, except arbitrarily.

Summary

This conclusion may be generalized: what happens to a firm's cash during any one accounting period is the joint result of all of its activities during that period and, in varying degrees, of all of the firm's past activities. These activities interact. Ordinarily changes in a firm's cash position cannot be associated with individual inputs, groups of inputs, individual activities, or groups of activities—except arbitrarily. *Thus it is of little significance to speak of the contribution to cash of a particular activity or period of time.* All one is usually entitled to say is that cash increased or decreased subsequent to a particular activity or during a particular period of time. But the extent to which that increase or decrease was caused by the activity or period (as contrasted with the extent to which it was caused by other activities or periods) usually cannot be known.

As we shall see, this conclusion has important implications for accounting theory. What is true here of cash is also true of profits: it is of little significance to speak of the contribution to profits made by an individual activity or by activities during a particular period of time.

Assignment Problems

Problem 6-A:

Refer to Problem 4-A (pages 228–229). Prepare a statement of sources and uses of cash for this entity for the fiscal year ending 6/30/X4. While you should use good form, the entity's balance sheet changes were simple enough that you will not need to use all of the cash statement subheadings that are illustrated in the text.

Problem 6-B:

As part of your training in accounting, you must become able to distinguish relevant from irrelevant information. Some of the data given in this and other problems, accordingly, is deliberately irrelevant. Part of your job is to determine what is pertinent and what is not.

Given below is the information necessary to determine all the summary balance sheet changes affecting the cash balance of Rowayton Corporation for 19X9. Do not concern yourself with the remaining changes; instead, you may assume that they have been (or will be) correctly recorded. All changes pertain to 19X9 only, unless stated otherwise. The company's 12/31/X8 cash balance was $49,920.

1. The company sold old equipment for $10,630, cash.
2. This equipment had a book value of $12,110 at the time of sale.
3. The company purchased new equipment for $48,390, cash.
4. The company made investments in affiliated companies totalling $41,300, cash (use the account title Investments in Affiliates).
5. The company issued $34,000 of capital stock, for cash.
6. The company paid $20,000 of long-term debt.
7. All sales are on account; sales totalled $320,380.
8. Collections on account totalled $316,570.
9. The company received $12,110 of dividends on its investments.
10. The company paid accounts payable totalling $54,480.
11. The company paid salaries totalling $83,480; salaries are recorded in a liability account called Payroll before being paid.
12. The company paid miscellaneous costs of operations totalling $112,610.
13. The company's interest payable account had a balance of $1,870 at 12/31/X8, and $2,120 at 12/31/X9; interest charges for 19X9 totalled $5,040.
14. The company paid $26,020 of taxes; taxes are recorded in a liability account called Taxes Payable before being paid.

Prepare the company's cash ledger account, and insert its 12/31/X8 balance. Journalize the foregoing balance sheet changes, and post those of them that affect cash to the cash ledger account; rule and balance this account. Use good form and suitable indexing.

Problem 6-C:

Refer to the data in Problem 6-B. Classify the balance sheet changes given for Rowayton Corporation according to whether they are operating or financial. If a change is financial, indicate whether it is noncurrent asset, noncurrent equity, or dividend. You may combine your answers for changes 1 and 2, and may omit changes 10, 11, and 12.

⁄ Problem 6-D:

Problem 6-B shows the information necessary to determine all of the summary balance sheet changes affecting the cash balance of Rowayton Corporation for 19X9. Prepare a statement of sources and uses of cash.

Problem 6-E:

As part of you training in accounting, you must become able to distinguish relevant from irrelevant information. Some of the data given in this and other problems, accordingly, is deliberately irrelevant. Part of your job is to determine which is pertinent and which is not.

Shown below are all the 19X5 summary balance sheet changes affecting the cash balances of Putnam Pharmaceutical Corporation, along with a few balance sheet changes that do *not* affect cash. Do not concern yourself with the remaining changes; instead, you may assume that they have been (or will be) correctly recorded. All changes described pertain to 19X5 only, unless stated otherwise. The last three zeros have been omitted from all figures; you should do likewise. (Other information concerning this company is given in Problems 4-C through 4-F, pages 231–236; however, the data given below provide all the information necessary to solve this problem.)

The company's cash balance was $12,481 on 12/31/X4, and $14,565 on 12/31/X5. The company's business is highly seasonal in nature. During the busy season the company borrows heavily on current notes payable to banks. During the slack season the company invests temporary cash surpluses in marketable securities and interest-bearing time deposits.

1. The company purchased patents for $3,050, cash.
2. The company purchased land and buildings for $5,042, on account.
3. The company purchased machinery and equipment for $8,211, on account. These liabilities are included in the amounts paid in change 4.
4. The company paid accounts payable totalling $142,528.
5. Depreciation of buildings totalled $2,185; depreciation of machinery and equipment totalled $5,464; amortization of goodwill and patents totalled $2,953.
6. The company issued $4\frac{1}{2}\%$ debentures (a kind of bonds payable) for $15,000, cash.
7. The company issued $894 of its own common stock to its employees, for cash.
8. The company declared $21,682 of dividends, and paid $20,883 of these.
9. The company made investments and deposits (a noncurrent asset) totalling $530, paying cash.
10. The company's sales totalled $502,524; all sales are made on account.
11. The company's estimated income taxes for the year totalled $39,163.
12. The company treats interest-bearing time deposits as a current investment, not as cash. During the year it made $34,632 of deposits and $20,119 of withdrawals from such time deposits; interest-bearing time deposits earned $1,382 of interest during the year.

13. The company bought $9,405 of current marketable securities, and sold $6,743 of such marketable securities; all such transactions were for cash.

14. The company collected $512,580 of receivables.

15. The company made $8,079 of current prepayments (purchases of prepaid assets).

16. The company issued current notes payable to banks totalling $5,828, and retired earlier notes totalling $32,665.

17. The company paid long-term debt totalling $1,747, and income taxes payable totalling $32,332.

18. The company paid various costs of current operations totalling $273,229.

Prepare a statement of sources and uses of cash for Putnam Pharmaceutical Corporation for the year ended 12/31/X5. Use good form.

Problem 6-F:

As part of your training in accounting, you must become able to distinguish relevant from irrelevant information. Some of the data given in this and other problems, accordingly, is deliberately irrelevant. Part of your job is to determine what is pertinent and what is not.

Shown below are all the 19X9 summary balance sheet changes affecting the cash balance of Trans Eastern Rhode Island Airlines. Do not concern yourself with the remaining changes; instead, you may assume that they have been (or will be) correctly recorded. All changes described pertain to 19X9 only, unless stated otherwise. The last three zeros have been omitted from all figures; you should do likewise. Prepare a statement of sources and uses of cash for Trans Eastern Rhode Island Airlines for the year ended 12/31/X9; use good form.

1. The company's cash balance was $3,672 on 12/31/X8, and $4,315 on 12/31/X9.

2. The company purchased investments and miscellaneous assets (noncurrent assets) for $689, cash.

3. The company purchased $32,180 of flight equipment on account, and $2,708 of other property and equipment on account. These liabilities are included in the amount paid in change 15.

4. The company made advance payments on flight equipment purchase contracts (a kind of noncurrent advances to suppliers) totalling $6,046.

5. Earlier advance payments on flight equipment purchase contracts totalling $7,320 were settled by delivery to the company of flight equipment.

6. The company sold old flight equipment on account for $186; this equipment had a book value of $203 at the time of sale. These receivables are included in the amount collected in change 11.

7. The company issued capital stock for $59 cash, long-term notes payable for $15,000 cash, and other long-term debt for $216 cash.

8. The company declared and paid dividends totalling $1,336.

9. The company paid long-term notes payable totalling $2,000, and debentures (a kind of bonds payable) totalling $749.

10. The company made $307 of sales for cash and $34,078 of sales on account. Customers made advance purchases of tickets for transportation totalling $58,539; of these purchases, $43,832 were for cash and $14,707 were on account.

11. Tickets purchased in advance totalling $58,146 were used by customers; receivables totalling $49,588 were collected.

12. The company has been undertaking a major acquisition of new flight equipment, which has required substantial liquid resources (cash and easily marketable securities). Rather than leave its money idle, the company has invested temporary cash surpluses in short-term investments. Such investments totalled $24,103; earlier temporary investments were liquidated for $41,484 during the year. Usually, purchases and sales of temporary investments would be treated as operating (since only current assets are involved). But these investments result from making nonoperating purchases of flight equipment; accordingly, treat the transactions in temporary investments as nonoperating.

13. The company made $522 of prepayments; $454 of prepayments expired during the year.

14. Most customers who wish to purchase tickets on account are required to make security deposits with the company, called "customer deposits on air travel plan." During the year such deposits totalled $20; earlier deposits totalling $17 were reclaimed by customers. These deposits are treated as a current liability.

15. The company paid $4,306 of federal income taxes, $2,325 of interest on long-term debt, and $107,770 of accounts payable and accrued liabilities.

Problem 6-G:

Illustration 4-2 (page 192) is an example of a columnar journal. In an actual columnar journal, however, the column at the left of Illustration 4-2 would be omitted as unnecessary, and only simple column totals would be shown at the bottom. Specialized columnar journals, devoted to recording specific kinds of balance sheet changes, also are often used—both by businesses and by private individuals. A common example is a cash disbursements (expenditures) journal.

Mr. and Mrs. H. H. Overgaard were married on June 27, 19X4, shortly after they graduated from college. Though both were employed, it became evident after the first few months of their married life that their expenditures tended to exceed their combined income. Concerned to see where their money was going, they decided to maintain a columnar cash disbursements journal. Each day they recorded their expenditures (initially on old envelopes; later, when this proved to be a nuisance, they used small pocket notebooks). Each evening (with occasional lapses), Mr. Overgaard entered this information in a columnar journal he had designed himself; it is reproduced below.

Separate columns were used for *Food, Drink and Tobacco, Entertainment,* and *Books, Records, Etc.* because the Overgaards suspected that they were overspending on these items. The *Tax* column was used to record the local 5% sales tax on almost all items (a few purchases, such as drugs, groceries, newspapers, transportation, and entertainment are excepted). Separate *Medical* and *Tax* columns were maintained for federal income tax purposes. The *Household* column was used to record such things as rent, utilities, laundry, and occasional purchase of such things as furniture and kitchen gadgets. All other expenditures were recorded in the *Miscellaneous Amounts* column, and the nature of these expenditures was explained in the wide column to the far right.

Date	Total Spent	Food	Drink and Tobacco	Enter- tainment	Books, Records, Etc.	House- hold	Trans- porta- tion	Medical	Tax	Miscellaneous	
										Amount	Explanation

The following is a day-by-day summary of the Overgaards' expenditures for the week ended 11/16/X4. Record these expenditures on a day-by-day basis in the cash disbursements journal. Calculate totals for the week, as of the end of the week.

11/10/X4 Purchased potato salad and pastrami from the neighborhood delicatessen for $.52. Paid bus fares of 60¢. Bought books costing $9.90, plus sales tax of 50¢. Bought cigarettes for $3.95, plus 20¢ tax. Restaurant meals cost $5.75, plus 29¢ tax. Purchased pocket comb for 39¢, plus 2¢ tax.

11/11/X4 Purchased $4.00 of subway tokens. Paid bus fares of 60¢. Restaurant meals cost $2.80, plus 14¢ tax. Bought 49¢ of crackers and $1.39 of beer from the neighborhood delicatessen. Bought a bottle of aspirin for 59¢. Bought $6.00 of postage stamps. Bought a birthday gift for Mrs. Overgaard's father for $14.98, plus 75¢ tax.

11/12/X4 Paid $2.00 into an office collection (for a baby shower to be given a secretary). Paid bus fares of $1.20. Restaurant meals cost $3.25, plus 17¢ tax. Paid shoe repair costs of $4.50, plus 23¢ tax. Paid taxi fare (plus tip) of $2.35. Bought shoe polish for 39¢, plus 2¢ tax.

11/13/X4 Paid bus fares of 60¢. Restaurant meals cost $2.90, plus 15¢ tax. Bought $8.05 of food from a neighborhood supermarket and 39¢ of potato chips from the delicatessen.

11/14/X4 Paid bus fares of 60¢. Restaurant meals cost $3.10, plus 16¢ tax. Bought a plastic storm window kit for $2.98, plus 15¢ tax. Bought light bulbs for $1.29, plus 7¢ tax. Paid laundry bill of $2.70, plus 14¢ tax. Purchased a small cactus in a planter (the planter was a statue of Kuan-yin, Goddess of Compassion, but the ensemble was sold as a Chinese Buddha Thorn Tree), for $3.98, plus 20¢ tax. Went to the movies at a local university at a cost of $3.00 for admission and 60¢ for popcorn.

11/15/X4 Went to museum, paying $2.00 admission, $1.20 bus fares, and $3.60 for lunch, plus 18¢ tax. Bought wine for $4.58, plus 23¢ tax. Paid drycleaning bill of $3.00, plus 15¢ tax. Paid magazine subscription of $6.25. Bought phonograph record for $4.69, plus 24¢ tax. Paid combined electricity and gas bill of $24.78, plus $1.24 tax. Paid doctor bill of $25.00. Bought cough drops for 10¢, plus 1¢ tax, and shampoo for $1.49, plus 8¢ tax.

11/16/X4 Bought Sunday paper for 30¢.

✓ ***Problem 6-H:***

As part of your training in accounting, you must become able to extend the concepts and techniques you have learned into situations that require different methods of analysis. This problem provides an opportunity to increase your flexibility and broaden your understanding. The background needed to solve this problem has been provided by the text, but the particular method of analysis required may at first seem unusual. Apply what you already have learned to this new situation.

On January 12, 19X1 the accountant for Irwin-North Haven Corporation, Mr. Marcus Oral Lempereur, failed to report to work. The company's management and auditors were concerned, since there had been indications of irregularities in his records for the previous year. A cash statement prepared by the accountant for the year ended 12/31/X0 is shown below. Subsequent investigation revealed the following additional information:

1. The company's sales were correctly recorded at $1,192,600. Of these sales, $277,500 were for cash and $915,100 on account; 19X0 collections of accounts receivable totalled $923,400.

2. Several years before, the company made an investment in 10,000 shares of the capital stock of Braskamp Mines, Incorporated. This investment had cost $97,500. During 19X0, Braskamp Mines, Incorporated, made a major ore discovery. Irwin-North Haven Corporation sold its shares on 9/10/X0 for $377,500, cash. On 9/13/X0, Braskamp Mines, Incorporated, paid a dividend of two dollars per share to stockholders who owned shares as of 8/30/X0. This was the first dividend that Braskamp Mines, Incorporated, had paid in three years.

Irwin-North Haven Corporation
Sources and Uses of Cash
For the Year 19X0

Sources:
Operations:
  Receipts:

Sales		$1,192,600
Expenditures:		
Salaries	$327,300	
Suppliers	507,100	
Interest	12,600	
Taxes	45,800	
Miscellaneous	197,500	1,100,300
Net Effect of Operations		$ 92,300
Proceeds from Sale of Noncurrent Assets:		
Equipment	$ 5,300	
Investments	377,500	382,800
Net Sources		$ 475,100
Uses:		
Purchase of Noncurrent Assets:		
Land	$ 50,000	
Buildings	179,300	
Equipment	242,100	$ 471,400
Dividends		30,000
Net Uses		$ 501,400
Decrease in Cash for the Year		$ 26,300
Cash at End of Year		112,800
Cash at Beginning of Year		$ 139,100

3. Irwin-North Haven Corporation employees earned a total of $327,300 during 19X0. The liability to employees for wages and salaries was $27,900 at the beginning of the year, and $34,800 at 12/31/X0.

4. Of the payments reported as made to suppliers, $6,300 were for bills that had been paid in full well in advance of when due, and then resubmitted by Mr. Lempereur for a second payment in full at their due date. Upon inquiry, the suppliers stated

that they had no record of receiving a second payment on these bills. It is suspected that Mr. Lempereur destroyed these checks and abstracted an equal amount of the company's cash.

5. Old equipment was traded in on new equipment with a list price of $242,100 during the year; the equipment supplier allowed a trade-in allowance of $12,700 on the old equipment. This old equipment had a book value of $5,300 at the time of sale. This was the only purchase of equipment during 19X0. The new equipment was paid for in cash.

6. The company maintains two bank accounts. The balance in one account was overstated at 12/31/X0 by $8,200—the amount of a check drawn upon it and deposited to the other bank account on 12/30/X0. The deposit was correctly reflected in the second bank account, but the related withdrawal was not recorded in the first bank account.

Prepare a corrected cash statement for the year ended 12/31/X0. If in doubt about any of the facts, make the most likely interpretation and state your assumptions. As a means of supporting your answer, you may find it convenient to prepare a schedule calculating the total effect of the accounting irregularities in the present cash statement.

Problem 6-I:

As part of your training in accounting, you must become able to extend the concepts and techniques you have learned into situations that require different methods of analysis. This problem provides such an opportunity to increase your flexibility and broaden your understanding. The background needed to solve this problem has been provided by the text, but the particular method of analysis required may at first seem unusual. Apply what you already have learned to this new situation.

Shown below are the comparative balance sheets of Perpetual Paper Products at 12/31/X0 and 12/31/X1, its cash statement for 19X1, some (but not all) of its summary journal entries for 19X1, and certain other data. You may assume that each journal entry given is a complete summary of its kind of 19X1 balance sheet change. For example, entry 1 records all of the other materials and supplies used in manufacturing forest product inventories during 19X1, and entry 3 records all the prepaid items exhausted in manufacturing forest product inventories during the year. No unusual balance sheet changes occurred during the year; instead, all changes were of the normal kinds discussed in this and previous chapters, and in the notes to the firm's balance sheet. The company's accountant made no errors. You may assume that all needed information has been given you. Determine all of the other summary journal entries for Perpetual Paper Products for 19X1 *except* those entries involving the cash account (these entries, of course, are implied in the cash statement). One possible line of attack in solving this problem would begin by organizing its data into T-accounts.

PERPETUAL PAPER PRODUCTS
BALANCE SHEET
(*thousands of dollars*)

	December 31			
	19X1		*19X0*	
ASSETS				
Current Assets				
Cash	$ 11,812		$ 11,885	
Receivables from customers	36,609		36,166	
Receivables from others	3,172		2,592	
Forest product inventories	48,748		46,945	
Other materials and supplies.	20,565		20,474	
Prepaid items	3,220	$124,126	3,170	$121,232
Plant Assets				
Land	$ 5,146		$ 4,922	
Buildings	52,438		50,514	
Machinery and equipment	247,214	304,798	238,650	294,086
Timber Resources		41,122		29,373
Investments and Other Assets		56,905		50,350
Total Assets		$526,951		$495,041
LIABILITIES AND SHAREHOLDERS'				
INVESTMENT				
Current Liabilities				
Payable to suppliers and others	$ 42,712		$ 37,452	
Loans and current maturities of long-term				
debt	22,847		21,774	
Dividends declared	10,248		10,009	
Estimated taxes on income	6,304	$ 82,111	5,649	$ 74,884
Long-Term Debt		107,682		101,690
Shareholders' Investment				
Common shares	$149,153		$145,414	
Reinvested earnings	188,005	337,158	173,053	318,467
Total Liabilities and Shareholders'				
Investment		$526,951		$495,041

Notes:

At the end of each year, the company follows the common practice of determining those portions of its long-term debt that will become payable in the next year, then reclassifying them as a current liability: current maturities of long-term debt. On its balance sheet, this current liability is combined with the company's current loans (from banks and others) into a single current liability account: loans and current maturities of long-term debt. Payment of current loans is an operating expenditure (as are almost all payments of current liabilities). But payment of current maturities of long-term debt is nonoperating, and is reflected in the section of the company's cash statement for retirement of noncurrent equities.

PERPETUAL PAPER PRODUCTS
SUMMARY OF CASH RECEIPTS AND DISBURSEMENTS
(*thousands of dollars*)
19X1

RECEIPTS
Operations

Collections of receivables—from customers	$470,937	
—from others	4,423	
Dividends received	2,465	
Amounts borrowed on current loans	24,776	$502,601
Less: Payments to suppliers and others	$376,800	
Payments of estimated taxes on income	27,698	
Cash payments of costs of marketing and distribution	1,038	
Prepayments made	3,059	
Cash purchases of forest products inventories	63	
Repayments of amounts borrowed on current loans	23,900	432,558
Cash from operations		$ 70,043

Sale of Noncurrent Assets

Buildings	$ 155	
Machinery and equipment	63	218
Issuance of Long-Term Debt		2,548
		$ 72,809

DISBURSEMENTS
Purchase of Long-Term Assets

Land	$ 224	
Buildings	3,868	
Machinery and equipment	32,694	
Investments	2,816	$ 39,602
Repayment of Long-Term Debt		9,606
Dividends		23,674
		$ 72,882
Net Decrease in Cash		$ 73
Cash—12/31/X1		11,812
Cash—12/31/X0		$ 11,885

Certain 19X1 journal entries made by the company:

1. Forest Product Inventories   13,205
   Other Materials and Supplies   13,205
   —To record other materials and supplies used in manufacturing forest product inventories.
2. Reinvested Earnings   11,895
   Other Materials and Supplies   11,895
   —To record cost of all other materials and supplies used by the company during the year.
3. Forest Product Inventories   2,177
   Prepaid Items   2,177
   —To record prepaid items exhausted in manufacturing forest product inventories.

4. Forest Product Inventories   1,498
     Timber Resources   1,498
     —To record amortization of timber resources used in manufacturing forest product inventories.

5. Reinvested Earnings   285,845
     Forest Product Inventories   285,845
     —To record cost of forest product inventories sold or used in research during the year.

6. Cash   155
     Buildings   133
     Reinvested Earnings   22
     —To record sale of old buildings. These buildings had a book value of $133 at the time that they were sold for $155.

7. Cash   63
     Reinvested Earnings   3
     Machinery and Equipment   66
     —To record sale of old machinery and equipment. This machinery and equipment had a book value of $66 at the time that it was sold for $63.

8. Reinvested Earnings   6,218
     Payable to Suppliers and Others   6,218
     —To record interest charges for the year.

9. Reinvested Earnings   79,946
     Payable to Suppliers and Others   79,946
     —To record various non-manufacturing costs of operations for the year.

10. Reinvested Earnings   1,897
     Estimated Taxes on Income   1,897
     —To record estimated state and foreign income taxes for the year.

11. Cash   2,465
     Reinvested Earnings   2,465
     —To record dividends received on investments.

Other data: all sales were on account, except for sales of old buildings, machinery, and equipment. Most sales are reflected in Receivables from Customers, but some are reflected in the account Receivables from Others (an account used to reflect unusual kinds of sales).

All purchases of prepaid items, land, buildings, machinery, and equipment were for cash.

All investments and other assets that were not purchased for cash were acquired by issuing common shares (capital stock).

All timber resources that were acquired during the year were acquired by issuing long-term debt. This and the issue of long-term debt reflected on the cash statement were the only reasons for which long-term debt was issued during the year. No long-term debt was paid prior to its maturity date.

All prepaid items that were exhausted during the year were either used in manufacturing forest product inventories or expired in furthering the company's other operations.

There were no sales of land, timber resources, or investments and other assets; no common shares were retired during the year.

The cost of the forest product inventories manufactured by the company is the sum of the following kinds of costs of goods used in manufacturing: timber resources used (trees, amortization of logging roads, etc.), logs purchased from outsiders for cash, other materials and supplies used, prepayments expired, and a variety of other goods (including other logs purchased from outsiders) purchased on account.

All Other Materials and Supplies were purchased on account.

In practice, the cost of forest product inventories ordinarily would include certain costs of depreciation; for simplicity this complication has been omitted. Similarly for simplicity, interest charges on long-term debt are ignored.

Problem 6-J:

As part of your training in accounting, you must become able to extend what you have learned into new situations. This problem provides such an opportunity to increase your flexibility and broaden your understanding. The text provides all background information needed to solve this problem, but the circumstances described will be unfamiliar. Apply what you already have learned to this new situation.

George A. Patton University is a state-supported institution that offers degrees through the doctorate. Each year, the State Legislature reviews the activities of the university, prior to making its annual appropriation. The following remarks were made recently by State Senator George V. George, Chairman of the Senate Higher Education Subcommittee, to Dr. William T. Russell, President of George A. Patton University:

"You guys are simply overpaying your full-rank professors! Every student pays tuition of $600 a year. If he takes ten courses, and that's pretty typical, this works out to $60 per course. I've been going through last year's statistics, and usually it's the young, low-ranking profs who teach the big sections with lots of students, while the high-rank professors teach small courses. Yet the high-ranking profs make at least half again as much as the low-rank ones. Here's an example: Paul Frishkoff, Assistant Professor of History; he's one of the university's real money-makers, yet I bet you don't even recognize his name."

"On the contrary, I recall him as being a young but promising expert on the history of West African trade."

"Well, last fall you had him teaching 1,200 students, including 1,120 in Survey of European History; that's $72,000 bucks he made for you. Now, compare J. Edward Murphy, Professor of Accounting; last fall he taught Advanced Accounting to 45 students and Seminar on Accounting Theory to 15, a total of 60 students. He made one twentieth the money for you that Frishkoff did, yet you're paying him twice as much!"

Comment. Defend your comments. You may assume that all three courses are required ones for the students who are taking them.

Problem 6-K:

Mrs. Roberta G. Derwinski is some nine inches shorter than her husband, Mr. John J. Derwinski. The family owns one automobile; both drivers use the rear-view mirror, but need to adjust it at different angles in order to see the road. Each time that Mr. Derwinski drives the car immediately after his wife has driven it, he must readjust the rear-view mirror. Attempts at this usually left the mirror at a slightly wrong angle, and subsequent adjustments had to be made in traffic. Once the honeymoon is over, most husbands find one or two annoying things about their wives; each time Mr. Derwinski readjusted the mirror, he could be heard to mutter something crude about midgets. Early in January, 19X8, his wife made the following suggestion:

"Dear, since it troubles you so, why don't you just put on a kind of button thinga-gummy, like on the radio? You know—you don't have to tune the radio just so when you want to change stations—you just set the button for your station once and for all, then when you *want* it . . . why are you stopping the car, dear?"

Six months later Mr. Derwinski had completed a working model of a rear-view automobile mirror that would automatically switch to any of three different positions, set in advance by its owner. He and his two brothers-in-law, Mr. Leonard R. Garland and Mr. Charles L. Ronan, then founded DGR Automatic Miracle Automirror Co. to patent, produce, and sell this new product. The founders invested a total of $80,000 cash, then spent the first three years in planning, developing production techniques to a point where the product was commercially feasible, and raising additional capital. Years four and five were devoted to intensive initial marketing efforts. The product was a success, and years six through ten were spent in a more gradual extension of markets; during these latter years, the founders withdrew cash dividends totalling $120,000. Finally, at the end of year ten, the founders sold their investment in the firm to a larger company, for $960,000, cash.

Comment on the effects on the founders' cash of the company's activities in each of the years one through ten. Defend your comments.

Problem 6-L:

Delaware Diurnal Corporation pays its employees a Christmas bonus based upon estimates of how productive they have been during the previous year. Mr. William L. O'Hara and Mr. Barrett Dawson are two employees who together manufacture a single product. Until this year they worked separately, but the company has discovered that they are much more efficient working as a team. Their bonus will be an excellent one, but the company is puzzled how to divide it between them. Past experience indicates that, working alone, O'Hara could make 450 units of product per day while Dawson could make only 250 units of product per day. Working together, they can make 1,050 units of product per day. O'Hara, who is older and in a higher skill classification, is paid regular wages of $6.00 an hour, compared to Dawson's $4.00 per hour.

What is the relative productivity of these two workers? You may answer this in terms of the number of units of daily output that should be attributed to each worker. Ignore any possible complications in union relations in your answer. At least eight different answers might plausibly be given to this question; provide at least six of these, together with appropriate supporting calculations.

Seven

Funds Statements

Financial Changes

All change reports specialize. As noted on pages 300–301, different change reports summarize different balance sheet changes. The cash statement summarizes all changes involving cash. The report to be considered in this chapter summarizes *financial changes*. Here are some of the questions that investors ask about a company's financial activities:

> How has the company been financing its activities? What has management been doing with the investment entrusted to it? Where's all the money going? Has the company been buying new noncurrent assets? Has it retired any of its old noncurrent debt? Has it issued or retired any capital stock?

Financial activities relate to noncurrent assets, noncurrent equities, and dividends (see pages 296–297). Balance sheet changes involving noncurrent assets, noncurrent liabilities, and capital stock are important for investor resource-allocation decisions, for these changes often involve major, semi-permanent commitments that help determine the operating-activity environment for years to come. Of course, investors are also interested in the company's dividend policy.

Some of these financial activities can be roughly discerned by comparing beginning and ending balance sheets. But if the investor is to obtain a complete, coherent picture of a company's financial activities, he needs a report in which (among other things) all major financial changes are described and summarized. Such a report primarily concerned with financial changes is often called a *funds statement*.

Funds statements and net working capital

In preparing a cash statement, the accountant can rely on the rule: report only those balance sheet changes that affect cash. There is a similar (though slightly more complicated) rule that can be used in preparing funds statements: *report only those changes that affect the balance of net working capital.* (Net working capital was defined on page 142; you should also be familiar with the distinction between the current/ noncurrent and the monetary/nonmonetary classifications emphasized on pages 113–114.)

If you follow this rule, you will obtain a change report that (with a few exceptions) discusses and summarizes all financial changes, but the truth of this is not immediately evident. In fact, most students are a little puzzled when they first learn of this rule. To illustrate why it is true, the 19X2 balance sheet changes of Instance, Inc., can be used. The data come from Problem 6-2 and its solution on pages 305–314. (If you are reading ahead and have not yet solved Problem 6-2, it would be wise to read no further until you are sure you understand it.)

Illustration 7-1 is a narrative summary of the company's 19X2 balance sheet changes. (This illustration repeats Illustration 6-7.) Illustration 7-2 gives the company's 19X2 simple summary journal entries.

Illustration 7-1

Instance, Inc.
Narrative Summary of Balance Sheet Changes
For the Year 19X2

1. The company purchased $3,960 of merchandise; all merchandise is purchased on account.
2. Sales for the year totalled $6,200; all sales were on account.
3. The company's 12/31/X2 physical count of merchandise on hand revealed that the company owned merchandise that had cost $460.
4. Salaries of $1,125 were paid in cash.
5. The company purchased $44 of supplies; all supplies are purchased on account.
6. The company's 12/31/X2 physical count of supplies on hand revealed that the company owned supplies that had cost $24.
7. Utility services costing $180 were purchased on account.
8. Consulting services were purchased for $153, cash; these services were entirely expended during the year.
9. Depreciation of buildings was $18.
10. Depreciation of store equipment was $144.
11. Depreciation of delivery equipment was $91.
12a. The company sold old store equipment for $42, cash.
12b. The cost (less accumulated depreciation) of the old store equipment sold was $36.
13a. The company sold an old building for $30, cash.
13b. The cost (less accumulated depreciation) of the old building sold was $48.
14. The company estimated that its liability for 19X2 taxes would be $207.
15. Interest payable of $23 accrued on the company's noncurrent liabilities.
16. The company's board of directors declared dividends of $135.
17. The company issued additional capital stock for $153, cash.
18. The company bought back and retired $21 of its bonds payable.
19. The company collected accounts receivable of $6,210.
20. The company paid $4,452 of accounts payable.
21. The company paid $216 of taxes payable.

22. The company paid $24 of interest payable.
23. The company paid $115 of dividends payable.
24. The company purchased $65 of delivery equipment on account.
25. The company purchased $200 of store equipment for cash.
26. The company purchased $23 of land on account.

Operating changes versus financial changes

To repeat, our goal is to demonstrate that a report limited to summarizing changes that affect the balance of net working capital will also summarize almost all *financial* changes. The first step in showing this is to distinguish Instance, Inc.'s financial changes from its operating changes. It will be convenient to concentrate on the operating changes first and then discuss their identifying characteristics. We will return to the financial changes a little later.

You will recall that Chapter Six (page 298) defined an operating balance sheet change as follows:

Operations are an entity's activities directly relating to providing and selling those products and services that it is "in business" to provide and sell.

An *operating change* is either (1) a change in an entity's current assets or current liabilities resulting from operations, or (2) a writedown of a noncurrent, nonmonetary asset to reflect services provided by that asset to current-period operations.

In Illustration 7-2, all entries meeting the definition of an operating entry have been marked "Op." If you are puzzled by anything in Illustration 7-2, you may wish to review the discussion of the operating/financial distinction on pages 297–298.

Illustration 7-2

Instance, Inc.
Simple Summary Journal Entries
For the Year 19X2

Op.	1.	Merchandise Inventory	3,960		Op.	11.	Retained Earnings	91	
		Accounts Payable		3,960			Delivery Equipment		91
Op.	2.	Accounts Receivable	6,200			12a.	Cash	42	
		Retained Earnings		6,200			Store Equipment		42
Op.	3.	Retained Earnings	4,070			12b.	Store Equipment	6	
		Merchandise Inventory		4,070			Retained Earnings		6
Op.	4.	Retained Earnings	1,125			13a.	Cash	30	
		Cash		1,125			Buildings		30
Op.	5.	Supplies	44			13b.	Retained Earnings	18	
		Accounts Payable		44			Buildings		18
Op.	6.	Retained Earnings	57		Op.	14.	Retained Earnings	207	
		Supplies		57			Taxes Payable		207
Op.	7.	Retained Earnings	180		Op.	15.	Retained Earnings	23	
		Accounts Payable		180			Interest Payable		23
Op.	8.	Retained Earnings	153			16.	Retained Earnings	135	
		Cash		153			Dividends Payable		135
Op.	9.	Retained Earnings	18			17.	Cash	153	
		Buildings		18			Capital Stock		153
Op.	10.	Retained Earnings	144			18.	Bonds Payable	21	
		Store Equipment		144			Cash		21

Op. 19. Cash	6,210		24. Delivery Equipment	65	
Accounts Receivable		6,210	Accounts Payable		65
Op. 20. Accounts Payable	4,452		25. Store Equipment	200	
Cash		4,452	Cash		200
Op. 21. Taxes Payable	216		26. Land	23	
Cash		216	Accounts Payable		23
Op. 22. Interest Payable	24				
Cash		24			
23. Dividends Payable	115				
Cash		115			

In general, all operating changes fall into one of two groups:

1. Those that relate to sales or the costs of making sales = those that directly affect profits = those that involve debits or credits to retained earnings.

2. Those that do not affect retained earnings, but reflect instead (a) replenishment of current assets used up in operations, or, (b) payment of current liabilities (other than dividends payable). It is usually possible to distinguish an operating change from a financial change by these characteristics.

Financial entries and net working capital

A financial change has been defined as any change that is not operating. Illustration 7-3 gives Instance, Inc.'s financial entries for 19X2. (Entries 12a through 13b are nonoperating because they relate to incidental sales of used noncurrent assets; Entries 16 and 23 are nonoperating because they relate to dividends—distributions of profits rather than profits themselves.)

Illustration 7-3

Instance, Inc.
Financial Entries
For the Year 19X2

Entries that affect the balance of net working capital			*Entries that do not affect the balance of net working capital*		
12a. Cash	42		12b. Store Equipment	6	
Store Equipment		42	Retained Earnings		6
13a. Cash	30		13b. Retained Earnings	18	
Buildings		30	Buildings		18
16. Retained Earnings	135		23. Dividends Payable	115	
Dividends Payable		135	Cash		115
17. Cash	153		(This last entry does not affect net		
Capital Stock		153	working capital because the decrease in		
18. Bonds Payable	21		Dividends Payable offsets the decrease		
Cash		21	in Cash.)		
24. Delivery Equipment	65				
Accounts Payable		65			
25. Store Equipment	200				
Cash		200			
26. Land	23				
Accounts Payable		23			

Illustration 7-3 also shows the relationship between Instance, Inc.'s financial entries and its net working capital. You will recall that *net working capital is the total of all current assets minus all current liabilities.* The balance of net working capital is the amount of that total. For example, the balance of Instance, Inc.'s net working capital at 12/31/X1 was $251 (see page 305):

Current Assets:

Cash	$100	
Accounts Receivable	368	
Merchandise Inventory	570	
Supplies	37	$1,075

Current Liabilities:

Accounts Payable	$676	
Taxes Payable	112	
Interest Payable	16	
Dividends Payable	20	824
Net Working Capital		$ 251

An increase in a current asset or a decrease in a current liability will increase net working capital. A decrease in a current asset or an increase in a current liability will decrease net working capital.

Now, consider Illustration 7-3. *Most of Instance, Inc.'s financial changes affect the balance of net working capital.* (Satisfy yourself that each of the eight entries listed as affecting net working capital actually does either increase or decrease the balance of net working capital.) A change report that discusses and summarizes all entries affecting net working capital will also discuss and summarize most financial changes. Moreover, all but one of the remaining financial changes affect retained earnings. *If the accountant prepares a statement of changes in net working capital and a statement of changes in retained earnings, he thereby discusses and summarizes almost all financial changes.*[1] The accountant thus prepares one change report—the funds statement—that discusses and summarizes all balance sheet changes affecting the balance of net working capital. He prepares another change report—the income statement—that discusses and summarizes all balance sheet changes affecting retained earnings.[2] Together, these two change reports discuss and summarize almost all financial changes.

---

[1] The only financial changes omitted are:

(a) Relatively unimportant ones involving payment of current nonoperating liabilities (such as dividends payable).

(b) Certain unusual transactions, such as the acquisition of noncurrent assets by direct issue of noncurrent equities, for example:

Land	XXX	
Capital Stock		XXX

This kind of transaction will be ignored in the present discussion. Financial changes of this kind should also be reported on funds statements; in a later chapter you will see how this can be accomplished.

[2] Students who have had previous exposure to accounting will be aware that the income statement can take several forms. The kind of income statement mentioned here is the one that includes a reconciliation of the beginning and ending balances of retained earnings.

Finally, notice in Illustration 7-3 that the financial changes not affecting net working capital are of relatively minor importance. This will usually be true, and the funds statement (statement of changes in net working capital) is therefore considered the main report of financial changes.

Steps in
Constructing a Funds Statement

The six steps in preparing a funds statement parallel the steps for preparing a cash statement (see pages 304–305):[3]

1. Put the entity's journal entries in simple summary form.

2. Select all entries that affect the balance of net working capital; ignore the rest.

3. Prepare separate lists of sources and uses. (A source of net working capital is a change that increases the balance of net working capital; a use of net working capital is a change that decreases the balance of net working capital.)

4. Subdivide both lists into operating, noncurrent asset, noncurrent equity, and dividend activities.

5. Combine all operating activities on one list.

6. Prepare suitable headings and footings.

Operating changes in net working capital

One final thing should be mentioned to prevent confusion later on. All that has been demonstrated is that a report summarizing changes that affect the balance of net working capital will incorporate most financial changes. But such a report will not be limited to financial changes; it will also include various operating changes. If you wish to prepare a report directed to financial changes, the operating changes that affect the balance of net working capital must be segregated. For example, a sale on account is an operating change:

Accounts Receivable   XXX
Retained Earnings   XXX

A sale on account also increases net working capital (by increasing current assets). Any simple operating change affecting both retained earnings and a current asset or liability also affects the balance of net working capital (by an amount equal to the

---

[3] Students who have had previous exposure to accounting also may be aware that the statement preparation techniques described below are somewhat more elaborate than those ordinarily used in practice. Detailed, step-by-step rules are given in what follows in order to develop your understanding of what a funds statement actually summarizes. Once you have become familiar with this statement, you can save time in its preparation by utilizing a shortcut method illustrated on pages 348–349. In turn, once you have become familiar with the relationships between funds statements and income statements, we will study another shortcut technique for funds statement preparation. The latter method, discussed in Chapter Nine, parallels techniques commonly used in actual practice.

change in the current account). All this means is that Step 2 in constructing a funds statement is insufficient by itself to group all financial changes in one place. In addition, it is necessary to apply steps 4 and 5 in order to separate the financial changes from those operating changes that affect the balance of net working capital. This will be demonstrated in detail in what follows.[4]

Step 1. Put the entity's journal entries in simple summary form. This step has already been performed in Illustration 7-2.

Step 2. Select all changes that affect the balance of net working capital.

(a) A change will increase the balance of net working capital if a current asset increases or a current liability decreases, and the other account affected is neither a current asset nor a current liability. A change will not affect the balance of net working capital if it affects two current accounts. Call these *double-effect changes.* Here are the company's double-effect changes:

1. Merchandise	3,960		21. Taxes Payable	216	
Accounts Payable		3,960	Cash		216
5. Supplies	44		22. Interest Payable	24	
Accounts Payable		44	Cash		24
19. Cash	6,210		23. Dividends Payable	115	
Accounts Receivable		6,210	Cash		115
20. Accounts Payable	4,452				
Cash		4,452			

In all cases, the debit increases the balance of net working capital, while the credit decreases this balance by an equal amount; the increases and decreases offset each other and net working capital is not affected.

Here are the changes that increase net working capital:

Op. 2.	Accounts Receivable	6,200		13a. Cash	30	
	Retained Earnings		6,200	Buildings		30
12a. Cash		42		17. Cash	153	
	Store Equipment		42	Capital Stock		153

For example, Entry 2 increases net working capital because a current asset has increased, along with a noncurrent equity (which is not part of net working capital). The effect of Entry 2 is:

Increase net working capital	6,200	
No effect on net working capital		6,200

---

[4] Students who have had previous exposure to accounting may also be aware that, in practice, a different line of attack is often used to calculate net operating changes in net working capital: the accountant adjusts the firm's profit for the year to exclude items (such as depreciation) that affect profit but do not affect the balance of net working capital, then shows the result as the overall effect of operations on net working capital. This procedure is not used in this chapter because, as is argued later, it leads to several misunderstandings about what the funds statement indicates and the status of the items excluded. However, both lines of attack are acceptable under current APB rules.

(Notice again that even though the funds statement is the main report on financial changes, the rules given here involve selecting some operating changes, such as Entry 2.)

(b) A change will decrease the balance of net working capital if a current asset decreases or a current liability increases, and the other account affected is neither a current asset nor a current liability. Here are the changes that decrease net working capital:

Op. 3.	Retained Earnings	4,070		Op. 15. Retained Earnings	23	
	Merchandise Inventory		4,070	Interest Payable		23
Op. 4.	Retained Earnings	1,125		16. Retained Earnings	135	
	Cash		1,125	Dividends Payable		135
Op. 6.	Retained Earnings	57		18. Bonds Payable	21	
	Supplies		57	Cash		21
Op. 7.	Retained Earnings	180		24. Delivery Equipment	65	
	Accounts Payable		180	Accounts Payable		65
Op. 8.	Retained Earnings	153		25. Store Equipment	200	
	Cash		153	Cash		200
Op. 14.	Retained Earnings	207		26. Land	23	
	Taxes Payable		207	Accounts Payable		23

Entry 3 decreases net working capital because a current asset has decreased, while the other account involved is not part of net working capital. Entry 26 decreases net working capital because a current liability has increased, while the other account involved is not part of net working capital. Once again, some changes affecting the balance of net working capital are operating changes; this system for constructing a funds statement is not designed to exclude operating changes, but to include all major financial changes.

Notice that an increase in net working capital always involves a debit to a current asset or current liability; a decrease in the balance of net working capital always involves a credit to a current asset or current liability. The balance of net working capital is affected whenever a *single* current asset or current liability changes.

Step 3. Prepare separate lists of sources and uses

You may find it helpful to turn back to Illustration 7-1 for the explanations of some of the following changes.

Sources and uses of net working capital are easy to identify. Increase changes are sources of net working capital; decrease changes are uses of net working capital:

Sources		*Uses*	
Op. 2. Sales*	$6,200	Op. 3. Cost of Merchandise	
12a. Sale of Old Store		Sold	$4,070
Equipment	42	Op. 4. Payment of Salaries	
13a. Sale of Old Building	30	(Cost of Employee	
17. Issue of Capital Stock	153	Services Used)	1,125
		Op. 6. Cost of Supplies Used	57
		Op. 7. Cost of Utility Services	
		Used	180
		Op. 8. Cost of Consulting	
		Services Used	153
		Op. 14. Cost of 19X2 Taxes	207

Uses

Op. 15.	Interest Charges	23
16.	Dividends Declared	135
18.	Retirement of Bonds Payable	21
24.	Purchase of Delivery Equipment	65
25.	Purchase of Store Equipment	200
26.	Purchase of Land	23

* *Ordinary operating sales of the firm's usual goods and services.*

Step 4. Subdivide both lists into operating, noncurrent asset, noncurrent equity, and dividend activities.

Sources			Uses		
Operating:			**Operating:**		
Op.	Sales	$6,200	Op.	Cost of Merchandise Sold	$4,070
			Op.	Cost of Employee Service Used	1,125
Noncurrent Asset:			Op.	Cost of Supplies Used	57
	Sale of Old Store Equipment	$ 42	Op.	Cost of Utility Services Used	180
	Sale of Old Building	30	Op.	Cost of Consulting Services Used	153
		$ 72	Op.	Cost of 19X2 Taxes	207
			Op.	Interest Charges	23
Noncurrent Equity:					$5,815
	Issue of Capital Stock	$ 153			

Noncurrent Asset:		
Purchase of Delivery Equipment		$ 65
Purchase of Store Equipment		200
Purchase of Land		23
		$ 288
Noncurrent Equity:		
Bonds Payable Retired		$ 21
Dividend:		
Declaration of Dividends		$ 135

Step 5. Combine all operating activities on one list.

Sources

Operating:			
Op.	Sales		$6,200
Op.	Cost of Merchandise Sold	$4,070	
Op.	Cost of Employee Services Used	1,125	
Op.	Cost of Supplies Used	57	
Op.	Cost of Utility Services Used	180	
Op.	Cost of Consulting Services Used	153	
Op.	Cost of 19X9 Taxes	207	
Op.	Interest Charges	23	5,815
			$ 385

continued on page 346

Noncurrent Asset:
  Sale of Old Store Equipment . . . . $ 42
  Sale of Old Building   30
                         $ 72

Noncurrent Equity:
  Issue of Capital Stock . . . . $ 153

Uses

Noncurrent Asset:
  Purchase of Delivery Equipment . . . . $ 65
  Purchase of Store Equipment   200
  Purchase of Land   23
                         $ 288

Noncurrent Equity:
  Bonds Payable Retired . . . . $ 21

Dividend:
  Declaration of Dividends . . . . $ 135

Step 6. Prepare suitable headings and footings.

Illustration 7-4

Instance, Inc.
Sources and Uses of Net Working Capital
For the Year 19X2

Sources:
Operations:
  Receipts:
    Sales $6,200
  Expenditures:
    Cost of Merchandise Sold $4,070
    Cost of Employee Services   1,125
    Cost of Supplies Used   57
    Cost of Utility Services   180
    Cost of Consulting Services   153
    Cost of 19X2 Taxes   207
    Interest Charges   23   5,815

Effect of Operations on Net Working Capital . . . . $ 385
Proceeds from Sale of Noncurrent Assets:
  Store Equipment . . . . $ 42
  Building   30   72

Proceeds from Issue of Noncurrent Equities:
  Capital Stock Issued   153

Net Sources . . . . $ 601

Uses:
Purchase of Noncurrent Assets:
  Delivery Equipment . . . . $ 65
  Store Equipment   200
  Land . . . .   23 $ 288

Retirement of Noncurrent Equities:
Bonds Payable Retired 21
Dividends Declared 135

Net Uses . . . . $ 444

Increase in Net Working Capital . . . . $ 166

Net Working Capital—12/31/X2:
Current Assets $1,071
Current Liabilities. . . . . 654 $ 417

Net Working Capital—12/31/X1:
Current Assets $1,075
Current Liabilities. 824 251

Increase in Net Working Capital . . . . $ 166

Illustration 7-4 uses the title "Sources and Uses of Net Working Capital" instead of "Funds Statement" or "Statement of Changes in Financial Position." Any of those titles would be acceptable, but the first is used here because it seems least subject to misinterpretation. Finally, the word "applications" often is substituted for "uses," so that funds statements frequently are called statements of "Sources and Applications of Funds."

The purpose of preparing a statement of sources and uses of net working capital is to obtain a report of all major financial changes. Illustration 7-4 provides just that, but, as you have seen, it also discusses and summarizes a number of operating changes. If you wish to restrict the funds statement to financial changes, just follow this rule: *Summarize all operating changes by a single figure.*[5] This figure is often labeled "funds from operations," as in Illustration 7-5.

Illustration 7-5

Instance, Inc.
Sources and Uses of Net Working Capital
For the Year 19X2

Sources:
Funds from Operations $385
Proceeds from Sale of Noncurrent Assets:
Store Equipment . . . . $ 42
Building 30 72

Proceeds from Issue of Noncurrent Equities:
Capital Stock Issued 153

Net Sources $610

Uses:
Purchases of Noncurrent Assets:
Delivery Equipment . . . . $ 65
Store Equipment 200
Land 23 $288

continued on page 348

---

[5] To repeat what was said in the previous footnote, this is a simplification of the actual practice, which is discussed in Chapter Nine.

Retirement of Noncurrent Equities:
Bonds Payable Retired. 21
Dividends Declared 135

Net Uses **$444**

Increase in Net Working Capital. **$166**

Net Working Capital—12/31/X2 . . . . **$417**
Net Working Capital—12/31/X1 251

Increase in Net Working Capital. **$166**

It should be emphasized again that Illustration 7-5 represents just one of several possible forms that might be used for a funds statement. You have already seen an alternative form on page 90. There is a great deal of variety in such forms, partly because the funds statement is one of the more recent reports developed by accountants and is still undergoing a good deal of experiment; the form in Illustrations 7-4 and 7-5 will be used for the remainder of this chapter, then modified slightly in Chapter Nine.

A possible shortcut

Pages 314–315 illustrated a possible shortcut method for preparation of cash statements. There is a similar shortcut method for the preparation of funds statements.

Begin by putting the firm's journal entries in simple, summary form. Label each operating change that affects the balance of net working capital either R or E, depending upon whether it is a receipt or expenditure. Label each financial change affecting the balance of net working capital S or U, depending upon whether it is a source or use of funds. All changes that remain unlabeled are to be ignored. Move directly from this labeled set of simple summary journal entries to the construction of the funds statement itself. This is illustrated below for the simple summary journal entries of Instance, Inc.

Illustration 7-6

Instance, Inc.
Shortcut Method for Preparing Funds Statement
For the Year 19X2

1.	Merchandise Inventory	3,960		8.	Retained Earnings	153
	Accounts Payable		3,960		Cash	153 ^{E}
2.	Accounts Receivable	6,200		9.	Retained Earnings	18
	Retained Earnings		6,200 ^{R}		Buildings	18
3.	Retained Earnings	4,070		10.	Retained Earnings	144
	Merchandise Inventory		4,070 ^{E}		Store Equipment	144
4.	Retained Earnings	1,125		11.	Retained Earnings	91
	Cash		1,125 ^{E}		Delivery Equipment	91
5.	Supplies	44		12a.	Cash	42
	Accounts Payable		44		Store Equipment	42 ^{S}
6.	Retained Earnings	57		12b.	Store Equipment	6
	Supplies		57 ^{E}		Retained Earnings	6
7.	Retained Earnings	180		13a.	Cash	30
	Accounts Payable		180 ^{E}		Buildings	30 ^{S}

13b. Retained Earnings	18			20. Accounts Payable	4,452	
Buildings		18		Cash		4,452
14. Retained Earnings	207			21. Taxes Payable	216	
Taxes Payable		207	E	Cash		216
15. Retained Earnings	23			22. Interest Payable	24	
Interest Payable		23	E	Cash		24
16. Retained Earnings	135		U	23. Dividends Payable	115	
Dividends Payable		135		Cash		115
17. Cash	153			24. Delivery Equipment	65	
Capital Stock		153	S	Accounts Payable		65 U
18. Bonds Payable	21			25. Store Equipment	200	
Cash		21	U	Cash		200 U
19. Cash	6,210			26. Land	23	
Accounts Receivable		6,210		Accounts Payable		23 U

Another example of a funds statement

The discussion of funds statements has been fairly involved, and another example will help tie things together. The example to be used is derived from Problem 5-3 and its solution (see pages 248, 251).

Illustration 7-7 gives the comparative balance sheets of Senner Home Repairs, Inc., at 12/31/X1 and 12/31/X2. Illustration 7-8 gives a narrative summary of the company's 19X2 balance sheet changes. From this information, a statement of sources and uses of net working capital will be constructed. If you understand the discussion up to this point, try solving the following example without looking at the solution. Feel free to use the shortcut approach if you believe that you understand this material. If you have no particular difficulties with this problem, feel free to skim Problems 7-1 and 7-2 and their solutions instead of actually solving them. However, you should study the other matters discussed in this chapter.

Illustration 7-7

Senner Home Repairs, Inc.
Comparative Balance Sheets
12/31/X1 and 12/31/X2

Assets

	12/31/X1	12/31/X2
Current Assets:		
Cash	$ 3,500	$ 5,300
Accounts Receivable	6,800	4,500
Supplies	11,200	9,800
Prepaid Insurance	900	500
Prepaid Taxes	1,300	1,400
Total Current Assets	$23,700	$21,500
Noncurrent Assets:		
Land	$ 5,000	$ 5,000
Building	24,900	23,500
Equipment	36,300	39,900
Total Noncurrent Assets	$66,200	$68,400
Total Assets	$89,900	$89,900

continued on page 350

Equities

Current Liabilities:		
Accounts Payable	$ 5,900	$ 7,500
Wages Payable	1,200	1,400
6% Note Payable—due 9/1/X2	10,000	–0–
Interest Payable.	300	–0–
Total Current Liabilities	$17,400	$ 8,900
Noncurrent Liabilities:		
Mortgage Payable	15,000	14,700
Total Liabilities	$32,400	$23,600
Stockholders' Equity:		
Capital Stock	$50,000	$50,000
Retained Earnings	7,500	16,300
Total Stockholders' Equity	$57,500	$66,300
Total Equities	$89,900	$89,900

Illustration 7-8

Senner Home Repairs, Inc.
Narrative Summary of Balance Sheet Changes
For the Year 19X2

1. Cash sales totalled $35,400.
2. Accounts receivable of $112,600 were collected.
3. Employees earned wages of $71,000. All wages are recorded as liabilities before being paid.
4. Supplies costing $43,800 were purchased on account.
5. Depreciation of equipment was $10,300.
6. Total cash payments of $300 were made to reduce the principal of the company's mortgage payable.
7. Total cash payments of $900 were made for interest charges on the company's mortgage payable. Mortgage interest is paid once per month, and none was owed at either 12/31/X1 or 12/31/X2.
8. During 19X1 the company had prepaid $1,300 of 19X2 taxes. All of these prepayments expired during the year.
9. During 19X2, the company paid an additional $6,000 of 19X2 taxes that had not been prepaid in 19X1.
10. The company paid $56,100 of accounts payable.
11. Sales on account totalled $110,300.
12. Wages payable of $70,800 were paid.
13. Supplies that had cost the company $45,200 were used.
14. Equipment costing $13,900 was purchased on account.
15. Depreciation of building was $1,400.
16. Prepaid insurance of $400 expired.
17. Interest charges for 19X2 on the company's 6% note payable were $400.
18. Total cash payments of $700 were made for interest payable on the company's 6% notes payable (this includes $300 of interest charges accrued in 19X1).
19. The company paid its 6% note payable of $10,000.
20. The company prepaid $1,400 of 19X3 taxes.

Although the shortcut method could be used in solving this problem, the more detailed method is shown below for the benefit of those readers who may be experiencing difficulties. The shortcut method is illustrated on pages 348–349.

Step 1. Express the company's journal entries in simple summary form.

Op.	1.	Cash	35,400		Op. 11.	Accounts Receivable	110,300	
		Retained Earnings		35,400		Retained Earnings		110,300
Op.	2.	Cash	112,600		Op. 12.	Wages Payable	70,800	
		Accounts Receivable		112,600		Cash		70,800
Op.	3.	Retained Earnings	71,000		Op. 13.	Retained Earnings	45,200	
		Wages Payable		71,000		Supplies		45,200
Op.	4.	Supplies	43,800		14.	Equipment	13,900	
		Accounts Payable		43,800		Accounts Payable		13,900
Op.	5.	Retained Earnings	10,300		Op. 15.	Retained Earnings	1,400	
		Equipment		10,300		Building		1,400
	6.	Mortgage Payable	300		Op. 16.	Retained Earnings	400	
		Cash		300		Prepaid Insurance		400
Op.	7.	Retained Earnings	900		Op. 17.	Retained Earnings	400	
		Cash		900		Interest Payable		400
Op.	8.	Retained Earnings	1,300		Op. 18.	Interest Payable	700	
		Prepaid Taxes		1,300		Cash		700
Op.	9.	Retained Earnings	6,000		19.	6% Notes Payable	10,000	
		Cash		6,000		Cash		10,000
Op. 10.		Accounts Payable	56,100		Op. 20.	Prepaid Taxes	1,400	
		Cash		56,100		Cash		1,400

Since the taxes involved in Entry 9 were 19X2 taxes, it follows that by the end of 19X2 they would no longer be prepaid. Therefore, the appropriate summary debit is to retained earnings instead of to prepaid taxes. Once again, all operating entries have been marked "Op.," even though it is not customary practice to do so.

Step 2. Select all changes that affect the balance of net working capital; ignore the rest.[6]

Increase changes				Decrease changes		
Op. 1. Cash	35,400		Op. 3. Retained Earnings	71,000	
Retained Earnings		35,400	Wages Payable		71,000
Op. 11. Accounts Receivable	110,300		6. Mortgage Payable	300	
Retained Earnings		110,300	Cash		300
			Op. 7. Retained Earnings	900	
			Cash		900
			Op. 8. Retained Earnings	1,300	
			Prepaid Taxes		1,300
			Op. 9. Retained Earnings	6,000	
			Cash		6,000
			Op. 13. Retained Earnings	45,200	
			Supplies		45,200
			14. Equipment	13,900	
			Accounts Payable		13,900
			Op. 16. Retained Earnings	400	
			Prepaid Insurance		400
			Op. 17. Retained Earnings	400	
			Interest Payable		400

[6] Here are the changes that do *not* affect the balance of net working capital. Regarding Entry 19, notice that the 6% note payable was a current liability (due in less than one year). Its retirement had the following form, which is a double-effect change:

Current liability	XXX	
Current asset		XXX

Double-effect changes			No-effect changes		
2. Cash	112,600		5. Retained Earnings	10,300	
Accounts Receivable		112,600	Equipment		10,300
4. Supplies	43,800		15. Retained Earnings	1,400	
Accounts Payable		43,800	Building		1,400
10. Accounts Payable	56,100				
Cash		56,100			
12. Wages Payable	70,800				
Cash		70,800			
18. Interest Payable	700				
Cash		700			
19. 6% Notes Payable	10,000				
Cash		10,000			
20. Prepaid Taxes	1,400				
Cash		1,400			

Steps 3 and 4. Prepare separate lists of sources and uses; subdivide both lists into operating, noncurrent asset, noncurrent equity, and dividend activities.

The increase changes shown above are the sources, and the decrease changes are the uses of net working capital, so Step 3 has already been performed. At this point, you may wish to refer back to Illustration 7-3 for explanation of some of the journal entries. Notice that there was no dividend activity for this company.

Sources		*Uses*	
Operating:		Operating:	
1. Cash Sales	$ 35,400	3. Cost of Employee Services	$ 71,000
11. Sales on Account	110,300	7. Interest Charges on Mortgage	900
	$145,700	8. Partial Cost of 19X2 Taxes	1,300
		9. Partial Cost of 19X2 Taxes	6,000
		13. Cost of Supplies Used	45,200
		16. Cost of Insurance Expired	400
		17. Interest Charges on 6% Note	400
			$125,200
		Noncurrent Assets:	
		14. Equipment Purchased	$ 13,900
		Noncurrent Equities:	
		6. Partial Payment of Mortgage	$ 300

Step 5. Combine all operating activities on a single list: summarize all operating changes by a single figure.

(Funds from operations = $145,700 − $125,200 = $20,500.)

Sources		*Uses*	
Funds from Operations	$20,500	Noncurrent Assets: Equipment Purchased	$13,900
		Noncurrent Equities: Payment on Mortgage	$ 300

As you can see, the resulting funds statement is going to be a very simple one because there were actually only two financial changes during 19X2—the purchase of equipment and the payment of mortgage principal.

Step 6. Prepare suitable headings and footings.

Illustration 7-9

Senner Home Repairs, Inc.
Sources and Uses of Net Working Capital
For the Year 19X2

Sources:
Funds from Operations $20,500

Uses:
Purchase of Noncurrent Assets:
  Equipment Purchased $13,900
Payment of Noncurrent Equities:
  Payment of Mortgage Payable Principal. 300

Net Uses $14,200

Increase in Net Working Capital for the Year . . . . $ 6,300

Net Working Capital—12/31/X2 . . . . $12,600
Net Working Capital—12/31/X1 6,300

Increase in Net Working Capital for the Year . . . . $ 6,300

Here is the shortcut method for preparing this funds statement:

Illustration 7-10

Senner Home Repairs, Inc.
Shortcut Method for Preparing Funds Statement
For the Year 19X2

1. Cash	35,400			11. Accounts Receivable	110,300		
Retained Earnings		35,400	R	Retained Earnings		110,300	R
2. Cash	112,600			12. Wages Payable	70,800		
Accounts Receivable		112,600		Cash		70,800	
3. Retained Earnings	71,000			13. Retained Earnings	45,200		
Wages Payable		71,000	E	Supplies		45,200	E
4. Supplies	43,800			14. Equipment	13,900		
Accounts Payable		43,800		Accounts Payable		13,900	U
5. Retained Earnings	10,300			15. Retained Earnings	1,400		
Equipment		10,300		Building		1,400	
6. Mortgage Payable	300			16. Retained Earnings	400		
Cash		300	U	Prepaid Insurance		400	E
7. Retained Earnings	900			17. Retained Earnings	400		
Cash		900	E	Interest Payable		400	E
8. Retained Earnings	1,300			18. Interest Payable	700		
Prepaid Taxes		1,300	E	Cash		700	
9. Retained Earnings	6,000			19. 6% Notes Payable	10,000		
Cash		6,000	E	Cash		10,000	
10. Accounts Payable	56,100			20. Prepaid Taxes	1,400		
Cash		56,100		Cash		1,400	

Notice the schedule of changes in net working capital appended to the foot of Illustration 7-9. The main purpose of this kind of appendage is to assure the reader that the figures reported in the main part of the statement are consistent with changes recorded in the company's balance sheets. In published financial statements this appendage becomes very elaborate, often appearing in a form like the following:

Changes in Net Working Capital

	12/31/X1	12/31/X2	Increase/ (De- crease)
Current Assets:			
Cash	$ 3,500	$ 5,300	$ 1,800
Accounts Receivable .	6,800	4,500	(2,300)
Supplies . . .	11,200	9,800	(1,400)
Prepaid Insurance .	900	500	(400)
Total Current Assets .	1,300	1,400	100
Total Current Assets . .	$23,700	$21,500	$ (2,200)
Current Liabilities:			
Accounts Payable .	$ 5,900	$ 7,500	$ 1,600
Wages Payable . .	1,200	1,400	200
6% Note Payable .	10,000	–0–	(10,000)
Interest Payable. .	300	–0–	(300)
Total Current Liabilities .	$17,400	$ 8,900	$ (8,500)
Net Working Capital .	$ 6,300	$12,600	$ 6,300

The Accounting Principles Board requires that all published funds statements contain an appendage of this kind, either as part of the statement itself or in a supporting schedule. The reasons for this requirement are not made entirely clear, but the Accounting Principles Board is an authoritative body and most firms comply with its opinions. Nonetheless, there are two main disadvantages to such an elaborate appendage:

1. It is redundant because it reports detailed information already given on the balance sheet.

2. It can lead readers to think that details of changes in year-end composition of current assets and current liabilities are the main thing reported by the funds statement. Actually, what is important in the funds statement is the information about financial changes in the noncurrent accounts. *The information about changes in the composition of year-end net working capital is the least important thing reported by the funds statement.* Consequently this book will keep the appendages to funds statements as brief as possible; your understanding of actual funds statements will not be hindered, and time and space will be saved.

Current maturation of long-term debt

One final technical matter relating to funds statement construction should be mentioned at this point, since references to it are occasionally made in published financial statements. As the maturity date of long-term debt approaches, a time eventually is reached at which the debt becomes due within one year. At that point, by definition, it becomes a current liability.

The *maturation* of a debt occurs when that debt becomes due; by analogy, this becoming-current sometimes is called the debt's *current maturation*. The effect of a debt's current maturation is to decrease net working capital:

	Effect on *Liabilities*	*Effect on* *Net Working Capital*
Current:	Increase	Decrease
Noncurrent:	Decrease	No effect

Since whatever happens to *non*current liabilities does not affect the balance of net working capital, the effect on net working capital of the current maturation of a noncurrent liability is solely to increase current liabilities and decrease its balance. This decrease would be reported on the funds statement as a use of funds. Similarly, the current maturation of a long-term receivable to a point where it became due within one year would be reported as a source of funds.

Example

In the following example, interest payments are ignored for brevity. On 3/1/X0 Mize-Ellsworth Corporation issued $1,000,000 of five-year, $7\frac{1}{2}\%$ bonds payable, due 3/1/X5. There was a $1,000,000 source of funds in 19X0 and no effect on net working capital during 19X1, 19X2, and 19X3. During 19X4 these bonds became a current liability—and should be so reported on the firm's 12/31/X4 balance sheet. If the firm wished, a journal entry similar to the following could be made as of 3/1/X4, but many firms would not bother to do this:

Bonds Payable	1,000,000	
Bonds Payable Due Within One Year		1,000,000

Regardless of whether such an entry were made, on 3/1/X4 the firm acquired a current liability in place of a noncurrent one, net working capital decreased by $1,000,000, and this should be reported as a use of funds. When, on 3/1/X5, the bonds are actually *paid,* there will be no effect on net working capital, since simultaneous decreases in a current liability and a current asset have occurred.

For simplicity, the remaining examples in the text itself ignore such current maturation of long-term debt. But there are other examples of it in some of the Assignment Problems.

Funds

When calling statements like those in Illustration 7-5 or 7-9 "funds statements," the word "funds" is being used in the technical sense of short-run economic power. When a company wishes to purchase something, in the short run, it can do so by paying cash—up to the point where its cash runs out. Another alternative is to buy on credit—up to the point where short-run credit becomes hard to obtain. Still another possibility is to wait until sales of its products or services have generated additional cash. Over the operating cycle, all current assets help generate cash, and all current liabilities (except advances from customers) are generally paid in cash. A company's short-run economic power is thus closely related to the balance of its current assets and current liabilities—its net working capital. *Call this short-run economic power the company's "command over funds."*

A company's command over funds usually exceeds its cash balance, though the latter is included in the former. As a student you also have a greater command of funds than of cash; that is, your short-run ability to purchase goods and services is usually greater than the total of your bank balance and currency holdings. You can buy some things on credit, borrow small sums from friends, and so forth. Similarly, when considering a company's short-run economic power, its command over funds is more significant than its bank balance, particularly since it is customary for companies to do most of their business on credit.

One index of a company's command over funds is its net working capital balance. There are other possible indexes of a company's command over funds. (One index is discussed in Chapter Nine). By using net working capital as an index, however, it is possible to answer several of the questions asked on page 337 of this chapter. Illustration 7-5 (Instance, Inc.) serves as a good example.

How has the company been financing its activities?

Instance, Inc.'s main source of new funds is its operations, but there have also been important sources of funds from financial activities. Over a third of the company's new funds come from such things as sales of old noncurrent assets and, more importantly, a new issue of capital stock. Illustration 7-5 shows the details.

What has management been doing with the investment entrusted to it?
Where's all the money going?

The balance sheet gives a summary answer to these questions by reporting the cumulative effects of management's actions to date. The statement of sources and uses of net working capital gives the details of what has happened during the current year. Management has used funds to retire long-term debt and to acquire noncurrent assets. It has built up its net working capital balance by $166, while declaring dividends of $135. Illustration 7-5 gives the details of these activities and answers such questions as the following:

Has the company been buying new noncurrent assets? Has it retired any of its old noncurrent debt? Has it issued or retired any capital stock?

While a detailed appendage showing changes in the composition of net working capital is superfluous, information about the overall change in net working capital is quite significant. This change represents a change in the company's capacity to raise the wherewithal to seize unexpected opportunities or respond to emergencies. In general, by using net working capital as an index of command over funds, it is possible to report upon a variety of matters of concern to investors.

Problems for Study and Self-Examination

If you were able to solve the previous illustration without difficulty, feel free to go on to page 369. If you did not solve this illustration by yourself, or if you found it difficult, solve Problem 7-1.

Problem 7-1:

This problem is designed to include a number of financial changes. Various simplifications have been employed to save you time, with the result that this problem is not completely realistic.

Illustration 7-11 gives the comparative balance sheets of Miami Corporation at 12/31/X1 and 12/31/X2. Illustration 7-12 is a narrative summary of the company's balance sheet changes for 19X2. Prepare a funds statement. Feel free to use the short-cut method. Use good form. Compare your answer with the "official" one before going on.

Illustration 7-11

Miami Corporation
Comparative Balance Sheets
December 31, 19X1 and 19X2

	December 31 19X1	December 31 19X2
Assets		
Current Assets:		
Cash	$ 200	$ 170
Accounts Receivable	350	390
Inventories	500	480
Total Current Assets	$1,050	$1,040
Noncurrent Assets:		
Land	$ 150	$ 90
Buildings	380	450
Equipment	1,200	1,330
Patents	400	430
Total Noncurrent Assets	$2,130	$2,300
Total Assets	$3,180	$3,340
Equities		
Current Liabilities:		
Accounts Payable	$ 250	$ 300
Other Payables	250	30
Total Current Liabilities	$ 500	$ 330
Noncurrent Liabilities:		
Bonds Payable	$1,000	$1,100
Mortgage Payable	500	200
Total Noncurrent Liabilities	$1,500	$1,300
Total Liabilities	$2,000	$1,630

continued on page 358

Stockholders' Equity:

Capital Stock	$1,000	$1,500
Retained Earnings.	180	210
Total Stockholders' Equity	$1,180	$1,710
Total Equities	$3,180	$3,340

Illustration 7-12

Miami Corporation
Narrative Summary of Balance Sheet Changes
For the Year 19X2

1. Sales on account totalled $2,160; all sales were on account.
2. In making these sales, the company used up inventories that had cost $1,200.
3. Accounts receivable totalling $2,120 were collected.
4. Miscellaneous costs of operations totalled $480; all related purchases were made on account (credit Other Payables).
5. Interest charges totalled $80; all interest is paid on the last day of each month.
6a. Equipment was sold for cash proceeds of $220.
6b. The equipment sold had a book value (cost less accumulated depreciation) of $300 at the time it was sold.
7. During the year, the company purchased $670 of equipment, all on account.
8. The company issued additional capital stock for $500, cash.
9. Depreciation of equipment totalled $240.
10. The company purchased a new building for $100, cash.
11. Total depreciation of buildings was $30.
12. The company purchased new patents for $80, cash.
13. Total amortization of patents was $50.
14a. Land was sold for total cash proceeds of $290.
14b. The land sold had cost the company only $60.
15. The company issued additional bonds payable for $100, cash.
16. The company made a $300 payment on the principal of its mortgage payable.
17. The company purchased inventories costing $1,180, all on account.
18. The company paid $700 of Other Payables.
19. The company paid $1,800 of accounts payable.
20. The company declared and paid $200 of dividends. Because payment was made immediately, the dividends were not first recorded as a liability.

Problem 7-2 (Optional):

Do not attempt this problem until you have made a serious effort to solve Problem 7-1 and have carefully reviewed its solution. If you found Problem 7-1 fairly easy, there is no reason for you to solve this problem; if Problem 7-1 proved difficult, this problem will serve as additional review.

Complete information concerning Campus Store for the period 7/1/X4 to 6/30/X5 is given below. Prepare a statement of sources and uses of net working capital. Feel free to use the shortcut method. Use good form.

Campus Store is a privately owned bookstore serving the students and faculty of a large university. The company prepares financial statements once a year, every

June 30. A summary of the company's balance sheet changes for the fiscal year 19X4–19X5 is given below, but certain details of the company's activities first need to be explained.

(a) The company, which has been gradually expanding, has become increasingly cramped in its present quarters. In April, 19X4, the company began construction of a new store building next door to its present one. To finance this project, the company obtained a $700,000 loan commitment from a life insurance company. Campus Store actually borrows only enough to pay for construction costs as they are incurred, although it expects to borrow the whole $700,000 before the building is completed. Interest is charged at a rate of 6 percent on amounts actually borrowed. The total loan is to be paid off over a 20-year period beginning July 1, 19X7.

(b) Amounts owed to the contractor who is erecting the new building are recorded in a special current liability account called "construction payable." All construction costs are recorded as a liability before being paid.

(c) Most company sales are for cash, but university faculty members are allowed to buy on account. In addition to books, the company sells some general merchandise: school supplies, toiletries, tobacco, etc.

(d) Store customers who save their cash register receipts are entitled to turn them in at the end of each fiscal year for a 5 percent patronage refund. The company finds that only about 60 percent of all cash register receipts are turned in for this refund.

(e) The company takes a physical inventory of merchandise and supplies once a year, every June 30, using the periodic inventory method (see page 207). It keeps separate track of the cost of books and the cost of general merchandise sold.

Shown below are the firm's comparative balance sheets as of 6/30/X4 and 6/30/X5, and a narrative summary of its balance sheet changes for the year ended 6/30/X5.

Campus Store
Comparative Balance Sheets
June 30, 19X4, and June 30, 19X5

Assets

	6/30/X4	6/30/X5
Current Assets:		
Cash	$ 97,200	$153,900
Accounts Receivable	19,400	23,800
Merchandise: Books	247,700	258,300
General	96,200	94,300
Store Supplies	3,500	3,200
Prepaid Insurance	5,700	8,300
Total Current Assets	$469,700	$541,800
Noncurrent Assets:		
Land	$ 27,600	$ 27,600
Building	142,500	135,000
Fixtures	64,500	58,200
Building Under Construction	6,700	208,600
Total Noncurrent Assets	$241,300	$429,400
Total Assets	$711,000	$971,200

continued on page 360

Equities

Current Liabilities:

Accounts Payable	$ 78,400	$ 75,100
Construction Payable	–0–	80,100
Taxes Payable	71,900	89,100
Salaries Payable	3,400	1,700
Interest Payable	–0–	2,100
Total Current Liabilities	$153,700	$248,100

Noncurrent Liabilities:

6% Notes Payable	–0–	105,000
Total Liabilities	$153,700	$353,100

Stockholders' Equity:

Capital Stock	$500,000	$500,000
Retained Earnings	57,300	118,100
Total Stockholders' Equity	$557,300	$618,100
Total Equities	$711,000	$971,200

Campus Store
Narrative Summary of Balance Sheet Changes for the Year Ended 6/30/X5

1. Cash sales totalled $1,625,900.
2. Sales on account totalled $166,800.
3. During the year, the company borrowed a total of $105,000 on its loan commitment from the insurance company. (Change 9 discusses the interest costs related to this borrowing.)
4. The company bought $10,600 of advertising (mostly newspaper advertising) on account. Following conventional accounting practice, the company wrote off the entire cost of advertising during the year of purchase.
5. The company bought $9,400 of utility services (water, heat, light, telephone) for cash.
6. Customers claimed and were paid patronage refunds totalling $53,700.
7. The company's income taxes for the year totalled $76,100; the company records all taxes as liabilities before they are paid.
8. The company's property taxes for the year totalled $16,800.
9. Interest charges on the firm's 6 percent loan commitment totalled $3,600. The company records all interest charges as liabilities before they are paid.
10. Dividends were declared totalling $15,000. These dividends were payable six weeks after their declaration date.
11. Miscellaneous costs of operations paid directly in cash totalled $4,800.
12. Miscellaneous costs of operations purchased on account totalled $6,400.
13. All salaries are recorded as liabilities before they are paid. Total salaries for the year were $174,200.
14. The company purchased $9,900 of fixtures (shelves and counters) on account.
15. Bills received from the contractor who is erecting the new store totalled $201,900.
16. Accounts receivable totalling $162,400 were collected.
17. Store supplies costing $13,300 were purchased on account.
18. Books costing $1,035,700 were purchased on account.
19. General merchandise costing $296,900 was purchased on account.

20. Insurance policies costing $7,000 were purchased for cash.
21. See Change 9. The company paid $1,500 of interest on its loan from the insurance company.
22. Salaries of $1,700 were owed employees at 6/30/X5.
23. Taxes payable of $75,700 were paid.
24. $15,000 of dividends payable were paid.
25. Bills from the contractor (for the new building) totalling $121,800 were paid.
26. Accounts payable of $1,376,100 were paid.
27. Prepaid insurance of $4,400 expired.
28. Store supplies that had cost the company $13,600 were consumed during the year.
29. Books that had cost the company $1,025,100 were sold during the year.
30. General merchandise that had cost the company $298,800 was sold during the year.
31. Depreciation of building totalled $7,500 for the year.
32. Depreciation of fixtures totalled $8,700 for the year.
33a. On 6/30/X5 old fixtures (owned on 6/30/X4) were sold for $4,300, cash. (You already have recorded 19X4–19X5 depreciation for these fixtures in Change 32.)
33b. The cost less accumulated depreciation of the fixtures sold in Change 33a was $7,500 at the time of sale.

Solutions

Solution 7-1:

Although the shortcut method could be used in solving this problem, the more detailed method will be shown first for the benefit of those readers who are experiencing difficulties. The shortcut method is illustrated on pages 364–365.

Step 1. Put all balance sheet changes in simple summary journal entries.

Op.	1.	Accounts Receivable	2,160		Op.	11.	Retained Earnings	30
		Retained Earnings		2,160			Buildings		30
Op.	2.	Retained Earnings	1,200			12.	Patents	80
		Inventories		1,200			Cash		80
Op.	3.	Cash	2,120		Op.	13.	Retained Earnings	50
		Accounts Receivable		2,120			Patents		50
Op.	4.	Retained Earnings	480			14a.	Cash	290
		Other Payables		480			Land		290
Op.	5.	Retained Earnings	80			14b.	Land	230
		Cash		80			Retained Earnings		230
	6a.	Cash	220			15.	Cash	100
		Equipment		220			Bonds Payable		100
	6b.	Retained Earnings	80			16.	Mortgage Payable	300
		Equipment		80			Cash		300
	7.	Equipment	670		Op.	17.	Inventories	1,180
		Accounts Payable		670			Accounts Payable		1,180
	8.	Cash	500		Op.	18.	Other Payables	700
		Capital Stock		500			Cash		700
Op.	9.	Retained Earnings	240		Op.	19.	Accounts Payable	1,800
		Equipment		240			Cash		1,800
	10.	Buildings	100			20.	Retained Earnings	200
		Cash		100			Cash		200

Entries 6a–b and 14a–b follow the rules developed on pages 246–247 for recording nonoperating sales of nonmonetary assets.

Step 2. Select all changes that affect the balance of net working capital: ignore the rest.[7]

		Increase changes					Decrease changes	
Op.	1.	Accounts Receivable	2,160		Op.	2.	Retained Earnings	1,200
		Retained Earnings		2,160			Inventories		1,200
	6a.	Cash	220		Op.	4.	Retained Earnings	480
		Equipment		220			Other Payables		480
	8.	Cash	500		Op.	5.	Retained Earnings	80
		Capital Stock		500			Cash		80
	14a.	Cash	290			7.	Equipment	670
		Land		290			Accounts Payable		670
	15.	Cash	100			10.	Buildings	100
		Bonds Payable		100			Cash		100
						12.	Patents	80
							Cash		80
						16.	Mortgage Payable	300
							Cash		300
						20.	Retained Earnings	200
							Cash		200

---

[7] The following changes are ignored: (*footnote continues on page 363*)

Steps 3 and 4. Prepare separate lists of sources and uses: subdivide both lists into operating, noncurrent asset, noncurrent equity, and dividend activities.

You may wish to refer back to Illustration 7-12 for explanations of some of the following changes.

Sources		Uses	
Operating:		**Operating:**	
Op. 1. Sales on Account . . .	$2,160	Op. 2. Cost of Inventories Used . .	$1,200
		Op. 4. Other Costs of Operations .	480
		Op. 5. Interest Charges	80
			$1,760
Noncurrent Asset:		**Noncurrent Asset:**	
6a. Proceeds from Sale of		7. Purchase of Equipment . .	$ 670
Equipment	$ 220	10. Purchase of Building . . .	100
14a. Proceeds from Sale of Land	290	12. Purchase of Patents . . .	80
	$ 510		$ 850
Noncurrent Equity:		**Noncurrent Equity:**	
8. Proceeds from Issue of		16. Payment Made on	
Capital Stock . . .	$ 500	Mortgage	$ 300
15. Proceeds from Issue of			
Bonds Payable . . .	100	**Dividend:**	
	$ 600	20. Dividends Declared . . .	$ 200

Step 5. Combine all operating activities on one list; summarize all operating changes by a single figure.

´Sources		Uses	
Funds from Operations*	$ 400	**Noncurrent Asset:**	
		Purchase of Equipment . . .	$ 670
Noncurrent Asset:		Purchase of Building	100
Sale of Equipment.	$ 220	Purchase of Patents	80
Sale of Land	290		$ 850
	$ 510		
		Noncurrent Equity:	
Noncurrent Equity:		Payment Made on Mortgage . .	$ 300
Issue of Capital Stock . . .	$ 500		
Issue of Bonds Payable . . .	100	**Dividend:**	
	$ 600	Dividends Declared	$ 200

* *$2,160 − $1,760 = $400.*

Double-effect changes				No-effect changes		
3. Cash	2,120		7b.	Retained Earnings	80	
Accounts Receivable		2,120		Equipment		80
17. Inventories	1,180		9.	Retained Earnings	240	
Accounts Payable		1,180		Equipment		240
18. Other Payables	700		11.	Retained Earnings	30	
Cash		700		Buildings		30
19. Accounts Payable	1,800		13.	Retained Earnings	50	
Cash		1,800		Patents		50
			14b.	Land	230	
				Retained Earnings		230

Step 6. Prepare suitable headings and footings.

Illustration 7-13

Miami Corporation
Sources and Uses of Net Working Capital
For the Year 19X2

Sources:

Funds from Operations		$ 400
Proceeds from Sale of Noncurrent Assets:		
Equipment Sold	$ 220	
Land Sold	290	510
Proceeds from Issue of Noncurrent Equities:		
Capital Stock Issued	$ 500	
Bonds Payable Issued.	100	600
Net Sources		$1,510

Uses:

Purchase of Noncurrent Assets:		
Equipment Purchased	$ 670	
Building Purchased	100	
Patents Purchased	80	$ 850
Retirement of Noncurrent Equities:		
Payment Made on Mortgage Principal		300
Dividends Declared		200
Net Uses		$1,350
Increase in Net Working Capital		$ 160

Net Working Capital—12/31/X2:		
Current Assets	$1,040	
Current Liabilities.	330	$ 710
Net Working Capital—12/31/X1:		
Current Assets	$1,050	
Current Liabilities.	500	550
Increase in Net Working Capital		$ 160

Here is the shortcut method of preparing this funds statement:

Illustration 7-14

Miami Corporation
Shortcut Method for Preparing Funds Statement
For the Year 19X2

1. Accounts Receivable	2,160		4. Retained Earnings	480	
Retained Earnings		2,160 R	Other Payables		480 E
2. Retained Earnings	1,200		5. Retained Earnings	80	
Inventories		1,200 R	Cash		80 E
3. Cash	2,120		6. Cash	220	
Accounts Receivable		2,120	Equipment		220 E

7. Retained Earnings	80		15. Cash	290	
Equipment		80	Land		290
8. Equipment	670		16. Land	230	
Accounts Payable		670	Retained Earnings		230
9. Cash	500		17. Cash	100	
Capital Stock		500	Bonds Payable		100
10. Retained Earnings	240		18. Mortgage Payable	300	
Equipment		240	Cash		300
11. Buildings	100		19. Inventories	1,180	
Cash		100	Accounts Payable		1,180
12. Retained Earnings	30		20. Other Payables	700	
Buildings		30	Cash		700
13. Patents	80		21. Accounts Payable	1,800	
Cash		80	Cash		1,800
14. Retained Earnings	50		22. Retained Earnings	200	
Patents		50	Cash		200

Solution 7-2:

Although the shortcut method could be used in solving this problem, the more detailed method will be employed instead, for the benefit of those readers who may be experiencing difficulties.

Step 1. Put the entity's journal entries in simple summary form.

1. Cash	1,625,900		18. Books	1,035,700	
Retained Earnings		1,625,900	Accounts Payable		1,035,700
2. Accounts Receivable	166,800		19. General Merchandise	296,900	
Retained Earnings		166,800	Accounts Payable		296,900
3. Cash	105,000		20. Prepaid Insurance	7,000	
6% Notes Payable		105,000	Cash		7,000
4. Retained Earnings	10,600		21. Interest Payable	1,500	
Accounts Payable		10,600	Cash		1,500
5. Retained Earnings	9,400		22. Salaries Payable	175,900	
Cash		9,400	Cash		175,900
6. Retained Earnings	53,700		23. Taxes Payable	75,700	
Cash		53,700	Cash		75,700
7. Retained Earnings	76,100		24. Dividends Payable	15,000	
Taxes Payable		76,100	Cash		15,000
8. Retained Earnings	16,800		25. Construction Payable	121,800	
Taxes Payable		16,800	Cash		121,800
9. Retained Earnings	3,600		26. Accounts Payable	1,376,100	
Interest Payable		3,600	Cash		1,376,100
10. Retained Earnings	15,000		27. Retained Earnings	4,400	
Dividends Payable		15,000	Prepaid Insurance		4,400
11. Retained Earnings	4,800		28. Retained Earnings	13,600	
Cash		4,800	Store Supplies		13,600
12. Retained Earnings	6,400		29. Retained Earnings	1,025,100	
Accounts Payable		6,400	Books		1,025,100
13. Retained Earnings	174,200		30. Retained Earnings	298,800	
Salaries Payable		174,200	General Merchandise		298,800
14. Fixtures	9,900		31. Retained Earnings	7,500	
Accounts Payable		9,900	Building		7,500
15. Building under			32. Retained Earnings	8,700	
Construction	201,900		Fixtures		8,700
Construction Payable		201,900	33a. Cash	4,300	
16. Cash	162,400		Fixtures		4,300
Accounts Receivable		162,400	33b. Retained Earnings	3,200	
17. Store Supplies	13,300		Fixtures		3,200
Accounts Payable		13,300			

Step 2. Select all changes that affect the balance of net working capital.

Increase Changes

Op. 1.	Cash	1,625,900	
	Retained Earnings		1,625,900
Op. 2.	Accounts Receivable	166,800	
	Retained Earnings		166,800
3.	Cash	105,000	
	6% Notes Payable		105,000
33a.	Cash	4,300	
	Fixtures		4,300

Double-effect changes are found in Entries 16 through 26. No-effect changes are found in Entries 31, 32, and 33b.

Decrease Changes

Op. 4.	Retained Earnings	10,600	
	Accounts Payable		10,600
Op. 5.	Retained Earnings	9,400	
	Cash		9,400
Op. 6.	Retained Earnings	53,700	
	Cash		53,700
Op. 7.	Retained Earnings	76,100	
	Taxes Payable		76,100
Op. 8.	Retained Earnings	16,800	
	Taxes Payable		16,800
Op. 9.	Retained Earnings	3,600	
	Interest Payable		3,600
10.	Retained Earnings	15,000	
	Dividends Payable		15,000
Op. 11.	Retained Earnings	4,800	
	Cash		4,800
Op. 12.	Retained Earnings	6,400	
	Accounts Payable		6,400
Op. 13.	Retained Earnings	174,200	
	Salaries Payable		174,200
14.	Fixtures	9,900	
	Accounts Payable		9,900
15.	Building Under Construction	201,900	
	Construction Payable		201,900
Op. 27.	Retained Earnings	4,400	
	Prepaid Insurance		4,400
Op. 28.	Retained Earnings	13,600	
	Store Supplies		13,600
Op. 29.	Retained Earnings	1,025,100	
	Books		1,025,100
Op. 30.	Retained Earnings	298,800	
	General Merchandise		298,800

Steps 3 and 4. Prepare separate lists of sources and uses; subdivide both lists into operating, noncurrent asset, noncurrent equity, and dividend activities.

You may wish to refer back to pages 360–361 for explanations of certain journal entries.

Sources		*Uses*	
Operating:		**Operating:**	
1. Cash sales	$1,625,900	4. Cost of Advertising . . .	$ 10,600
2. Sales on Account	166,800	5. Cost of Utilities.	9,400
	$1,792,700	6. Cost of Patronage Refunds .	53,700
		7. Cost of Taxes	76,100
Noncurrent Asset:		8. Cost of Taxes	16,800
33a. Proceeds from Sale of Fixtures	$ 4,300	9. Interest Charges. . . .	3,600
		11. Miscellaneous Costs of	
Noncurrent Equity:		Operations	4,800
3. Proceeds from Issue of 6%		12. Miscellaneous Costs of	
Notes Payable	$ 105,000	Operations	6,400
		13. Cost of Salaries	174,200
		27. Cost of Insurance Expired . .	4,400
		28. Cost of Supplies Used . . .	13,600
		29. Cost of Books Sold . . .	1,025,100
		30. Cost of General Merchandise	
		Sold	298,800
			$1,697,500
		Noncurrent Asset:	
		14. Purchase of Fixtures . . .	$ 9,900
		15. Construction of New Building.	201,900
			$ 211,800
		Dividends:	
		10. Dividends Declared. . . .	$ 15,000

Step 5. Combine all operating activities on one list; summarize all operating changes by a single figure.

Sources		*Uses*	
Funds from Operations*	$ 95,200	**Noncurrent Asset:**	
		Purchase of Fixtures.	$ 9,900
Noncurrent Asset:		Construction of New Building . .	201,900
Sale of Fixtures	$ 4,300		$ 211,800
Noncurrent Equity:		**Dividend:**	
Issue of 6% Notes Payable . . .	$ 105,000	Dividends Declared	$ 15,000

---

* *$1,792,700 − $1,697,500 = $95,200.*

Step 6. Prepare suitable headings and footings.

Notice that a decrease in net working capital is reported in much the same way as an increase.

Campus Store
Sources and Uses of Net Working Capital
For the Year Ended 6/30/X5

Sources

Funds from Operations	$ 95,200
Proceeds from Sale of Noncurrent Assets:	
Fixtures Sold	4,300
Proceeds from Issue of Noncurrent Equities:	
6% Notes Payable Issued	105,000
Net Sources	$204,500

Uses

Purchase of Noncurrent Assets:		
Fixtures Purchased	$ 9,900	
Construction of New Building	201,900	$211,800
Dividends		15,000
Net Uses		$226,800
Decrease in Net Working Capital		$ 22,300
Net Working Capital—6/30/X4:		
Current Assets	$469,700	
Current Liabilities	153,700	$316,000
Net Working Capital—6/30/X5:		
Current Assets	$541,800	
Current Liabilities	248,100	293,700
Decrease in Net Working Capital		$ 22,300

Appendix

***Another Way to
Study the Funds Statement***

The funds statement summarizes certain journal entries while ignoring others. As indicated on page 643–644, the rule governing the choice of entries is simple: *Choose all changes that affect the balance of net working capital.* This process could have been described another way—by representing the set of all possible balance sheet accounts as follows:

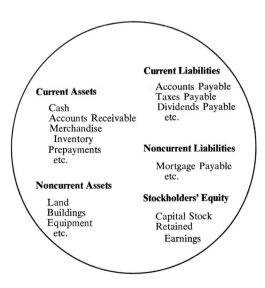

In using this method, as further developed below, the accountant acts as though he had divided, or "partitioned," the set into two subsets—one containing the current accounts, the other containing the noncurrent accounts:

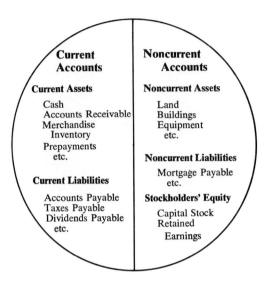

Under this system, balance sheet changes can be represented by double-headed arrows. For example, the straight arrow in the next figure might represent a purchase of land for cash (or the proceeds of a cash sale of land, depending upon whether the change was positive or negative). The curved arrow might represent a purchase of merchandise on account:

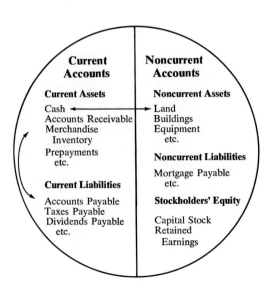

This way of looking at balance sheet changes reduces them to the three basic types shown below. (For added clarity, details have been simplified in subsequent figures.)

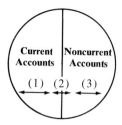

Type-1 changes debit one current account and credit another current account, such as:

| Merchandise Inventory | XXX | | Taxes Payable | XXX | |
| Accounts Payable | | XXX | Cash | | XXX |

These are *double-effect changes.*

Type-3 changes debit one noncurrent account and credit another noncurrent account, such as:

| Retained Earnings | XXX | | Land | XXX | |
| Equipment | | XXX | Retained Earnings | | XXX |

These are *no-effect changes.* Both Type-1 and Type-3 changes occur entirely within their respective partitioned areas.

Type-2 changes cross the partition. Of the two accounts affected, one is current and the other is noncurrent. Here are some cross-partition changes:

Accounts Receivable	XXX		Equipment	XXX	
Retained Earnings		XXX	Accounts Payable		XXX
Cash	XXX		Retained Earnings	XXX	
Bonds Payable		XXX	Supplies		XXX

These are *increase* and *decrease changes.* Each has one foot in the current subset and one foot in the noncurrent subset. *The rule for preparing funds statements has been to choose all cross-partition changes* or, if you prefer, to choose every change having a debit in one subset and a credit in the other subset.[8]

---

[8] An exception to this rule will be examined in Chapter Nine: acquisitions of noncurrent assets by issuing noncurrent equities are Type-3 transactions. Yet they, and certain similar changes, are reported on funds statements.

Other change reports

This same rule was followed in constructing the cash statement, but the balance sheet was partitioned differently:

Since we have used only one cash account, there can be no double-effect changes with this partitioning. Here are the two remaining basic kinds of changes:

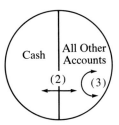

In preparing the cash statement the rule (see page 305) has been to choose all cross-partition changes—all changes that increased or decreased cash and affected some noncash account. All within-partition changes have been ignored.

The main difference between a cash statement and a funds statement is in the decision as to where the partition will be placed. Otherwise, the rules for constructing the two statements are almost identical.

Some people refer to funds statements as "cash statements" or "cash-flow statements," or use similar "cash" language for funds statements. This is a careless way to talk, for cash statements and funds statements are not the same thing; they are based in different partitionings and, therefore, report and summarize different changes. Unfortunately, this loose language is well established. The next chapters will discuss some additional misconceptions about funds statements.

All change reports can be viewed as resulting from some kind of partitioning of the balance sheet accounts, together with a set of rules similar to those developed in the last two chapters. The change report discussed in the next chapter is called an *income statement*. It results from the following partitioning of the balance sheet accounts:

Assignment Problems

Problem 7-A:

Shown below are the balance sheet changes of Gadsden Co. for the month of January, 19X2, and its 12/31/X1 balance sheet.

Gadsden Co.
Balance Sheet
December 31, 19X1

Assets

Current Assets:

Cash	$ 2,000	
Accounts Receivable	4,500	
Merchandise Inventory	8,000	
Prepaid Insurance	500	$15,000

Noncurrent Assets:

Land	$ 2,300	
Buildings	5,200	
Equipment	11,500	19,000

Total Assets		$34,000

Equities

Current Liabilities:

Accounts Payable	$ 4,200	
Dividends Payable	700	
Interest Payable.	200	
Other Payables	1,100	$ 6,200

Noncurrent Liabilities:

Bonds Payable—6%		10,000

Total Liabilities		$16,200

Stockholders' Equity:

Capital Stock	$12,000	
Retained Earnings	5,800	17,800

Total Equities		$34,000

1. The company bought $43,000 of merchandise on account.
2. The company made cash sales of $5,000.
3. The company made sales on account totalling $43,800.
4. The cost to the company of merchandise sold in changes 2 and 3 totalled $39,700.
5. Accounts receivable totalling $44,100 were collected.
6. Dividends payable totalling $700 were paid.
7. Accounts payable totalling $42,180 were paid.
8. Other payables totalling $1,100 were paid.
9. Equipment was purchased for $2,000, cash.
10. Building depreciation totalled $50.
11. Equipment depreciation totalled $375.
12. $20 of prepaid insurance expired.
13. Interest charges of $50 accrued on the company's bonds payable.

Indicate which of these balance sheet changes are operating and which are financial.

Problem 7-B:

The balance sheet changes of Gadsden Co. for the month of January, 19X2, and its 12/31/X1 balance sheet are shown in Problem 7-A. Assume that a statement of sources and uses of net working capital is to be prepared. Indicate which of these balance sheet changes is a double-effect change, which is a no-effect change, and which is a cross-partition change.

Problem 7-C:

Shown below are the balance sheet changes of Gathings Variety Store for the month of October, 19X1, and its 10/1/X1 balance sheet. Indicate which of these balance sheet changes are operating and which are financial.

1. The company paid accounts payable totalling $237,000.
2. The company paid dividends payable totalling $4,000.
3. The company estimates that its taxes for the month will be $3,200.
4. During the month, the company paid $18,500 of taxes payable.
5. Depreciation of furniture and fixtures for the month was $1,100.
6. Depreciation of buildings for the month was $500.
7. The company purchased $200,000 of merchandise during the month, all on account.
8. Merchandise that had cost the company $225,000 was used in operations.
9. The company declared a $6,000 dividend, to be paid on 1/15/X2.
10. The company's employees earned $83,000 during the month.
11. Salary payments to company employees totalled $91,000.
12. On 10/31/X1, the company purchased furniture for $8,000, cash. No depreciation was taken on this furniture for October, 19X1.
13. The company employs a delivery service to deliver merchandise to its customers. This delivery service charged Gathings Variety Store $19,200 for October, 19X1, deliveries. The company paid in cash (without ever bothering to record a liability).
14. The company consumed supplies costing $7,000 during the month.
15. Supplies costing $11,400 were purchased on account.
16. October sales of the company's products were all for cash and totalled $353,000.
17a. On 10/1/X1, the company sold some old chairs that had been used in the store for $680, cash.
17b. At the time of sale, the chairs sold had book value of $800.

Gathings Variety Store
Balance Sheet
October 1, 19X1

Assets

Current Assets:
Cash	$ 40,000	
Merchandise Inventory	190,000	
Supplies	6,000	$236,000

Noncurrent Assets:
Buildings	$120,000	
Furniture and Fixtures	70,000	190,000

Total Assets	$426,000

Equities

Current Liabilities:
Accounts Payable	$ 80,000	
Salaries Payable	17,000	
Dividends Payable	4,000	
Taxes Payable	19,000	$120,000

Stockholders' Equity:
Capital Stock	$200,000	
Retained Earnings	106,000	306,000

Total Equities	$426,000

Problem 7-D:

The balance sheet changes of Gathings Variety Store for the month of October, 19X1, and its 10/1/X1 balance sheet are shown in Problem 7-C. Assume that a statement of sources and uses of net working capital is to be prepared. Indicate which of these balance sheet changes is a double-effect change, which is a no-effect change, and which is a cross-partition change.

Problem 7-E:

The balance sheet changes of Gathings Variety Store for the month of October, 19X1, and its 10/1/X1 balance sheet are shown in Problem 7-C. Prepare a statement of sources and uses of net working capital for the month of October, 19X1.

Problem 7-F:

As part of your training in accounting, you must become able to distinguish relevant from irrelevant information. Some of the data given in this and other problems, accordingly, is deliberately irrelevant. Part of your job is to determine which is pertinent and which is not.

The following problem, though self-contained, is based on the data employed in Problems 5-G through 5-I, and 6-F (pages 280–283, 326–327). The comparative balance sheet of Trans Eastern Rhode Island Airlines for 12/31/X8 and 12/31/X9 is given below. This balance sheet has been designed to incorporate certain accounts and reporting practices that were not discussed in the text; where necessary, these variations are discussed in the notes to the balance sheet. The last three zeros have been omitted from all figures; you should do likewise in your answers.

Trans Eastern Rhode Island Airlines
Statements of Financial Position
(In Thousands)
For the Years Ended December 31

ASSETS	19X9		19X8	
CURRENT ASSETS:				
Cash	$ 4,315		$ 3,672	
Temporary investments	–0–		17,381	
Receivables	10,886		10,087	
Parts inventory	4,389		3,682	
Maintenance and operating supplies	805		756	
Prepayments	697	$ 21,092	629	$ 36,207
NONCURRENT ASSETS:				
Flight equipment	$80,598		$47,879	
Advances on flight equipment purchase contracts	10,696		11,970	
Other property and equipment	12,187		9,975	
Investments and miscellaneous	1,195	104,676	569	70,393
		$125,768		$106,600

LIABILITIES AND STOCKHOLDERS' EQUITY	19X9		19X8	
CURRENT LIABILITIES:				
Debentures maturing within one year	$ 754		$ 749	
Accounts payable and accrued liabilities. . .	13,193		11,142	
Customer deposits under Air Travel Plan . .	631		628	
Advance sale of tickets for transportation . .	2,444		2,051	
Accrued federal income taxes	928		727	
Accrued interest on long-term debt	759	$ 18,709	551	$ 15,848
LONG-TERM DEBT:				
Debentures payable	$23,269		$24,023	
Notes payable	33,000		20,000	
Other long-term debt	2,064	58,333	1,848	45,871
STOCKHOLDERS' EQUITY:				
Common stock	$26,056		$25,997	
Retained earnings	22,670	48,726	18,884	44,881
		$125,768		$106,600

Notes:

When new aircraft are purchased, there usually is well over a year's delay between placement of the order and receipt of the aircraft by the company. Accordingly, the advances made by the company to the aircraft manufacturer are treated as noncurrent assets.

Debentures are a kind of bonds payable. Some bonds are secured with a claim upon specific assets owned by the company—usually land and buildings. In contrast, a debenture is secured only by the general credit of the firm. The company has issued debentures with varying maturity dates. At the end of each year it follows the practice of reclassifying debentures due within the next year as a current liability, by making a journal entry of the form:

Debentures Payable	XXX	
Debentures Maturing within One Year		XXX

Both customer deposits under air travel plan and advance sale of tickets for transportation may be regarded as kinds of advances from customers. The former represents security deposits of customers who wish to purchase tickets on account.

Here is a partial list of the company's balance sheet changes for the year ended 12/31/X9. All changes described pertain to 19X9 only, unless stated otherwise. Do not concern yourself with any changes not described below. Instead, you may assume that they have been (or will be) correctly recorded. Similarly, do not worry if there appear to be insufficient amounts in certain accounts to allow certain changes to occur—such apparent impossibilities arise because various other balance sheet changes have been omitted to save you time.

1. The company purchased investments and miscellaneous assets for $689, cash.

2. The company purchased $32,180 of flight equipment, and $2,708 of other property and equipment, on account.

3. The company made advance payments on flight equipment purchase contracts (a kind of noncurrent advances to suppliers) totalling $6,046.

4. Earlier advance payments on flight equipment purchase contracts totalling $7,320 were settled by delivery of flight equipment to the company.

5. The company sold old flight equipment on account for $186; this equipment had a book value of $203 at the time of sale.

6. The company issued capital stock for $59 cash, long-term notes payable for $15,000 cash, and other long-term debt for $216 cash.

7. The company declared and paid dividends totalling $1,336.

8. The company paid long-term notes payable totalling $2,000, and debentures totalling $749. Debentures totalling $754 will become due next year.

9. The company made $307 of sales for cash, and $34,078 of sales on account. Customers made advance payments totalling $58,539; of these ticket purchases, $43,832 were for cash and $14,707 were on account.

10. Tickets purchased in advance totalling $58,146 were used by customers; receivables totalling $49,588 were collected.

11. The company paid $4,306 of federal income taxes, $2,325 of interest on long-term debt, and $107,770 of accounts payable and accrued liabilities. Federal income taxes for 19X9 totalled $4,507; interest charges for 19X9 totalled $2,533.

12. The company bought $13,695 of parts inventories and $12,935 of maintenance and operating supplies on account.

13. Costs were incurred on account for the activities indicated below. None of these costs resulted in the company's acquiring assets:

Flying and ground operations	$42,630
Maintenance	3,069
Sales and advertising	9,169
General and administrative	3,357
Miscellaneous nonoperating	78

14. Current assets were utilized in operations, as indicated below. None of these activities resulted in the company acquiring new assets.

	Total	Parts Inventory	Maintenance and Operating Supplies	Prepayments
Flight and ground operations . . .	$ 4,365	$3,217	$1,083	$ 65
Maintenance	11,179	9,771	1,408	–0–
Sales and advertising. . .	291	–0–	109	182
General and administrative . . .	493	–0–	286	207

ς 15. Interest on the company's investments is recognized as a receivable before being collected. Such interest totalled $1,416; contrary to what is done in the text, the firm treats this interest as nonoperating.

Prepare a statement of sources and uses of net working capital.

Problem 7-G:

As part of your training in accounting, you must become able to extend the concepts and techniques you have learned into situations that require different methods of analysis. This problem provides an opportunity to increase your flexibility and broaden your understanding. The background needed to solve this problem has been provided by the text, but the particular method of analysis required may at first seem unusual. Apply what you already have learned to this new situation.

This is a self-contained problem, based on the materials in Problems 4-C through 4-F, and Problem 6-E (see pages 231–235, 325–326). Shown below are the comparative balance sheets of Putnam Pharmaceutical Corporation at 12/31/X5 and 12/31/X4, the company's 19X5 cash statement, and some (but not all) of the company's summary journal entries for 19X5. The financial statements have been designed to incorporate certain accounts and reporting practices that were not discussed in the text; where necessary, these variations are discussed in the notes. No unusual balance sheet changes occurred during the year; instead, all changes were of the normal kinds discussed in this and previous chapters and in the notes to the firm's balance sheet. The last three zeros have been omitted from all figures; you should do likewise in your answers. Prepare a statement of sources and uses of net working capital for Putnam Pharmaceutical Corporation for the year ended 12/31/X5; use good form. (One possible line of attack in solving this problem would be to prepare the general outline of a funds statement, leaving considerable space between captions; then fill in the details of this statement as you learn them from the problem data, using T-account analysis only where essential. If you emerge with a funds statement entirely consistent with the problem data, do not worry about possible balance sheet changes about which you have not been told.)

19X5 Summary Journal Entries:

1. Notes and Accounts Receivable   5,120
       Retained Earnings   403
          Land and Buildings   5,523
          —To record sale of land and buildings with a book value of $5,523, for $5,120.
2. Notes and Accounts Receivable   3,243
       Retained Earnings   742
          Machinery and Equipment   3,985
          —To record sales of machinery and equipment with a book value of $3,985, for $3,243.
3. Land and Buildings   1,823
       Machinery and Equipment   1,762
          Notes Payable—Foreign   3,585
          —To record overseas purchase of noncurrent assets.

(continued on page 382)

Putnam Pharmaceutical Corporation
Financial Position
(In Thousands)

	12/31/X5		12/31/X4	
Current Assets				
Cash	$14,565		$12,481	
Time deposits—interest-bearing	35,579		19,684	
Marketable securities	8,534		5,872	
Notes and accounts receivable	73,622		70,445	
Inventories	93,762		93,559	
Prepaid expenses and other current assets	8,712	$234,774	5,959	$208,000
Current Liabilities				
Notes payable to banks	$ 5,828		$32,665	
Current portion of long-term debt	525		1,747	
Accounts payable, trade	18,414		14,222	
Other payables and accrued expenses	34,374		29,846	
United States and foreign income taxes	26,516	85,657	19,685	98,165
Working capital		$149,117		$109,835
Investments and Deposits		3,690		3,160
Land and Buildings		61,265		62,108
Machinery and Equipment		54,014		53,490
Goodwill and Unamortized Cost of Patents		13,503		13,406
		$281,589		$241,999
Long-Term Debt				
$4\frac{1}{4}\%$ debentures	$10,000		$10,000	
$4\frac{1}{2}\%$ debentures	15,000		–0–	
$4\frac{1}{4}\%$ sinking fund notes	6,475		7,000	
Notes payable—foreign	3,585	35,060	–0–	17,000
Net assets represented by stockholders' equity		$246,529		$224,999
Stockholders' Equity				
Common stock		$ 88,001		$ 87,107
Retained earnings		158,528		137,892
Total stockholders' equity		$246,529		$224,999

Notes:

"Prepaid expenses" is another name for what the text calls "prepayments" or "prepaid services." When the firm purchases one of these assets, ordinarily it does so on account (despite the word "prepaid" in the account title). For example, when the firm purchases insurance it makes the following entry when it receives a bill from the insurance agency:

Prepaid Expenses	XXX	
Accounts Payable		XXX

It pays cash only when the bill is due.

The company has made deposits with airlines and certain suppliers. These deposits are intended to be of a relatively permanent nature, and therefore are classified as noncurrent. The company chooses to combine these deposits with its incidental investments in other companies into a single account, "investments and deposits."

Debentures are a kind of bonds payable. Some corporation bonds are secured by a mortgage or other legal claim upon specific noncurrent assets of the company. In contrast, a debenture is a corporation bond that is unsecured by mortgage or any other specific claim to assets, but is secured by the general credit of the company.

The company's $4\frac{1}{4}\%$ sinking fund notes have various maturity dates. Each year a new group of these notes becomes due. At the end of each year, the company transfers the amount that must be paid next year (which thus has become a current liability) from the noncurrent liability "$4\frac{1}{4}\%$ sinking fund notes" to the current liability "current portion of long-term debt."

Putnam Pharmaceutical Corporation
Sources and Uses of Cash
(In Thousands of Dollars)
For the Year 19X5

Sources
Operations:
  Receipts:

Collection of Accounts Receivable	$512,580	
Withdrawal of Time Deposits	20,119	
Sale of Marketable Securities	6,743	
Issue of Current Notes Payable to Banks	5,828	$545,270

  Expenditures:

Payment of Costs of Current Operations	$273,229	
Payment of Suppliers	129,275	
Payment of Income Taxes	32,332	
Prepayments Made	8,079	
Time Deposits Made	34,632	
Marketable Securities Purchased	9,405	
Payment of Current Notes to Banks	32,665	519,617

Net Effect of Operations on Cash		$ 25,653
Proceeds from Issue of Noncurrent Equities:		
$4\frac{1}{2}\%$ Debentures Issued	$ 15,000	
Common Stock Issued	894	15,894
Net Sources		$ 41,547

Uses
Purchase of Noncurrent Assets:

Land and Buildings Purchased	$ 5,042	
Machinery and Equipment Purchased.	8,211	
Patents Purchased	3,050	
Investments and Deposits Made	530	$ 16,833

Retirement of Noncurrent Equities:		
Payment of Long-Term Debt		1,747
Dividends		20,883
Net Uses		$ 39,463
Increase in Cash for the Year		$ 2,084

Cash—12/31/X5		$ 14,565
Cash—12/31/X4		12,481
Increase in Cash for the Year		$ 2,084

Notes:
    The payments for land, buildings, machinery, and equipment have been separated from the other payments of accounts payable. In the text, such payments were treated as operating, for simplicity. This would be an acceptable alternate presentation.

4. Retained Earnings   21,682

    Other Payables and Accrued Expenses   21,682

    —To record declaration of dividends.

5. 4¼% Sinking Fund Notes   525

    Current Portion of Long-Term Debt   525

    —To record portion of sinking fund notes that will become due in 19X6.

6. Notes and Accounts Receivable   502,524

    Retained Earnings   502,524

    —To record ordinary sales.

7. Time Deposits   1,382

    Notes and Accounts Receivable   4,870

    Retained Earnings   6,252

    —To record interest on time deposits, royalties, etc.

8. Retained Earnings   199,664

    Inventories   199,664

    —To record the cost of goods sold by the company during the year.

9. Retained Earnings   212,961

    Inventories   16,034

    Prepaid Expenses and Other Current Assets   8,603

    Other Payables and Accrued Expenses   166,721

    Accounts Payable   21,603

    —To record the company's marketing, administrative, and general costs for the year. The credit to inventories in large part reflects samples given to doctors.

10. Retained Earnings   2,923

    Other Payables and Accrued Expenses   2,923

    —To record interest charges for the year.

11. Retained Earnings   39,163

    United States and Foreign Income Taxes   39,163

    —To record income taxes for the year.

Problem 7-H:

As part of your training in accounting, you must become able to extend the concepts and techniques you have learned into situations that require different methods of analysis. This problem provides an opportunity to increase your flexibility and broaden your understanding. The background needed to solve this problem has been provided by the text, but the particular method of analysis required may at first seem unusual. Apply what you already have learned to this new situation.

Shown below are the comparative balance sheets of Trimble Hotel Corp. at 12/31/X1 and 12/31/X2, the company's 19X2 cash statement and 19X2 funds statement, a few of its summary journal entries for 19X2, and certain other data. You may assume that each journal entry given is a complete summary of its kind of 19X2 balance sheet changes. For example, Entry 1 records all room rentals made on account. No unusual balance sheet changes occurred during the year; instead, all changes were of the normal kinds discussed in this and previous chapters. You may assume that all needed information has been given. The last three zeros have been omitted from all figures; you should do likewise in your answers.

Determine all of the other summary journal entries for Trimble Hotel Corp. for 19X1 *except* those reflected in the cash statement or the funds statement. (One possible line of attack in solving this problem would begin by organizing its data into T-accounts.)

Trimble Hotel Corp.
Comparative Balance Sheets
December 31, 19X1 and 19X2

Assets

	December 31 19X1	December 31 19X2
Current Assets:		
Cash	$ 8,272	$ 5,631
Accounts Receivable	1,244	1,226
Inventories	1,043	1,021
Prepaid Advertising	448	472
Other Current Assets	893	910
Total Current Assets	$11,900	$ 9,260
Noncurrent Assets:		
Land	$ 9,763	$10,414
Buildings	50,317	63,345
Furniture and Equipment	15,020	16,522
Total Noncurrent Assets	$75,100	$90,281
Total Assets	$87,000	$99,541

Equities

	December 31 19X1	December 31 19X2
Current Liabilities:		
Accounts Payable	$ 2,812	$ 3,075
Wages and Salaries Payable	986	723
Taxes Payable	3,179	1,870
Interest Payable	618	646
Other Current Payables	1,405	1,321
Total Current Liabilities	$ 9,000	$ 7,635
Noncurrent Liabilities:		
Bank Loans	$ 6,800	$ 6,926
5½% Bonds Payable	40,000	37,000
Total Noncurrent Liabilities	$46,800	$43,926
Total Liabilities	$55,800	$51,561
Stockholders' Equity:		
Capital Stock	$ 9,676	$25,676
Retained Earnings	21,524	22,304
Total Stockholders' Equity	$31,200	$47,980
Total Equities	$87,000	$99,341

Trimble Hotel Corp.
Sources and Uses of Cash
For the Year 19X2

Sources:
Operations:
  Receipts:

Room Rentals	$14,804	
Store and Office Rentals	2,052	
Other Sales	32,884	
Collection of Accounts Receivable	18,743	$68,483

  Expenditures:

Payment of Wages and Salaries	$25,911	
Payment of Other Accounts Payable	6,379	
Payment of Interest	2,580	
Payment of Taxes	8,039	
Payment of Accounts Payable	23,213	66,122

Cash from Operations		$ 2,361
Proceeds from Issue of Noncurrent Equities:		
Proceeds from Issue of Capital Stock	$16,000	
Proceeds from Bank Loans	126	16,126
Net Sources		$18,487

Uses:
Purchase of Noncurrent Assets:

Land Purchased	$ 670	
Buildings Purchased	16,942	$17,612

Retirement of Noncurrent Equities:		
Payments Made to Retire 5% Bonds Payable		3,060
Dividends Paid		456
Net Uses		$21,128

Decrease in Cash During Year	$ (2,641)
Cash—12/31/X1	8,272
Cash—12/31/X2	$ 5,631

Trimble Hotel Corp.
Sources and Uses of Net Working Capital
For the Year 19X2

Sources:
Operations:
  Receipts:

Room Rentals	$33,464	
Store and Office Rentals	2,052	
Other Sales	32,884	$68,400

  Expenditures:

Cost of Salaries and Wages	$25,648	
Cost of Goods Sold	11,012	
Property Operating Costs	10,200	
Prepaid Advertising Expired	2,340	
Interest Charges	2,608	
Cost of Property Taxes	4,180	
Cost of Income Taxes	2,550	58,538

Funds from Operations		$ 9,862

Proceeds from Sale of Land		65
Proceeds from Issue of Noncurrent Equities:		
Issue of Capital Stock	$16,000	
Additional Bank Loans	126	16,126
Net Sources		$26,053

Uses:

Purchase of Noncurrent Assets:		
Land Purchased	$ 670	
Buildings Purchased	16,942	
Furniture and Equipment Purchased.	6,200	$23,812
Retirement of Noncurrent Equities:		
Cost of Retiring 5½% Bonds Payable		
(Including Call Premium of $60)		3,060
Dividends Declared		456
Net Uses		$27,328
Decrease in Net Working Capital		$ 1,275

Net Working Capital—12/31/X1:		
Current Assets	$11,900	
Current Liabilities	9,000	$ 2,900
Net Working Capital—12/31/X2:		
Current Assets	$ 9,260	
Current Liabilities	7,635	1,625
Decrease in Net Working Capital		$ 1,275

19X2 Summary Journal Entries:

1. Accounts Receivable   18,660
        Retained Earnings   18,660
        —To record room rentals made on account.
2. Retained Earnings   10,200
        Inventories   760
        Other Current Assets   3,145
        Other Current Payables   6,295
        —To record property operation costs for the year.
3. Accounts Receivable   65
        Land   19
        Retained Earnings   46
        —To record sale of land that had cost the company $19, for $65.
4. Bonds Payable   3,000
        Retained Earnings   60
        Cash   3,060
        —To record payment of 5½% bonds payable.

Other data: during 19X2, the company retired $3,000 principal value of bonds in advance of their maturity date; under the contract between the company and its bondholders, the company is required to pay the bondholders a 2% call premium (penalty for early payment) on all bonds retired before their maturity date; this premium amounted to $3,000 × 2% = $60.

Wages and salaries, interest, and taxes are always recorded as liabilities before being paid.

Despite its title, prepaid advertising is purchased on account.

The account other current payables was employed only for recording those balance sheet changes summarized in Entry 2 above (and, of course, to record payment of other current payables).

Problem 7-I:

Refer to Miami Corporation's 19X2 funds statement (page 364) and its comparative balance sheets (pages 357–358). Describe the company's financial activities for the year in ordinary English, as though you were explaining them to someone who had no training in accounting. You may, of course, use figures in your answer, but avoid accounting jargon.

Problem 7-J:

Refer to the data concerning Campus Store on pages 358–361 and 368. After studying only the firm's comparative balance sheets, Bernard J. Monagan, M.D., a stockholder in Campus Store, made a few calculations, then turned to you and remarked:

"You've studied accounting, haven't you? I thought so. How's about bailing me out here—there's a couple things I don't understand. Look, their cash went up by $56,700 during the year, but retained earnings went up by $60,800. That's a $4,100 difference. I thought at first it might be because of dividends, but they paid $15,000 in dividends last year. Where'd that $4,100 *go?*

"Another thing: how come with a $60,800 increase in retained earnings, they paid only $15,000 in dividends? Heck, they paid over $50,000 in patronage refunds to customers last year. What are they doing—holding back on the stockholders?"

Answer Dr. Monagan's questions; describe the company's financial activities in ordinary English. You may, of course, use figures in your answer, but avoid accounting jargon.

Problem 7-K:

This is a self-contained problem based on the material in Problem 5-P (pages 289–292). Shown below are the comparative balance sheets of Simplified Textiles, Inc., at 12/31/X5 and 12/31/X6, together with the company's summary journal entries for 19X6. Three zeros have been omitted from all figures; you should do likewise in your answer.

Prepare the firm's 19X6 statement of sources and uses of net working capital.

Simplified Textiles, Inc.
Balance Sheet
(In Thousands)
December 31, 19X5 and 19X6

		12/31/X6		12/31/X5	
ASSETS:					
Current assets:					
Cash		$ 4,354		$ 4,686	
Receivables		23,013		20,211	
Inventories		44,017		37,708	
Miscellaneous		794	$ 72,178	845	$ 63,450
Noncurrent assets:					
Investments		$ 852		$ 852	
Land and improvements		2,694		2,406	
Buildings		26,504		22,113	
Machinery and equipment		58,924	88,974	49,767	75,138
Total			$161,152		$138,588
LIABILITIES AND STOCKHOLDERS' EQUITY					
Current liabilities:					
Notes payable		$ 16,261		$ 8,197	
Accounts payable		3,640		3,739	
Accrued liabilities		2,804	$ 22,705	2,472	$ 14,408
Noncurrent liabilities			17,500		–0–
Stockholders' equity:					
Common stock		$ 5,081		$ 4,381	
Retained earnings		115,866	120,947	119,799	124,180
Total			$161,152		$138,588

1. Accounts Payable   70,560
       Cash   70,560
   —To record payment of accounts payable.
2. Receivables   100
       Buildings   80
       Retained Earnings   20
   —To record sale of old buildings at an amount in excess of their book value.
3. Buildings   5,434
       Accounts Payable   5,434
   —To record purchase of buildings.
4. Retained Earnings   2,848
       Cash   2,848
   —To record declaration and payment of dividends.
5. Receivables   589
       Retained Earnings   589
   —To record accrual of interest on investments.

6. Machinery and Equipment   14,614
    Accounts Payable   14,614
    —To record purchase of machinery and equipment.

7. Cash   128,130
    Receivables   128,130
    —To record collections of accounts receivable.

8. Retained Earnings   50
    Land and Improvements   50
    —To record amortization of land improvements.

9. Inventories   119,971
    Accounts Payable   49,555
    Accrued Liabilities   70,416
    —To record cost of inventories acquired during the year.

10. Retained Earnings   571
    Miscellaneous Current Assets   571
    —To record cost of miscellaneous current assets consumed in operations.

11. Cash   17,116
    Notes Payable   17,116
    —To record issue of notes payable.

12. Retained Earnings   11,234
    Cash   685
    Accrued Liabilities   10,549
    —To record miscellaneous costs of operations.

13. Receivables   130,243
    Retained Earnings   130,243
    —To record sales on account.

14. Retained Earnings   113,662
    Inventories   113,662
    —To record the cost of goods sold.

15. Miscellaneous Current Assets   520
    Accounts Payable   520
    —To record purchases of miscellaneous current assets.

16. Land and Improvements   338
    Accounts Payable   338
    —To record purchases of land and land improvements.

17. Retained Earnings   963
    Buildings   963
    —To record depreciation of buildings.

18. Retained Earnings   5,457
    Machinery and Equipment   5,457
    —To record depreciation of machinery and equipment.

19. Notes Payable   9,052
    Cash   9,052
    —To record payment of notes payable.

20. Accrued Liabilities   80,633
      Cash   80,633
      —To record payment of accrued liabilities.
21. Cash   17,500
      Noncurrent Liabilities   17,500
      —To record issue of noncurrent liabilities.
22. Cash   700
      Common Stock   700
      —To record issue of common stock.

Problem 7-L:

The text provides all the background needed to solve this problem, but the statement required will be unfamiliar; apply what you already have learned to this new requirement.

Refer to the Appendix to Chapter Seven (page 369–373). All change reports can be viewed as resulting from some kind of partitioning of the balance sheet accounts, together with a set of rules similar to those employed in preparing a funds statement. But the reverse is true, too. *Any* partitioning of the balance sheet accounts, together with a set of rules similar to those employed in preparing a funds statement, will generate a change report. Most such change reports are of little significance, but a few are of potential interest to readers of financial statements.

Problem 7-K gives the comparative balance sheets of Simplified Textiles, Inc., at 12/31/X5 and 12/31/X6, together with the company's summary journal entries for 19X6.

Prepare a statement of the changes in the company's noncurrent assets for 19X6. Use the same construction rules as in preparing a funds statement, except do not compress all operating changes into a single figure.

Problem 7-M:

Refer to the first three paragraphs of Problem 7-L, only prepare instead a statement of the changes in the company's retained earnings for 19X6. Use the same construction rules as in preparing a funds statement, except do not compress all operating changes into a single figure.

Recreational Problem:

Refer to the first three paragraphs of Problem 7-L, only prepare instead a statement of the changes in those accounts whose titles begin with a vowel (Inventories, Investments, Accounts Payable, and Accrued Liabilities) for 19X6. Use the same construction rules as in preparing a funds statement, except do not compress all operating changes into a single figure.

Eight

Income Statements

Income statements try to answer the following investor questions, which we first saw on page 23:

"How profitable has the company been? Have profits been increasing or decreasing?"

Suppose a businessman is trying to answer these questions about his own business —a shoe store. Roughly speaking, his "profits" equal the difference between the cash (or other assets) he receives from sales and what he gives up in making these sales (this in effect is the usage we have been following since page 49).

His journal entries would show him the total shoe sales:

Cash	XXX			Accounts Receivable	XXX	
Retained Earnings		XXX		Retained Earnings		XXX

These journal entries would also show what the shoes sold had cost him:

Retained Earnings	XXX	
Shoes (or Merchandise)		XXX

But shoes aren't the only things the shoe-store owner gives up in making sales. He also has to pay his salesmen:

Retained Earnings	XXX			Retained Earnings	XXX	
Salaries Payable		XXX		Commissions Payable		XXX

In addition, he uses various supplies. If the shoe-store owner is renting his store building, he is also using up the building services obtained by his rental payments. His insurance policies are slowly expiring. Eventually he will have to pay taxes on his business activities. Costs for advertising, heat, light, telephone services, and other things needed in the day-by-day operation of his business are adding up. All these things are additional costs of the sales:

Retained Earnings	XXX		Retained Earnings	XXX	
Supplies		XXX	Taxes Payable		XXX
Retained Earnings	XXX		Retained Earnings	XXX	
Prepaid Rent		XXX	Accounts Payable		XXX
Retained Earnings	XXX		Retained Earnings	XXX	
Prepaid Insurance		XXX	Cash		XXX

Looking ahead, the shoe-store owner's shelves, store furniture, and equipment are gradually releasing their services. Consider the chairs his customers sit in. With reasonable luck, their total service life may be five years. (Ignore possible scrap values.) Part of what he gives up to make the sales of any one year is one-fifth of the total services originally offered by these chairs. Similarly, one of the costs of the sales made in any one month is $1/60$ of the cost of these chairs ($1/5 \times 1/12 = 1/60$). The same is true of any other depreciable assets: they have limited service lives and are gradually releasing their services. The cost of the services they release is part of the cost of making sales.

Retained Earnings	XXX		Retained Earnings	XXX
Furniture and Fixtures		XXX	Equipment	XXX

As was indicated on page 149, one of the two senses of the word "matching" in accounting is employed here: accountants allocate the costs of various inputs to the periods in which economic benefits are received. Here, the economic benefits are the sales to customers, and what we have just seen is that the accountant "matches" recording of these sales by recording all of the costs of making these sales, too.

Product versus period costs

A distinction that was made on page 78 may help clarify what this matching involves. Sometimes it is convenient to act as though there were two different kinds of costs: (1) *product costs*—ones that can readily be associated with individual sales, such as the cost of shoes sold in the previous example, and (2) *period costs*—ones that help cause the sales of a year as a whole but that cannot be traced, except arbitrarily, to the making of individual sales; the rent and insurance costs in the previous example are instances of these.

Some accounting writers emphasize this distinction, yet it does not appear to be inherent in the nature of the costs themselves. Instead, whether a particular cost is a product or period one often depends upon the accounting system employed and the amount of information the accountant wants about cost behavior. For example, in Chapter Thirteen it will become clear that depreciation expense may be either a product or a period expense, depending upon whether the accountant has gathered the information needed to associate the expiration of an asset's services with some single measure of physical output. Accordingly, I prefer to use the distinction between primary and secondary measurements introduced in Chapter Four, and would say that some matching involves direct primary measurement of expenditures that result in particular sales, while other matching involves indirect secondary attribution of costs to the sales of particular periods of time—and that these secondary measurements (which include what would be classified as period costs) are much more difficult and much less clear-cut than the primary ones.

The profits of a service enterprise

The profits of an enterprise that sells a service instead of a product are determined in much the same way: once again profits will equal the difference between the assets received from sales and what is given up to make sales (including the costs of the received services of long-lived assets during the period). For example, a dry-cleaning shop receives cash for its services; it makes expenditures for salaries and utilities; it expends various supplies and the services provided by its equipment; its profit for the year is the difference between the inflow of cash from sales and the expenditures of assets (or incurrences of liabilities) involved in making these sales.

Determination of the profits of a company that sells a product is slightly more complicated than determination of the profits of a company that sells only services, simply because, in the former case, one must keep track of the cost of goods sold as well as the sales themselves. Accordingly, most of the discussion in this and the remaining chapters will concern firms that sell products.

Retained earnings and profits

For a company to be profitable, the assets received from customers must be greater in amount than the matched assets given up (or liabilities incurred) in making the sales. For the shoe store, the total dollar value of the cash and accounts receivable obtained from sales must be greater than the total dollar cost of shoes, supplies, prepaid rent, prepaid insurance, services of furniture, fixtures, and equipment, *plus* the total dollar value of the various liabilities incurred for other services. This may be phrased more concisely: call the difference between the company's total assets and total liabilities its *net worth* (see page 126 for this usage). For a company to be profitable, its sales activity must increase its net worth. Notice that the profitability of a company is a matter of changes in its assets and liabilities. If the net dollar amount of assets minus liabilities (net worth) is greater after the company's sales, those sales were profitable; if net worth is not greater after sales, sales were not profitable.

There is another side to this, however. The total assets of a company must equal the total rights of investors in that company. Assets must equal equities. The total amount reported for assets must be equalled by the total amount reported for sources of assets. If net worth (which reflects all liabilities) has increased, then this increase must be assigned to the only remaining source: stockholders' equity—the reasons for this were given on pages 131–133. The capital stock portion of stockholders' equity is not affected by sales of the company's product or services because it is simply an historical record of direct stockholder investments. Therefore, the source assigned to any increase in net worth resulting from sales is retained earnings, the only remaining part of stockholders' equity. This makes good sense, for the retained earnings account reflects the changes in residual rights of stockholders. If a company is profitable, the stockholders are entitled to the profits; their equity (the expression of their rights to company assets) should increase. If the company runs at a loss, the stockholders must absorb that loss, and their equity will diminish.

Even though profits and losses are a matter of changes in assets and liabilities, these changes are reflected in the retained earnings account. You can see this by glancing over the sample entries given for the shoe store. This suggests that *it is possible to prepare a complete report about a company's profits by preparing a statement of changes in retained earnings.* Such a report is called an *income statement.*[1] Changes in retained earnings reflect all of the asset and liability changes that make up profits.

Using a statement of changes in retained earnings as a report on operating activity is similar to using a statement of changes in net working capital as a report on financial activity. All financial changes are changes in noncurrent assets and noncurrent equities; yet these changes are reflected in changes in the current accounts. You can prepare a report about financial changes in noncurrent accounts by preparing a statement of changes in current accounts! Similarly, profits involve changes in assets and liabilities, but you can prepare a report of profits—an income statement— by preparing a statement of changes in the account that reflects these changes: retained earnings.[2]

---

[1] Students who have had prior exposure to accounting may be slightly puzzled to see the income statement depicted as a statement of changes in retained earnings. As you will see below, the reason it is possible to do this is that I develop the discussion in terms of the kind of income statement that includes a statement of changes in retained earnings at its end. The alternate system, whereby such things as dividends are reported separately from the income statement, is discussed on pages 408–409.

The combined income/retained earnings form of income statement is emphasized in this book because its construction is the most consistent with that of other change reports, and it best illustrates that an income statement is merely a report of changes in asset and liability accounts, as reflected in the retained earnings account.

[2] If you have studied linear programming, the following comment may be useful. If you have not studied linear programming, simply ignore what follows.

The partitioning of the balance sheet described in the Appendix to Chapter Seven and the decision to report only cross-partition changes in change reports means that any change report may be regarded as constructed of simple summary journal entries, each of which:

(a) has one line affecting the things about which the report is concerned (for example, cash, financial changes in noncurrent accounts, or profits), and

(b) has another line affecting something in which the primary change is reflected (for example, a noncash account, net working capital, or retained earnings). This latter effect is simply the dual of the former.

Both the funds statement and the income statement are prepared in terms of the duals of those things about which these reports are really concerned. (This is not true of the cash statement.) The funds statement is concerned about financial changes in noncurrent accounts, but it is prepared in terms of the dual of these changes—changes in net working capital. The income statement is concerned with profit changes in assets and liabilities, but is prepared in terms of the dual of these changes—changes in retained earnings.

How to Prepare
an Income Statement

Students who have had previous exposure to accounting may be aware that the statement preparation techniques described below are somewhat more elaborate than those ordinarily used in practice. Detailed step-by-step rules are given in what follows in order to develop your understanding of what an income statement actually summarizes. Once you have become familiar with this statement, you can save time in its preparation by utilizing a shortcut method illustrated on pages 410–411.

Statement of changes in retained earnings

Illustration 8-1 is a narrative summary of the balance sheet changes of Nadir Caves Souvenir Shoppe for the week ended May 7, 19XI. Illustration 8-2 gives these changes as simple summary journal entries. The data here are the same as those in Chapter Four (pages 187–193).

Illustration 8-1

Nadir Caves Souvenir Shoppe
Narrative Summary of Balance Sheet Changes
For the Week May 1–7, 19X1

1. Stockholders invested $10,000, cash.
2. The company prepaid one month's rent of $6,000.
3. The company purchased $3,000 of curios for cash.
4. The company bought an additional $6,500 of curios on account.
5. The company bought $800 of supplies on account.
6. Sales to customers totalled $3,950; all sales were for cash.
7. The curios sold in Change 6 had cost the company $1,900.
8. The company paid $4,200 of its accounts payable.
9. Prepaid rent of $1,400 expired.
10. Supplies that had cost the company $117 were consumed.

Step 1. Express all balance sheet changes as simple summary journal entries.

Illustration 8-2

Nadir Caves Souvenir Shoppe
Simple Summary Journal Entries
May 1–7, 19X1

1. Cash	10,000		6. Cash	3,950	
Capital Stock		10,000	Retained Earnings		3,950
2. Prepaid Rent	6,000		7. Retained Earnings	1,900	
Cash		6,000	Merchandise Inventory		1,900
3. Merchandise Inventory	3,000		8. Accounts Payable	4,200	
Cash		3,000	Cash		4,200
4. Merchandise Inventory	6,500		9. Retained Earnings	1,400	
Accounts Payable		6,500	Prepaid Rent		1,400
5. Supplies	800		10. Retained Earnings	117	
Accounts Payable		800	Supplies		117

Step 2. Select all changes that affect retained earnings; ignore the rest.

Only four of these balance sheet changes affected retained earnings:

6. Cash	3,950		9. Retained Earnings	1,400	
Retained Earnings		3,950	Prepaid Rent		1,400
7. Retained Earnings	1,900		10. Retained Earnings	117	
Merchandise Inventory		1,900	Supplies		117

In constructing a statement of changes in retained earnings, you can follow the same general rules that were employed in preparing cash statements and funds statements (see pages 304–305, 342–343). It happens that all of Nadir Caves Souvenir Shoppe's changes affecting retained earnings were operating changes, which simplifies matters.

Steps 3 and 4. Prepare separate lists of changes that increase and changes that decrease retained earnings; subdivide both lists into operating and nonoperating (financial) activities.

Increase		Decrease	
Operating:		*Operating:*	
6. Cash sales	$3,950	7. Cost of merchandise sold .	$1,900
		9. Cost of prepaid rent expired .	1,400
		10. Cost of supplies used . . .	117
			$3,417

Step 5. Combine all operating activities on one list.

Increase			Decrease
			(None)
Operating:			
Cash sales.		$3,950	
Cost of merchandise sold . .	$1,900		
Cost of prepaid rent expired .	1,400		
Cost of supplies used . . .	117	3,417	
		$ 533	

Since the retained earnings statement is intended to be a report of operating changes, do not summarize all operating changes by a single figure. To do so would be to throw away the details of these operating changes.

Step 6. Prepare suitable headings and footings.

Illustration 8-3

Nadir Caves Souvenir Shoppe
Statement of Changes in Retained Earnings
For the Week May 1–7, 19X1

Receipts:		
Sales		$3,950
Expenditures:		
Cost of Merchandise Sold	$1,900	
Cost of Prepaid Rent Expired	1,400	
Cost of Supplies Used	117	3,417
Increase in Retained Earnings		$ 533

You can verify that retained earnings increased by $533 during the week by looking at the company's May 7, 19X1 balance sheet (Illustration 4-3, page 192). When the company was founded on 5/1/X1, there were no retained earnings. By 5/7/X1, total stockholders' equity was $10,533. Since $10,000 of this was capital stock, retained earnings must have increased by $533 during the week.

Some technical terminology

Now is a good time to introduce some technical language that accountants have developed for retained earnings changes. When speaking of changes in assets and liabilities, it is usually considered proper to use the words *receipts* and *expenditures*. But the retained earnings statement reports the reflection of asset and liability changes in an account that itself is neither an asset nor a liability. This has led accountants to use special language to distinguish retained earnings changes from changes in assets and liabilities (even though the two kinds of changes result from the same transactions and internal changes). If an operating change in assets or liabilities increases retained earnings, call the retained earnings change a *revenue*. If an operating change in assets or liabilities decreases retained earnings, call the retained earnings change an *expense*.

A *revenue* is the reflection in retained earnings of the assets a company receives from selling the products or services in which it ordinarily deals. The revenues of a shoe store arise from its sales of shoes and such items as shoe laces, shoe polish, and so forth. The revenues of a movie theater arise from its sales of admissions, popcorn, advertising services for local merchants, and so forth.

An *expense* is the reflection in retained earnings of the costs of obtaining revenues —the matched costs of the assets sold, used, or expired, and the amounts of liabilities incurred in selling the products or services in which the company deals. With respect to nonmonetary assets, notice that *expenditures* (which are reported on funds statements) occur at the time the nonmonetary asset is purchased; *expenses* occur as the asset yields its services.

Finally, *operating income* is the accountant's technical name for the difference between total revenues and total expenses. A company's operating income is the reflection in retained earnings of that company's profit from operations—of the changes

	What Is Reported on	
	Funds Statement	Income Statement
Inflows of assets or reductions of liabilities* resulting from selling ordinary goods and services	Receipt	Revenue
Inflow does not affect net working capital	(nothing)	Revenue†
Outflows of assets, exhaustion of asset services, and incurrence of liabilities resulting from selling ordinary goods and services	Expenditure	Expense
Outflow does not affect net working capital	(nothing)	Expense
Difference between reported inflows and outflows	Funds from operations	Net income from operations

* These latter are mainly sales involving satisfaction of advances from customers (see page 129) who prepaid for the product or service which they received. The related entry would have the following form:

Advances From Customers   XXX
    Retained Earnings   XXX

† Transactions of this kind are rare. The only examples that come to mind are certain kinds of barter deals occasionally conducted in international trade, and unusual sales where the seller accepts the buyer's long-term notes.

in the company's net worth resulting from its dealings in its ordinary products or services. Instead of operating income, the accountant will often speak of *net income from operations*. These mean exactly the same thing. We will see later that some kinds of income are nonoperating; but if all income is operating income, the accountant will speak simply of "net income." Instead of calling his profit report a statement of changes in retained earnings, the accountant usually calls it an *income statement*.

The main distinctions between funds-statement and income-statement terminology may be diagrammed as shown on the opposite page.

Here is the Nadir Caves Souvenir Shoppe report using this new language.

Illustration 8-4

Nadir Caves Souvenir Shoppe
Statement of Income and Retained Earnings
For the Week May 1–7, 19X1

Revenues:		
Sales		$3,950
Expenses:		
Cost of Merchandise Sold	$1,900	
Rent Expense	1,400	
Supplies Expense	117	3,417
Net Income		$ 533
Retained Earnings—4/30/X1		–0–
Retained Earnings—5/7/X1		$ 533

The language for supplies and prepaid rent has been greatly abbreviated. *Rent expense* means "the effect on retained earnings of prepaid rent expiring in operations." *Supplies expense* means "the effect on retained earnings of using up supplies in the course of selling the company's regular products or services."

The language for merchandise has not been abbreviated quite this much. Instead of "merchandise expense," accountants say *cost of merchandise sold* or even *cost of goods sold*. This inconsistency in the language for merchandise expense appears to be a matter of convention.

Strictly speaking, it is redundant to use the titles *rent expense* and *supplies expense* when you've already used the caption *expenses*. That is, the expenses section of this income statement might instead appear as follows:

Expenses:		
Cost of Merchandise Sold	$1,900	
Rent	1,400	
Supplies	117	3,417

Some firms use this latter style, some use the style in Illustration 8-4, and others use a mixture of both styles (see, for example, the income statement on page 658).[3]

---

[3] The reason this book usually employs the style exemplified in Illustration 8-4 is that it corresponds neatly with the "nominal account" titles that will be discussed in Chapter Ten.

Another example of an income statement

Here is another example of income statement construction. If you had no difficulty with the previous example, feel free to skim the material between here and the discussion of dividends on page 402; otherwise, you may wish to use this example for review. Some of the data in what follows are employed in later examples.

Illustration 8-5 gives Nadir Caves Souvenir Shoppe's balance sheet changes for the week ended May 14, 19X1. (The original data may be found in Problem 4-2, pages 194–195.)

Illustration 8-5

Nadir Caves Souvenir Shoppe
Narrative Summary of Balance Sheet Changes
For the Week May 8–14, 19X1

1. The company bought $270 of curios for cash.
2. The company bought $1,475 of curios on account.
3. The company bought $79 of supplies on account.
4. The company declared and paid a $300 cash dividend to its stockholders.
5. The company made cash sales of $4,460.
6. The curios sold in Change 5 cost the company $2,103.
7. Supplies that cost $121 were consumed in operations.
8. One week's prepaid rent costing $1,400 expired.
9. The company paid accounts payable of $2,760.

The following solution is quite detailed, to provide maximum help for students who are having difficulties; if you don't need this much help, feel free to skim some of these details.

Step 1. Express all balance sheet changes as simple summary journal entries.

1. Merchandise Inventory	270		6. Retained Earnings	2,103	
Cash		270	Merchandise Inventory		2,103
2. Merchandise Inventory	1,475		7. Retained Earnings	121	
Accounts Payable		1,475	Supplies		121
3. Supplies	79		8. Retained Earnings	1,400	
Accounts Payable		79	Prepaid Rent		1,400
4. Retained Earnings	300		9. Accounts Payable	2,760	
Cash		300	Cash		2,760
5. Cash	4,460				
Retained Earnings		4,460			

Step 2. Select all changes that affect retained earnings; ignore the rest.

4. Retained Earnings	300		7. Retained Earnings	121	
Cash		300	Supplies		121
5. Cash	4,460		8. Retained Earnings	1,400	
Retained Earnings		4,460	Prepaid Rent		1,400
6. Retained Earnings	2,103				
Merchandise Inventory		2,103			

Step 3. Prepare separate lists of changes that increase and changes that decrease retained earnings.

Increase		*Decrease*	
5. Cash sales	$4,460	4. Dividends declared	$ 300
		6. Cost of goods sold	2,103
		7. Cost of supplies used . . .	121
		8. Cost of prepaid rent expired .	1,400

Step 4. Subdivide both lists into operating and nonoperating activities.

Since the income statement is mainly a report of operating changes, it does not distinguish between different kinds of financial changes; it merely classifies all of them as "nonoperating," whether they are noncurrent asset, noncurrent equity, or dividend activities. However, unlike the funds statement, the type of income statement emphasized in this chapter does not summarize all nonoperating changes by a single figure; instead, it reports them all at the bottom of the income statement (as demonstrated in subsequent examples).

Increase		*Decrease*	
Operating:		*Operating:*	
Cash Sales	$4,460	Cost of goods sold	$2,103
		Cost of supplies used . . .	121
		Cost of prepaid rent expired .	1,400
			$3,624
		Nonoperating:	
		Dividends declared	$ 300

Step 5. Combine all operating activities on one list.

Increase			*Decrease*	
Operating:			*Nonoperating:*	
Cash sales.		$4,460	Dividends declared	$ 300
Cost of goods sold .	$2,103			
Cost of supplies used	121			
Cost of prepaid rent				
expired . . .	1,400	3,624		
		$ 836		

Step 6. Prepare suitable headings and footings; employ suitable descriptive language.

Illustration 8-6

Nadir Caves Souvenir Shoppe
Statement of Income and Retained Earnings
For the Week May 8–14, 19X1

Revenues:		
Sales		$4,460
Expenses:		
Cost of Goods Sold	$2,103	
Rent Expense	1,400	
Supplies Expense	121	3,624
Net Income		$ 836
Dividends		300
Increase in Retained Earnings		$ 536
Retained Earnings—5/7/X1		533
Retained Earnings—5/14/X1		$1,069

Dividends are distributions to owners. They have nothing directly to do with the company's dealings in its main products or services, which is why they are financial rather than operating activities. For the same reason, *dividends are not an expense*: expenses are costs of obtaining revenues; dividends have nothing whatever to do with obtaining revenues. Instead they merely concern the entity's dealings with its stockholders.

Even though dividend declarations don't affect the calculation of operating profits, they lead to *distributions* of profits—distributions to owners of cash (or, occasionally, of other assets) equal to some of the increase in net worth resulting from profitable operations of the present period or earlier periods.[4] Accordingly, the effect on retained earnings of declaring dividends often is reported on the income statement, but the effect is reported after the net income figure so that readers will not confuse the dividend information with the report on profitability.

Order of items on the income statement

This raises the question: In what order does the accountant list things on the income statement? As with the balance sheet, there are a variety of ways to set up an income statement, but here is a good style to follow:

Show revenues first; then show expenses. Under expenses, if the company sells a product, show cost of merchandise sold (or cost of goods sold) as the first expense. (If the company sells only services, salaries expense is often shown first.) Show expenses in any order you like thereafter. There seems to be some tendency to show larger expenses first and such expenses as miscellaneous expenses and taxes expense last, but there are no firm rules here. The difference between revenues and expenses is net income from operations.

---

[4] The only exception to this would be "liquidating dividends," such as the final distribution of residual assets by a company that is going out of business.

Below that, show any nonoperating gains and losses. Revenues are the reflection in retained earnings of the assets that a firm receives from selling the products or services in which it ordinarily deals; expenses are the costs of obtaining revenues. *Nonoperating gains and losses* are the reflections in retained earnings of other activities that affect profits but that do not directly relate to selling the products or services in which the firm ordinarily deals. These gains and losses include such things as the effect on retained earnings of incidental sales of noncurrent assets. Two examples of these were shown in the Miami Corporation illustration in the last chapter (see Problem 7-1 and its solution, pages 357–358, 362–365):

6a. Equipment was sold for total cash proceeds of $220.
6b. The equipment sold in Change 6a had a book value of $300 at the time it was sold.
14a. Land was sold for total cash proceeds of $290.
14b. The land sold in Change 14a had cost the company only $60.

6a. Cash	220		14a. Cash	290	
Equipment		220	Land		290
6b. Retained Earnings	80		14b. Land	230	
Equipment		80	Retained Earnings		230

In Entry 6b, a decrease of $80 in the value of equipment was recognized (together with a related $80 decrease in retained earnings) at the time the equipment was sold. Call this kind of nonoperating decrease a *loss*. In Entry 14b, an increase of $230 in the value of land was recognized (together with a related $230 increase in retained earnings) at the time the land was sold. Call this kind of nonoperating increase a *gain*.

The total of net income from operations and any nonoperating gains and losses is simply called *net income*. Net income = Revenues − Expenses + Nonoperating gains − Nonoperating losses. It should be noticed that the accounting definition of *net income* is dependent upon the definitions of revenues, expenses, nonoperating gains, and nonoperating losses. Net income is a residual of these rather than something with a separate, independent definition.[5]

If there are no nonoperating gains and losses, net income from operations will equal net income. When this occurs, label net income from operations as "net income." This has been done in Illustrations 8-4 and 8-6. Dividends are reported after net income. If more than one nonoperating gain or loss is reported, a subheading called "nonoperating gains and losses" could be used on the income statement. Here, then, is one possible layout of an income statement:

---

[5] The reader is warned that this observation may be controversial. Various *theories* of accounting income have been proposed by academic authors, but these have not yet been reflected in actual accounting practice, which instead relies upon complicated rules for revenue and expense recognition.

Illustration 8-7

Name of Company
Statement of Income and Retained Earnings
Period Concerned

Revenues:
  Sales . . . . $XXX
  Other Revenues (if any) . . . . XXX $XXX

Expenses:
  Cost of Goods Sold . . . . $XXX
  Other Expenses XXX
  ———————————. XXX
  ———————————. XXX
  ———————————. XXX
  Other Expenses . . . . XXX XXX

Net Income from Operations . . . . $XXX
Nonoperating Gains and Losses:
  ——————————————. . . . . $XXX
  ——————————————. XXX
  ——————————————. . . . . XXX XXX

Net Income . . . . $XXX
  Dividends XXX

Increase in Retained Earnings for the Period . . . . $XXX
Retained Earnings—Beginning of Period XXX

Retained Earnings—End of Period . . . . $XXX

It's customary to combine income-statement items that have similar causal explanations. For example, all sales are usually represented by a single figure, even though some may have been for cash and others on account. Often building depreciation and equipment depreciation are combined into a single "depreciation expense" figure, and so forth. The reason for doing this is to avoid overwhelming the reader with detail. Readers of financial statements use these statements for predicting what will happen to the company in the future. If different kinds of revenues and expenses are apt to behave differently from each other, the income statement should distinguish them from each other. If not, then like items might as well be combined and a shorter report prepared.

This parallels one reason why the income statement reports much more detail about operating changes than it does about nonoperating changes. The latter occur much more erratically than do operating changes; nonoperating changes are much harder to predict. If we know the trend of a firm's cost of goods sold over the last several years we may be in a fairly good position to predict its cost of goods sold for next year. But similar predictions of losses and gains from sales of used noncurrent assets are subject to a much wider margin of error. We saw on pages 26–27 that most financial statements are used in attempts to predict future economic attributes of the firm. Since nonoperating gains and losses cannot be accurately predicted, they might as well be reported as concisely as possible.

There are additional reasons for summarizing nonoperating gains and losses instead of reporting their details. The firm is "in business" to make profits from operations; its main concern is not with such incidental nonoperating activities. These gains and losses often arise when the book values of depreciable assets differ from their current market values. If the asset is sold at a date or a scrap value different from that employed in the original depreciation estimates, a correction is required, and this correction affects retained earnings. But the related underdepreciation or overdepreciation of an asset has occurred over its *entire life,* not just in the current year. This makes the presence of such a gain or loss on the present year's income statement of less significance than the information given about operating activities. (The problem of the correct treatment of underdepreciation and overdepreciation is discussed in more detail in Chapter Thirteen.) Finally, nonoperating gains and losses are usually of minor significance to the company's profit-seeking activities.

For these reasons, the practice is to report single net figures for nonoperating gains or losses instead of reporting details.

This decision in turn underlies the rule, which we have been following since page 184, for breaking up compound journal entries into simple ones:

Operating entry: Break up the compound entry in such a way that retained earnings appears in as many simple entries as possible.

Nonoperating entry: Break up the compound entry in such a way that retained earnings appears in no more than one simple entry.

The effect of this rule is to record as well as report single net figures for nonoperating gains and losses instead of recording details. If details are not to be reported, there is little point in recording them.

Extraordinary items

The previous discussion has indicated that there are important differences between revenues and expenses on the one hand, and nonoperating gains and losses on the other. Yet you will rarely observe this exact language in actual published income statements. Instead, large nonoperating gains and losses are usually reported under the heading *Extraordinary Items.* Such extraordinary items include:

1. Gains and losses from the sale of investments in other firms, whenever it had initially been intended that these investments were to be long-term ones and the investments had not been made with the expectation of reselling them.

2. Losses resulting from legal condemnation of the firm's properties, expropriation of properties by foreign governments, or similar acts.

3. Major gains and losses from revaluations of foreign currencies.

Most such gains and losses involve technical matters which are best reserved for an advanced course. The main thing to emphasize here is that if a nonoperating gain or loss is to be treated as an extraordinary item, it must be *large* in comparison to the firm's net income. For example, if a loss on the sale of buildings and equipment is to be reported as an extraordinary item, a substantial amount of buildings and equipment must be sold, perhaps an entire plant.

If the nonoperating gain or loss is relatively insignificant in comparison to net income, usually it simply is included among that year's miscellaneous revenues or expenses. This is done for convenience and to avoid cluttering the income statement with extra detail (which, as we already have seen, isn't very useful for investor prediction purposes, anyway). Extraordinary items are generally accompanied by detailed footnote explanations; this by itself would suffice to encourage practicing accountants to treat insignificant nonoperating gains and losses as though they were operating—the extra work required to treat them as extraordinary items just isn't warranted. All of this is a good example of what is often called the accountants' *materiality rule*: treat minor items in convenient, expedient, ways.

Accordingly, in practice the form employed for income statements is more apt to resemble that in Illustration 8-8 than that in Illustration 8-7.

Illustration 8-8

Name of Company
Statement of Income and Retained Earnings
Period Concerned

Revenues:
Sales	$XXX	
Other Revenues (including minor nonoperating gains).	XXX	$XXX

Expenses:
Cost of Goods Sold	$XXX	
———————————	XXX	
———————————	XXX	
———————————	XXX	
———————————	XXX	
Other Expenses (including minor nonoperating losses)	XXX	XXX

Income Before Extraordinary Items		$XXX
Extraordinary Items:		
———————————	$XXX	
———————————	XXX	XXX

Net Income	$XXX
Retained Earnings—Beginning of Period	XXX
Retained Earnings—End of Period	$XXX

Nonetheless, the operating/nonoperating distinction is sufficiently important to the significance of the income statement that we will continue to use it here and there in the remainder of this book. Doing so is easily reconciled with present accounting practice: *an "extraordinary item" is merely a nonoperating gain or loss that the accountant believes should be reported separately from the calculation of net income from operations.*

Gross margin

On page 89, you were given an alternate form of income statement. There are a number of correct ways to prepare an income statement, just as there are a number of ways to prepare other financial statements. One way that is frequently used gives a special treatment to cost of goods sold. Cost of goods sold (merchandise expense) is often the most important single expense on the income statement. Many accountants (and many investors) subtract cost of goods sold directly from the figure for sales to get a subtotal called *gross margin* or *gross profit,* from which the other expenses are then subtracted to obtain net income from operations.[6] Illustration 8-9 shows how this would be done for Nadir Caves Souvenir Shoppe for the week ended May 14, 19X1.

Illustration 8-9

Nadir Caves Souvenir Shoppe
Statement of Income and Retained Earnings
For the Week May 8–14, 19X1

Sales		$4,460
Less: Cost of Goods Sold		2,103
Gross margin		$2,357
Rent Expense	$1,400	
Supplies Expense	121	1,521
Net Income		$ 836
Dividends		300
Increase in Retained Earnings		$ 536
Retained Earnings—5/7/X1		533
Retained Earnings—5/14/X1		$1,069

Both forms of income statement shown in Illustrations 8-6 and 8-9 are widely used in practice. To emphasize that cost of goods sold is an expense similar to any other expense, this book will use the general form employed in Illustration 8-6 in subsequent income statements, although you will see many published income statements using the gross margin form employed in Illustration 8-9.

Net income and profits

Profits were defined (on pages 49, 189–192, and 391) as the effect on net worth (all assets minus all liabilities) of the entity's sales and their related costs. Each of these changes in assets and liabilities also affects retained earnings. Accordingly, income was defined (on pages 393–394) as this effect of profits on retained earnings. This can be generalized by saying that the income statement reports the effects on retained earnings of changes in net worth resulting from operations, nonoperating gains and losses, and dividends. Illustration 8-10 shows the assets and liabilities of Nadir Caves Souvenir Shoppe at May 7 and May 14, 19X1:

---

[6] Of course, this applies only to companies that sell a product; companies that sell services (such as theaters) would not use this kind of income statement (unless popcorn and soft drink sales were their major source of revenue).

Illustration 8-10

Nadir Caves Souvenir Shoppe
Net Worth
May 7 and May 14, 19X1

	5/7/X1	5/14/X1
Assets:		
Cash	$ 750	$ 1,880
Merchandise Inventory	7,600	7,242
Supplies	683	641
Prepaid Rent	4,600	3,200
	$13,633	$12,963
Liabilities:		
Accounts Payable	3,100	1,894
Net Worth	$10,533	$11,069

It happens that both assets and liabilities decreased during the week. But liabilities decreased faster, so the company's net worth increased by $536 ($11,069 − $10,533 = $536). This simple illustration was constructed so that all balance sheet changes affecting net worth would be either operating changes or dividends.[7] The $536 increase in net worth is thus reflected in a $536 increase in retained earnings.

Other statements of changes in retained earnings

For many companies, this very simple income statement will also serve as a complete statement of changes in retained earnings. But in an advanced accounting course, you would discover that there are certain rather technical balance sheet changes that affect retained earnings but do not fit into the "profit" framework we have developed here.[8] Such changes may be included on the income statement, but sometimes they are reflected on a separate statement of changes in retained earnings. Similarly, although dividends often are reported on the income statement, it also is common for them to be reported on a separate statement of changes in retained earnings instead. An example of this is given below.

The "combined" income statement illustrated in this book is an acceptable one whose rules of construction correspond well with those of other change reports. For simplicity, the income statements in the rest of this book will serve as complete statements of changes in retained earnings. These usually are called by such diverse

---

[7] *Last* week there was a change that increased net worth without affecting retained earnings—the company issued capital stock for $10,000, cash (Illustration 8-1).

[8] Here is an example. Corporations are under no obligation to buy back shares of capital stock from their stockholders, but (as we saw in Chapter Five) sometimes they du just that. If a profitable company buys back its own shares, it stands to reason that the price it pays will usually be greater than the amount the company received when it first issued these shares. This can affect retained earnings. Yet the accountant would insist that the corporation exists to serve the interests of its stockholders, not to make profits from dealings with them. Because of the special nature of the relationship between stockholders and their corporation, if the reacquisition of shares of a company's own capital stock affects retained earnings, it would be regarded as a "nonprofit" transaction and would not be reported on the income statement.

names as "combined statement of income and changes in retained earnings," "statement of income and retained earnings," "summary of income earned and retained," "statement of income and surplus" (a misnomer, as was indicated on page 262), and others. For brevity and simplicity, the simplest acceptable name—"income statement"—will be used in the bulk of this book, though actual statements will be headed Statement of Income and Retained Earnings.

An example of a separate retained earnings statement

Page 89 gives the income statement of C. M. de Céspedes Cigar Co. It would be possible to break up this statement into two smaller statements. One of these, the income statement, could end with the amount of the firm's 19X5 net income; the other could show the changes in the firm's retained earnings for the year. In this particular case, the only things that affected retained earnings during 19X5 were profits and dividends. But had there been other matters that affected retained earnings but not profits, these also could be reflected in the retained earnings statement.

The shortened income and retained earnings statements of C. M. de Céspedes Cigar Co. are shown below.

C. M. de Céspedes Cigar Co.
and Subsidiary Companies

Consolidated Statement of Income

For the Year Ended December 31, 19X5

Net sales and other revenues		$165,701,527
Costs and expenses:		
Cost of goods sold	$132,706,749	
Selling, administrative, and general expenses	26,178,638	
Interest expense	2,622,296	
Income taxes	1,357,631	162,865,314
Net income		$ 2,836,213

C.M. de Céspedes Cigar Co.
and Subsidiary Companies

Consolidated Statement of Retained Earnings

For the Year Ended December 31, 19X5

Retained earnings at beginning of year	$ 21,192,517
Net income	2,836,213
	$ 24,028,730
Dividends (per share: common—$1, preferred—$6)	1,857,599
Retained earnings at end of year	$ 22,171,131

Summary

1. An income statement is a report on profits. It shows:
    (a) The kinds and amounts of profits a company has had (operating income, nonoperating gains and losses).
    (b) What has happened to profits (the amount of dividends, the amount of net income retained).

2. An income statement is a change report of the same general kind, though slightly different in form, as those discussed in Chapters Six and Seven. Here is how an income statement is prepared:
    (a) Express all balance sheet changes as simple summary journal entries.
    (b) Select all changes that affect retained earnings; ignore the rest.
    (c) Prepare separate lists of changes that increase and changes that decrease retained earnings.
    (d) Subdivide both lists into operating and nonoperating activities.
    (e) Combine all operating activities on one list.
    (f) Prepare suitable headings and footings; employ suitable descriptive captions. Combine all like items; for example, report all sales as a single figure.

3. The accountant's "income" is the reflection in retained earnings of operating and nonoperating profits (and losses). Take the case of profits: if a company is operating at a profit, its assets will be increasing faster (or decreasing slower) than its liabilities. As a result, some of the total amount reported for the firm's assets will need to be assigned to a source other than a liability. The amount needing such assignment will equal the amount of profits, less any dividends paid or declared.[9] The source assigned must be (by elimination) stockholders' equity and, in particular, retained earnings.

A possible shortcut

Pages 314 and 348 illustrated possible shortcut methods for preparation of cash and funds statements. There is a similar shortcut method for the preparation of income statements, which can speed your work once you understand them.

Begin by putting the firm's journal entries in simple, summary form. Label all operating changes that affect retained earnings R or E, depending upon whether they are revenues or expenses. Label all nonoperating changes G, L, or D, depending upon whether they are gains, losses, or dividend declarations. All remaining changes (which are unlabeled) are to be ignored. Move directly from this labeled set of simple summary entries to the construction of the income statement itself. Illustration 8-11 shows the shortcut method based on Nadir Caves Souvenir Shoppe's journal entries for the period May 1-7, 19X1 (which does not happen to include any nonoperating changes). The firm's income statement is on page 399. A more complicated example of this shortcut method is given on page 418.

---

[9] It is assumed here that capital stock is neither issued nor retired during the period involved.

Illustration 8-11

Nadir Caves Souvenir Shoppe
Shortcut Method for Preparing an Income Statement
For the Week May 1–7, 19X1

1. Cash	10,000		6. Cash	3,950		
Capital Stock		10,000	Retained Earnings		3,950 ^{R}	
2. Prepaid Rent	6,000		7. Retained Earnings	1,900		
Cash		6,000	Merchandise		1,900 ^{E}	
3. Merchandise	3,000		8. Accounts Payable	4,200		
Cash		3,000	Cash		4,200 ^{E}	
4. Merchandise	6,500		9. Retained Earnings	1,400		
Accounts Payable		6,500	Prepaid Rent		1,400 ^{E}	
5. Supplies	800		10. Retained Earnings	117		
Accounts Payable		800	Supplies		117 ^{E}	

Statement construction in practice

In the last three chapters a technique of constructing cash, funds, and income statements from a firm's underlying summary journal entries has been illustrated. This technique accurately reflects the essence of what occurs when these statements are prepared, and it accurately indicates the nature of the different transactions and internal changes summarized on each statement.

But this technique is a simplification of actual statement construction practices. It is impractical for most firms to organize the thousands of balance sheet changes recorded during the year into the narrative summaries from which we have constructed these statements. A firm that employs a computerized accounting system *could* use our process, but in practice other techniques are employed. Cash statements are constructed from an analysis of changes in the cash account. Funds statements are constructed in part from income statements and in part from analyses of the firm's noncurrent assets and equities (the techniques for this are illustrated in Chapter Nine). Finally, the income statement itself is constructed from a set of specialized accounts (which are discussed in Chapter Ten) that group together similar changes in retained earnings.

But until you understand the cash, funds, and income statements (and how they are related to each other), these practical statement construction techniques tend to obscure the true nature of what these statements report and what really is going on during their construction. That is why, up to this point, this book has used simplified statement construction methods. An additional reason for using the simplified methods is that, by combining all similar balance sheet changes into summary changes for the year, it has been possible to introduce a number of realistic cases modeled upon actual published financial statements without swamping you in detail. For this latter reason these simplifications will still be used for presentation of certain new material in the remainder of this book.

Problems for Study and Self-Examination

Problem 8-1:

Illustration 8-12 gives the balance sheet of Gathings Variety Store as of 10/1/X1. Illustration 8-13 is a narrative summary of the company's balance sheet changes for

October, 19X1. The order in which items have been listed in this summary is deliberately scrambled. Prepare an income statement for October, 19X1. Feel free to use the shortcut method.

Illustration 8-12

Gathings Variety Store
Balance Sheet
October 1, 19X1

Assets

Current Assets:
Cash	$ 40,000	
Merchandise Inventory	190,000	
Supplies	6,000	$236,000

Noncurrent Assets:
Buildings	$120,000	
Furniture and Fixtures	70,000	190,000

Total Assets $426,000

Equities

Current Liabilities:
Accounts Payable	$ 80,000	
Salaries Payable	17,000	
Dividends Payable	4,000	
Taxes Payable	19,000	$120,000

Stockholders' Equity:
Capital Stock	$200,000	
Retained Earnings	106,000	306,000

Total Equities $426,000

Illustration 8-13

Gathings Variety Store
Narrative Summary of Balance Sheet Changes
October 19X1

1. The company paid accounts payable totalling $237,000.
2. The company paid dividends payable totalling $4,000.
3. The company estimates that its taxes for the month will be $3,200.
4. During the month, the company paid $18,500 of taxes payable.
5. Depreciation of furniture and fixtures for the month was $1,100.
6. On 10/1/X1, the company's buildings had a remaining estimated service life of $18\frac{1}{2}$ years. The company estimates that these buildings will have a scrap value of $9,000 on retirement.
7. The company purchased $200,000 of merchandise during the month, all on account.
8. The company took a physical count of merchandise on hand at 10/31/X1 and found that it still owned merchandise that had cost $165,000.

9. The company declared a $6,000 dividend, to be paid on 1/15/X2.
10. The company's employees earned $83,000 during the month.
11. Salary payments to company employees totalled $91,000.
12. On 10/31/X1, the company purchased furniture for $8,000, cash. No depreciation was taken on this furniture for October, 19X1.
13. The company employs a delivery service to deliver merchandise to its customers. This delivery service charged Gathings Variety Store $19,200 for October, 19X1, deliveries. The company paid in cash (without ever bothering to record a liability).
14. The company consumed supplies costing $7,000 during the month.
15. Supplies costing $11,400 were purchased on account.
16. October sales of the company's products were all for cash and totalled $353,000.
17a. On 10/1/X1, the company sold some old chairs that had been used in the store for $680, cash.
17b. At the time of sale, the chairs sold in Change 17a had book value of $800. Changes 17a and 17b are given the same index number because they are simple changes that form a single compound transaction when combined.

Problem 8-2 (Brain-teaser):

This problem uses the same data as Problem 4-5 (pages 211–212).

Udall Stores prepares financial statements once a year on December 31. As of that day, the company takes a physical count of merchandise and supplies on hand and determines from this the cost of merchandise and supplies that have been consumed in the year's operations (i.e. it uses the periodic inventory method discussed on page 207).

Shown below are some errors the company's accountant made during 19X1. These errors are unrelated to each other. Dollar figures have deliberately been omitted, since you don't need them. For each error, indicate the effects (if any) of that error on the company's 19X1 funds statement and the company's 19X1 income statement. Be sure to list all effects. You may assume that funds from operations were positive, that there was an increase in net working capital for the year, that net income and net income from operations were both positive, and that there was an increase in retained earnings for the year.

1. Merchandise was purchased on account from a supplier in late December, 19X1. Although the goods had been delivered to the company at 12/31/X1, they had not yet been unloaded. Neither the merchandise nor the related account payable was recorded until early 19X2.

2. The company forgot to record a sale on account that was made on 12/28/X1. The related merchandise was delivered to the customer on the day of the sale.

3. During October, 19X1, the company issued a $6\frac{1}{4}\%$ note payable whose principal and interest are due on 3/15/X2. The company recorded the issue of the note correctly, but forgot to accrue interest at 12/31/X1.

4. During November, 19X1, the company bought a 3-year fire insurance policy for cash. The purchase of this policy was recorded correctly; however, the company did not write off any of the cost of this policy at 12/31/X1 (or at any other time during 19X1).

5. The company bought a storage building in April, 19X1. The purchase was recorded correctly, but, in calculating depreciation, the building's total service life was underestimated.

6. The company purchased some merchandise on account during November, 19X1, recording the purchase correctly. In early December (before the goods had been paid for) this merchandise was returned as defective. The company never paid the related account payable, but it neglected to record the return.

Solutions

Solution 8-1:

Compare your answer to this problem with the income statement on page 417. If the two agree, you should feel free to move on to the next problem after reading page 418; if not, the details of the construction of this statement are given below.

Calculations:

Entry 6: The buildings are to be written down from $120,000 to $9,000 over the next 222 months. (18½ years = 222 months.) This total decline of $111,000 ($120,000 − $9,000 = $111,000) will be at a rate of $500 a month ($111,000/222 = $500). The October depreciation charge for buildings is $500.

Entry 8: Merchandise Inventory—10/1/X1	$190,000
October 19X1 Purchases (see Entry 7)	200,000
	$390,000
Merchandise Inventory—10/31/X1	165,000
Cost of Merchandise Sold during Month	$225,000

Although the shortcut method could be used in solving this problem, the more detailed method will be shown for the benefit of those readers who may be experiencing difficulties. The shortcut method is illustrated on page 418.

Step 1. Express all balance sheet changes as simple summary journal entries.

1.	Accounts Payable	237,000		IF 10.	Retained Earnings	83,000	
	Cash		237,000		Salaries Payable		83,000
2.	Dividends Payable	4,000		11.	Salaries Payable	91,000	
	Cash		4,000		Cash		91,000
IF 3.	Retained Earnings	3,200		F 12.	Furniture and Fixtures	8,000	
	Taxes Payable		3,200		Cash		8,000
4.	Taxes Payable	18,500		IF 13.	Retained Earnings	19,200	
	Cash		18,500		Cash		19,200
I 5.	Retained Earnings	1,100		IF 14.	Retained Earnings	7,000	
	Furniture and Fixtures		1,100		Supplies		7,000
I 6.	Retained Earnings	500		15.	Supplies	11,400	
	Buildings		500		Accounts Payable		11,400
7.	Merchandise Inventory	200,000		IF 16.	Cash	353,000	
	Accounts Payable		200,000		Retained Earnings		353,000
IF 8.	Retained Earnings	225,000		F 17a.	Cash	680	
	Merchandise Inventory		225,000		Furniture and Fixtures		680
IF 9.	Retained Earnings	6,000		I 17b.	Retained Earnings	120	
	Dividends Payable		6,000		Furniture and Fixtures		120

Notice how Entries 17a and 17b have the combined effect of reflecting the $800 book value of the furniture sold ($680 + $120 = $800).

The entries from the above group to be used in preparing the income statement are marked with an "I"; those entries that would be used in preparing a funds statement are marked with an "F." Although there is considerable overlap between these two subsets of entries, the overlap is not complete. For example, the funds statement discusses *purchases* of noncurrent assets (expenditures), as in Entry 12, whereas the income statement discusses *depreciation* of noncurrent assets (expenses), as in Entries 5 and 6. The funds statement discusses the *proceeds* from the sale of old furniture (Entry 17a), whereas the income statement discusses the *loss* on that sale (Entry 17b).

Steps 2 and 3. Select all changes that affect retained earnings; prepare separate lists of changes that increase and changes that decrease retained earnings.

	Increase				*Decrease*	
16. Cash	353,000		3.	Retained Earnings	3,200	
Retained Earnings		353,000		Taxes Payable		3,200
			5.	Retained Earnings	1,100	
				Furniture and Fixtures		1,100
			6.	Retained Earnings	500	
				Buildings		500
			8.	Retained Earnings	225,000	
				Merchandise Inventory		225,000
			9.	Retained Earnings	6,000	
				Dividends Payable		6,000
			10.	Retained Earnings	83,000	
				Salaries Payable		83,000
			13.	Retained Earnings	19,200	
				Cash		19,200
			14.	Retained Earnings	7,000	
				Supplies		7,000
			17b.	Retained Earnings	120	
				Furniture and Fixtures		120

Step 4. Subdivide both lists into operating and nonoperating activities.

(You may wish to refer back to Illustration 8-13 for explanations of certain journal entries.)

Increase		*Decrease*	
Operating:		*Operating:*	
16. Cash sales	$353,000	3. Estimated cost of taxes	$ 3,200
		5. Depreciation of furniture and fixtures	1,100
		6. Depreciation of buildings	500
		8. Cost of goods sold	225,000
		10. Cost of salaries earned	83,000
		13. Cost of delivery services	19,200
		14. Cost of supplies used	7,000
			$339,000
		Nonoperating:	
		9. Dividends declared	$ 6,000
		17b. Loss on sale of furniture	120

Step 5. Combine all operating activities on one list.

The order of operating decreases is slightly changed in what follows, because of a personal preference for showing larger expenses first; however, any number of possible account orders would be correct.

	Increase			*Decrease*	
Operating:			*Nonoperating:*		
Cash sales		$353,000	Loss on sale		
Cost of goods sold	$225,000		of furniture		$ 120
Cost of salaries earned	83,000		Dividends		
Cost of delivery services	19,200		declared		6,000
Depreciation of furniture					
and fixtures	$1,100				
Depreciation of buildings	500	1,600			
Cost of supplies used		7,000			
Estimated cost of taxes		3,200	339,000		
			$ 14,000		

Step 6. Prepare suitable headings, footings, and descriptive captions; combine all like items.

Illustration 8-14

Gathings Variety Store
Statement of Income and Retained Earnings
For the Month of October, 19X1

Revenues:		
Sales		$353,000
Expenses:		
Cost of Goods Sold	$225,000	
Salaries Expense	83,000	
Delivery Expense	19,200	
Depreciation Expense	1,600	
Supplies Expense	7,000	
Taxes Expense	3,200	339,000
Net Income from Operations		$ 14,000
Loss on Sale of Furniture		120*
Net Income		$ 13,880
Dividends		6,000
Increase in Retained Earnings		$ 7,880
Retained Earnings—10/1/X1		106,000
Retained Earnings—10/31/X1		$113,880

* This is an example of the kind of minor nonoperating loss that ordinarily would not be reported separately (as it is here) but that would instead be treated as a miscellaneous expense (see pages 405–406).

Just for comparison, Illustration 8-15 gives the company's October funds statement. (The appended schedule of changes in net working capital has been omitted.)

Illustration 8-15

Gathings Variety Store
Sources and Uses of Net Working Capital
For the Month of October, 19X1

Sources:

Funds from Operations	$15,600
Proceeds from Sale of Noncurrent Assets:	
Proceeds from Sale of Furniture	680
Net Sources	$16,280

Uses:

Purchase of Noncurrent Assets:	
Purchase of Furniture	$ 8,000
Dividends Declared	6,000
Net Uses	$14,000
Increase in Net Working Capital.	$ 2,280

Here is the shortcut method for solving this problem. The simple journal entries are explained on page 415.

Illustration 8-16

Gathings Variety Store
Shortcut Method for Preparing an Income Statement
For the Month of October, 19X1

1.	Accounts Payable	237,000		10.	Retained Earnings	83,000
	Cash		237,000		Salaries Payable	83,000^E
2.	Dividends Payable	4,000		11.	Salaries Payable	91,000
	Cash		4,000		Cash	91,000
3.	Retained Earnings	3,200		12.	Furniture and Fixtures	8,000
	Taxes Payable		3,200^E		Cash	8,000
4.	Taxes Payable	18,500		13.	Retained Earnings	19,200
	Cash		18,500		Cash	19,200^E
5.	Retained Earnings	1,100		14.	Retained Earnings	7,000
	Furniture and Fixtures		1,100^E		Supplies	7,000^E
6.	Retained Earnings	500		15.	Supplies	11,400
	Buildings		500^E		Accounts Payable	11,400
7.	Merchandise Inventory	200,000		16.	Cash	353,000
	Accounts Payable		200,000		Retained Earnings	353,000^R
8.	Retained Earnings	225,000		17.	Cash	680
	Merchandise Inventory		225,000^E		Furniture and Fixtures	680
9.	Retained Earnings	6,000		18.	Retained Earnings	120
	Dividends Payable		6,000^D		Furniture and Fixtures	120^L

Solution 8-2 (Brain-teaser):

1. The entry that should have been made (but wasn't) is:[10]

> Merchandise Inventory   XXX
> Accounts Payable   XXX

Funds statement: no effect. Merchandise is understated and accounts payable is understated; the errors offset each other in their effects on net working capital.

Income statement: no effect. The error does not affect retained earnings.

2. There is no error in recording merchandise, given the company's inventory methods. The entry that should have been made was:

> Accounts Receivable   XXX
> Retained Earnings   XXX

Funds statement: Funds from operations were understated; net sources of funds were understated; the increase in funds for the year was understated.

Income statement: Sales were understated; so were net income from operations, net income, and the increase in retained earnings for the year.

3. The entry that should have been made was:

> Retained Earnings   XXX
> Interest Payable   XXX

Let + represent overstated and − represent understated:

Funds statement: Funds from operations   +
                     Net sources of funds   +
                     Increase in net working capital +
Income statement: Interest expense   −
                     Total expenses   −
                     Net income from operations   +
                     Net income   +
                     Increase in retained earnings   +

4. The entry that should have been made was:

> Retained Earnings   XXX
> Prepaid Insurance   XXX

Funds statement: Funds from operations   +
                     Net sources of funds   +
                     Increase in net working capital +

---

[10] See the solution to Problem 4-5 (pages 214–215) if any of these explanations puzzle you.

Income statement: Insurance expense   −

Total expenses   −

Net income from operations   +

Net income   +

Increase in retained earnings   +

5. Underestimating the service life led to recording too high a figure for building depreciation.

Funds statement: No effect; the only accounts affected are buildings and retained earnings.

Income statement: Depreciation expense   +

Total expenses   +

Net income from operations   −

Net income   −

Increase in retained earnings   −

6. As you will recall from Problem 4-5, this is tricky. Under the company's inventory method, this merchandise would be regarded as having been sold. The basic relationship is:

$$\underset{\substack{\text{Error has} \\ \text{no effect}}}{\frac{\text{Beginning}}{\text{Inventory}}} + \underset{\text{Overstated}}{\frac{\text{Purchases for}}{\text{the Year}}} = \underset{?}{\frac{\text{Merchandise}}{\text{Sold}}} + \underset{\substack{\text{Error has} \\ \text{no effect}}}{\frac{\text{Ending}}{\text{Inventory}}}$$

In effect, total purchases have been overstated, and accordingly so has cost of goods sold. Since 12/31/X1 merchandise is stated at the correct figure, the error is now in accounts payable (overstated) and retained earnings (understated).

Funds statement: Funds from operations   −

Net sources of funds   −

Increase in net working capital −

Income statement: Cost of goods sold   +

Total expenses   +

Net income from operations   −

Net income   −

Increase in retained earnings   −

Consolidated Income Statements

Chapter Three contained a brief discussion of consolidated balance sheets and the eliminations from parent and subsidiary company figures that must be made to prepare such statements (see pages 152–156). Consolidated income and funds statements are also prepared for consolidated entities; this section is a brief discussion of the former.[11]

---

[11] Consolidated funds statements usually are prepared directly from consolidated income statements in the manner described in the next chapter. Accordingly, consolidated funds statements are not discussed separately.

Elimination of intercompany revenues, expenses, and profits

It is common for parent and subsidiary companies to buy from and sell to each other in much the same manner that they deal with outsiders. Accordingly, the financial statements of both firms may reflect revenues, expenses, and profits resulting from intercompany sales. First, consider the balance sheet. If one company owns goods sold to it by the other company, any intercompany profit in the recorded cost of these goods to the buyer should be eliminated in preparing the consolidated balance sheet. Why? Because it is meaningless to speak of an entity making a profit in dealing with itself, and it is equally meaningless to include such a profit as part of the cost reported for an asset.[12]

As a parallel example, suppose that a wife owns several investments in her own name, and that her husband buys two shares of stock from her. These shares cost her $60 apiece when she bought them, but he pays her their current market value of $75 apiece, or a total of $150. A few weeks later, he sells one of these shares to a broker (an outsider) for $80. From the standpoint of their *individual* records, the wife made a $30 gain [$150 − ($60 × 2) = $30], and the husband made a $5 gain ($80 − $75 = $5), for a total gain of $35 ($30 + $5 = $35). But the *family* has made a combined gain of only $20. They began with two shares that cost a total of $120 ($60 × 2 = $120); they now have only one share that cost $60, and $80 in cash; the total family gain is $60 + $80 − $120 = $20. A simpler way to calculate this consolidated gain is to take the individual total gains of $35, and eliminate the intrafamily profit of $15 on the share that has not yet been sold to outsiders ($75 − $60 = $15).

On a family balance sheet prepared after these transactions, the remaining share should be reported at the $60 that the family has paid for it, not the $75 for which it sold within the family, even though $75 would be the correct amount on the husband's individual records. Similarly, from the standpoint of the combined entity, the only genuine sale is the sale to the outside broker. The entire intrafamily sale between the wife and husband should be eliminated when preparing a combined income statement for the family; so should the intrafamily cost of goods sold and the effects of the intrafamily sale on net income and retained earnings. (The details of this would be worked out in an advanced course, but are not necessary here.) For if one *didn't* eliminate the intrafamily sale, it eventually would be counted twice: once within the family and once when the shares were sold to outsiders. The rule, then, is to regard only sales to outsiders as genuine for consolidated income statement purposes, and to eliminate all others.

Similarly, in preparing consolidated financial statements for corporations, any intercompany sales (between parent and subsidiary or between two subsidiaries) are treated as fictitious on the consolidated income statement, and any intercompany profit is eliminated from ending inventories on the balance sheet. Under the same reasoning, intercompany dividend charges and dividend revenues are eliminated on the income statement, and intercompany dividends receivable and dividends payable are eliminated on the balance sheet.

---

[12] This is the conventional reasoning on this matter, and is based in historical cost accounting. Under some current market value approaches (see the next section of this chapter) such profit recognition would be entirely appropriate.

As far as the matters discussed in this text are concerned, you may treat consolidated income statements (and funds statements) in the same ways that you would the financial statements of individual firms. Accordingly little reference to this topic will be made in subsequent chapters.

A Detailed Look at the
Accountant's Rules for Reporting Revenue

In this section we will examine the accountant's rules for reporting revenue and, in the process, complete our earlier discussion of the historical cost rule for reporting nonmonetary assets on the balance sheet (see pages 146–147, and 148). This discussion will be fairly detailed, so an outline of it might be useful at the start.

1. First, I will describe the accountant's actual practices, since it is important to have a clear understanding of them before considering alternative practices.

2. Given the accountant's actual practices, it becomes possible to discuss the significance of the resulting figures reported on financial statements. It will become evident that these figures are not as informative as they might be.

3. Next, I will discuss possible alternatives to present accounting practices, and will indicate why accountants follow their present practices.

4. Up to this point, the discussion will be conventional in the sense that most accounting theorists would agree in substance with what is said. But at this point it becomes appropriate to draw on the discussion of allocation in Chapter Six (pages 318–323) in an attempt to describe a problem that underlies all attempts by accountants to report revenues—a problem that is often insoluble on strictly theoretical grounds.

5. But in practice the accountant *must* report revenue. Accordingly, I will conclude with a fairly conventional discussion of the practical ways in which accountants might solve some of their revenue-reporting difficulties.

1. Actual Practices

The accountant's preference for reporting nonmonetary assets at their historical costs (historical purchase prices less accumulated depreciation or other amortization) has had a profound effect on his *rules for revenue recognition*—rules for deciding when to report that a firm has had a revenue or a gain (or, for that matter, a loss). For simplicity, the discussion in this section will assume that all recorded revenues and gains result from situations in which cash or a receivable is received. This ignores the advances from customers case, in which the revenue relates to a decrease in liabilities.[13] This discussion also ignores a few special industry situations (such as

---

[13] When an advance is received from a customer, the related journal entry has the following form:

Cash	XXX	
Advances from Customers		XXX

(continues on next page)

those of gold mines, construction companies, and certain agricultural firms) where the accepted rules conflict with those discussed below. Finally, during most of the discussion the case of losses is ignored, as are "conservative" writedowns of assets held for sale or retirement to lower market values. These omissions simplify our discussion of the accountant's revenue-recognition rules without significantly distorting the picture.

Gains on the sale of noncurrent nonmonetary assets

The accountant's rules for calculating gains and losses on the sale of noncurrent nonmonetary assets are simple enough to provide a good starting point. These sales occur, for example, when the company retires old buildings and equipment or sells off unneeded land. The asset's amortized historical cost (*book value*) at the time of the sale is calculated. This book value is compared with the proceeds from the sale. If these proceeds are greater than the book value, the difference represents a gain; otherwise it represents a loss. As an example, suppose that nine years ago a firm bought a machine for $10,000, expecting it to have a ten-year service life and a zero scrap value upon retirement. Its book value now is $1,000 [$10,000 − ($10,000 × 9/10) = $1,000]. If it were sold to a dealer in used equipment for $1,300 cash, there would be a $300 gain on this sale:

Cash	1,300	
Equipment		1,000
Retained Earnings		300

If it were sold for only $600, cash, there would be a $400 loss:

Cash	600	
Retained Earnings	400	
Equipment		1,000

Recognition of gains on nonmonetary assets

Suppose that a firm owns a nonmonetary asset that it does not wish to sell and whose market value has increased since the company purchased it. Suppose also that the accountant wishes to reflect this increase in market value by recognizing a gain. To do so, he would have to make an entry of the form:

Nonmonetary Asset	XXX	
Retained Earnings		XXX

When the liability to the customer is extinguished by delivering merchandise or performing services for the customer, the related journal entry has the form:

Advances from Customers	XXX	
Retained Earnings		XXX

This is just as legitimate a sale as any other. From the standpoint of the firm, it makes little difference whether a sale results in its receiving cash, obtaining a receivable, or discharging one of its liabilities. Either way, its net working capital is increased.

That is, he would have to recognize an increase in the amount at which the asset itself is reported. The accountant's rule of reporting nonmonetary assets at their historical costs implies that he will not recognize any increase in the market values of nonmonetary assets nor any related gains as long as the firm owns the asset. This in turn means that *the accountant reports gains on nonmonetary assets only when these assets are sold.*

Take Miami Corporation's land as an example of this (the sale of this land was described in Illustration 7-12, changes 14a and 14b, page 358). Miami Corporation bought this land for $60 and later sold it for $290. Suppose that the firm had purchased this land 23 years prior to the date of its sale. Presumably the $290 − $60 = $230 increase in market value did not occur only in 19X2, but instead occurred over the entire 23-year period that the firm owned the land. This increase occurred at an average rate of $230 ÷ 23 = $10 per year (though probably more in some years than in others). The $230 gain is applicable to the entire 23-year period; yet under generally accepted revenue recognition rules, Miami Corporation does not report any of this gain on its income statement until 19X2, the year the land is sold. And when it does report the gain, it reports it all at once, as though it were entirely applicable to management's actions in 19X2.

Recognition of losses on nonmonetary assets

The accountant's rules for recognition of losses on nonmonetary assets are somewhat more liberal than his rules for the recognition of gains. As we saw on page 148, under the rule of *conservatism,* if an asset is being held for resale or retirement and its current market value is significantly lower than its amortized historical cost, the accountant will write the asset down to the lower market value, recognizing a loss in the process. The related journal entry will have the form:

> Retained Earnings   XXX
>   Nonmonetary Asset   XXX

Most nonmonetary assets do not experience drastic losses in value, so the accountant's usual rule is to use historical costs; accordingly, the accountant's loss-recognition rule ordinarily is the same as his rule for recognizing gains—nothing is reported until the asset is sold or retired.

The realization rule

Accountants have a technical name for this rule that gains or losses on nonmonetary assets are not to be recognized until the time of sale or retirement: they call this *the realization rule.* They would say that, although the $230 gain on Miami Corporation's land may have existed before the sale, it existed only as a potential that wasn't *realized* until the sale captured it.

If a nonmonetary asset has increased in current market value, the realization and historical cost rules become different aspects of the same basic rule. Consider again the entry that would have to be made to record the increase in the nonmonetary asset's current market value (and the related gain) prior to sale:

Nonmonetary Asset   XXX
Retained Earnings[14]   XXX

The historical cost rule specifies that one should not make the debit to this entry, while the realization rule specifies that one should not make the credit; either rule would be sufficient to prevent making the entry and recognizing current market values and gains prior to sale.

This relationship between the realization rule and the historical cost rule is not surprising. Revenues and gains are the reflection in retained earnings of changes in assets. Any rule for recognizing changes in retained earnings might be expected to be closely related to the rules for recognizing changes in assets. In much of what follows, rules for revenue recognition and rules for the amounts at which assets are reported will be discussed as one and the same things; either the revenue aspect or the asset aspect (whichever is the more convenient) will be stressed. Therefore, it is important that you remember that *a rule for determining the amounts at which assets are reported is implicitly a revenue-recognition rule, and vice-versa.*

Revenues from services

The realization rule usually is also followed by firms that deal only in services. The drycleaning shop mentioned at the beginning of this chapter would report its assets at amortized historical cost figures. No matter how stable its business is, nor how easy it is to predict future sales, the drycleaning shop would not recognize revenues before sales to customers are actually made. The only difference between firms that sell products and firms that sell services in this respect is that the former have one more kind of nonmonetary asset to report and to amortize: goods that are being held for sale.

The sole exception to these observations occurs with certain contractual services, such as interest. These exceptions are discussed in a later subsection.

The realization rule (rough definition): Recognize revenues, gains, and losses from nonmonetary assets and services only at the time of sale or retirement.

Inventories

Manufactured inventories provide a particularly good example of how the realization rule works. A manufactured inventory usually results from a long process that

---

[14] Such occasional exceptions to the historical cost rule as are acceptable in financial accounting practice usually credit a special stockholders' equity account (similar to Premium on Capital Stock—see page 265) instead of Retained Earnings in an attempt to sidestep the realization rule. For instance, an investment in the common stock of another firm is a nonmonetary asset (it is not monetary since it is neither cash nor a right to receive a specific amount of cash at a specific time). Certain kinds of firms whose business it is to invest in other companies, called "mutual funds," report common stock investments at their market values, whether or not these are higher than historical cost; other investment firms, so-called "closed end investment companies," report investments in common stock at either historical cost or current market value, with parenthetical disclosure of the other. When current market values are reported by any of these firms a special stockholders' equity account is used to reflect the difference between historical costs and current market values.

begins with a decision to make the product. Equipment must be acquired. Raw materials must be purchased. Inventories must be produced and packaged. Marketing activities, some of which may even predate the decision to make the product, must be performed.

This book is an extreme example of a manufactured inventory; perhaps its history will help bring the revenue-recognition issue into focus. I began actively writing this book in the spring of 1966. Even after the manuscript had been completed, tested in several preliminary editions and revised several times, it took the publisher and the printer months to get it edited, typeset, printed, and bound. The instructor at your school had to be persuaded that this was the book he wanted to use, which required a complicated marketing effort. Copies had to be distributed to book stores. All in all, years of effort went into this book; yet no revenue was recognized until after you went to the book store and bought a copy (or, if you're reading a used copy, until the original owner bought it).

Obviously, the revenue was earned over the entire project in the sense that it resulted from all of the activities of the several years. But the accountant would not recognize any revenue until the time of sale. As we have repeatedly seen, any costs associated with the project would be reported as an asset, since the benefits (revenues) from these costs will not be recognized until a future period. The amount reported for this asset will be no greater than the total of the historical costs incurred by the publisher for this book. Earning revenue is a continuous process, but the realization rule makes the accountant act as though the total revenue was earned all at once, at the point of sale.

Matching

Once the sale does occur, an entry of the form:

| Monetary Asset | XXX | |
| Retained Earnings | | XXX |

is made; this entry, of course, records the current market value (selling price) of the goods involved. As we saw earlier, during this single accounting period, all accumulated historical costs of generating this sale are written off to expense, using entries of the form:

| Retained Earnings | XXX | |
| Nonmonetary Asset | | XXX |

The combined effect of these two entries is to compare the current market value (equal to the revenue) with the historical cost (expense) of the good in question. In this sense, the accountant speaks of "matching" costs with revenues, and another rule almost as widely cited by accountants as the realization rule is the *matching rule*: once revenues have been recognized, all expenses of earning these revenues should be recognized, too, whether these be cost of goods sold, supplies used, building services exhausted, or other costs.[15] Of course, the obverse of this rule is that, conservatism

---

[15] Remember, though, that there is another sense of "matching," discussed on page 149, in which instead of matching costs with revenues, revenues (or cash inflows) are matched with inputs to determine the contributions of those inputs to profits or to cash.

ignored, costs should not be charged to expenses *until* the related revenues have been received; this is why the accountant records costs of assets when he believes that they can be objectively and reliably associated with future revenues.

Contractual service revenues

When discussing revenues from services, I commented that the realization rule is not applied to certain revenues from contractual services. We already have seen examples of this with interest and rent revenues. For example, suppose that on 11/1/X8, Lender Co. lends Borrower Co. $6,000 on its 9-month, 8% note receivable, and that no interest is payable on this note until maturity of the loan. Lender Co. closes its books once a year, every December 31. It could be argued that whatever corresponds to a "sale" in this case occurs either at 11/1/X8 or at the maturity date. Yet Lender Co. would record no revenue on 11/1/X8 but would accrue *part* of its total interest revenue as of 12/31/X8, long before maturity:

$$\text{Interest Receivable} \quad 80$$
$$\text{Retained Earnings} \quad\quad\quad 80$$
$$(\$6,000 \times 8\% \times 2/12 = \$80)$$

The same thing is done with rent: the accountant recognizes revenue at times other than when the contract is signed or a monetary asset is explicitly given by a customer. In general, whenever a firm contracts with its customers to provide services (such as the services of money or property) at a constant rate and at a constant cost over time, the accountant feels free to accrue revenue on this contract without worrying about the realization rule (see pages 129–130 for an earlier discussion of this kind of accrual). The reasons for making this exception should become clearer after we have discussed the reasons why the accountant usually follows the realization rule; these reasons are given in section 3, below. Meanwhile, though, here is a summary of the accountant's rules for recognizing revenues, gains, and losses:

> Recognize revenues, gains, and losses from nonmonetary assets and services only at the time of sale or retirement. There are two exceptions to this "realization" rule:
> 1. Losses on nonmonetary assets may be recognized prior to sale or retirement when conservatism so dictates;
> 2. Revenues for contractual services may be accrued proportionately to the provision of these services if the contract is legally enforceable, the charge for these services is specific (and usually constant), and these services are provided at a constant rate.

In a nutshell, one could say that, ignoring conservatism, *revenues from assets are recognized at the time of sale, and revenues from services are recognized at the time they are provided.*

Recording unconsolidated subsidiaries

There is one major exception to the foregoing rule: investments in unconsolidated subsidiaries are not recorded at historical cost (except at the time of purchase, or by coincidence). The general principles of consolidated financial statement preparation have been briefly outlined in this chapter and in Chapter Three. But parent firms are not always required to prepare consolidated statements. Indeed, if the parent's ownership interest is 50% or less, or if the subsidiary is in a line of business drastically different from that of the parent, consolidation is considered to be improper. (An example of the latter situation arises when a manufacturer of an expensive consumer product, such as automobiles or prefabricated houses, owns a subsidiary that finances purchases of these products; such finance company subsidiaries usually are not consolidated with the parent's financial statements.) In general, firms tend to consolidate some subsidiaries and not consolidate others.

If the investment in a subsidiary is not consolidated, it will be reflected in the firm's investments. There are two ways to do this. One, the method you would expect from the foregoing, would be to report the investment at its historical cost to the firm (therefore it is called the *cost* method).

But in practice an alternate method is used. A parent company is in a position to control the activities of its subsidiary and, in particular, the subsidiary's dividends. For simplicity, it will be assumed that the subsidiary's dividends during any year never exceed its net income for that year. A parent has a right to its proportionate share in all of the subsidiary's profits. If the subsidiary company's cash position permits, it could withdraw dividends equal to those profits. (Indeed, if the subsidiary doesn't have enough cash, the parent could loan it the necessary amount to cover any desired dividends!) Alternately, the parent could choose to have the subsidiary pay no dividends whatever (subject only to certain legal considerations that can be ignored here).

Under the cost method, any dividends received from the subsidiary will be reflected in the parent's revenues and net income. Accordingly, if the parent is using the cost method of reporting investments in unconsolidated subsidiaries and if the subsidiary has been profitable, the parent is in an excellent position to manipulate the amounts that will be reported for its own revenues and net income. If its net income needs improvement, it may require the subsidiary to pay a dividend; if it would prefer not to increase its reported net income for the year, the parent may tell the subsidiary *not* to pay any dividends.

The way to avoid such possibilities of manipulation is to require that the parent firm adjust the amount at which its investment in the unconsolidated subsidiary is reported by the amount of its proportionate share in any subsidiary profits (or losses) that have not been reflected in dividend payments. This approach is called the *equity* method of reporting investments in unconsolidated subsidiaries, since the parent is reflecting the change in the subsidiary's residual equity in its own investment account.

Suppose that the subsidiary is profitable, that its net income exceeds its dividends, and that the parent uses the equity method. Then the amount reported for the parent's investment will grow, and will exceed the historical cost of that investment by the parent's proportionate share of the subsidiary's undistributed profits; moreover, the parent's proportionate share will be reflected in the parent's revenues—a clear violation of the realization rule. In general, under the equity method an asset is written up and a revenue recognized without conducting a sale. This violation of the usual rules is acceptable to accountants because it avoids something worse: the possibilities for income manipulation inherent in the cost method. However, the equity method *is* an exception to the accountant's usual rules; it therefore will be ignored in the remainder of this chapter.

The Accounting Principles Board requires that all investments in unconsolidated subsidiaries be recorded on the equity basis, as well as all other ownership investments in which the investing firm owns a 20% or greater interest. (Certain technical aspects of these APB requirements are omitted for brevity.) Smaller investments may be reported on the cost basis; small temporary investments usually should be reported on the cost basis, in consistency with the realization rule (but they may, of course, be reported at market value if this is significantly lower than cost).

2. The Significance of Reported Figures

Any expenditure or purchase on account by a company will result in the company's obtaining either (a) an expense, (b) an offset to a gain, (c) a loss, or (d) an asset. Ignore monetary assets and credit purchases for the moment. Regard the expenditure as resulting in an expense if it is one of the costs of obtaining a revenue being reported on the current income statement. If the expenditure relates to a nonoperating gain being reported, it will appear buried in the net figure reported for that gain. If no revenue or gain is recognized, the expenditure is considered to have resulted in a loss, unless future services are expected to flow from it. If such future services are expected, the expenditure is viewed as resulting in the acquisition of an asset. The figure reported for the asset will be reduced as these services are received, and the related costs either matched with gains or revenues, or reported as losses.

Assets, expenses, and losses all involve expenditures. Since the services provided by assets are the obtaining of revenues and gains, an expense reflects an expenditure whose revenue has been recognized in the present accounting period; a loss reflects a barren expenditure that will not result in revenue; and an asset is an expenditure whose revenues are yet to be recognized.

So far, revenues have been looked upon as reflecting changes in assets, but we could turn this around and say that a nonmonetary asset is simply a set of costs waiting for recognition of the revenues they will help generate. During this waiting period, the realization rule prohibits any upward change in the figures reported for the asset, although downward changes (loss recognition) are permitted where appropriate. The only nonmonetary asset for which this *isn't* true is site land, because it is perceived as not yielding up its services.[16] If we ignore land and the possibility of losses, we can put this in a nutshell. *A nonmonetary asset is a cost of expected future sales.*

Limitations of accounting reports

One reason for studying accounting is to become aware of its limitations—what it doesn't do as well as what it does. Accountants record nonmonetary assets at their historical costs and, relatedly, record revenues and gains on these assets as they are

---

[16] "Site land" is land used for buildings, parking lots, outdoor storage, and so on. Its main service is to support tangible assets, and this service is not expected to be exhausted. In contrast, mining land yields up its services as ore is mined.

sold or retired, instead of as they develop; the main alternative to this would be, as we saw earlier, to report nonmonetary assets at *current market values*—estimated figures representing the prices that the firm might get if it sold the assets or the prices it might pay if it bought the same assets now (or, possibly, at the times the assets' services will be received).[17]

As we saw earlier (pages 145–147), one result of the prevailing use of amortized historical costs is that the balance sheet reports the firm's economic position only in a highly specialized sense that has nothing to do with the values of its nonmonetary assets. Instead, the amounts reported for many nonmonetary assets will be lower than what those assets are worth. At times, this downward bias can be considerable, as when a firm owns land and buildings purchased in the 1930s that have since multiplied many times in market value. Finally, we saw that historical cost magnitudes reported for assets may be less significant for some prediction purposes than current market values would be.

Similarly, the use of historical costs on the income statement delays the recognition of revenues and gains and some losses, in comparison to what would occur if the realization rule were not followed. In some cases—Miami Corporation's land, for instance—the use of historical costs seems to result in distortion of the figures reported on the firm's income statement (another result is severe understatement of amounts reported on the firm's balance sheet). The Miami Corporation example may be generalized: the accountant does not report revenues and gains on nonmonetary assets during the periods in which they develop. Instead, he reports them in the periods in which they are sold. This tends to make the reported net incomes of earlier periods lower than they otherwise would be, and the reported net income figure of the period of sale is higher than it otherwise would be. This delay misleadingly results in reporting profits that have emerged over a long period of time as though they had resulted from management's activities in a single year. (Of course, any one company is likely to own a number of nonmonetary assets on which gains are developing, and a number of inventories in the revenue-earning process. This makes the effect of delaying recognition of revenues and gains hard to predict. Any one year will get the credit for all gains and revenues on assets and services sold during that year, even though many of these gains and revenues may relate to prior years. On the other hand, gains and revenues resulting from this year's efforts will not be reported unless these efforts have resulted from sales by year-end. By coincidence, these two effects may offset each other; ordinarily, though, they will either increase or decrease reported net income.)

Finally, use of historical costs results in income statement matching of unlike magnitudes: *current* revenues are matched with *historical* costs, some of which are quite old. For example, if a firm bought its buildings twenty years ago, this year's income statement will subtract stale twenty-year-old depreciation expenses from recent revenues to obtain net income—a process akin to subtracting apples from

---

[17] As this suggests, there are a variety of things that might be considered as current market values. Distinction among these is important in an advanced course in accounting theory but, for simplicity, it will not be attempted here. Unless indicated otherwise, you may assume that the current market value of an asset is the maximum amount for which the firm could sell that asset in today's markets.

oranges. It could be plausibly argued that elementary arithmetic and statistical considerations demand subtracting *current* costs from current revenues—i.e., subtracting like from like.

3. Why Accountants
Report Historical Costs

Given these criticisms, accountants must have strong reasons for reporting historical costs instead of current market values if they are to justify their present rules. Accountants believe that they do have strong reasons and that, whatever the deficiencies of historical costs, there are serious objections to reporting current market values. We saw some of these reasons on pages 55–56.

1. Current values require subjective estimates and suffer from personal bias and error. Usually there is a range of possible current market value figures for an asset; if current values are reported in a firm's financial statements, management can select figures from either the high or the low side of that range, thereby manipulating the amount reported for net income.

2. Current values are unstable because market prices fluctuate. In contrast, historical costs are stable matters of record. An unrealized gain on a nonmonetary asset may disappear before the asset is sold; for example, land that has increased in market value during a period of general business expansion may drastically decline in market value during a recession. It seems pointless to report a gain (and the related increase in asset value) until a sale *captures* it.

3. Many current values seem irrelevant to investor decisions. An example of this is the current selling prices of assets that the firm should not sell (for instance, the land under its plant).

Accrual of contractual revenues

Notice in passing that none of these objections pertains to the practice of accruing contractual revenues, discussed above. Here, the necessary calculations can be made objectively, the amounts involved do not fluctuate, and there are no problems of relevance. Presumably, this is why accountants are willing to accrue such contractual revenues, even though they are not willing to recognize other kinds of service revenues prior to sale.

Prediction

The accountant would have several responses to the claim that current values are more useful for prediction than are historical costs. First, the accountant is in no position to know what predictions his readers make, nor the data needed for these predictions. He does know, though, that different users of his reports do considerably different things with them, and that what is suitable for one reader may be inappropriate for another. In contrast, historical costs are required for a variety of institutional purposes and are used by many readers.

This can be summarized by saying that the accountant's knowledge of the information needs of his readers is limited, but that he *does* know that historical cost data are in demand; there is no similar demand for current market value data, and therefore no practical reason to believe that he is depriving his readers of anything they need in order to make predictions.

Finally, many of the readers of financial statements lack sophistication and knowledge of business affairs. The accountant believes that he has a special responsibility to avoid building up erroneous favorable impressions of the firm through reporting unrealized increases in asset values and unrealized gains in his reports; his sense of responsibility here is reinforced by various laws, regulations, and other restrictions that society places upon him—"institutional" constraints.

Doubts

I have already expressed doubts about the adequacy of these reasons on pages 25–27 and 56–57. First, it should be evident from the discussion of allocation in Chapter Six (pages 318–323) that a high percentage of accounting's allocations are inevitably arbitrary even under historical-cost accounting; we will see further examples of this in section 4, below, and in Chapter Thirteen. Thus, the seeming objectivity of historical costs is often illusory.

Second, historical purchase prices are stable for the same reason that Napoleon no longer offers the world any surprises: both are dead. Today's historical costs were yesterday's current market values—how can historical costs be inherently more stable than current market values? All that the stability argument boils down to is an assertion that historical costs can be known with greater objectivity than current market values—and as we have seen, that is at best only partly true.

Arguments that claim current market values are irrelevant to some assets and may be inappropriate for some purposes have buried in them an implicit assumption that only one kind of market price should be reported in accounting, that either everything should be reported at historical cost or everything should be reported at a current market value. Yet, once it is identified, this assumption seems to be unmotivated: why not report *both*? Section 5, below, examines this possibility.

Finally, the accountant's reluctance to create unduly favorable impressions should be accompanied by some corresponding reluctance to do what is exemplified by the reports concerning Miami Corporation's land: first creating unduly *un*favorable impressions, then in a single year creating a much more favorable impression of management's performance for that year than is warranted. Accountants should try to minimize distortion, not to create one kind of distortion in preference to another.

4. The Basic Problem
of Revenue Recognition

But I believe that it is possible to cut through all of these arguments and get to the essence of the accountant's revenue-recognition problem. Moreover, having done this it will become evident that *neither* historical costs nor current values can lead to a fully satisfactory way of calculating income, and that there is no way to conclusively demonstrate that either the realization rule or the current-value methods of revenue recognition gives clearly preferable results. Unfortunately, showing this requires departing from conventional opinion. The reader is warned that in the rest of this section, I am expressing what still is a minority viewpoint.

Primary measurements of income

There is a kind of life cycle to anything sold by a firm. Business enterprises sell either products or services, or both; because of technology, fashion, and other changes, each product or service has a finite economic life. First, there is a period in which plans are made, then a period of preparation for sales, then a period of initial marketing effort. If the product or service is successful, there then will be a period in which it is selling well with relatively moderate marketing effort. Finally, though, as technologies or tastes change, sales will decline and eventually the product or service will be discontinued.

On pages 226–227, the notion of *primary measurements* was introduced (counts of physical quantities or observations of market prices—simple straightforward measurements that offer no difficulties to the financial accountant). These were contrasted with *secondary measurements,* of which allocations (such as depreciation and patent amortization) are an example. Secondary measurements are much harder to make than primary ones, partly because there are no conclusively defensible, clear-cut ways to make them.

Over the entire economic life of a product or service, it may be possible to calculate its total contribution to income by use of primary measurements only. Suppose, for example, that a firm organizes a division with its own plant, officers, and employees, to manufacture and sell a new product in an industry other than the one in which the firm usually operates. This is an experimental venture for the firm—if profits are high enough, the firm will remain in this new industry; if not, it will withdraw. The firm spends two and a half years preparing to introduce this product. During the next three and a half years, its sales are adequate to cover costs, but the product is not nearly so profitable as had been hoped; moreover, competitors in the new industry have begun to reduce the firm's share of the market. Finally, six years after the venture began, the firm abandons its efforts in this area and sells the new product division to a large, diversified manufacturer. The firm initially invested $8,000,000 in the new product division; during the next six years cash receipts from the new product exceeded expenditures by $2,700,000. At the end of six years the diversified manufacturer paid $6,300,000 for the division. Therefore, the total income of the division during the six-year period was $1,000,000:

Net inflow of assets:		
From operations	$2,700,000	
From liquidation	6,300,000	$9,000,000
Initial outflow of assets		8,000,000
Total income for six years		$1,000,000

The total six-year income on this venture can be determined by simple primary measurements of inflows and outflows of cash.

The income allocation problem

Unfortunately, there is no clear-cut way, defensible against all alternatives, in which this million-dollar six-year income can be allocated to the individual six years. Pages 318–323 argued that when a firm's inputs interact (when the results of combined inputs differ from the results that separate inputs would have produced), then it is impossible to determine the contribution to cash made by an individual input or group of inputs (such as the activities of an individual year). For exactly the same reasons, it is impossible to specify (in any non-arbitrary way) the contribution to the total million-dollar six-year income made by any individual input or by the total activities of any given individual year.[18] The planning activity influences the results of all subsequent activities; so does the period of preparation for sales; so does the initial marketing effort; so do all of the other activities relating to the product. Any allocation of the million-dollar six-year income to individual years is bound to be arbitrary.

Removal of simplifications

And, of course, this example was highly simplified. The typical firm is simultaneously engaged in a large number of ventures at different stages in their economic lives, involving sale of a variety of different products and services. These ventures interact with each other—for example, the success of one product may be significantly affected by how well the firm's other products are selling. Many of the firm's activities, such as marketing and administration, are designed to benefit all products and services jointly.

All ventures tend to interact with all other ventures. What happens to a firm during any one period is a joint result of the activities that occur during that period and during all prior periods. If a company is founded, does business for a number of years, then finally is liquidated, it is possible to calculate its total net income over its entire life in the same way as in the previous divisional example. But any attempt to allocate this total lifetime net income and to determine the net incomes of individual years is bound to be arbitrary.

The revenue-recognition controversy may at present be insoluble

Of course, the same conclusion holds for revenues. The accountant cannot wait until the end of a firm's life to prepare income statements; he must prepare them at least once per year. But the amounts he reports for revenues are inevitably arbitrary. The process of earning a particular revenue begins long before any sale is made, and it may continue long afterwards. One could plausibly argue that the revenue-earning process begins at that point when the firm first conceives of the individual product or

---

[18] As a matter of fact, the teaching assistant example on pages 319, and 321–322 is just as good a demonstration of the difficulties of income allocation as it is of the difficulties of cash allocation, since in that example it happened that the cash inflow *equalled* the combined income of the two graders (and, for that matter, their combined revenue). Once again, remember that the factors that may allow the teaching assistants to reach a mutually satisfactory allocation are rarely present among the readers of financial accounting reports as a group. This is why the arbitrariness of financial accounting's cash and income allocations is important.

service. It extends through the planning period, the initial marketing effort, and all subsequent activities up through the point of sale. But if the sale is for credit, the company's activities are not yet over; it still must collect from its customers, and it may also have servicing or warranty obligations. Moreover, since one sale often leads to other sales, the particular sale may have beneficial effects continuing far into the future.

Accountants wish to pick some *one* point in time at which to recognize revenue. But the discussion here and in Chapter Six indicates that, because of the interaction of the firm's activities, such an allocation of the total revenue to any one point in time is inevitably arbitrary. Whatever point of time one chooses, someone else could choose another point and defend his choice just as well (or as badly). In particular, this means that there seems to be no final way in which to resolve the controversies between those who wish to recognize current values and those who wish to employ the realization rule—these controversies boil down to questions of whether one recognizes revenue before or at the point of sale.[19] If this conclusion is correct, it helps explain why these disputes have not yet been settled: *both* sides are equally right . . . or equally wrong.

Allocation to specific inputs

One final comment should be made here. This section has devoted itself almost entirely to the problems of allocating income and revenue to the groups of inputs that make up the activities of individual accounting periods. But the same conclusions pertain to allocations of income or revenues to specific individual inputs, such as depreciable assets. These allocations are arbitrary, too, for the same reasons that similar allocations of cash were arbitrary. This is an important point, because the amortization of nonmonetary assets depends upon determination of the economic benefits that these assets provide to the firm. It will be demonstrated in Chapter Thirteen that these "economic benefits" must be reducible to beneficial effects on the firm's cash or income. This in turn means that it must be possible to allocate a firm's total cash inflows or its income to the inputs that "caused" them. But what we have seen indicates that this kind of allocation will be arbitrary. Accordingly, the accountant's rules for amortizing nonmonetary assets suffer from grave theoretical deficiencies, and the accountant has an expense allocation problem corresponding to his cash, income, and revenue allocation problems. This expense allocation problem, though, may be saved for Chapter Thirteen.[20]

---

[19] Alternately, the difference between the historical cost and the market price of a manufactured inventory also is an interaction effect—one that results only because the firm's various inputs have combined to create together something that would not have occurred separately. Conventional financial accounting allocates this interaction effect to the period in which the related product is sold; those who wish to recognize current market values would prefer to allocate it to an earlier period or periods. But, again, such allocations are arbitrary.

[20] Another implication of the matters discussed in this section may be of interest to readers who are concerned with international trade, who are nationals of countries in which multinational firms operate, or who simply would like to see another application of the allocation discussions in this book: see my "Transfer Prices of the Multinational Firm: When Will They Be Arbitrary?" *Abacus* 7 (June, 1971) pages 40–53.

5. Practical Remedies

To summarize the previous two sections, there are arguments for using current market values in financial accounting. The objections of those who favor historical costs seem to demonstrate little more than that current market values should not be used exclusively, and there seems to be no way at present to settle the dispute between these revenue recognition rules. Yet, since there is a practical requirement that financial statements be prepared, *some* decision must be made about what method should be used—one or the other, or both.

Institutional uses of financial accounting

In Chapter One, a very important distinction was made between two uses of accounting, institutional and resource-allocation:

Institutional: various laws, judicial decisions, and regulatory commission decisions require that financial accounting reports be prepared in certain ways; besides these, most users expect that accounting statements will be prepared in a conventional manner, and these expectations are an important institutional constraint.

Resource-allocation: those who use financial statements usually do so in order to make better-informed economic decisions; data most appropriate for an individual's resource-allocation purposes are not necessarily those required for institutional purposes.

For institutional purposes, revenue must be recognized on a historical cost basis. The main exceptions (page 427) involve either revenues from contractual services or situations in which the accountant, on grounds of "conservatism," recognizes current market values when these are lower than amortized historical costs. Other than that, under existing laws and regulations the accountant has no *practical* problem whatever in determining which revenue recognition rule to follow: he chooses the realization rule. By doing so he satisfies the expectations of most of his readers: historical costs are so thoroughly entrenched as *the* standard method of recording assets that most readers automatically expect that the parallel realization rule will be employed for revenues.

Resource-allocation uses of financial accounting data

Yet the individual user of financial accounting data may find that rules appropriate for institutional purposes are inappropriate for his particular resource-allocation purposes—it all depends upon what his purposes *are*.

An example of this was given earlier: the American Accounting Association's 1966–68 Committee on External Reporting considered a hypothetical stockholder who was trying to use a firm's financial statements in order to predict its future dividends. They listed eight things this stockholder might wish to estimate in his attempts to predict these future dividends (page 26). All eight related to the future, not to the past. The Committee then asked what kinds of accounting information would be the most useful to the purposes of this particular investor (if one disregarded all institutional constraints). In the Committee's opinion, the revenues recognized under the realization rule should be of considerable significance for the prediction purposes of this stockholder, *but so, in the Committee's opinion, should the current values of many of the firm's assets.* For example, it noted that dividends will be affected by proceeds from the sale of retired assets, costs of new assets, and net proceeds from the firm's operations (its dealings in products and services). Since historical costs relate to the past, the Committee believed that current market values gave a better indication of these *future* proceeds and costs than do historical costs. Various other examples are given in this Committee's report of purposes for which current market values are more relevant to investor's purposes than are historical costs.

Reporting both kinds of information

For resource-allocation purposes, then, a compromise solution might be to prepare financial accounting statements on *both* realization and current-value bases, resulting in two sets of figures. Some of the problems that accountants have had over revenue recognition may result from the accountant's wish to report things according to a single, consistent system. There are great advantages to using a single system of reporting—if nothing else, doing so saves money and eliminates a large potential cause of confusion. But the arguments in this book indicate that no one revenue recognition method is "right," because there is no one conclusively defensible way to allocate revenues to periods of time. If this is true, then the advantages of reporting revenues on more than one basis may outweigh the resulting confusions and additional costs.[21] Under present accounting practices, income statements pretend much greater precision than they actually possess—reporting only one revenue figure misleadingly implies that a single revenue figure is appropriate for all purposes. Reporting two (or more) revenue figures would make income statements more candid.

Meanwhile, present institutional constraints on financial accounting specify that reports utilizing the realization rule *must* be prepared. Although there is nothing preventing management from also publishing reports prepared on a current-value basis, auditors are at present unwilling to audit such reports, and company managements themselves have yet to show much enthusiasm for the idea. This need not be discouraging to those who favor reporting of current market values; even among academic accountants, the acceptance of current-value accounting has been widespread only during the last decade. Its general acceptance by practitioners may be *expected* to take considerably longer.

But there is another consequence of the allocation problem in financial accounting: notions of so-called "cash-flow income," which are gaining rapid acceptance among certain users of financial statements. This phenomenon, which most accountants regard as unfortunate, will be discussed in the next chapter.

---

[21] You are reminded that the question of which type of current values should be reported was deliberately neglected. The previous arguments demonstrate that no one type will be suitable for all reader purposes. Conceivably, more than one might be reported, but fears of reader confusion are apt to prevent this.

Problem for Study and Self-Examination

Problem 8-3 (*Brain-teaser*):

Shown below are some, but not all, of the account balances of Highly Simplified, Inc. at 12/31/X1 and 12/31/X2:

	Account Balances	
	12/31/X1	*12/31/X2*
Cash	$917	$1,419
Merchandise Inventory	714	500
Accounts Payable	809	410

The following (admittedly unrealistic) statements apply to the company's 19X2 operations:

1. All merchandise is purchased on account.
2. Merchandise is the *only* thing that is purchased on account.
3. All expenditures of cash are payments of accounts payable.
4. All cash receipts come from sales. Sales provide the only revenue.
5. No sales are made on account; there are no advances from customers.
6. Cost of goods sold is the only expense. In 19X2, cost of goods sold totalled $2,315. There were no nonoperating gains or losses.

Calculate the company's 19X2 net income. An appropriate line of attack for solving this problem would be to prepare T-accounts for this firm, post all information given in this problem (including beginning and ending balances), then reconstruct missing elements.

Solution

Solution 8-3:

The following solution is quite detailed, for the sake of providing maximum help to students who are having difficulties; if you don't need this much help, feel free to skim some of these details.

From the information given, first calculate total 19X2 purchases of merchandise:

19X2 cost of goods sold (6)	$2,315
Merchandise Inventory—12/31/X2	500
Total merchandise that must have been provided either by purchases or by the 12/31/X1 inventory[22]	$2,815
Merchandise Inventory—12/31/X1	714
Total 19X2 purchases of merchandise	$2,101

Since all merchandise purchases are on account (1), and merchandise is the only thing purchased on account (2), total 19X2 purchases on account must also be $2,101. Knowing this, calculate total payments of accounts payable for the year:

Total 19X2 purchases on account	$2,101
Accounts Payable—12/31/X1	809
Total accounts payable either paid in 19X2 or owed at 12/31/X2	$2,910
Accounts Payable—12/31/X2	410
Total 19X2 payments of accounts payable	$2,500

Since all cash expenditures are made on account (3), total 19X2 cash expenditures must also equal $2,500. Knowing this, you can calculate total 19X2 cash receipts:

Total 19X2 cash expenditures	$2,500
Cash—12/31/X2	1,419
Total cash that must have been provided either by 19X2 receipts or by the 12/31/X1 cash balance	$3,919
Cash—12/31/X1	917
Total 19X2 cash receipts	$3,002

Since all cash receipts come from sales (4), total 19X2 sales must also be $3,002. Since sales is the only revenue (4), and cost of goods sold is the only expense (6), and there are no nonoperating gains or losses (6), net income must be $687:

Sales	$3,002
Cost of Goods Sold	2,315
Net Income	$ 687

---

[22] This is often called the *cost of goods available for sale.*

Personally, I would use ledger accounts to solve this kind of problem. Here's how they could be employed, given the following information (beginning and ending balances have been inserted in their proper places):

Cash		Merchandise Inventory		Accounts Payable	
✓ 917		✓ 714	2,315		✓ 809
	✓ 1,419		✓ 500	✓ 410	

From the problem data, all of the credits to the merchandise account are known, so total merchandise credits can be written in as follows:

Cash		Merchandise Inventory		Accounts Payable	
✓ 917		✓ 714	2,315		✓ 809
	✓ 1,419		✓ 500	✓ 410	
			2,815		

But, in the ruled ledger account, total credits must equal total debits:

Cash		Merchandise Inventory		Accounts Payable	
✓ 917		✓ 714	2,315		✓ 809
	✓ 1,419		✓ 500	✓ 410	
		2,815	2,815		

This leaves the accounts payable accounts $2,101 out of balance. From the problem data you know that this must represent purchases on account:

Cash		Merchandise Inventory		Accounts Payable	
✓ 917		✓ 714	2,315		✓ 809
	✓ 1,419	2,101 ✓	500	✓ 410	2,101
		2,815	2,815		

The solution eventually works out the same way as before. I find it much easier and quicker to use ledger accounts than schedules, even though ledger accounts take up more space when one tries to show how to use them in a book. Like myself, you may find that you are less apt to subtract when you should add, or get otherwise confused when using ledger accounts, but individual preferences vary here; use schedules if you prefer them.

Losses and Deficits

Most of our illustrations have involved firms whose retained earnings increase, but decreases in retained earnings also are possible. For example, Illustration 8-17 shows comparative balance sheets of Instance, Inc., that reflect a $15 decrease in retained earnings ($49 − $34 = $15).

The underlying data for this firm were presented on pages 305–307 and 313–314. These data result in the firm operating at a profit. (Retained earnings decreased because dividends were greater than that profit.) Let us change the data so that the company suffers a loss. You can do this by changing just three of the summary balance sheet changes on pages 306–307 and summary journal entries on pages 308–309.

Suppose that sales had been for $200 less. Entry 2 then becomes:

> 2′ Accounts Receivable   6,000
>   Retained Earnings   6,000

Since there is now a loss, it is unlikely that the company would declare any dividends. Eliminate entry 16 and change entry 23 to:

> 23′ Dividends Payable   20
>   Cash   20

Illustration 8-17

Instance, Inc.
Comparative Balance Sheets
December 31, 19X1 and 19X2

Assets

	December 31	
	19X1	*19X2*
Current Assets:		
Cash	$ 100	$ 229
Accounts Receivable	368	358
Merchandise Inventory	570	460
Supplies	37	24
Total Current Assets	$1,075	$1,071
Noncurrent Assets:		
Land	$ 140	$ 163
Buildings	260	194
Store Equipment	720	740
Delivery Equipment	170	144
Total Noncurrent Assets	$1,290	$1,241
Total Assets	$2,365	$2,312

continued on page 442

Equities

Current Liabilities:		
Accounts Payable	$ 676	$ 496
Taxes Payable	112	103
Interest Payable	16	15
Dividends Payable	20	40
Total Current Liabilities	$ 824	$ 654
Noncurrent Liabilities:		
Bonds Payable	$ 392	$ 371
Long-Term Notes Payable	100	100
Total Noncurrent Liabilities	$ 492	$ 471
Total Liabilities	$1,316	$1,125
Stockholders' Equity:		
Capital Stock	$1,000	$1,153
Retained Earnings	49	34
Total Stockholders' Equity	$1,049	$1,187
Total Equities	$2,365	$2,312

This suffices to pay the company's beginning-of-year dividend liability. Illustrations 8-19 and 8-20 show the company's revised 19X2 income statement and 12/31/X2 balance sheet.

The revised 12/31/X2 balance of retained earnings is negative. Such a negative retained earnings balance is often called a *deficit*. The interests of stockholders are reflected in both of the stockholders' equity accounts, and if the total of the two remains positive, stockholders continue to have a positive interest in the company; in such cases, deficits are simply *subtracted* from capital stock in determining total stockholders' equity. This is done in Illustration 8-19. (It is also possible for a deficit to be so great as to exceed the total of the other stockholders' equity accounts, thereby wiping out the interests of stockholders and impairing the interests of creditors; this book will not explore such extreme situations.)

Illustration 8-18

Instance, Inc.
Revised Statement of Income and Retained Earnings
For the Year 19X2

Revenues:		
Sales		$6,000
Expenses:		
Cost of Goods Sold	$4,070	
Salaries Expense	1,125	
Supplies Expense	57	
Utilities Expense	180	
Consulting Services Expense	153	
Depreciation Expense	253	
Taxes Expense	207	
Interest Expense	23	$6,068
Net Loss from Operations		$ (68)

Nonoperating Gains and Losses:

Loss on Sale of Building	$ 18	
Gain on Sale of Store Equipment	6	12
Net Loss		$ (80)
Retained Earnings—12/31/X1		49
Retained Earnings—12/31/X2†		$ (31)

† *Deficit.*

Illustration 8-19

Instance, Inc.
Revised Balance Sheet
December 31, 19X2

Assets

Current Assets:		
Cash	$ 324 (1)*	
Accounts Receivable	158 (2)*	
Merchandise Inventory	460	
Supplies	24	$ 966*
Noncurrent Assets:		
Land	$ 163	
Buildings	194	
Store Equipment	740	
Delivery Equipment	144	1,241
Total Assets		$2,207*

Equities

Current Liabilities:		
Accounts Payable	$ 496	
Taxes Payable	103	
Interest Payable	15	$ 614*
Noncurrent Liabilities:		
Bonds Payable	$ 371	
Long-Term Notes Payable	100	471
Total Liabilities		$1,085*
Stockholders' Equity:		
Capital Stock	$1,153	
Retained Earnings†	(31)*	1,122*
Total Equities		$2,207*

* *Figures that have changed from those in Illustration 8-17.*
† *Deficit.*

Notes:

1. This is $95 higher than before because $95 less dividends were paid in Entry 23′ than in Entry 23. ($115 − $20 = $95)

2. This is $200 lower than before because sales in Entry 2′ were $200 lower than in Entry 2. ($6,200 − $6,000 = $200)

Assignment Problems

Problem 8-A:

Refer to Problem 4-A (pages 228–230). Prepare a statement of sources and uses of net working capital for this entity, using the form that does *not* compress all of the operating changes into a single figure. Prepare an income statement for this entity. Describe the differences between the two statements.

Problem 8-B:

Problem 7-A (page 374) gives the balance sheet changes of Gadsden Co. for the month of January, 19X2, and its 12/31/X1 balance sheet.

1. Indicate which of these balance sheet changes would be incorporated in a funds statement for January, 19X2.

2. Indicate which of these balance sheet changes would be incorporated in an income statement for January, 19X2.

Problem 8-C:

Problem 7-A (page 374) gives the balance sheet changes of Gadsden Co. for the month of January, 19X2, and its 12/31/X1 balance sheet. Prepare an income statement for January, 19X2.

Problem 8-D:

The comparative balance sheets of Senner Home Repairs, Inc., for 12/31/X1 and 12/31/X2 are given on pages 349–350 of the text; a narrative summary of the company's 19X2 balance sheet changes and the related summary journal entries are given on page 350. Prepare an income statement for 19X2.

Problem 8-E:

Problem 7-K (pages 386–389) gives the comparative balance sheets of Simplified Textiles, Inc. for 12/31/X5 and 12/31/X6, together with the company's summary journal entries for 19X6. Prepare an income statement for 19X6. Treat interest on the company's investments as a nonoperating revenue.

Problem 8-F:

The comparative balance sheets of Campus Store for 6/30/X4 and 6/30/X5 are given below; so is a narrative summary of the company's balance sheet changes for the year ended 6/30/X5, and the related summary journal entries. This information is based on material discussed on pages 358–361 of the text.

Prepare an income statement for the year ended 6/30/X5. Show patronage refunds as a direct subtraction from sales. Use the "gross margin" form of income statement illustrated on page 407 of the text.

Campus Store
Comparative Balance Sheets
June 30, 19X4, and June 30, 19X5

	6/30/X4	6/30/X5
Assets		
Current Assets:		
Cash	$ 97,200	$153,900
Accounts Receivable	19,400	23,800
Merchandise: Books	247,700	258,300
General	96,200	94,300
Store Supplies	3,500	3,200
Prepaid Insurance	5,700	8,300
Total Current Assets	$469,700	$541,800
Noncurrent Assets:		
Land	$ 27,600	$ 27,600
Building	142,500	135,000
Fixtures	64,500	58,200
Building Under Construction	6,700	208,600
Total Noncurrent Assets	$241,300	$429,400
Total Assets	$711,000	$971,200
Equities		
Current Liabilities:		
Accounts Payable	$ 78,400	$ 75,100
Construction Payable	–0–	80,100
Taxes Payable	71,900	89,100
Salaries Payable	3,400	1,700
Interest Payable	–0–	2,100
Total Current Liabilities	$153,700	$248,100
Noncurrent Liabilities:		
6% Notes Payable	–0–	105,000
Total Liabilities	$153,700	$353,100
Stockholders' Equity:		
Capital Stock	$500,000	$500,000
Retained Earnings	57,300	118,100
Total Stockholders' Equity	$557,300	$618,100
Total Equities	$711,000	$971,200

Campus Store
Narrative Summary of Balance Sheet Changes
For the Year Ended 6/30/X5

1. Cash sales totalled $1,625,900.
2. Sales on account totalled $166,800.
3. During the year the company borrowed (by issuing notes payable) a total of $105,000 on its loan commitment from the insurance company (Change 9 discusses the interest costs related to this borrowing).

4. The company bought $10,600 of advertising (mostly newspaper advertising) on account. Following conventional accounting practice, the company writes off the entire cost of advertising during the year of purchase.
5. The company bought $9,400 of utility services (water, heat, light, telephone) for cash.
6. Customers claimed and were paid patronage refunds totalling $53,700.
7. The company's income taxes for the year totalled $76,100; the company records all taxes as liabilities before they are paid.
8. The company's property taxes for the year totalled $16,800.
9. Of the $105,000 that the company borrowed on its 6% loan commitment (see Change 3), $30,000 was borrowed on 9/30/X4 and $75,000 on 12/31/X4. The company records all interest charges as liabilities before they are paid.
10. Dividends were declared totalling $15,000. These dividends were payable six weeks after their declaration date.
11. Miscellaneous costs of operations paid directly in cash totalled $4,800.
12. Miscellaneous costs of operations purchased on account totalled $6,400.
13. All salaries are recorded as liabilities before they are paid. Total salaries for the year were $174,200.
14. The company purchased $9,900 of fixtures (shelves and counters) on account.
15. Bills received from the contractor who is erecting the new store totalled $201,900.
16. Accounts receivable totalling $162,400 were collected.
17. Store supplies costing $13,300 were purchased on account.
18. Books costing $1,035,700 were purchased on account.
19. General merchandise costing $296,900 was purchased on account.
20. Insurance policies costing $7,000 were purchased for cash.
21. See Change 9. The company paid interest on its loan from the insurance company through 3/1/X5.
22. Salaries of $1,700 were owed employees at 6/30/X5.
23. Taxes payable of $75,700 were paid.
24. All dividends payable were paid.
25. Bills from the contractor for the new building totalling $121,800 were paid.
26. Accounts payable of $1,376,100 were paid.
27. Prepaid insurance of $4,400 expired.

The company's physical count at 6/30/X5 revealed that the following merchandise and supplies were on hand (still owned by the company):
28. Store supplies that had cost the company $3,200.
29. Books that had cost the company $258,300.
30. General merchandise that had cost the company $94,300.

31. The company will not take any depreciation on the new store building until it is completed. The old store building had an estimated service life of 23 years (with no estimated scrap value on retirement) when it was purchased on 7/1/X0.
32. The fixtures owned on 6/30/X4 had been purchased on 7/1/X1. At that time they had an estimated service life of 10 years and an estimated scrap value on retirement of $5,000. The fixtures purchased this year should be depreciated at a rate of $800 a year; they were purchased on 4/1/X5 and put into service immediately.
33a. On 6/30/X5 old fixtures (owned on 6/30/X4) were sold for $4,300, cash. (You already have recorded 19X4–19X5 depreciation for these fixtures in Change 32.)
33b. The book value (cost less accumulated depreciation) of the fixtures sold was $7,500 at the time of sale.

Campus Store
Simple Summary Journal Entries
7/1/X4–6/30/X5

1.	Cash	1,625,900		18.	Books	1,035,700	
	Retained Earnings		1,625,900		Accounts Payable		1,035,700
2.	Accounts Receivable	166,800		19.	General Merchandise	296,900	
	Retained Earnings		166,800		Accounts Payable		296,900
3.	Cash	105,000		20.	Prepaid Insurance	7,000	
	6% Notes Payable		105,000		Cash		7,000
4.	Retained Earnings	10,600		21.	Interest Payable	1,500	
	Accounts Payable		10,600		Cash		1,500
5.	Retained Earnings	9,400		22.	Salaries Payable	175,900	
	Cash		9,400		Cash		175,900
6.	Retained Earnings	53,700		23.	Taxes Payable	75,700	
	Cash		53,700		Cash		75,700
7.	Retained Earnings	76,100		24.	Dividends Payable	15,000	
	Taxes Payable		76,100		Cash		15,000
8.	Retained Earnings	16,800		25.	Construction Payable	121,800	
	Taxes Payable		16,800		Cash		121,800
9.	Retained Earnings	3,600		26.	Accounts Payable	1,376,100	
	Interest Payable		3,600		Cash		1,376,100
10.	Retained Earnings	15,000		27.	Retained Earnings	4,400	
	Dividends Payable		15,000		Prepaid Insurance		4,400
11.	Retained Earnings	4,800		28.	Retained Earnings	13,600	
	Cash		4,800		Store Supplies		13,600
12.	Retained Earnings	6,400		29.	Retained Earnings	1,025,100	
	Accounts Payable		6,400		Books		1,025,100
13.	Retained Earnings	174,200		30.	Retained Earnings	298,800	
	Salaries Payable		174,200		General Merchandise		298,800
14.	Fixtures	9,900		31.	Retained Earnings	7,500	
	Accounts Payable		9,900		Building		7,500
15.	Building under			32.	Retained Earnings	8,700	
	Construction	201,900			Fixtures		8,700
	Construction Payable		201,900	33a.	Cash	4,300	
16.	Cash	162,400			Fixtures		4,300
	Accounts Receivable		162,400	33b.	Retained Earnings	3,200	
17.	Store Supplies	13,300			Fixtures		3,200
	Accounts Payable		13,300				

Problem 8-G:

As part of your training in accounting, you must become able to extend the concepts and techniques you have learned into situations that require different methods of analysis. This problem provides an opportunity to increase your flexibility and broaden your understanding. The background needed to solve this problem has been provided by the text, but the particular method of analysis required may at first seem unusual. Apply what you already have learned to this new situation.

Shown below is the cash statement of Crestview Circle Corp. for 19X3, plus certain other data. Prepare an income statement for 19X3.

Crestview Circle Corp.

Sources and Uses of Cash
(000 omitted)

For the Year 19X3

Sources

Operations:
  Receipts:
    Cash sales $2,507
    Collections on account   9,287
    Collections of royalties 228 $12,022

  Expenditures:
    Payments of accounts payable incurred for inventories $5,197
    Payments of salaries   2,109
    Payments of interest   330
    Other payments   2,833   10,469

        Net effect of operations on cash . . . . $ 1,553
Proceeds from Sale of Noncurrent Assets:
  Land . . . . $ 412
  Buildings   1,817   2,229

Net Sources . . . . $ 3,782

Uses

Purchase of Noncurrent Assets:
  Equipment . . . . $ 441
Retirement of Noncurrent Equities:
  Bonds payable retired   2,937
Dividends   531

Net Uses . . . . $ 3,909

Decrease in Cash for the Year . . . . $ 127

Other data:

All salaries and dividends are recorded as liabilities before being paid.

All inventories are purchased on account; these purchases totalled $5,203 during 19X3.

During the year, the company took advantage of depressed prices on the bond market to purchase and retire $3,000 of its own bonds payable for $2,937.

The company receives royalties on patented processes that it has developed, which other firms are licensed to use.

All expenses other than cost of goods sold, salaries expense, depreciation expense, and interest expense are paid directly in cash (this is unrealistic, but is assumed to simplify your calculations); these expenses totalled $2,833, and consisted mainly of tax payments.

The land that was sold had cost the company $215; the buildings that were sold had a book value of $1,958 at the time of sale.

Here are some of the company's account balances:

	12/31/X3	12/31/X2
Salaries Payable	$ 82	$ 93
Accounts Receivable	1,703	1,776
Inventories	701	643
Royalties Receivable	75	62
Interest Payable	87	80
Dividends Payable	112	123
Retained Earnings	15,328	14,612

No unusual balance sheet changes occurred during the year; all changes were of the normal kinds discussed in this and previous chapters.

One possible line of attack in solving this problem would be to prepare the general outline of an income statement, leaving considerable space between captions, then fill in the details of this statement as you learn them from the problem data; use T-account analysis only where essential. If you emerge with an income statement entirely consistent with the problem data, do not worry about possible balance sheet changes of which you have not been told.

Problem 8-H:

During the 60 years prior to 19X3, Berwyn Watch and Clock Corporation enjoyed a well-deserved reputation for manufacturing unusually accurate wrist watches, table clocks, and other small timepieces. Upon the 8/17/X2 death of the founder's son, Mr. R. Owen Berwyn, Jr., the company passed into new ownership. The new management believed that it was long overdue for the company to enter the low-priced wristwatch field. Accordingly, it drastically reduced the quality of the firm's product while simultaneously reducing prices (though perhaps to a lesser extent). The firm's 19X0–19X3 net incomes were reported to be:

> 19X0: $4,280,000
> 19X1: 4,315,000
> 19X2: 3,970,000
> 19X3: 7,240,000

During 19X3 and 19X4 the market price of the company's common stock increased dramatically as a result of the increase in the firm's reported earnings. 19X4 sales declined somewhat from the level achieved in 19X3.

Comment. Defend your comments.

Problem 8-I:

Zia Teresa Kitchens' market research indicated that there was a good potential market for Italian casserole pasta dishes among housewives who loved Italian cooking, but did not have the time to prepare it properly. After four years of extensive research, the company perfected a disposable reinforced-foil casserole that was inexpensive, yet almost indestructible under supermarket and home conditions. In late 19X7, the company introduced a gourmet line of six different kinds of frozen bake-and-serve lasagne, cannelloni, and manicotti. These products were even more successful than anticipated, and the company's 19X8 and 19X9 net income increased substantially. In late 19X9, the company entered into an agreement with 'Tricia-Sue Foods, one of the industry giants, whereby 'Tricia-Sue Foods would manufacture the disposable foil casseroles for a line of its own economy, American-style frozen main dishes; Zia Teresa Kitchens was to receive large royalties under this agreement.

Shortly thereafter an article in the financial press attributed the company's increased profitability to the "... less tradition-bound management of the new team led by Frank Sacci, one of the youngest company presidents in the Convenience Food Industry." The founder and first president of Zia Teresa Kitchens, Mr. Raffaello S. Sacci, had retired on 12/31/X7. The new president, his son Frank, had had no previous business experience except for an undergraduate degree in business administration. The elder Mr. Sacci was slightly annoyed by the article. Why? Discuss the general implications of your answer for financial accounting.

Problem 8-J:

Mr. John S. McDowell, Jr., a stockholder of House of Mendax, Inc., is puzzled by its 3/31/X3 balance sheet, and asks you the following question:

"According to the balance sheet, on March 31, 19X3, the company's net worth was $83,240,000. There were almost exactly one million shares of common stock outstanding on that date. So, the common stock was worth about $83.24 per share. Yet Mendax stock has been selling at over $110 since December, 19X2. I don't think it's been as low as eighty-three and a quarter for the past five or six years. Who's wrong—the market or the company?"

Answer Mr. McDowell's question. In doing so, describe concisely but clearly the significance of the main groups of figures reported on the balance sheet.

Problem 8-K:

As part of your training in accounting, you must become able to extend what you have learned into new situations. This problem provides an opportunity to increase your flexibility and broaden your understanding. The text provides all background information needed to solve this problem, but the circumstances described will be unfamiliar. Apply what you already have learned to this new situation.

On 1/1/X3, Grabowski Corporation completed its Waterbury installation of new machinery and production facilities for manufacture of one of its principal products, at a total cost of $7,800,000. It was estimated that this installation would have a ten-year service life, and a negligible scrap value upon retirement.

During 19X6 and 19X7 there was a technological breakthrough in the company's industry. Entirely different automatic equipment was introduced, making it possible to manufacture the product involved at much lower cost and with much greater control over quality. The company's president, Mr. Chris B. Grabowski, made the following observation in August, 19X8:

"We've got a real hassle. Everybody down the line keeps telling me we should scrap the Waterbury installation and put in that new equipment. The engineers and cost accountants say that the cost savings will more than cover the cost of the new equipment in the first two years. The sales department says if we *don't* put in the new equipment, the competition is going to murder us on price.

"So why not? I'll tell you why not. Each of these guys sees his own little corner of the operation, but he doesn't see the broad picture. Two years ago our profits fell off a bit. Last year was even worse, and we've been catching Old Nick from the stockholders ever since. This year we've finally turned the corner—we'll be able to report profits five to ten percent higher than they were in 19X4. But if we scrap the Waterbury installation, we'd have to report almost a $4,000,000 loss—and that'd knock our profits back below where they were last year! Sure, we've got to replace the equipment. We'll be all set up to do it by the end of the year. But I'm not *about* to scrap the Waterbury equipment until next January."

Comment. Defend your comments.

Problem 8-L:

The Kozy Korner Restaurant had been in business for a number of years. On 8/31/X2 its owner, Miss Gladys B. Harris, sold the property to Mr. Donald J. Sikes. Mr. Sikes redecorated the restaurant, and re-opened it as The Bristol Cozy Corner on 1/1/X3. Mr. Sikes had invested his life's savings of $40,000, plus $60,000 borrowed from a local bank, in this enterprise. At 1/1/X3 the business had net working capital (mostly inventories) of $3,800. The company's noncurrent assets cost a total of $96,200 (including accumulated costs of redecorating); of these, $17,000 pertained to land; the rest pertained to assets with an average service life of eight years. On 1/1/X4, Mr. Sikes' brother-in-law asked, in a conversational manner, "So, how's business?" He received the following reply:

"Slow. Oh, I guess I shouldn't complain. Not for the first year. Look: I've been working up some figures on it. I pulled $9,000 out of the business last year, including the $1,500 for Alice's operation. Yet, even after taxes, I'm exactly $2,000 ahead of where I was last year, cashwise. That's about an eleven percent return. I suppose we'll get by, if the neighborhood doesn't change too much."

On 12/31/X3 the business' net working capital totalled $5,800, and its noncurrent liabilities still totalled $60,000. Comment. Defend your comments. (Hint: Mr. Sikes is overlooking something.)

Problem 8-M:

As part of your training in accounting, you must become able to extend what you have learned into new situations. This problem provides an opportunity to increase your flexibility and broaden your understanding. The text provides all background information needed to solve this problem, but the circumstances described will be unfamiliar. Apply what you already have learned to this new situation.

Mr. Rajwant Singh lives in a nation with a simple graduated income tax. Income is calculated on the basis of receipts of cash or other valuable property, no deductions or exemptions whatever are allowed, and income is taxed at the following rates (the table is expressed in the local currency, the Or):

Annual Income	Tax rate
First Ø500,000	0%
Next Ø500,000	15%
Next Ø500,000	25%
Next Ø500,000	45%
Thereafter	60%

As a standard of comparison, an inexpensive American automobile costs Ø500,000. During the years 19X0 through 19X3, Mr. Singh went to college, majoring in business. His education prepared him well for success; his reported income and tax payments for the next few years were as follows:

Year	Income	Tax
19X0	Ø 50,000	Ø –0–
19X1	30,000	–0–
19X2	80,000	–0–
19X3	120,000	–0–
19X4	900,000	60,000
19X5	1,200,000	125,000
19X6	1,600,000	245,000
19X7	2,100,000	485,000
	Ø6,080,000	Ø915,000

Mr. Singh contends that he is being taxed unfairly. Comment. Defend your comments.

Problem 8-N:

As part of your training in accounting, you must become able to extend what you have learned into new situations. This problem provides an opportunity to increase your flexibility and broaden your understanding. The text provides all background information needed to solve this problem, but the circumstances described will be unfamiliar. Apply what you already have learned to this new situation.

The Herb Garden is a shopping complex located in a quiet rural area approximately 30 miles from a large city. The business began in the 1950s as a simple country restaurant, selling a few preserves and spices as a sideline. However, it acquired an affluent clientele attracted by its excellent food, and it soon began to expand. The complex now boasts a greatly enlarged version of the original restaurant, a specialty foods shop, three clothing stores, a toy shop, an art gallery with several resident artists, a book store, a record store, an automobile service center, and a nightclub serving soft drinks and catering to teenagers. A large motel is at present being constructed upon the site. The original owners have retained control of the enterprise by leasing all of the shops other than the restaurant to outside concessionaires. Under the terms of the lease, these concessionaires pay the firm a minimum rent plus a percentage of their total sales.

During 19X7 the management of The Herb Garden began to worry about declining revenues in the specialty foods shop. This store forms the entrance to the restaurant itself, and sells preserves, dried herbs, spices, herb teas, health foods, condiments, baked goods, and so on, over half of which are grown or manufactured locally. The 19X5 specialty foods shop revenues were approximately 5% lower than those of 19X4; 19X6 revenues were 8% lower still. The 19X5 results were not surprising, since that year had been a poor one for the complex as a whole due to unfavorable economic conditions (resulting from closure of a nearby military base) and general unwillingness by the well-to-do individuals who patronized the complex to spend as freely as usual. But in 19X6 the revenues of the complex as a whole increased by 18%.

In part, this was the result of a successful gamble. The company had become increasingly concerned that most of its clientele was middle-aged; in hope of sharing in the growing youth market, they agreed to the erection of the teen nightclub. Since 19X4, its concessionaire has booked popular regional bands and an occasional group with a national reputation. The management of The Herb Garden feared initially that restaurant revenues would be harmed by the change in image created by the new emphasis upon youth; but after a worrisome decline in 19X5, restaurant revenues in 19X6 were actually 2% higher than in 19X4. The restaurant has even become quite popular among the younger crowd, who refer to it as "The Grass Garden," and they seem to have enormous amounts of money to spend.

The contract of the concessionaire who operates the specialty foods shop comes up for renewal in the middle of 19X7. First-quarter reports indicate a further decline in specialty foods shop sales. Management is considering not renewing this contract, and replacing the concessionaire with someone who is a bit more competent. The next group booked into the teen nightclub is a promising regional one named Sulfur Dioxide and the Floating Particles.

Comment. Defend your comments.

Problem 8-O:

The following remarks were made by the president of *Outdoor Tiger*, The Magazine For Men, Inc., to his chief accountant:

"Jake, the figure you're reporting for last year's net income is going to mislead everyone who reads it. Sure, I know that you followed the rules, and that the auditors approved the income statement. But facts are facts. We show a net income of about $100,000. Yet in the last year we built up our subscriptions by $600,000 over what they were a year ago—and we're at a point now where half of any new subscription is pure profit. Your realization rule says we can't report any of these subscriptions as income until the point that we actually mail copies out to the subscribers. Yet there's no doubt we *will* mail them out, there's no trouble in estimating things here, and we know what the price is—we've already got the money! Besides, you know darn well that getting new subscriptions is the hardest part of the whole job—putting the mag itself out is easy by comparison.

"We should have reported net income almost four times as large as we did last year: the $100,000 that we *did* report, plus nearly $300,000 on those extra subscriptions. Yes, yes, I *know* we'll report the extra income in the next two or three years, as we fill the subscriptions. But what's that going to do for the poor stockholder who looked at our low profit figure for last year, then sold his stock? Answer me that! That's what I mean when I say our income statement is so blasted misleading."

Comment. Defend your comments.

Problem 8-P:

General Diversified Corporation of Birmingham is not merely the largest employer in the city of Birmingham, Nebraska, but dominates the economy of four adjacent counties. The company acquired its site land in 1897 from the local government for a nominal fee of $1.00. It has reported the land at this figure on its balance sheet ever since. Recently, company officials have wondered whether this practice is not unduly conservative. A reputable firm of appraisers has estimated that similar site land would sell for between $60,000,000 and $80,000,000. The company is making active use of all of its land (indeed, it is negotiating for adjacent property), and does not intend to sell any of it.

Comment and defend your comments. Do not restrict your comments to the "official" position of American accounting practitioners. (Warning: the situation outlined in this problem is less open-and-shut than might appear on first glance; for example, does the significance of a current market value depend upon what one intends to do with the related asset?)

Nine

Relationships between and within Financial Statements

*Expenses and Expenditures,
Revenues and Cash Receipts*

Cash and income statements are very different from each other (compare pages 302–305, 391–397). The previous chapter demonstrates that, in particular, expenses (income statement) and expenditures (cash statement) differ, yet people confuse the two. The phrase "making money," for example, signifies "earning income"; when someone asks "How much money did the company make last year?" he means income, but he talks as though he meant cash.

It is worth stressing that *revenues are not cash*. Revenues are the effect on retained earnings of receiving cash, receiving a monetary asset, or extinguishing a nonmonetary liability by making a sale.[1] In Problem 4-1 (pages 194, 196–198), for instance, only $1,800 (less than 45 percent) of Martin Co.'s sales were for cash.

It should also be stressed that *expenses are not cash*. Expenses are the effect on retained earnings of giving up, using, or receiving the services of assets in connection with earning revenues. The only Martin Co. expense involving direct cash payment in Problem 4-1 was the salaries expense of $410 (less than 11 percent of total expenses).

Of course all revenues eventually involve cash receipts, either before the sale (advances from customers), at the time of sale (cash sales), or after the sale (sales on account). Similarly, all expenses eventually involve cash expenditure. Buildings and equipment are usually paid for long before the sales that they help generate. Inventories bought on credit are often not paid for until after they have been sold, but cash is eventually paid for them. The point to be emphasized here is that the timing of cash receipts and sales is *different*: they aren't the same thing. The timing of cash expenditures and expenses is also different. Regarding the income statement as a kind of cash statement can only lead to confusion.

---

[1] If this latter source of revenue puzzles you, see footnote 13 on pages 422–423.

Accrual accounting

If income accounting is not cash accounting, what is it? The technical name for the process of preparing an income statement is *accrual accounting*. In Chapters Three and Eight, the word "accrual" was used in a slightly narrower sense (see pages 130 and 427): a monetary asset or liability was "accrued" if the accountant recognized part of it at some point before it was technically a legal claim to receive or pay cash.

Here are two examples. Suppose first that a company is preparing financial statements for the year 19X2. The company estimates that the taxes on its 19X2 income will be $35,000. These taxes will not be due until April 15, 19X3. But the accountant recognizes these taxes as of 12/31/X2, even though the taxing authority does not yet have a legal claim to receive cash on that date:

Retained Earnings	35,000	
Taxes Payable		35,000

The accountant reports $35,000 of taxes expense on the income statement and $35,000 of taxes payable on the balance sheet. The taxes are "accrued" because cash is not yet due on them.

Similarly, assume that the company owns a 6 percent note receivable for $1,000, which it acquired on 3/31/X2. The note is due on 3/31/X3, and all interest is to be paid on that date. As of 12/31/X2, no cash is yet due for interest, but the accountant accrues interest receivable (and interest revenue) for the nine months and reports both on his financial statements ($1,000 × 6% × 9/12 = $45):

Interest Receivable	45	
Retained Earnings		45

In general, the accountant pays little attention to the date cash is legally due or to the exact timing of cash receipts when he is recognizing monetary assets and liabilities (or related revenues and expenses). He attaches little importance to these things because he believes that he can better represent the actual economic situation of the company by accruing than by waiting until the entire claim is legally receivable or payable in cash.[2] The use of the word "accrual" in the foregoing is consistent with the meaning given this word in Chapters Three and Eight, but now the meaning of accrual can be expanded. The following broader definition will be used hereafter:

> *Accrual accounting* designates that system of accounting in which the accountant bases his concept of "income" in changes in net worth (assets minus liabilities) rather than in changes in cash. All income changes in net worth are reflected by changes in Retained Earnings, therefore, alternately, you might say that accrual accounting results from the accountant's recognizing revenues and expenses when Retained Earnings changes rather than when Cash changes.

---

[2] Note in passing that another way to put a main point of Chapter Eight's discussion of revenue-recognition rules is that although accountants are willing to accrue certain monetary assets in this sense of "accrual," they are not willing to accrue nonmonetary assets.

Problem for Study and Self-Examination

Problem 9-1:

This problem has a twofold purpose:

1. To help you understand the interrelationships among balance sheet accounts.

2. To give you a deeper understanding of the relationships between cash receipts and expenditures and the information reported on income statements.

As part of your training in accounting, you must become able to extend the concepts and techniques you have learned into situations that require different methods of analysis. This problem provides an opportunity to increase your flexibility and broaden your understanding. The background needed to solve this problem has been provided by the text, but the particular method of analysis required may at first seem unusual. Apply what you already have learned to this new situation.

Mills and Kensett Co. operates a chain of small department stores and does an extensive mail order business. The company has three kinds of sales:

1. Cash sales at retail stores.

2. Sales on account—mostly installment account sales from its mail order catalogs.

3. Ordinary mail order sales. These involve customers paying cash with their orders, thereby creating a liability "due customers," which is later settled by shipping the customers their goods.

The company prepares financial statements once a year as of January 31. On that day, its spring mail-order catalog has just been published, but not mailed. All costs of this catalog are shown as a current asset at this date. Except where explicitly indicated otherwise, assume that the company had no unusual balance sheet changes during the year; instead, its changes may be assumed to have been the normal kinds discussed in this and previous chapters. The company's accountant made no mistakes. The figures given in this problem have been abbreviated by omitting the last three digits—$9,008 signifies $9,008,000, and so forth. This is indicated in the last line of the statement title.

Illustration 9-1 gives the comparative balance sheets for this company at January 31, 19X2 and 19X3. Illustration 9-2 is the company's cash statement for the year. Illustration 9-3 gives other data about the company's activities. From this information, determine the company's income statement for the year ended 1/31/X3. To assist you, here is the general layout of this company's income statement:

Mills and Kensett Co.
Statement of Income and Retained Earnings
For the Year Ended 1/31/X3
(000 omitted)

Revenues:		
Sales		$XXX
Expenses:		
Cost of Goods Sold	$XXX	
Salaries Expense	XXX	
Advertising Expense	XXX	
Depreciation Expense	XXX	
Taxes Expense	XXX	
Interest Expense	XXX	
Other Expense	XXX	XXX

continued on page 458

Net Income from Operations	$XXX
Loss on Sale of Equipment	XXX
Net Income	$XXX
Dividends	XXX
Increase in Retained Earnings	$XXX
Retained Earnings—1/31/X2	XXX
Retained Earnings—1/31/X3	$XXX

Illustration 9-1

Mills and Kensett Co.
Comparative Balance Sheets
January 31, 19X2 and 19X3
(000 omitted)

Assets

	1/31/X2	1/31/X3
Current Assets:		
Cash	$ 9,008	$ 7,287
Accounts Receivable	11,257	13,156
Merchandise Inventory	49,532	48,240
Prepaid Catalog Costs	2,998	2,946
Other Current Assets	2,253	1,462
Total Current Assets	$75,048	$73,091
Noncurrent Assets:		
Land	$ 2,892	$ 3,626
Buildings	8,535	8,909
Fixtures and Equipment	11,843	13,364
Total Noncurrent Assets	$23,270	$25,899
Total Assets	$98,318	$98,990

Equities

	1/31/X2	1/31/X3
Current Liabilities:		
Accounts Payable	$10,406	$12,700
Due Customers	1,341	1,273
Taxes Payable	2,810	2,205
Other Accrued Payables	4,600	3,198
Total Current Liabilities	$19,157	$19,376
Noncurrent Liabilities:		
Long-Term Notes Payable	9,000	8,000
Total Liabilities	$28,157	$27,376
Stockholders' Equity:		
Capital Stock	$25,067	$25,567
Retained Earnings	45,094	46,047
Total Stockholders' Equity	$70,161	$71,614
Total Equities	$98,318	$98,990

Illustration 9-2

Mills and Kensett Co.
Sources and Uses of Cash
For the Year Ended 1/31/X3
(000 omitted)

Sources
Operations:
Receipts:

Cash Sales	$155,327	
Advances from Customers	67,622	
Collections on Account	93,421	$316,370

Expenditures:

Payment of Accounts Payable	$196,096	
Payment of Salaries	81,320	
Payment of Catalog Costs	11,864	
Payment of Interest	510	
Payment of Taxes	5,748	
Payment of Other Accrued Payables	6,625	
Purchase of Other Current Assets	9,454	311,617

Net Cash from Operations		$ 4,753
Proceeds from Sale of Equipment		135
Proceeds from Issue of Capital Stock		500
Net Sources of Cash		$ 5,388

Uses
Purchase of Noncurrent Assets:

Land Purchased	$ 734	
Buildings Purchased	662	
Fixtures and Equipment Purchased	2,909	$ 4,305

Retirement of Long-Term Notes Payable		1,000
Dividends Paid		1,804
Net Uses of Cash		$ 7,109

Decrease in Cash for the Year		$ (1,721)
Cash—1/31/X2		9,008
Cash—1/31/X3		$ 7,287

Illustration 9-3

Mills and Kensett Co.
Other Data

Salaries, interest, and dividends are always paid directly in cash, without previously setting up liabilities for the amounts to be paid.

The account "other accrued payables" is exclusively used to accrue certain "other expenses;" the remaining "other expenses" result from writedowns of "other current assets."

All "other current assets" are purchased for cash.

All merchandise is purchased on account. Merchandise purchases for the year totalled $189,670.

All noncurrent assets are purchased for cash. No land or buildings were sold. Equipment having a net book value of $343 was sold for cash.

All catalog costs are paid directly in cash. All other advertising is purchased on account; such purchases totalled $8,720 for the year.

All taxes are recorded as liabilities before being paid.

In the "official" solution to this problem, a schedule technique is used for the necessary calculations. But another appropriate line of attack for solving this problem would be one similar to that used in Problem 5-3 (pages 248–250, 251–252). Prepare T-accounts for this firm; post all information given in this problem, including beginning and ending balances, then reconstruct the missing elements in the T-accounts. Typically, very active accounts (such as cash and retained earnings) will have too many elements missing for this line of attack to work with them, but it is efficient with other accounts.

Solution

Solution 9-1:

The following solution is quite detailed, for the sake of providing maximum help to students who are having difficulties; if you don't need this much help, feel free to skim some of these details.

Illustration 9-4

Mills and Kensett Co.
Statement of Income and Retained Earnings
For the Year Ended 1/31/X3
(000 omitted)

Revenues:		
Sales		$318,337
Expenses:		
Cost of Goods Sold	$190,962	
Salaries Expense	81,320	
Advertising Expense	20,636	
Depreciation Expense	1,333	
Taxes Expense	5,143	
Interest Expense	510	
Other Expense	15,468	315,372
Net Income from Operations		$ 2,965
Loss on Sale of Equipment		208
Net Income		$ 2,757
Dividends		1,804
Increase in Retained Earnings		$ 953
Retained Earnings—1/31/X2		45,094
Retained Earnings—1/31/X3		$ 46,047

Calculations:

Illustration numbers in parentheses indicate sources of information used in calculations.

Sales:

Cash sales (Ill. 9-2)		$155,327
Sales on account:		
Accounts receivable—1/31/X3 (Ill. 9-1)	$ 13,156	
Collections on account (Ill. 9-2)	93,421	
	$106,577	
Accounts receivable—1/31/X2 (Ill. 9-1)	11,257	95,320
Ordinary mail order sales:		
Due customers—1/31/X2 (Ill. 9-1)	$ 1,341	
Advances from customers (Ill. 9-2)	67,622	
	$ 68,963	
Due customers—1/31/X3 (Ill. 9-1)	1,273	67,690
Total sales		$318,337

continued on page 462

Cost of Goods Sold:

Merchandise inventory—1/31/X2 (Ill. 9-1)	$ 49,532
Merchandise purchases (Ill. 9-3)	189,670
	$239,202
Merchandise inventory—1/31/X3 (Ill. 9-1)	48,240
Cost of goods sold	$190,962

Salaries Expense:

    All salaries are paid directly in cash (Ill. 9-3). Therefore, salaries expense equals total cash payments for salaries = $81,320 (Ill. 9-2).

Advertising Expense:

Prepaid catalog costs—1/31/X2 (Ill. 9-1)	$ 2,998	
Payment of catalog costs (Ill. 9-2)	11,864	
	$14,862	
Prepaid catalog costs—1/30/X3 (Ill. 9-1)	2,946	$11,916
Other advertising expense (Ill. 9-3)		8,720
Total advertising expense		$20,636

Depreciation Expense:

Buildings:

No buildings were sold (Ill. 9-3)				
Buildings—1/31/X2 (Ill. 9-1)		$ 8,535		
Purchases of buildings (Ill. 9-2, 9-3)		662		
		$ 9,197		
Buildings—1/31/X3 (Ill. 9-1)		8,909	$ 288	
Furniture and equipment:				
Furniture and equipment—1/31/X2 (Ill. 9-1)		$11,843		
Furniture and equipment purchased (Ill. 9-2)		2,909		
		$14,752		
Book value of furniture and equipment sold (Ill. 9-3) . .	$ 343			
Furniture and equipment—1/31/X3 (Ill. 9-1)	13,364	13,707	1,045*	
Total depreciation expense			$1,333	

---

    * Here is another way to calculate the depreciation of furniture and equipment:

Furniture and Equipment

Balance—1/31/X2 (Ill. 9-1) . . .	*11,843*	*Depreciation*	*?*
Purchases (Ill. 9-2)	*2,909*	*Book value of assets sold (Ill. 9-3)* .	*343*
		Balance—1/31/X3 (Ill. 9-1) . .	*13,364*
	14,752		*14,752*

Taxes Expense:

Taxes payable—1/31/X3 (Ill. 9-1).	$2,205
Payment of taxes (Ill. 9-2).	5,748
	$7,953
Taxes payable—1/31/X2	2,810
Taxes expense	$5,143

This can be calculated another way: We know from Illustration 9-3 that all taxes are recorded as a liability before being paid. This liability (taxes payable) decreased by only $605 during the year ($2,810 − $2,205 = $605), despite tax payments of $5,748. Taxes expense must have been $5,748 − $605 = $5,143.

Interest Expense:
     Interest is always paid directly in cash (Ill. 9-3), so there were no accruals of interest at year end, and cash payments of interest (Ill. 9-2) equal interest expense = $510.

Other Expense: (See Ill. 9-3)
Accrued:

Other accrued payables—1/31/X3 (Ill. 9-1)	$ 3,198	
Payment of other accrued payables (Ill. 9-2)	6,625	
	$ 9,823	
Other accrued payables—1/31/X2 (Ill. 9-1)	4,600	$ 5,223
Writedowns of other current assets:		
Other current assets—1/31/X2 (Ill. 9-1)	$ 2,253	
Purchases of other current assets (Ill. 9-2)	9,454	
	$11,707	
Other current assets—1/31/X3 (Ill. 9-1)	1,462	10,245
Total other expenses		$15,468

Loss on Sale of Equipment:

Book value of equipment sold (Ill. 9-3)	$343
Proceeds from sale of equipment (Ill. 9-2)	135
Loss on sale of equipment.	$208

Dividends:
     Dividends are always paid directly in cash (Ill. 9-3), so, total cash payments for dividends (Ill. 9-2) equal total dividends = $1,804.

This was an unusually difficult problem—the hardest so far in this book. Yet it is important that you begin to acquire the kind of understanding of the relationships among accounts that this problem demands. If you had trouble calculating all of the figures for the income statement (and most students do), you would benefit from trying to work this problem again. Wait a day or so until the problem is no longer fresh in your memory; then try to solve it again without looking at the answers.

Relationships Between
Income Statements and Funds Statements

This section will seek a deeper understanding of the relationships between the income statement and the funds statement. It will also discuss a technique used in practice for constructing funds statements from income statements. You already know that the operating changes chosen for these two reports overlap. Since the funds statement is primarily a report on financial changes, you have been responding to this overlap by summarizing all operating changes in the funds statement by a single figure. Now it is time to look at these funds statement operating changes more closely. Miami Corporation will serve as the example here. Illustration 9-5 gives a narrative summary of Miami Corporation's balance sheet changes for 19X2; Illustration 9-6 expresses these changes as simple summary journal entries. (The underlying data can be found in Problem 7-1 and its solution; see pages 695–697 and 698–702.)

Illustration 9-5

Miami Corporation
Narrative Summary of Balance Sheet Changes
For the Year 19X2

1. Sales on account totalled $2,160; all sales were on account.
2. In making these sales, the company used up inventories that had cost $1,200.
3. Accounts receivable totalling $2,120 were collected.
4. Miscellaneous costs of operations totalled $480; all related purchases were made on account (credit Other Payables).
5. Interest charges totalled $80; all interest is paid on the last day of each month.
6a. Equipment was sold for cash proceeds of $220.
6b. The equipment sold had a book value (cost less accumulated depreciation) of $300 at the time it was sold.
7. During the year the company purchased $670 of equipment, all on account.
8. The company issued additional capital stock for $500, cash.
9. Depreciation of equipment totalled $240.
10. The company purchased a new building for $100, cash.
11. Total depreciation of buildings was $30.
12. The company purchased new patents for $80, cash.
13. Total amortization of patents was $50.
14a. Land was sold for total cash proceeds of $290.
14b. The land sold had cost the company only $60.
15. The company issued additional bonds payable for $100, cash.
16. The company made a $300 payment on the principal of its mortgage payable.
17. The company purchased inventories costing $1,180, all on account.
18. The company paid $700 of other payables.
19. The company paid $1,800 of accounts payable.
20. The company declared and paid $200 of dividends. Because payment was made immediately, the dividends were not first recorded as a liability.

Illustration 9-6

Miami Corporation
Simple Summary Journal Entries
For the Year 19X2

FI	1.	Accounts Receivable	.	2,160			I	11.	Retained Earnings.	.	30	
		Retained Earnings	.		2,160				Buildings.	. . .		30
FI	2.	Retained Earnings.	.	1,200			F	12.	Patents		80	
		Inventories	. . .		1,200				Cash			80
	3.	Cash.	.	2,120			I	13.	Retained Earnings.	.	50	
		Accounts Receivable			2,120				Patents			50
FI	4.	Retained Earnings.	.	480			F	14a.	Cash.		290	
		Other Payables .	.		480				Land			290
FI	5.	Retained Earnings.	.	80			I	14b.	Land		230	
		Cash			80				Retained Earnings	.		230
F	6a.	Cash.		220			F	15.	Cash.		100	
		Equipment . . .			220				Bonds Payable . .			100
I	6b.	Retained Earnings.	.	80			F	16.	Mortgage Payable .	.	300	
		Equipment . . .			80				Cash			300
F	7.	Equipment		670				17.	Inventories		1,180	
		Accounts Payable	.		670				Accounts Payable	.		1,180
F	8.	Cash.		500				18.	Other Payables	. .	700	
		Capital Stock	. .		500				Cash			700
I	9.	Retained Earnings.	.	240				19.	Accounts Payable .	.	1,800	
		Equipment . . .			240				Cash			1,800
F	10.	Buildings		100			FI	20.	Retained Earnings.	.	200	
		Cash			100				Cash			200

In Illustration 9-6, entries that are summarized on the funds statement are marked "F"; entries that are summarized on the income statement are marked "I."

Changes that are never reported

First of all, notice that several of the company's balance sheet changes are not summarized on either change report:

3.	Cash	2,120		18.	Other Payables	700	
	Accounts Receivable		2,120		Cash		700
17.	Inventories	1,180		19.	Accounts Payable	1,800	
	Accounts Payable		1,180		Cash		1,800

These are the company's day-to-day operating-cycle transactions (defined on page 296), whereby inventories and supplies are purchased, cash is collected on receivables, current liabilities are paid, and so forth. At present, *these kinds of routine operating-cycle transactions usually are not reported on published financial statements.*[3] The apparent reason for this is that they are routine, and regarded as of little interest to investors. Yet the total dollar value of these transactions is quite significant.

---

[3] Transactions 3, 18, and 19 would be reported if cash statements were included among published financial statements. However as indicated earlier, cash statements are used mainly for the internal purposes of the firm, and are not usually published

Overlapping in the income statement and the funds statement

Five of the entries in Illustration 9-6 "overlap," that is, they are chosen for both the income statement and the funds statement:

1. Accounts Receivable	2,160		(Sales)
Retained Earnings		2,160	
2. Retained Earnings	1,200		(Cost of goods sold)
Inventories		1,200	
4. Retained Earnings	480		(Miscellaneous expense)
Other Payables		480	
5. Retained Earnings	80		(Interest expense)
Cash		80	
20. Retained Earnings	200		(Dividends)
Cash		200	

The income statement and the funds statement (statement of sources and uses of net working capital) report exactly the same information about operations *insofar as operations affect the current accounts*. The income statement reports this information because each of the underlying balance sheet changes affects retained earnings. The funds statement reports this information because each of the underlying balance sheet changes also affects net working capital. The income statement and the statement of sources and uses of net working capital will always overlap: *both will always include the same information about current operations*.

These overlaps will occur whenever a revenue reflects a source of funds, such as a receipt of current assets (as most revenues do) or a reduction in a current liability (as in the case of advances from customers), or where an expense is accompanied by a use of funds, such as an expenditure of current assets or an increase in a current liability. However, as you have already seen with cash entries, many funds statement and income statement changes do not overlap.

Funds Statement Changes		*Related Income Statement Changes*	
6a. Proceeds from sale of equipment—*source* . . .	$220	6b. Loss on sale of equipment— *loss*	$ 80
7. Purchase of new equipment— *use*	$670	9. Depreciation of old equipment —*expense*	$240
10. Purchase of new building—*use*	$100	11. Depreciation of old building— *expense*	$ 30
12. Purchase of new patents—*use* .	$ 80	13. Amortization of old patents— *expense*	$ 50
14a. Proceeds from sale of land— *source*	$290	14b. Gain on sale of land—*gain* .	$230
8. Proceeds from issue of capital stock—*source*	$500		
15. Proceeds from issue of bonds payable—*source*	100		
16. Payment made on mortgage payable—*use*	300	There are no related income statement changes for changes 8, 15, and 16.	

Illustrations 9-7 and 9-8 give the 19X2 funds and income statements for Miami Corporation. In this case, none of the operating changes chosen for the funds statement have been summarized. Overlaps are indicated by asterisks.

Illustration 9-7

Miami Corporation
Sources and Uses of Net Working Capital
For the Year 19X2

Sources:
Funds from Operations:
 Receipts:
  Sales $2,160*
 Expenditures:
  Cost of Goods Sold $1,200*
  Miscellaneous Costs of Operations 480*
  Interest Charges 80*   1,760*

Funds from Operations . . . . $ 400*
Proceeds from Sale of Noncurrent Assets:
 Equipment Sold . . . . $ 220
 Land Sold   290   510

Proceeds from Issue of Noncurrent Equities:
 Capital Stock Issued . . . . $ 500
 Bonds Payable Issued   100   600

Net Sources $1,510

Uses:
Purchase of Noncurrent Assets:
 Equipment Purchased . . . . $ 670
 Building Purchased   100
 Patents Purchased . . . .   80 $ 850

Retirement of Noncurrent Equities:
 Payment Made on Mortgage Principal   300
Dividends Declared 200*

Net Uses $1,350

Increase in Net Working Capital. . . . . $ 160
Net Working Capital—12/31/X1:
 Current Assets $1,050
 Current Liabilities   500   550

Net Working Capital—12/31/X2:
 Current Assets $1,040
 Current Liabilities . . . .   330 $ 710

* Overlaps between income statement and funds statement for Miami Corporation.

Illustration 9-8

Miami Corporation
Statement of Income and Retained Earnings
For the Year 19X2

Revenues:
 Sales $2,160*
Expenses:
 Cost of Goods Sold $1,200*
 Miscellaneous Expense 480*
 Interest Expense 80*   1,760*

continued on page 468

Net Income from Current Operations		$ 400*
Depreciation Expense	$ 270	
Amortization of Patents	50	320
Net Income before Extraordinary Items		$ 80
Extraordinary Items:		
Gain on Sale of Land	$ 230	
Loss on Sale of Equipment	80	150
Net Income		$ 230
Dividends		200*
Increase in Retained Earnings		$ 30
Retained Earnings—12/31/X1		180
Retained Earnings—12/31/X2		$ 210

* Overlap between income statement and funds statement for Miami Corporation.

Illustration 9-8 is in conformity with previous income statements, except for the additional subtotal "net income from current operations." This is *not* a standard subtotal that you would find on a published income statement, but the use of it here demonstrates a limited way in which funds statements can be used as reports on company profits.

The funds statement as a short-run profits report

The following observation was made in Chapter Six (page 296):

> Operating-cycle changes involve only current assets and current liabilities; however, they occur in an environment of services provided by the entity's noncurrent nonmonetary assets—its buildings, equipment, and the like. These noncurrent nonmonetary asset services help the company sell those things that it is in business to sell. For instance, few customers would buy from a store that did not have counters, display racks, or some kind of furniture or fixtures. Depreciation charges and other noncurrent asset writeoffs reflect the services that noncurrent nonmonetary assets provide during a particular year.

For income statement purposes, such relatively long-run matters as the expenditure of depreciable asset services must be taken into consideration. But the income statement does not provide the only way to look at profits.

As commented several times before, almost all investors are interested in how successful the company has been in providing and selling its particular products or services. Investor questions can be answered on several levels of sophistication and in more than one dimension: the accountant can report on how well the company is doing in the short run or the long run. *In the short run, he can discuss company profitability without paying much attention to what is happening to noncurrent assets.*

This is exactly what the operating portion of a funds statement does. It provides a sort of net income from *current* operations, in which the effects on noncurrent assets (depreciation and amortization) are ignored.[4] For some purposes, a report on profits from current operations can be useful.

As an example, I once knew an elderly couple who owned the grocery store in a small Michigan community. The husband had bought the business with his life's savings when he retired from his previous work. The store did little business, but enough to cover current costs and provide for the couple's needs. Meanwhile, the store building was slowly growing older. From a long-run standpoint, the accountant would have to reflect this in discussing the success of the store's operations: the couple was receiving services from the building, and those services were slowly being exhausted. The interests of the couple, however, were *not* long-run. They were only interested in having the building outlast them. For this reason, they were mainly concerned with the success of the store's current operations.

College students are often in a similar position. While in school, a student's income is apt to be much lower than after graduation. If the student is trying to decide whether he can afford to stay in school until he graduates, he may treat the problem as involving short-run considerations. For example, he may ignore the facts that his car and clothing are slowly wearing out. He worries about them only if they must actually be replaced. Both this and the example of the elderly couple involve a short-run notion of success. From a long-run standpoint (that of the elderly couple's heirs, for example), operations might appear less successful.

But these examples involve special cases. Are there any ordinary situations in which a short-run concept of operating profit is appropriate? Short-term creditors provide such a case. The short-term creditor (one who extends credit to the company for less than a year) needs to predict what will happen to the company over the period that the company owes him money. If the company prepares financial statements once a year, most of the creditor's predictions can relate to a one-year interval. Unless the creditor is developing a close long-run relationship with the company, he can ignore long-run considerations. He need not worry whether the company's buildings and equipment are slowly being exhausted, so long as their services will not be exhausted during the life of his investment (and so long as he knows that the company will give priority to paying current debts before it buys any new buildings and equipment). Owners and long-term creditors must take the long view, but the short-term creditor does not and should not take the long view. *The operating portion of a funds statement can provide short-term creditors and investors complete information about the company's short-run operating profitability*—its short-run success in dealing in the products and services that it is in business to produce and sell.

In those cases where information about short-run operating profitability would be useful to some readers of a company's financial statements, the accountant should consider reporting the details of operating changes on the funds statement instead of summarizing them in a single figure. Other reasons for doing this are given below.

---

[4] Many accountants, including the Accounting Principles Board, object to speaking of any sort of net income as being reported on the funds statement. What is said in this subsection is not standard opinion. As pointed out later in this chapter, accountants are quite concerned that the funds statement is presently being treated by some investors as though it were an income statement. Funds statements are not income statements, even though, as demonstrated here, the operating section of a funds statement does report net income from current operations.

Another consequence of overlap: " adding back" on the funds statement

The Miami Corporation funds statement (Illustration 9-7) excludes from the calculation of funds from operations certain balance sheet changes *that are perfectly good expenses, but that do not affect net working capital.* This suggests another way in which funds from operations could be calculated, exemplified in Illustration 9-9.

Illustration 9-9

Miami Corporation
Sources and Uses of Net Working Capital
For the Year 19X2

Sources:

Funds from Operations:		
Net Income from Operations		$ 80*
Add: Depreciation Expense	$ 270*	
Amortization of Patents	50*	320*
Funds from Operations		$ 400
Proceeds from Sale of Noncurrent Assets:		
Equipment Sold	$ 220	
Land Sold	290	510
Proceeds from Issue of Noncurrent Equities:		
Capital Stock Issued	$ 500	
Bonds Payable Issued	100	600
Net Sources		$1,510

Uses:

Purchase of Noncurrent Assets:		
Equipment Purchased	$ 670	
Building Purchased	100	
Patents Purchased	80	$ 850
Retirement of Noncurrent Equities:		
Payment Made on Mortgage Principal		300
Dividends Declared		200
Net Uses		$1,350
Increase in Net Working Capital.		$ 160
Net Working Capital—12/31/X1:		
Current Assets	$1,050	
Current Liabilities	500	550
Net Working Capital—12/31/X2:		
Current Assets	$1,040	
Current Liabilities	330	$ 710

* *Changes from Illustration 9-7.*

The calculation of *net income from operations* from *funds from current operations* requires taking into consideration certain long-run matters (like depreciation) that the current operations figure omits. Similarly, calculating *funds from current operations* from *net income from operations* requires that you exclude certain long-run matters (like depreciation). Since these matters are subtractions in arriving at net income from operations, you exclude them *by adding them back*. In Illustration 9-9, $320 of long-run expenses are excluded this way, so as to get funds from *current* operations instead of net income from operations.

This method of calculating funds from operations by "adding back" is used on most published funds statements. The motive may be a belief that operating revenue and expense activities are so important as a source of funds that the relationships between the funds and income statements should be explicitly indicated on the former. Unfortunately, such adding back of irrelevant expenses to net income in order to obtain funds from operations leads untrained readers into serious misunderstandings. Here are a few common misconceptions that grow out of funds statements like Illustration 9-9:

Misunderstanding 1: the false belief that depreciation is a source of funds

Adding depreciation back to net income from operations has the same arithmetic effect as adding in such items as the cash proceeds from sales of noncurrent assets or the issuance of capital stock. The latter are sources of funds, so readers are tempted to regard depreciation (and other writedowns of long-lived assets) as being sources of funds, too. This can go so far that occasionally people start believing they can improve their funds situation by increasing their depreciation rates. Actually (excluding certain tax considerations) depreciation and funds have nothing whatever to do with each other, *which is exactly why depreciation is excluded from funds statements!* But excluding depreciation by adding it back to net income from operations makes it look as though depreciation were a source of funds.

Misunderstanding 2: the false belief that depreciation is irrelevant

If the untrained reader grasps that depreciation is being excluded, he may begin to wonder whether depreciation is actually important. All too often depreciation is regarded as a "bookkeeping activity" that has little to do with what has really happened to the company. Yet depreciation is just as much a cost of obtaining sales as is any other expense. It is excluded from the funds statement because depreciation isn't a cost of current operations. The funds statement takes a short-run view of operating profitability. To do this, it is necessary to exclude long-run considerations like depreciation. But as soon as you take a longer view, you must recognize that part of the costs to be matched with revenues are the costs of the services of noncurrent assets used in earning those revenues.

Misunderstanding 3: the false belief that "cash-flow income" can be obtained

The final misconception relates to the previous two misconceptions and was discussed briefly in the last chapter. Some readers and financial analysts assert that it is possible to obtain a sort of "cash-flow income" by taking the reported net income figure (*not* net income from operations) and adding back depreciation and other writeoffs of noncurrent assets. Sometimes it is claimed that the resulting figure has all the virtues of net income while being free of unnecessary bookkeeping conventions. From time to time, you may find stock salesmen saying such things as,

"Granted, this company's net income is unsatisfactory, but look at its cash flow!" The Accounting Principles Board has expressed strong opposition to such language; certainly it involves serious misconceptions:

First of all, these calculations are not really an attempt to measure a cash magnitude; instead, they are attempts to determine funds from operations plus, perhaps, proceeds from the sale of noncurrent assets. But they often are imprecise calculations of this since the income statement is affected differently from the funds statement by such things as sales of noncurrent assets. For example, the sale of Miami Corporation's old equipment resulted in a fund *receipt* (positive), but an income statement *loss* (negative). (See Entries 6a and 6b in Illustration 9-6.) Merely adding back depreciation and other noncurrent asset writeoffs will not compensate for such differences, and the resulting "cash-flow" income figure may not correspond to any figure on a funds statement.

Second, even when this approach does yield an approximation to a figure reported on a funds statement, the result represents short-run profitability. As pointed out before, such a figure may be very useful to a creditor, *but stockholders' interests are usually more long-run than this.* In any event, it is quite misleading to act as though funds from operations and net income reflect the same thing. One is an index of short-run profitability; the other is an index of long-run profitability.

By now these misconceptions are firmly enough entrenched that it will take a long time and much education of investors to eliminate them. Nevertheless, some of the temptation to make these mistakes could be removed by using an alternative approved by the APB. Instead of using the "add-back" form of funds statement, accountants could use the "subtraction" form, which calculates funds from operations by subtracting from sales only those expenses that involve expenditures of net working capital. This form was exemplified in Illustration 7-4, page 346:

Receipts:		
Sales		$6,200
Expenditures:		
Cost of Merchandise Sold	$4,070	
Cost of Employee Services	1,125	
Cost of Supplies Used	57	
Cost of Utility Services	180	
Cost of Consulting Services	153	
Cost of 19X2 Taxes	207	
Interest Charges	23	5,815
Funds from Operations		$ 385

If the accountant preferred, revenue and expense nomenclature could be employed instead of net working capital nomenclature (for instance, "utilities expense" instead of "cost of utility services"). If the foregoing seems too detailed, it easily could be abbreviated to:

Sales	$6,200
Less: Expenses that decrease net working capital	5,815
Funds from operations	$ 385

The effect of using this "subtraction" method of calculating funds from operations would be to satisfy the goal of stressing the relationship between the funds and income statements, while avoiding the misunderstandings caused by the "add-back" method. The "subtraction" method has the additional virtue of reflecting the real nature of funds from operations by indicating that these are the impact of the firm's profit-seeking activities on its current accounts, instead of a kind of bastardized version of net income. This is a main reason why the "subtraction" method was used in Chapter Seven.

In (partial) defense of "cash-flow income"

Although "cash-flow income" involves a serious misconception and is not an acceptable concept to the Accounting Principles Board (or to most other accountants, for that matter) one is not entitled to dismiss the concept as a mistake and simply forget about it. Instead, attempts to calculate cash-flow income are symptomatic of a very serious limitation to financial accounting (it has been discussed in Chapters Six and Eight and will be discussed in more detail in Chapter Thirteen).

In the final section of Chapter Six (pages 318–323), it was argued that the contribution to cash made by an individual input to a firm is impossible to determine. In Chapter Eight (pages 432–438), it was argued that the same is true of income: it is usually impossible to determine the contribution to income made by an individual input to a firm. As you will remember, this is because the firm's inputs interact, producing different amounts of cash and income together than they would alone; there is an unlimited variety of ways in which the resulting cash and income could be attributed to these inputs, yet there is no defensible way to choose one allocation over the others. Accordingly, the concept of "the contribution of an input to cash or income" is arbitrary.

But we have seen that accountants wish to amortize nonmonetary assets by estimating both the total economic benefits that they can be expected to provide and the economic benefits yielded during the current period, then calculating amortization for the period as follows (zero scrap values are assumed):

Amortization for period	=	Historical acquisition price	×	Estimated services yielded during the period	÷	Estimated total services

But, as is argued in the first section of Chapter Thirteen, it can be easily shown that the estimated services of an asset must be reducible to the asset's effects upon the firm's cash, or to related notions of effects on income.[5] Since the asset's contribution

---

[5] One reason for this is that the amortization magnitudes must be incorporated, as expenses, on income statements and used in the calculation of net income. Another reason is that, as the final section in Chapter Four indicated, the amounts reported in financial accounting are constructed out of a set of simple primary measurements of cash, counts of quantities of monetary assets and liabilities shown at figures corresponding to equivalent amounts of cash, and counts of quantities of nonmonetary assets and liabilities shown at figures corresponding to cash-equivalent market prices (or portions thereof). Another, more complicated, reason for this is given in Chapter Thirteen.

to cash or income usually can be calculated only in an arbitrary way, the accountant's amortization calculation inevitably is arbitrary, too:

$$\begin{matrix} \text{Amortization} \\ \text{for} \\ \text{period} \end{matrix} = \begin{matrix} \text{Historical} \\ \text{acquisition} \\ \text{price} \end{matrix} \times \begin{matrix} \text{Arbitrary} \\ \text{amount} \end{matrix} \div \begin{matrix} \text{Arbitrary} \\ \text{amount} \end{matrix}$$

The result, as Chapter Thirteen also indicates, has been a mess. Contemporary financial accounting rules allow a great variety of amortization methods (you've seen only a small sample of them so far), and each is no more defensible than any other. The most conspicuous example of this has been depreciation—the range of conflicting depreciation alternatives allowed a firm is wide enough to have significant effects upon the reported incomes of firms. Some financial analysts, accordingly, have come to believe that depreciation figures are simply unreliable and should be disregarded— that the information content of the income statement can be improved by ignoring depreciation. As indicated above, the effects of depreciation may be removed from net income by adding back the depreciation charge. It is a misconception to call the result "income." But if the depreciation figure *is* sufficiently arbitrary to be more confusing than informative, ignoring depreciation would be appropriate for resource-allocation uses of accounting. On this reasoning, one may deplore the practice of calculating net-income-plus-depreciation and labeling the result "cash-flow income," yet sympathize with what the user of the financial statements was trying to do when he made his mistake. We will return to these matters in Chapter Thirteen.

Funds Statement Reporting of Transactions That Do Not Affect Net Working Capital

The main purpose of a funds statement is to summarize and report the major financial activities of the firm during the accounting period: its purchases of noncurrent assets, and its issuing and retirement of long-term debt and capital stock. As the discussion on pages 337–342 indicated, most of these transactions are reflected in changes in net working capital; accordingly, it is practical to use a statement of changes in net working capital as a report on major financial transactions.

But certain major financial transactions are not reflected by changes in net working capital. Typically, these involve large acquisitions of noncurrent assets wherein the buyer issues capital stock or long-term debt in payment for the assets acquired. As an example, suppose that Findley Industrial Products, Inc., has decided to contract its operations by discontinuing unprofitable manufacturing activities at its Pittsfield plant. The company disposes of its Pittsfield equipment in various ways with which we are not concerned; it sells its Pittsfield land and buildings to Gray Mfg. Co. for $1,800,000. Instead of paying cash, Gray issues shares of its own common stock having a market value of $1,800,000. Gray records this transaction as follows:

Land	700,000	
Buildings	1,100,000	
Common Stock		1,800,000

Finally, assume that, from the standpoint of Gray Mfg. Co., this is a sufficiently important transaction to be reported to stockholders.

How to report such transactions

There is no difficulty in reporting such transactions on funds statements. All that's needed is a slight revision in those rules for constructing funds statements that were given on pages 342–344. Our rule has been that once all of the firm's journal entries have been put in simple summary form, one should select all changes that affect the balance of net working capital, ignoring the rest. To report financial transactions not reflected by changes in net working capital, this rule should be modified to the following:

2a. Select all entries that affect the balance of net working capital.

2b. Also select all entries that affect two noncurrent accounts *if* neither of these accounts is retained earnings.

2c. Ignore all other entries.

The reason for ignoring simple entries involving retained earnings and some other noncurrent account (for example, entries recording depreciation) is that these entries are already reflected on the income statement, so that nothing is gained by an additional funds statement recording.

Finally, for all selected entries that affect two noncurrent accounts, the account debited should be treated as a use of net working capital and the item credited should be treated as a source of net working capital. In the example discussed above, Gray Mfg. Co.'s simple summary entries would include the following:

Land	700,000	
Common Stock		700,000
Buildings	1,100,000	
Common Stock		1,100,000

Gray Mfg. Co.'s next funds statement would include an $1,800,000 issue of common stock among its sources of funds, and purchases of $700,000 of land and $1,100,000 of buildings among its uses of funds. Doing this violates the strict logic of funds statement construction discussed in the appendix to Chapter Seven, but it is done so that the funds statement will reflect *all* financial transactions, including those relatively rare ones that do not affect net working capital. The Accounting Principles Board has required that all such financial transactions involving only noncurrent accounts be reported on published funds statements as involving simultaneous sources and uses of funds.

Other transactions of this kind

The following are the main kinds of financial transactions affecting only noncurrent accounts that might be reported on a funds statement:

1. Purchases of noncurrent plant assets, in which the buyer issues shares of its common stock in payment.

2. Purchases of noncurrent plant assets, in which the buyer issues noncurrent debt in payment.

3. Acquisition of permanent investments in the common stock of other firms, in which the buyer issues shares of its own common stock in payment.

In addition, occasionally firms receive gift assets or swap plant and equipment with each other. All such transactions are handled in the same way as the purchase of land and buildings described above.

Example

For simplicity, there will be no further discussion of financial transactions affecting only noncurrent accounts, but a final example of such transactions is given below. The following is a summary of West Frankfort Component Corporation's financial activities for 19X3:

1. The firm issued common stock for $207,000, cash.

2. The firm also issued common stock having a market value of $3,500,000 for the entire common stock of Springer Electronics, Inc. The firm intends to hold the Springer stock as a permanent investment.

3. The firm purchased equipment costing $1,200,000 on account.

4. The firm purchased a building for $4,000,000; it did so by issuing a $4,000,000, 10% note payable to the seller. The principal of this note is due in four equal annual installments, beginning on 6/30/X5.

5. The firm paid dividends totalling $523,000.

6. 19X3 funds from operations totalled $809,000.

7. Net working capital was $2,140,000 on 12/31/X2 and $1,433,000 on 12/31/X3. The firm's 19X3 funds statement is shown below.

West Frankfort Component Corporation
Sources and Uses of Net Working Capital
For the Year 19X3
(000 omitted)

Sources:

Funds from Operations		$ 809
Proceeds from Issue of Noncurrent Equities:		
Notes Payable	$4,000	
Capital Stock ($207 + $3,500)	3,707	7,707
Net Sources		$8,516

Uses:

Purchase of Noncurrent Assets:		
Investments	$3,500	
Building	4,000	
Equipment	1,200	$8,700
Dividends		523
Net Uses		$9,223
Decrease in Net Working Capital		$ (707)
Net Working Capital—12/31/X2		2,140
Net Working Capital—12/31/X3		$1,433

You will notice that no attempt is made in this funds statement to distinguish transactions affecting the balance of net working capital from those that affect only noncurrent accounts.

Other Kinds of Funds Statements

The statement of sources and uses of net working capital is one of several possible funds statements. The cash statement is sometimes presented as another kind of funds statement. More importantly, in recent years, accounting writers have given considerable attention to another form—the statement of sources and uses of *net current monetary accounts,* sometimes called *net quick assets.* A company's "current monetary accounts" refer to its cash and current claims to receive and pay cash. The main difference between net working capital and net current monetary accounts is that the latter excludes such nonmonetary accounts as Inventories, Supplies, Advances to Suppliers, and Advances from Customers. Illustration 9-10 gives Miami Corporation's current monetary accounts at the two balance sheet dates. (See Illustration 7-11, pages 357–358, for the underlying data.)

The statement of sources and uses of net current monetary accounts is constructed in much the same way as the statement of sources and uses of net working capital, with the exception of the rule for choosing balance sheet changes. The statement of sources and uses of net working capital chooses all simple changes that affect the balance of net working capital. The statement of sources and uses of net current monetary accounts chooses all simple changes that affect the balance of net current monetary accounts: current monetary assets and current monetary liabilities, instead of current assets and current liabilities.

Illustration 9-10

Miami Corporation
Current Monetary Accounts
December 31, 19X1 and 19X2

	December 31 19X1	19X2
Current Monetary Assets:		
Cash	$200	$170
Accounts Receivable	350	390
Total Current Monetary Assets	$550	$560
Current Monetary Liabilities:		
Accounts Payable	$250	$300
Other Payables	250	30
Total Current Monetary Liabilities	$500	$330
Net Current Monetary Accounts	$ 50	$230

In preparing a net current monetary accounts fund statement for Miami Corporation, the only difference (as compared with Illustration 9-7) will be in the treatment given inventories. Entry 2, recording the cost of goods sold, does not affect net current monetary accounts because inventories are not monetary. But *purchases* of inventory do affect net current monetary accounts. Consider Entry 17 in Illustration 9-6:

17. Inventories	1,180	
Accounts Payable		1,180

A current monetary liability is increased, whereas the other half of the entry does not affect current monetary accounts.

All other changes in Illustration 9-6 affecting net working capital also affect net current monetary accounts, and vice-versa. Thus the only difference between the respective funds statements is in the treatments given to inventories and, of course, the resulting differences in the subtotals. In Illustration 9-11, these differences are indicated by asterisks. (Compare Illustration 9-7.) Illustration 9-11 uses the "subtraction" method 'of calculating funds from operations. The "add-back" method is particularly awkward with this kind of funds statement unless purchases of inventories are listed among the purchases of noncurrent assets.

Illustration 9-11

Miami Corporation
Sources and Uses of Net Current Monetary Accounts
For the Year 19X2

Sources:
Funds from Operations:
  Receipts:

Sales			$2,160
Expenditures:			
Purchases of Inventories		$1,180*	
Miscellaneous Costs of Operations		480	
Interest Charges		80	1,740*
Funds from Operations			$ 420*
Proceeds from Sale of Noncurrent Assets:			
Equipment Sold		$ 220	
Land Sold		290	510
Proceeds from Issue of Noncurrent Equities:			
Capital Stock Issued		$ 500	
Bonds Payable Issued		100	600
Net Sources			$1,530*

Uses:

Purchase of Noncurrent Assets:			
Equipment Purchased		$ 670	
Building Purchased		100	
Patents Purchased		80	$ 850

Retirement of Noncurrent Equities:

Payment Made on Mortgage Principal	300
Dividends Declared	200
Net Uses	$1,350
Increase in Net Current Monetary Accounts	$ 180*
Net Current Monetary Accounts—12/31/X1	50*
Net Current Monetary Accounts—12/31/X2	$ 230*

* *Changes from Illustration 9-7.*

Usually the differences between the net working capital and the net current monetary accounts funds statements will be slight. The main reason for briefly discussing net current monetary accounts funds statements is to demonstrate that funds statements are still undergoing experimentation and are fairly flexible reports that can be designed in different ways to meet different needs.[6]

Problem for Study and Self-Examination

Problem 9-2:

As part of your training in accounting, you must become able to extend the concepts and techniques you have learned into situations that require different methods of analysis. This problem provides an opportunity to increase your flexibility and broaden your understanding. The background needed to solve this problem has been provided by the text, but the particular method of analysis required may at first seem unusual. Apply what you already have learned to this new situation.

Illustration 9-12 gives the comparative balance sheets of Berryville Co. at December 31, 19X1 and 19X2. Illustration 9-13 gives the company's 19X2 income statement. The company had a bad year in 19X2. Illustration 9-14 provides some additional information (not all of which is relevant) about the company's 19X2 balance sheet changes.

Prepare a statement of sources and uses of net working capital. Summarize all operating changes by a single figure.

---

[6] The main advantage of the net current monetary accounts funds statement over the net working capital funds statement relates to matters we discussed on pages 473–474. Suppose that someone who was deeply disenchanted with financial accounting's allocations of nonmonetary assets wished to substitute a funds statement for the income statement—or at least wished to use such a funds statement for some of the purposes that currently are served by income statements. He would wish to use a funds statement that included as few allocations of nonmonetary assets as possible. In the net working capital funds statement, the calculation of funds from operations includes allocations of inventories and prepayments. In contrast, no such allocations appear on a statement of sources and uses of net current monetary accounts. Instead, this statement reports *purchases* of inventories and prepayments. These purchase figures usually are reliable and well-authenticated. If one were distressed by the arbitrariness of allocations of nonmonetary assets, he should prefer the net current monetary accounts funds statement.

Illustration 9-12

Berryville Co.
Comparative Balance Sheets
December 31, 19X1 and 19X2

Assets

	December 31 19X1	December 31 19X2
Current Assets:		
Cash	$ 37,800	$ 24,200
Accounts Receivable	51,200	29,300
Notes Receivable—6%	5,000	6,000
Interest Receivable	100	150
Advances to Suppliers	4,300	5,600
Merchandise Inventory	90,600	77,600
Supplies	7,400	5,300
Prepaid Rent	7,200	7,200
Prepaid Insurance	6,300	3,900
Total Current Assets	$209,900	$159,250
Noncurrent Assets:		
Land	$ 10,000	$ 10,000
Building	85,000	80,000
Equipment	54,000	59,000
Total Noncurrent Assets	$149,000	$149,000
Total Assets	$358,900	$308,250

Equities

	December 31 19X1	December 31 19X2
Current Liabilities:		
Accounts Payable	$ 39,200	$ 24,000
Wages and Salaries Payable	3,700	4,300
Taxes Payable	12,400	1,050
Interest Payable	1,250	1,250
Dividends Payable	1,700	–0–
Advances from Customers	7,800	6,400
Total Current Liabilities	$ 66,050	$ 37,000
Noncurrent Liabilities:		
Long-Term Notes Payable—5%	150,000	150,000
Total Liabilities	$216,050	$187,000
Stockholders' Equity:		
Capital Stock	$100,000	$105,000
Retained Earnings	42,850	16,250
Total Stockholders' Equity	$142,850	$121,250
Total Equities	$358,900	$308,250

Illustration 9-13

Berryville Co.
Statement of Income and Retained Earnings
For the Year 19X2

Revenues:
Sales	$315,000	
Interest Revenue	350	$315,350

Expenses:
Cost of Goods Sold	$203,400	
Wages and Salaries Expense	74,900	
Depreciation Expense	13,000	
Insurance Expense	3,100	
Rent Expense	14,400	
Supplies Expense	17,600	
Taxes Expense	1,050	
Utilities Expense	4,500	
Interest Expense	7,500	339,450

Net Loss from Operations	$ (24,100)
Loss on Sale of Equipment	2,500*
Net Loss	$ (26,000)
Retained Earnings—12/31/X1	42,850
Retained Earnings—12/31/X2	$ 16,250

* *In practice this nonoperating loss probably would be classified as a miscellaneous expense;*
it is separately indicated here for clarity.

Illustration 9-14

Berryville Co.
Additional Information

1. During 19X2, $27,000 of sales were for cash; $7,800 related to 12/31/X1 advances from customers; $280,200 were on account.
2. The $4,300 of merchandise on which the company had paid advances to suppliers as of 12/31/X1 was all received during 19X2. All other merchandise received during 1969 was purchased on account.
3. The 6% notes receivable on the 12/31/X1 balance sheet were 12-month notes due 8/31/X2. The 6% notes receivable on the 12/31/X2 balance sheet were 9-month notes due 4/30/X3. Interest on all notes receivable is due at the time of maturity. The 12/31/X2 notes came onto the company's books by the following journal entry:

Notes Receivable—6%	6,000	
Accounts Receivable		6,000

   A customer who had made a purchase on account was unable to pay his account receivable when it became due; the company accepted his interest-bearing note instead.
4. Interest payments on the long-term notes payable are due every April 30 and October 31. The notes themselves are due on 4/30/X7.

5. Every June 30, the company pays one year's rent in advance.
6. The building and equipment owned at 12/31/X1 were all purchased seven years prior to that date. At that time, the building had an estimated total service life of 24 years, and the equipment had an estimated total service life of 13 years. Equipment with a book value of $6,000 was sold (for cash) on 1/1/X2. New equipment costing $19,000 was purchased (on account) on 12/31/X2. There were no sales or purchases of land or buildings during the year.
7. Accounts payable totalling $235,800 were paid during the year.
8. The utilities expense was paid in cash.

Solution

Solution 9-2:

Operations were so unsuccessful this year that they resulted in a net *use* of funds, rather than in a net source of funds. Receipts and revenues overlap completely for this company, and so do expenditures and expenses, *except* depreciation expense, which does not affect net working capital.

Receipts:		
Sales	$315,000	
Interest Earned	350	$315,350
Expenditures:		
Cost of Goods Sold	$203,400	
Cost of Wages and Salaries.	74,900	
Insurance Expired	3,100	
Rent Expired	14,400	
Supplies Used	17,600	
Cost of Taxes	1,050	
Cost of Utilities	4,500	
Interest Charges	7,500	326,450
Net Decrease in Funds Resulting from Operations		$ 11,100

The proceeds of the sale of equipment were $3,500:

Book Value of Equipment Sold	$ 6,000	
Loss on Sale of Equipment	2,500	
Proceeds from Sale of Equipment	$ 3,500	

Judging from the balance sheet, $5,000 of capital stock was issued during the year.

From Item 6 of Illustration 9-14, $19,000 of equipment was purchased during the year. This can be reasoned as follows. Item 6 indicates that the entire $5,000 19X2 decrease in buildings was the result of depreciation (this is the only remaining possibility, since there were no purchases or sales of buildings during the year). Therefore, we know that the following is true:

Total 19X2 depreciation (from Illustration 9-13)	$13,000
Depreciation of buildings	5,000
Depreciation of equipment	$ 8,000
Book value of equipment that was sold	6,000
Effect of above events upon equipment—a decrease of	$14,000

But equipment *increased* by $5,000 during 19X2; therefore there must have been a $14,000 + $5,000 = $19,000 purchase of equipment during the year.

There are no indications of any other balance sheet changes affecting the balance of net working capital. Apparently, the funds statement is the simple one shown below:

Berryville Co.
Sources and Uses of Net Working Capital
For the Year 19X2

Sources:		
Proceeds from Sale of Equipment		$ 3,500
Proceeds from Issue of Capital Stock		5,000
Net Sources		$ 8,500
Uses:		
Net Decrease in Funds Resulting from Operations		$ 11,100
Purchase of Equipment		19,000
Net Uses		$ 30,100
Decrease in Net Working Capital		$ 21,600
Net Working Capital—12/31/X1:		
Current Assets	$209,900	
Current Liabilities	66,050	$143,850
Net Working Capital—12/31/X2:		
Current Assets	$159,250	
Current Liabilities	37,000	122,250
Decrease in Net Working Capital		$ 21,600

Appendix

*Relationships Between
and Within Statements: Ratios*

How profitable has the company been? The income statement provides most of the answer to this question, which we first asked on page 23, but not the whole answer. Suppose you are told that a company earned $100,000 last year and are given an income statement supplying the details. How would you determine profitability? A lot will depend on the size of the company. How much has been invested in it? If the company is small, $100,000 may represent an excellent return on this investment. If the company is large, a $100,000 net income may represent a dismal performance. One major purpose in evaluating the profitability of a company is to determine how effectively its management has utilized the resources that have been entrusted to it; this can't be done until net income has been compared with these resources—until you have related the company's net income to its *size*. Here's a parallel example: A landlord buys a single-family house and an apartment house at the same time. He pays $20,000 for the single-family house and $200,000 for the apartment house. After repairs, taxes, and other costs, he clears $1,000 a year on the single-family house and $8,000 a year on the apartment house. Which building is more profitable?

The apartment house yields $7,000 more a year in profits than the single-family house, but it *cost* more. In figuring out which house is more profitable, it would be fairly logical to divide the net income by the cost of the investment. (An even more logical approach might be to divide net income by the cost, less accumulated depreciation; however, this raises a lot of side issues that are better avoided for now.)

	Single Family House	Apartment House
Rental Income	$ 1,000	$ 8,000
Cost	20,000	200,000
Profit Rate on Cost	5%	4%

Dollar for dollar, the single-family house is more profitable an investment than the apartment house. *You can apply the same logic to companies.* To compare the profitability of two different-sized companies, simply divide each company's net income (before any distribution of profits) by some index of its size. In what follows, assume that the company's accounting period is one year.

One of the best indexes of a company's size is the average total amount of its equities—the amount that investors as a whole have invested in the company. If you use amount of equities as an index of size, you must use a consistent measure of income. "Income" should be profits *before* any dividend distributions to investors. Since total equities (all investors) are involved, it also should be profits *before interest charges.* From the standpoint of creditors, interest fees are just as much a distribution to investors as dividends are to stockholders. The measure of company profitability should be:

$$\frac{\text{Rate of return on}}{\text{total investment}} = \frac{\text{(Net income)} + \text{(Interest Expense)}^7}{\text{(Average total equities)}}$$

How do you calculate average total equities? To be precise, you should determine total equities at the end of each month, each week, or each day; then work out the exact average. As a practical matter, however, it usually will suffice to take beginning and ending total equities, add them, and divide by two:

$$\frac{\text{Rate of return on total}}{\text{investment (approximate)}} = \frac{\text{(Net income)} + \text{(Interest Expense)}}{\text{(Beginning total equities} + \text{Ending total equities)}/2}$$

If the rates of return of two firms are to be compared meaningfully, the time periods involved in the calculation of these rates must be identical. It is customary to calculate rates of return in terms of one-year periods—and up to now we have been assuming that each company's accounting period is one year. If it happens to be a shorter period than that, you must turn the rate of return into an annual rate. This is easily enough done: just multiply the rate calculated for the shorter period *by the number of these periods in one year.* Here is a complete formula for this approximate calculation of rate of return on total investment:

Let
- Y = Net income
- X = Interest expense
- B = Total equities, beginning of period
- E = Total equities, end of period
- N = Number of accounting periods in one year

$$\frac{\text{Rate of return on total}}{\text{investment (approximate)}} = \left(\frac{Y + X}{(B + E)/2}\right) \times N$$

---

[7] Interest expense is added back to net income so as to get net income before interest charges. Interest expense is a subtraction in arriving at net income, so the way to exclude interest expense is to reverse this subtraction by adding it back.

Two examples are given below. The first is based on the Mills and Kensett Co. data in Problem 9-1 (pages 457–465). The second is based on the following Trimble Hotel Corp. financial statements:

Trimble Hotel Corp.
Comparative Balance Sheets
December 31, 19X1 and 19X2

Assets

	December 31	
	19X1	19X2
Current Assets:		
Cash	$ 8,272	$ 5,631
Accounts Receivable	1,244	1,226
Inventories	1,043	1,021
Prepaid Advertising	448	472
Other Current Assets	893	910
Total Current Assets	$11,900	$ 9,260
Noncurrent Assets:		
Land	$ 9,763	$10,414
Buildings	50,317	63,345
Furniture and Equipment	15,020	16,522
Total Noncurrent Assets	$75,100	$90,281
Total Assets	$87,000	$99,541

Equities

	19X1	19X2
Current Liabilities:		
Accounts Payable	$ 2,812	$ 3,075
Wages and Salaries Payable	986	723
Taxes Payable	3,179	1,870
Interest Payable	618	646
Other Current Payables	1,405	1,321
Total Current Liabilities	$ 9,000	$ 7,635
Noncurrent Liabilities:		
Bank Loans	$ 6,800	$ 6,926
$5\frac{1}{2}\%$ Bonds Payable	40,000	37,000
Total Noncurrent Liabilities	$46,800	$43,926
Total Liabilities	$55,800	$51,561
Stockholders' Equity:		
Capital Stock	$ 9,676	$25,676
Retained Earnings	21,524	22,304
Total Stockholders' Equity	$31,200	$47,980
Total Equities	$87,000	$99,541

Trimble Hotel Corp.
Statement of Income and Retained Earnings
For the Year 19X2

Revenues:

Room Rentals	$33,464	
Store and Office Rentals	2,052	
Other Sales	32,884	$68,400

Expenses:

Wages and Salaries Expense	$25,648	
Cost of Goods Sold	11,012	
Property Operating Expenses	10,200	
Advertising Expense	2,340	
Depreciation Expense	8,612	
Interest Expense	2,608	
Property Taxes	4,180	
Income Taxes	2,550	67,150

Net Income from Operations		$ 1,250
Nonoperating Gains and Losses:		
Loss on Retirement of Bonds Payable	$ 60	
Gain on Sale of Land	46	14
Net Income		$ 1,236
Dividends		456
Increase in Retained Earnings		$ 780
Retained Earnings—12/31/X1		21,524
Retained Earnings—12/31/X2		$22,304

	Mills and Kensett Co.*	Trimble Hotel Corp.*
Net income for the year	$ 2,757,000	$ 1,236,000
Add back interest expense	510,000	2,608,000
Net income before distribution of profits to any investors = (1).	$ 3,267,000	$ 3,844,000
Total equities—beginning of year	$ 98,318,000	$ 87,000,000
Total equities—end of year	98,990,000	99,541,000
	$197,308,000	$186,541,000
	÷ 2	÷ 2
Average total equities = (2)	$ 98,654,000	$ 93,270,500
Rate of return on average total investment = (1)/(2)	3.3%	4.1%

* *The last three digits were omitted in the original data.*

Dollar for dollar, Trimble Hotel Corp. was slightly more profitable than Mills and Kensett Co. during 19X2. In comparison with both of these companies, here are the figures for Student Services, Inc. (The related financial statements are shown below. A full discussion of this company's 19X2 activities is given in the next chapter, but at this point, the financial statements will suffice; advance vacation payments are advances from customers.)

	Student Services, Inc.
Net income for the year	$ 11,130
Add back interest expense	–0–
Net income before distribution of profits to any investors = (1)	$ 11,130
Total equities—beginning of year	$ 86,510
Total equities—end of year	99,650
	$186,160
	÷ 2
Average total equities = (2)	$ 93,080
Rate of return on average total investment = (1)/(2)	12.0%

Student Services, Inc.
Comparative Balance Sheets
December 31, 19X1 and 19X2

	12/31/X1	*12/31/X2*
Current Assets:		
Cash	$24,300	$14,200
Accounts Receivable	15,430	16,020
Supplies	6,190	7,010
Prepaid Rent	560	560
Prepaid Insurance	420	220
Total Current Assets	$46,900	$38,010
Noncurrent Assets:		
Equipment	39,610	61,640
Total Assets	$86,510	$99,650
Current Liabilities:		
Accounts Payable	$ 4,010	$ 5,690
Wages Payable	3,780	1,980
Advance Vacation Payments	90	150
Taxes Payable	5,110	7,180
Total Liabilities	$12,990	$15,000
Stockholders' Equity:		
Capital Stock	$50,000	$50,000
Retained Earnings	23,520	34,650
Total Stockholders' Equity	$73,520	$84,650
Total Equities	$86,510	$99,650

Student Services, Inc.
Statement of Income and Retained Earnings
For the Year 19X2

Revenues:
Sales $179,780

Expenses:
Wages Expense	$112,300	
Supplies Expense	31,480	
Depreciation Expense	6,470	
Transportation Expense	2,730	
Taxes Expense	12,270	
Insurance Expense	200	
Rent Expense.	1,680	
Miscellaneous Expense	1,520	168,650

Net Income . . . . $ 11,130
Retained Earnings—12/31/X1. 23,520

Retained Earnings—12/31/X2. . . . . $ 34,650

Even though Student Services, Inc. has a much smaller net income than either of the other two companies, dollar-for-dollar it was much more profitable, at least in 19X2. Every dollar invested in Student Services, Inc. earned about 12¢ in profits, as contrasted with only about 3½¢ for the larger companies. Call the rate of return on average total investment the *all-investor earnings rate*.

Additional significance of this earnings ratio

Assets equal equities, so this particular earnings ratio measures more than just a rate of return on total investment. It also measures the rate of return on a company's total assets, and this is an index of how profitably management is employing the assets entrusted to it.[8] The all-investor earnings rate thus reflects the general economic efficiency of the company. Given some idea of the degree of risk in the company's industry, you can use the all-investor earnings rate to estimate the company's relative effectiveness as a user of society's resources.

To appreciate the significance of the all-investor earnings rate, it is important to remember that this ratio also represents the rate of return on total company assets ("all-asset earnings rate"), and that the two concepts have the same meaning. This is merely to say that the investor's concern about the company's general profitability may be perceived in either of two ways:

1. Are investors receiving an adequate return on their aggregate investment (all-investor earnings rate)?

---

[8] The reasoning here goes like this: assets = equities, therefore:

$$\text{All-investor earnings rate} = \frac{\text{Net income} + \text{Interest expense}}{\text{Average total equities}}$$

$$= \frac{\text{Net income} + \text{Interest expense}}{\text{Average total assets}}$$

$$= \frac{\text{Rate of return on average total}}{\text{assets employed in the company}}$$

2. Is management earning an adequate return on the assets that have been entrusted to it (all-asset earnings rate)?

As the previous discussion indicates, the particular ratio that has been calculated is pertinent to *both* questions. Accordingly, it will hereafter be referred to as the *all-investor (all-asset) earnings rate,* even though this terminology is slightly cumbersome.

Rate of return on stockholders' equity

Besides calculating a company-wide rate of return on total investor equities, you could also ask: how, in particular, is stockholder investment doing? To determine this, you need to calculate a rate of return on average stockholders' investment:

$$\text{Rate of return to stockholders} = \frac{\text{Net income}}{\text{Average stockholders' equity}}$$

Here, the appropriate measure of size is average stockholders' equity. Since stockholders are the only investors being discussed, the appropriate profit figure is simply net income. (You should not add back interest charges this time; interest expense is an appropriate charge against income when determining the amount of profits available to *stockholders.*) Here are the calculations for the same three companies:

	Mills and Kensett Co.	Trimble Hotel Corp	Student Services, Inc.
Net income for the year—(3)	$ 2,757,000	$ 1,236,000	$ 11,130
Stockholders' equity—beginning of year. . .	$ 70,161,000	$31,200,000	$ 73,520
Stockholders' equity—end of year	71,614,000	47,980,000	84,650
	$141,775,000	$79,180,000	$158,170
	÷2	÷2	÷2
Average stockholders' equity—(4)	$ 70,887,500	$39,590,000	$ 79,085
Rate of return to stockholders—(3)/(4) . . .	3.9%	3.1%	14.1%

Stockholders in Mills and Kensett Co. are receiving a better return per dollar of invested capital than are stockholders in Trimble Hotel Corp., despite the fact that the rate of return to Mills and Kensett Co. investors as a whole is slightly inferior to the rate of return to Trimble Hotel Corp. investors as a whole. Neither group of stockholders is doing as well as stockholders in Student Services, Inc.

Notice that Stockholders in Mills and Kensett Co. and in Student Services, Inc. are doing slightly better than investors as a whole in their companies. It is easy to see why this is so: Student Services, Inc. serves as a good example. The rate of return to investors as a whole is an *average* of the rate of return to stockholders and the rate of return to creditors. The return to creditors is measured by a company's interest expense. Since Student Services, Inc. had no interest expense, its return to creditors is zero.[9] Since zero is less than the 12 percent average return to all investors, the remaining investors (stockholders) must have received more than the average 12 percent rate of return. Call the rate of return on average stockholders' equity the *stockholders' earnings rate.*

You can figure the rate of return to creditors in much the same way that you figured the stockholders' earnings rate: divide that part of total profits to which creditors are entitled (interest expense) by average creditor equities:

$$\text{Rate of return to creditors} = \frac{\text{Interest expense}}{\underset{\text{(Average total creditor equities)}}{\text{Average total liabilities}}}$$

Considered by itself, the rate of return to creditors is of little use in analyzing the company's financial statements. Its significance lies in indicating *why* the stockholders' earnings rate differs from the all-investor (all-asset) earnings rate. Here are the calculations for all three companies (income taxes are ignored in what follows):

	Mills and Kensett Co.	Trimble Hotel Corp.	Student Services, Inc.
Interest expense—(5)	$ 510,000	$ 2,608,000	$ –0–
Total liabilities—beginning of year	$28,157,000	$ 55,800,000	$12,990
Total liabilities—end of year	27,376,000	51,561,000	15,000
	$55,533,000	$107,361,000	$27,990
	÷2	÷2	÷2
Average total liabilities—(6)	$27,766,500	$ 53,680,500	$13,995
Rate of return to creditors—(5)/(6)	1.8%	4.9%	0.0%

Of course, some creditors did better than these *average* rates of return indicate, while others—the holders of non-interest-bearing debts—fared worse.

	Summary of Earnings Ratios		
	Mills and Kensett Co.	Trimble Hotel Corp.	Student Services, Inc.
Average rate of return to all investors (all-investor, all-asset earnings rate) . . .	3.3%	4.1%	12.0%
Average rate of return to stockholders (stockholders' earnings rate)	3.9%	3.1%	14.1%
Average rate of return to creditors	1.8%	4.9%	0.0%

---

[9] Actually, supplier-creditors probably do receive an indirect return, insofar as the prices they charge are, on the average and for their industries as a whole, higher than they would be were suppliers not extending credit to their customers. But this probably would not be true of their sales to any *one* company, and the true rate of return to creditors would be very difficult to estimate with any assurance. For lack of objective reliable figures, such indirect returns to creditors are usually ignored by accountants, though they can be significant in economic theory.

The company-wide rate of return for Mills and Kensett Co. was 3.3 percent; every thousand dollars invested in the company earned, on the average, $33 in profits. If this thousand dollars were invested by creditors, their share in profits (on the average) was only $18. Thus, for every average $1,000 invested by creditors, $15 of the profits earned on their investment went instead to stockholders ($33 − $18 = $15). This is what makes the position of being a stockholder attractive: the rights of creditors to profits are limited by the interest rates on the debts owed them; stockholders, as residual equity holders, get whatever is left over.

Of course, all this can work to the stockholders' disadvantage whenever the company-wide rate of return is less than the average rate of return to creditors. This is exactly what happened with Trimble Hotel Corp. Every thousand dollars invested in the company earned, on the average, $41 in profits. If this thousand dollars were invested by creditors, their share in profits (on the average) was $49. Therefore, on the average, each $1,000 from creditors cost the stockholders $8 in profits ($49 − $41 = $8).

	Profits	Group's Average Investment	Rate of Return to Group
Total amount available to all Trimble investors (net income before interest expense) . . .	$3,844,000 ÷	$93,270,000 ≈	4.1%
Total amount going to Trimble creditors (interest expense)	2,608,000 ÷	53,680,000 ≈	4.9%
Total amount going to Trimble stockholders (net income)	$1,236,000 ÷	$39,590,000 ≈	3.1%

Gross profit and operating ratios

Investors often calculate additional ratios. Chapter Eight (page 407) showed that many accountants (and investors) subtract cost of goods sold directly from the figure for sales to get a subtotal called "gross margin" or "gross profit," from which the other expenses are then subtracted to obtain net income from operations. Ordinarily, a company's ratio of gross profits to sales is fairly stable from year to year, though of course it may vary widely from one company to another. Variations in this gross-profit-to-sales ratio often are a symptom of conditions worth further investigation.

The ratio of net income from operations to total revenues is also of interest to investors.[10] For example, consider a company that has been unusually profitable and

---

[10] Notice that this is the ratio of net income *from operations* to total revenues. The ratio of net income to sales is also calculated by many investors, but has major defects:

1. Total revenues may include revenues other than sales: dividend revenue and interest revenue are good examples. We took the ratio of gross profit to sales because sales was the only revenue related to cost of goods sold. All revenues are related to net income from operations, so the correct comparison is with total revenues, not merely with the sales component of total revenues.

2. Net income is affected by nonoperating gains and losses. These occur in an erratic manner, making the ratio of net income to sales comparatively unstable. This ratio can change dramatically when, as far as the company as a whole is concerned, little of permanent significance has changed.

(*continued on page 494*)

is expanding its activities. Elementary economic theory warns that, if management is not making effective effort to the contrary, each dollar of company sales may become progressively less profitable as time passes. Two phenomena contribute to this:

1. If a company has been unusually profitable, it tends to attract competition.

2. As a company expands, there is a tendency to tap successively less-profitable segments of the company's potential markets.

If these economic phenomena occur, the company's total net income from operations may continue to increase for a while since sales are increasing, but the ratio of net income from operations to sales will decline. The ratio, therefore, gives a truer picture of what is happening to company profitability than the net income from operations itself.

In general, both the ratio of gross profits to sales and the ratio of net income from operations to total revenues will indicate changes in the company's activities, environment, or success from one year to the next—changes that may be worth further investigation. These ratios are called the *gross profit ratio* and the *operating ratio,* respectively.

$$\text{Gross profit ratio} = \frac{\text{Sales} - \text{Cost of goods sold}}{\text{Sales}}$$

$$\text{Operating ratio} = \frac{\text{Net income from operations}}{\text{Total revenues}}$$

Here are these ratios for Mills and Kensett Co., Trimble Hotel Corp., and Student Services, Inc. (Student Services, Inc. doesn't have a cost of goods sold; Trimble Hotel Corp. has a cost of goods sold, but it's relatively unimportant. A gross profit ratio would not be calculated for either of these companies, nor for any other company that deals primarily in services.)

	Mills and Kensett Co.	Trimble Hotel Corp.	Student Services, Inc.
Sales = (7)	$318,337,000		
Cost of goods sold	190,962,000		
Gross profit = (8)	$127,375,000		
Gross profit ratio = (8)/(7)	40.0%		
Net income from operations = (9)	$ 2,965,000	$ 1,250,000	$ 11,130
Total revenues = (10)	318,337,000	68,400,000	179,780
Operating ratio = (9)/(10)	0.93%	1.8%	6.2%

3. This ratio matches unrelated things: for example, sales are an operating revenue; the nonoperating gains and losses that go into the calculation of net income often have little to do with sales.

This isn't to say that the ratio of net income to sales is worthless; however, changes in the ratio of net income from operations to sales will usually be a better indicator of significant change in the company's activities, environment, or success than changes in the ratio of net income to sales.

Neither the operating ratio nor the gross profit ratio is of much use in comparing companies from different industries because these ratios vary greatly from one industry to another. For example, grocery stores usually have very low operating ratios, but they make up for it by having a great volume of business. Furniture stores do a comparatively small volume of business and therefore need relatively high operating ratios. *To compare the profitability of two companies in different industries, you must use their stockholders' earnings ratios or their all-investor (all-asset) earnings ratios.* The earnings rate on invested capital (assets) is the fundamental concern when determining profitability, not the earnings rate on sales. In the following exaggerated example, the two imaginary companies are equally profitable, but they have very different operating and gross profit ratios. (Assume that neither company had nonoperating gains or losses.)

	Company A	*Company B*
Average total equities for the year = (a)	$1,000,000	$ 200,000
Average stockholders' equity for the year = (b)	$ 400,000	$ 80,000
Sales = (c)	$2,000,000	$4,000,000
Cost of goods sold	1,700,000	2,400,000
Gross profit = (d)	$ 300,000	$1,600,000
Interest expense = (e)	$ 20,000	$ 4,000
Other expenses	240,000	1,588,000
	$ 260,000	$1,592,000
Net income from operations = net income = (f)	$ 40,000	$ 8,000
Net income before interest expense = [(f) + (e)] = (g)	$ 60,000	$ 12,000
Gross profit ratio = (d)/(c)	15%	40%
Operating ratio = (f)/(c)	2%	0.2%
Stockholders' earnings rate = (f)/(b)	10%	10%
All-investor (all-asset) earnings rate = (g)/(a)	6%	6%

Other earnings ratios

One of the most widely calculated earnings ratios is *earnings per share* (and a related ratio comparing this with the market price of the company's capital stock in the stock market). Earnings per share is calculated as follows:[11]

$$\text{Earnings per share} = \frac{\text{Net income}}{\text{Average number of outstanding shares of capital stock}}$$

---

[11] This formula for earnings per share is relevant only for common shares, and it implicitly assumes that the firm has not issued any other kinds of stock, such as preferred stock. Once this simplifying assumption is removed, the calculation of earnings per share can become complicated; these complications are best reserved for an advanced text.

Notice the use of "net income" instead of "net income before interest expense." This is a *stockholders'* ratio. Assume that during 19X2 our three companies had the following average numbers of shares outstanding (published financial statements always provide this information):

	Average Number of Shares Outstanding[12]
Mills and Kensett Co.	2,500,000
Trimble Hotel Corp.	170,000
Student Services, Inc.	5,000

You could calculate net income per share in the manner shown below:

	Mills and Kensett Co.	*Trimble Hotel Corp.*	*Student Services, Inc.*
Net income = (11)	$2,757,000	$1,236,000	$11,130
Average number of shares = (12)	2,500,000	170,000	5,000
Net income per share = (11)/(12)	$ 1.10	$ 7.27	$ 2.23

Investors calculate a number of other ratios besides the ones mentioned here. Dividends per share are just as important to stockholders as earnings per share; similarly, *the percentage* of earnings paid out in dividends is of interest to stockholders.

Indexes of ability to pay liabilities

Finally, there are several other ratios that sometimes are symptomatic of the general stability or economic health of the firm. One of these was discussed on page 143—the *current ratio*:

$$\text{Current ratio} = \frac{\text{Current assets}}{\text{Current liabilities}}$$

It was indicated that this ratio is often used as a test of the firm's ability to pay its current debts when they come due. Another ratio sometimes used for the same purpose is the *quick ratio*:

$$\text{Quick ratio} = \frac{\text{Current monetary assets}}{\text{Current liabilities}}$$

---

[12] You will recall that there is no reason to expect the individual shares of one company to have the same market value as the individual shares of another, even if the two companies are of about the same size and are equally profitable. For example, two companies might each have total stockholders' equity of $1,000,000. Yet one might represent this by 50,000 ($20) shares and the other by 10,000 ($100) shares. In the three-company example, Mills and Kensett Co.'s shares are worth much less individually than Trimble Hotel Corp.'s shares, even though the total Mills and Kensett Co.'s stockholders' equity is about double the total Trimble Hotel Corp.'s stockholders' equity.

The logic for using the quick ratio instead of the current ratio as an index of debt-paying ability is that some current assets, such as inventories, take a relatively long time to become transformed into cash via the operating cycle (see pages 140–143)—a longer time than creditors may allow for payment of liabilities. And certain other current assets, such as prepayments, never *are* directly exchanged for cash. In contrast, current monetary assets are either cash itself or assets that usually can easily be converted into cash before current liabilities become due. The quick ratio sometimes is called the *acid test* or the *acid test ratio* by its proponents.

Both the current ratio and the quick ratio are short-run in significance. The firm's long-run ability to pay its debts as they mature often is tested by the *debt ratio*:

$$\text{Debt ratio} = \frac{\text{Total liabilities}}{\text{Total equities}}$$

or, by its complement, the *stockholders' equity ratio*:

$$\text{Stockholders' equity ratio} = \frac{\text{Stockholders' equity}}{\text{Total equities}} = 1 - (\text{debt ratio}).$$

Except in extreme circumstances, none of these ratios are as reliable predictors of a firm's ability to pay its liabilities when they mature as one would like. Empirical research indicates that the debt ratio (or related stockholders' equity ratio) may be a better predictor of inability to pay debts than are the current or quick ratios.[13]

Receivables and inventory ratios

The general economic health of a firm is also reflected in the average ages of its receivables and inventories. Most accounts receivable are non-interest bearing; a firm's investment in them is sterile. Even interest-bearing notes receivable often earn interest at lower rates than the rate of profit the firm could earn by investing additional cash in its operations. Accordingly, it is to the firm's advantage to keep its investment in receivables as low as is consistent with whatever are the practices in its industry for granting credit to customers. If it is unable to do this, the explanation may lie in any of several directions, such as inefficiency in collecting amounts owed the firm, or generally unfavorable business conditions within the industry—but this failure is something investors should know about.

Similarly, inventories earn no profits until they are sold; the firm's investment in inventories is also sterile, and management should do its best to make sure that inventories are held to those minimum quantities necessary to fill customer orders and satisfy internal needs for supplies, raw materials, components, and the like, promptly. Moreover, an increase in the amount invested in inventories may be symptomatic of a buildup of obsolete, unsaleable goods.

Some method is needed whereby investors can test for significant changes in the firm's general levels of receivables and inventories. At least three different approaches,

---

[13] For example, see William H. Beaver, "Alternative Accounting Measures as Predictors of Failure," *The Accounting Review* XLIII (January, 1968), pages 113–122.

each related to the others, have evolved. Just as with earnings, the absolute amounts of these assets held by the firm are not as significant as the relationships of these amounts to the firm's overall scale of activities. Accordingly, all three methods compare receivables levels with sales, and inventory levels with cost of goods sold. (The comparisons are *receivables–sales* and *inventories–cost of goods sold* so that like magnitudes are compared with like: the former two both contain an element of profit; the latter two do not.) One method of comparison results in the *receivables-to-sales ratio* and the *inventories-to-goods-sold ratio*:

$$\text{Receivables-to-sales ratio} = \frac{\text{Average receivables}}{\text{Total sales on account}^{[14]}}$$

$$\text{Inventories-to-goods-sold ratio} = \frac{\substack{\text{Average inventories of goods} \\ \text{held for manufacture or sale}}}{\text{Total cost of goods sold}}$$

The reciprocals of these two ratios are often called the receivables and inventory *turnover ratios*. They indicate how many times (on the average) the related asset was exhausted and replenished ("turned over") during the related accounting period.

$$\text{Receivables turnover} = \frac{\text{Total sales on account}}{\text{Average receivables}}$$

$$\text{Inventories turnover} = \frac{\text{Total cost of goods sold}}{\substack{\text{Average inventories of goods} \\ \text{held for manufacture or sale}}}$$

Finally, a third method of comparison yields the *average age of receivables* and the *average age of inventories*:

$$\substack{\text{Average age of} \\ \text{receivables (in days)}} = \left(\substack{\text{Number of days} \\ \text{in period}}\right) \times \left(\frac{\text{End-of-period receivables}}{\text{Total sales on account}}\right)$$

$$\substack{\text{Average age of} \\ \text{inventories (in days)}} = \left(\substack{\text{Number of days} \\ \text{in period}}\right) \times \left(\frac{\substack{\text{End-of-period inventories of goods} \\ \text{held for manufacture or sale}}}{\text{Total cost of goods sold}}\right)$$

Generally speaking, decreases in the turnover ratios and increases in the other four ratios are danger signals or, at minimum, indications that things are happening to the firm's operations that might be of interest to investors.

Example

Summarized 19X4 and 19X5 financial statement data of London Mills Auto Parts Co. are given below. Following these, the firm's debt, receivables, and inventories ratios are calculated.

---

[14] For convenience, the figure for total sales often is substituted here.

		December 31		
		19X5		*19X4*
Cash .	(a)	$ 7,582		
Marketable securities	(b)	56,205		
Accounts receivable	(c)	17,463	(d)	$15,943
Inventories of goods held for sale	(e)	28,639	(f)	26,731
Prepayments and supplies .	(g)	919		
Total current assets .	(h)	$110,808		
Noncurrent assets .	(i)	32,335		
Total assets .	(j)	$143,143		
Current monetary liabilities	(k)	$ 30,484		
Current nonmonetary liabilities	(l)	923		
Total current liabilities .	(m)	$ 31,407		
Noncurrent liabilities .	(n)	14,366		
Total liabilities .	(o)	$ 45,773		
Stockholders' equity	(p)	97,370		
Total equities	(q)	$143,143		
Sales .	(r)	$170,791		
Cost of goods sold .	(s)	81,563		

$$\text{Current ratio} = \frac{(h)}{(m)} = \frac{\$110,808}{\$31,407} \approx \underline{3.5}$$

$$\text{Quick ratio} = \frac{(a) + (b) + (c)}{(m)} = \frac{\$81,250}{\$31,407} \approx \underline{2.6}$$

$$\text{Debt ratio} = \frac{(o)}{(q)} = \frac{\$45,773}{\$143,143} \approx \underline{32\%}$$

$$\text{Stockholders' equity ratio} = \frac{(p)}{(q)} = \frac{\$97,370}{\$143,143} \approx \underline{68\%}$$

$$\text{Receivables-to-sales ratio} = \frac{(c) + (d)}{2(r)} = \frac{\$33,406}{\$341,582} \approx \underline{10\%}$$

$$\text{Inventories-to-goods-sold ratio} = \frac{(e) + (f)}{2(s)} = \frac{\$55,370}{\$163,126} \approx \underline{34\%}$$

$$\text{Receivables turnover} = \frac{2(r)}{(c) + (d)} = \frac{\$341,582}{\$33,406} \approx \underline{10 \text{ times}}$$

$$\text{Inventories turnover} = \frac{2(s)}{(e) + (f)} = \frac{\$163,126}{\$55,370} = \underline{2.9 \text{ times}}$$

$$\text{Average age of receivables} = \frac{365(c)}{(r)} = \frac{\$6,373,995}{\$170,791} \approx \underline{37 \text{ days}}$$

$$\text{Average age of inventories} = \frac{365(e)}{(s)} = \frac{\$10,453,235}{\$81,563} \approx \underline{128 \text{ days}}$$

A final comment on ratios

The significance of ratios depends on their context, as is easily seen with earnings per share. A 30-cent earnings per share will have very different implications if the company's stock is selling in the stock market for $1 a share than if it is selling for $100 a share. What might be an attractive investment in the first case will probably be much less attractive in the second case.

But the same is also true of the all-investor (all-asset) earnings rate and the stockholders' earnings rate. The significance of these ratios depends on other things about the company: What industry is the company in? How risky is its business? (In relatively risk-free industries, such as electric power, a 6 percent rate of return might be considered adequate; in less stable industries it would not be considered adequate.) What has the rate of return been in previous years? Has it been increasing or decreasing? Similar comments might be made concerning the other ratios discussed in this chapter.

In general, all ratios attempt to pack a great deal of information into a single figure. This is a worthwhile endeavor, but the resulting figures often are so *compressed* that they can be misleading without the following additional information:

1. The trend of the ratio in successive periods.
2. Typical behavior of the company's industry.
3. Details of events that affected the company during the year.

Problems for Study and Self-Examination

Problem 9-3:

For each of the three companies shown below, calculate the following ratios:

1. All-investor (all-asset) earnings rate
2. Stockholders' earnings rate
3. Average rate of return to creditors
4. Gross profit ratio
5. Operating ratio
6. Earnings per share

Express all ratios in *annual* terms. If rounding is necessary, round to two significant digits.

	Jones Co.	Scottsboro Co.	Rivers Co.
Length of accounting period	Year	Year	Month
Sales = (a)	$1,600,000	$127,300	$ 180,000
Other revenue = (b)	–0–	16,200	–0–
Total revenue for period = (c)	$1,600,000	$143,500	$ 180,000
Cost of goods sold = (d)	$1,440,000	$ 76,000	$ 127,000
Interest expense = (e)	40,000	2,400	1,350
Other expenses = (f)	104,000	60,000	42,650
Total expenses for period = (g)	$1,584,200	$138,400	$ 171,000

Net income from operations for period = (h) . .	$ 15,800	$ 5,100	$ 9,000
Nonoperating loss = (i)	3,200	–0–	–0–
Net income for period = (j)	$ 12,600	$ 5,100	$ 9,000
Average liabilities during period = (k)	$1,000,000	$ 40,000	$ 900,000
Average stockholders' equity during period = (l) . .	790,000	85,000	1,080,000
Average total equities during period = (m) . . .	$1,790,000	$125,000	$1,980,000
Average number of shares outstanding during period = (n)	3,400	8,000	450,000

Problem 9-4:

For both of the firms shown below calculate the following ratios as of 12/31/X7:
1. Current ratio
2. Quick ratio
3. Debt ratio
4. Stockholders' equity ratio
5. Receivables-to-sales ratio
6. Inventories-to-goods-sold ratio
7. Average age of receivables
8. Average age of inventories
9. Receivables turnover
10. Inventories turnover

If rounding is necessary, round to two significant digits.

	Michel Co.	*Schisler Co.*
Length of accounting period	*Year*	*Year*
Sales—19X7 (a)	$618,799	$22,633
Cost of goods sold—19X7 (b)	382,935	11,336
Current monetary assets—12/31/X7 (c)	$216,633	$ 8,632
Current nonmonetary assets—12/31/X7 (d)	219,649	3,913
Current assets—12/31/X7 (e)	$436,282	$12,545
Receivables—12/31/X7 (f)	$159,592	$ 2,782
Receivables—12/31/X6 (g)	130,909	2,405
Inventories of goods held for sale—12/31/X7 (h)	213,197	3,783
Inventories of goods held for sale—12/31/X6 (i)	191,571	3,081
Current monetary liabilities—12/31/X7 (j)	$129,889	$ 5,889
Current nonmonetary liabilities—12/31/X7 (k)	16,617	–0–
Current liabilities—12/31/X7 (l)	$146,506	$ 5,889
Noncurrent liabilities—12/31/X7 (m)	76,287	338
Total liabilities—12/31/X7 (n)	$222,793	$ 6,227
Stockholders' equity—12/31/X7 (o)	324,018	15,522
Total equities—12/31/X7 (p)	$546,811	$21,749

Solutions

Solution 9-3:

	Jones Co.	Scottsboro Co.	Rivers Co.
1. All-investor (all-asset) earnings rate = ((j) + (e)/(m))	2.9%	6.0%	6.3%
2. Stockholders' earnings rate = (j)/(l)	1.6%	6.0%	10.0%
3. Average rate of return to creditors = (e)/(k)	4.0%	6.0%	1.8%
4. Gross profit ratio = [(a) − (d)/(a)]	10.0%	40.0%	29.0%
5. Operating ratio = (h)/(c)	0.99%	3.6%	5.0%
6. Earnings per share = (j)/(n)	$3.70	$0.64	$0.24

Monthly income statement data were given for Rivers Co.; thus, in ratios 1, 2, 3, and 6, the numerator of the related fraction is also in monthly terms. These four ratios must each be multiplied by 12 in order to express them in annual terms (this has been done above). Ratios 4 and 5 do not require this correction because *both* parts of the fraction are in monthly terms, causing the difference from annual data to cancel out.

The least profitable company (Jones Co.) has the highest earnings per share. Earnings per share depend as much on number of shares outstanding as upon the amount of net income.

Solution 9-4:

	Michel Co.	Schisler Co.
1. Current ratio = (e)/(l).	3.0	2.1
2. Quick ratio = (c)/(l)	1.5	1.5
3. Debt ratio = (n)/(p)	41%	29%
4. Stockholders' equity ratio = (o)/(p).	59%	71%
5. Receivables-to-sales ratio = [(f) + (g)]/2(a)	23%	11%
6. Inventories-to-goods-sold ratio = [(h) + (i)]/2(b) .	53%	30%
7. Average age of receivables = 365(f)/(a).	94 days	45 days
8. Average age of inventories = 365(h)/(b)	203 days	122 days
9. Receivables turnover = 2(a)/[(f) + (g)].	4.3 times	8.7 times
10. Inventories turnover = 2(b)/[(h) + (i)] .	1.9 times	3.3 times

Assignment Problems

Problem 9-A:

Shown below are the comparative balance sheets of Coral Gables Sugar Corp. as of 12/31/X2 and 12/31/X1, the company's 19X2 income statement, and certain other data. For clarity, a minor nonoperating loss has been reported separately on the income statement instead of being included among the firm's expenses while other expense details have been combined and simplified. The last three zeros have been omitted from all figures; you should do likewise in your answer. No unusual balance sheet changes occurred during the year; all changes were of the normal kinds discussed in this and previous chapters.

Prepare the company's 19X2 statement of sources and uses of net working capital. Show all of your calculations. (One possible line of attack in solving this problem would be to prepare the general outline of a funds statement, leaving considerable space between captions, then fill in the details of this statement as you learn them from the problem data, using T-account analysis only where essential. If you emerge with a funds statement entirely consistent with the problem data, do not be concerned with possible balance sheet changes about which you have not been told.)

Coral Gables Sugar Corp.
Balance Sheets
December 31, 19X2 and 19X1
(000 omitted)

	19X2	19X1
Assets		
Current Assets		
Cash and marketable securities	$ 6,940	$ 4,360
Accounts receivable	23,300	20,897
Inventories		
Raw cane sugar	19,499	14,207
Stock in process	4,524	4,442
Finished cane-sugar products	7,572	8,175
Finished beet-sugar products	7,131	2,792
Supplies	11,190	12,226
Prepaid expenses, deferred charges, and deposits	3,844	4,569
Total current assets	$ 84,000	$ 71,668
Plant and Equipment		
Land	$ 8,060	$ 5,837
Buildings and structures	34,983	31,336
Machinery and equipment	91,727	85,722
Total plant and equipment	$134,770	$122,895
	$218,770	$194,563
Liabilities and Shareholders' Investment		
Current Liabilities		
Notes payable	$ 11,604	$ 1,803
Payable to suppliers and others	23,284	21,313
Accrued expenses	5,530	5,117
Federal income taxes	975	1,504
Total current liabilities	$ 41,393	$ 29,737

continued on page 504

Long-term Debt		
4.95% notes	$ 35,520	$ 36,420
5.30% subordinated debentures	40,600	29,600
Total long-term debt	$ 76,120	$ 66,020
Shareholders' Investment		
Capital stock	$ 49,545	$ 49,519
Income retained for use in business	51,712	49,287
Total stockholders' equity	$101,257	$ 98,806
	$218,770	$194,563

Coral Gables Sugar Corp.
Statement of Income, and Income Retained for Use in Business
19X2
(000 omitted)

Net Sales and Operating Revenues	$353,725
Costs and Expenses	
Product costs	$309,991
Selling, general and administrative expenses	25,033
	$335,024
	$ 18,701
Other Income (Expense)	
Interest on long-term debt	(3,641)
Interest and miscellaneous income	86
Income from Operations before Provision for Federal Income Taxes	$ 15,146
Provision for Federal Income Taxes	6,760
Net Income from Operations	$ 8,386
Loss on Sale of Plant and Equipment	495
Net Income	$ 7,891
Dividends declared	(5,466)
Income retained for use in business—1/1/X2	49,287
Income retained for use in business—12/31/X2	$ 51,712

Other data: no capital stock was retired during the year; all capital stock that was issued was purchased by employees under an incentive plan.

No long-term notes were issued and no debentures were retired. No land was sold.

The company's Costs and Expenses included $941 of depreciation on buildings and structures, and $7,008 of depreciation on machinery and equipment.

Purchases of buildings and structures totalled $5,268; machinery and equipment with a book value of $691 was sold during the year. There was a $187 loss on sales of buildings and structures, and a $308 loss on sales of machinery and equipment.

There were no unusual balance sheet changes in 19X2 that you have not been told about.

Problem 9-B:

The 12/31/X2 and 12/31/X1 balance sheets of Coral Gables Sugar Corp. and the company's 19X2 income statement are given in Problem 9-A, those of Instance, Inc., are given below. Compute the ratios indicated below for both companies.

You may assume that Coral Gables Sugar Corp. had an average of 7,071,000 shares of capital stock outstanding during 19X2, and that Instance, Inc., had an average of 107,500 shares of capital stock outstanding in 19X2. Coral Gables Sugar Corp.'s sales totalled $350,212,000; its cost of goods sold totalled $267,104,000.

Round all ratios to two significant digits, except for earnings per share (which should be calculated to the nearest penny).

1. 19X2 all-investor earnings rate
2. 19X2 rate of return to stockholders
3. 19X2 rate of return to creditors
4. 19X2 gross profit ratio
5. 19X2 operating ratio
6. 19X2 earnings per share
7. 12/31/X2 current ratio
8. 12/31/X2 quick ratio
9. 12/31/X2 debt ratio
10. 12/31/X2 stockholders' equity ratio
11. 19X2 receivables turnover
12. 19X2 inventories turnover
13. 12/31/X2 average age of receivables
14. 12/31/X2 average age of inventories

Assume that the capital stock of these two companies is selling for approximately the same price per share. Which company appears to be the better stock investment? Justify your answer. What else would you like to know to answer this question?

Instance, Inc.
Comparative Balance Sheets
December 31, 19X1 and 19X2
(000 omitted)

Assets

	December 31	
	19X1	*19X2*
Current Assets:		
Cash	$ 100	$ 229
Accounts Receivable	368	358
Merchandise Inventory	570	460
Supplies	37	24
Total Current Assets	$1,075	$1,071
Noncurrent Assets:		
Land	$ 140	$ 163
Buildings	260	194
Store Equipment	720	740
Delivery Equipment	170	144
Total Noncurrent Assets	$1,290	$1,241
Total Assets	$2,365	$2,312

continued on page 506

Equities

Current Liabilities:

Accounts Payable	$ 676	$ 496
Taxes Payable	112	103
Interest Payable	16	15
Dividends Payable	20	40
Total Current Liabilities	$ 824	$ 654

Noncurrent Liabilities:

Bonds Payable	$ 392	$ 371
Long-Term Notes Payable	100	100
Total Noncurrent Liabilities	$ 492	$ 471
Total Liabilities	$1,316	$1,125

Stockholders' Equity:

Capital Stock	$1,000	$1,153
Retained Earnings	49	34
Total Stockholders' Equity	$1,049	$1,187
Total Equities	$2,365	$2,312

Instance, Inc.
Income Statement
For 19X2
(000 omitted)

Revenues:

Sales		$6,200

Expenses:

Cost of Goods Sold	$4,070	
Salaries Expense	1,125	
Supplies Expense	57	
Utilities Expense	180	
Consulting Services Expense	153	
Depreciation Expense	253	
Taxes Expense	207	
Interest Expense	23	6,068
Net Income from Operations		$ 132

Non-Operating Gains and Losses:

Loss on Sale of Buildings	$ 18	
Gain on Sale of Store Equipment	6	12
Net Income		$ 120
Dividends		135
Decrease in Retained Earnings		$ (15)
Retained Earnings—12/31/X1		49
Retained Earnings—12/31/X2		$ 34

Problem 9-C:

Shown below are the comparative balance sheets of Pepper Enterprises for 12/31/X3 and 12/31/X2, the company's 19X3 income statement, and certain other data. For clarity, nonoperating gains and losses are reported separately on the income statement. The last three zeros have been eliminated from all figures reported; you should do likewise in your answer. No unusual balance sheet changes occurred during the year; instead, all changes were of the normal kinds discussed in this and previous chapters, and in the notes to the balance sheet of this firm. Prepare the company's 19X3 funds statement. Show all of your calculations. (One possible line of attack in solving this problem would be to prepare the general outline of a funds statement, leaving considerable space between captions, then fill in the details of this statement as you learn them from the problem data, using T-account analysis only where essential. If you emerge with a funds statement entirely consistent with the problem data, do not be concerned with possible balance sheet changes about which you have not been told.)

Pepper Enterprises
Comparative Balance Sheets
(In Thousands)
12/31/X3 and 12/31/X2

Assets	19X3	19X2
Current Assets:		
Cash and marketable securities	$ 6,029	$ 4,202
Receivables	27,118	27,725
Inventories	29,061	33,153
Prepaid expenses, deposits, etc.	1,016	925
Total current assets	63,224	66,005
Property:		
Land	4,170	2,832
Buildings and improvements	8,851	8,449
Machinery and equipment	48,925	47,454
Patents and license agreements	1,410	1,658
Total property	63,356	60,393
Total	126,580	126,398

Liabilities	19X3	19X2
Current Liabilities:		
Notes payable—banks	3,446	5,795
Current maturities of long-term debt	1,280	1,842
Accounts payable	6,932	5,951
Income taxes payable	3,052	3,719
Accrued expenses	11,250	9,101
Total current liabilities	25,960	26,408
Long-Term Debt	16,650	29,125
Stockholders' Equity:		
Common stock	66,567	60,595
Retained earnings	17,403	10,270
Total stockholders' equity	83,970	70,865
Total	$126,580	$126,398

Notes:
   The financial statement form employed by this company differs from the one used in the text.

(continued on page 508)

The company's long-term debt has various maturity dates. Each year, some of this debt becomes due. At the end of each year, the company transfers the amount that must be paid next year (which thus has become a current liability) from long-term debt to the current liability "Current maturities of long-term debt." These transfers amounted to $1,280 at 12/31/X3. In addition, $11,195 of long-term debt was called in for advance redemption in 19X3. The company paid a $336 call premium (penalty) for the right to retire this debt in advance of its maturity, paying a total of $11,531.

The company describes accrued current liabilities as "accrued expenses."

The company's inventories included supplies totalling $827 at 12/31/X3 and $614 at 12/31/X2.

Pepper Enterprises
Statement of Income
(In Thousands)
For the Year Ended 12/31/X3

Net Revenues		$173,936
Costs and Expenses		
Cost of sales and services	$133,057	
Depreciation and amortization expense	12,577	
Interest expense	1,933	
Other expenses	11,806	159,373
Operating Income before Income Taxes		14,563
Provision for Income Taxes		5,635
Operating Income		8,928
Nonoperating Gains and Losses		
Loss on retirement of long-term debt	336	
Loss on sale of machinery	181	
	517	
Gain on sale of patents	428	89
Net Income		8,839
Dividends		(1,706)
Retained earnings—12/31/X2		10,270
Retained earnings—12/31/X3		$ 17,403

Other data: the company's costs and expenses include depreciation of buildings and improvements totalling $645, depreciation of machinery and equipment totalling $11,744, and amortization of patents and license agreements totalling $188. Costs of sales and services includes $10,320 of costs of services performed for customers.

There were no sales of land, buildings, or improvements, and no purchases of patents and license agreements during the year. No long-term debt was issued during the year; no common stock was retired. All purchases of properties were made on account.

Patents that were almost fully amortized on 12/31/X2 and that had originally cost the company $227 became fully amortized at the ends of their legal lives, and expired during the year. Other patents (whose book value is deliberately not given) were sold.

Machinery and equipment that had a book value of $428 was sold during the year (the cost of machinery and equipment purchased during the year is deliberately not given).

There were no unusual balance sheet changes during the year that you have not been told about.

Problem 9-D:

Refer to the data in Problem 9-C. You may assume that Pepper Enterprises had an average of 1,271,000 shares of common stock outstanding during 19X3. Calculate the ratios indicated below. Express these ratios as fractions instead of dividing them out (for instance, the meaningless ratio of receivables to inventories should be given as 27,118/29,061, not as 0.93+).

1. 19X3 all-investor earnings rate
2. 19X3 rate of return to stockholders
3. 19X3 rate of return to creditors
4. 19X3 gross profit ratio
5. 19X3 operating ratio
6. 19X3 earnings per share
7. 12/31/X3 current ratio
8. 12/31/X3 quick ratio
9. 12/31/X3 debt ratio
10. 12/31/X3 stockholders' equity ratio
11. 19X3 receivables-to-sales ratio
12. 19X3 inventories-to-goods-sold ratio
13. 12/31/X3 average age of receivables
14. 12/31/X3 average age of inventories

Problem 9-E:

Some of the 19X1 balance sheet changes of Nadir Caves Souvenir Shoppe were discussed in Chapters Four and Eight. This company sells curios. It has no noncurrent assets; instead, it rents its store building and equipment from the owners of the cave. The rental fee covers all costs except those of the curios themselves, supplies, salaries, and taxes.

By 19X3, the company was paying rent of $250 per day (in the form of an entire month's rent at the beginning of each month) during the tourist season. Shown below is certain information relating to the company's operations for June, 19X3.

All sales are for cash; $165 of supplies were purchased for cash; all other supplies and merchandise were purchased on account. Salaries and taxes are always recorded as a liability before being paid; no taxes were paid during the month, but $820 of salaries were paid during the month. Dividends totalling $1,600 were declared and paid during the month.

After the accounts had been ruled and balanced at the end of the month, debits to cash totalled $31,350, and credits to supplies totalled $1,089; that is, the two T-accounts had the forms:

Cash		Supplies	
31,350			1,089

Nadir Caves Souvenir Shoppe
Comparative Balance Sheets
5/31/X3 and 6/30/X3

Assets		6/30/X3	5/31/X3
Cash		$ 9,672	$ 8,608
Merchandise		11,091	10,323
Supplies		497	876
Total Assets		$21,260	$19,807

Equities			
Accounts Payable		$ 7,402	$ 7,300
Salaries Payable		85	165
Estimated Taxes Payable		2,206	1,012
Capital Stock		10,000	10,000
Retained Earnings		1,567	1,330
Total Equities		$21,260	$19,807

There were no unusual balance sheet changes during the month; instead, all changes were of the normal kinds discussed in this and previous chapters. You have been told (directly or indirectly) all that you need to know in order to solve this problem. Prepare the company's income statement for June, 19X3. (One possible line of attack in solving this problem would begin by organizing its data into T-accounts.)

Problem 9-F:

Problem 7-K (pages 386–389) gives the comparative balance sheets of Simplified Textiles, Inc. at 12/31/X5 and 12/31/X6, together with the company's summary journal entries for 19X6. Three zeros have been omitted from all figures; you should do likewise in your answer.

Prepare a statement of sources and uses of net current monetary accounts (a net-quick-assets funds statement). You may assume that "miscellaneous current assets" are nonmonetary. Use the "subtraction" method to determine funds from operations.

Problem 9-G:

Shown below, in comparative form, are the 19X7 income statements of Bennett Enterprises and Jacksonville Corporation. For simplicity, information about changes in retained earnings has been omitted, and many expense details have been combined.

	Bennett Enterprises		Jacksonville Corporation	
Sales		$5,073,268		$5,102,919
Cost of Goods Sold		3,845,019		3,581,096
Gross Margin		$1,228,249		$1,521,823
Depreciation Expense	$714,267		$207,990	
Other Expenses	470,770	1,185,037	976,732	1,184,722
Net Income		$ 43,212		$ 337,101

The two companies had approximately equal average total assets and approximately the same average stockholders' equity during 19X7. Mr. Claude D. Fascell, a stockholder in both companies, made the following observation:

"I know that, on first glance, the Bennett Enterprises report looks poor, by comparison with the Jacksonville Corporation report. But there's a big difference between the two companies. Bennett uses a lot less labor and a lot more machinery in its operations than Jacksonville does. Bennett had total depreciation charges of $714,267 during 19X7; Jacksonville's depreciation totalled only $207,990. That means that Bennett Enterprises had a cash flow of $757,479, compared with Jacksonville Corporation's cash flow of only $545,091. Now, I know that cash flow income isn't quite the same as regular income, but it certainly counts for *something*—especially when the difference is as great as it is here."

Comment. Defend your comments.

Problem 9-H:

As part of your training in accounting, you must become able to extend what you have learned into new situations. This problem provides such an opportunity to increase your flexibility and broaden your understanding. The text provides all background information needed to solve this problem, but the circumstances described will be unfamiliar. Apply what you already have learned to this new situation.

Examples are given in the text of situations in which it is more appropriate to obtain one's information about an entity's success by looking at the funds from operations portion of a funds statement than by looking at an income statement. Most municipal governments prepare what effectively is either a cash statement or a funds statement, as a report upon their operations (instead of preparing an income statement as a report upon their operations). Why? Try to give more than just the first, obvious answer.

Problem 9-I:

Pages 358–361 and 365–368 show how the Campus Store statement of sources and uses of net working capital for the year ended 6/30/X5 was constructed. In particular, the firm's narrative summary of balance sheet changes is on pages 360–361 and its simple summary journal entries on page 365.

Suppose that instead you wished to construct a statement of sources and uses of net current monetary accounts. What would be *different* from the previous net-working-capital funds statement in this net-quick-assets funds statement—besides the changes in the heading?

Don't prepare the net-quick-assets funds statement; just indicate the differences.

Problem 9-J:

As part of your training in accounting, you must become able to extend the concepts and techniques you have learned into situations that require different methods of analysis. This problem provides an opportunity to increase your flexibility and broaden your understanding. The background needed to solve this problem has been provided by the text, but the particular method of analysis required may at first seem unusual. Apply what you already have learned to this new situation.

Shown below is information concerning the operations of Middletown Enterprises for ten weeks during 19X4. All of the company's sales are made on account. For simplicity, you may assume that the company collects 70% of its sales four weeks after they are made, and the other 30% of its sales six weeks after they are made. The company buys all of its inventories on account and pays for them three weeks after they are purchased. All "other expenses" are paid in cash during the week incurred.

Prepare comparative cash statements and comparative income statements for the weeks seven, eight, nine, and ten. Omit beginning and ending balances of Cash and Retained Earnings. An example of the appropriate form for such statements is given below. Discuss the relationship between the cash statements and the income statements in this simplified example.

Middletown Enterprises
Comparative Statements of Sources and Uses of Cash
Weeks Seven Through Ten

	Week Seven	Week Eight	Week Nine	Week Ten
Cash from Operations:				
Receipts:				
Collections on Account	$XXX	$XXX	$XXX	$XXX
Expenditures:				
Payments for Inventories	$XXX	$XXX	$XXX	$XXX
Other Expenditures	XXX	XXX	XXX	XXX
Total	$XXX	$XXX	$XXX	$XXX
Net Increase (Decrease) in Cash	$XXX	$XXX	$XXX	$XXX

Week	Sales	Cost of Goods Sold	Purchases of Inventories	Depreciation Expense	Other Expenses
One	$50,000	$30,000	$32,000	$4,000	$10,000
Two	55,000	33,000	37,000	4,000	10,000
Three	60,000	36,000	38,000	4,000	11,000
Four	65,000	39,000	46,000	4,000	12,000
Five	75,000	45,000	53,000	4,000	12,500
Six	90,000	54,000	46,000	4,000	14,000
Seven	75,000	45,000	38,000	4,000	16,000
Eight	65,000	39,000	37,000	4,000	13,000
Nine	60,000	36,000	32,000	4,000	12,500
Ten	55,000	33,000	31,000	4,000	12,000

Problem 9-K:

As part of your training in accounting, you must become able to extend what you have learned into new situations. This problem provides such an opportunity to increase your flexibility and broaden your understanding. The text provides all background information needed to solve this problem, but the circumstances described will be unfamiliar. Apply what you already have learned to this new situation.

In 1925, the Herlong Corporation paid $19,800,000 for a 99-year lease on a building site in Manhattan (such leases were common during this period). The company has been amortizing this lease at a rate of $19,800,000 ÷ 99 = $200,000 per year. In 19X1, the company's net income (after all expenses, including the $200,000 amortization) was $175,319. Mr. A. Sydney Rogers, one of the stockholders of the Herlong Corporation, makes the following observations to you:

"I don't mind charging off depreciation as an expense. Sure, depreciation doesn't mean that you're out of pocket—you know, you don't have to pay any cash for it. But the accountant's got to keep his books balanced, and I can see why he's got to do *something* with the depreciation.

"However, I sort of draw the line at this amortization of the lease. By the time that that lease runs out, I'm going to be long dead. And, the way things are going, the whole country will have turned Socialist by then, anyhow!"

Comment. Defend your comments. Are there any misconceptions in Mr. Rogers' remarks? Is amortization appropriate when the period of amortization extends beyond an individual's time horizon?

Part IV

Refinements and Complications

Ten

Nominal and Valuation Accounts

Nominal Accounts

The last several chapters have shown how journals and ledgers can be used as devices for accumulating and classifying financial accounting information and preparing various financial statements. Chapter Four characterized this system as "hand operated" (see footnote on page 200). This is a fair description, for despite the use of accounting machines to speed along repetitive parts of the job, the kind of accounting described in this book is largely carried out by hand. With pen and ink, someone has to write down the entries that go into the journal, and then physically post these entries to the different accounts in the ledger.

Hand-operated accounting systems are now technologically obsolete, for more and more companies are using computers to accumulate and classify their financial accounting data.[1] Computerized financial accounting systems have proved much more efficient and better adapted to preparing special reports than hand-operated systems. Unless you work for a fairly small company, you may never even *see* a hand-operated system.

So far, this hasn't caused any difficulties since the primary concern in this book has been to show what the accountant reports on financial statements. How the

---

[1] Even companies that are not yet using computers are making increasing use of book-keeping machines, unit record equipment, and other mechanized methods for recording and summarizing accounting data.

accountant accumulates and classifies data has been studied only to the extent necessary to explain how the accountant develops financial statements. Thus the discussion has ignored data-processing techniques that would be discussed in a more traditional text. Here's the reasoning behind this simplified approach:

1. It's much easier for most students to see what is going on in a hand-operated system than in a computerized system.

2. The characteristics of the hand-operated system parallel those of most computerized systems, so by studying a hand-operated system you are also learning what happens in a computerized system.

This chapter, however, is a partial exception to this, for it explains something invented by accountants to help them keep track of the significance of data being processed through hand-operated (and partially mechanized) systems. There are still parallels to this invention in computerized systems, but it's much more important in hand-operated systems. This invention gives changes in the retained earnings account special memorandum names to remind the accountant why the change occurred. In practice, this is done by substituting a variety of specially named accounts called "nominal accounts" for the retained earnings account. Here are three reasons for becoming familiar with nominal accounts:

1. Accountants think in terms of nominal accounts. The computer has become important in accounting only since the 1950s. Most accountants have been trained in hand-operated systems that use nominal accounts. Most writing on accounting matters is conducted in nominal-account language.

2. Nominal accounts are convenient. Their use will speed up the exposition in later chapters.

3. Nominal accounts are related to another invention that is very helpful in financial statements—an invention called "valuation accounts."

The basic framework of financial accounting has been presented in the last nine chapters.[2] Nominal accounts are not as fundamental to accounting as the balance sheet accounts you have studied up to now. However, such refinements can be important—as a parallel, the basic problems of automobile design had all been solved by World War I, but a modern car is much better than a 1914 model.

Illustration 10-1 shows the 19X2 retained earnings ledger account of Instance, Inc., together with the simple summary journal entries that affected it. (The underlying data for this illustration come from Illustrations 7-1 and 7-2, pages 338 and 339.) For the moment, try to forget what you remember of the company's balance sheet changes and look at these entries with fresh eyes. Suppose you wish to prepare an income statement from this information, or that you simply want to learn about some aspect of the company's 19X2 operations, and that the 19X2 income statement hasn't yet been prepared (either because it's still 19X2 or because it's early in 19X3 and the time-consuming job of preparing statements hasn't been completed).

---

[2] The only major exception to this is the material on manufacturing accounting in Chapter Twelve. Actually, we've even discussed the basic ideas of manufacturing accounting in earlier chapters, without labeling the discussion as such (see, for example, the discussion on page 48, in which the cost of shelves included the wages of the employee who constructed them).

Illustration 10-1

Instance, Inc.
*19X2 Journal Entries Affecting Retained Earnings
and Related Ledger Account*

	Increase				*Decrease*		
2. Accounts Receivable	6,200			3. Retained Earnings	4,070		
Retained Earnings		6,200		Merchandise Inventory		4,070	
12b. Store Equipment	6			4. Retained Earnings	1,125		
Retained Earnings		6		Cash		1,125	
				6. Retained Earnings	57		
				Supplies		57	
				7. Retained Earnings	180		
				Accounts Payable		180	
				8. Retained Earnings	153		
				Cash		153	
				9. Retained Earnings	18		
				Buildings		18	
				10. Retained Earnings	144		
				Store Equipment		144	
				11. Retained Earnings	91		
				Delivery Equipment		91	
				13b. Retained Earnings	18		
				Buildings		18	
				14. Retained Earnings	207		
				Taxes Payable		207	
				15. Retained Earnings	23		
				Interest Payable		23	
				16. Retained Earnings	135		
				Dividends Payable		135	

Retained Earnings

(3)	4,070	√		49
(4)	1,125	(2)		6,200
(6)	57	(12b)		6
(7)	180			
(8)	153			
(9)	18			
(10)	144			
(11)	91			
(13b)	18			
(14)	207			
(15)	23			
(16)	135			
√	34			
	6,255			6,255
		√		34

Unless you have been given additional information, the retained earnings ledger account will not be very useful to you, nor would much of the journal. You *could* guess that Entry 6 refers to supplies expense:

> 6. Retained Earnings   57
>   Supplies   57

But what is the significance of an entry like Entry 7?

> 7. Retained Earnings   180
>   Accounts Payable   180

If you go back to the original information, you discover that the $180 is utilities expense. Yet it's a nuisance to have to keep going back to the original information.

Besides, remember that the information shown in Illustration 10-1 is *summary* information for the year. It summarizes what may have been thousands of day-by-day journal entries. If a company actually used the system presented in this book to record changes in retained earnings, its journal and ledger would be very uninformative during the year, and very hard to summarize at the end of the year. Imagine trying to prepare an income statement at the end of the year when confronted with a retained earnings ledger account containing hundreds of unexplained figures, and a journal containing hundreds or thousands of opaque entries like the following:

Retained Earnings	XXX		Retained Earnings	XXX	
Cash		XXX	Accounts Payable		XXX

We've been able to get away with this so far because examples have been kept simple and have dealt only with summary entries. But as soon as the situation becomes realistically complicated, we no longer can manage without some way of labeling retained earnings entries. As was indicated on page 411, accountants have developed a practical solution to this problem, which it now is time to discuss.

A change occurs in retained earnings because some asset or liability changes. If an increase in an asset or a decrease in a liability is involved, the change in retained earnings reflects some specific kind of revenue or gain. If an asset decreases or a liability increases, the change in retained earnings reflects some specific kind of expense, loss, or dividend. If you make retained earnings entries the way we've been making them, the specific information about the *kind* of revenue, gain, expense, or loss is often sacrificed. You've already seen that Entry 7 throws away the information that the change in retained earnings involves a utility expense. Consider Entry 4:

4. Retained Earnings	1,125	
Cash		1,125

There is nothing in this entry to indicate that a salaries expense is involved. Consider Entry 8:

8. Retained Earnings	153	
Cash		153

A consulting services expense is involved here, but from all you can tell, this might just as well be a payment of sales commissions.

Memorandum titles

One way to escape these ambiguities is to add some memorandum information to the journal entries. For example, a few words might be added to the retained earnings title to indicate why retained earnings changed:

4. Retained Earnings—Salaries Expense	1,125	
Cash		1,125
7. Retained Earnings—Utilities Expense	180	
Accounts Payable		180
8. Retained Earnings—Consulting Services Expense	153	
Cash		153

All this does is to *label* each appearance of retained earnings with the description of the change that would appear on an income statement. Entry 4 might be a summary entry for hundreds of salaries expense entries made during the year. At the end of the year, there would be no difficulty in bringing all salaries expense entries together, for they all would show debits to "retained earnings—salaries expense." If, during the year, someone were curious to know the total of salaries expense for the year, he could simply run a quick adding-machine tape of all entries labeled "retained earnings—salaries expense." Even better, the accountant could make up a special ledger account called "retained earnings—salaries expense," and post all such entries to it. Once the accountant began labeling some retained earnings entries with additional memorandum information, it would be natural to label them all. This would eliminate any possibility of confusion. Illustration 10-2 does just that.

Illustration 10-2

Instance, Inc.
19X2 Journal Entries Affecting Retained Earnings
Causal Explanations Added for Retained Earnings Changes

2.	Accounts Receivable	6,200	
	Retained Earnings—Sales		6,200
3.	Retained Earnings—Cost of Goods Sold	4,070	
	Merchandise Inventory		4,070
4.	Retained Earnings—Salaries Expense	1,125	
	Cash		1,125
6.	Retained Earnings—Supplies Expense	57	
	Supplies		57
7.	Retained Earnings—Utilities Expense	180	
	Accounts Payable		180
8.	Retained Earnings—Consulting Services Expense	153	
	Cash		153
9.	Retained Earnings—Depreciation Expense	18	
	Buildings		18
10.	Retained Earnings—Depreciation Expense	144	
	Store Equipment		144
11.	Retained Earnings—Depreciation Expense	91	
	Delivery Equipment		91
12b.	Store Equipment	6	
	Retained Earnings—Gain on Sale of Store Equipment		6
13b.	Retained Earnings—Loss on Sale of Buildings	18	
	Buildings		18
14.	Retained Earnings—Taxes Expense	207	
	Taxes Payable		207
15.	Retained Earnings—Interest Expense	23	
	Interest Payable		23
16.	Retained Earnings—Dividends	135	
	Dividends Payable		135

Each change in retained earnings is accompanied by an appropriate descriptive caption. These captions are identical with the language used to describe the different changes on the income statement.

As remarked earlier, accountants have developed a special language for income statement captions. For instance, accountants say "salaries expense" instead of "salaries expenditure." All of the descriptive captions used in Illustration 10-2 are uniquely income statement captions. In turn, an income statement is one that reports changes in retained earnings. Illustration 10-2 accompanies each change in retained earnings with a descriptive caption used only for retained earnings changes.

This means that you don't have to say "retained earnings"! The descriptive caption is used *only* for retained earnings changes. If you use such a caption and also say "retained earnings," you are just repeating yourself, so you might as well save space and effort by using only the descriptive caption. For example, you can write Entry 4 as:

4. Salaries Expense	1,125	
Cash		1,125

Anyone familiar with income statements knows that "salaries expense" is an income statement caption. He *knows* that income statements are reports of changes in retained earnings and that this entry means a debit to retained earnings and a credit to cash. Similarly, Entry 7 can be written:

7. Utilities Expense	180	
Accounts Payable		180

Anyone familiar with income statements knows that this entry is the equivalent of:

7. Retained Earnings—Utilities Expense	180	
Accounts Payable		180

The words "utilities expense" form an income statement caption implying retained earnings. Similarly, you can write Entry 8 as simply:

8. Consulting Service Expense	153	
Cash		153

Special names

What we're doing here is giving different kinds of changes in retained earnings different names. There's nothing very unusual about doing this. Consider a parallel case; imagine an accounting professor whose legal name is John Hamilton Doe. Professor Doe may have a variety of additional names to go with the various different roles he plays in the world. To his children, he is "Daddy" and "Pop." To his wife, he usually is "Honey." To his next door neighbor, he is "Jack." To his older brother, he is "Ham" (a name he dislikes intensely and has been trying to escape for years). To his mother-in-law, he is "John." To the secretaries at the university he is "Dr. Doe." To some of his students, he is "Professor Doe." To his lodge brothers, he is "Grand Exalted Alligator." In each different role, John Hamilton Doe is called a different name.

Much the same thing is happening here with retained earnings. Each different kind of change in retained earnings is called a different name—a name that, in this case, stems from an income statement caption. You substitute the descriptive name for the words "retained earnings." As a result, instead of one retained earnings account, you have a whole set of descriptive-name accounts—salaries expense, utility expense, dividend income. Call these descriptive-name accounts *nominal accounts*.

When Professor Doe is called Daddy, Jack, and Grand Exalted Alligator, he is still John Hamilton Doe. Similarly, when changes in retained earnings are called by a variety of nominal account titles, they are still changes in retained earnings. It's very important to remember this. Up until now, all account titles have referred to different assets and equities. Call these *balance sheet account titles* to distinguish them from *nominal account titles*. "Cash" does not refer to the same asset as "supplies"; "accounts payable" does not refer to the same equity as "wages payable." But nominal accounts are different: for instance, "salaries expense," "utility expense," and "dividend income" all refer to just *one* equity—retained earnings. If you forget this, you'll be tempted to think of nominal accounts the way you think of balance sheet accounts and develop a confused impression that nominal accounts refer to different assets and equities. They don't. "Supplies expense" is not supplies (or a decrease in supplies); instead, it is a name for a change in retained earnings that reflects a particular kind of decrease in supplies (one occurring as a cost of the revenues recognized during the period). Salaries expense is *not* the salaries themselves, but a name for a change in retained earnings that reflects the cash paid (or the liability incurred) for salaries.

Illustration 10-3 shows all of Instance, Inc.'s 19X2 balance sheet changes, with those involving retained earnings written in nominal account style and marked with a star. Before going any further, be sure that you understand all starred entries. The rest of the entries do not involve retained earnings and are unchanged from the way they originally appeared in Illustration 7-2 (pages 339–340).

Illustration 10-3

Instance, Inc.
Simple Summary Journal Entries for 19X2
Nominal Accounts Used for Retained Earnings Changes

1.	Merchandise Inv.	3,960		*11.	Depreciation Expense	91	
	Accounts Payable		3,960		Delivery Equipment		91
*2.	Accounts Receivable	6,200		12a.	Cash	42	
	Sales		6,200		Store Equipment		42
*3.	Cost of Goods Sold	4,070		*12b.	Store Equipment	6	
	Merchandise Inv.		4,070		Gain on Sale of Store		
*4.	Salaries Expense	1,125			Equipment		6
	Cash		1,125		13a.	Cash	30
5.	Supplies	44			Buildings		30
	Accounts Payable		44	*13b.	Loss on Sale of Buildings	18	
*6.	Supplies Expense	57			Buildings		18
	Supplies		57	*14.	Taxes Expense	207	
*7.	Utilities Expense	180			Taxes Payable		207
	Accounts Payable		180	*15.	Interest Expense	23	
*8.	Consulting Services				Interest Payable		23
	Expense	153		*16.	Dividends	135	
	Cash		153		Dividends Payable		135
*9.	Depreciation Expense	18		17.	Cash	153	
	Buildings		18		Capital Stock		153
*10.	Depreciation Expense	144		18.	Bonds Payable	21	
	Store Equipment		144		Cash		21

(continued on page 524)

19.	Cash	6,210		23.	Dividends Payable	115	
	Accounts Receivable		6,210		Cash		115
20.	Accounts Payable	4,452		24.	Delivery Equipment	65	
	Cash		4,452		Accounts Payable		65
21.	Taxes Payable	216		25.	Store Equipment	200	
	Cash		216		Cash		200
22.	Interest Payable	24		26.	Land	23	
	Cash		24		Accounts Payable		23

* Nominal account.

Problem for Study and Self-Examination

Problem 10-1:

A narrative summary of the balance sheet changes of Nadir Caves Souvenir Shoppe for the period May 1–7, 19X1, is given below. Make all necessary journal entries. Use appropriate nominal accounts corresponding to the captions on the company's income statements (sales, cost of goods sold, rent expense, supplies expense).

Nadir Caves Souvenir Shoppe
Narrative Summary of Balance Sheet Changes
May 1–7, 19X1

1. Stockholders invested $10,000, cash.
2. The company prepaid one month's rent of $6,000.
3. The company purchased $3,000 of curios for cash.
4. The company bought an additional $6,500 of curios on account.
5. The company bought $800 of supplies on account.
6. Sales to customers totalled $3,950; all sales were for cash.
7. The curios sold in Change 6 had cost the company $1,900.
8. The company paid $4,200 of its accounts payable.
9. Prepaid rent of $1,400 expired.
10. Supplies that had cost the company $117 were consumed.

Solution

Solution 10-1:

1. Cash	10,000			6. Cash	3,950		
Capital Stock		10,000		Sales		3,950	
2. Prepaid Rent	6,000			7. Cost of Goods Sold	1,900		
Cash		6,000		Merchandise Inventory		1,900	
3. Merchandise Inventory	3,000			8. Accounts Payable	4,200		
Cash		3,000		Cash		4,200	
4. Merchandise Inventory	6,500			9. Rent Expense	1,400		
Accounts Payable		6,500		Prepaid Rent		1,400	
5. Supplies	800			10. Supplies Expense	117		
Accounts Payable		800		Supplies		117	

Nominal Accounts
in the Ledger; Closing Entries

Up until now, you have used the ledger to classify and organize balance sheet changes, and you may continue to do this, adding a set of nominal accounts to the balance sheet accounts. Take Nadir Caves Souvenir Shoppe, May 1–7, 19X1, as the example. Here's how you have been showing the company's ledger:

		Cash					*Supplies*					*Capital Stock*	
(1)	10,000	(2)	6,000		(5)	800	(10)	117				(1)	10,000
(6)	3,950	(3)	3,000										
		(8)	4,200				*Prepaid Rent*					*Retained Earnings*	

		Merchandise Inventory			(2)	6,000	(9)	1,400		(7)	1,900	(6)	3,950
(3)	3,000	(7)	1,900							(9)	1,400		
(4)	6,500						*Accounts Payable*			(10)	117		
					(8)	4,200	(4)	6,500					
							(5)	800					

The use of nominal accounts involves splitting up and labeling the changes recorded in the retained earnings account as follows:

Retained Earnings

	Cost of Goods Sold			*Sales*	
(7)	1,900			(6)	3,950
	Rent Expense				
(9)	1,400				
	Supplies Expense				
(10)	117				

After adding nominal accounts, the ledger of Nadir Caves Souvenir Shoppe would look like this on May 7, 19X1, just before the financial statements are prepared:

Cash				*Prepaid Rent*				*Sales*		
(1)	10,000	(2)	6,000	(2)	6,000	(9)	1,400		(6)	3,950
(6)	3,950	(3)	3,000							
		(8)	4,200	*Accounts Payable*				*Cost of Goods Sold*		
Merchandise Inventory				(6)	4,200	(4)	6,500	(7)	1,900	
						(5)	800			
(3)	3,000	(7)	1,900					*Rent Expense*		
(4)	6,500			*Capital Stock*						
						(1)	10,000	(9)	1,400	
Supplies										
				Retained Earnings				*Supplies Expense*		
(5)	800	(10)	117					(10)	117	

There was no beginning balance in retained earnings for this first period, so, the retained earnings ledger account is temporarily empty. (Usually it would contain the beginning balance.) To summarize, nominal accounts were invented as a way to organize and label retained earnings changes so that (1) preparation of income statements would be easier, and (2) information about specific kinds of retained earnings changes would be easily available *during* the accounting period, before the income statement is prepared.[3]

Once the income statement has been prepared, these reasons no longer apply and nominal accounts become unnecessary. Besides, to prepare the balance sheet, you need one figure for retained earnings, not several. Consequently, you must find a way to transfer back to the parent retained earnings account the information that has been split off into nominal accounts. Here's one way to do this:

Retained Earnings			
(7)	1,900	(6)	3,950
(9)	1,400		
(10)	117		

The main objection to transferring the retained earnings information in this way is that doing so violates a basic rule of bookkeeping. Paralleling the conventions discussed on page 244, *a ledger account balance can be changed only by making a journal*

---

[3] You might ask: "Why wasn't a similar set of nominal accounts set up for funds statements?" Probably there are two main reasons that nominal accounts were not invented for funds statements: (1) The labeling would be much more complicated with funds statements; more than one account is involved, so you couldn't do the equivalent of leaving out the words "Retained Earnings." (2) Funds statements have been recognized as important only in recent years; thus there hasn't been time for nominal accounts to develop.

entry, and posting it to the ledger. You must invent journal entries that will reduce the nominal accounts to zero balances and transfer all the information they contain back to the retained earnings account. This is very easily done. Consider, for example, the sales account:

	Sales	
	(6)	3,950

You want to end up with a zero balance in sales, while showing a $3,950 credit to retained earnings. To make the balance in sales zero, all you need to do is *debit* sales for $3,950. To show a $3,950 credit to retained earnings, *credit* retained earnings for $3,950. Here is how this journal entry looks:

I. Sales	3,950	
Retained Earnings		3,950[4]

This changes the ledger accounts to:

Retained Earnings		*Sales*	
I. 3,950	I. 3,950	(6) 3,950

Similarly, consider cost of goods sold:

Cost of Goods Sold	
(7) 1,900	

To end up with a zero balance in this account while showing the $1,900 as a reduction to retained earnings, simply *credit* cost of goods sold and *debit* retained earnings:

II. Retained Earnings	1,900	
Cost of Goods Sold		1,900

This changes the ledger accounts to:

Retained Earnings		*Cost of Goods Sold*	
II. 1,900	I. 3,950	(7) 1,900	II. 1,900

Admittedly, this is an odd way to transfer information. You move a figure from place X to place Y by putting the *opposite* of that figure in place X and the figure itself in place Y.

---

[4] My wife proofread this book for me while it was in manuscript form. At this particular point she said, "I hate accounting!" She is a patient woman most of the time.

But the transfer method works. It gets the information back into the retained earnings account through the use of journal entries and ledger postings. Here are Nadir Caves Souvenir Shoppe's nominal-account-to-retained-earnings entries on May 7, 19X1. Such entries usually are called *closing entries*. The process involved is usually called "closing the nominal accounts to retained earnings," or "closing the books." After the closing entries, the company's ruled and balanced ledger accounts are shown. First, here are the closing entries:

I. Sales	3,950		III. Retained Earnings	1,400	
Retained Earnings		3,950	Rent Expense		1,400
II. Retained Earnings	1,900		IV. Retained Earnings	117	
Cost of Goods Sold		1,900	Supplies Expense		117

The purpose of these closing entries is to transfer the information about changes in retained earnings back from the "kind of retained earnings change accounts" (nominal accounts) to retained earnings itself. Entry I is not a reduction or cancellation of revenues; it's just a transfer of information from one information-accumulation device to another. Similarly, Entry II is not a reduction or cancellation of merchandise expense, but simply a transfer.

	Cash					*Prepaid Rent*					*Sales*		
(1)	10,000	(2)	6,000	(2)	6,000	(9)	1,400	I.	3,950	(6)	3,950
(6)	3,950	(3)	3,000			√	4,600		══		══
		(8)	4,200								
		√	750		6,000		6,000		*Cost of Goods Sold*		
	13,950		13,950	√	4,600			(7)	1,900	II.	1,900
√	750								══		══

Accounts Payable

(6)	4,200	(4)	6,500		*Rent Expense*
√	3,100	(5)	800	(9)	1,400	III.	1,400

Merchandise Inventory

(3)	3,000	(7)	1,900
(4)	6,500	√	7,600
	9,500		9,500
√	7,600		

Accounts Payable:

	7,300		7,300
		√	3,100

Supplies Expense

(10)	117	IV.	117

Capital Stock

| √ (1) | 10,000 |

Supplies

(5)	800	(10)	117
		√	683
	800		800
√	683		

Retained Earnings

II.	1,900	I.	3,950
III.	1,400		
IV.	117		
√	533		
	3,950		3,950
		√	533

From the previous discussion it is evident that closing entries have two related effects, both of which are necessary for the functioning of the financial accounting system:

1. All revenues, expenses, gains, losses, and dividends of the previous period are reflected in the retained earnings account, thereby bringing it up to date as of the end of the accounting period.

2. Balances in all nominal accounts are reduced to zero, thereby ensuring that at the end of the next accounting period the totals recorded in the nominal accounts will reflect the total revenues, expenses, gains, losses, and dividends of *that* period.

Closing entries, in practice

In this book, the method used for making closing entries is a slight simplification of the methods used in actual practice, though it is faithful to the real effect of such entries. In practice, retained earnings nominal accounts often are closed to one or more special *closing accounts*; these in turn are later closed to retained earnings. For example, all revenues and expenses might first be closed to an account called "revenue and expense summary" (or income summary, or operating summary, or profit and loss); this account will later be closed to retained earnings. Dividends and nonoperating gains and losses might be closed directly to retained earnings, to some other closing account(s), or to the first closing account. If the firm operates a number of divisions, separate closing accounts may be used for each division.

Closing accounts provide some minor bookkeeping convenience; it may be, though, that their continued employment by firms is at least in part best explained as a historical survival from an earlier period when it was common in British accounting practice for the closing account to be an important permanent record (and for the income statement to be prepared in a form resembling a closing account). In any event, special closing accounts fail to enhance one's understanding of closing entries and will not be discussed in the remainder of this book.

An Additional Example (Optional)

If you had any difficulties with the previous discussion, you may wish to use the following additional example of nominal accounts and closing entries. Otherwise, feel free to move on to Problem 10-2.

Shown below are the balance sheet accounts of Nadir Caves Souvenir Shoppe for the week ended May 14, 19X1. Set up ledger accounts for this company. Prepare journal entries for all balance sheet changes, using appropriate nominal accounts. Post all of these journal entries to the ledger. Make closing entries. Post all closing entries to the ledger. Rule and balance the ledger.

Nadir Caves Souvenir Shoppe
Narrative Summary of Balance Sheet Changes
May 8–14, 19X1

1. The company bought $270 of curios for cash.
2. The company bought $1,475 of curios on account.
3. The company bought $79 of supplies on account.
4. The company declared and paid a $300 cash dividend to its stockholders.
5. The company made cash sales of $4,460.
6. The curios sold in Change 5 cost the company $2,103.
7. Supplies that cost $121 were consumed in operations.
8. One week's prepaid rent, costing $1,400, expired.
9. The company paid accounts payable of $2,760.

Optional Example Solution

Here are the journal entries for the firm's balance sheet changes.

1. Merchandise Inventory	270			6. Cost of Goods Sold	2,103		
Cash		270		Merchandise			
2. Merchandise Inventory	1,475			Inventory		2,103	
Accounts Payable		1,475		7. Supplies Expense	121		
3. Supplies	79			Supplies		121	
Accounts Payable		79		8. Rent Expense	1,400		
4. Dividends	300			Prepaid Rent		1,400	
Cash		300		9. Accounts Payable	2,760		
5. Cash	4,460			Cash		2,760	
Sales		4,460					

Here is the firm's ledger after all May 8–14 balance sheet changes have been posted, but before closing entries.

	Cash				Prepaid Rent				Sales	
✓	750	(1)	270	✓	4,600	(8)	1,400		(5)	4,460
(5)	4,460	(4)	300							
		(9)	2,760		*Accounts Payable*				*Cost of Goods Sold*	
	Merchandise Inventory			(9)	2,760	✓	3,100	(6)	2,103	
✓	7,600	(6)	2,103			(2)	1,475			
(1)	270					(3)	79		*Rent Expense*	
(2)	1,475				*Capital Stock*			(8)	1,400	
	Supplies					✓	10,000		*Supplies Expense*	
✓	683	(7)	121		*Retained Earnings*			(7)	121	
(3)	79					✓	553		*Dividends*	
								(4)	300	

Notice that, at this point, the only figure in the retained earnings account is the beginning balance. Why? Because *all* changes in retained earnings are shown in the nominal accounts.

Here are the closing entries on May 14, 19X1, followed by the company's ruled and balanced ledger accounts.

I. Sales	4,460			IV. Retained Earnings	121		
Retained Earnings		4,460		Supplies Expense		121	
II. Retained Earnings	2,103			V. Retained Earnings	300		
Cost of Goods Sold		2,103		Dividends		300	
III. Retained Earnings	1,400						
Rent Expense		1,400					

		Cash		
√	750	(1)		270
(5)	4,460	(4)		300
		(9)		2,760
		√		1,880
	5,210			5,210
√	1,880			

		Merchandise Inventory		
√	7,600	(6)		2,103
(1)	270			
(2)	1,475	√		7,242
	9,345			9,345
√	7,242			

		Supplies		
√	683	(7)		121
(3)	79	√		641
	762			762
√	641			

		Prepaid Rent		
√	4,600	(8)		1,400
		√		3,200
	4,600			4,600
√	3,200			

		Accounts Payable		
(9)	2,760	√		3,100
		(2)		1,475
√	1,894	(3)		79
	4,654			4,654
		√		1,894

		Capital Stock		
		√		10,000

		Retained Earnings		
II.	2,103	√		553
III.	1,400	I.		4,460
IV.	121			
V.	300			
√	1,089			
	5,013			5,013
		√		1,089

		Sales		
I.	4,460	(5)		4,460

		Cost of Goods Sold		
(6)	2,103	II.		2,103

		Rent Expense		
(8)	1,400	III.		1,400

		Supplies Expense		
(7)	121	IV.		121

		Dividends		
(4)	300	V.		300

Problem for Study and Self-Examination

Problem 10-2:

This problem is based on Problem 9-2 and its solution (pages 479–484). Illustration 10-4 gives the comparative balance sheets of Berryville Co. at December 31, 19X1 and 19X2. Illustration 10-5 gives a narrative summary of the company's 19X2 balance sheet changes. Illustration 10-6 gives the company's 19X2 income statement.

Set up ledger accounts for retained earnings and all nominal accounts; the retained earnings account should contain its 1/1/X2 beginning balance. Prepare journal entries for all 19X2 balance sheet changes; post these to the retained earnings and nominal accounts (but don't worry about their effects on other accounts). Prepare closing entries and post these to the ledger accounts. Compare your final 12/31/X2 retained earnings balance with the $16,250 one on the firm's balance sheet.

(Keep in mind that, during the accounting period, the company will leave the retained earnings account inactive at its beginning-of-period balance of $42,850. All changes in retained earnings should be recorded in the nominal accounts during the period; at the end of the period, retained earnings will be changed as the balances of the nominal accounts are closed to it.)

Illustration 10-4

Berryville Co.
Comparative Balance Sheets
December 31, 19X1 and 19X2

Assets	19X1	19X2
Current Assets:		
Cash	$ 37,800	$ 24,200
Accounts Receivable	51,200	29,300
Notes Receivable—6%	5,000	6,000
Interest Receivable	100	150
Advances to Suppliers	4,300	5,600
Merchandise Inventory	90,600	77,600
Supplies	7,400	5,300
Prepaid Rent	7,200	7,200
Prepaid Insurance	6,300	3,900
Total Current Assets	$209,900	$159,250
Noncurrent Assets:		
Land	$ 10,000	$ 10,000
Building	85,000	80,000
Equipment	54,000	59,000
Total Noncurrent Assets	$149,000	$149,000
Total Assets	$358,900	$308,250

Equities	19X1	19X2
Current Liabilities:		
Accounts Payable	$ 39,200	$ 24,000
Wages and Salaries Payable	3,700	4,300
Taxes Payable	12,400	1,050
Interest Payable	1,250	1,250
Dividends Payable	1,700	–0–
Advances from Customers	7,800	6,400
Total Current Liabilities	$ 66,050	$ 37,000
Noncurrent Liabilities:		
Long-Term Notes Payable—5%	150,000	150,000
Total Liabilities	$216,050	$187,000
Stockholders' Equity:		
Capital Stock	$100,000	$105,000
Retained Earnings	42,850	16,250
Total Stockholders' Equity	$142,850	$121,250
Total Equities	$358,900	$308,250

Illustration 10-5

Berryville Co.
Narrative Summary of Balance Sheet Changes
For the Year 19X2

1. The company issued additional capital stock for $5,000, cash.
2. Cash sales totalled $27,000.
3. Sales of $280,200 were made on account.
4. Additional sales of $7,800 resulted when 12/31/X1 advances from customers were settled.
5. Other customers paid the company $6,400 in advance for goods to be delivered in 19X3.
6. Accounts receivable of $296,100 were collected in cash.
7. Merchandise costing $186,100 was purchased on account.
8. All 12/31/X1 interest receivable ($100) was collected.
9. An additional $200 of interest was earned and collected by the company in 19X2.
10. The $5,000 six percent note receivable reported on the 12/31/X1 balance sheet was collected.
11. On 7/31/X2, the company acquired *another* six percent note receivable, in settlement of a $6,000 account receivable. The principal amount of this new note was $6,000. It is due on 4/30/X3.
12. A total of $4,300 of merchandise, upon which the company had paid advances to suppliers in 19X1, was received during 19X2. (This is in addition to the merchandise received in Change 7.)
13. The company paid $5,600 of advances to suppliers for merchandise to be delivered in 19X3.
14. The company bought $15,500 of supplies on account.
15. Every June 30, the company pays one year's rent ($14,400) in advance.
16. The company purchased two insurance policies for a total of $700.
17a. The company sold old equipment for $3,500, cash.
17b. The equipment sold had a book value of $6,000. (All 19X2 depreciation of equipment is discussed in Change 33. The book value of $6,000 reflects depreciation on this equipment up through the date it was sold.)
18. The company bought $19,000 of equipment on account.
19. The company paid $235,800 of accounts payable.
20. The company paid wages and salaries payable of $3,700; these were the wages and salaries owed at 12/31/X1.
21. The company paid $70,600 of wages and salaries expense, in cash.
22. The company paid $12,400 of taxes payable. These were the taxes owed at 12/31/X1.
23. The company paid the 12/31/X1 interest payable of $1,250.
24. The company paid an additional $6,250 for interest charges on its five percent long-term notes payable through 10/31/X2.
25. The company paid its 12/31/X1 dividends payable of $1,700.
26. The company paid $4,500 of utilities expense, in cash.
27. Cost of goods sold was $203,400.
28. Supplies expense was $17,600.
29. See Change 11. No interest had been collected on the new $6,000 note receivable by 12/31/X2; $150 of interest had accrued.
30. See Change 15. Rent expense for the year was $14,400.

31. Insurance expense for the year was $3,100.
32. Building depreciation totalled $5,000.
33. Equipment depreciation totalled $8,000.
34. See Changes 20 and 21. At the end of the year, the company owed its employees an additional $4,300 for wages and salaries earned during 19X2 but not paid until 19X3.
35. The company estimates that its 19X2 taxes will be $1,050. These taxes will be paid in 19X3.
36. See Change 24. At 12/31/X2, the company owed an additional two months' interest (of $1,250) on its five percent long-term notes payable.

Changes 17a and 17b are given the same index number because they are simple changes that form a single compound transaction when combined.

Illustration 10-6

Berryville Co.
Statement of Income and Retained Earnings
For the Year 19X2

Revenues:		
Sales	$315,000	
Interest Revenue	350	$315,350
Expenses:		
Cost of Goods Sold	$203,400	
Wages and Salaries Expense	74,900	
Depreciation Expense	13,000	
Insurance Expense	3,100	
Rent Expense	14,400	
Supplies Expense	17,600	
Taxes Expense	1,050	
Utilities Expense	4,500	
Interest Expense	7,500	339,450
Net Loss from Operations		$ (24,100)
Loss on Sale of Equipment		2,500
Net Loss		$ (26,600)
Retained Earnings—12/31/X1		42,850
Retained Earnings—12/31/X2		$ 16,250

Solution

Solution 10-2:

Illustration 10-7

Berryville Co.
Simple Summary Journal Entries
For the Year 19X2

1.	Cash	5,000		18.	Equipment	19,000	
	Capital Stock		5,000		Accounts Payable		19,000
2.	Cash	27,000		19.	Accounts Payable	235,800	
	Sales		27,000		Cash		235,800
3.	Accounts Receivable	280,200		20.	Wages and Salaries		
	Sales		280,200		Payable	3,700	
4.	Advances from				Cash		3,700
	Customers	7,800		21.	Wages and Salaries		
	Sales		7,800		Expense	70,600	
5.	Cash	6,400			Cash		70,600
	Advances from			22.	Taxes Payable	12,400	
	Customers		6,400		Cash		12,400
6.	Cash	296,100		23.	Interest Payable	1,250	
	Accounts Receiv-				Cash		1,250
	able		296,100	24.	Interest Expense	6,250	
7.	Merchandise Inven-				Cash		6,250
	tory	186,100		25.	Dividends Payable	1,700	
	Accounts Pay-				Cash		1,700
	able		186,100	26.	Utilities Expense	4,500	
8.	Cash	100			Cash		4,500
	Interest Receivable		100	27.	Cost of Goods Sold	203,400	
9.	Cash	200			Merchandise		
	Interest Revenue		200		Inventory		203,400
10.	Cash	5,000		28.	Supplies Expense	17,600	
	Notes Receiv-				Supplies		17,600
	able—6%		5,000	29.	Interest Receivable	150	
11.	Notes Receivable—6%	6,000			Interest Revenue		150
	Accounts Receivable		6,000	30.	Rent Expense	14,400	
12.	Merchandise Inventory	4,300			Prepaid Rent		14,400
	Advances to Sup-			31.	Insurance Expense	3,100	
	pliers		4,300		Prepaid Insurance		3,100
13.	Advances to Suppliers	5,600		32.	Depreciation Expense	5,000	
	Cash		5,600		Building		5,000
14.	Supplies	15,500		33.	Depreciation Expense	8,000	
	Accounts Payable		15,500		Equipment		8,000
15.	Prepaid Rent	14,400		34.	Wages and Salaries		
	Cash		14,400		Expense	4,300	
16.	Prepaid Insurance	700			Wages and		
	Cash		700		Salaries Payable		4,300
17a.	Cash	3,500		35.	Taxes Expense	1,050	
	Equipment		3,500		Taxes Payable		1,050
17b.	Loss on Sale of			36.	Interest Expense	1,250	
	Equipment	2,500			Interest Payable		1,250
	Equipment		2,500				

Here are the retained earnings and nominal accounts after Entries 1 through 36 have been posted:

Retained Earnings		*Depreciation Expense*		*Utilities Expense*	
	✓　42,850	(32)　5,000		(26)　4,500	
		(33)　8,000			

Sales		*Insurance Expense*		*Interest Expense*	
	(2)　27,000	(31)　3,100		(24)　6,250	
	(3)　280,200			(36)　1,250	
	(4)　7,800				

Rent Expense

(30)　14,400

Cost of Goods Sold		*Interest Revenue*	
(27)　203,400			(9)　200
			(29)　150

Supplies Expense

(28)　17,600

Wages and Salaries Expense		*Taxes Expense*		*Loss on Sale of Equipment*	
(21)　70,600		(35)　1,050		(17b)　2,500	
(34)　4,300					

Illustration 10-8

Berryville Co.
Closing Entries
12/31/X2

A.	Sales	315,000		G.	Retained Earnings	17,600
	Retained Earnings		315,000		Supplies Expense		17,600
B.	Retained Earnings	203,400		H.	Retained Earnings	1,050
	Cost of Goods Sold		203,400		Taxes Expense		1,050
C.	Retained Earnings	74,900		I.	Retained Earnings	4,500
	Wages and Salaries Expense		74,900		Utilities Expense		4,500
D.	Retained Earnings	13,000		J.	Retained Earnings	7,500
	Depreciation Expense		13,000		Interest Expense		7,500
E.	Retained Earnings	3,100		K.	Interest Revenue	350
	Insurance Expense		3,100		Retained Earnings		350
F.	Retained Earnings	14,400		L.	Retained Earnings	2,500
	Rent Expense		14,400		Loss on Sale of Equipment		2,500

This closing procedure could be speeded up by using compound entries instead of simple two-line entries. You could use one compound entry for all revenues, another for all expenses, and a third for all nonoperating gains and losses:

I.	Sales	315,000		II. Retained Earnings	339,450	
	Interest Revenue	350		Cost of Goods Sold		203,400
	Retained Earnings		315,350	Wages and Salaries		
				Expense		74,900
III.	Retained Earnings	2,500		Depreciation Expense		13,000
	Loss on Sale of			Insurance Expense		3,100
	Equipment		2,500	Rent Expense		14,400
				Supplies Expense		17,600
				Taxes Expense		1,050
				Utilities Expense		4,500
				Interest Expense		7,500

In addition to saving time, this way of closing yields several of the subtotals needed for the income statement: compare the $315,350, $339,450, and $2,500 retained earnings figures with the subtotals in Illustration 10-6.

Finally, the retained earnings and nominal accounts after the closing entries have been posted and all accounts have been ruled and balanced are shown on page 539.

Valuation Accounts

The accountant uses nominal accounts to distinguish among different kinds of changes in retained earnings, but retained earnings is not the only account that is handled in this way. For instance, the accountant uses something similar to nominal accounts for the inventories of manufacturers. There are a variety of different kinds of costs that go into a manufactured inventory. Chapter Twelve examines a system of special-name accounts that the accountant employs to distinguish among different kinds of manufacturer's inventory costs.

This section will discuss a different kind of special-name account used for depreciable assets.[5] (You have already seen one example of these in the balance sheet on page 88.) You will recall from page 145 that the *book value* of a depreciable asset is its cost less depreciation to date. Refer to the Berryville Co. data in Problem 10-2 (pages 532–535). The company's building had a book value of $85,000 at 12/31/X1; suppose that it had been purchased ten years prior to 12/31/X1 for $135,000 and had been estimated to have a 25-year service life with a scrap value of $10,000 upon

---

[5] This discussion will assume that no serious errors in depreciation estimates are made by the firm, so that no corrections for errors in depreciation are necessary; such corrections are discussed in Chapter Thirteen.

	Retained Earnings		
B.	203,400	√	42,850
C.	74,900	A.	315,000
D.	13,000	K.	350
E.	3,100		
F.	14,400		
G.	17,600		
H.	1,050		
I.	4,500		
J.	7,500		
L.	2,500		
√	16,250		
	358,200		358,200
		√	16,250

Wages and Salaries Expense

(21)	70,600	C.	74,900
(34)	4,300		
	74,900		74,900

Depreciation Expense

(32)	5,000	D.	13,000
(33)	8,000		
	13,000		13,000

Sales

A.	315,000	(2)	27,000
		(3)	280,200
		(4)	7,800
	315,000		315,000

Insurance Expense

(31)	3,100	E.	3,100

Rent Expense

(30)	14,400	F.	14,400

Cost of Goods Sold

(27)	203,400	B.	203,400

Supplies Expense

(28)	17,600	G.	17,600

Taxes Expense

(35)	1,050	H.	1,050

Utilities Expense

(26)	4,500	I.	4,500

Interest Expense

(26)	6,250	J.	7,500
(36)	1,250		
	7,500		7,500

Interest Revenue

K.	350	(9)	200
		(29)	150
	350		350

Loss on Sale of Equipment

(17b)	2,500	L.	2,500

retirement.[6] Following the method used so far, the summary entry for year 1 depreciation on this building would be:

Depreciation Expense   5,000
  Buildings   5,000

At the end of the first year the buildings ledger account would look as follows:

Buildings

✓	135,000		
		✓	5,000
		✓	130,000
	135,000		135,000
✓	130,000		

Similarly, the account would look as follows two years later:

Buildings

✓	135,000		
		✓	5,000
		✓	130,000
	135,000		135,000
✓	130,000		
		✓	5,000
		✓	125,000
	130,000		130,000
✓	125,000		
		✓	5,000
		✓	120,000
	125,000		125,000
✓	120,000		

The accountant finds two main drawbacks to this system of recording:

1. After the first year, it is impossible to tell from the reported figure how much the building cost; it is also impossible to tell from the figure reported on the balance sheet how much of the total services originally estimated for the building has been provided.

2. The cost of the building is something known with a high degree of assurance, whereas its depreciation is a matter of estimate—estimated service life, estimated

---

[6] These figures are consistent with the $5,000 a year depreciation given for the building in Change 32 of Illustration 10-5 (see page 535). (($135,000 − $10,000)/25 = $5,000 a year.) At 12/31/X1, when the building was 10 years old, it would have a book value of $85,000 ($135,000 − (10 × $5,000) = $85,000), the figure reported for the building on that date in Illustration 10-4 (see page 533).

scrap value. The book value reported for the partly depreciated building is a mixture of known and estimated data. The accountant prefers to keep objective, high-assurance data (such as costs of buildings) uncontaminated by subjective, low-assurance estimates.[7]

There is a simple way to do this: *the accountant merely uses a special-name account to accumulate all of the depreciation writedowns.* On December 31 of the first year, instead of making the following entry:

Depreciation Expense   5,000
     Buildings   5,000

the accountant makes this entry:

Depreciation Expense   5,000
     Buildings—Accumulated Depreciation   5,000

His buildings account would then look like this:

Buildings		Buildings— Accumulated Depreciation	
✓ 135,000			5,000

Similarly, the building account would look as shown below two years later:

Buildings		Buildings— Accumulated Depreciation	
✓ 135,000		✓	5,000
		✓ 10,000	5,000
		10,000	10,000
		✓	10,000
		✓ 15,000	5,000
		15,000	15,000
		✓	15,000

As you can see, the total of all depreciation recorded since acquisition of the building is progressively reflected in the accumulated depreciation account.

The figure for the $135,000 cost of the building has been preserved. Estimates are not mingled with objective data. Yet the building is still recorded at the correct figure of $120,000 at the end of the third year, so long as you understand the system

---

[7] Personally, I have never felt that these drawbacks were terribly serious, which is why they have been ignored up to now. However, as you will see, the device used by the accountant to overcome these drawbacks is so simple and convenient that it is worth using whenever possible.

and are aware that the correct figure for the building can be obtained only by combining the two accounts.

Here is how these accounts would be reported on Berryville Co.'s balance sheet at the end of the third year:

Noncurrent Assets:

Land		$ XXX
Buildings—at cost	$135,000	
Less: Accumulated Depreciation	15,000	120,000

Notice that the account, "buildings—accumulated depreciation," is not closed to the account, "buildings," the way a nominal account is closed to retained earnings, for that would defeat the whole purpose. Partly for this reason, accounts such as "buildings—accumulated depreciation" are given a different designation. They are called *valuation* accounts. In turn, the buildings account would often be called a *parent account*.

You have already seen examples of valuation accounts without knowing it. On pages 264–266, "premium on capital stock" and "discount on capital stock" are valuation accounts to capital stock. In both cases, legal considerations require that the account capital stock be shown at an amount that differs from the true permanent investment of stockholders. If the amount reported for capital stock is less than this permanent investment, the premium account is used to correct figures upwards; if the amount reported for capital stock is greater than this permanent investment the discount account is used to correct figures downward. Almost all of the accounts discussed toward the end of Chapter Five are valuation accounts to either capital stock, preferred stock, or retained earnings. You will see additional examples of valuation accounts in subsequent chapters.

By 12/31/X1 (ten years after the purchase of the building), a total of $50,000 will have built up in the "building—accumulated depreciation" account (10 × $5,000 = $50,000). Here are the related ledger accounts at 12/31/X1 (these ledger accounts are abridged so as to show only 19X1 data):

Buildings		Buildings— Accumulated Depreciation	
√ 135,000		√ 50,000	√ 45,000
			5,000
		50,000	50,000
			√ 50,000

Here is how these accounts would be reported on the company's 12/31/X1 balance sheet (compare with Illustration 10-4, page 533):

Noncurrent Assets:

Land		$10,000
Buildings—at cost	$135,000	
Less: Accumulated Depreciation	50,000	85,000

Why do accountants use valuation accounts? The main reason is that they add great flexibility to recording and reporting. They allow reporting something in one fashion, then modifying it to report simultaneously in another. In the previous example, use of the accumulated depreciation valuation account allows the building to be reported at both its historical cost and its book value. In the next chapter you will see that use of valuation accounts allows reporting of accounts receivable at both the amounts legally owed to the firm and the amounts that the firm actually expects to collect—and that, similarly, their use allows reporting both the amount owed at the maturity of a long-term debt and the amount that is currently owed. In general, valuation accounts are employed to increase the amount of data that may be expressed by an accounting system.

Two things are worth stressing here:

1. Valuation accounts are *balance sheet accounts*. They appear on the balance sheet and are not closed to the parent account before preparing financial statements. These accounts do not appear on the income statement.

2. Once you use valuation accounts, you cannot answer such questions as "What is the book value of the building?" without considering *both* the parent account and the valuation account. But this is to be expected, for a single account has simply been broken up into special-name accounts. You saw earlier with nominal accounts that there is really only one retained earnings account, even though changes in it are given a variety of special names. Similarly with valuation accounts: at 12/31/X1, *there really is only one buildings account*, with a balance of $85,000.[8]

Retirements of depreciable assets

Retirements of depreciable assets are recorded in much the same way using valuation accounts as we have recorded them in previous chapters. The only difference is that an additional account must be employed. For example, suppose that a machine was purchased nine years ago for $10,000, and that it was estimated to have a total service life of ten years and a zero scrap value upon retirement. If depreciation has been brought up to date, accumulated depreciation on this machine will total ($10,000 ÷ 10) × 9 = $9,000. If this machine were now to be sold to a dealer in used equipment for $1,300, cash, the appropriate journal entry would be:

Cash	1,300	
Equipment—Accumulated Depreciation	9,000	
Equipment		10,000
Gain on Sale of Equipment		300

Notice that when recording the retirement of a depreciable asset it is important to reflect the retirement in both its parent and valuation accounts. Once again, the reason for this is that the parent and valuation accounts are not independent of each other; they merely are parts of a single account—Equipment.

---

[8] Nomenclature of valuation accounts varies a good deal from one set of published financial statements to another. "Buildings—Accumulated Depreciation" is often called "Buildings—Allowance for Depreciation," or "Buildings—Reserve for Depreciation." All three of these names mean the same thing.

Nominal accounts and valuation accounts may be distinguished by the following characteristics:

Nominal accounts are used to record specific kinds of changes in a balance sheet account during a specific accounting period. For example, expense and revenue accounts are used to record different kinds of changes in retained earnings during the year. When the accounting period ends, the nominal accounts are closed to the balance sheet accounts. Nominal accounts do not appear on the balance sheet.

Valuation accounts are used when the accountant wishes or is required to report some particular amount for an asset or equity, yet that amount differs from what *should* be reported. For example, a firm is required to report the total par value of its capital stock in the parent account Capital Stock. But if stockholders paid more than the par value for their shares, the firm may use the valuation account Premium on Capital Stock to help record the actual amount received. Valuation accounts do appear on the balance sheet.

These differences may be diagrammed as follows:

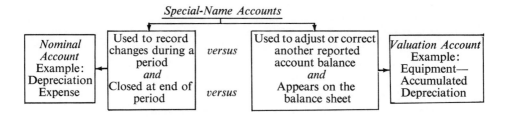

Problem for Study and Self-Examination

Problem 10-3:

This continues the illustration for Berryville Co. (pages 538–542). The $54,000 of equipment owned by the company at 12/31/X1 was made up of the following:

Group One: $7,000 of two-year-old equipment that had cost $10,000 on 1/1/X0 (at which time it had an estimated service life of 6 years and an estimated scrap value on retirement of $1,000).

Group Two: $47,000 of four-year-old equipment that had cost $69,000 when it was purchased (at which time it had an estimated service life of 12 years and an estimated scrap value on retirement of $3,000).

Using valuation accounts:

1. Prepare the appropriate summary journal entries for 19X1 equipment depreciation; post this entry to the appropriate ledger accounts (your depreciation expense account should already show $5,000 of building depreciation).

2. Prepare the noncurrent asset section of the company's 12/31/X1 balance sheet.

Problem 10-4:

Before doing this problem, check your solution to Problem 10-3 to be sure that you understand it. The following is the complete information concerning changes in Berryville Co.'s noncurrent assets during 19X2:

1. There were no changes in Land.
2. No buildings were purchased or sold.
3. On 6/30/X2, equipment costing $19,000 was purchased on account. It was estimated that this equipment would have a total service life of five years and a scrap value of $4,000 upon retirement.
4. On 9/1/X2, all of the Group One equipment was sold for $3,500, cash.

A. Prepare the following ledger accounts, entering 12/31/X1 balances: Land, Buildings, Equipment, Buildings—Accumulated Depreciation, Equipment—Accumulated Depreciation, Depreciation Expense, and Loss on Sale of Equipment.

B. Make appropriate journal entries for the following:
    (1) Purchase of new equipment on 6/30/X2.
    (2) Retirement of old equipment on 9/1/X2. In making journal entries for this, you should:
        (a) Be sure to bring depreciation expense on the old equipment up to date (the company received services from this equipment for 8 months in 19X2).
        (b) Remove the *entire* $10,000 historical cost of the old equipment from the company's records (the company no longer owns these assets).
        (c) Remove the *entire* accumulated depreciation on this old equipment from the company's records (for the same reason as above).
    (3) 19X2 depreciation on the new equipment purchased on 6/30/X2.
    (4) 19X2 depreciation on the old Group Two equipment.
    (5) 19X2 depreciation on buildings.
    (6) Closing entries for depreciation expense and loss on sale of equipment.

C. Post all journal entries to the ledger accounts. Rule and balance the ledger accounts.

D. Prepare the noncurrent asset section of the company's 12/31/X2 balance sheet. Compare this with Illustration 10-4 (page 533). Compare your depreciation expense account with that in the solution to Problem 10-2 (page 536).

Solutions

Solution 10-3:

Group One equipment is being depreciated at a rate of $1,500 a year (($10,000 − $1,000)/6 = $1,500). Group Two equipment is being depreciated at a rate of $5,500 a year (($69,000 − $3,000)/12 = $5,500). Therefore, 19X1 depreciation charges totalled $7,000 ($1,500 + $5,500 = $7,000).

Depreciation Expense	7,000	
Equipment—Accumulated Depreciation		7,000

At 12/31/X0 the balance in Equipment—Accumulated Depreciation was $18,000

Group One: One year × $1,500	$ 1,500
Group Two: Three years × $5,500	16,500
	$18,000

At 12/31/X0 the balance in the equipment account was $79,000 ($10,000 + $69,000 = $79,000). Here are the related ledger accounts for 19X1:

Equipment		Equipment—Accumulated Depreciation	
✓ 79,000		✓ 18,000	
	✓ 25,000		7,000
Depreciation Expense		25,000	25,000
5,000			✓ 25,000
7,000			

Here is the noncurrent asset section of the company's 12/31/X1 balance sheet:

Noncurrent Assets:

Land		$10,000	
Buildings—at cost	$135,000		
Less: Accumulated Depreciation	50,000	85,000	
Equipment—at cost	$ 79,000		
Less: Accumulated Depreciation	25,000	54,000	$149,000

Solution 10-4:

The following solution is quite detailed, for the sake of providing maximum help to students who are having difficulties; if you don't need this much help, feel free to skim some of these details.

A. The solution to step A will be found as part of the solution to step C.

B. (1) *Purchase of new equipment on 6/30/X2:*

Equipment	19,000	
Accounts Payable		19,000

(2) *Retirement of old Group One equipment on 9/1/X2:*
   (a) *Bring depreciation expense up to date.*
       This equipment is being depreciated at a rate of $1,500 a year. For eight months, $1,500 × 8/12 = $1,000.

Depreciation Expense	1,000	
Equipment—Accumulated Depreciation		1,000

   (b) *Remove the entire $10,000 historical cost of the equipment sold.*

Cash	3,500	
Equipment		3,500
Loss on Sale of Equipment	6,500	
Equipment		6,500

   (c) *Remove the entire accumulated depreciation of the equipment sold.*
       At 12/31/X1, the accumulated depreciation of the Group One equipment was $3,000. It is now $4,000—see (a) above: $3,000 + $1,000 = $4,000.

Equipment—Accumulated Depreciation	4,000	
Loss on Sale of Equipment		4,000

You could have recorded the sale of the old equipment by a single compound entry instead of the previous string of simple entries:

Depreciation Expense	1,000	
Cash	3,500	
Equipment—Accumulated Depreciation	3,000	
Loss on Sale of Equipment	2,500	
Equipment		10,000

Satisfy yourself that this single compound entry has exactly the same effect as the four previous simple entries:

	Simple Entries	Compound Entry
Depreciation Expense	+ $1,000	= + $ 1,000
Cash	+ $3,500	= + $ 3,500
Equipment—Accumulated Depreciation	+ $1,000 − $4,000	= − $ 3,000
Loss on Sale of Equipment . . .	+ $6,500 − $4,000	= + $ 2,500
Equipment	− $3,500 − $6,500	= − $10,000

There are circumstances in which it is simpler to make a compound entry than a series of simple ones.

(3) *19X2 depreciation of the new equipment:*
The company received six months' service from the new equipment in 19X2; $(($19,000 - $4,000)/5) \times 6/12 = \underline{$1,500.}$

Depreciation Expense	1,500	
Equipment—Accumulated Depreciation		1,500

(4) *19X2 depreciation of the old Group Two equipment:*
Same as 19X1 (see page 544).

Depreciation Expense	5,500	
Equipment—Accumulated Depreciation		5,500

(5) *19X2 depreciation of buildings:*
Same as 19X1 (see page 542).

Depreciation Expense	5,000	
Buildings—Accumulated Depreciation		5,000

(6) *Closing entries:*

Retained Earnings	13,000	
Depreciation Expense		13,000
Retained Earnings	2,500	
Loss on Sale of Equipment		2,500

Here are the company's ledger accounts for 19X2:
  C.

Land			*Buildings*			*Equipment*			
√	10,000		√	135,000		√ (1)	79,000 19,000	(2b) (2b) √	3,500 6,500 88,000
							98,000		98,000
Depreciation Expense			*Buildings— Accumulated Depreciation*			√	88,000		
(2a) (3) (4) (5)	1,000 1,500 5,500 5,000	(6) 13,000	√	55,000	√ (5)	50,000 5,000				
	13,000	13,000		55,000		55,000	*Equipment— Accumulated Depreciation*		
					√	55,000	(2c)	4,000	√ 25,000
Loss on Sale of Equipment								(2a) (3) (4)	1,000 1,500 5,500
(2b)	6,500	(2c) 4,000 (6) 2,500					√	29,000	33,000
	6,500	6,500							√ 29,000

Notice that depreciation expense comes to the same $13,000 total as before; nothing really has been changed by the use of valuation accounts. The noncurrent asset section of the 12/31/X2 balance sheet would appear as follows:

D.

Noncurrent Assets:

Land		$10,000	
Buildings—at cost	$135,000		
Less: Accumulated Depreciation	55,000	80,000	
Equipment—at cost	$ 88,000		
Less: Accumulated Depreciation	29,000	59,000	$149,000

Except for the use of valuation accounts, this is identical with the figures reported in Illustration 10-4.

Generally speaking, whenever the accountant wishes to distinguish between different kinds of changes in a single balance sheet account, he uses one or more valuation accounts, just as he uses various kind-of-change nominal accounts to record changes in retained earnings. You will see other examples of valuation accounts and another kind of nominal accounts in later chapters.

The Accounting Cycle

Recall the following definitions from Chapter Four (page 180):

Transaction:
> Any change in an entity's assets or equities that is accompanied by a related change in the assets or equities of some other entity.

Exchange:
> A complete transaction—a purchase or sale that takes place in some kind of market.

Accrual:
> An incomplete transaction that is given partial recognition by the accountant.

Internal Change:
> Any balance sheet that change is not a transaction and that therefore involves only the entity and its owners (in their capacity as residual equity holders).

Different companies have different-length accounting periods—different intervals between formal financial statements. Berryville Co. and Trimble Hotel Corp. prepare financial statements once a year, so their accounting periods are one year in length; Gadsden Co. prepares statements once a month, ¬o it has a one-month accounting period. Nominal accounts will always be closed to retained earnings at least once a year, and will usually be closed each time formal financial statements are prepared if the company's accounting period is shorter than one year. (Occasional exceptions to this will be ignored in what follows.) In contrast, balance sheet accounts, including valuation accounts, tend to go on from one period to the next. When balance sheet accounts are reduced to zero (as was Berryville Co.'s dividends payable account), this reduction has nothing to do with the end of an accounting period.

The totality of financial accounting activities occurring during a company's accounting period is often referred to as the company's *accounting cycle*. During the accounting cycle, balance sheet changes occur every day. The company makes numerous day-by-day journal entries to record these changes. Journal entries are then posted to the ledger, sometimes every day, sometimes once a week, sometimes once a month (systems differ from one company to another). The balance sheet changes recorded during the period are mostly exchanges—current operating transactions and other changes involving receipt or expenditure of funds.

A number of accruals and internal changes that must eventually be recorded in a company's financial statements are not recorded during the accounting period. Instead, the accountant waits until the end of the period to record them. Call these *adjusting entries*. By and large, the accountant will delay recording anything about which information is not needed during the period. For example, interest receivable (and interest revenue) may be accruing over the entire period. Unless cash is collected on the interest receivable, however, the accountant is apt to wait until the end of the period to record the information (by an adjusting entry). The accountant could accrue on a daily basis, but, as noted on page 190, this would make extra work for him without serving any real purpose. (There's not much that anyone would do with daily information about interest although, in total, it's important information to have on the financial statements at the end of the period.) If cash is collected, the accountant will record the interest information at that point, for the company needs to know what its cash balance is at all times during the year; and if he's going to record the cash part of the transaction, he must record the rest of the transaction to keep debits equal to credits.

Similarly, there is no particular advantage to recording depreciation for a store on a daily basis because there is ordinarily no use for this information during the accounting period. But, as shown in Problem 10-6, depreciation expense must be brought up to date when a depreciable asset is sold or retired, and of course it must be recorded at the end of the accounting period, since depreciation information is very important for income statements. Thus, the accountant minimizes his work by recording depreciation on sold or retired assets at the time of sale or retirement, and on the remaining depreciable assets just once a period, by an adjusting entry made at the end of the period (for the whole length of time between successive financial statements).

You can see that *the main difference between ordinary journal entries and adjusting journal entries is in the time they are made.* Other than this, they're pretty much alike; there's nothing special about adjusting entries. In fact, it is possible for some journal entries to be made either during the period or at the end of the period, depending on the company's system of accounting. Inventories provide a good example of this: some companies figure cost of goods sold each time a sale is made (perpetual inventory method). For these companies, cost of goods sold is an ordinary day-to-day entry. Other companies wait until the end of the accounting period to record the cost of goods sold (periodic inventory method). At this time, they count the ending inventory, determine what it cost, then subtract this ending inventory figure from the sum of the cost of their beginning inventory and the cost of the inventories that they purchased during the period. The difference gives the cost of the inventories sold during the period:

(Beginning Inventory) + (Purchases) = (Ending Inventory) + (Cost of Goods Sold)

If the company waits until the end of the accounting period to record decreases in inventories, cost of goods sold becomes an adjusting entry.

By now you should be aware that *there is nothing new about adjusting entries*—we have been making them throughout this book, ever since the discussion of interest receivable in Chapter One. All that is being done now is to point out that some journal entries with which you already are familiar are made during the accounting period ("ordinary entries"), while others ("adjusting entries") are made at period end. Shown below are some typical examples of ordinary entries and adjusting entries. Be aware that in unusual accounting systems, exceptions can be found to some of these examples.

Ordinary Entries Typical events recorded during the accounting period	*Adjusting Entries* Typical events recorded only at the end of the accounting period
Sales of any kind	Accrual of unpaid interest payable
Purchases of nonmonetary assets	Accrual of unpaid interest receivable
Collections of receivables	Depreciation
Payments of liabilities	Amortization of patents
Advances to suppliers	Accrual of miscellaneous liabilities for
Advances from customers	services rendered the company
Payments for services	Accrual of tax liability
Borrowing of money and other issuing of	Supplies expense
noncurrent equities	Expiration of prepaid rent, prepaid
Declaration of dividends	insurance

A few additional adjusting entries are discussed in later chapters.

In summary, here are the three main kinds of journal entries:
1. *Ordinary:* Made during the accounting period; these record exchanges and certain related changes.
2. *Adjusting:* Made at the end of the accounting period; they record corrections, accruals, and internal changes.
3. *Closing:* Made at the end of the accounting period *last* of all; these do *not* record genuine balance sheet changes, but simply transfer information from the nominal accounts to the retained earnings account.

Example of an accounting cycle

We will use Gadsden Co.'s January, 19X2 activities as an example of a company's activities over its entire accounting cycle. Assume that this company records cost of goods sold at the time each sale is made (perpetual inventory method). Illustration

10-9 gives its balance sheet at 1/1/X2, followed by its ordinary January, 19X2, journal entries.

Illustration 10-9

Gadsden Co.
Balance Sheet
December 31, 19X1

Assets

Current Assets:

Cash	$ 2,000	
Accounts Receivable	4,500	
Merchandise Inventory	8,000	
Prepaid Insurance	500	$15,000

Noncurrent Assets:

Land		$ 2,300	
Buildings—at cost	$10,000		
Less: Accumulated Depreciation	4,800	5,200	
Equipment—at cost	$20,500		
Less: Accumulated Depreciation	9,000	11,500	19,000

Total Assets	$34,000

Equities

Current Liabilities:

Accounts Payable	$ 4,200	
Dividends Payable	700	
Interest Payable.	200	
Other Payables	1,100	$ 6,200

Noncurrent Liabilities:

Bonds Payable—6%	10,000

Total Liabilities	$16,200

Stockholders' Equity:

Capital Stock	$12,000	
Retained Earnings	5,800	17,800

Total Equities	$34,000

1. Merchandise Inventory	43,000	6. Dividends Payable	700
Accounts Payable	43,000	Cash	700
2. Cash	5,000	7. Accounts Payable	42,180
Sales	5,000	Cash	42,180
3. Accounts Receivable	43,800	8. Other Payables	1,100
Sales	43,800	Cash	1,100
4. Cost of Goods Sold	39,700	9. Equipment	2,000
Merchandise Inventory	39,700	Cash	2,000
5. Cash	44,100		
Accounts Receivable	44,100		

Remember that these are *summaries* of the company's ordinary journal entries during the month. There may have been dozens of purchases of merchandise making up the $43,000 figure shown in Entry 1 and hundreds of sales making up the figures in Entries 2 and 3, etc. Illustration 10-10 gives the company's ledger as it would look before any adjusting entries are made; it is here termed the "unadjusted ledger," although this is not standard usage.

Illustration 10-10

Gadsden Co.
Unadjusted Ledger
1/31/X2

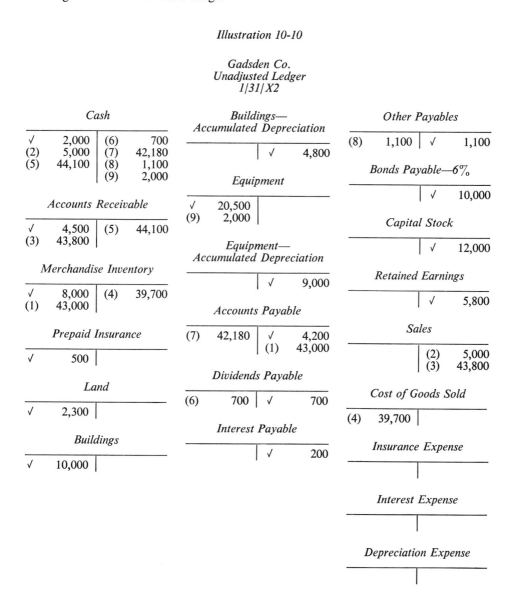

Before making adjustments, a company using a hand-operated accounting system usually tests to see whether its recording of ordinary journal entries has been clerically accurate. After all, a great number of such entries are made and posted during the period, leaving ample room for error. If these errors are not detected early, they may complicate the adjusting and closing process.

Among the tests that the accountant performs is one called preparing a *trial balance*. A trial balance is an arithmetic check to see whether the total debits equal the total credits in the ledger. If debits and credits are not equal, the accountant knows that a clerical error has been made during the period and will try to locate it before going any further.

Here is one of several ways to prepare a trial balance:

1. Prepare a sheet of paper with one line for each of the company's accounts; write the name of each account at the left of its line. Then draw two columns, one for debit balances and the other for credit balances.

2. Without ruling the accounts, determine the balance in each account and write it in the appropriate column.

3. Total the columns and make sure that debits equal credits.

Illustration 10-11 gives the unadjusted trial balance for Gadsden Co. It is called an "*un*adjusted trial balance" because adjusting entries have not been made. Since this is not a formal document, but merely a check on the accountant's accuracy, there is no need for a heading or dollar signs.

Illustration 10-11

Gadsden Co.

	Unadjusted Trial Balance 1/31/X2	
	Debit	*Credit*
Cash	5,120	
Accounts Receivable	4,200	
Merchandise Inventory	11,300	
Prepaid Insurance	500	
Land	2,300	
Buildings	10,000	
Buildings—Accumulated Depreciation		4,800
Equipment	22,500	
Equipment—Accumulated Depreciation		9,000
Accounts Payable		5,020
Dividends Payable		–0–
Interest Payable		200
Other Payables		–0–
Bonds Payable—6%		10,000
Capital Stock		12,000
Retained Earnings		5,800
Sales		48,800
Cost of Goods Sold	39,700	
Insurance Expense	–0–	
Interest Expense	–0–	
Depreciation Expense	–0–	
Total	95,620	95,620

Here are the company's adjusting entries. Illustration 10-12 gives the ledger as it would appear after all adjusting entries have been posted, but before closing entries have been made. At this stage, the ledger is called the "adjusted ledger."

10.	Depreciation Expense	50	12.	Insurance Expense	20
	Buildings—Accumulated			Prepaid Insurance	20
	Depreciation	50	13.	Interest Expense	50
11.	Depreciation Expense	375		Interest Payable	50
	Equipment—Accumulated				
	Depreciation	375			

Illustration 10-12

Gadsden Co.
Adjusted Ledger
1/31/X2

Cash

✓	2,000	(6)	700
(2)	5,000	(7)	42,180
(5)	44,100	(8)	1,100
		(9)	2,000

Accounts Receivable

✓	4,500	(5)	44,100
(3)	43,800		

Merchandise Inventory

✓	8,000	(4)	39,700
(1)	43,000		

Prepaid Insurance

✓	500	(12)	20

Land

✓	2,300	

Buildings

✓	10,000	

Buildings—Accumulated Depreciation

		✓	4,800
		(10)	50

Equipment

✓	20,500	
(9)	2,000	

Equipment—Accumulated Depreciation

		✓	9,000
		(11)	375

Accounts Payable

(7)	42,180	✓	4,200
		(1)	43,000

Dividends Payable

(6)	700	✓	700

Interest Payable

		✓	200
		(13)	50

Other Payables

(8)	1,100	✓	1,100

Bonds Payable—6%

		✓	10,000

Capital Stock

		✓	12,000

Retained Earnings

		✓	5,800

Sales

		(2)	5,000
		(3)	43,800

Cost of Goods Sold

(4)	39,700	

Insurance Expense

(12)	20	

Interest Expense

(13)	50	

Depreciation Expense

(10)	50	
(11)	375	

Often, a trial balance is prepared at this point to check the clerical accuracy of the adjusting process. This is called the *adjusted trial balance*. In Illustration 10-13, the adjusted trial balance is placed alongside the unadjusted trial balance so that you can compare them. Ordinarily these two trial balances would be kept separate.

Illustration 10-13

Gadsden Co.

	Unadjusted Trial Balance 1/31/X2 Debit	Unadjusted Trial Balance 1/31/X2 Credit	Adjusted Trial Balance 1/31/X2 Debit	Adjusted Trial Balance 1/31/X2 Credit
Cash	5,120		5,120	
Accounts Receivable	4,200		4,200	
Merchandise Inventory	11,300		11,300	
Prepaid Insurance	500		480	
Land	2,300		2,300	
Buildings	10,000		10,000	
Buildings—Accumulated Depreciation		4,800		4,850
Equipment	22,500		22,500	
Equipment—Accumulated Depreciation		9,000		9,375
Accounts Payable		5,020		5,020
Dividends Payable		–0–		–0–
Interest Payable		200		250
Other Payables		–0–		–0–
Bonds Payable—6%		10,000		10,000
Capital Stock		12,000		12,000
Retained Earnings		5,800		5,800
Sales		48,800		48,800
Cost of Goods Sold	39,700		39,700	
Insurance Expense	–0–		20	
Interest Expense	–0–		50	
Depreciation Expense	–0–		425	
Total	95,620	95,620	96,095	96,095

Notice that, even at this late stage, the balance in the retained earnings account is still the company's beginning (12/31/X1) balance. Ordinarily, the retained earnings account will change only when the nominal accounts are closed at the end of the period.

If we use compound entries, there are only two closing entries needed in this simple example:

A. Sales	48,800			B. Retained Earnings	40,195	
Retained Earnings		48,800		Cost of Goods Sold		39,700
				Insurance Expense		20
				Interest Expense		50
				Depreciation Expense		425

Illustration 10-14 shows the way the company's ledger would look after closing entries have been posted and the accounts ruled and balanced. The ledger is now termed the "closed ledger."

Illustration 10-14

Gadsden Co.
Closed Ledger
1/31/X2

Cash

√	2,000	(6)	700
(2)	5,000	(7)	42,180
(5)	44,100	(8)	1,100
		(9)	2,000
		√	5,120
	51,100		51,100
√	5,120		

Accounts Receivable

√	4,500	(5)	44,100
(3)	43,800	√	4,200
	48,300		48,300
√	4,200		

Merchandise Inventory

√	8,000	(4)	39,700
(1)	43,000	√	11,300
	51,000		51,000
√	11,300		

Prepaid Insurance

√	500	(12)	20
		√	480
	500		500
√	480		

Land

√	2,300	

Buildings

√	10,000	

Buildings— Accumulated Depreciation

		√	4,800
√	4,850	(10)	50
	4,850		4,850
		√	4,850

Equipment

√	20,500		
(9)	2,000	√	22,500
	22,500		22,500
√	22,500		

Equipment— Accumulated Depreciation

		√	9,000
√	9,375	(11)	375
	9,375		9,375
		√	9,375

Accounts Payable

(7)	42,180	√	4,200
√	5,020	(1)	43,000
	47,200		47,200
		√	5,020

Dividends Payable

(6)	700	√	700

Interest Payable

		√	200
√	250	(13)	50
	250		250
		√	250

Other Payables

(8)	1,100	√	1,100

Bonds Payable—6%

		√	10,000

Capital Stock

		√	12,000

Retained Earnings

B.	40,195	√	5,800
√	14,405	A.	48,800
	54,600		54,600
		√	14,405

Sales

A.	48,800	(2)	5,000
		(3)	43,800
	48,800		48,800

Cost of Goods Sold

(4)	39,700	B.	39,700

Insurance Expense

(12)	20	B.	20

Interest Expense

(13)	50	B.	50

Depreciation Expense

(10)	50	B.	425
(11)	375		
	425		425

Some companies like to prepare a final trial balance before making up the financial statements to test whether any clerical errors have been made in the closing and balancing process. (I made an error at this point myself—misread my own handwriting and indicated a total of $270 for interest payable. This threw my final trial balance $20 off. Discovering this allowed me to correct my error before going any further.) Illustration 10-15 shows a final trial balance.

Illustration 10-15

Gadsden Co.

	Unadjusted Trial Balance 1/31/X2		Adjusted Trial Balance 1/31/X2		Final Trial Balance 1/31/X2	
	Debit	*Credit*	*Debit*	*Credit*	*Debit*	*Credit*
Cash	5,120		5,120		5,120	
Accounts Receivable.	4,200		4,200		4,200	
Merchandise Inventory . . .	11,300		11,300		11,300	
Prepaid Insurance .	500		480		480	
Land	2,300		2,300		2,300	
Buildings	10,000		10,000		10,000	
Buildings—Accumulated Depreciation		4,800		4,850		4,850
Equipment . . .	22,500		22,500		22,500	
Equipment—Accumulated Depreciation . .		9,000		9,375		9,375
Accounts Payable .		5,020		5,020		5,020
Dividends Payable .						
Interest Payable . .		200		250		250
Other Payables . .						
Bonds Payable—6%.		10,000		10,000		10,000
Capital Stock. . .		12,000		12,000		12,000
Retained Earnings .		5,800		5,800		14,405
Sales		48,800		48,800		
Cost of Goods Sold .	39,700		39,700			
Insurance Expense .			20			
Interest Expense . .			50			
Depreciation Expense			425			
Total	95,620	95,620	96,095	96,095	55,900	55,900

The totals of the final trial balance are smaller than the other totals because the large nominal account debits and credits have been netted into a single smaller credit to retained earnings.

Gadsden Co.'s 1/31/X2 balance sheet is shown as Illustration 10-16.

Illustration 10-16

Gadsden Co.
Balance Sheet
January 31, 19X2

Assets

Current Assets:

Cash		$ 5,120	
Accounts Receivable		4,200	
Merchandise Inventory		11,300	
Prepaid Insurance		480	$21,100

Noncurrent Assets:

Land		$ 2,300	
Buildings—at cost	$10,000		
Less: Accumulated Depreciation	4,850	5,150	
Equipment—at cost	$22,500		
Less: Accumulated Depreciation	9,375	13,125	20,575
Total Assets			$41,675

Equities

Current Liabilities:

Accounts Payable		$ 5,020	
Interest Payable.		250	$ 5,270

Noncurrent Liabilities:

Bonds Payable—6%		10,000
Total Liabilities		$15,270

Stockholders' Equity:

Capital Stock		$12,000	
Retained Earnings		14,405	26,405
Total Equities			$41,675

Summary

The accounting cycle of a firm that uses a hand-operated accounting system consists essentially of the following activities (this description has been slightly simplified to save space—certain details of internal checks on accuracy have been omitted):

During the accounting period:

1. The accountant analyzes source documents (such as bills from suppliers, payroll data, records of sales, etc.), determines which accounts have changed, and makes ordinary journal entries.

2. These ordinary journal entries are posted to ledger accounts.

At the end of the accounting period:

3. The unadjusted balances of all ledger accounts are computed.

4. An unadjusted trial balance is prepared from the unadjusted ledger account balances.

5a. It is determined whether total debits equal total credits on the unadjusted trial balance. Other tests of the accuracy of the work done during the period are made. Correcting entries are prepared.

5b. Simultaneously, other adjusting entries are also being prepared.

6. Correcting and other adjusting entries are entered in the journal.

7. These entries are posted to the ledger.

8. The adjusted balances of all ledger accounts are computed.

9. An adjusted trial balance is prepared from the adjusted ledger balances.

10. Closing entries are prepared.

11. Closing entries are entered in the journal.

12. These entries are posted to the ledger.

13. The final balances of all ledger accounts are determined.

14. A final trial balance is prepared from the final ledger balances.

15. Financial statements are prepared. Usually the income statement is prepared from either the adjusted trial balance or the closing entries; the balance sheet is prepared from the final trial balance.

16. The process of recording ordinary balance sheet changes (of the next year) is begun all over again.

Step 16 indicates why all of this is called an accounting *cycle*: by the time the next-to-last step (preparing financial statements) is being performed, the firm already is well into the next year and is preparing ordinary journal entries again.

The activities that are performed during the accounting cycle may be diagrammed, to indicate (by arrows) the order in which they are performed and to show the relationships of one document to another. This is done in Illustration 10-17. Heavy arrows signify repetitive ordinary activities performed during the period. Light arrows indicate end-of-period accounting cycle activities. The kind of diagram in Illustration 10-17 is often called a *flowchart*. Here the reason for the name should be clear: Illustration 10-17 indicates the sequence (or flow) of activities in the accounting cycle.

Notice how end-of-period changes repeatedly pass through the journal and the ledger. It is assumed in Illustration 10-17 that the income statement is prepared from the adjusted trial balance. Numbers on arrows correspond to index numbers above.

At the start of this chapter, it was pointed out that some activities in a hand-operated system do not pertain to computerized accounting systems. In a computerized system, trial balances are not needed to check clerical accuracy. The account-balancing process is done automatically. (However, some kind of printout of account balances is often helpful at different points in the end-of-period work; and, of course there must be some feature of the computer program insuring that debits will equal credits at all times.)

Yet most things talked about in this chapter do apply to a computerized system. The input to a computerized system (punch cards, tape, or whatever else is used) can be regarded as the journal of the system, and the information storage of the computer (tape, disk, drum, data cell, or whatever) as the ledger. Ordinary entries are recorded during the accounting period, and adjustments are made at the end of the period whether or not the system is computerized. These entries are made in much the same way under either kind of system. The published financial statements are also the same no matter which system is used.

Illustration 10-17

Flowchart of the Accounting Cycle
of a Firm That Uses a Hand-Operated Accounting System

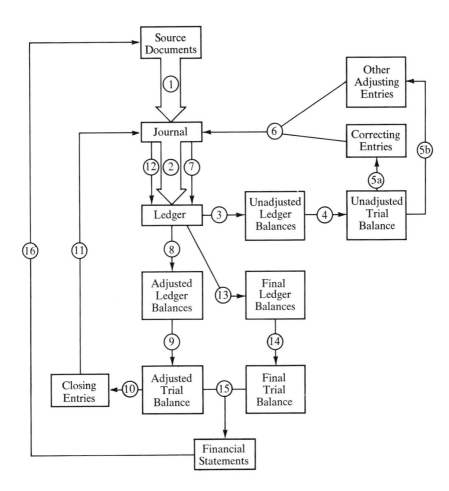

Problem for Study and Self-Examination

Problem 10-5:

Student Services, Inc., does business in a university community. The company originally specialized in major household cleaning jobs: walls, rugs, drapes, "spring cleaning," and so forth. More recently, it has diversified into general handyman work: minor maintenance, lawn care, gardening, snow removal, and the like. Most of the company's employees are college students who work part time. The company provides the necessary materials and supplies, coordinates activities, and supervises the quality of work performed.

Illustration 10-18 gives the company's balance sheet at 12/31/X1. Illustration 10-19 is a narrative summary of the company's ordinary 19X2 balance sheet changes. Illustration 10-20 gives information relating to the adjusting entries that the company made as of 12/31/X2.

1. Prepare the company's ledger, posting all 12/31/X1 balances. Here are the accounts that you should use and the number of lines to allow for each account:

Account	No. of Lines	Account	No. of Lines
Cash	10	Capital Stock	2
Accounts Receivable	5	Retained Earnings	5
Supplies	5	Sales	4
Prepaid Rent	5	Wages Expense	2
Prepaid Insurance	5	Supplies Expense	2
Equipment	5	Depreciation Expense	4
Equipment—Accumulated		Transportation Expense	2
Depreciation	6	Taxes Expense	4
Accounts Payable	6	Insurance Expense	2
Wages Payable	5	Rent Expense	2
Advance Vacation Payments	5	Miscellaneous Expense	2
Taxes Payable	6		

2. Make summary journal entries for all ordinary balance sheet changes recorded during the year.

3. Post these ordinary journal entries to the ledger.

4. Prepare an unadjusted trial balance.

5. Make all necessary adjusting entries as of 12/31/X2.

6. Post these adjusting entries to the ledger.

7. Prepare an adjusted trial balance.

8. Make closing entries as of 12/31/X2. (You can do this by making just two closing entries—one to close sales revenues to retained earnings, and one compound entry to close all expenses to retained earnings.)

9. Post closing entries to the ledger.

10. Rule and balance the ledger.

11. Prepare a final trial balance.

12. Prepare the company's 19X2 income statement.

13. Prepare the company's 12/31/X2 balance sheet.

Illustration 10-18

Student Services, Inc.
Balance Sheet
December 31, 19X1

Assets

Current Assets:

Cash	$24,300	
Accounts Receivable	15,430	
Supplies	6,190	
Prepaid Rent	560	
Prepaid Insurance	420	$46,900

Noncurrent Assets:

Equipment—at cost	$72,300	
Less: Accumulated Depreciation	32,690	39,610
Total Assets		$86,510

Equities

Current Liabilities:

Accounts Payable	$ 4,010	
Wages Payable	3,780	
Advance Vacation Payments	90	
Taxes Payable	5,110	$12,990

Stockholders' Equity:

Capital Stock	$50,000	
Retained Earnings	23,520	73,520
Total Equities		$86,510

Illustration 10-19

Student Services, Inc.
Narrative Summary of Ordinary Balance Sheet Changes
For the Year 19X2

1. The company's employees earned wages totalling $112,300. Wages are always recorded as a liability before being paid.
2. Wage payments to employees totalled $114,100.
3. The company bought $28,500 of new equipment on account.
4. The company bought $32,300 of supplies on account.
5. The company expects its employees to provide their own cars, but reimburses their transportation costs (at a flat rate of 7¢ per mile). During 19X2, such payments totalled $2,730.
6. The company runs a vacation service whereby employees will drop by a customer's house (once or twice a day) when the customer is on vacation, to feed pets, take in the mail, inspect the premises, and so forth. This is the second year that this service has been offered. Customers pay in advance for this service. Such advance payments totalled $1,860 in 19X2.
7. The company completed $1,800 of such vacation contracts in 19X2.
8. Except for vacation contracts, all customers are billed after they have received services, and are given one month in which to pay. Bills for services *other* than vacation services totalled $177,980 in 19X2.
9. The company always records taxes as a liability before paying them. During 19X2, the company paid $10,200 of taxes payable.
10. During 19X2, the company recognized $5,800 of tax expense (the remaining 19X2 taxes expense was recognized by an adjustment as of 12/31/X2—see adjusting item 18).
11. The company pays one year's rent on its premises ($1,680) in advance every September 1.
12. Miscellaneous expenses (paid in cash) totalled $1,520.
13. Accounts receivable of $177,390 were collected.
14. Accounts payable of $59,120 were paid.

Illustration 10-20

Student Services, Inc.
Information Relating to Adjusting Entries
As of 12/31/X2

15. The new equipment purchased during 19X2 (see Change 3) was purchased and put into service on May 1, 19X2. It was estimated that this equipment would have a total service life of ten years and a $1,500 scrap value on retirement.

16. The equipment owned at 12/31/X1 had been bought seven years before. At that time it was estimated to have a total service life of 15 years and a scrap value of $2,250 on retirement.

17. The company made a physical count of the supplies that it owned at 12/31/X2 and discovered that it owned supplies costing $7,010.

18. As of 12/31/X2, the company recognized an additional liability of $6,470 for 19X2 taxes.

19. As of 12/31/X2, it was recognized that one year's prepaid rent had expired.

20. As of 12/31/X2, it was recognized that $200 of prepaid insurance had expired.

Solution

Solution 10-5:

Illustration 10-21

Student Services, Inc.
Ordinary Summary Journal Entries
For the Year 19X2

1. Wages Expense	112,300	
Wages Payable		112,300
2. Wages Payable	114,100	
Cash		114,100
3. Equipment	28,500	
Accounts Payable		28,500
4. Supplies	32,300	
Accounts Payable		32,300
5. Transportation Expense	2,730	
Cash		2,730
6. Cash	1,860	
Advance Vacation Payments		1,860
7. Advance Vacation Payments	1,800	
Sales		1,800
8. Accounts Receivable	177,980	
Sales		177,980
9. Taxes Payable	10,200	
Cash		10,200
10. Taxes Expense	5,800	
Taxes Payable		5,800
11. Prepaid Rent	1,680	
Cash		1,680
12. Miscellaneous Expense	1,520	
Cash		1,520
13. Cash	177,390	
Accounts Receivable		177,390
14. Accounts Payable	59,120	
Cash		59,120

Illustration 10-22 shows the company's ledger after all ordinary journal entries have been posted. Illustration 10-23 is the company's unadjusted trial balance.

Illustration 10-22

Student Services, Inc.
Unadjusted Ledger
12/31/X2

Cash			
√	24,300	(2)	114,100
(6)	1,860	(5)	2,730
(13)	177,390	(9)	10,200
		(11)	1,680
		(12)	1,520
		(14)	59,120

Accounts Receivable			
√	15,430	(13)	177,390
(8)	177,980		

Supplies		
√	6,190	
(4)	32,300	

Prepaid Rent		
√	560	
(11)	1,680	

Prepaid Insurance		
√	420	

Equipment		
√	72,300	
(3)	28,500	

Equipment—
Accumulated Depreciation

		√	32,690

Accounts Payable			
(14)	59,120	√	4,010
		(3)	28,500
		(4)	32,300

Wages Payable			
(2)	114,100	√	3,780
		(1)	112,300

Advance
Vacation Payments

(7)	1,800	√	90
		(6)	1,860

Taxes Payable			
(9)	10,200	√	5,110
		(10)	5,800

Capital Stock

		√	50,000

Retained Earnings

		√	23,520

Sales			
		(7)	1,800
		(8)	177,980

Wages Expense	
(1)	112,300

Depreciation Expense

Transportation Expense	
(5)	2,730

Taxes Expense	
(10)	5,800

Insurance Expense

Rent Expense

Miscellaneous Expense	
(12)	1,520

Illustration 10-23

Student Services, Inc.
Unadjusted Trial Balance
12/31/X2

	Debit	Credit
Cash	14,200	
Accounts Receivable	16,020	
Supplies	38,490	
Prepaid Rent	2,240	
Prepaid Insurance	420	
Equipment	100,800	
Equipment—Accumulated Depreciation .		32,690
Accounts Payable		5,690
Wages Payable		1,980
Advance Vacation Payments		150
Taxes Payable		710
Capital Stock		50,000
Retained Earnings		23,520
Sales		179,780
Wages Expense	112,300	
Supplies Expense	–0–	
Depreciation Expense	–0–	
Transportation Expense	2,730	
Taxes Expense	5,800	
Insurance Expense	–0–	
Rent Expense	–0–	
Miscellaneous Expense	1,520	
Total	294,520	294,520

These balances are calculated from the T-accounts on page 566. For example, the balance for cash is calculated as follows on a scratch sheet or an adding machine:

24,300	114,100
1,860	2,730
177,390	10,200
203,550	1,680
	1,520
	59,120
189,350←	189,350
14,200	

Illustration 10-24

Student Services, Inc.
Adjusting Entries
As of 12/31/X2

15. The new equipment was used for 8 months in 19X2, so its 19X2 depreciation would be:
$$((\$28,500 - \$1,500)/10) \times 8/12 = \$1,800$$

Depreciation Expense	1,800	
Equipment—Accumulated Depreciation		1,800

16. One year's depreciation on the old equipment would be:
$$(\$72,300 - \$2,250)/15 = \$4,670$$

Depreciation Expense	4,670	
Equipment—Accumulated Depreciation		4,670

17.

Supplies—12/31/X1	$ 6,190
19X2 purchase of supplies	32,300
	$38,490
Supplies—12/31/X2	7,010
Supplies expense	$31,480

Supplies Expense	31,480	
Supplies		31,480

18.

Taxes Expense	6,470	
Taxes Payable		6,470

19.

Rent Expense	1,680	
Prepaid Rent		1,680

20.

Insurance Expense	200	
Prepaid Insurance		200

Illustration 10-25 shows the company's ledger after all adjusting entries have been posted. Illustration 10-26 is the company's adjusted trial balance.

Illustration 10-25

Student Services, Inc.
Adjusted Ledger
12/31/X2

Cash

√	24,300	(2)	114,100
(6)	1,860	(5)	2,730
(13)	177,390	(9)	10,200
		(11)	1,680
		(12)	1,520
		(14)	59,120

Accounts Receivable

√	15,430	(13)	177,390
(8)	177,980		

Supplies

√	6,190	(17)	31,480
(4)	32,300		

Prepaid Rent

√	560	(19)	1,680
(11)	1,680		

Prepaid Insurance

√	420	(20)	200

Equipment

√	72,300		
(3)	28,500		

Equipment— Accumulated Depreciation

		√	32,690
		(15)	1,800
		(16)	4,670

Accounts Payable

(14)	59,120	√	4,010
		(3)	28,500
		(4)	32,300

Wages Payable

(2)	114,100	√	3,780
		(1)	112,300

Advance Vacation Payments

(7)	1,800	√	90
		(6)	1,860

Taxes Payable

(9)	10,200	√	5,110
		(10)	5,800
		(18)	6,470

Capital Stock

		√	50,000

Retained Earnings

		√	23,520

Sales

		(7)	1,800
		(8)	177,980

Wages Expense

(1)	112,300	

Supplies Expense

(17)	31,480	

Depreciation Expense

(15)	1,800	
(16)	4,670	

Transportation Expense

(5)	2,730	

Taxes Expense

(10)	5,800	
(18)	6,470	

Insurance Expense

(20)	200	

Rent Expense

(19)	1,680	

Miscellaneous Expense

(12)	1,520	

Illustration 10-26

Student Services, Inc.
Trial Balances

	Unadjusted Trial Balance 12/31/X2		Adjusted Trial Balance 12/31/X2	
	Debit	Credit	Debit	Credit
Cash	14,200		14,200	
Accounts Receivable	16,020		16,020	
Supplies	38,490		7,010	
Prepaid Rent	2,240		560	
Prepaid Insurance	420		220	
Equipment	100,800		100,800	
Equipment—Accumulated Depreciation		32,690		39,160
Accounts Payable		5,690		5,690
Wages Payable		1,980		1,980
Advance Vacation Payments . . .		150		150
Taxes Payable		710		7,180
Capital Stock		50,000		50,000
Retained Earnings		23,520		23,520
Sales		179,780		179,780
Wages Expense	112,300		112,300	
Supplies Expense			31,480	
Depreciation Expense			6,470	
Transportation Expense	2,730		2,730	
Taxes Expense	5,800		12,270	
Insurance Expense			200	
Rent Expense			1,680	
Miscellaneous Expense	1,520		1,520	
Total	294,520	294,520	307,460	307,460

As in Illustration 10-24, these balances are calculated from the firm's T-accounts, in this case those on page 596.

Illustration 10-27

Student Services, Inc.
Closing Entries
As of 12/31/X2

A. Sales	179,780		B. Retained Earnings	168,650	
Retained			Wages Expense		112,300
Earnings		179,780	Supplies Expense		31,480
			Depreciation Expense		6,470
			Transportation Expense		2,730
			Taxes Expense		12,270
			Insurance Expense		200
			Rent Expense		1,680
			Miscellaneous Expense		1,520

Illustration 10-28

Student Services, Inc., Closed Ledger, 12/31/X2

Cash

√	24,300	(2)	114,100
(6)	1,860	(5)	2,730
(13)	177,390	(9)	10,200
		(11)	1,680
		(12)	1,520
		(14)	59,120
		√	14,200
	203,550		203,550
√	14,200		

Accounts Receivable

√	15,430	(13)	177,390
(8)	177,980	√	16,020
	193,410		193,410
√	16,020		

Supplies

√	6,190	(17)	31,480
(4)	32,300	√	7,010
	38,490		38,490
√	7,010		

Prepaid Rent

√	560	(19)	1,680
(11)	1,680	√	560
	2,240		2,240
√	560		

Prepaid Insurance

√	420	(20)	200
		√	220
	420		420
√	220		

Equipment

√	72,300		
(3)	28,500	√	100,800
	100,800		100,800
√	100,800		

Equipment—Accumulated Depreciation

		√	32,690
		(15)	1,800
√	39,160	(16)	4,670
	39,160		39,160
		√	39,160

Accounts Payable

(14)	59,120	√	4,010
		(3)	28,500
√	5,690	(4)	32,300
	64,810		64,810
		√	5,690

Wages Payable

(2)	114,100	√	3,780
√	1,980	(1)	112,300
	116,080		116,080
		√	1,980

Advance Vacation Payments

(7)	1,800	√	90
√	150	(6)	1,860
	1,950		1,950
		√	150

Taxes Payable

(9)	10,200	√	5,110
		(10)	5,800
√	7,180	(18)	6,470
	17,380		17,380
		√	7,180

Capital Stock

	√	50,000

Retained Earnings

B.	168,650	√	23,520
√	34,650	A.	179,780
	203,300		203,300
		√	34,650

Sales √

A.	179,780	(7)	1,800
		(8)	177,980
	179,780		179,780

Wages Expense √

(1)	112,300	B.	112,300

Supplies Expense √

(17)	31,480	B.	31,480

Depreciation Expense √

(15)	1,800	B.	6,470
(16)	4,670		
	6,470		6,470

Transportation Expense √

(5)	2,730	B.	2,730

Taxes Expense √

(10)	5,800	B.	12,270
(18)	6,470		
	12,270		12,270

Insurance Expense √

(20)	200	B.	200

Rent Expense √

(19)	1,680	B.	1,680

Miscellaneous Expense √

(12)	1,520	B.	1,520

Illustration 10-28 shows the company's ledger after closing entries have been posted and all accounts have been ruled and balanced. Illustration 10-29 shows the company's final trial balance. Illustration 10-30 is the company's income statement; Illustration 10-31 is the company's 12/31/X2 balance sheet.

Illustration 10-29

Student Services, Inc.
Trial Balances

	Unadjusted Trial Balance 12/31/X2		Adjusted Trial Balance 12/31/X2		Final Trial Balance 12/31/X2	
	Debit	*Credit*	*Debit*	*Credit*	*Debit*	*Credit*
Cash	14,200		14,200		14,200	
Accounts Receivable	16,020		16,020		16,020	
Supplies	38,490		7,010		7,010	
Prepaid Rent	2,240		560		560	
Prepaid Insurance	420		220		220	
Equipment	100,800		100,800		100,800	
Equipment— Accumulated Depreciation		32,690		39,160		39,160
Accounts Payable		5,690		5,690		5,690
Wages Payable		1,980		1,980		1,980
Advance Vacation Payments		150		150		150
Taxes Payable		710		7,180		7,180
Capital Stock		50,000		50,000		50,000
Retained Earnings		23,520		23,520		34,650
Sales		179,780		179,780		
Wages Expense	112,300		112,300			
Supplies Expense			31,480			
Depreciation Expense			6,470			
Transportation Expense	2,730		2,730			
Taxes Expense	5,800		12,270			
Insurance Expense			200			
Rent Expense			1,680			
Miscellaneous Expense	1,520		1,520			
Total	294,520	294,520	307,460	307,460	138,810	138,810

Illustration 10-30

Student Services, Inc.
Statement of Income and Retained Earnings
For the Year 19X2

Revenues:		
Sales		$179,780
Expenses:		
Wages Expense	$112,300	
Supplies Expense	31,480	
Depreciation Expense	6,470	
Transportation Expense	2,730	
Taxes Expense	12,270	
Insurance Expense	200	
Rent Expense	1,680	
Miscellaneous Expense	1,520	168,650
Net Income		$ 11,130
Retained Earnings—12/31/X1		23,520
Retained Earnings—12/31/X2		$ 34,650

Illustration 10-31

Student Services, Inc.
Balance Sheet
December 31, 19X2

Assets

Current Assets:		
Cash	$ 14,200	
Accounts Receivable	16,020	
Supplies	7,010	
Prepaid Rent	560	
Prepaid Insurance	220	$38,010
Noncurrent Assets:		
Equipment—at cost	$100,800	
Less: Accumulated Depreciation	39,160	61,640
Total Assets		$99,650

Equities

Current Liabilities:		
Accounts Payable	$ 5,690	
Wages Payable	1,980	
Advance Vacation Payments	150	
Taxes Payable	7,180	$15,000
Stockholders' Equity:		
Capital Stock	$ 50,000	
Retained Earnings	34,650	84,650
Total Equities		$99,650

Assignment Problems

Problem 10-A:

The comparative balance sheets of Senner Home Repairs, Inc., for 12/31/X1 and 12/31/X2 are given on page 349 of the text, a narrative summary of the company's 19X2 summary journal entries on page 350, and the company's 19X2 income statement below. These have been simplified to avoid the use of valuation accounts.

Senner Home Repairs, Inc.
Statement of Income and Retained Earnings
For the Year 19X2

Revenues:		
Sales		$145,700
Expenses:		
Salaries Expense	$71,000	
Depreciation Expense.	11,700	
Interest Expense	1,300	
Taxes Expense.	7,300	
Supplies Expense	45,200	
Insurance Expense	400	136,900
Net Income		$ 8,800
Retained Earnings—12/31/X1		7,500
Retained Earnings—12/31/X2		$ 16,300

Other data: on 12/31/X1 the company had the following account balances: building—allowance for depreciation, $29,300; equipment—allowance for depreciation, $30,600.

Record the company's 19X2 balance sheet changes in summary journal entries, employing valuation and nominal accounts. Prepare the noncurrent assets section of the company's 12/31/X2 balance sheet.

Problem 10-B:

Problem 9-C (pages 506–509) gives the balance sheets of Pepper Enterprises for 12/31/X2 and 12/31/X3, in a simplified form that does not employ valuation accounts. In solving this problem, you are to employ valuation and nominal accounts.

The costs of property owned at 12/31/X2 were as follows: land, $2,832; buildings and improvements, $19,356; machinery and equipment, $83,252; patents and license agreements, $3,054. The following changes affecting property accounts occurred during 19X3:

1. Purchases on account: land, $1,338; buildings and improvements, $1,047; machinery and equipment, $13,643.

2. Machinery was sold that had cost the company $3,565; accumulated depreciation on this machinery at the time of sale was $3,137. Accumulated depreciation on this machinery at 12/31/X2 had been $3,009. This machinery was sold (on account) for $247.

3. Patents that had cost the company $227 reached the end of their 17-year legal life and expired during 19X3. Accumulated amortization on these patents was $216 at 12/31/X2.

4. Other patents (also with 17-year legal lives) that had cost the company $85 were sold on 5/26/X3 (2/5 of the way through 19X3) for $488, cash. These patents were exactly 5 years old at 5/26/X3.

5. The company made the following year-end adjustments for depreciation and amortization. These are in addition to those discussed or implied in changes 2, 3, and 4: buildings and improvements, $645; machinery and equipment, $11,616; patents and license agreements, $175.

Prepare ledger accounts as of 12/31/X2 for all property accounts and the following nominal accounts: depreciation expense, amortization expense, loss on sale of machinery, gain on sale of patents. Record all changes given in journal entries. Do not prepare closing entries. Post all entries made to the ledger. Rule and balance the property accounts, then prepare the property section of the company's 12/31/X3 balance sheet. Compare your result with that on page 507.

Problem 10-C:

The comparative balance sheets of Campus Store for 6/30/X4 and 6/30/X5 are given in Problem 8-F (pages 444–447), as is a narrative summary of the company's balance sheet changes for the year ended 6/30/X5 and the related simple summary journal entries. These have been simplified to avoid the use of nominal and valuation accounts. Shown below is the company's income statement and certain other data.

Campus Store
Statement of Income and Retained Earnings
For the Year Ended 6/30/X5

Sales ($1,625,900 + $166,800) .		$1,792,700	
Less: Patronage Refunds		53,700	$1,739,000
Cost of Goods Sold:			
Books .		$1,025,100	
General Merchandise .		298,800	1,323,900
Gross Margin .			$ 415,100
Salaries Expense .		$ 174,200	
Advertising Expense .		10,600	
Utilities Expense .		9,400	
Supplies Expense .		13,600	
Insurance Expense .		4,400	
Taxes Expense ($76,100 + $16,800) .		92,900	
Depreciation Expense ($7,500 + $8,700) .		16,200	
Interest Expense .		3,600	
Miscellaneous Expense ($4,800 + $6,400) .		11,200	336,100
Net Income from Operations .			$ 79,000
Loss on Sale of Equipment .			3,200

continued on page 576

Net Income	$ 75,800
Dividends	15,000
Increase in Retained Earnings	$ 60,800
Retained Earnings—6/30/X4	57,300
Retained Earnings—6/30/X5	$ 118,100

Other data: on 6/30/X4 the company had the following account balances: building—accumulated depreciation, $113,400; fixtures—accumulated depreciation, $76,200. The fixtures sold in changes 33a and 33b had accumulated depreciation of $21,300 at the time of sale. The new fixtures purchased in change 14 were paid for by 12/31/X5.

Prepare summary journal entries, employing appropriate nominal and valuation accounts. To save time, prepare *only* those journal entries requiring the use of nominal or valuation accounts.

Problem 10-D:

See Problem 10-C. Prepare closing entries. Also, prepare the noncurrent asset section of the company's 6/30/X5 balance sheet.

Problem 10-E:

The following information summarizes some (but not all) of the economic activity of Haley's of West Palm Beach for the fiscal year ended 9/30/X0. Three zeros have been omitted from the figures; you should do likewise in your answers. Prepare journal entries, but not closing entries, using appropriate nominal and valuation accounts.

1. Sales totalled $3,047; of these, $2,891 were on account; the rest were for cash.

2. The only other revenue was dividend income, which totalled $19 during the year. The company recognizes a receivable for dividends when they are declared.

3. Salaries are recorded as a liability before being paid. The company owed its employees $20 for salaries at the beginning of the year, and $26 at year end. Payments of salaries totalled $605.

4. Depreciation of furniture and equipment totalled $62, of vehicles—$8, and of building—$46. (This is exclusive of depreciation on the fixtures sold in change 8.)

5. The company's beginning and ending inventories of merchandise totalled $304 and $287, respectively. The company purchased $1,726 of merchandise during the year, on account.

6. Taxes are recorded as a liability before being paid. These taxes totalled $207 during the year.

7. Miscellaneous expenses (credit *Various*) totalled $189.

8. On 3/31/X0 the company sold used fixtures for $23, cash. These fixtures had been purchased exactly $7\frac{1}{2}$ years earlier, at which time they cost $106, and had an estimated service life of 8 years and an estimated scrap value upon retirement of $10.

9. Dividends, paid in cash, totalled $88.

Problem 10-F:

Problem 10-E gives some (but not all) of the balance sheet changes of Haley's of West Palm Beach for the fiscal year ended 9/30/X0. Prepare closing entries as of 9/30/X0. Which of the company's nominal and valuation accounts should show balances before the closing entries? After the closing entries?

Problem 10-G:

Sarasota Globetrotter Corporation closes its books once a year, every December 31st. The company records depreciation as an end-of-year adjusting entry. The only exception to this occurs when depreciable assets are sold during the year. At 12/31/X8, the noncurrent asset section of the company's balance sheet appeared as follows.

Noncurrent assets:

Land		$ 100,300
Buildings—at cost	$ 986,700	
Less: Accumulated depreciation	402,600	584,100
Equipment—at cost	$2,670,200	
Less: Accumulated depreciation	1,310,900	1,359,300
Total noncurrent assets		$2,043,700

The following is a summary of all 19X9 changes affecting company noncurrent assets:

1. The company bought equipment on account at a total cost of $327,100 on 9/1/X9.

2. This equipment is estimated to have a 17-year service life, and a scrap value of $10,900 upon retirement.

3. On 5/31/X9, the company sold old equipment for $24,300. This equipment had cost $217,600 when it was purchased on 2/1/X0. At that time it was estimated to have a service life of 11 years and a scrap value of $6,400 upon retirement.

4. On 6/30/X9 the company completed demolition of an old building that had housed the machinery sold in change 3. This building had been constructed 49 years prior to 1/1/X9 for a total cost of $90,000. At that time it was estimated to have a service life of 50 years and no scrap value upon retirement. The wreckers paid the company $2,100 for the old bricks.

5. Depreciation of building and equipment owned at 12/31/X8 and not retired during 19X9 were $25,600 and $245,300, respectively.

Make all appropriate ordinary and adjusting journal entries, employing nominal and valuation accounts. Do not make closing entries. Prepare all necessary ledger accounts as of 1/1/X9; post the journal entries to the ledger. Do not bother to prepare ledger accounts for cash and accounts payable. Prepare the noncurrent asset section of the company's 12/31/X9 balance sheet.

Problem 10-H:

As part of your training in accounting, you must become able to extend the concepts and techniques you have learned into situations that require different methods of analysis. This problem provides such an opportunity to increase your flexibility and broaden your understanding. The background needed to solve this problem has been provided by the text, but the particular method of analysis required may at first seem unusual. Apply what you already have learned to this new situation. Four zeros are omitted from the figures in the following problem. You should do likewise in your answer.

Several years after graduation, you become assistant comptroller of a medium-sized manufacturing firm. On December 30, 19X8 (a Saturday), you brought home the company's 19X7 and 19X8 accounting records pertaining to its noncurrent assets, intending to make the related 19X8 year-end adjusting entries the next day. Summary information about all 19X8 changes in these noncurrent assets will be needed by the auditors when they arrive at 8:00 A.M. on Monday, 1/1/X9. You are working at home on Sunday (instead of working at the office) because you promised to babysit your precocious three-year-old son while your wife makes preparations for the New Year's Eve party that you are giving on Sunday night.

Your son spent most of Sunday morning engrossed in a picture book about ships. Because of this, you were able to finish work shortly after lunch, and then watch the ball games. The party that evening was very successful. But when the last guest departed at 3:30 A.M. on January 1st, you were surprised to hear water splashing in the children's bathroom. This was particularly startling because, to the best of your knowledge, this room had not been used by any of your guests.

Throwing the door open, you find your son standing next to the bathtub, which is filled to the brim. "Thips, Daddy!" he crows, a radiant smile on his little face, "Thee the pwetty thips!"

There in the bathtub are all the noncurrent asset records. Evidently the child put them to soak early in the evening, for the ink is gone from most of them. Besides, most of the paper has disintegrated as a result of long and vigorous stirring (for this, your son used your golf clubs). Taking sudden stock of yourself, it is only too clear that you enjoyed the party enough that you are unable to remember any of the noncurrent asset figures reliably. After a desperate search, your wife reminds you that all your scratch paper was used in lighting a fireplace fire.

The records themselves can eventually be reconstructed from underlying documents, though at some cost in time. But it will be very inconvenient if you do not have the summary information relating to 19X8 changes in noncurrent assets by 8:00 A.M.—really by 7:00 A.M., since that is when you must leave for work. Accordingly, you set to salvaging whatever you can from the tub. Here is what you have learned by 6:00 A.M.:

The company owns only three kinds of noncurrent assets. Here is what has survived of the related ledger accounts. All figures that survived are complete—none were *partially* washed away.

Land		Buildings		Equipment	
√		√ 3,480		√ 4,327	530
	√		√		√
	278		4,686		5,127

Buildings— Accumulated Depreciation		Equipment— Accumulated Depreciation	
	√		√
√		√	
1,718			2,526

There were no purchases or sales of buildings or equipment during 19X7. On 3/31/X8, the company purchased land and buildings on account for a combined price of $1,248. The buildings had an estimated service life of 25 years, with an estimated scrap value upon retirement of $100. On 9/1/X8, the company purchased equipment (on account) with an estimated service life of 9 years and an estimated scrap value upon retirement of $17. There were no other purchases of noncurrent assets.

The company uses straight-line depreciation. Depreciation charges for 19X7 (the previous year) were as follows: buildings, $116; equipment, $361.

All noncurrent assets that were retired during 19X8 were sold. On 6/30/X8, old equipment was sold for cash. This equipment had been purchased on 6/30/X0, at which time it had an estimated service life of 12 years, and an estimated scrap value upon retirement of $50. There was a $27 loss on this sale. The company records such retirements by a single compound journal entry of the form:

```
Depreciation Expense  . . . . . . . .  . . .  XXX
Equipment—Accumulated Depreciation .  . . .  XXX
Loss on Retirement of Equipment   . . . . .  XXX
Cash  . . . . . . . . . . . . . . . . . . .  XXX
    Equipment . . . . . . . . . . . . .          XXX
```

There were no other sales of noncurrent assets during 19X8, and no noncurrent assets became fully depreciated during either 19X7 or 19X8. You are quite sure that there were no unusual transactions involving noncurrent assets during 19X8.

You have one hour left. Reconstruct all 19X8 summary journal entries involving noncurrent assets, and complete the related ledger accounts (including beginning and ending balances). One possible line of attack would begin by organizing your data into T-accounts.

Problem 10-I:

As part of your training in accounting, you must become able to extend what you have learned into new situations. This problem provides an opportunity to increase your flexibility and broaden your understanding. The text provides all background information needed to solve this problem, but the circumstances described will be unfamiliar. Apply what you already have learned to this new situation.

For many years Matthews Enterprises had no significant difficulty in collecting its accounts receivable. However, in 19X3 the company introduced a new line of products in a new industry. Trade association statistics for this industry indicated that the company should expect 1% of all credit sales of the new line to prove uncollectible. Cash sales are uncommon in this industry. The new line was profitable enough to more than cover such bad debts.

During the last half of 19X3, related credit sales totalled $3,207,000. The company did not recognize any sales as uncollectible during 19X3, but it has been having difficulty collecting certain accounts. As of 12/31/X3, the company's accounts receivable total $9,320,000, of which $1,013,000 are from the new product line. The company believes that the trade association predictions are correct—that approximately $3,207,000 × 1% ≈ $32,000 of new product accounts receivable will prove to be uncollectible.

This leads to a predicament. On the one hand, the company wishes to report that $9,320,000 of receivables are legally owed to it. On the other hand, it wishes to report that its receivables are *worth* only about $9,320,000 − $32,000 = $9,288,000. Comment. Defend your comments. (Hint: this chapter has indicated a way to report an amount and an adjustment or qualification to this amount simultaneously.)

Problem 10-J:

Shown below are the 12/31/X2 balance sheet of Leesburg-Morris Chemicals and the general form of the company's income statement, followed by some (but not all) of the company's summary balance sheet changes for the year 19X3. Three zeros have been omitted from all figures; you should do likewise in your answers. Prepare appropriate journal entries, employing nominal and valuation accounts.

Leesburg-Morris Chemicals
Consolidated Balance Sheet
(000 omitted)
December 31, 19X2

Assets

Current Assets:

Cash	$ 10,668	
Marketable securities and time deposits	31,141	
Accounts and notes receivable:		
Trade	86,111	
Miscellaneous	36,705	
Inventories	86,620	$251,245

Investments and Non-Current Receivables:

Non-consolidated subsidiaries	$ 88,169	
Sundry	59,184	147,353

Property:

	Cost	Accumulated Depreciation	
Land	$ 11,828	$ –0–	11,828
Land and waterway improvements	11,884	6,377	5,507
Buildings	72,344	33,411	38,933
Machinery and other equipment	569,032	318,603	250,429
Wells and brine systems	13,102	7,516	5,586
Furniture and fixtures	6,227	3,442	2,785
Other	9,905	3,767	6,138
Construction in progress	62,221	–0–	62,221
Deferred Charges and Other Assets			8,223

Total	$790,248

Liabilities

Current Liabilities:

Notes payable	$ 70,214	
Long-term debt due within one year	1,877	
Accounts payable	37,745	
United States and foreign taxes on income	18,291	
Accrued and other current liabilities	39,857	$167,984

Long-Term Debt:

Promissory notes.	$ 90,000	
Debentures	38,232	
Notes payable under revolving credit agreements	73,060	
Other	18,960	220,252

Stockholders' Equity:

Common stock	$256,466	
Earned surplus	145,546	402,012
Total		$790,248

Leesburg-Morris Chemicals
Consolidated Statement of Income and Earned Surplus
(000 omitted)
For the Year Ended December 31, 19XX

Sales and Other Revenues:

Sales	$XXX	
Dividends received	XXX	
Interest income	XXX	
Other income	XXX	$XXX

Costs and Other Charges:

Cost of sales	$XXX	
Provision for depreciation and depletion	XXX	
Selling and administrative expenses	XXX	
Interest expense	XXX	
Other income charges.	XXX	XXX
Income before provision for taxes on income		$XXX
Provision for taxes on income		XXX
Net Income		$XXX
Balance of earned surplus at beginning of the year		XXX
		$XXX
Deduct—Cash dividends		XXX
Balance of earned surplus at end of the year		$XXX

Notes:

As was emphasized in the text, "Earned Surplus" is an obsolete title account; nonetheless the firm uses it.

The company's debentures payable and notes payable under revolving credit agreements have various maturity dates. Each year a new group of these becomes due. At the end of each year, the company transfers the amount that must be paid next year (which thus has become a current liability) from the respective long-term debt accounts to the current liability "long-term debt due within one year."

The company employs the expense account "provision for depreciation and depletion" even though it employs no accumulated depletion accounts.

(continued on page 582)

The company's financial statements have been consolidated with those of several other companies it owns. Certain other companies owned by Leesburg-Morris Chemicals have not been consolidated in this fashion; instead, the purchase price of the company's investment in them is reported among the investments on the balance sheet. (The general principles of consolidated financial statements are discussed in Chapters Three and Eight.)

Gains on sales of noncurrent assets are recorded in the account "other income"; losses on sales of noncurrent assets are recorded in the account "other income charges."

The firm's income statement is somewhat compressed. Expenses such as salaries expense, insurance expense, and utilities expense are combined under the single title "selling and administrative expenses."

1. The company issued common stock for $3,962, cash.

2. The company acquired investments in nonconsolidated subsidiaries costing a total of $8,379, by issuing "other long-term debt."

3. Sales totalled $642,617; of these, $580,312 were on ordinary trade accounts and notes receivable, and $62,305 were on miscellaneous other accounts and notes receivable.

4. Ordinary trade accounts and notes receivable totalling $551,566 were collected; miscellaneous other accounts and notes receivable totalling $90,362 were collected.

5. $19,377 of selling and administrative expenses were incurred on ordinary trade accounts payable; another $60,787 of selling and administrative expenses accrued or arose through other current liabilities.

6. Dividends totalling $18,756 were declared and paid.

7. Other income charges totalling $1,186 were incurred on ordinary trade accounts payable.

8. The company issued $80,000 of short-term notes payable, for cash.

9. The company sold machinery and equipment on miscellaneous accounts receivable for $2,554; this machinery and equipment cost the company $59,881, and had accumulated depreciation of $57,418 at the time of sale.

10. The company sold "other property" on miscellaneous accounts receivable for $2,316; this "other property" cost the company $5,171, and had accumulated depreciation of $2,769 at the time of sale.

11. $49,422 of construction in progress was completed and transferred to the following properties accounts: buildings, $19,611; land and waterway improvements, $2,524; machinery and other equipment, $27,287.

12. Land costing $7,382 was acquired under short-term notes payable; machinery and other equipment costing $35,139 were acquired on ordinary trade accounts payable.

Problem 10-K:

Problem 10-J gives the 12/31/X2 balance sheet of Leesburg-Morris Chemicals, and the general form of the company's income statement. Shown below are some (but not all) of the company's summary balance sheet changes for 19X3. Three zeros have been omitted from all figures; you should do likewise in your answers. Prepare appropriate journal entries, employing nominal and valuation accounts.

(a) The company issued $39,823 of debentures and $18,890 of other long-term debt, for cash.

(b) Expenditures for deferred charges and other assets (all on ordinary trade accounts payable) totalled $2,896.

(c) Taxes are recorded as a liability before being paid; $18,315 of United States and foreign taxes on income were recognized during the year.

(d) Interest charges of $14,791 were recognized as having accrued during the year.

(e) The company invested $67,840, cash, in marketable securities and time deposits; it sold $58,410 of such investments, for cash.

(f) Interest and dividends on such investments are initially recorded as miscellaneous accounts receivable; interest of $7,319 and dividends of $3,971 were recognized during the year.

(g) $129,711 of inventories were acquired under ordinary trade accounts payable; $298,584 of inventories were acquired under accrued and other current liabilities.

(h) The following liabilities were paid: short-term notes payable, $94,447; long-term debt due within one year, $1,877; accounts payable, $187,242; United States and foreign taxes on income, $21,224; accrued and other current liabilities, $446,191.

(i) The company sold furniture and fixtures on miscellaneous accounts receivable for $394; these furniture and fixtures cost the company $2,400, and had accumulated depreciation of $1,961 at the time of sale.

(j) $1,341 of construction in progress was completed and transferred to the following properties accounts: wells and brine systems, $518; other property, $823.

(k) $5,085 of furniture and fixtures and $6,087 of construction in progress were acquired on ordinary trade accounts payable.

(l) $4,032 of other properties and $31,417 of construction in progress were acquired under short-term notes payable.

(m) $44,712 of construction in progress was acquired under accrued and other current liabilities.

Problem 10-L:

Refer to the data in Problems 10-J and 10-K; these describe all of the company's balance sheet changes that were recorded during 19X3 (as distinguished from those recorded at year end). Prepare an unadjusted trial balance for Leesburg-Morris Chemicals, as of December 31, 19X3.

Problem 10-M:

Problem 10-J gives the 12/31/X2 balance sheet of Leesburg-Morris Chemicals and the general form of the company's income statement. Problems 10-J and 10-K give the company's summary balance sheet changes that were recorded during 19X3. Shown below are the balance sheet changes that the company recorded by adjusting entries as of 12/31/X3. Prepare appropriate adjusting entries, employing nominal and valuation accounts.

A. $1,662 of sundry investments were sold at cost, on miscellaneous accounts receivable. This transaction occurred on 12/30/X3. It was necessary to record it as an adjusting entry because, by oversight, it was not recorded on the date on which it occurred.

B. The following long-term debt will mature during 19X4: debentures, $2,310; notes payable under revolving credit agreements, $11,200.

C. 19X3 expirations of deferred charges and other assets resulted in transfers of costs to the following accounts: provision for depreciation and depletion, $372; inventories, $303; selling and administrative expenses, $776.

D. $6,707 of interest expense was accrued as of 12/31/X3; so were $7,157 of selling and administrative expenses, $17,673 of costs of inventories, $5,607 of taxes on income, $613 of interest income, $1,404 of other income charges, and $990 of other income (miscellaneous accounts receivable are used to record accruals of interest and other income).

E. Inventories were utilized as follows: selling and administrative expenses, $3,465; construction in progress, $1,126; cost of goods sold, $417,768.

F. It was discovered that (through a clerical error) 19X3 sales on ordinary trade accounts receivable totalling $189 had been recorded twice.

G. At year end, completion of construction in progress totalling $4,009 was recognized; these costs were transferred to the following properties accounts: buildings, $3,086; machinery and other equipment, $923.

H. 19X3 depreciation was as follows: land and waterway improvements, $839; buildings, $6,012; machinery and other equipment, $49,057; wells and brine systems, $171; furniture and fixtures, $3,311; other properties, $3,003.

Problem 10-N:
   Refer to the data in Problems 10-J, 10-K, and 10-M. Prepare an adjusted trial balance for Leesburg-Morris Chemicals as of 12/31/X3.

Problem 10-O:
   Refer to the data in Problems 10-J, 10-K, and 10-M. Prepare closing entries for Leesburg-Morris Chemicals as of 12/31/X3.

Problem 10-P:
   Refer to the data in Problems 10-J, 10-K, and 10-M. Prepare a final trial balance for Leesburg-Morris Chemicals as of 12/31/X3.

Problem 10-Q:
   Refer to the data in Problems 10-J, 10-K, and 10-M. Prepare a balance sheet for Leesburg-Morris Chemicals as of 12/31/X3.

Problem 10-R:
   Refer to the data in Problems 10-J, 10-K, and 10-M. Prepare an income statement for Leesburg-Morris Chemicals for the year ended 12/31/X3.

Eleven

Receivables, Payables, and Compound Interest

The remaining chapters of this book will concentrate on certain technical features of financial accounting that you must understand in order to comprehend published financial statements. Many of the matters discussed also serve as foundations for your work in advanced courses. Chapters Twelve and Thirteen are concerned with special problems of reporting nonmonetary assets. This chapter discusses two major phenomena with which accountants must contend when reporting monetary items:

1. Some receivables inevitably turn out to be uncollectible.

2. The proceeds obtained from issuing debt often differ from its *maturity value*—the amount to be paid at its due date, exclusive of any amount explicitly designated as interest charges.

Up to now we have been assuming the use of simple interest for interest-bearing debt. In dealing with this second phenomenon, the accountant may make calculations that employ *compound* interest (wherein interest is charged upon accumulated interest payable as well as upon the amount initially borrowed). Because of this, and because a knowledge of compound interest will be useful in many of your other courses, this chapter also contains an introductory discussion of compound interest. It should be emphasized, however, that it is not the purpose of this chapter to provide a thorough discussion of any of these three topics—thorough discussion must be left to a more advanced text. Instead, the aim of what follows is merely to provide that minimum introduction needed to understand financial statements.

Receivables: Uncollectible Accounts

Before we consider uncollectible accounts receivable, a brief review of material that was discussed earlier would be appropriate. Let us consider the case of a manufacturer selling its finished goods. Such goods usually are sold on credit—few manufacturers sell directly for cash. Therefore, in exchange for finished goods, the manufacturer obtains a receivable:

$$
\begin{array}{lll}
\text{Accounts Receivable} & \text{XXX} & \\
\quad \text{Sales} & & \text{XXX}
\end{array}
$$

(This entry records the acquisition of a receivable and the related revenue.)

$$
\begin{array}{lll}
\text{Cost of Goods Sold} & \text{XXX} & \\
\quad \text{Finished Goods} & & \text{XXX}
\end{array}
$$

(This entry records giving up of finished goods and the related merchandise expense.)

Once the accountant has decided which revenues he will recognize for a particular year, he tries to report, as expenses of that year, all the costs of obtaining these revenues. This is called the *matching* process. For instance, suppose that the manufacturer made a practice of paying all freight charges on shipments to its customers. The accountant would then report all freight charges on 19X1 sales as a 19X1 expense.

Significance of this for uncollectibles

Almost any company that sells on credit will sometimes discover that it is unable to collect an account receivable, usually because the customer has experienced unexpected financial difficulties. The risk of uncollectibles is one that few companies can escape; a company that demands direct cash payment from its customers will ordinarily lose far more profits than are lost through uncollectibles, simply because it will lose most of its customers! Uncollectibles, or "bad debts," are a common, if regrettable, business expense.[1]

If expenses are to be matched with the revenues they help generate, the bad debts that result from a particular year's sales should be reflected in that year's expenses. *At the end of the year, however, the accountant is unable to tell exactly which sales will prove to be uncollectible.*

Example of uncollectible accounts receivable

Hagen-Los Angeles Corporation was founded in 19X1. During its first year of operations, it sold to approximately 14,000 customers, all sales on account. Total 19X1 sales were $15,100,000:

$$
\begin{array}{lll}
\textit{During 19X1:} \ \text{Accounts Receivable} & 15,100,000 & \\
\quad \text{Sales} & & 15,100,000
\end{array}
$$

---

[1] Some accountants prefer instead to describe bad debts as a correction of the sales figures, on the grounds that if a receivable turns out to be uncollectible, the company was mistaken in thinking that a genuine sale had taken place. This book rejects that interpretation mainly because the "expense" interpretation of bad debts is much more commonly found in practice.

Total 19X1 collections on account were $14,100,000.

> *During 19X1:* Cash   14,100,000
>   Accounts Receivable   14,100,000

At 12/31/X1, $1,000,000 of accounts receivable resulting from 19X1 sales were still outstanding (15,100,000 − 14,100,000 = 1,000,000). The company established the policy of trying to collect overdue accounts receivable until an account became a year old, at which time the company felt forced to admit that the account was uncollectible. During 19X2, $970,000 of 19X1 accounts receivable were collected.

> *During 19X2:* Cash   970,000
>   Accounts Receivable   970,000

The remaining $30,000 of accounts receivable resulting from 19X1 sales were judged to be uncollectible (1,000,000 − 970,000 = 30,000). The company might make the following entry in 19X2:

> *During 19X2:* Bad Debts Expense   30,000
>   Accounts Receivable   30,000

Such an entry would be partly correct. Uncollectible accounts should be eliminated from accounts receivable (as is done by this entry), but the bad debts expense is shown as a 19X2 expense, even though the related sales were made in 19X1. Therefore, the entry violates the matching rule by associating the bad debts expense with the wrong year's revenues.

Estimating uncollectibles

Usually, there is a simple way to avoid violating the matching rule. At the end of each year, the accountant merely estimates the total uncollectibles that will result from that year's sales. Two ways of making these estimates are illustrated later.

If the company has been in business for several years, it has ordinarily had enough experience with its customers to make reliable estimates. If it is a new company (like Hagen-Los Angeles Corporation), its industry trade association may be able to provide the necessary data, or its experienced employees may be able to draw on their background with other companies. Suppose that at the end of 19X1, the Hagen-Los Angeles Corporation accountant estimates that $30,200 of accounts receivable arising from 19X1 sales will be uncollectible; then the following entry should be made as of *December 31, 19X1*:

> *As of 12/31/X1:* Bad Debts Expense   30,200
>   Accounts Receivable—Estimated
>   Uncollectibles   30,200

You might immediately ask: "Why not just credit accounts receivable? Why use this other account? After all, the accountant is estimating that $30,200 of accounts receivable will be uncollectible, and the appropriate thing to do with uncollectible accounts is to write them off."

The answer is simple. "Accounts receivable—estimated uncollectibles" is a *valuation account* (see page 544) to accounts receivable (just as "equipment—accumulated depreciation" is a valuation account to equipment). There are two reasons for using a valuation account here instead of accounts receivable:

1. The $30,200 is an *estimate*. The $1,000,000 figure for accounts receivable is a firm figure, known with precision. Accountants are reluctant to mingle estimated figures with relatively exact ones; instead, they use separate accounts for the estimates (earlier, you saw that a valuation account is used for accumulated depreciation for exactly the same reason).

2. There is also a technical reason resulting from the way most firms keep their books. The accounts receivable account serves as a summary of detailed records in which the accounts of each customer are maintained separately, and it gives the total amount owed by all customers according to these records. At 12/31/X1, the accountant is unable to tell which of the individual customer accounts will go bad, so he must include all of them in his detailed records. Were the accounts receivable account credited, its total would no longer equal the sum of the individual customer accounts in the detailed records.

19X2 entries

During 19X2, whenever it is determined that an individual customer account is uncollectible, this account will be removed from the detailed records, and the accounts receivable ledger account correspondingly reduced. But no expense will be recognized, since this was already done as of 12/31/X1. Instead, the accountant will reduce (debit) the valuation account because "accounts receivable—estimated uncollectibles" is an estimate of total uncollectibles; once an amount of uncollectibles is known, the estimate should be reduced by a corresponding amount. Assuming again that accounts totalling $30,000 actually proved uncollectible, the summary 19X2 entry would be:

During 19X2: Accounts Receivable—Estimated Uncollectibles   30,000
                    Accounts Receivable   30,000

Uncollectibles had been estimated as $30,200; actual uncollectibles were $30,000. What is done with the "extra" $200? Ordinarily, nothing is done with the extra $200, for it is *expected* that estimates will err. As long as the cumulative error remains small, it may be ignored. A large cumulative error would call for a correction entry, and we shall see an example of such an entry in Chapter Thirteen. Often, however, estimation errors in successive years tend to cancel each other, and no cumulative problem arises.

Balance sheet presentation

The valuation account, "accounts receivable—estimated uncollectibles," is presented on the balance sheet in exactly the same way as is the account, "equipment—

accumulated depreciation." On Hagen-Los Angeles Corporation's 12/31/X1 balance sheet, you would see something similar to one of the following:

Current Assets:

Cash		$ XXX
Accounts Receivable	$1,000,000	
Less: Estimated Uncollectibles	30,200	969,800
Inventories		XXX

or,

Current Assets:

Cash	$ XXX
Accounts Receivable (net of $30,200 estimated uncollectibles)	969,800
Inventories	XXX

Acceptable alternate titles for "accounts receivable—estimated uncollectibles" include "accounts receivable—estimated bad debts," "accounts receivable—allowance for bad debts," and so forth. You sometimes see the account title "reserve for bad debts." But, as indicated in Chapter Five (pages 268–270), the word "reserve" is confusing in this context, since it also refers to restrictions of retained earnings. An alternative presentation, which parallels the second one above, was given on page 88.

Estimation techniques

Two main lines of attack are followed in estimating uncollectible accounts receivable. Either estimation technique can be used as a partial check on the accuracy of the other.

A. *Percentage of credit sales.* One approach requires the accountant to estimate the percentage of *total* credit sales that may prove uncollectible. This percentage figure may be derived from the company's past experience or from the general experience of the company's industry. For example, the Hagen-Los Angeles Corporation accountant might determine that, in his industry, uncollectibles tend to be from 1/10 to 1/4 percent of credit sales. Taking into consideration the particular circumstances of his company, he might believe that 2/10 percent of Hagen-Los Angeles Corporation's credit sales will prove uncollectible. His estimate of 19X1 uncollectibles would be:

Total 19X1 credit sales	$15,100,000
Estimated percentage uncollectible	2/10%
Estimated 19X1 bad debts expense	$ 30,200

and he would make the entry:

Bad Debts Expense	30,200	
Accounts Receivable—Estimated Uncollectibles		30,200

Notice that this approach is used to estimate what the bad debts expense for the year will be. In contrast, the next method looks to the other half of this journal entry and attempts to estimate what the year-end balance of accounts receivable—estimated uncollectibles should be.

B. *Aging.* Instead, the accountant might prefer to examine the individual outstanding accounts receivable *at December 31, 19X1,* to determine which ones look doubtful. Here is one way he could do this. Past experience might tell him that the odds are as follows: approximately half of all accounts more than 60 days overdue, a quarter of accounts 30 to 60 days overdue, and 5 percent of accounts 1 to 29 days overdue will be uncollectible. Suppose that, upon analysis, the status of the individual 12/31/X1 accounts proves to be:

Not overdue	$ 679,200
1–29 days overdue	270,000
30–60 days overdue	34,800
More than 60 days overdue	16,000
Total	$1,000,000

It then would be possible to estimate 12/31/X1 uncollectibles as follows:

Days Overdue	Amount	Estimated Percentage Uncollectible	Total Estimated Uncollectible at 12/31/X1
Under 30	$270,000	5%	$13,500
30–60	34,800	25%	8,700
Over 60	16,000	50%	8,000
Estimated 12/31/X1 Balance of Accounts Receivable—Estimated Uncollectibles			$30,200

This particular technique is called *aging* the ending balance of accounts receivable. The example was artificially constructed so that the percentage-of-credit-sales approach and the aging approach yield exactly the same results. Of course, you can expect at least minor differences. Any major difference is a signal that at least one of these estimation approaches is giving erroneous results.[2]

---

[2] At this point a question may occur to some students. The aging technique is based upon year-end accounts receivable balances. If some of these accounts arose in earlier years, how can the calculated expense magnitude relate solely to the current year's sales? Won't the effort to match costs with related revenues be defeated?

Two things should be emphasized in reply. First, the aging method compares the amount that should be in accounts receivable—estimated uncollectibles with what is there before adjustment; a credit balance in the latter (the balance that should on average be present if the firm's estimates are correct) reflects estimated uncollectibles of prior years that have not yet been definitively identified. The current year's charge to expense is the difference between these two amounts and, accordingly, is *net* of these prior-year amounts. Second, and more importantly, both the aging and the percentage-of-credit-sales approaches are attempts to *estimate* figures for uncollectibles; it is not improper to estimate one magnitude by examining changes in another magnitude, even when the latter is partly unrelated to the former, as long as changes in the latter allow satisfactory predictions of changes in the former (and as long as we understand why these predictions from partly unrelated data "work"). Many scientific measurements are made in this way.

As in the percentage-of-credit-sales case, the accountant who uses aging would make the entry:

Bad Debts Expense	30,200	
Accounts Receivable—Estimated Uncollectibles		30,200

But under the aging method, he is estimating the appropriate balance of estimated uncollectibles to report at year-end, rather than the bad debts expense for the year. The $30,200 credit to accounts receivable—estimated uncollectibles serves to raise the balance of that account from zero to the estimated amount of $30,200.

Virtually all firms that sell on credit age their accounts receivable on a regular basis in order to determine which accounts are overdue and require extra collection effort. Thus, the information needed for the aging method of estimating uncollectibles usually is readily available as a byproduct of the firm's ordinary credit control activities. Because of this, the aging method of estimating uncollectibles is more widely used in practice than is the percentage-of-credit-sales method.

19X2 events

This distinction becomes important when there is a remaining balance in accounts receivable—estimated uncollectibles at year end after all accounts specifically identified as uncollectible have been written off, but before the adjusting entry recording bad debts expense has been made. The percentage-of-credit-sales method will ignore this remaining balance, but the aging approach must take it into consideration. Hagen-Los Angeles Corporation's 19X2 accounts receivable activity will be used to illustrate this:

1. 19X2 sales, all on account, totalled $17,300,000.

Accounts Receivable	17,300,000	
Sales		17,300,000

2. $970,000 of accounts receivable originating in 19X1 sales were collected; in addition, $16,150,000 of accounts receivable originating in 19X2 sales were collected ($970,000 + $16,150,000 = $17,120,000).

Cash	17,120,000	
Accounts Receivable		17,120,000

3. $30,000 of accounts receivable, which originated in 19X1 sales, proved to be uncollectible.

Accounts Receivable—Estimated Uncollectibles	30,000	
Accounts Receivable		30,000

Notice that when individual accounts are specifically identified as actually being uncollectible, the debit is made to the estimated uncollectibles valuation account rather than to bad debts expense.

After these three entries have been posted, the ledger accounts will appear as follows:

	Accounts Receivable				Accounts Receivable—Estimated Uncollectibles			
√	1,000,000	(2)	17,120,000	(3)	30,000	√	30,200
(1)	17,300,000	(3)	30,000				
		√	1,150,000				
	18,300,000		18,300,000				

Finally, upon analysis, the status of the individual 12/31/X2 accounts was determined to be:

Not overdue	$ 768,600
1–29 days overdue	322,000
30–60 days overdue	42,000
More than 60 days overdue	17,400
Total	$1,150,000

A. *Percentage of credit sales.* Under the percentage-of-credit-sales approach, 19X2 bad debts expense would be calculated as follows:

Total 19X2 credit sales	$17,300,000
Estimated percentage uncollectible	2/10%
Estimated 19X2 bad debts expense	$ 34,600

and the following journal entry would be made (without reference to the balance in the accounts receivable—estimated uncollectibles account):

4a.	Bad Debts Expense	34,600	
	Accounts Receivable—Estimated Uncollectibles		34,600

yielding the following result:

	Accounts Receivable—Estimated Uncollectibles			
(3)	30,000	√	30,200
√	34,800	(4a)	34,600
	64,800		64,800

Notice that the ending balance in the valuation account exceeds the bad debts expense for the year by the $200 overage in last year's estimate of uncollectibles ($30,200 − $30,000 = $200).

B. *Aging.* Under the aging approach, the 12/31/X2 valuation account balance would be estimated as $35,300, but the journal entry required to obtain this balance would be for only $35,100:

Days Overdue	Amount	Estimated Percentage Uncollectible	Total Estimated Uncollectibles at 12/31/X2
Under 30	$322,000	5%	$16,100
30–60	42,000	25%	10,500
Over 60	17,400	50%	8,700

Estimated 12/31/X2 balance of Accounts Receivable—Estimated Uncollectibles . .	$35,300
Actual balance before adjusting entry ($30,200–$30,000)	200
Adjustment to be made	$35,100

The valuation account should have a balance of $35,300, but it *already* contains a $200 balance, so the accountant would make the entry:

4b. Bad Debts Expense   35,100
   Accounts Receivable—Estimated Uncollectibles   35,100

yielding the following result:

Accounts Receivable—
Estimated Uncollectibles

(3)	30,000	✓	30,200
✓	35,300	(4b)	35,100
	65,300		65,300

For greater realism, the 19X2 figures were chosen so that the bad debts expense and the ending valuation account balances differ slightly depending upon whether the percentage of credit sales or the aging method is used.

Problem for Study and Self-Examination

Problem 11-1:

 Montebello Mart is a large suburban department store. Part of its sales are for cash, and part on regional and national credit card plans. The company also offers its own "Courtesy Charge" plan to customers who meet certain minimum credit standards. This problem is concerned *only* with sales under the Courtesy Charge plan.

At the beginning of 19X1, the company's Courtesy Charge accounts receivable totalled $567,000 (a very high figure, reflecting Christmas sales). Accounts receivable—estimated uncollectibles totalled $10,000. In the past, the company had assumed that 2 percent of Courtesy Charge sales would prove uncollectible. However, in the last two years there has been a tendency for national and regional credit card plans to attract the more reliable customers. Therefore, the average quality of customers using the Courtesy Charge plan has deteriorated somewhat. The company's credit manager believes that a bad debts rate of 3 percent might be expected on 19X1 Courtesy Charge sales.

During 19X1, Courtesy Charge sales totalled $1,600,000. Accounts totalling $1,480,000 were collected. Other accounts totalling $50,000 were written off as uncollectible.

1. Prepare appropriate 19X1 journal entries. Post these entries to the two accounts receivable accounts.

2. At the end of 19X1, the company's controller was concerned. He had analyzed the company's $637,000 ending balance of accounts receivable, as follows:

Months Overdue	Amount
0	$517,000
1	52,000
2	30,000
3	18,000
Over 3	20,000
Total	$637,000

In his experience, the likelihood of an account being uncollectible increases sharply with its age:

Months Overdue	Likelihood of Uncollectibility
0	1%
1	5%
2	10%
3	30%
Over 3	60%

Prepare an alternate calculation of the amount that should be reported for estimated uncollectibles as of 12/31/X1. Assume that the entries in step 1 have already been made. If the controller accepts this alternate calculation, what additional adjusting entry (or entries) should be made?

Solution

Solution 11-1:

A. *During 19X1:*

1.	Accounts Receivable	1,600,000	
	Sales		1,600,000
2.	Cash	1,480,000	
	Accounts Receivable		1,480,000
3.	Accounts Receivable—Estimated		
	Uncollectibles	50,000	
	Accounts Receivable		50,000

As of 12/31/X1:

4.	Bad Debts Expense	48,000	
	Accounts Receivable—Estimated		
	Uncollectibles		48,000

($1,600,000 × 3% = $48,000)

Accounts Receivable					*Accounts Receivable—* *Estimated Uncollectibles*			
√	567,000	(2)	1,480,000		(3)	50,000	√	10,000
(1)	1,600,000	(3)	50,000		√	8,000	(4)	48,000
		√	637,000					
						58,000		58,000
	2,167,000		2,167,000					
							√	8,000
√	637,000							

B.

Months Overdue	Amount	Likelihood of Uncollectibility	Estimated Uncollectibles
0	$517,000	1%	$ 5,170
1	52,000	5%	2,600
2	30,000	10%	3,000
3	18,000	30%	5,400
Over 3	20,000	60%	12,000
Total			$28,170

It appears that estimated uncollectibles should be increased by approximately $20,000. Technically, at least part of this $20,000 must result from underestimation in previous years, since the quality of these accounts gradually deteriorated (and the estimated percentage of uncollectibles became increasingly wide of the mark). Ordinarily, the entire $20,000 would be charged to the expense of the current year, if only because allocation of this $20,000 among years would be very difficult. In practice, rounded figures usually would be used for the adjustment ($20,000 instead of $20,170), since the adjustment is also an estimate; however unrounded figures are used here for consistency.

As of	Bad Debts Expense	20,170	
12/31/X1:	Accounts Receivable—Estimated Uncollectibles		20,170

Premium and Discount on Debt

A problem, illustrated by the following example, arises with noncurrent debt when the amount received by the borrower differs from the maturity value of the debt. On 1/1/X1, Borrower Company issued an 8 percent note[3] for $10,000 to Lender Company; the principal and interest on this note are both due in three years.[4] Lender Company believed that 8 percent was an insufficient interest rate, considering the particular degree of risk that this loan involved. Instead of asking Borrower Company to prepare a new note at a higher rate of interest, Lender Company compensated for the otherwise unsatisfactory interest rate by paying less than $10,000 for the note. This is entirely legitimate, as long as Borrower Company agrees to accept less than $10,000. (As an analogy, were you to consider buying a used car and discover before the deal was concluded that the car needed minor repairs, you could either ask the owner to make these repairs himself or reduce your offer by their estimated cost.) Suppose that in this case the parties agreed that Lender Company would pay only $9,575.08 for the note (later in this chapter we will see how this amount might have been calculated). The $424.92 difference ($10,000.00 − $9,575.08 = $424.92) is called a *discount* on the note.

You saw on page 266 that this same "discount" term is used when capital stock is issued at a price less than its par or stated value, and that it is customary for such capital stock to be reported at its full par or stated value, with a valuation account employed to reflect the discount. A similar practice is followed with debt: the note is recorded at its full maturity value, with the discount recorded in a valuation account. Borrower Company would make the following entry when the note was issued:

Cash	9,575.08	
Discount on Notes Payable	424.92	
Notes Payable		10,000.00

Were Borrower Company to prepare a balance sheet at this point, the following would be an acceptable presentation of the note and discount:

Noncurrent Liabilities:
Notes Payable	$10,000.00	
Less: Discount	424.92	$9,575.08

Notice that "discount on notes payable" is a valuation account to notes payable, not an asset.

---

[3] As has been true throughout this book, you may assume that when no time period is specified for an interest rate, the rate is an annual one. Accordingly, interest on this note is calculated at 8 percent *per year*.

[4] With most such notes, interest would be paid once per year; payment at maturity was chosen here merely to simplify the following discussion, and does not affect the points to be made.

A valuation account isn't a necessity here; instead, the following entry would be acceptable for recording the issue of the note:

Cash	9,575.08	
Notes Payable		9,575.08

The note could be reported at its $9,575.08 net amount on the balance sheet, too, since $9,575.08 *is* the amount actually borrowed at the issue date, not $10,000.00. But since the method that uses a valuation account is the one most commonly followed, it will be used in the rest of this chapter.

Premium on debt

It is equally possible for the interest rate on a note to be higher than deemed necessary by the lender, and for the note to be issued at a *premium*—an amount in excess of the note's maturity value. Once again, a premium on debt is analogous to a premium on capital stock. For example, suppose instead that Lender Company would have been satisfied with less than 8 percent interest on the note, and that it was willing to lend to Borrower Company at a lower rate. Since it is getting more interest than it requires, Lender Company will be willing to pay more than $10,000.00 for the note; let us suppose that it pays $10,122.09. Then Borrower Company will make the following entry when it issues the note:

Cash	10,122.09	
Premium on Notes Payable		122.09
Notes Payable		10,000.00

Premium on notes payable is another valuation account to notes payable. Borrowers often misjudge the interest rates that lenders desire; situations involving premiums and discounts on debt are common in the business world.

Entries on Lender Company's books

As was emphasized in Chapter Three (pages 126–128), a liability on one entity's books usually corresponds to an asset on some other entity's books. In this case the other entity is Lender Company and the asset is a note receivable. Lenders rarely employ valuation accounts for their investments. In the discount case above, Lender Company would have made the following journal entry upon receipt of the note:

Notes Receivable	9,575.08	
Cash		9,575.08

or the debit might be to an investment account instead of to notes receivable. Similarly, in the premium case, Lender Company's entry would be:

Notes Receivable	10,122.09	
Cash		10,122.09

Calculation of the interest charge

The *total interest charge* on a loan is the difference between the amount that was actually borrowed by the borrower and the total amount that will be paid to the lender. If you borrow $200 and repay $218, the total interest charge is $18, no matter how that $18 is described nor when the $218 is paid. This total interest charge should be distinguished from the "official" or *nominal* interest charge, which is calculated from the rate formally stated in the loan contract itself. For instance, in the previous discount example, the nominal interest charge was $10,000 × 8% = $800 per year, for a total of $2,400 over the three years ($800 × 3 = $2,400). But total interest is greater than $2,400:

Total amount to be paid to Lender Company:		
Nominal interest	$ 2,400.00	
Maturity value of note	10,000.00	$12,400.00
Amount borrowed by Borrower Company		9,575.08
Total interest charge		$ 2,824.92

Similarly, over the entire three-year period, Lender Company's total interest revenue is $2,824.92. As mentioned in Chapter Eight (pages 425–427), accountants depart from their historical cost and realization rules to accrue interest receivable and interest revenue in such cases. How should this $2,824.92 be allocated to each of the three years?

In Chapter Eight (pages 432–434) I examined a situation in which the total income of a firm over a period of six years could be determined without ambiguity, but in which the net income of any individual year could not be calculated, except arbitrarily. The situation here is similar: the $2,824.92 interest charge arises because, after considering the *total* three-year contract, both parties agreed that Lender Company would pay $9,575.08 for the note. The $2,824.92 may be associated unambiguously with the entire three-year period, but any allocation of it to individual years is bound to be arbitrary.[5]

There are several possible ways to perform this arbitrary allocation. The simplest way, which also is the traditional one, is to allocate one third of the $2,824.92 to each year. For example, the following entry might be made on Lender Company's books for each of the three years, 19X1, 19X2, and 19X3 ($2,824.92 ÷ 3 = $941.64):

Interest Receivable	800.00	(nominal interest)
Notes Receivable	141.64	(amortization of discount)
Interest Revenue		941.64

---

[5] Be aware that this is a controversial statement. Many accountants and experts on finance consider the *constant rate* method of allocating interest (discussed later in this chapter) not to be arbitrary—just as many regard recognition of revenue at the time of sale to be a non-arbitrary approach to revenue recognition. Arguments about why the constant rate method is arbitrary, too, may be found in *The Allocation Problem in Financial Accounting Theory* (American Accounting Association, 1969), especially pages 80–82.

The total discount was $424.92, and this entry has the effect of amortizing one third of the discount each year ($424.92 ÷ 3 = $141.64), so that by the end of the third year, the discount will have been entirely written off and the note will be correctly reported at its full maturity value of $10,000.00.

Entries on Borrower Company's books

Similar amortization of the discount could be made on Borrower Company's books; the entry at the ends of 19X1, 19X2, and 19X3 would be:

Interest Expense	941.64	
Interest Payable		800.00
Discount on Notes Payable		141.64

On successive balance sheets of Borrower Company, this note would appear as follows:

Noncurrent Liabilities:			*1/1/X1*
Notes Payable		$10,000.00	
Less: Discount.		424.92	$ 9,578.08
Noncurrent Liabilities:			*12/31/X1*
Notes Payable		$10,000.00	
Less: Discount.		283.28	$ 9,716.72
Noncurrent Liabilities:			*12/31/X2*
Notes Payable		$10,000.00	
Less: Discount.		141.64	$ 9,858.36
Noncurrent Liabilities:			*12/31/X3*
Notes Payable		$ 10,000	
Less: Discount.		-0-	$10,000.00

and Borrower Company's current liabilities would report the following interest payable:

1/1/X1:	$ -0-
12/31/X1:	800.00
12/31/X2:	1,600.00
12/31/X3:	2,400.00

Finally, at maturity Borrower Company would make the following entry to record the payment of note and interest:

Notes Payable	10,000.00	
Interest Payable	2,400.00	
Cash		12,400.00

Lender Company's figures

Corresponding amounts would be reported for Lender Company's notes receivable and interest receivable:

	1/1/X1	*12/31/X1*	*12/31/X2*	*12/31/X3*
Notes receivable	$9,575.08	$9,716.72	$9,858.36	$10,000.00
Interest receivable	–0–	800.00	1,600.00	2,400.00

and at maturity Lender Company would make the entry:

Cash	12,400.00	
Notes Receivable		10,000.00
Interest Receivable		2,400.00

A premium could be written off in the same way. This approach to amortization of a discount or premium on debt and the allocation of the total interest charge to individual years may be called *straight-line* amortization of premium and discount. (It is so called because, when expressed graphically, the equal annual amortization would be reflected in a straight line.) Although the foregoing example involved notes payable and notes receivable, premiums and discounts are common with other kinds of debt, bonds being the most common example; the straight-line method of amortizing premium and discount is also potentially applicable to these situations.

"Asset" reporting of discount

It should be clear from the foregoing that, if discount on a liability is separately recorded, the discount account is a valuation account to the liability. However, some firms perceive discount as a kind of prepaid interest (arising from the firm's accepting less than the principal amount when issuing the debt, rather than from the firm's actually paying any cash in advance). Under this interpretation, the discount is reported as an asset—either as a prepayment or as part of a "miscellaneous assets" category. This practice is illustrated in the balance sheet on page 88; there is nothing terribly misleading about it, but it nonetheless involves a misconception: a borrower does not acquire an asset merely because it has received less than the principal amount when it issues a debt. Instead, the only change is that, in addition to the nominal interest charged over the life of the debt, interest equal to the difference between the principal and the amount received at issue will also be charged. That the resulting discount account has a debit balance does not make it an asset, any more than accumulated depreciation is a liability because it has a credit balance.

A draw-back to the straight-line method

Despite its simplicity, often the straight-line method is not used in practice. Instead, the Accounting Principles Board has required use of another method for amortizing premium and discount and for allocating the total interest charge to different years. One introduction to this other approach involves making use of a general concept developed in the previous chapter—the *rate of return*. Only instead of the rate of return on the assets or equities of the firm as a whole, we shall be concerned with the rates of return on individual debt obligations.

Suppose that, in the discount example above, Lender Company used straight-line amortization. At all times its total investment in Borrower Company debt will be the sum of the note receivable and the interest receivable owed it:

Illustration 11-1

Lender Company
Investment in Borrower Company Debt at Various Dates
(Assuming Straight-Line Amortization of Discount)

	1/1/X1	*12/31/X1*	*12/31/X2*	*12/31/X3*
Notes receivable	$9,575.08	$ 9,716.72	$ 9,858.36	$10,000.00
Interest receivable	–0–	800.00	1,600.00	2,400.00
Total investment	$9,575.08	$10,516.72	$11,458.36	$12,400.00

Strictly speaking, if we wish to calculate the reported rate of return on this investment during each of the three years, we should compare the interest revenue recognized during each year with the average total investment during the year. In practice, though, rates of return for individual investments usually are calculated on beginning-of-year or beginning-of-period total investment amounts—mainly because certain time-saving mathematical tables (which will be introduced in the next section) traditionally have been set up on a beginning-of-period basis:

$$\begin{matrix} \text{Rate of return on an investment} \\ \text{(as usually calculated for} \\ \text{practical purposes)} \end{matrix} = \frac{\text{(Revenue from the investment during period)}}{\text{(Total investment at beginning of period)}}$$

Here, then, are the rates of return on Lender Company's investment in Borrower Company's debt during the three years, if Lender Company uses straight-line amortization of discount:

Year	*Revenue*	÷	*Total Investment at Beginning of Year*	≈	*Rate of Return for Year*
19X1	$ 941.64		$ 9,575.08		9.8%
19X2	941.64		10,516.72		9.0
19X3	941.64		11,458.36		8.2
	$2,824.92				

The rate of return declines in successive years because reported revenue remains constant while the total investment increases. To avoid this effect, the Accounting Principles Board requires use of a method that gives a constant rate of return in each year. They call this approach the *interest method* but, for clarity, I will use an acceptable alternate name: the *constant rate* method. It can be demonstrated that only one pattern of interest allocation will yield such a constant rate; in this case the pattern is 19X1—$861.76, 19X2—$939.32, 19X3—$1,023.84:

Year	Revenue	÷	Total Investment at Beginning of Year	≈	Rate of Return for Year
19X1	$ 861.76		$ 9,575.08		9.0%
19X2	939.32		10,436.84		9.0
19X3	1,023.84		11,376.16		9.0
	$2,824.92				

The details of the constant rate method, such as how the pattern of interest charges is calculated and what the related journal entries are, will be given after the next section of this chapter. But the constant rate method is a compound interest technique, and before you can understand it, you must understand the fundamentals of compound interest calculations.[6] This is to your advantage, anyway: compound interest technique is one of the basic mathematical tools of economic analysis; you will encounter a number of additional applications in managerial accounting and finance courses.

Accordingly, in the next section, questions of amortization of debt premium and discount will be temporarily ignored. The discussion will concentrate solely on compound interest calculations. Later in the chapter, the two topics will be combined.

Compound Interest Calculations

Suppose that you were to deposit $100.00 in a bank for three years at 6% interest,[7] and you didn't make any withdrawals during this three-year period; how much money would you have in the bank at the end? The answer depends on whether the bank pays interest on accumulated interest and, if so, how often. Let's begin with the simplest case and suppose, contrary to usual bank practice, that the bank pays 6% interest on the original $100.00 deposit, but not on accumulated interest. In that event, as Illustration 11-2 demonstrates, your investment will have grown to $118.00 by the end of three years.

---

[6] If you are familiar with compound interest calculations, feel free to bypass the next section. If you've had previous exposure to such calculations but are unsure of your ability to handle them, test your understanding with the Problems for Study and Self-Examination at the end of the next section. The necessary present-value tables are to be found on pages 625–632.

[7] You are reminded that since no time period is specified for the interest rate, this means 6% interest per year.

Illustration 11-2

Accumulation of $100 at 6% Simple Interest

Year	Sum upon Which Interest Is Calculated	Interest Rate	Interest for Year	Original Deposit Plus Accumulated Interest
1	$100.00	6%	$6.00	$106.00
2	100.00	6	6.00	112.00
3	100.00	6	6.00	118.00

As we saw in Chapter One, this kind of interest, figured on only the initial amount borrowed, regardless of how much interest receivable has accrued, is called *simple interest*. Simple interest is widely employed with short-term debt for relatively small sums of money. But when the principal of the debt is large or the time period over which money is loaned is great, the lender's investment in accumulated interest receivable may become increasingly significant. Then it is more and more likely that borrower and lender will agree that interest will be charged on interest receivable as well as upon the initial principal. This latter arrangement results in *compound interest*. In theory, there are an infinite number of compound interests, depending upon how frequently the calculation of interest on accumulated interest receivable is performed. Here, two of the many possibilities will be exemplified.

Illustration 11-3 is an example of *annual compounding*. By the beginning of the second year, principal plus accumulated interest receivable total $106.00; this, instead of the $100.00 principal, is used to determine the $6.36 interest charge for the second year [($100.00 × 6%) + ($6.00 × 6%) = $6.36]. Thus, by the beginning of the third year, the combined investment is $112.36, and the third year's interest charge is calculated upon this $112.36.

Illustration 11-3

Accumulation of $100 at 6% Interest
Compounded Annually

Year	Sum upon Which Interest Is Calculated	Interest Rate	Interest for Year	Original Deposit Plus Accumulated Interest
1	$100.00	6%	$6.00	$106.00
2	106.00	6	6.36	112.36
3	112.36	6	6.7416	119.1016

Notice that by calculating interest on the total investment (principal plus accumulated interest receivable) as of the beginning of the year, it appears in Illustration 11-3 that no interest was earned during the year, but only at year end—otherwise, some of the current year's interest would enter into the calculation of the total current-year interest charge.

Alternatively, one might calculate interest on accumulated interest receivable every six months. To do so, an interest rate of 6% × 6/12 = 3% will be used; Illustration 11-4 shows how such *semiannual compounding* works.

Illustration 11-4

Accumulation of $100 at 6% Interest
Compounded Semiannually
(Amounts rounded to two decimal places)

Year	Period	Sum upon Which Interest Is Calculated	Interest Rate	Interest for Period	Original Deposit Plus Accumulated Interest
1	1	$100.00	3%	$3.00	$103.00
	2	103.00	3	3.09	106.09
2	3	106.09	3	3.18	109.27
	4	109.27	3	3.28	112.55
3	5	112.55	3	3.38	115.93
	6	115.93	3	3.48	119.41

Quarterly, monthly, daily, and hourly compounding are equally possible.[8] Notice that as soon as one shifts to semiannual compounding, it becomes necessary to use two interest periods per year. Similarly, quarterly compounding requires four interest periods per year, monthly compounding requires twelve, and so forth.

Present values

Each of these illustrations has concerned the amount to which an investment of $100.00 would accumulate. It turns out that for many business purposes, including the premium and discount purposes that are discussed in the next section, a decision maker is apt to ask a slightly different form of question. Instead of knowing what he has to invest and wanting to know how large that investment will grow, the decision maker has information about a sum to be received in the *future,* and he needs to know how much must be invested now to accumulate to that future amount. As a simplified illustration, an investor might need $10,000.00 in three years' time and have an opportunity to invest money in a bank that compounded interest annually, at year end. The investor would want to know how much he must invest now, as a single deposit, to attain his $10,000.00 goal on schedule. This may be calculated from Illustration 11-3, but doing so requires a little work:

We know that if $100.00 were deposited now, by the end of three years the investor would have $119.1016. But he doesn't want $119.1016; he wants $10,000.00. Therefore, he must invest a sum equal to $10,000 × ($100.00 ÷ 119.1016) ≈ $8,396.19. Illustration 11-5 verifies this calculation.

---

[8] The limiting (most extreme) case, which corresponds to compounding over infinitesimal intervals of time, is called *continuous compounding,* and its calculations require the use of calculus, instead of the simple arithmetic used above.

Illustration 11-5

Accumulation of $8,396.19 at 6% Interest
Compounded Annually

Year	Sum upon Which Interest Is Calculated	Interest Rate	Interest for Year	Original Deposit Plus Accumulated Interest
1	$8,396.19	6%	$503.77	$ 8,899.96
2	8,899.96	6	534.00	9,433.96
3	9,433.96	6	566.04	10,000.00

In technical language, $8,396.19 is the *present value* (or *present worth, discounted present value, discounted present worth, discounted value,* etc.) of $10,000.00 in three periods' time at 6% interest per period. Because many decisions in accounting and finance require use of present values, tables have been prepared for various periodic interest rates and periods of time; this eliminates the need for calculating present value factors. For arithmetic convenience, all such tables indicate the decimal amount that must be invested to accumulate to *one dollar.* Then, if a sum other than one dollar is involved, one merely multiplies the amount given in the table by the amount desired to determine the sum that must be invested. Similarly, such tables are set up in terms of interest rates per *period,* rather than per year, because interest often is compounded monthly or quarterly.

Table A (page 625) in the Appendix to this chapter is such a present value table, rounded to four significant digits[9] and showing present values for commonly used interest rates and time periods. Each column of Table A reflects a different possible interest rate; each row represents a different future period-end date. For instance, look at the intersection of the *Period 3* row with the 6% column. This indicates that to accumulate $1.00 in three periods at 6% interest per period, one must invest $0.8396 now. From this it follows that if one wished to accumulate $10,000.00 now, it would be necessary to invest $10,000.00 × 0.8396 = $8,396.00. This agrees, to four significant digit accuracy, with the answer of $8,396.19 that was calculated above. (Tables that are accurate to only four significant digits are used to save time in your calculations; should you ever need them, more accurate tables are readily available in library reference rooms or through standard computer programs—both Tables A and B were prepared from such a program. Besides, later in this chapter I will show you an expedient to enhance the effective accuracy of such tables.)

---

[9] For those who have forgotten exactly what is meant by *significant digits,* we speak of a decimal being accurate to *n* significant digits when the first *n* digits of the number, read from left to right, and ignoring all zeros before the first non-zero digit, are accurate. When we round to *n* significant digits, we discard all remaining digits. For example, here are three numbers, each rounded to four significant digits:

Number	Number as Rounded
1,032,467.91	1,032,000.00
22.500	22.50
0.007601432	0.007601

Examples

Here are three more examples of how Table A might be used. If you believe that you understand the foregoing material, use these examples to test your understanding.

1. Mr. W. Johnson Arends, Jr. has the opportunity to invest money at 10% interest, compounded annually at year-end. In five years he wishes to buy a house that he estimates will cost $32,500. How much must he invest now in order to have this sum available at the end of five years?

To answer this, look at the intersection of the *Period 5* row and the *10%* column; this indicates that to obtain a dollar in five years at 10% interest per year compounded annually, one must invest $0.6209. Accordingly, to obtain $32,500 instead of one dollar, it is necessary to invest $32,500 × 0.6209 ≈ $20,180. Actually $32,500 × 0.6209 = $20,179.25, but since Table A is accurate only to four significant digits, this answer should be rounded to four significant digits, too. Any attempt at greater precision would be illusory (as is evidenced by the fact that a more exact answer, computed on my desk calculator and rounded to the nearest penny, is $20,179.94).

2. Honolulu Jack and Levelling Corporation has been offered a note due in three years by one of its customers who wishes long-term credit. The total amount to be received at the maturity of this note (including interest) is $14,520; no interest is to be paid until maturity. Honolulu Jack and Levelling Corporation believes that it should earn a minimum of 9%, compounded annually, on a loan with this degree of risk. The customer intends to purchase goods costing $12,000. How much cash in addition to the note should Honolulu Jack and Levelling Corporation require from its customer?

The intersection of the *Period 3* row and 9% column is 0.7722; therefore Honolulu Jack and Levelling Corporation should regard the customer's note as being worth $14,520 × 0.7722 ≈ $11,210, and should require $12,000 − $11,210 = $790 additional cash. If the firm regards the note as worth more than $11,210, its rate of return will be less than 9% compounded annually. Of course if the firm can persuade its customer to accept a lower present value for the note, it may wish to do so—all the present-value calculation does here is to determine the *maximum* value that Honolulu Jack and Levelling Corporation should place on the note.

3. On 1/1/X7 Pine Mountain Enterprises was offered an investment that would pay $1,000.00 on each of 7/1/X7, 1/1/X8, 7/1/X8 and 1/1/X9. Pine Mountain Enterprises wishes to earn a minimum of 9%, compounded semiannually, on any investment with this degree of risk. What is the maximum that the firm should be willing to pay for this investment?

Nine percent per year, compounded semiannually, is equivalent to $4\frac{1}{2}$% per six-month period, compounded semiannually.[10] Accordingly, the investment offers four single payments of $1,000.00 each, which may be valued as follows:

---

[10] Nine percent per year, compounded *annually,* is not equivalent to 9% per year compounded semiannually, nor to $4\frac{1}{2}$% per six-month period compounded semiannually. Instead, the latter is equivalent to 9.2025% per year, compounded annually. For example, an investment of $10,000.00 compounded semiannually at a semiannual rate of $4\frac{1}{2}$% will grow as follows:

First six months: $10,000.00 × 1.045 = $10,450.00
Second six months: $10,450.00 × 1.045 = $10,920.25

Period	4½% Present-Value Factor	Amount of Single Payment	Present Value of Single Payment
1	0.9569	$1,000.00	$ 956.90
2	0.9157	1,000.00	915.70
3	0.8763	1,000.00	876.30
4	0.8386	1,000.00	838.60
	3.5875 ×	$1,000.00 =	$3,587.50

and $3,587.50 is the maximum that Pine Mountain Enterprises should be willing to pay for this investment.

Annuities

In this last situation, a shortcut calculation is possible, because each of the single payments is the same size ($1,000.00) as the others. Instead of determining the present value of each single payment, we could calculate the total of the 4½% present-value factors for periods 1 through 4, then multiply the result (3.5875) by $1,000.00 to obtain the correct answer. This is done on the bottom line of the previous calculation.

Such a series of equal payments is called an *annuity*. To be more precise, an *annuity* is any series of equal payments that are evenly spaced in time (a year apart, six months apart, etc.). Annuities are sufficiently common in accounting and finance that special shortcut present-value tables have been designed for dealing with them. Table B in the Appendix to this chapter is an annuity present value table, one that corresponds to single-payment present-value Table A.

In the previous example, the present value of the four-period annuity was shortcut calculated by determining the sum of the four single payment present values (3.5875). *Every present-value factor in Table B is calculated in the same way.* For instance, the *Period 3, 7%* figure in Table B (2.6243) is calculated as follows:

	Period	Present-Value Factor for a Single Payment
From	1	0.9346
Table	2	0.8734
A	3	0.8163
Total, on Table B	3	2.6243

Similarly, the Table B factor for a 5-period annuity at 3% per period (4.5797) is the sum of the following five single payment 3% present-value factors from Table A:

Period	Present-Value Factor
1	0.9709
2	0.9426
3	0.9151
4	0.8885
5	0.8626
Total	4.5797

Notice that the amounts in Table B are accurate to five or six significant digits. This means that calculations that are based on Table B may appropriately be rounded to five or six significant digits instead of four.

Examples

Here are three examples of present-value calculations that involve annuities:

1. Mr. Leslie C. Deschler is considering an investment that would pay $380.00 per month for two years, beginning one month from the present date. Mr. Deschler wishes to earn a minimum of 6%, compounded monthly, on any investment with this degree of risk. What is the maximum that he should be willing to pay for this investment?

Since a monthly annuity and monthly compounding are involved, we must use periods of one month in our calculations. Six percent per year, compounded monthly, is equivalent to $\frac{1}{2}$% per month, compounded monthly. According to Table B, the present value of a 24-period annuity of $1.00 at $\frac{1}{2}$% per period is 22.5629. Therefore Mr. Deschler should be willing to pay a maximum of 22.5629 × $380.00 ≈ $8,573.90 for this investment.

2. Alternative Culture Corporation is considering buying a machine that would yield it cash savings of $13,000 a year at the end of each of the next eight years. In addition, this machine will have a cash scrap value of $5,000 at the end of the eighth year. Alternative Culture Corporation wishes to earn a minimum of 12%, compounded annually, on investments with this degree of risk. What is the maximum that it should be willing to pay for this machine?

Investments in machinery may be treated in the same way as any other kinds of investments as long as the firm feels able to predict the effects on cash of owning the machinery. Notice that, from the standpoint of the firm, cash savings are just as desirable as are receipts of interest.

This particular investment involves an eight-period annuity of $13,000 and a single payment in eight years of $5,000. Its present value at 12% interest may be calculated as follows:

	Present Value Factor	Amount	Present Value
Annuity (Table B)	4.9676	$13,000.00	$64,579.00
Single payment (Table A)	0.4039	5,000.00	2,019.00
Total			$66,598.00

Accordingly, Alternative Culture Corporation will receive a 12% return on this investment (assuming that its predictions are correct) if it pays $66,598.00 for the machine, and less than 12% if it pays more than $66,598.00.

3. Mr. G. Elliott O'Neal is considering an investment that will pay $40 every six months for the next ten years, in twenty installments starting six months from the present date. Also, at the end of ten years, this investment will pay an additional $1,000 as a single payment. Mr. O'Neal wishes to earn a rate of return of 7%, compounded semiannually, on investments of this kind. What is the maximum that he should be willing to pay for this investment?

This investment offers a 20-period annuity of $40 and a single payment, in 20 periods, of $1,000. Since the annuity is received semiannually and compounding is to be semiannual, we must use periods of six months' length and an interest rate of $7\% \times 6/12 = 3\frac{1}{2}\%$. Accordingly, the present value of the investment as a whole is:

	$3\frac{1}{2}\%$ Present-Value Factor	Amount	Present Value
Annuity	14.2124	$ 40.00	$ 568.496
Single payment	0.5026	1,000.00	502.60
Amount Mr. O'Neal should be willing to pay			$1,071.10

Notice that twenty periods are used in this calculation instead of ten years, because of the semiannual receipt of the $40 annuity and the semiannual compounding.

This example provides a bridge to the discussion of the amortization of premium and discount on debt. For, as the next section will emphasize, Mr. O'Neal's investment has the characteristics of a ten-year, 8%, $1,000 bond; and the calculation indicates that an investor who would be satisfied with a 7% rate of return compounded semiannually on this bond should be willing to pay a $1,071.10 − $1,000.00 = $71.10 premium for it.

Problems for Study and Self-Examination

Problem 11-2:

In September, 19X3, Miss Teena K. Boggs expects to enroll as a freshman at Columbus State University. Her goals are to major in Business Administration and, thereby, to find a suitable husband. Her uncle, Carl Albert Boggs, MD, wishes to provide for all costs of her education and marriage by making a single deposit into a savings account on 6/1/X3. The bank pays 6% interest, compounded quarterly.

Dr. Boggs estimates that Teena will need to withdraw $1,250 every three months for her college expenses, beginning on 9/1/X3, with the final withdrawal on 3/1/X7. He anticipates that her wedding will cost $5,000, and that this sum will be needed on 6/1/X7. How much should Dr. Boggs deposit in the bank on 6/1/X3 to allow all of these withdrawals with nothing left over at the end?

Problem 11-3:

Mr. Winfield K. McCormack is considering purchasing a fifteen-year, $10,000, 7.4% bond. This investment will pay $370 every six months for a total of thirty installments, beginning six months from now. In addition, this investment will make a single payment of $10,000 exactly fifteen years from now. Mr. McCormack wishes to earn 8%, compounded semiannually, on investments of this kind. What is the maximum that he should be willing to pay for this bond?

Solutions

Solution 11-2:

There will be an annuity of fifteen $1,250 withdrawals, followed by a single withdrawal of $5,000 at the end of the sixteenth period. The savings bank is paying interest at a rate of $1\frac{1}{2}\%$ per quarterly period. The necessary deposit may be calculated as follows:

	$1\frac{1}{2}\%$ Present-Value Factor	*Amount*	*Present Value*
Annuity (Table B)	13.3432	$1,250.00	$16,679.00
Single payment (Table A)	0.7880	5,000.00	3,940.00
Total deposit needed			$20,619.00

Quarterly periods are used in this calculation because of the quarterly nature of the withdrawals and the quarterly compounding.

Solution 11-3:

There will be a thirty-period annuity of $370 per semiannual period and a single payment in thirty periods of $10,000. The appropriate periodic interest rate is $8\% \times 6/12 = 4\%$. The amount Mr. McCormack should be willing to pay may be calculated as follows:

	4% Present-Value Factor	*Amount*	*Present Value*
Annuity	17.2920	$ 370.00	$6,398.04
Single payment	0.3083	10,000.00	3,083.00
Total			$9,481.04

The Constant Rate Method

We are now prepared to return to considering constant rate amortization of premium and discount on debt. Let us suppose that Matsunaga Corporation has borrowed money by issuing bonds payable. For our initial example, I will simplify things drastically by assuming that only one bond is issued and that it has only a two-year life. Of course, in practice, bond issues run to millions of dollars and lives of 10 to 40 years are typical, but this simplified example illustrates all that is needed to understand the more complicated cases.

Therefore, suppose that on 12/31/X7 Matsunaga Corporation issued a two-year, 6%, $1,000 bond to Jasper Enterprises. Interest on this bond is due every June 30th and December 31st, and the principal is due on 12/31/X9. Jasper Enterprises believed that, considering the risk involved in this investment, it should earn 7%, compounded semiannually, instead of 6%.

Let us first consider these two interest rates. All bonds make two kinds of cash payments to bondholders: an annuity of interest payments (usually made every six months) and a single payment at maturity. In this case the interest annuity is $30 every six months ($1,000 × 6% × 6/12 = $30). This interest annuity is determined by the 6% "official" rate on the bond. Such a 6% rate is given the technical name of the *nominal* or *coupon* rate on the bond. *The main significance of the nominal rate on a bond is that it determines the amount of the interest annuity:*

$$\text{Maturity value of bond} \times \text{Nominal rate} \times 6/12 = \frac{\text{Amount of cash interest paid}}{\text{on bond every six months}}$$

The 7% rate that was desired by the lender is called the *effective rate, market rate, yield to maturity* or *yield rate,* of interest on the bond. The effective rate both helps determine the amount the lender will pay for the bond and dominates the amortization calculations under the constant rate approach. Finally, the maturity value of a bond often is called its *par value.*

(In what follows you might reasonably wonder why bonds so often are issued at effective rates that differ from their nominal rates. This isn't just a device to make added work for students. While a full explanation requires lengthy discussion of the legal and institutional details of issuing bonds, the essence is that the nominal rate must be decided upon before the date on which the bonds are issued. Meanwhile, the interest rate demanded by the market and/or the market's appraisal of the firm will often change, and the effective rate eventually demanded by the market will equal the nominal rate only by coincidence or inspired guessing.)

Calculation of issue price

In the previous section we saw a way to calculate the price that Jasper Enterprises will be willing to pay for this bond. Jasper Enterprises will receive a four-period annuity of $30 and a $1,000 single payment at the end of the fourth period. The amount that Jasper Enterprises will be willing to pay for these rights equals their combined present value at the 7% × 6/12 = $3\frac{1}{2}$% per period effective rate of interest that Jasper Enterprises desires:

	$3\frac{1}{2}$% Present-Value Factor	Amount	Present Value
Annuity	3.6731	$ 30.00	$ 110.19
Single payment	0.8714	1,000.00	871.40
Amount that Jasper Enterprises would pay			$ 981.59
Maturity value of bond			1,000.00
Discount at issue			$ (18.41)

A more accurate, shortcut, calculation

There is a shortcut way to make the previous calculation. Jasper Enterprises is buying this bond at a discount because the bond's nominal interest rate is less than the desired effective rate. We may calculate the total amount of this discount directly, by determining the extent to which actual interest payments fall short of what the lender wants, and then calculating the present value of this deficiency.

In this case interest payments at the nominal rate are $30.00 every six months. Were the nominal rate equal to the 7% effective rate, semiannual interest payments would be $1,000.00 × 7% × 6/12 = $35.00. Therefore, the actual semiannual interest annuity is $35.00 − $30.00 = $5.00 less than the lender wishes. *The present value of this deficiency will equal the discount at the issue date.* Since the $5.00 deficiency occurs as an annuity, a present-value factor from Table B should be applied to it:

	Amount	$3\frac{1}{2}\%$ Present- Value Factor	Present Value (= Discount at Issue)
Deficiency in annuity	$5.00	3.6731	$18.37

This $18.37 corresponds, except for rounding, to the $18.41 discount in the earlier calculation. Not merely is the issue price calculated more rapidly this way than by the previous method, but it is accurate to one more decimal place (because the annuity factors are accurate to at least five significant digits and present-value factors are being applied to a smaller number than before). Accordingly, all subsequent issue price calculations in this chapter will use this shortcut method.

A premium example

The shortcut method works equally well with premiums. Suppose instead that Jasper Enterprises wished to receive only a 4% rate of return on this kind of investment. If the nominal rate were equal to this new 4% effective rate, semiannual interest would be $1,000.00 × 4% × 6/12 = $20.00. Instead, it is $30, so the interest annuity is $10 per period higher than the lender demands. In calculating the premium that the lender would pay, we must remember to use the new effective rate, 2% instead of $3\frac{1}{2}\%$, and the new 2% present-value factor of 3.8077:

$$\$10.00 \times 3.8077 \approx \$38.08$$

Accordingly, if Jasper Enterprises was satisfied to earn only 4% on this investment, it would be willing to pay $1,000.00 + $38.08 = $1,038.08 for this bond. The parallel longer way to calculate this (and this is the last time the longer method will be used) is:

	2% Present- Value Factor	Amount	Present Value
Annuity	3.8077	$ 30.00	$ 114.23
Single payment	0.9238	1,000.00	923.80
Amount that Jasper Enterprises would pay			$1,038.03
Maturity value of bond			1,000.00
Premium at issue			$ 38.03

Amortization under the constant rate method

Given all of the foregoing, the constant rate method is elegantly simple. During any period, the balance of the lender's investment in debt is considered to be equal to the maturity value of the debt plus any unamortized premium or less any unamortized discount at the *beginning* of that period. The interest charge for any period equals the lender's investment during the period times the *effective* interest rate for the period:

$$Interest\ Charge = \left[\begin{pmatrix} Maturity \\ Value \\ of\ Debt \end{pmatrix} \pm \begin{pmatrix} Unamortized\ Premium \\ or\ Discount\ at \\ Beginning\ of\ Period \end{pmatrix} \right] \times \begin{pmatrix} Effective \\ Interest \\ Rate \end{pmatrix}$$

This results in the interest charge being consistent at all times with the effective interest rate sought by the lender.

Premium example

I will use the premium case of the previous illustration as an example. If Jasper Enterprises purchased the $1,000, 6%, two-year bond at a price to yield an effective interest rate of 4%, compounded semiannually, the entry on Matsunaga Corporation's books at the issue date would be:

12/31/X7	Cash	1,038.08	
	Bonds Payable		1,000.00
	Premium on Bonds Payable		38.08

On the first interest date, Matsunaga Corporation would pay $30.00 of interest, but would calculate interest expense as being only $1,038.08 × 2% = $20.76. The difference of $30.00 − $20.76 = $9.24 is amortization of the premium:

6/30/X8	Interest Expense	20.76	
	Premium on Bonds Payable	9.24	
	Cash		30.00

During the second period, Jasper Enterprises' investment will have decreased to the extent that the premium was amortized during the first period (you may regard $9.24 of the $30.00 interest received by Jasper Enterprises on 6/30/X8 as a partial repayment of its $1,038.08 investment). Therefore, the interest charge for the second period will be less, too; it will equal:

Original investment in bond	$1,038.08
Less: amortization of premium through 6/30/X8	9.24
Investment at beginning of period	$1,028.84
Effective interest rate per period	× 2%
Interest charge for period	$ 20.58

The entry at the end of the second period will be:

12/31/X8	Interest Expense	20.58	
	Premium on Bonds Payable	9.42	
	Cash		30.00

During the third period, the interest charge will be $1,028.84 - $9.42 = $1,019.42 \times 2\% = $20.39, and the entry at the end of the third period will be:

6/30/X9	Interest Expense	20.39	
	Premium on Bonds Payable	9.61	
	Cash		30.00

During the fourth period, the same calculation yields an interest charge of ($1,019.42 - $9.61) \times 2\% = $20.20. By now a one-cent cumulative rounding error has crept into the calculation: the correct amount is $20.19. The interest entry at the end of the fourth period will be:

12/31/X9	Interest Expense	20.19	
	Premium on Bonds Payable	9.81	
	Cash		30.00

The premium account has been reduced to zero (or to one penny, if the cumulative rounding error has not been corrected). The final 12/31/X9 entry, recording payment of the bond's principal, will be:

12/31/X9	Bonds Payable	1,000.00	
	Cash		1,000.00

A further shortcut

Once you understand the constant rate method of amortizing premium or discount, a further shortcut is possible for calculating the amount of periodic amortization. Under the constant rate method, at the end of each period the amount reported for a debt will be the present value of the *remaining* amounts to be received by the lender, discounted at the effective rate. For example, at the end of the first period (6/30/X8) there will be three remaining interest payments on the Matsunaga Corporation bonds. The 2% annuity factor for three periods is 2.8839; if we multiply this by the $10.00 interest superiority we obtain $28.84—the unamortized premium at the end of the first period. We have already seen that the unamortized premium at the beginning of the first period equals the 2% annuity factor for four periods, 3.8077, times the $10.00 interest superiority. Accordingly, the *amortization* of premium for the period equals the $10.00 interest superiority times the difference between the two annuity figures, or $10.00 \times (3.8077 - 2.8839) = $10.00 \times 0.9238 \approx $9.24.

But we saw at the outset that the annuity tables are merely the cumulations of the related single payment tables. Therefore, we could obtain the 0.9238 figure directly by looking at the related 2% single-payment present value figure for period four. This results in the following simplified formula for the amortization of premium or discount during any period:

$$\text{Amortization} = \begin{array}{c} \text{Interest} \\ \text{superiority} \\ \text{or inferiority} \end{array} \times \begin{array}{c} \text{Present value of a single payment} \\ \text{of \$1.00 to be received at the} \\ \text{maturity date of the bond} \end{array}$$

Here is how this shortcut method would be used to calculate all four of the previous amortization amounts:

Interest Date	Interest Superiority per Period	Present Value at the Effective Rate of a Single Payment of $1.00 to be Received at Maturity	Amortization of Premium for Period
6/30/X8	$10.00	0.9238	$9.24
12/31/X8	10.00	0.9423	9.42
6/30/X9	10.00	0.9612	9.61
12/31/X9	10.00	0.9804	9.80

These are the same amounts as before, even to the one-cent rounding error.

A discount example

One final example should be given—in this case, a more realistic one. Suppose that on 4/1/X3 American Greening Company issued $1,000,000 of 6.6%, five-year bonds at a price that yielded an effective rate of 7%. Interest on these bonds is payable every April and October first. Every six months, $1,000,000 × 6.6% × 6/12 = $33,000 of interest will be paid. Had the nominal rate equalled the yield rate, this semiannual payment would have been $1,000,000 × 7% × 6/12 = $35,000. Therefore the interest annuity is deficient by $35,000 − $33,000 = $2,000 per period. Table B gives the present value of a ten-period, $3\frac{1}{2}$% annuity of a dollar as 8.3166; therefore, the discount at the issue date must have been $2,000 × 8.3166 ≈ $16,633.

4/1/X3	Cash	983,367	
	Discount on Bonds Payable	16,633	
	Bonds Payable		1,000,000

Discount amortization will first be calculated the long way, then corresponding calculations under the shortcut method will be given. The interest expense for the first period will be $983,367 × $3\frac{1}{2}$% ≈ $34,418:

10/1/X3	Interest Expense	34,418	
	Discount on Bonds Payable		1,418
	Cash		33,000

The interest expense for the second period will be $983,367 + $1,418 = $984,785 × $3\frac{1}{2}$% ≈ $34,467:

4/1/X4	Interest Expense	34,467	
	Discount on Bonds Payable		1,467
	Cash		33,000

—and so forth. Illustration 11-6 indicates the interest expense and amortization of discount at each of the interest dates during the bond's life.

Illustration 11-6

Amortization of Bond Discount by the Constant Rate Method

Interest Date	Maturity Value Less Unamortized Discount at Beginning of Period	× Effective Rate	= Interest Charge	− Cash Payment	= Discount Amortization for Period	Maturity Value Less Unamortized Discount at End of Period
10/1/X3	$983,367	3.5%	$34,418	$33,000	$ 1,418	$ 984,785
4/1/X4	984,785	3.5	34,467	33,000	1,467	986,252
10/1/X4	986,252	3.5	34,519	33,000	1,519	987,771
4/1/X5	987,771	3.5	34,572	33,000	1,572	989,343
10/1/X5	989,343	3.5	34,627	33,000	1,627	990,970
4/1/X6	990,970	3.5	34,684	33,000	1,684	992,654
10/1/X6	992,654	3.5	34,743	33,000	1,743	994,397
4/1/X7	994,397	3.5	34,804	33,000	1,804	996,201
10/1/X7	996,201	3.5	34,867	33,000	1,867	998,068
4/1/X8	998,068	3.5	34,932	33,000	1,932	1,000,000

Total amortization of discount $16,633

Shortcut Method

Interest Date	Interest Superiority per Period	Present Value at the Effective Rate of a Single Payment of $1.00 to be Received at Maturity	Amortization of Premium for Period
10/1/X3	$2,000	0.7089	$1,418
4/1/X4	2,000	0.7337	1,467
10/1/X4	2,000	0.7594	1,519
4/1/X5	2,000	0.7860	1,572
10/1/X5	2,000	0.8135	1,627
4/1/X6	2,000	0.8420	1,684
10/1/X6	2,000	0.8714	1,743
4/1/X7	2,000	0.9019	1,804
10/1/X7	2,000	0.9335	1,867
4/1/X8	2,000	0.9662	1,932

As you can see from Illustration 11-6, over the five-year period the entire $16,633 discount is amortized, so that the entry to record repayment of the bonds at maturity will simply be:

$$4/1/X8 \quad \text{Bonds Payable} \quad 1,000,000$$
$$\text{Cash} \qquad\qquad\qquad 1,000,000$$

Problems for Study and Self-Examination

Problem 11-4:

See pages 610–612. Prepare a table, similar to Illustration 11-6, for Matsunaga Corporation's single 6% bond, assuming that it was issued at an $18.37 discount.

Problem 11-5:

On 2/1/X3 Mink Mfg. Corp. issued $2,400,000 of $6\frac{1}{2}$%, 20-year bonds, at a price to yield an effective interest rate of 6%. Interest is payable on these bonds every February and August 1st. The firm uses the constant rate method of amortizing premium and discount. Make appropriate journal entries as of 2/1/X3, 8/1/X3, and 2/1/X4. You may ignore any year-end accruals of interest payable. Round your answers to the nearest dollar.

Problem 11-6:

Same as Problem 11-5, except that you should assume that the company uses the straight-line method of amortizing premium and discount.

Solution 11-4:

Interest Date	Maturity Value Less Unamortized Discount at Beginning of Period	× Effective Rate	= Interest Charge	− Cash Payment	= Discount Amortization for Period	Maturity Value Less Unamortized Discount at End of Period
6/30/X8	$981.63	3.5%	$34.36	$30.00	$ 4.36	$ 985.99
12/31/X8	985.99	3.5	34.51	30.00	4.51	990.50
6/30/X9	990.50	3.5	34.67	30.00	4.67	995.17
12/31/X9	995.17	3.5	34.83	30.00	4.83	1,000.00

Total amortization of discount $18.37

Shortcut Method

Interest Date	Interest Superiority per Period	Present Value at the Effective Rate of a Single Payment of $1.00 to be Received at Maturity	Amortization of Premium for Period
6/30/X8	$5.00	0.8714	$4.36
12/31/X8	5.00	0.9019	4.51
6/30/X9	5.00	0.9335	4.67
12/31/X9	5.00	0.9662	4.83

Solution 11-5:
These bonds pay a 40-period interest annuity of $2,400,000 × 6½% × 6/12 = $78,000. Had the nominal rate equalled the 6% effective rate, this annuity would have been only $2,400,000 × 6% × 6/12 = $72,000. The present value of a 40-period annuity of one dollar at 3% per period is 23.1148. Accordingly, the premium on these bonds at the date of issue must have been $78,000 − $72,000 = $6,000 × 23.1148 ≈ $138,689; and the entry at issue must have been:

```
2/1/X3   Cash                              2,538,689
             Bonds Payable                              2,400,000
             Premium on Bonds Payable                     138,689
```

Premium amortization will be as follows:

Interest Date	Interest Superiority	3% Present-Value Factor	Amortization
8/1/X3	$6,000	0.3066 (40 period)	$1,840
2/1/X4	6,000	0.3158 (39 period)	1,895

Therefore, the two remaining journal entries will be:

```
8/1/X3   Interest Expense                  76,160
         Premium on Bonds Payable           1,840
             Cash                                        78,000

2/1/X4   Interest Expense                  76,105
         Premium on Bonds Payable           1,895
             Cash                                        78,000
```

Solution 11-6:

Total amount to be paid to bondholders:
Nominal interest ($78,000 × 40) $3,120,000
Maturity value of bonds 2,400,000 $5,520,000
Amount borrowed by Mink Mfg. Corp. 2,538,689
Total interest charge $2,981,311

For each six-month period, the interest charge will be $74,533 ($2,981,311/40 ≈ $74,533), and the amortization of premium will be $3,467 ($138,689/40 ≈ $3,467). The entry at issue will be identical to the one in Problem 11-5:

```
2/1/X3   Cash                              2,538,689
             Bonds Payable                              2,400,000
             Premium on Bonds Payable                     138,689
```

The entries for interest charges, however, will be different:

8/1/X3 and 2/1/X4	Interest Expense	74,533	
	Premium on Bonds Payable	3,467	
	Cash		78,000

Receivables and Payables Other Than Bonds

Applicability of the constant rate approach

The previous section was concerned exclusively with bonds payable. But the constant rate approach is applicable to a wide variety of other noncurrent payables and receivables, such as notes payable, investments in notes receivable, bonds receivable, mortgages payable, and so on. The Accounting Principles Board has required employment of the constant rate method for all such receivables and payables. However, any other method that gives results approximating those of the constant rate method is also acceptable. The straight-line method fits this description whenever the life of the obligation is relatively short or the difference between the nominal and effective rates is small. Therefore, the straight-line method often will satisfy APB requirements, too. The straight-line approach is generally acceptable for current receivables and payables.

"Non-interest-bearing" notes

In particular, the constant rate method is applicable to so-called *non-interest-bearing notes*. Non-interest-bearing notes are ones in which no explicit charge is made for interest, but in which the borrower receives less when the note is issued than the amount that must be paid at maturity; the entire effective interest charge is reflected in a discount on the note. Here is an example.

Let us suppose that on 1/1/X6 Mère Tirésias' Unisex Boutiques borrowed $8,734.39 from Glendale General Corporation, issuing a note that is due on 1/1/X8. No specific provision is made for interest, but Mère Tirésias' Unisex Boutiques must pay Glendale General Corporation $10,000.00 at maturity. From Table A we see that the present value of one dollar in two periods at 7% interest per period is 0.8734 (had Table A been accurate to six significant digits, the present-value factor would have been 0.873439). Accordingly, the proceeds received when the note was issued correspond to an effective rate of 7%, compounded annually, on this loan. Assuming that Mère Tirésias' Unisex Boutiques closes its books once per year, every December 31st, it should make the following entries during the life of this note. (For clarity, a separate valuation account for discount is used in what follows; however some firms would record this note at a single net figure.)

1/1/X6	Cash	8,734.39	
	Discount on Notes Payable	1,265.61	
	Notes Payable		10,000.00

Interest charges during 19X6 will be $8,734.39 \times 7\% = \$611.41$:

12/31/X6	Interest Expense	611.41	
	Discount on Notes Payable		611.41

Interest charges during 19X7 will be $8,734.39 + \$611.41 = \$9,345.80 \times 7\% = \$654.20$ (corrected for a one-cent cumulative rounding error):

12/31/X7	Interest Expense	654.20	
	Discount on Notes Payable		654.20

The discount has now been entirely amortized ($611.41 + \$654.20 = \$1,265.61$), and the payment of the note may be recorded by the entry:

12/31/X7	Notes Payable	10,000.00	
	Cash		10,000.00

In more complicated situations, an approach that parallels the shortcut approach to calculating bond discount amortization may be used with non-interest-bearing notes.

Parallel entries should be made by Glendale General Corporation, though many lenders would carry their investments in such notes at single, net, amounts instead of using a valuation account for discount.

Other applications of the constant rate approach

Three other common applications of the constant rate approach should be mentioned in passing:

1. When a firm has received a note from another entity, it may want to sell it to some third party prior to the note's maturity date, so as to obtain immediate cash. This process is called *discounting* the note receivable. If the entity acquiring the note is a bank, it will usually employ a form of compound interest calculation, instead of a simple interest calculation, to determine how much it will pay for the note; the calculation involved parallels the longer form of bond issue price calculation, illustrated in the previous section. Banks also use the constant rate approach with various other kinds of notes.

2. Accountants treat the liability that arises from a long-term lease on land, buildings, or equipment as interest bearing, even when (as usually is the case) the lease involves no explicit charge for interest. The techniques used here correspond in a general way to the constant rate treatment of non-interest-bearing notes.

3. Calculations similar to those for determining the issue prices of bonds are widely recommended for *capital budgeting*—the managerial accounting process whereby decisions are made concerning which depreciable assets to purchase, which new projects to begin, which old projects to terminate, and so on. A simple example of such a capital budgeting calculation was given in the Alternative Culture Corporation example on page 608.

Finally, there are all sorts of technical complications in accounting for liabilities, which are reserved for an advanced course: for instance—what to do when bonds are issued at a date other than exactly six months from an interest date, how to calculate the effective rate when you aren't told what it is, what to do when the effective rate is an uneven amount, and so forth. The subject of receivables and payables can become quite involved (and engrossing). The discussion in this chapter has outlined those main points you need to understand in order to comprehend published financial statements, but you should not regard it as anything more than an introduction.

Problems for Study and Self-Examination

Problem 11-7:

On 1/1/X6 Walpahu Tool and Die Company borrowed from Springer Corporation, issuing a $4,500 non-interest-bearing note due in three years. Springer Corporation believes that 8% interest, compounded annually, would be appropriate for a note offering this degree of risk. Both firms close their books once a year, every December 31st, and employ the constant rate method of amortizing premium and discount.

1. Indicate the journal entries that Walpahu Tool and Die Company should make at 1/1/X6, 12/31/X6, and 12/31/X7. You may assume that Walpahu Tool and Die Company uses a valuation account to reflect discount.

2. Indicate the journal entries that Springer Corporation should make at 12/31/X7, 12/31/X8, and 1/1/X9. You may assume that Springer Corporation records such notes at net amounts.

Problem 11-8:

Same as Problem 11-7, except that both firms use the straight-line method of amortizing premium and discount.

Solution

Solution 11-7:

Table A indicates that the present value of one dollar in three periods at 8% interest per period is 0.7938. Therefore, we could calculate what Springer Corporation must have paid for the note as follows: $4,500 \times 0.7938 \approx \$3,572$. However, if you were ingenious, you may have recognized that a more exact answer may be obtained by an approach similar to the shortcut approach for bonds. If the note had paid 8% explicit interest, it would have paid an annuity of $4,500 \times 8\% = \$360.00$ each year; instead, it paid an annuity of zero—$360.00 per year deficient. The present value of this deficiency may be obtained by taking the present value of a three-period, 8% annuity from Table B, 2.5771:

$$\$360.00 \times 2.5771 \approx \$927.76$$

Accordingly, Springer Corporation must have paid $4,500.00 - \$927.76 = \$3,572.24$. Interest charges and discount amortization on the books of both parties should be as follows:

Year	*Interest Deficiency*	*8% Present-Value Factor*	*Interest Charge (Equals Amortization of Discount)*
19X6	$360.00	0.7938	$285.80
19X7	360.00	0.8573	308.60
19X8	360.00	0.9259	333.30
Cumulative rounding error			0.06
Total discount			$927.76

1. *Walpahu Tool and Die Company's books:*

1/1/X6	Cash	3,572.24	
	Discount on Notes Payable	927.76	
	Notes Payable		4,500.00
12/31/X6	Interest Expense	285.80	
	Discount on Notes Payable		285.80
12/31/X7	Interest Expense	308.60	
	Discount on Notes Payable		308.60

2. *Springer Corporation's books:*

12/31/X7	Notes Receivable*	308.60	
	Interest Revenue		308.60

12/31/X8   Notes Receivable*   333.36
    Interest Revenue   333.36
(Includes cumulative rounding error of $0.06)

1/1/X9   Cash   4,500.00
    Notes Receivable*   4,500.00

---

* *Or, Investment in Notes Receivable.*

Solution 11-8:

Total amount to be repaid to Springer:
  Nominal interest . . . . $ –0–
  Maturity value 4,500.00 $4,500.00

Amount borrowed by Walpahu 3,572.24

Total interest charge . . . . $ 927.76

Annual interest charge and discount amortization on the books of both firms will be $309.25 ($927.76 ÷ 3 ≈ $309.25).

1. *Walpahu Tool and Die Company's books:*

1/1/X6   Cash   3,572.24
    Discount on Notes Payable   927.76
      Notes Payable   4,500.00

12/31/X6   Interest Expense   309.25
and   Discount on Notes Payable   309.25
12/31/X7

2. *Springer Corporation's books:*

12/31/X7   Notes Receivable*   309.25
    Interest Revenue   309.25

12/31/X8   Notes Receivable*   309.26
    Interest Revenue   309.26
(Includes cumulative rounding error of $0.01)

1/1/X9   Cash   4,500.00
    Notes Receivable*   4,500.00

---

* *Or, Investment in Notes Receivable.*

Table A
Present Value of a Single Payment of One Dollar

Interest rate per period (%)

Period	0.5	1.0	1.5	2.0	2.5	3.0	3.5	4.0	4.5	5.0
1	0.9950	0.9901	0.9852	0.9804	0.9756	0.9709	0.9662	0.9615	0.9569	0.9524
2	0.9901	0.9803	0.9707	0.9612	0.9518	0.9426	0.9335	0.9246	0.9157	0.9070
3	0.9851	0.9706	0.9563	0.9423	0.9286	0.9151	0.9019	0.8890	0.8763	0.8638
4	0.9802	0.9610	0.9422	0.9238	0.9060	0.8885	0.8714	0.8548	0.8386	0.8226
5	0.9754	0.9515	0.9283	0.9057	0.8839	0.8626	0.8420	0.8219	0.8025	0.7835
6	0.9705	0.9420	0.9145	0.8880	0.8623	0.8375	0.8135	0.7903	0.7679	0.7462
7	0.9657	0.9327	0.9010	0.8706	0.8413	0.8131	0.7860	0.7599	0.7348	0.7107
8	0.9609	0.9235	0.8877	0.8535	0.8207	0.7894	0.7594	0.7307	0.7032	0.6768
9	0.9561	0.9143	0.8746	0.8368	0.8007	0.7664	0.7337	0.7026	0.6729	0.6446
10	0.9513	0.9053	0.8617	0.8203	0.7812	0.7441	0.7089	0.6756	0.6439	0.6139
11	0.9466	0.8963	0.8489	0.8043	0.7621	0.7224	0.6849	0.6496	0.6162	0.5847
12	0.9419	0.8874	0.8364	0.7885	0.7436	0.7014	0.6618	0.6246	0.5897	0.5568
13	0.9372	0.8787	0.8240	0.7730	0.7254	0.6810	0.6394	0.6006	0.5643	0.5303
14	0.9326	0.8700	0.8118	0.7579	0.7077	0.6611	0.6178	0.5775	0.5400	0.5051
15	0.9279	0.8613	0.7999	0.7430	0.6905	0.6419	0.5969	0.5553	0.5167	0.4810
16	0.9233	0.8528	0.7880	0.7284	0.6736	0.6232	0.5767	0.5339	0.4945	0.4581
17	0.9187	0.8444	0.7764	0.7142	0.6572	0.6050	0.5572	0.5134	0.4732	0.4363
18	0.9141	0.8360	0.7649	0.7002	0.6412	0.5874	0.5384	0.4936	0.4528	0.4155
19	0.9096	0.8277	0.7536	0.6864	0.6255	0.5703	0.5202	0.4746	0.4333	0.3957
20	0.9051	0.8195	0.7425	0.6730	0.6103	0.5537	0.5026	0.4564	0.4146	0.3769
21	0.9006	0.8114	0.7315	0.6598	0.5954	0.5375	0.4856	0.4388	0.3968	0.3589
22	0.8961	0.8034	0.7207	0.6468	0.5809	0.5219	0.4692	0.4220	0.3797	0.3418
23	0.8916	0.7954	0.7100	0.6342	0.5667	0.5067	0.4533	0.4057	0.3634	0.3256
24	0.8872	0.7876	0.6995	0.6217	0.5529	0.4919	0.4380	0.3901	0.3477	0.3101
25	0.8828	0.7798	0.6892	0.6095	0.5394	0.4776	0.4231	0.3751	0.3327	0.2953

Table A, continued

Interest rate per period (%)

Period	0.5	1.0	1.5	2.0	2.5	3.0	3.5	4.0	4.5	5.0
26	0.8784	0.7720	0.6790	0.5976	0.5262	0.4637	0.4088	0.3607	0.3184	0.2812
27	0.8740	0.7644	0.6690	0.5859	0.5134	0.4502	0.3950	0.3468	0.3047	0.2678
28	0.8697	0.7568	0.6591	0.5744	0.5009	0.4371	0.3817	0.3335	0.2916	0.2551
29	0.8653	0.7493	0.6494	0.5631	0.4887	0.4243	0.3687	0.3207	0.2790	0.2429
30	0.8610	0.7419	0.6398	0.5521	0.4767	0.4120	0.3563	0.3083	0.2670	0.2314
31	0.8567	0.7346	0.6303	0.5412	0.4651	0.4000	0.3442	0.2965	0.2555	0.2204
32	0.8525	0.7273	0.6210	0.5306	0.4538	0.3883	0.3326	0.2851	0.2445	0.2099
33	0.8482	0.7201	0.6118	0.5202	0.4427	0.3770	0.3213	0.2741	0.2340	0.1999
34	0.8440	0.7130	0.6028	0.5100	0.4319	0.3660	0.3105	0.2636	0.2239	0.1904
35	0.8398	0.7059	0.5939	0.5000	0.4214	0.3554	0.3000	0.2534	0.2143	0.1813
36	0.8356	0.6989	0.5851	0.4902	0.4111	0.3450	0.2898	0.2437	0.2050	0.1727
37	0.8315	0.6920	0.5764	0.4806	0.4011	0.3350	0.2800	0.2343	0.1962	0.1644
38	0.8274	0.6852	0.5679	0.4712	0.3913	0.3252	0.2706	0.2253	0.1878	0.1566
39	0.8232	0.6784	0.5595	0.4619	0.3817	0.3158	0.2614	0.2166	0.1797	0.1491
40	0.8191	0.6717	0.5513	0.4529	0.3724	0.3066	0.2526	0.2083	0.1719	0.1420
41	0.8151	0.6650	0.5431	0.4440	0.3633	0.2976	0.2440	0.2003	0.1645	0.1353
42	0.8110	0.6584	0.5351	0.4353	0.3545	0.2890	0.2358	0.1926	0.1574	0.1288
43	0.8070	0.6519	0.5272	0.4268	0.3458	0.2805	0.2278	0.1852	0.1507	0.1227
44	0.8030	0.6454	0.5194	0.4184	0.3374	0.2724	0.2201	0.1780	0.1442	0.1169
45	0.7990	0.6391	0.5117	0.4102	0.3292	0.2644	0.2127	0.1712	0.1380	0.1113
46	0.7950	0.6327	0.5042	0.4022	0.3211	0.2567	0.2055	0.1646	0.1320	0.1060
47	0.7910	0.6265	0.4967	0.3943	0.3133	0.2493	0.1985	0.1583	0.1263	0.1009
48	0.7871	0.6203	0.4894	0.3865	0.3057	0.2420	0.1918	0.1522	0.1209	0.0961
49	0.7832	0.6141	0.4821	0.3790	0.2982	0.2350	0.1853	0.1463	0.1157	0.0916
50	0.7793	0.6080	0.4750	0.3715	0.2909	0.2281	0.1791	0.1407	0.1107	0.0872

Table A, continued

Interest rate per period (%)

Period	6.0	7.0	8.0	9.0	10.0	11.0	12.0	13.0	14.0	15.0
1	0.9434	0.9346	0.9259	0.9174	0.9091	0.9009	0.8929	0.8850	0.8772	0.8696
2	0.8900	0.8734	0.8573	0.8417	0.8264	0.8116	0.7972	0.7831	0.7695	0.7561
3	0.8396	0.8163	0.7938	0.7722	0.7513	0.7312	0.7118	0.6931	0.6750	0.6575
4	0.7921	0.7629	0.7350	0.7084	0.6830	0.6587	0.6355	0.6133	0.5921	0.5718
5	0.7473	0.7130	0.6806	0.6499	0.6209	0.5935	0.5674	0.5428	0.5194	0.4972
6	0.7050	0.6663	0.6302	0.5963	0.5645	0.5346	0.5066	0.4803	0.4556	0.4323
7	0.6651	0.6227	0.5835	0.5470	0.5132	0.4817	0.4523	0.4251	0.3996	0.3759
8	0.6274	0.5820	0.5403	0.5019	0.4665	0.4339	0.4039	0.3762	0.3506	0.3269
9	0.5919	0.5439	0.5002	0.4604	0.4241	0.3909	0.3606	0.3329	0.3075	0.2843
10	0.5584	0.5083	0.4632	0.4224	0.3855	0.3522	0.3220	0.2946	0.2697	0.2472
11	0.5268	0.4751	0.4289	0.3875	0.3505	0.3173	0.2875	0.2607	0.2366	0.2149
12	0.4970	0.4440	0.3971	0.3555	0.3186	0.2858	0.2567	0.2307	0.2076	0.1869
13	0.4688	0.4150	0.3677	0.3262	0.2897	0.2575	0.2292	0.2042	0.1821	0.1625
14	0.4423	0.3878	0.3405	0.2992	0.2633	0.2320	0.2046	0.1807	0.1597	0.1413
15	0.4173	0.3624	0.3152	0.2745	0.2394	0.2090	0.1827	0.1599	0.1401	0.1229
16	0.3936	0.3387	0.2919	0.2519	0.2176	0.1883	0.1631	0.1415	0.1229	0.1069
17	0.3714	0.3166	0.2703	0.2311	0.1978	0.1696	0.1456	0.1252	0.1078	0.0929
18	0.3503	0.2959	0.2502	0.2120	0.1799	0.1528	0.1300	0.1108	0.0946	0.0808
19	0.3305	0.2765	0.2317	0.1945	0.1635	0.1377	0.1161	0.0981	0.0829	0.0703
20	0.3118	0.2584	0.2145	0.1784	0.1486	0.1240	0.1037	0.0868	0.0728	0.0611
21	0.2942	0.2415	0.1987	0.1637	0.1351	0.1117	0.0926	0.0768	0.0638	0.0531
22	0.2775	0.2257	0.1839	0.1502	0.1228	0.1007	0.0826	0.0680	0.0560	0.0462
23	0.2618	0.2109	0.1703	0.1378	0.1117	0.0907	0.0738	0.0601	0.0491	0.0402
24	0.2470	0.1971	0.1577	0.1264	0.1015	0.0817	0.0659	0.0532	0.0431	0.0349
25	0.2330	0.1842	0.1460	0.1160	0.0923	0.0736	0.0588	0.0471	0.0378	0.0304

Table A, continued

Interest rate per period (%)

Period	6.0	7.0	8.0	9.0	10.0	11.0	12.0	13.0	14.0	15.0
26	0.2198	0.1722	0.1352	0.1064	0.0839	0.0663	0.0525	0.0417	0.0331	0.0264
27	0.2074	0.1609	0.1252	0.0976	0.0763	0.0597	0.0469	0.0369	0.0291	0.0230
28	0.1956	0.1504	0.1159	0.0895	0.0693	0.0538	0.0419	0.0326	0.0255	0.0200
29	0.1846	0.1406	0.1073	0.0822	0.0630	0.0485	0.0374	0.0289	0.0224	0.0174
30	0.1741	0.1314	0.0994	0.0754	0.0573	0.0437	0.0334	0.0256	0.0196	0.0151
31	0.1643	0.1228	0.0920	0.0691	0.0521	0.0394	0.0298	0.0226	0.0172	0.0131
32	0.1550	0.1147	0.0852	0.0634	0.0474	0.0355	0.0266	0.0200	0.0151	0.0114
33	0.1462	0.1072	0.0789	0.0582	0.0431	0.0319	0.0238	0.0177	0.0132	0.0099
34	0.1379	0.1002	0.0730	0.0534	0.0391	0.0288	0.0212	0.0157	0.0116	0.0086
35	0.1301	0.0937	0.0676	0.0490	0.0356	0.0259	0.0189	0.0139	0.0102	0.0075
36	0.1227	0.0875	0.0626	0.0449	0.0323	0.0234	0.0169	0.0123	0.0089	0.0065
37	0.1158	0.0818	0.0580	0.0412	0.0294	0.0210	0.0151	0.0109	0.0078	0.0057
38	0.1092	0.0765	0.0537	0.0378	0.0267	0.0190	0.0135	0.0096	0.0069	0.0049
39	0.1031	0.0715	0.0497	0.0347	0.0243	0.0171	0.0120	0.0085	0.0060	0.0043
40	0.0972	0.0668	0.0460	0.0318	0.0221	0.0154	0.0107	0.0075	0.0053	0.0037
41	0.0917	0.0624	0.0426	0.0292	0.0201	0.0139	0.0096	0.0067	0.0046	0.0032
42	0.0865	0.0583	0.0395	0.0268	0.0183	0.0125	0.0086	0.0059	0.0041	0.0028
43	0.0816	0.0545	0.0365	0.0246	0.0166	0.0112	0.0076	0.0052	0.0036	0.0025
44	0.0770	0.0509	0.0338	0.0226	0.0151	0.0101	0.0068	0.0046	0.0031	0.0021
45	0.0727	0.0476	0.0313	0.0207	0.0137	0.0091	0.0061	0.0041	0.0027	0.0019
46	0.0685	0.0445	0.0290	0.0190	0.0125	0.0082	0.0054	0.0036	0.0024	0.0016
47	0.0647	0.0416	0.0269	0.0174	0.0113	0.0074	0.0049	0.0032	0.0021	0.0014
48	0.0610	0.0389	0.0249	0.0160	0.0103	0.0067	0.0043	0.0028	0.0019	0.0012
49	0.0575	0.0363	0.0230	0.0147	0.0094	0.0060	0.0039	0.0025	0.0016	0.0011
50	0.0543	0.0339	0.0213	0.0134	0.0085	0.0054	0.0035	0.0022	0.0014	0.0009

Table B
Present Value of an Annuity of One Dollar Per Period

Interest rate per period (%)

Period	0.5	1.0	1.5	2.0	2.5	3.0	3.5	4.0	4.5	5.0
1	0.9950	0.9901	0.9852	0.9804	0.9756	0.9709	0.9662	0.9615	0.9569	0.9524
2	1.9851	1.9704	1.9559	1.9416	1.9274	1.9135	1.8997	1.8861	1.8727	1.8594
3	2.9702	2.9410	2.9122	2.8839	2.8560	2.8286	2.8016	2.7751	2.7490	2.7232
4	3.9505	3.9020	3.8544	3.8077	3.7620	3.7171	3.6731	3.6299	3.5875	3.5460
5	4.9259	4.8534	4.7826	4.7135	4.6458	4.5797	4.5151	4.4518	4.3900	4.3295
6	5.8964	5.7955	5.6972	5.6014	5.5081	5.4172	5.3286	5.2421	5.1579	5.0757
7	6.8621	6.7282	6.5982	6.4720	6.3494	6.2303	6.1145	6.0021	5.8927	5.7864
8	7.8230	7.6517	7.4859	7.3255	7.1701	7.0197	6.8740	6.7327	6.5969	6.4632
9	8.7791	8.5660	8.3605	8.1622	7.9709	7.7861	7.6077	7.4353	7.2688	7.1078
10	9.7304	9.4713	9.2222	8.9826	8.7521	8.5302	8.3166	8.1109	7.9127	7.7217
11	10.6770	10.3676	10.0711	9.7868	9.5142	9.2526	9.0016	8.7605	8.5289	8.3064
12	11.6189	11.2551	10.9075	10.5753	10.2578	9.9540	9.6633	9.3851	9.1186	8.8633
13	12.5562	12.1337	11.7315	11.3484	10.9832	10.6350	10.3027	9.9856	9.6829	9.3936
14	13.4887	13.0037	12.5434	12.1062	11.6909	11.2961	10.9205	10.5631	10.2228	9.8986
15	14.4166	13.8651	13.3432	12.8493	12.3814	11.9379	11.5174	11.1184	10.7395	10.3797
16	15.3399	14.7179	14.1313	13.5777	13.0550	12.5611	12.0941	11.6523	11.2340	10.8378
17	16.2586	15.5623	14.9076	14.2919	13.7122	13.1661	12.6513	12.1657	11.7072	11.2741
18	17.1728	16.3983	15.6726	14.9920	14.3534	13.7535	13.1897	12.6593	12.1600	11.6896
19	18.0824	17.2260	16.4262	15.6785	14.9789	14.3238	13.7098	13.1339	12.6933	12.0853
20	18.9874	18.0456	17.1686	16.3514	15.5892	14.8775	14.2124	13.5903	13.0079	12.4622
21	19.8880	18.8570	17.9001	17.0112	16.1845	15.4150	14.6980	14.0292	13.4047	12.8212
22	20.7841	19.6604	18.6208	17.6580	16.7654	15.9369	15.1671	14.4511	13.7844	13.1630
23	21.6757	20.4558	19.3309	18.2922	17.3321	16.4436	15.6204	14.8568	14.1478	13.4886
24	22.5629	21.2434	20.0304	18.9139	17.8850	16.9355	16.0584	15.2470	14.4955	13.7986
25	23.4456	22.0232	20.7196	19.5235	18.4244	17.4131	16.4815	15.6221	14.8282	14.0939

Table B, continued

Interest rate per period (%)

Period	0.5	1.0	1.5	2.0	2.5	3.0	3.5	4.0	4.5	5.0
26	24.3240	22.7952	21.3986	20.1210	18.9506	17.8768	16.8904	15.9828	15.1466	14.3752
27	25.1980	23.5596	22.0676	20.7069	19.4640	18.3270	17.2854	16.3296	15.4513	14.6430
28	26.0677	24.3164	22.7267	21.2813	19.9649	18.7641	17.6670	16.6631	15.7429	14.8981
29	26.9330	25.0658	23.3761	21.8444	20.4535	19.1885	18.0358	16.9837	16.0219	15.1411
30	27.7941	25.8077	24.0158	22.3965	20.9303	19.6004	18.3920	17.2920	16.2889	15.3725
31	28.6508	26.5423	24.6461	22.9377	21.3954	20.0004	18.7363	17.5885	16.5444	15.5928
32	29.5033	27.2696	25.2671	23.4683	21.8492	20.3888	19.0689	17.8736	16.7889	15.8027
33	30.3515	27.9897	25.8790	23.9886	22.2919	20.7658	19.3902	18.1476	17.0229	16.0025
34	31.1955	28.7027	26.4817	24.4986	22.7238	21.1318	19.7007	18.4112	17.2468	16.1929
35	32.0354	29.4086	27.0756	24.9986	23.1452	21.4872	20.0007	18.6646	17.4610	16.3742
36	32.8710	30.1075	27.6607	25.4888	23.5563	21.8323	20.2905	18.9083	17.6660	16.5469
37	33.7025	30.7995	28.2371	25.9695	23.9573	22.1672	20.5705	19.1426	17.8622	16.7113
38	34.5299	31.4847	28.8051	26.4406	24.3486	22.4925	20.8411	19.3679	18.0500	16.8679
39	35.3531	32.1630	29.3646	26.9026	24.7303	22.8082	21.1025	19.5845	18.2297	17.0170
40	36.1722	32.8347	29.9158	27.3555	25.1028	23.1148	21.3551	19.7928	18.4016	17.1591
41	36.9873	33.4997	30.4590	27.7995	25.4661	23.4124	21.5991	19.9931	18.5661	17.2944
42	37.7983	34.1581	30.9941	28.2348	25.8206	23.7014	21.8349	20.1856	18.7235	17.4232
43	38.6053	34.8100	31.5212	28.6616	26.1664	23.9819	22.0627	20.3708	18.8742	17.5459
44	39.4082	35.4555	32.0406	29.0800	26.5038	24.2543	22.2828	20.5488	19.0184	17.6628
45	40.2072	36.0945	32.5523	29.4902	26.8330	24.5187	22.4955	20.7200	19.1563	17.7741
46	41.0022	36.7272	33.0565	29.8923	27.1542	24.7754	22.7009	20.8847	19.2884	17.8801
47	41.7932	37.3537	33.5532	30.2866	27.4675	25.0247	22.8994	21.0429	19.4147	17.9810
48	42.5803	37.9740	34.0426	30.6731	27.7732	25.2667	23.0912	21.1951	19.5356	18.0772
49	43.3635	38.5881	34.5247	31.0521	28.0714	25.5017	23.2766	21.3415	19.6513	18.1687
50	44.1428	39.1961	34.9997	31.4236	28.3623	25.7298	23.4556	21.4822	19.7620	18.2559

Table B, continued

Interest rate per period (%)

Period	6.0	7.0	8.0	9.0	10.0	11.0	12.0	13.0	14.0	15.0
1	0.9434	0.9346	0.9259	0.9174	0.9091	0.9009	0.8929	0.8850	0.8772	0.8696
2	1.8334	1.8080	1.7833	1.7591	1.7355	1.7125	1.6901	1.6681	1.6467	1.6257
3	2.6730	2.6243	2.5771	2.5313	2.4869	2.4437	2.4018	2.3612	2.3216	2.2832
4	3.4651	3.3872	3.3121	3.2397	3.1699	3.1024	3.0373	2.9745	2.9137	2.8550
5	4.2124	4.1002	3.9927	3.8897	3.7908	3.6959	3.6048	3.5172	3.4331	3.3522
6	4.9173	4.7665	4.6229	4.4859	4.3553	4.2305	4.1114	3.9975	3.8887	3.7845
7	5.5824	5.3893	5.2064	5.0330	4.8684	4.7122	4.5638	4.4226	4.2883	4.1604
8	6.2098	5.9713	5.7466	5.5348	5.3349	5.1461	4.9676	4.7988	4.6389	4.4873
9	6.8017	6.5152	6.2469	5.9952	5.7590	5.5370	5.3282	5.1317	4.9464	4.7716
10	7.3601	7.0236	6.7101	6.4177	6.1446	5.8892	5.6502	5.4262	5.2161	5.0188
11	7.8869	7.4987	7.1390	6.8052	6.4951	6.2065	5.9377	5.6869	5.4527	5.2337
12	8.3838	7.9427	7.5361	7.1607	6.8137	6.4924	6.1944	5.9176	5.6603	5.4206
13	8.8527	8.3577	7.9038	7.4869	7.1034	6.7499	6.4235	6.1218	5.8424	5.5831
14	9.2950	8.7455	8.2442	7.7862	7.3667	6.9819	6.6282	6.3025	6.0021	5.7245
15	9.7122	9.1079	8.5595	8.0607	7.6061	7.1909	6.8109	6.4624	6.1422	5.8474
16	10.1059	9.4466	8.8514	8.3126	7.8237	7.3792	6.9740	6.6039	6.2651	5.9542
17	10.4773	9.7632	9.1216	8.5436	8.0216	7.5488	7.1196	6.7291	6.3729	6.0472
18	10.8276	10.0591	9.3719	8.7556	8.2014	7.7016	7.2497	6.8399	6.4674	6.1280
19	11.1581	10.3356	9.6036	8.9501	8.3649	7.8393	7.3658	6.9380	6.5504	6.1982
20	11.4699	10.5940	9.8181	9.1285	8.5136	7.9633	7.4694	7.0248	6.6231	6.2593
21	11.7641	10.8355	10.0168	9.2922	8.6487	8.0751	7.5620	7.1016	6.6870	6.3125
22	12.0416	11.0612	10.2007	9.4424	8.7715	8.1757	7.6446	7.1695	6.7429	6.3587
23	12.3034	11.2722	10.3711	9.5802	8.8832	8.2664	7.7184	7.2297	6.7921	6.3988
24	12.5504	11.4693	10.5288	9.7066	8.9847	8.3481	7.7843	7.2829	6.8351	6.4338
25	12.7834	11.6536	10.6748	9.8226	9.0770	8.4217	7.8431	7.3300	6.8729	6.4641

Table B, continued

Interest rate per period (%)

Period	6.0	7.0	8.0	9.0	10.0	11.0	12.0	13.0	14.0	15.0
26	13.0032	11.8258	10.8100	9.9290	9.1609	8.4881	7.8957	7.3717	6.9061	6.4906
27	13.2105	11.9867	10.9352	10.0266	9.2372	8.5478	7.9426	7.4086	6.9352	6.5135
28	13.4062	12.1371	11.0511	10.1161	9.3066	8.6016	7.9844	7.4412	6.9607	6.5335
29	13.5907	12.2777	11.1584	10.1983	9.3696	8.6501	8.0218	7.4701	6.9830	6.5509
30	13.7648	12.4090	11.2578	10.2737	9.4269	8.6938	8.0552	7.4957	7.0027	6.5660
31	13.9291	12.5318	11.3498	10.3428	9.4790	8.7331	8.0850	7.5183	7.0199	6.5791
32	14.0840	12.6466	11.4350	10.4062	9.5264	8.7686	8.1116	7.5383	7.0350	6.5905
33	14.2302	12.7538	11.5139	10.4644	9.5694	8.8005	8.1354	7.5560	7.0482	6.6005
34	14.3681	12.8540	11.5869	10.5178	9.6086	8.8293	8.1566	7.5717	7.0599	6.6091
35	14.4982	12.9477	11.6546	10.5668	9.6442	8.8552	8.1755	7.5856	7.0700	6.6166
36	14.6210	13.0352	11.7172	10.6118	9.6765	8.8786	8.1924	7.5979	7.0790	6.6231
37	14.7368	13.1170	11.7752	10.6530	9.7059	8.8996	8.2075	7.6087	7.0868	6.6288
38	14.8460	13.1935	11.8289	10.6908	9.7327	8.9186	8.2210	7.6183	7.0937	6.6338
39	14.9491	13.2649	11.8786	10.7255	9.7570	8.9357	8.2330	7.6268	7.0997	6.6380
40	15.0463	13.3317	11.9246	10.7574	9.7791	8.9511	8.2438	7.6344	7.1050	6.6418
41	15.1380	13.3941	11.9672	10.7866	9.7991	8.9649	8.2534	7.6410	7.1097	6.6450
42	15.2245	13.4524	12.0067	10.8134	9.8174	8.9774	8.2619	7.6469	7.1138	6.6478
43	15.3062	13.5070	12.0432	10.8380	9.8340	8.9886	8.2696	7.6522	7.1173	6.6503
44	15.3832	13.5579	12.0771	10.8605	9.8491	8.9988	8.2764	7.6568	7.1205	6.6524
45	15.4558	13.6055	12.1084	10.8812	9.8628	9.0079	8.2825	7.6609	7.1232	6.6543
46	15.5244	13.6500	12.1374	10.9002	9.8753	9.0161	8.2880	7.6645	7.1256	6.6559
47	15.5890	13.6916	12.1643	10.9176	9.8866	9.0235	8.2928	7.6677	7.1277	6.6573
48	15.6500	13.7305	12.1891	10.9336	9.8969	9.0302	8.2972	7.6705	7.1296	6.6585
49	15.7076	13.7668	12.2122	10.9482	9.9063	9.0362	8.3010	7.6730	7.1312	6.6596
50	15.7619	13.8007	12.2335	10.9617	9.9148	9.0417	8.3045	7.6752	7.1327	6.6605

Assignment Problems

Problem 11-A:

For several years, Callaway Connecticut Corporation has employed the aging technique for estimating uncollectible accounts receivable. The company bills customers at the beginning of each month and performs aging calculations at each month end, using the following estimation percentages:

Age of account (in months)	Estimated percentage uncollectible
1	2.1%
2	5.4%
3	13.3%
4	33.3%
over 4	100.0%

The Controller of Callaway Connecticut Corporation, Ms. Georgia H. Mackay, is interested in comparing the results of the aging technique with the results that would be obtained by charging a flat 2% of all credit sales to bad debts expense. On 12/31/X3 the balances of the company's accounts receivable and allowance for bad debts were $424,014 and $23,157, respectively. The following data is from the company's records for 19X4 and 19X5:

	19X4	19X5
Year-end Accounts Receivable:		
1 month old	$ 310,300	$ 343,200
2 months old	104,212	145,189
3 months old	52,803	48,399
4 months old	19,100	21,228
Over 4 months old	4,077	9,376
Total	$ 490,492	$ 567,392
Cash sales	105,277	122,316
Credit sales	2,809,200	3,285,600
Actual uncollectible accounts written off	54,117	55,124

Compare the company's bad debts expenses and ending balances of allowance for bad debts under the two estimation approaches, for 19X4 and 19X5.

Problem 11-B:

The following data pertain to Fissile Corporation of Atlanta's sales and collections for the years 19X1 through 19X3. All of this company's sales are on account. At 12/31/X0, the company's accounts receivable and allowance for bad debts were $27,000 and $2,200, respectively.

	19X1	*19X2*	*19X3*
Accounts Receivable, at December 31:			
Age in days: 0–29	$ 11,000	$ 14,000	$ 16,000
30–59	10,000	10,000	12,000
60–89	5,800	5,000	4,000
90–120	2,400	1,500	2,000
over 120	800	1,500	1,000
Total	$ 30,000	$ 32,000	$ 35,000
Sales	250,000	280,000	300,000
Uncollectible accounts receivable actually written off .	2,500	2,700	3,400
Collections on account	244,500	275,300	293,600

Calculate the company's bad debts expense and year-end balances of allowance for bad debts for 19X1 through 19X3. Prepare the company's 19X1 journal entries (omitting closing entries) insofar as you have the data to do so. You may assume that the company employs an aging approach for estimating uncollectible accounts receivable, using the following rates:

Age in days	*Estimated Percentage Uncollectible*
0–29	1%
30–59	6%
60–89	10%
90–120	32%
over 120	80%

Problem 11-C:

Refer to the data in Problem 11-B. Assume instead that the company estimates bad debts as 1.1% of sales. Calculate the company's bad debts expense and year-end balances of allowance for bad debts for 19X1 through 19X3. Prepare the firm's 19X1 journal entries (omitting closing entries) insofar as you have the data to do so.

Problem 11-D:

On 6/30/X3 Maston Paul Mfg. Company issued $8,000,000 of 7.5%, 15-year bonds. Interest is payable on these bonds every June 30th and December 31st, beginning 12/31/X3. Maston Paul Mfg. Company employs the constant rate method for amortizing premium and discount.

1. Assume that these bonds were sold at a price that yielded an effective interest rate of 7%, compounded semiannually. What entries should the firm make as of 6/30/X3, 12/31/X3, and 6/30/X4?

2. Assume that these bonds were sold at a price that yielded an effective interest rate of 8%, compounded semiannually. What entry should the firm make on 6/30/X4?

3. Assume that these bonds were sold at a price that yielded an effective interest rate of 7.5%, compounded semiannually. What entries should the firm make on 6/30/X3 and 6/30/X7?

Problem 11-E:

Refer to the data in Problem 11-D. Assume instead that the company employs the straight-line method for amortizing premium and discount. Answer the questions contained in Problem 11-D.

Problem 11-F:

On 6/30/X2 Stephens Business Machinery Corp. issued $7,300,000 of 7%, twenty-year bonds. Interest is payable on these bonds every June 30th and December 31st, beginning 12/31/X2. The company employs the constant rate method of amortizing premium and discount.

1. Assume that these bonds were sold at a price that yielded an effective interest rate of 8%, compounded semiannually. What journal entries should the firm have made on 6/30/X2, 12/31/X2, and 6/30/X3?

2. Suppose instead that these bonds were sold at a price that yielded an effective rate of 6%, compounded semiannually. What journal entry should the firm have made on 6/30/X3?

3. Same as 2, but suppose that the firm suffered severe financial reverses during 19X5–19X8. On 12/31/X8, these bonds were being traded among investors at a price that yielded an effective interest rate of 28%, compounded semiannually.

   (a) What was the market price of a $1,000 bond on 12/31/X8 (ignore brokerage commissions)?

   (b) What effect did this increase in the effective rate have on the firm's 19X8 interest expense? Do not make any calculations; just indicate the general nature of the effect.

Problem 11-G:

In answering the following questions, assume the firm uses the constant rate method of amortizing premium and discount, and calculate (where appropriate) the amount of premium or discount at the issue date by using an approach similar to the shortcut approach for bonds, which was illustrated in the solution to Problem 11-7.

1. On 4/1/X3 Coco Robichaud Co. issued an eighteen-month, $8,000 non-interest-bearing note to Zeake Real Properties, Inc., at an amount that yielded Zeake Real Properties, Inc., an effective rate of 10%, compounded quarterly. Coco Robichaud Co. closes its books once a year, every December 31st. It accrues interest on obligations of this kind as an end-of-year adjusting entry (as well as, of course, at maturity). What journal entries should Coco Robichaud Co. make on 4/1/X3, 12/31/X3, and 10/1/X4?

2. Same as 1, except that the $8,000 note bears 6% interest, payable quarterly. Indicate the entries that Coco Robichaud Co. should make on 4/1/X3, 7/1/X3, and 10/1/X3.

3. Same as 1, except that the $8,000 note bears 10% interest. What will be the issue price of this note if the interest is:

   (a) Payable quarterly?

   (b) Simple interest payable at maturity?

4. Same as 1, except that the $8,000 note bears 10.65% simple interest payable at maturity. What will be its issue price?

Problem 11-H:

Ignore taxes in answering the following questions.

1. Florida-Hawaii Company is considering purchasing a machine that would offer it cost savings (at year end) of $13,500 a year for six years, at the end of which

the machine would be retired with no scrap value. The firm wishes to earn a minimum of 12% interest, compounded annually, on any such investment. What is the maximum that the firm should be willing to pay for this machine?

2. Same as 1, but assume that the machine is expected to have a $4,000 scrap value at the end of six years.

3. Same as 2. Alternatively, the company could buy a machine that offered no scrap value and no cost savings for the first five years; but this alternate machine would offer a single $113,561 cost saving at the end of the sixth year. The firm cannot buy both machines—they are incompatible. If the firm buys one of them, which one should it be? Defend your answer.

Problem 11-I:

Each of the following questions except number 5 should be given a numerical answer, but you need not multiply or divide. Instead, you may leave your answer in to-be-calculated form. As an example, suppose that your answer was 8 times 15 divided by 6. The correct result, of course, is 20; but you may leave it in the form $(8 \times 15) \div 6$. Question 5 should be multiplied (or divided) out because it is somewhat unwieldy in to-be-calculated form.

1. What amount would an investor pay for the right to receive $400 per month for seven months, starting one month from now, if the appropriate effective interest rate on such investments is 1% per month, compounded monthly?

2. To how much will a single deposit of $750 accumulate in five years if it is invested at 6%, compounded quarterly?

3. Suppose that you can invest money at a rate of 7%, compounded semiannually, and that you wish to have $10,000 in six years' time. How much must you invest now, as a single deposit, to accomplish this?

4. Suppose that an investor makes equal quarterly deposits of $300 into a savings bank that pays interest at the rate of 8%, compounded quarterly. The investor makes his first deposit on 2/1/X1 and his last deposit on 8/1/X1. To how much will his bank balance have accumulated by 11/1/X1?

5. On 3/1/X1 an investor deposited $2,000 into a bank that pays 6%, compounded quarterly. He exhausted this bank deposit by making equal withdrawals on 3/1/X3, 6/1/X3, 9/1/X3 and 12/1/X3. How big was any one such withdrawal?

Problem 11-J:

See Problem 11-2. Miss Teena K. Boggs got married right on schedule. Her uncle is still concerned for her welfare, especially since after a year of work following graduation, her husband has decided to go to graduate school. At her uncle's encouragement, Teena and her husband have rented an apartment in Play-Pair 'Partments, an apartment complex that caters to young couples and provides a swimming pool, gymnasium, sauna baths, and an intense, if hectic, social life.

The two-year lease that the couple signed calls for a down payment of $550 on 9/1/X8, followed by 22 monthly payments of $275, beginning on 10/1/X8. Teena's uncle is now dealing with a bank that pays 6% interest, compounded monthly.

1. Suppose that he wished to make a single deposit in the bank on 8/1/X8 that would provide for all of the payments required under the lease. How much should he deposit?

2. As part of your training in accounting, you must become able to extend what you have learned into new situations. This question provides an opportunity to increase your flexibility and broaden your understanding. Suppose that Teena's uncle had sufficient foresight to be able to make this single deposit as a wedding present on 6/1/X7. How much should he have deposited?*

---

* It is inappropriate to reply that if her uncle had the foresight to make the deposit on 6/1/X7, he should also have had the foresight to know how much to deposit.

Problem 11-K:

In answering the first and second questions, calculate the amount of premium or discount at the issue date by using an approach similar to the shortcut approach for bonds, which was illustrated in the solution to Problem 11-7.

1. On 7/1/X0 Indianapolis Krypton Company issued a three-year, $11,500 non-interest-bearing note to Altoona Spee-Dee Pressure Corporation, at an amount that yielded Altoona Spee-Dee Pressure Corporation an effective rate of 8%, compounded semiannually. Indianapolis Krypton Company closes its books once a year, every December 31st. It accrues interest on obligations of this kind as an end-of-year adjusting entry (as well as, of course, at maturity) and employs the constant rate method of amortizing premium and discount. What entries should Indianapolis Krypton Company make on 7/1/X0, 12/31/X0, and 12/31/X1?

2. Same as 1, except assume instead that the firm employs the straight-line method of amortizing premium and discount.

3. On 1/1/X5 Jacobs-Gross Multispan issued a 30-month, $16,000 non-interest-bearing note to Greigg & Greigg Enterprises, for $12,840. Greigg & Greigg Enterprises compounds interest semiannually. What was the yield rate on this note?

4. On 10/1/X9, Kansas Conglomerate Corporation issued a $7,000, non-interest-bearing note to Smith Bandstra, Incorporated, for $5,692, a price that yielded Smith Bandstra, Incorporated, 12%, compounded quarterly. What was the life of this note?

5. On 6/30/X3, Marion Waterloo Ferrate, Inc., issued a 27-month, non-interest-bearing note to Industrial Credit of Sioux City for $9,368, a price that yielded Industrial Credit of Sioux City 10%, compounded quarterly. What is the maturity value of this note?

Problem 11-L:

1. On 6/30/X7, Iowa City Iron and Steel issued $4,000,000 of 25-year bonds at a price of $3,249,044; the effective interest rate on these bonds is 9%, compounded semiannually. Interest is payable every June 30th and December 31st, beginning 12/31/X7. What was the nominal rate on these bonds?

2. On 4/1/X9, United Gree-Gree issued $5,200,000 of 6.8% bonds at a price of $4,701,337; the effective interest rate on these bonds is 8%, compounded semiannually. Interest is payable every April 1st and October 1st, beginning 10/1/X9. What is the life of these bonds?

3. On 8/15/X8, Manning Edison issued 7.4%, 15-year bonds at a price of $3,214,030; the effective interest rate on these bonds was 7%, compounded semiannually. Interest is payable on these bonds every August 15th and February 15th, beginning 2/15/X9. What is the maturity value of these bonds?

4. On 3/15/X4, Thoth-Hansen Company issued $6,500,000 of 7.7%, 10-year bonds at a price of $6,823,332. Interest is payable every March 15th and September 15th, beginning 9/15/X4. What is the effective interest rate on these bonds?

Problem 11-M:

As part of your training in accounting, you must become able to extend the concepts and techniques you have learned into situations that require different methods of analysis. This problem provides an opportunity to increase your flexibility and broaden your understanding. The background needed to solve this problem has been provided by the text, but the particular method of analysis required may at first seem unusual. Apply what you already have learned to this new situation.

For a number of years, Davis Friendly Products has been estimating uncollectible accounts receivable as a percentage of credit sales. The company's Controller, Mr. John W. Tuten, has become interested in the possibility of using the aging technique instead.

The company mails out its bills on the first of every month. Payment is due on the tenth of the following month. If a bill is not paid by the end of the sixth month, it is effectively uncollectible—at least Mr. Tuten does not recall a case in which the amount recovered from such a bill equalled the costs of collecting it. The company's collection experience has been fairly stable over the last several years, and Mr. Tuten has done a study of how long customers have taken to pay their bills. This study gives the following results:

Months elapsed after billing before payment received	Percentage of all bills
0–1	5%
1–2	70%
2–3	12%
3–4	6%
4–5	3%
5–6	1%
Uncollectible	3%
	100%

Determine the appropriate estimated-percentage-uncollectible figures to use in an aging schedule for this company. If you need to round, do so to the nearest 1%. You may assume that aging calculations will be made at month-ends only.

Problem 11-N:

As part of your training in accounting, you must become able to extend the concepts and techniques you have learned into situations that require different methods of analysis. This problem provides an opportunity to increase your flexibility and broaden your understanding. The background needed to solve this problem has been provided by the text, but the particular method of analysis required may at first seem unusual. Apply what you already have learned to this new situation.

All of Brunswick Boar Brand's sales are on account, and the company estimates uncollectible accounts receivable as 2% of sales. The company's Controller, Mr. Spark M. Landrum, has completed a comparison of the results of the company's present estimation methods with those that would have occurred had it employed an aging approach. Based on the following fragmentary information, reconstruct all of the company's accounts receivable activities for 19X1 and 19X2, under both the aging and the percentage-of-sales approaches. You may assume that no unusual activities occurred and that all company calculations were performed properly.

Accounts receivable—12/31/X0	$151,514
—12/31/X1	170,680
—12/31/X2	192,270
Allowance for bad debts—12/31/X0	9,382
19X1 bad debts expense—under aging approach	10,873
—under percentage-of-sales approach.	10,460
Total 19X2 debits to allowance for bad debts, under aging approach*	20,827
12/31/X1 allowance for bad debts, under percentage of sales approach	9,767
Amount by which 19X1 writeoffs of accounts actually uncollectible exceeded 19X2 writeoffs	394

* *That is, after its 12/31/X2 ruling, the allowance for bad debts account appeared as follows:*

Allowance for Bad Debts

20,827	

Total bad debts expense over the two-year period was $200 higher under the aging approach than under the percentage-of-sales approach.

Problem 11-O:

As part of your training in accounting, you must become able to extend what you have learned into new situations. This problem provides an opportunity to increase your flexibility and broaden your understanding. The text provides all background information needed to solve this problem, but the circumstances described will be unfamiliar. Apply what you already have learned to this new situation.

1. Deserving Space-Age Products, Inc., has experienced severe financial difficulties and is in danger of going out of business. Since it is a major regional employer, the government wishes to help it survive. On 3/1/X3 the government purchased $1,000,000 of the firm's 20-year, 6% bonds at a price to yield an effective rate of zero percent interest, compounded semiannually. Interest is payable on these bonds every six months, beginning on 9/1/X3. The firm employs the constant rate method of amortizing premium and discount.

    (a) How much did the government pay for these bonds on 3/1/X3?

    (b) What journal entry should the firm make on 9/1/X4?

2. On 6/30/X8, Hermes Trismegistus Corporation issued $2,000,000 of 50-year, 7.5% bonds at a price to yield an effective rate of 7%, compounded semiannually.

Interest is payable on these bonds every June 30th and December 31st, beginning 12/31/X8. What journal entry (or entries) should Hermes Trismegistus Corporation make on its *final* interest payment date assuming that it employs the constant rate method of amortizing premium and discount? (It is possible to give an exact answer to this question without making extensive calculations.)

3. The present-value tables in this book go up to only 50 periods and 14%. But suppose that there was a 100% column in Table B. What would be its present-value factors for the first three periods? For period ten billion?

Problem 11-P:

Flynt Griffin Metals is considering using either the percentage-of-credit-sales or the aging approach to estimating uncollectible accounts receivable. Mr. Howard A. Weitner, president of the company, makes the following suggestion:

"When you get right down to the nitty-gritties, there's a trade-off either way. Percentage-of-sales is good income statement matching—it gives you a realistic bad debts expense figure to compare with the sales figure. Aging gives you a good net receivables figure for the balance sheet. OK, you've got to decide which statement's the most important. To me it's pretty obvious that the main thing is to put out a good income statement—which means using the percentage-of-sales approach."

Comment. Defend your comments.

Problem 11-Q:

As part of your training in accounting, you must become able to extend what you have learned into new situations. This problem provides an opportunity to increase your flexibility and broaden your understanding. The text provides all background information needed to solve this problem, but the circumstances described will be unfamiliar. Apply what you already have learned to this new situation.

Summerville Athens Corporation produces and sells a single product that requires considerable servicing and adjustment for the first two years after it is sold. The company offers a 24-month warranty covering most such work. Depending upon the particular model involved, the product sells for from $800 to $1,400 apiece. On the average, warranty work costs about $100 per product, regardless of model. This relationship has been quite stable for several years. The bulk of all warranty work falls between the 6th and 18th months of ownership. Sales have been expanding—from approximately 8,000 units in 19X5 to approximately 10,000 units in 19X7. A summary of the company's 19X7 income statement is given below. Warranty work is done in the Service Division of the Sales Department; warranty work costs are included in selling expenses.

Summerville Athens Corporation
Income Statement
For 19X7

Sales .		$10,253,530
Cost of Goods Sold	$6,152,188	
Selling, General, and Administrative Expenses .	3,075,989	9,228,177
Net Income .		$ 1,025,353

What accounting treatment should the company give costs of warranty work? Defend your answer.

Problem 11-R:

Mr. Stanley L. Dole is a student at Atchison State University. Shortly before the beginning of his sophomore year, Mr. Dole wished to purchase an automobile. He made arrangements with a local lending agency (which advertised loans to students) to finance his purchase, then bought a suitable car for $2,106.48. He then went back to the lending agency to make final arrangements for the loan, speaking with Mr. John R. Russell, the firm's College Credit Coordinator. Mr. Dole indicated that he intended to work summers to pay for his car and would, therefore, prefer to pay for it in annual installments instead of the customary monthly ones. Mr. Russell nodded his head sympathetically and replied:

"Sure, and I'll wager you're on a tight budget; most students are. Look, in three years you'll be making a lot more money than you are now. We have a special plan for college students whereby you pay a low rate of interest while you're in school, then a high one after you graduate. Here, I'll make some scratch calculations to show you what we can do for you:

Year	(a) Loan Balance at Beginning of Year	Interest Rate	(b) Interest Cost	(c) Payment Made at End of Year	Loan Balance at End of Year (a) + (b) − (c)
1	$2,106.48	5.00%	$105.32	$1,000.00	$1,211.80
2	1,211.80	5.00%	60.59	1,000.00	272.39
3	272.39	267.12%	727.61	1,000.00	–0–

Mr. Dole remained polite, but he was deeply unwilling to pay 267.12% interest. After further discussion he and Mr. Russell agreed upon a contract whereby he borrowed $2,106.48, then paid principal and interest in three equal annual installments, beginning in one year, at 20% interest, compounded annually. In answering the following questions you may assume that 20% is a fair interest rate for this kind of loan, and may ignore any tax or legal issues raised by this problem. The present value of a three-period annuity of one dollar at 20% per period is 2.10648.

1. Was Mr. Dole any better off as a result of the loan contract that he actually signed than he would have been under the contract that he rejected? Prove your answer.

2. The text claims that all methods of allocating interest charges to the individual time periods included in a multi-period loan are arbitrary, and that in particular the constant rate method is arbitrary. Relate your answer to part 1 to this contention.

Twelve

Nonmonetary
Assets: Cost Accumulation

For simplicity, the discussion of nonmonetary assets has ignored some aspects of the treatment normally given nonmonetary assets in published financial statements. You will gain a deeper understanding of these reports if these simplifications are removed and a close examination is made of the two main problems that complicate accounting for nonmonetary assets:

1. It has been assumed that the cost of a nonmonetary asset is easy to determine. Actually, this cost may be the sum of many separate components, which leads to problems of *cost accumulation* to be discussed in this chapter.

2. Very simple methods have been used for the writedown, or *cost amortization,* of nonmonetary assets as they yield their services to operations. We have assumed straight-line depreciation of depreciable assets and have sidestepped any factors that could complicate inventory amortization. But several different depreciation and inventory methods are actually employed in published financial statements. These methods are examined in Chapter Thirteen.

Noncurrent Assets

A simple example of cost accumulation

Although the following example is a simple one, it raises several of the main issues involved in any cost accumulation. Across the room as I write this book is a three-speed, twelve-inch table fan that I purchased from a mail-order catalog. The vendor's price for this fan was $19.50. In addition, I had to pay $1.05 for postage from the vendor's Seattle warehouse. What was the cost of this fan to me? Obviously, the cost was \$20.55—the *total* that I had to pay to acquire the fan (\$19.50 + \$1.05 = \$20.55). Why should the shipping costs be included in the total cost of the asset? Shipping costs should be included because one requirement that a good must fulfill to be considered an asset is that it provide benefits to the entity concerned. While the fan was in its Seattle warehouse, it was of little benefit to me. Part of the cost of obtaining its benefits was the cost of transporting it from Seattle. This suggests a rough definition of an asset's cost. The following refers to an asset's *original* cost, avoiding involvement in problems of depreciation and other amortization.

> The original *cost of a nonmonetary asset* to an entity is the total market value of all that the entity gave up to obtain the benefits of that asset; it is the sum of all necessary or normal costs of obtaining that asset in a place and condition suitable for it to provide the services for which the entity purchased it.[1]

Often, more than shipping costs must be added to the catalog price. I purchased the fan in Oregon, which did not have a state sales tax at that time; had I lived in California, I would have had to pay an additional 98¢ in sales taxes. There would have been no legal way to buy that fan without paying the 98¢—it would have been a necessary cost of acquiring the fan and its services. Therefore, a California fan owner should include the 98¢ in the total cost of his fan. This illustrates two further points:

1. The costs of two identical assets may legitimately differ if they are bought by different buyers under different circumstances. The cost of an asset is not an absolute thing, existing independently and of itself. The cost of an asset is relative to the entity receiving its services, and it cannot be discussed independently of that entity. This is why the previous definition made reference to the cost of a nonmonetary asset *to an entity*. Were someone to ask "What's a fan like that cost?" you really should reply, "That depends on who's buying it."

2. The shipping costs were in payment for something of direct benefit to me— having the fan transported from Seattle to my home. There is no similar direct benefit from a sales tax. Yet if the tax is a necessary cost of obtaining the fan, it should be included as part of that fan's cost. For a business firm purchasing assets to be used for business purposes, inclusion of the sales tax in the asset's cost may also be defended via the "matching" principle (see page 426). The tax is a necessary cost of obtaining future revenue (not just current revenues); therefore instead of being expensed in the present year, this cost should be deferred and given asset status.

Installation costs are also part of the total cost of many assets. Suppose that, instead of a table fan, I bought an attic fan. If I merely leaned such a fan against a window, then turned it on, the machine would fly off and either break or unplug itself. For the fan to provide its intended services, it must be installed. For it to function at top efficiency, it must be installed carefully. Clearly, installation costs should be included in the total costs of such a fan.

Though we've been considering mainly assets purchased by private individuals, the same things are true of assets purchased by corporations. Part of the total cost of

---

[1] In this sense, *monetary* assets are not reported at cost. As you will recall, a monetary asset will either be cash itself or a right to receive cash. In either case, the figure at which the monetary asset is reported will reflect the amount of cash involved, rather than the value given up to acquire the asset.

a machine to a company is the freight cost of having the machine delivered to its plant. Most machines used in industry must be installed; such installation costs are another element in the machine's total cost. The cost of any nonmonetary asset to a business enterprise is the totality of all necessary or normal costs of obtaining that asset in a place and condition suitable for its intended use. The adding together of the individual costs of that total may be called a process of *cost accumulation.*

Other costs

The necessity and normality of a cost are judged in terms of lenient standards that reflect the uncertainty of actual business life. Quite a variety of different costs may be accumulated as part of the total cost of the asset. Here are some examples.

1. The price quoted by the vendor or, often, the price arrived at through negotiation between the vendor and the purchaser—for brevity, call this the *vendor's list price,* even though it may be a negotiated price less than the price given in his catalog or quoted by his salesmen.

2. The costs of transporting the machine from the vendor's warehouse or plant to the buyer. Some or all of these costs may already be included in the list price, since different vendors handle freight charges in different ways.[2]

3. Installation costs. Besides the costs of foundations and hardware, installation costs include the wages of company employees involved in the installation (for the actual number of hours that they worked) and depreciation of company equipment used. Until now, we have been treating the costs of employee services and depreciation as *expenses.* But, as observed in Chapter One (pages 48–49), an expense will be recognized only when no new asset results from receiving the services of the employees or the depreciable assets. Here, there is a new asset: the new machine. *Accumulated in its cost will be the costs of all services expended to obtain it* (this applies to used machines as well). Remember the rough definition at the start of this chapter:

> The original cost of a nonmonetary asset to an entity is the total market value of all that the entity gave up to obtain the benefits of that asset. . . .

The cost of the nonmonetary asset includes *all* that was given up, whether money or services. Indeed, when a company constructs a building for itself, the greater part of the asset's accumulated cost may consist of the costs of such services.

4. Many other costs may be included in the total cost accumulation: insurance on the machine (for the period during which it was being shipped and installed), and any taxes directly related to its acquisition. If the machine is of a new, unfamiliar type, there may be costs of learning how to operate it; these are sometimes included in the machine's total cost. Whenever purchasing costs can be clearly associated with a particular asset, there is theoretical justification for including them in the cost

---

[2] There are two main ways in which freight charges are handled: A sale may be made "f.o.b. seller," a technical term indicating that the list price does not include freight charges; or a sale may be made "f.o.b. buyer," in which case the list price includes the freight. Although mail-order companies don't employ this language, those who advertise, "We pay the postage," are selling f.o.b. buyer; all other mail-order companies sell f.o.b. seller. (The initials "f.o.b." are variously explained as meaning "freight on board" or "free on board"; it doesn't matter which is correct, since all you ever see are the initials, anyway.)

accumulation for that asset. For example, before buying a house, you'll probably have it appraised by a professional appraiser; his fee will properly be part of the cost of the house to you. Of course there are limits to how far you can go in accumulating minor cost components—accounting costs money, too!

Interest costs

What about interest costs? Suppose that when a company buys a machine, it borrows the necessary money by issuing a three-year note payable, and that total interest charges on this note will be $21,600. Is this $21,600 part of the cost of the machine? On first thought it might seem to be, but not when you reflect upon the matter.

As shown in earlier chapters, any profitable company will generate funds from operations—funds that can be used to pay dividends, to retire long-term debt, or to purchase new noncurrent assets.[3] If these new funds are insufficient to meet all of the company's needs, the company may borrow. This borrowing, however, is the result of *all* the company's uses of funds, not just particular uses. For this reason, it is illogical to associate any interest charges related to this borrowing with any *one* use of funds (such as individual purchases of noncurrent assets). As an example, Illustration 12-1 gives the 19X2 funds statement of Harris Corporation. Assume that the $20,000 of notes payable were issued in connection with the purchase of buildings.

Illustration 12-1

Harris Corporation
Sources and Uses of Net Working Capital
For the Year 19X2

Sources:		
Funds from Operations		$127,200
Issue of Noncurrent Equities:		
6% 24-Month Notes Payable Issued	$ 20,000	
Capital Stock Issued.	100,000	120,000
Net Sources		$247,200
Uses:		
Purchase of Noncurrent Assets:		
Land Purchased	$ 40,000	
Building Purchased	110,000	
Equipment Purchased	80,400	$230,400
Dividends		30,000
Net Uses.		$260,400
Decrease in Net Working Capital		$ 13,200

---

[3] Technically, this is true not only of profitable companies, but of any company whose operating losses are less than the total of those of its expenses that do not involve any decrease in funds (such as depreciation expense)—any company that has positive funds from operations, whether or not it operates at a profit.

Total interest charges on these 6 percent, 24-month notes payable will be $2,400 ($20,000 × 6% × 24/12 = $2,400). Obviously Harris Corporation had to borrow the $20,000 to meet *all* of its needs for funds. The company's net uses of funds totalled $260,400. This total was provided by obtaining $127,200 of new funds from operations, drawing down the company's net working capital balance by $13,200, issuing $100,000 of capital stock, *and* issuing $20,000 of interest-bearing notes. But no one source of funds resulted from any one use of funds. If *any* use of funds had been $20,000 less, the money would not have had to be borrowed and there would have been no interest charges at all.

It is never logical to associate an individual equity with an individual asset because equities are interests in *total* assets. Nor is it logical to associate the interest charges on one or more liabilities with any one asset.[4] Interest charges are costs of a company's total financing, not costs of individual nonmonetary assets.

Another example

An additional example should carry this point home. Suppose that you buy an automobile and happen to be able to pay cash. In exchange for a certain amount of money you receive a certain amount of future transportation services, pride of ownership, aesthetic delight, and/or whatever else an automobile provides for you.

Contrast this with buying an identical automobile under an installment contract that involves borrowing part of the car's purchase price and paying interest. In this case you exchange what eventually is a larger total amount of cash for the identical services from the car plus the right to borrow a sum of money. In an example this simple, it is clear that you are purchasing two things under the installment contract: the benefits of the car and the services of money—and that only the portion of the installment contract that relates to the car's services is part of the cost of the car. The previous subsection is merely a demonstration that the same general considerations pertain to business borrowing, too: that interest charges are not properly classified as part of the costs of assets bought on contracts involving payment of interest.[5]

Excessive costs

Certain other kinds of costs should be excluded from the total cost of a nonmonetary asset. For example, while installing a heavy machine, the crane operator makes a mistake, the machine swings free, then falls. Should all of the resulting

---

[4] This is true even when, for the security of the lender, the lender acquires a special claim on an asset in the event that the borrower defaults on the loan (as is the case with a mortgage)—unless, of course, there *is* a default. As shown in Chapter One (pages 52–53), the accountant is more concerned with the economic realities of the situation than with legal technicalities.

[5] There is one major exception to this rule in actual accounting practice. When a firm is building major facilities for its own use and borrows money to finance the construction, interest charges during the period of construction are added to the cost of the facilities. There are two main reasons for this exception. First, were the firm to have purchased the facilities from outsiders instead of constructing them itself, their purchase price presumably would have included interest charges. Second, and perhaps more persuasive, the matching rule suggests that until the facilities are completed and thus able to generate revenue, expenses should not be charged against them. In any event, this exception pertains only to interest charges during the period of construction; no *subsequent* interest charges on the debt are included in the cost of the facilities.

repair costs be included in the total cost of the machine? Some minor damage is normal in any heavy installation. But in cases of serious damage, the accountant would recognize a loss, rather than add the repair costs to the total cost of the machine.

This can involve difficult matters of judgment. It is easy to know what to do in extreme cases. If the entire machine must be replaced, the original cost will be treated as a loss. If the damage can be repaired for only a few dollars, the repair costs will be included in the accumulated costs of the machine. Unfortunately, in real-life situations, matters are not always so clear-cut. For example, suppose the vendor's list price for the machine was $150,000; freight costs were an additional $2,000; installation costs were $5,000; and the repair costs were $4,000. You could find accountants with unequivocal opinions about the correct treatment of this $4,000, but these opinions would conflict. Some accountants would say to *capitalize* the $4,000, that is, include it in the total accumulated cost of the machine. Others would suggest treating it as a loss. Still other accountants might contend that the $4,000 should be treated as a current operating expense. Personally, I doubt that there is any hard and fast way to decide how the $4,000 should be treated. Much would depend on the exact facts of the case. Suppose, for instance, that $1,700 of the $4,000 represented the book value of an empty forklift truck demolished by the machine when it fell; then it is likely that at least $1,700 of the damage would be treated as a loss. It isn't normal for unrelated equipment to be destroyed when a machine is installed, but even here you could find reputable accountants who would prefer a different treatment. And what of the remaining $2,300 ($4,000 − $1,700 = $2,300)? Its treatment would depend upon the judgment of the company's management or accountant. It would be possible for management to decide upon any one of several possible treatments, depending upon the effect upon the company as a whole. There is a wide gray area in what is considered a "necessary or normal" cost of an asset.

Paying more than necessary

Assume that a company buys a machine, intending to obtain certain services, and soon afterward discovers that it could have acquired these services at a lower price. Presuppose that the company could have bought an equivalent machine for less, or that the job of installation could have been performed less expensively. Should the cost at which the asset is reported be the total amount paid or the lesser amount that *might* have been paid (and the difference reported as some kind of loss)?

In almost all cases, the accountant would report the machine at its actual purchase price and not worry about "might-have-beens." Any company should try to spend its money as efficiently as possible and pay no more than necessary to meet its needs. *But the effort to save money costs money, too.* There is a point at which the costs of investigating alternatives and the costs of delays in deciding exceed the resulting savings. The efficient company will try to keep the *total* cost of its purchases *and its purchasing* to a minimum. Therefore, from time to time, an efficient company may pay more for an asset than is actually necessary. Any enterprise operates under conditions of uncertainty and insufficient information, in which numerous mistaken decisions are to be expected. An error has to be enormous before the accountant will record a loss resulting from a decision about what to purchase.

An illustration of cost accumulation of nonmonetary assets

An example at this point might help tie things together. El Dorado Company is a manufacturer. Most of its sales are in the Midwest, yet in recent years the company has been doing more and more business on the West Coast. These sales have become extensive enough that the company needs West Coast warehouse facilities. Since its needs are specialized, it has decided to build its own warehouse building. Illustration 12-2 is a narrative summary of some of the company's related 19X2 activities.

Illustration 12-2

El Dorado Company
19X2 Warehouse-Building Activities

1. The company investigated several possible Northern California sites for its new warehouse. It finally narrowed the possibilities down to two sites—one in San Jose and one in Alameda. The company purchased 60-day options on both sites, paying each property owner $3,000 for agreeing not to sell their land to anyone else for 60 days.
2. At the end of 60 days, the company purchased the San Jose site, paying cash of $150,000 (in addition to the cost of options).
3. Before any new buildings could be constructed on this site, the existing buildings had to be removed. The removal was performed by professional wreckers at a total cost of $18,000.
4. The new warehouse was constructed by an independent contractor, assisted by El Dorado Company engineers. The contractor's total bill was $2,800,000. Salaries of El Dorado Company engineers involved in the construction project totalled $126,400.
5. During construction of the new warehouse, a load of steel I-beams was accidentally dropped upon two employee automobiles. No one was injured, but the cars were destroyed. The company settled the resulting claims for $3,000; all but $600 of this was covered by the company's insurance.
6. Legal fees, survey costs, title insurance, and additional charges pertaining to the site totalled $9,300. Legal fees, permits, insurance, and additional charges pertaining to the warehouse itself totalled $21,800.
7. The company financed the construction of this warehouse by issuing $3,000,000 of $6\frac{1}{4}$ percent notes payable, due 3/1/X7. Interest charges for 19X2 on these notes totalled $156,250.

There are two different assets being purchased by this company: land and a building. It is important to distinguish between the costs of the two—the building will be depreciated, while the land will not. These distinctions are made in the following entries:

1. Options are bought to allow the purchaser enough time to make a careful decision. It is quite normal for companies to take out options on more than one site. The cost of options to El Dorado Company (including the cost of the option on the land that was not purchased) is a cost of the decision-making process that resulted in

buying the land, and forms part of the total cost of that land. At the time El Dorado Company purchased the two options, the following entry would have been made:

Options	6,000	
Cash		6,000

2. Upon purchase of the actual site, the El Dorado Company's accountant would have made the following entries:

Land	6,000	
Options		6,000
Land	150,000	
Cash		150,000

3. Removal of the old buildings was necessary to make the land suitable for its intended use. Costs of removing old buildings thus became part of the cost of the land (*not* part of the cost of the new buildings), just as costs of removing brush and rocks would have been part of the cost of the land.

Land	18,000	
Accounts Payable		18,000

Had any part of the $150,000 paid for the land in Change 2 been a cost of these old buildings, the whole $150,000 would *still* have been included in the accumulated cost of the land, since the company had wanted only the land, not the old buildings.

4. The appropriate entries would have been:

Buildings	2,800,000	
Accounts Payable		2,800,000
Buildings	126,400	
Salaries Payable		126,400

5. Accidents are a regrettable, but normal feature of some construction projects. Since $2,400 was recoverable from the insurance company, the following (compound) entry would have been appropriate:

Insurance Receivable	2,400	
Buildings	600	
Cash		3,000

6. In the compound entry below, many different accounts are symbolized by the word "Various." The company itself would have credited the actual accounts involved.

Land	9,300	
Buildings	21,800	
Various		31,100

7. The following entries would have been appropriate for the notes payable:

Cash	3,000,000	
6¼% Notes Payable		3,000,000
Interest Expense	156,250	
Interest Payable		156,250

Illustration 12-3 is a summary of the total costs of the land and building.

Illustration 12-3

El Dorado Company
Summary of Costs of Land and Building

	Land	Building
1. Options	$ 6,000	–0–
2. Site	150,000	–0–
3. Site Preparation	18,000	–0–
4. Contractor's Fee	–0–	$2,800,000
Engineering Salaries	–0–	126,400
5. Net Cost of Accident	–0–	600
6. Miscellaneous Costs	9,300	21,800
7. Notes and Interest	–0–	–0–
Total	$183,300	$2,948,800

Repairs and Maintenance

A nonmonetary asset is an object or right offering future economic benefits to the firm, purchased by the firm for a known price. The dollar amount of this price, which is used to represent the asset, can be reduced in some accepted way as parts of these benefits are determined to have been yielded.

We must look briefly at one other fundamental problem of cost accumulation. The foregoing definition of a nonmonetary asset has been used throughout this book, and for most purposes this definition suffices. But occasionally we need to be more precise. Sometimes it is not clear whether an expenditure results in the acquisition of a new asset or in an expense for the repair of an old asset.

Eventually, any depreciable asset will wear out or become obsolete. In addition, during its life, other kinds of deterioration will occur that can be corrected by maintenance or repair.[6] For example, an automobile's fan belt will wear out and need to be

---

[6] The distinction between repairable and unrepairable deterioration is not as clear-cut as one might wish. During World War II, for example, private automobiles were kept in service for years longer than was usual, partly through unusually extensive repairs and maintenance; in a sense, repair expense was substituted for depreciation expense. But, *taking the company's depreciation and retirement policies as given,* the two phenomena can be distinguished.

replaced one or more times during the car's service life. Should the expenditure for the new belt be treated as an expense of the current period's operations? Or should the expenditure be *capitalized*—that is, recorded as resulting in the acquisition of a new depreciable asset (together with the retirement of an old asset), and charged in part to future years? In a sense, the new belt offers benefits that extend over the entire remaining service life of the car—because if the fan belt is *not* replaced, the car's engine soon will be destroyed.[7] Yet accountants record the replacement of a fan belt as maintenance.

In part, the reason for this involves the degree of detail in the accountant's records (also the amount of expenditure, as will be discussed later). Here is an example: when I bought my present car, I recorded the purchase of one asset. When I make depreciation calculations, I continue to regard it as a single asset with a five-year life. Actually, this car is constructed of a large number of distinct parts. But in terms of the transportation services that I wanted, the combination of all these parts into one vehicle is far more important than are the individual components. Accordingly, my personal accounting system does not need to show fine-enough detail that the individual fan belt would appear as a separate asset. Instead of recording the retirement of an old fan belt and its replacement by a new asset, I would record the expenditure as resulting in an expense. This suggests the following definition:

> *Repairs and maintenance* involve expenditures to replace or correct defects in *components* of nonmonetary assets—defects that have developed during the period the asset has been providing its services to the firm. Whether a good is an asset or a component of another asset depends in part upon the amount of detail employed in the firm's accounting system. For an expenditure to be regarded as repairs or maintenance, the correction or replacement must not significantly alter the nature of the services provided by the original asset, nor extend its service life beyond the period that it originally offered.

You will notice that at least three things in this definition are left to the subjective judgment of the accountant or management. Unfortunately, this is an area in which hard and fast objective rules, desirable though they might be, simply are not available.

1. Degree of detail in accounting system

This book has stressed that there is a general principle in accounting practice that expenditures benefitting future periods should be regarded as resulting in assets. Yet now it turns out that this depends in part on the degree of detail in the firm's accounting system.

For example, when a trucking firm buys a fleet of trucks, it is apt to set up accounts for at least four different kinds of assets: engines and transmissions, cabs, tires, and bodies. When a set of tires is replaced, this is recorded as the retirement of an old asset and acquisition of a new one. Assuming no trade-ins, and no gain or loss

---

[7] Using the language that was developed in earlier chapters, almost the entire output of the car is an interaction effect of the fan belt and the car's other components.

on the retirement and that depreciation on these tires has been brought up to date, the related journal entries would be of the following form:

> Tires—Accumulated Depreciation XXX
> Tires   XXX
> —To record retirement of old tires.

> Tires   XXX
> Accounts Payable   XXX
> —To record purchase of new tires.

But if instead the firm's accounting system records just a single asset—Trucks—then the purchase of new tires will merely result in an expense:

> Repairs and Maintenance Expense XXX
> Accounts Payable   XXX

Similarly, when a company builds a new building, it may either record all of the costs of the building in a single asset account—Building—or record detail. Many firms identify major components of the building that will need to be replaced during its overall service life, then record these components as separate assets. When these components are replaced, the costs of doing so will be capitalized; otherwise these costs would be treated as an expense of the year of replacement.

Accordingly, the treatment given the expenditure depends on the firm's accounting system. The underlying facts are the same in either event, *and there are no rules governing the amount of detail that must be employed in an accounting system.* Management may choose whichever treatment it prefers. This is a slightly disturbing result, one similar to matters that will be discussed in the next chapter: management is free to manipulate whether or not an expenditure will be treated as an expense.

2. *Alteration of asset services*

Another decision, at least partly subjective, must be made: has the expenditure significantly altered the services provided by the original asset? Suppose, for instance, that the horn in your car burns out and you replace it with a much more powerful (or sensuous) one. Would this be a repair? Or would such an expenditure involve, at least in part, the purchase of a new asset?

A lot depends upon which services of the original asset are important to the entity. The answer here is not clear-cut, but one approach would be to find out what it would have cost to replace the old horn with an identical horn, treat *that* cost as a repair expense, then regard the remainder as the cost of a new asset.

3. *Addition to service life*

Similarly, sometimes the replacement of a major component with a new improved one will add to the service life that the asset initially offered (even though the *nature* of the services provided may not have been significantly affected). In such situations, some decision must be made concerning how much of the cost of the new component should be treated as repair expense and how much should be capitalized. As before, the decision must be based at least in part upon subjective judgments.

Materiality

Many of the problems discussed in this section have their roots in differing standards of what is important. What is a significant difference in the services or service life of an asset? When is a component important or distinct enough to be recorded as a separate asset? There are vast gray areas here.

The accountant usually expresses his subjective judgments on such matters in terms of something he calls *materiality*. Something is considered to be material if reporting it would be likely to alter a decision made by a trained, intelligent reader of the accountant's report. Excessive detail in accounting costs money; the intention underlying the materiality notion is to avoid wasting time and intellectual resources worrying about the correct treatment of minor matters. But the notion is hard to apply—what *is* minor? Obviously, materiality is a relative notion—what is not material for a large firm may be quite material for a small one. But, again, there are large gray areas.

For example, most minor expenditures to correct defects are regarded as not material, on the grounds that it makes no difference to investors how these expenditures are recorded. Therefore, such expenditures are charges to expense—both because of conservatism and because it's simpler than capitalizing them then depreciating them later on. But this just pushes the problem back one step: how big can an expenditure be before the treatment given it could affect an investor's decision? Some accountants use the rules of thumb that an item must amount to at least 10% of the amount previously recorded for the asset, or at least 10% of the firm's current net income before it is material. Others (including myself) argue that this is not the kind of thing that lends itself to simple rules, nor can it be answered satisfactorily in the abstract. (Surprisingly little research has been done into what *does* affect investor decisions; but even after more data are available, the eventual decision as to what is important may still depend upon individual subjective judgments.)

Expense Accumulation on Condensed Income Statements

Before we examine cost accumulation for manufactured inventories, it will be helpful to take a brief detour and examine a similar accumulation process that is conducted on many published income statements: expense accumulation. Often, expense data are grouped according to whether the expense relates to the cost of goods sold, the company's selling effort, or the general management of the firm; then a condensed income statement is prepared. An example will show how this might be done. Illustration 12-4 is the 19X2 income statement of Berryville Co., in familiar form (Illustration 12-4 is identical to Illustration 9-13, page 481).

Illustration 12-4

Berryville Co.
Statement of Income and Retained Earnings
For the Year 19X2

Revenues:
Sales	$315,000	
Interest Revenue	350	$315,350

Expenses:
Cost of Goods Sold	$203,400	
Wages and Salaries Expense	74,900	
Depreciation Expense	13,000	
Insurance Expense	3,100	
Rent Expense	14,400	
Supplies Expense	17,600	
Taxes Expense	1,050	
Utilities Expense	4,500	
Interest Expense	7,500	339,450

Net Loss from Operations	$ (24,100)
Loss on Sale of Equipment	2,500
Net Loss	$ (26,600)
Retained Earnings—12/31/X1	42,850
Retained Earnings—12/31/X2	$ 16,250

Broadly speaking, the expenses of a manufacturer may be divided into three main categories: (1) costs of manufacturing products that have been sold, (2) costs of selling these products, and (3) costs of the general administration of the business—planning, accounting, billing, fund raising, hiring, etc. To these might be added a fourth category: taxes expenses.

These distinctions correspond closely with the organizational divisions of the firm, which were discussed on page 20: costs of goods sold are the primary responsibility of the firm's vice president in charge of manufacturing; selling expenses are the primary responsibility of the vice president in charge of marketing; administrative expenses are the responsibilities of the president, treasurer, and controller. Many firms wish to accumulate expenses under these categories in much the same way that El Dorado Company accumulated various costs under the categories *land* and *buildings*.

Cost of goods sold already is accumulated into a single figure. The same can be done with selling and administrative expenses. The Berryville Co. accountant should be able to estimate how much of the company's expenses relate to the general administration of the company and how much relate to selling activities. For example, the accountant might analyze the payroll and determine that of the $74,900 wages and salaries expense, $30,200 related to general administration and $44,700 to selling effort. Suppose that the accountant analyzes all expenses (except taxes expense and cost of goods sold) and obtains the following results:[8]

	Total	Selling	General Adminis- tration
Wages and Salaries Expense	$ 74,900	$44,700	$30,200
Depreciation Expense.	13,000	10,900	2,100
Insurance Expense	3,100	2,300	800
Rent Expense	14,400	7,700	6,700
Supplies Expense	17,600	14,300	3,300
Utilities Expense	4,500	2,500	2,000
Interest Expense	7,500	–0–	7,500
Total	$135,000	$82,400	$52,600

This analysis and regrouping lets you see not only the *nature* of the company's expenses but also to some extent, their *purpose*. Such an analysis tells you something that you did not know before: the company spent $82,400 in its selling efforts and $52,600 for general management and financing. Illustration 12-5 shows how the company's income statement could be prepared to report expense information by the purpose of each expense.

Illustration 12-5

Berryville Co.
Statement of Income and Retained Earnings
For the Year 19X2

Revenues:			
Sales		$315,000	
Interest Revenue		350	$315,350
Expenses:			
Cost of Goods Sold		$203,400	
Selling Expenses:			
Wages and Salaries	$44,700		
Depreciation	10,900		
Insurance	2,300		
Rent	7,700		
Supplies	14,300		
Utilities	2,500	82,400	

[8] The details of these calculations can be complicated and are best reserved for a more advanced course—such as a course in cost accounting. But the basic principles are simple. Wages and salaries would be allocated on the basis of the duties performed by the individuals involved. Depreciation of depreciable assets used solely by those doing general administration or solely by those doing selling would be allocated to the respective activities—for example, depreciation of automobiles used by salesmen would be allocated to selling expenses. Depreciation of depreciable assets used in common would be allocated to both on some plausible-seeming basis; for example, building depreciation might be allocated to the administrative and selling activities within that building on the basis of relative floor space utilized. Methods can be found or developed to allocate any expenses in this general way, although some of these allocations will be arbitrary.

General Administrative Expenses:

Wages and Salaries	$30,200	
Depreciation	2,100	
Insurance	800	
Rent	6,700	
Supplies	3,300	
Utilities	2,000	
Interest	7,500	52,600
Taxes Expense		1,050	339,450

Net Loss from Operations	$(24,100)
Loss on Sale of Equipment	2,500
Net Loss	$(26,600)
Retained Earnings—12/31/X1	42,850
Retained Earnings—12/31/X2	$ 16,250

To obtain a condensed income statement, you need merely eliminate the subsidiary details under general administrative expenses and selling expenses. This is done in Illustration 12-6. As the discussion on page 405 indicated, further compression usually would be achieved by treating the $2,500 nonoperating loss as an expense.

Illustration 12-6

Berryville Co.
Statement of Income and Retained Earnings
For the Year 19X2

Revenues:

Sales	$315,000	
Interest Revenue	350	$315,350

Expenses:

Cost of Goods Sold	$203,400	
Selling Expenses	82,400	
General Administrative Expenses	52,600	
Taxes Expense	1,050	339,450

Net Loss from Operations	$(24,100)
Loss on Sale of Equipment	2,500
Net Loss	$(26,600)
Retained Earnings—12/31/X1	42,850
Retained Earnings—12/31/X2	$ 16,250

Certainly, you obtain a slightly clearer picture of the nature of company activities if the data are grouped by the purpose of each expense. But why condense the resulting grouped income statement into one like Illustration 12-6? There seem to be two main reasons for doing this.

1. Many accountants wish to avoid confusing their readers with excessive detail. This is a genuine danger, particularly if readers are not trained in accounting. As

more and more detail is given, a point is eventually reached where the reader understands less and less. The question here is whether the reader is *so* easily confused that Illustration 12-6 is therefore preferable to Illustration 12-5.

2. Even more important, perhaps, many companies wish to avoid giving secrets away to competitors. The less detail on the income statement, the less danger of secrets leaking out. For instance, a statement showing the details of a company's production costs is almost never included in any set of published financial statements, even though it might be of considerable interest to readers. Most companies do not want outsiders to know the details of their business.

Would the kind of detail given in a statement like Illustration 12-5 really be dangerous to the company? Perhaps not, but the fear of damaging the company by reporting too much detail is widespread. This, together with the fear of confusing readers, make condensed income statements resembling Illustration 12-6 very common. Comparative income statements of Wadsworth Publishing Company, Inc. (the publishers of this book) provide a good illustration of condensed income statements. Notice the following:

1. The company employs different language than that used in the illustrations in this book.

2. The company combines selling, general, and administrative expenses under a single heading, but reports depreciation and interest separately. (Some companies include depreciation in the accumulated totals for other expense groups, then indicate the total amount of depreciation by a footnote.)

Both of these dissimilarities illustrate the variety allowed in good income statement practice. The following statements have been slightly simplified.

Illustration 12-7

Wadsworth Publishing Company, Inc. and Subsidiaries
Statement of Consolidated Income and Retained Earnings
For the Years Ended December 31, 1970 and 1969

	1970	1969
Net Sales	$10,032,568	$8,459,105
Costs and Expenses:		
Production costs	5,388,450	4,441,353
Selling, general, and administrative expenses	2,493,757	2,091,410
Interest	103,595	77,828
Depreciation (straight-line method)	36,888	33,572
Total Costs and Expenses	8,022,690	6,644,163
Income Before Taxes on Income	2,009,878	1,814,942
Taxes on Income:		
Federal	898,000	884,297
State	100,000	72,143
Total Taxes on Income	998,000	956,440
Net Income	1,011,878	858,502
Retained Earnings at Beginning of Year	2,806,554	1,948,052
Retained Earnings at End of Year	$ 3,818,432	$2,806,554

Costs of Manufactured Inventories

A quick overview

In this section we will see that there are four main inventory accounts reported on the balance sheets of manufacturing firms: raw materials, supplies, work in process, and finished goods. The first two reflect the costs of inventories on hand that have not yet been used in manufacturing; the third reflects the costs of inventories that are in the process of manufacture but not yet completed; the fourth reflects the costs of completed products not yet sold to customers. We will see that the costs of work in process and finished goods are the results of often complicated processes of cost accumulation, whereby various charges for things such as wages, utilities, and depreciation, are combined with costs of raw materials and supplies to determine product costs.

Inventory cost accumulation

Inventory costs are accumulated in the same way as are costs of land, buildings, and equipment. The cost of an inventory is the sum of all necessary and normal costs that the company incurred to obtain that inventory in a place and condition appropriate for it to provide its services. (Of course, if the inventory is of salable merchandise or a manufactured product, the service that it provides is that of being sold to a customer.) For example, the cost of a fountain pen displayed in a stationery store is the sum of the manufacturer's list price, plus any additional freight or postage necessary to transport the pen to the store. The cost of an automobile to a new car dealer is the sum of the manufacturer's price, the cost of shipping the car from the plant to the dealer's showroom, plus any additional costs necessary to get the car ready to be sold. (Automobiles often arrive at the dealer's with minor defects requiring correction; industry custom requires the dealer to bear many of these costs. If, for example, a dealer must replace a cracked wing window at his own expense, this expenditure becomes part of the cost of his new car inventory.)

The same rule applies to any *manufactured* inventory: its cost is the sum of all necessary and normal costs of manufacturing it. But a manufactured inventory involves a much greater *variety* of costs than anything so far considered. The cost accumulation for a manufactured inventory is so much more complicated than that for noncurrent assets or retail inventories that accountants have been forced to develop special techniques for recording manufacturing costs. Here are some examples of the kinds of costs that make up the total cost of a manufactured inventory:

Direct materials: These include raw materials, purchased components, and any other materials that end up in the final product. The direct materials used in manufacturing a shoe would include the leather (including any leather unavoidably wasted in cutting), heels, nails, glue, thread, laces, eyelets, lining, preservatives, wax, and dye. Before the shoe is sold it must be boxed. The completed product of a shoe manufacturer is not just a shoe, but a shoe in a shoe box, so direct materials would also include the shoe box and the tissue paper in which the shoes are wrapped.

Direct labor: These costs consist of the wages and salaries of all individuals directly involved in making or assembling the product and its components. Shoe making includes specialized jobs, and there may be a different individual employed in each stage of the shoe's construction. A portion of each individual's wages would be accumulated in the total cost of the shoe.

Overhead (often called *burden*)*:* This is a technical term signifying all manufacturing costs other than direct materials and direct labor. Just as the cost of a purchased machine is the total of all costs necessary to obtain its intended services, so the cost of a manufactured inventory is the total of all factory costs of manufacturing it. "Overhead" includes the following:

1. "Indirect materials and supplies"—costs of materials and supplies that do not end up in the final product: machine oil, light bulbs used to illuminate the factory, sweeping compound used to keep it clean, forms and pencils used in the factory office, etc.

2. "Indirect labor"—costs of wages and salaries of factory employees not directly involved in making or assembling the product and its components: the plant superintendent, foremen, sweepers, maintenance men, quality control inspectors, etc.

3. Depreciation of the factory building, factory machinery, tools and fixtures—any depreciable asset used in the factory.

4. Factory heat, light, and power costs; factory telephone and water costs; property taxes on factory land, buildings, and equipment; insurance on the factory and its contents—this list could be continued almost indefinitely.

As a rule, manufactured products are not produced one at a time, but in batches. It is usually possible to associate the direct costs of a manufactured inventory with individual batches of finished product without falling into serious ambiguities. As an illustration, the direct materials used in manufacturing a particular lot of shoes may be determined by some simple paperwork: this is accomplished by merely requiring foremen to request the materials they need from the company's storeroom on requisition forms indicating the lot of shoes involved. Direct labor costs can similarly be traced to the individual lot of shoes manufactured by requiring that time cards be prepared indicating how much time each employee spends on each lot. (The details of this pertain to managerial accounting rather than to financial accounting, and will not be discussed here.)

Overhead costs are another matter. *Many overhead costs relate to factory activities as a whole.* We saw in Chapters Six and Eight that allocations of cash flows, income, and revenues to individual inputs usually were unavoidably arbitrary (see pages 318–323, 432–438). Similar difficulties are apt to arise with attempts to allocate overheads to individual batches of product. An allocation method may be developed that is satisfactory for the internal purposes of the firm (just as the teaching assistants on page 321 developed a mutually satisfactory allocation method for their purposes), but the odds are that this allocation will appear arbitrary to many individuals outside the firm who are affected by the firm's financial statements. This problem is severe enough and there are so many such allocations that, in contrast to the claims of those who prefer historical costs over current market values, the historical cost of a manufactured product may be a good bit more subjective than its current market value and may offer greater possibilities for manipulation of reported income (compare pages 431–432).

Take the property taxes on the factory building as an example. These are costs of *all* manufacturing activities going on in the building during the whole year, and the company may be making hundreds of different products. There is no fully satisfactory way to trace these costs to the individual products made in the building. Instead, some arbitrary allocation of tax costs must be made. Rather than allocate overhead items one at a time, accountants often speed up their work by making a combined allocation of all overhead costs to the various individual products made. (If you cannot be precise, you can at least be efficient.)

The methods employed in these overhead allocations are an important part of that phase of managerial accounting known as *cost accounting*. As indicated on page 29, since we are discussing *financial accounting,* we will not go into these details; instead, we will do what the financial accountants of many actual companies do— rely on the overall figures provided by cost accountants without inquiring into their calculations.

Special manufacturing accounts

The financial accountant receives his information on the costs of manufactured inventories in whatever form the cost accountant finds convenient. There are several cost accumulation systems used by cost accountants. Under one system, all costs of direct materials requisitioned are initially recorded in a single account called "direct materials"; all costs of direct labor are initially gathered into a single account called "direct labor"; and all overhead costs are initially recorded in a single account called "factory overhead." Costs are accumulated in these accounts before the direct costs are traced to individual batches of product and the overhead costs are allocated. (This allows the cost accountant to trace and allocate periodically—perhaps once a week—instead of constantly assigning costs to batches.)

Most multiproduct companies try to schedule their production so that individual products are manufactured in batches as large as possible (it's inefficient to change such things as tool settings more often than necessary). As a result of such extended production runs, a particular batch is often incomplete when factory costs *are* traced and allocated to individual products. Thus it is common at the time of tracing and allocating costs to use a special account for incomplete batches called "work in process inventory." Then, when the production run ends, all costs accumulated in the work in process inventory account are transferred to an account called "finished goods."[9]

In other firms the product may be physically incomplete at the end of an accounting period, in which case "work in process inventory" summarizes the costs to date. For example, there was a stage in the manufacture of this book when its pages had been printed but not yet been bound in hard covers. If the publisher's accounting period had happened to end at this point, all of the manufacturing costs incurred on this book up to that date would have been reflected in "work in process inventory."

---

[9] The foregoing remarks assume that the individual unit of product does not take long to make; when it does take a long time, the transfer of costs from work in process inventory to finished goods inventory may occur upon completion of individual units of product. The manufacture of expensive furniture is an example of such a product.

Once the book was completed and bound, these costs would then be transferred to Finished Goods Inventory.

> *Work in Process Inventory* = Incompletely manufactured inventory (where either the individual items are incomplete, or the batch is incomplete, or both).

The following diagram summarizes the relationships among the various accounts introduced in this section.

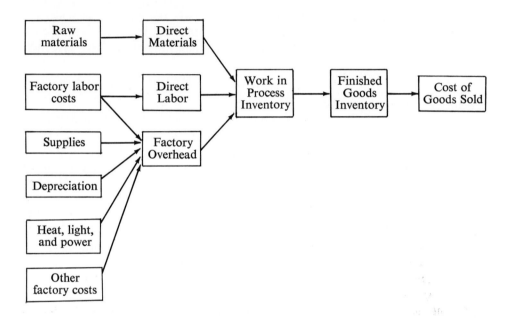

Costs of raw materials used are transferred to the account Direct Materials; in contrast, costs of supplies used are transferred to Factory Overhead. Costs of direct labor are transferred to Direct Labor, whereas costs of indirect labor are transferred to Factory Overhead. All other costs of the factory are transferred to Factory Overhead. Periodically, Direct Materials, Direct Labor, and Factory Overhead are closed to Work in Process Inventory in essentially the same way that the expense and revenue accounts are periodically closed to Retained Earnings. When manufactured goods have been completed, their costs are transferred from Work in Process Inventory to Finished Goods Inventory. Finally, when finished goods are sold, their costs are transferred to Cost of Goods Sold. In the diagram, all of these transfers are represented by arrows.

An example of cost accumulation of manufactured inventories

We will use a simplified example to help clarify the way costs of manufactured inventories are recorded. It should be emphasized that the system illustrated in what follows is only one of several possible cost accounting systems, and that there is great variety among actual systems, depending on the nature of the company's products, the information needs of management, and other circumstances that vary from company to company. However, the system illustrated below is a common one and reflects the main features (so far as financial accounting problems go) of most other systems.

San Jose Home Art Company manufactures a line of decorative hardware. The following summarizes the company's 19X2 transactions and internal changes so far as these affected the company's 19X2 income statement. The company prepares a condensed form of income statement. For simplicity, certain 19X2 changes (such as purchases of equipment) are ignored in this example (though of course the company would actually record them).

1. A total of $226,700 of raw materials and supplies were consumed during 19X2. Of these, $195,300 were direct materials used in manufacturing, $26,100 were indirect factory materials and supplies, $3,100 were supplies used in the company's administrative offices, and $2,200 were supplies used in the company's selling activities.

2. Wages and salaries during 19X2 totalled $369,000. These consisted of $220,800 of direct labor, $47,300 of indirect labor, $42,000 of administrative salaries, and $58,900 of sales salaries.

3. Power, water, and other utilities were purchased on account at a total cost of $18,800. Of this, $14,300 pertained to the factory, $2,700 to administration of the company, and $1,800 to selling activities.

4. Depreciation of buildings totalled $24,200. Of this, $15,100 pertained to the factory, $5,200 to the company's administrative offices, and $3,900 to its sales offices.

5. Equipment depreciation totalled $32,800. Of this, $26,800 pertained to factory equipment, $4,700 to equipment used in the company's administrative offices, and $1,300 to sales equipment.

6. All other costs were paid in cash and totalled $45,400, made up as follows: $29,200 of factory costs, $8,300 of administrative costs, and $7,900 of selling costs.

7. On 12/31/X1, the company's inventories included finished goods costing $49,300 and work in process costing $21,900.

8. During 19X2, inventories costing a total of $577,200 were completed.

9. Sales for 19X2 totalled $758,300, all on account. The goods sold had cost the company $571,800 to manufacture.

19X2 journal entries

Recording these data requires *reclassifying* them. The data are initially accumulated in what often are called "natural cost categories"—costs of wages and salaries, raw materials, supplies, utilities, depreciation, and so forth. The accountant must rearrange the data into administrative, selling, and factory costs. This rearrangement resembles taking a pack of cards that have been sorted by number, then re-sorting it by suit. The pack of cards remains the same, but its organization becomes different. Similarly, when data are reclassified from natural categories into those of a condensed income statement or a cost accounting schedule, the data themselves are not affected, but their organization is quite different.

1. The costs of raw materials and supplies consumed may be recorded by the following compound summary journal entry:

Direct Materials	195,300	
Factory Overhead	26,100	
Administrative Expenses	3,100	
Selling Expenses	2,200	
Raw Materials and Supplies		226,700

Notice that indirect materials and supplies are charged to factory overhead.

2. The summary entry for wages and salaries would be:

Direct Labor	220,800	
Factory Overhead	47,300	
Administrative Expenses	42,000	
Selling Expenses	58,900	
Wages and Salaries Payable		369,000

Before going any further, what is the nature of the accounts that have been debited in the two previous entries? Administrative expenses and selling expenses are merely retained earnings nominal accounts and will be closed to retained earnings at the end of the accounting period, but what about direct materials, direct labor, and factory overhead? These also are nominal accounts. *Instead of being retained earnings nominal accounts, however, they are inventory nominal accounts.* (Strictly speaking, they are nominal accounts to one specific inventory account: work in process. For, as we shall see in Entry 7 below, they are closed to work in process in the same way that expense and revenue accounts are closed to retained earnings.)

As was indicated on pages 522–523, revenue and expense nominal account titles are just special names for different kinds of changes in retained earnings. Similarly, the direct materials, direct labor, and factory overhead account titles are special names for different components of a total change in manufactured inventories, and will be closed to the balance sheet account, work in process inventory, as soon as it is determined how much of each cost should be allocated to each batch of product.[10]

Illustration 12-8 shows some, but not all, of the company's ledger accounts that will be affected by the journal entries the company will make. Omitted amounts are signified by "XXX." The first two entries have been posted, and the allocations involved are indicated by arrows.

---

[10] You should be warned that most accountants are not accustomed to viewing these inventory accounts as nominal accounts. I am using a highly simplified system of inventory nominal accounts, whereas many accountants employ much more detail. In particular, many accountants break the factory overhead account into a number of different accounts for different kinds of overhead costs, and establish separate *sets* of manufacturing accounts for each department in the factory. It is not uncommon for an accountant to use more than a hundred different inventory nominal accounts.

Illustration 12-8

San Jose Home Art Co.
Ledger

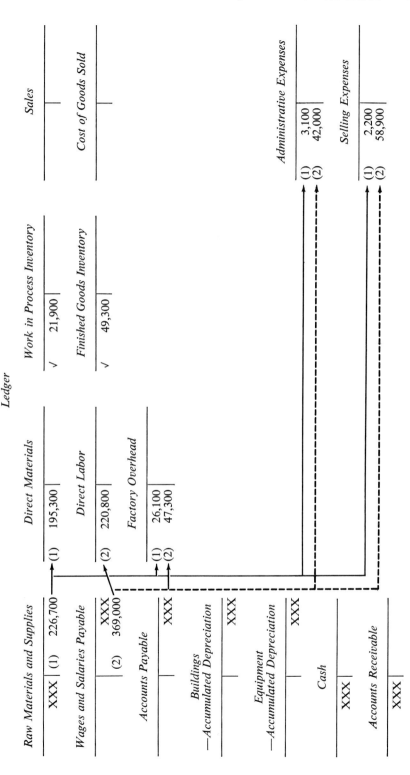

The next four entries require no supplementary comment:

```
3. Factory Overhead          14,300
   Administrative Expenses     2,700
   Selling Expenses            1,800
      Accounts Payable                    18,800
4. Factory Overhead                      15,100
   Administrative Expenses                5,200
   Selling Expenses                       3,900
      Buildings—Accumulated Depreciation          24,200
5. Factory Overhead                      26,800
   Administrative Expenses                4,700
   Selling Expenses                       1,300
      Equipment—Accumulated Depreciation          32,800
6. Factory Overhead          29,200
   Administrative Expenses     8,300
   Selling Expenses            7,900
      Cash                                45,400
```

Illustration 12-9 shows the affected ledger accounts after the first six entries have been posted.

7. At various times during the year, all amounts in the inventory nominal accounts are closed to Work in Process Inventory, as the proper allocation of these amounts to individual batches is determined. The following entry summarizes these transfers:

```
Work in Process Inventory    574,900
   Direct Materials                     195,300
   Direct Labor                         220,800
   Factory Overhead                     158,800
```

(Unlike the other entries, this one is not intended to correspond with the similarly numbered items of information on page 663; instead, item 7 on page 663 is reflected in the work in process inventory and finished goods inventory ledger accounts on the next page.)

8. The following entry summarizes the various transfers of the costs of completed production to the finished goods inventory account.

```
Finished Goods Inventory     577,200
   Work in Process Inventory            577,200
```

9. Here are the summary entries for the year's sales and cost of goods sold:

```
Accounts Receivable          758,200
   Sales                                758,200

Cost of Goods Sold           571,800
   Finished Goods Inventory             571,800
```

Illustration 12-9
San Jose Home Art Co.
Ledger

Raw Materials and Supplies

XXX	(1) 226,700

Direct Materials

(1) 195,300	√ 21,900

Work in Process Inventory

Sales

Wages and Salaries Payable

	XXX
	(2) 369,000

Direct Labor

(2) 220,800	√ 49,300

Finished Goods Inventory

Cost of Goods Sold

Accounts Payable

	XXX
	(3) 18,800

Factory Overhead

(1)	26,100
(2)	47,300
(3)	14,300
(4)	15,100
(5)	26,800
(6)	29,200

Buildings
—Accumulated Depreciation

	XXX
	(4) 24,200

Equipment
—Accumulated Depreciation

	XXX
	(5) 32,800

Administrative Expenses

(1)	3,100
(2)	42,000
(3)	2,700
(4)	5,200
(5)	4,700
(6)	8,300

Cash

XXX	(6) 45,400

Accounts Receivable

XXX	

Selling Expenses

(1)	2,200
(2)	58,900
(3)	1,800
(4)	3,900
(5)	1,300
(6)	7,900

Illustration 12-10
San Jose Home Art Co.
Ledger

Sales

	(9) 758,200

Cost of Goods Sold

(9) 571,800	

Administrative Expense*

(1) 3,100	
(2) 42,000	
(3) 2,700	
(4) 5,200	
(5) 4,700	
(6) 8,300	

Selling Expense†

(1) 2,200	
(2) 58,900	
(3) 1,800	
(4) 3,900	
(5) 1,300	
(6) 7,900	

Work in Process Inventory

√ 21,900	(8) 577,200
(7) 574,900	√ 19,600
596,800	596,800
√ 19,600	

Finished Goods Inventory

√ 49,300	(9) 571,800
(8) 577,200	√ 54,700
626,500	626,500
√ 54,700	

Direct Materials

(1) 195,300	(7) 195,300

Direct Labor

(2) 220,800	(7) 220,800

Factory Overhead

(1) 26,100	(7) 158,800
(2) 47,300	
(3) 14,300	
(4) 15,100	
(5) 26,800	
(6) 29,200	
158,800	158,800

Raw Materials and Supplies

XXX	(1) 226,700

Wages and Salaries Payable

	XXX
	(2) 369,000

Accounts Payable

	XXX
	(3) 18,800

Buildings
—Accumulated Depreciation

	XXX
	(4) 24,200

Equipment
—Accumulated Depreciation

	XXX
	(5) 32,800

Cash

XXX	(6) 45,400

Accounts Receivable

XXX	
(9) 758,200	

* debits total $66,000.   † debits total $76,000.

Illustration 12-10 shows the effects of these last entries on the ledger. Arrows indicate the transfers of inventory costs. Inventory accounts and inventory nominal accounts have been ruled and balanced. Notice that the balance in each of the inventory nominal accounts (the second column of accounts from the left) is now zero; the inventory nominal accounts have been closed.

The final step is to prepare closing entries for the *retained earnings* nominal accounts, and then to prepare an income statement. (Administrative expenses and selling expenses figures in the following were obtained from Illustration 12-10.)

A.	Sales	758,200	
	Retained Earnings		758,200
B.	Retained Earnings	713,800	
	Cost of Goods Sold		571,800
	Administrative Expenses		66,000
	Selling Expenses		76,000

Illustration 12-11

San Jose Home Art Company
Statement of Income and Retained Earnings
For the Year 19X2

Revenues:		
Sales		$758,200
Expenses:		
Cost of Goods Sold	$571,800	
Administrative Expenses	66,000	
Selling Expenses	76,000	713,800
Net Income		$ 44,400

Statement of cost of goods manufactured and sold

The parallel between the retained earnings and inventory nominal accounts may be carried a step further. Just as the income statement reflects the changes in retained earnings, so there is a statement that reflects all of the changes in manufactured inventories. Illustration 12-12 shows how the San Jose Home Art Company's 19X2 statement of cost of goods manufactured and sold might look. (For brevity, this statement is often called merely a statement of "cost of goods manufactured"—a practice I will occasionally follow, too.) This particular kind of statement is almost never included in published financial statements, apparently for fear of giving damaging information to competitors and other outsiders.[11] But such statements are

---

[11] Before writing this chapter I was curious about this and examined a group of 300 randomly selected sets of financial statements published by companies large enough to have active markets for their common stocks. None of these companies published a statement of production costs resembling Illustration 12-12. Yet I know from my experience as an auditor that many manufacturing companies prepare such statements for internal use.

prepared by many companies for internal use. There is no standard form for a statement of cost of goods manufactured and sold, though one modeled after Illustration 12-12 would be suitable for most purposes.[12]

Illustration 12-12

San Jose Home Art Company
Cost of Goods Manufactured and Sold
For the Year 19X2

Direct Materials .		$195,300
Direct Labor .		220,800
Factory Overhead:		
Indirect Materials and Supplies .	$26,100	
Indirect Labor .	47,300	
Power, Water, and Other Utilities .	14,300	
Depreciation—Buildings .	15,100	
—Equipment .	26,800	
Other Factory Overhead Costs .	29,200	158,800
Total Manufacturing Costs .		$574,900
Work in Process Inventory—12/31/X1 .		21,900
Total .		$596,800
Work in Process Inventory—12/31/X2 .		19,600
Cost of Goods Manufactured .		$577,200
Finished Goods Inventory—12/31/X1 .		49,300
Total .		$626,500
Finished Goods Inventory—12/31/X2 .		54,700
Cost of Goods Sold .		$571,800

Finally, it should be emphasized that *three* inventory accounts will appear on the 12/31/X2 balance sheet. In previous chapters we reported *two* different inventory accounts on the balance sheet of a retailer—merchandise inventory and supplies. In contrast, a manufacturer might report four different inventory accounts: raw materials, work in process inventory, finished goods inventory, and supplies. San Jose Home Art Company has chosen to combine two of these. None of these inventory accounts are nominal accounts for the simple reason that they are not closed to any other account by the end of the accounting period; instead, they are reported on the balance sheet like any other assets. Using what figures we have, and representing missing figures by "XXX," Illustration 12-13 gives the current asset section of the company's 12/31/X2 balance sheet.

---

[12] Illustration 12-12 may be regarded as a change statement just like any other change statement. It is based upon a partitioning of the balance sheet in which Work in Process Inventory constitutes one subset, and the remaining balance sheet accounts the other. (See the Appendix to Chapter Seven for background.) Under this interpretation, the portion of Illustration 12-12 extending below the total manufacturing cost of $574,900 forms an elaborate "tail" (reconciliation schedule) to the main body of the statement.

Illustration 12-13

San Jose Home Art Company
Balance Sheet
12/31/X2

Assets

Current Assets:
Cash . . . . $XXX
Accounts Receivable   XXX
Inventories:
Raw Materials and Supplies . . . . $ XXX
Work in Process Inventory   19,600
Finished Goods Inventory   54,700   XXX
Prepayments   XXX

Total Current Assets   XXX

Many companies condense all three inventory figures into a single balance sheet figure labeled "inventories."

The natures of the accounts introduced in this section may be expressed by the following diagram:

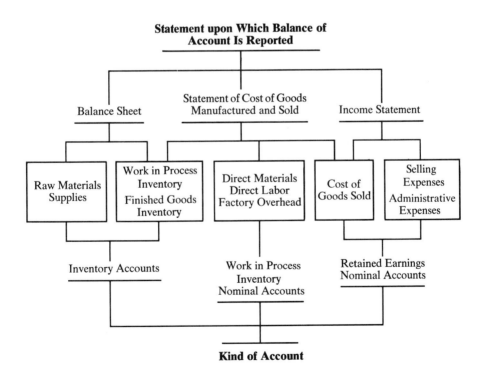

This diagram indicates the statements upon which the balance of each account is reported; with nominal accounts, this must be interpreted as the balance just prior to the closing of these accounts to work in process inventory or retained earnings.

In contrast, the transfers most frequently made among these accounts may be diagrammed as follows. Dotted lines signify closing entries, regular lines signify other entries (contrast the related diagram on page 671).

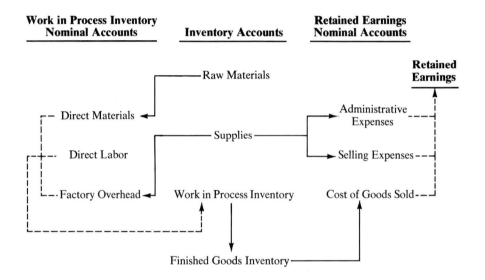

Summary of how balance sheet changes are reported

Finally, we now are in a position to describe completely how balance sheet changes are reported in financial accounting. (For simplicity, the net-working-capital funds statement is the only kind of funds statement considered in what follows.)

1. All balance sheet changes are reflected on the next balance sheet that is prepared by the firm.

2. All simple changes affecting the cash ledger account are reflected on the cash statement.

3. All simple changes affecting the balance of net working capital, plus all simple changes affecting two noncurrent accounts other than retained earnings, are reflected on the funds statement.

4. All simple changes affecting the retained earnings ledger account (or its related nominal accounts) are reflected on the income statement.

5. All simple changes affecting the work in process inventory ledger account (or its related nominal accounts) are reflected on the statement of cost of goods manufactured and sold.

6. All simple changes not included in one or more of categories 2 through 5 are reflected only on the balance sheet.

These relationships may be diagrammed as follows. For brevity, the following symbols will be used:

B = reflected on the balance sheet
C = reflected on the cash statement
F = reflected on the funds statement
I = reflected on the income statement
M = reflected on the statement of cost of goods manufactured and sold

		Affects Retained Earnings	Does not affect Retained Earnings	
			Affects two noncurrent accounts	Other
Affects net working capital	Affects Cash	B C F I		B C F
	Affects Work in Process Inventory	B F I M	No changes fit these descriptions	B F M
	Other	B F I		B F
Does not affect net working capital	Affects Cash	B C I		B C
	Affects Work in Process Inventory	B I M		B M
	Other	B I	B F	B

Problems for Study and Self-Examination

Problem 12-1:

As part of your training in accounting, you must become able to extend what you have learned into new situations. This problem provides an opportunity to increase your flexibility and broaden your understanding. The text provides all background information needed to solve this problem, but the circumstances described will be unfamiliar. Apply what you have already learned to this new situation.

The manufacturing process employed by Carcosa Corporation generates considerable smoke, and over the years, there has been increasing public concern about air pollution and increasing pressure on the company to install smoke elimination devices.

In July of 19X0, pressure brought to bear by the state sanitary commission and the general public combined to persuade the company to do something about its smoke emission. The company spent the next year conducting studies of the best ways to meet the problem. These preliminary studies cost $14,300. The company decided that the most efficient approach would be to install a device known as a

Cohelan precipitator in each of its smoke stacks. Eight of these devices were purchased, at a vendor's list price of $25,000 apiece. Freight charges on these precipitators totalled $3,200. This purchase was financed by the company's issuing a three-year, 6 percent note for $180,000 to the vendor, and paying the remaining $20,000 in cash. The precipitators had to be slightly modified by the company's engineers before they were installed, at a cost of $800 in salaries, $2,600 in materials, and $500 in miscellaneous costs. Direct costs of installation totalled $22,000, as follows:

Labor and salaries	$12,000
Materials	3,200
Depreciation of equipment	900
Other	5,900
Total	$22,000

Installing the precipitators also involved shutting down different parts of the company's plant so that smoke stacks could be entered. The company estimated that direct costs of these shutdowns totalled $9,600, and that profits of $30,000 were lost through idleness. Because of the hazardous nature of the installation, additional insurance had to be carried, at a cost of $1,100. There was one serious accident that caused $13,200 worth of damage; all but $2,600 of this damage was covered by insurance.

During 19X2, it became apparent that more smoke than the maximum specified by the state sanitary commission was still being emitted. The company was able to persuade the commission that its standards were excessively strict, but costs of doing so totalled $12,400. (Most of these costs were legal fees, though $800 represented the cost of bringing commission personnel and certain members of the state legislature to a conference at the company's headquarters.)

Even under the new, relaxed standards, the company was forced to spend an additional $16,100 modifying the precipitators so that they would function effectively. Had these modifications been made before the precipitators were installed, they would have cost only $7,000. It was also discovered that the precipitators demanded delicate adjustment to work efficiently. As a result, cleaning and maintenance costs were as follows:

> 19X1: $ 2,000
> 19X2: 13,300
> 19X3: 14,100

Originally, the company had estimated that cleaning and maintenance costs would average about $4,000 a year.

No further costs were incurred through the end of 19X3. At what cost should the smoke elimination equipment be reported on the company's 12/31/X3 financial statements? Ignore depreciation of the smoke elimination equipment. There are some debatable matters in this problem; justify your answer.

Problem 12-2:

Talcott Tube Co. is a manufacturer of industrial tubing. Illustration 12-14 gives the company's 12/31/X1 balance sheet. Notice that, for simplicity, the company combines the following things into single accounts:

a. Raw materials and supplies
b. All prepayments (prepaid insurance, prepaid rent, etc.)
c. All accumulated depreciation, whether on buildings or equipment
d. A number of minor current liabilities

Illustration 12-14

Talcott Tube Co.
Balance Sheet
December 31, 19X1
(000 omitted)

Assets

Current Assets:			
Cash		$ 2,940	
Accounts Receivable		21,360	
Inventories:			
Finished Goods	$ 6,990		
Work in Process	9,300		
Raw Materials and Supplies	17,610	33,900	
Prepayments		1,180	$59,380
Noncurrent Assets:			
Land	$ 1,660		
Buildings	8,230		
Equipment	31,060	$40,950	
Less: Accumulated Depreciation		20,020	20,930
Total Assets			$80,310

Equities

Current Liabilities:		
Notes Payable to Bank	$14,390	
Accounts Payable	13,530	
Other Liabilities (payroll, taxes, and others)	7,060	
Federal Income Taxes Payable	4,030	$39,010
Noncurrent Liabilities:		
6% Notes Payable—due 9/1/X4		6,100
Total Liabilities		$45,110
Stockholders' Equity:		
Capital Stock	$ 2,700	
Retained Earnings	32,500	35,200
Total Equities		$80,310

Illustration 12-15 gives a narrative summary of the company's 19X2 transactions and internal changes.

1. Journalize all 19X2 transactions and internal changes; feel free to use compound journal entries whenever it seems efficient to do so. Besides the accounts shown on the company's 12/31/X1 balance sheet, you are to use the following accounts only:

Sales	Loss on Sale of Equipment
Cost of Goods Sold	Dividends
Selling and Advertising Expense	Direct Materials
General and Administrative Expense	Direct Labor
Federal Income Tax Expense	Factory Overhead

2. Post all 19X2 journal entries for transactions and internal changes to the ledger.

3. Prepare closing entries as of 12/31/X2, the firm's balance sheet, its 19X2 income statement, and its 19X2 statement of cost of goods manufactured and sold.

Illustration 12-15

Talcott Tube Co.
Narrative Summary of Transactions and Internal Changes
For the Year 19X2
(000 omitted)

1. Sales totalled $140,570; all sales were made on account.
2. Purchases of raw materials and supplies totalled $66,330; all such purchases were made on account.
3. Direct materials used in manufacturing cost $64,670; an additional $2,960 of materials and supplies were used in the factory; $110 of supplies were used in the company's sales offices, and $270 of supplies were used in general administration.
4. Direct labor cost $26,320; other factory wages and salaries totalled $6,490; sales salaries totalled $3,780, and administrative salaries were $4,690. All salaries are recorded as an "other liability" before being paid.
5. Land costing $440, buildings costing $870, and equipment costing $7,400 were purchased on account.
6. Equipment with an original historical cost of $2,900 was sold; accumulated depreciation on this equipment totalled $2,310 at the time of sale; cash of $350 was received for this equipment (19X2 depreciation charges on this equipment are included in the $5,160 total immediately below).
7. Depreciation of building and equipment totalled $5,160; of this, $4,550 pertained to the factory, $290 to the company's sales offices and equipment, and $320 to general administration.
8. Costs of utility services totalled $4,430; $4,250 of this applied to the factory, $50 to selling activities, and $130 to general administration. All utility costs are recorded as other liabilities before being paid.
9. Repairs and maintenance to factory equipment cost $2,030, paid in cash.
10. Taxes, other than federal income taxes, cost a total of $1,380; $1,070 of this applied to manufacturing, the rest to the general administration of the company. Such taxes are recorded as other liabilities before being paid.
11. Prepayments totalling $980 were made.
12. The cost of prepayments expired totalled $950; $720 of this pertained to the factory, $60 to selling activities, and $170 to general administration.

13. Advertising costs totalled $2,870; interest charges totalled $1,220. All such costs are recorded as other liabilities before being paid.
14. Miscellaneous operating costs totalled $1,520; $970 of this pertained to the factory, $320 to selling activities, and $230 to general administration. All such costs are recorded as other liabilities before being paid.
15. At various times during the year, all costs initially recorded as direct materials, direct labor, and factory overhead were transferred to work in process.
16. Goods costing $112,300 were completed during the year.
17. The total cost of goods sold was $111,910.
18. Federal income taxes totalled $6,780; all federal income taxes are recorded as a liability before being paid.
19. Dividends, paid in cash, totalled $1,710.
20. The following liabilities were paid: notes payable of $14,390; accounts payable of $74,600; other liabilities of $52,900; federal income taxes payable of $5,520.
21. The company collected $138,680 from its customers, and borrowed $13,500 on notes payable that it issued to its bank.

Problem 12-3 (*Brain-teaser*):

As part of your training in accounting, you must become able to extend the concepts and techniques you have learned into situations that require different methods of analysis. This problem provides such an opportunity to increase your flexibility and broaden your understanding. The background needed to solve this problem has been provided by the text, but the particular method of analysis required may at first seem unusual. Apply what you have already learned to this new situation.

West Memphis Discount Store closes its books once a year, every December 31st. The following information was taken from the firm's ledger after all adjusting entries had been posted (including those establishing year-end merchandise inventory balances and cost of goods sold), but before closing entries had been made. There were no unusual transactions or internal changes during the year, and you may assume that the data given below provide all of the information that is needed to solve this problem.

	31 December 19X1	31 December 19X2
Cash	$ 819	$1,735
Merchandise Inventory	1,012	930
Accounts Payable (owed to merchandise supplier)	1,330	414
Taxes Payable	230	?
Sales	?	?
Cost of Goods Sold	?	2,288
Selling and Administrative Expenses	?	1,160
Total current assets	1,831	2,665

Other information:

1. All merchandise is purchased on account. The merchandise supplier sells merchandise only.

2. All selling and administrative expenses are paid directly in cash. The only expenses are those shown above and taxes expense. There were no nonoperating gains or losses in either year.

3. All taxes are on income. The tax rate is 30 percent of net income before taxes. Cash payments for taxes are always in payment of taxes accrued the previous calendar year.

4. There were no transactions affecting both cash and any account not explicitly mentioned above.

Calculate the company's 19X2 taxes expense. As in previous problems involving incomplete data, an appropriate line of attack for solving this problem would be to prepare T-accounts for the firm, post all information given in this problem (including beginning and ending account balances), then reconstruct missing elements.

Solutions

Solution 12-1:

I would favor reporting the smoke elimination equipment at a total cost of $285,200, calculated as follows:

Preliminary studies			$ 14,300
Eight Cohelan precipitators			200,000
Freight charges			3,200
Initial modifications: Salaries		$ 800	
Materials		2,600	
Other		500	3,900
Direct costs of installation			22,000
Direct costs of shutdowns			9,600
Cost of additional insurance			1,100
Cost of accident (to extent uninsured)			2,600
Cost of adjusting state sanitary commission standards			12,400
Cost of additional modifications			16,100
Total cost			$285,200

Obviously, the invoice cost of the eight precipitators should be counted, as should costs of freight and insurance, and the direct costs of installation (for the reasons given in the text). The uninsured cost of the accident does not seem unusually large for a project of this kind; probably most accountants would regard it as a normal cost of such an installation, though the matter is debatable. Had the uninsured cost of the accident been considerably higher, it would have been recorded as a loss.

The modifications made in the precipitators seem to have altered characteristics of the precipitators' original design, rather than corrected defects that emerged during use. Therefore, I would regard the cost of modifications as part of the cost of this equipment rather than as a repair. Here is a parallel: after buying an automobile, the buyer finds that the manufacturer's springs should be replaced with heavy-duty springs because of the load the buyer carries. The cost of new springs seems properly a part of the total accumulated cost of the car, but this also is debatable.

Another possibility in the Carcosa Corporation illustration would be to treat the $3,900 and $7,000 of initial modifications as part of the cost of the equipment, while treating the remaining $9,100 of additional modification costs as a loss resulting from not making appropriate modifications at the outset. (Yet *some* inefficiencies are inevitable in any project of this kind, especially when the engineering problems have not been completely solved.)

Similarly, it is not at all unusual for preliminary studies to be performed for such a project, and their cost is part of the total cost of the equipment, just as architects' fees form part of the cost of a building.

Any direct costs of shutdowns would be part of the costs of installation. Evidently it was impossible to install the precipitators while the plant was operating, and shutdown costs were a necessary part of the total cost. Estimated lost profits are another matter. Including lost profits in the accumulated cost of the equipment would require an entry of the following form:

Equipment	30,000	
Retained Earnings (some kind of nominal account)		30,000

But, as we have seen in earlier chapters, accountants consistently refuse to recognize revenues (and profits) until there has been a sale or other marketplace exchange. Accountants do not recognize profits (or any similar retained earnings change) upon the acquisition of an asset, and there has been no sale and no marketplace exchange in this case—just an estimate by management.

The most debatable thing included in my $285,200 accumulated total is the $12,400 cost of adjusting state sanitary commission standards. Out of "conservatism," most accountants would probably treat this cost as a 19X2 expense. Yet the acquisition of the equipment took place in a legal and regulatory context in which such expenditures are common. Here's a parallel example: suppose that, in building a home, you wish to erect it closer to one edge of the lot than local zoning ordinances allow. The legal costs of obtaining a zoning variance so that you could go ahead with your plans certainly would be part of the total cost of the house. Similarly, the legal costs of obtaining relaxed standards seem an appropriate cost of the smoke elimination equipment, although the matter is arguable.

Interest costs on the $180,000 loan should not be included in the total cost of the equipment, for the reasons explained earlier in the chapter. Even when they are unexpectedly large, maintenance costs should be reported as expenses, rather than added to the cost of the related equipment.

Solution 12-2:

This is a straightforward problem. The various costs of operations would be allocated as follows. (This schedule is prepared merely as a convenient way of summarizing some of the information in the problem; you need not have prepared such a schedule yourself.)

	Direct Materials	Direct Labor	Factory Overhead	Selling and Advertising Expense	General and Administrative Expense
3. Raw Materials and Supplies	$64,670	$ –0–	$ 2,960	$ 110	$ 270
4. Wages and Salaries . .	–0–	26,320	6,490	3,780	4,690
7. Depreciation	–0–	–0–	4,550	290	320
8. Utility Services . . .	–0–	–0–	4,250	50	130
9. Repairs and Maintenance	–0–	–0–	2,030	–0–	–0–
10. Taxes	–0–	–0–	1,070	–0–	310
12. Expiration of Prepayments . . .	–0–	–0–	720	60	170
13. Interest Charges . . .	–0–	–0–	–0–	–0–	1,220
13. Advertising	–0–	–0–	–0–	2,870	–0–
14. Other Costs	–0–	–0–	970	320	230
Total	$64,670	$26,320	$23,040	$7,480	$7,340

Illustration 12-16 gives the company's ordinary and adjusting journal entries; Illustration 12-17 gives its closing entries. Illustration 12-18 is the company's ledger for the year; Illustration 12-19 is its 12/31/X2 balance sheet; Illustration 12-20 is the company's 19X2 income statement; and Illustration 12-21 is its 19X2 statement of cost of goods manufactured and sold.

Illustration 12-16

Talcott Tube Co.
Ordinary and Adjusting Journal Entries
For the Year 19X2
(000 omitted)

1. Accounts Receivable	140,570	
Sales		140,570
2. Raw Materials and Supplies	66,330	
Accounts Payable		66,330
3. Direct Materials	64,670	
Factory Overhead	2,960	
Selling and Advertising Expense	110	
General and Administrative Expense	270	
Raw Materials and Supplies		68,010
4. Direct Labor	26,320	
Factory Overhead	6,490	
Selling and Advertising Expense	3,780	
General and Administrative Expense	4,690	
Other Liabilities		41,280
5. Land	440	
Buildings	870	
Equipment	7,400	
Accounts Payable		8,710
6. Cash	350	
Accumulated Depreciation	2,310	
Loss on Sale of Equipment	240	
Equipment		2,900
7. Factory Overhead	4,550	
Selling and Advertising Expense	290	
General and Administrative Expense	320	
Accumulated Depreciation		5,160
8. Factory Overhead	4,250	
Selling and Advertising Expense	50	
General and Administrative Expense	130	
Other Liabilities		4,430
9. Factory Overhead	2,030	
Cash		2,030
10. Factory Overhead	1,070	
General and Administrative Expense	310	
Other Liabilities		1,380
11. Prepayments	980	
Cash		980
12. Factory Overhead	720	
Selling and Advertising Expense	60	
General and Administrative Expense	170	
Prepayments		950
13. Selling and Advertising Expense	2,870	
General and Administrative Expense	1,220	
Other Liabilities		4,090
14. Factory Overhead	970	
Selling and Advertising Expense	320	
General and Administrative Expense	230	
Other Liabilities		1,520
15. Work in Process	114,030	
Direct Materials		64,670
Direct Labor		26,320
Factory Overhead		23,040
16. Finished Goods	112,130	
Work in Process		112,130

17. Cost of Goods Sold	111,910	
Finished Goods		111,910
18. Federal Income Tax Expense	6,780	
Federal Income Taxes Payable		6,780
19. Dividends	1,710	
Cash		1,710
20. Notes Payable to Bank	14,390	
Accounts Payable	74,600	
Other Liabilities	52,900	
Federal Income Taxes Payable	5,520	
Cash		147,410
21. Cash	152,180	
Accounts Receivable		138,680
Notes Payable to Bank		13,500

Illustration 12-17

Talcott Tube Co.
Closing Entries, For the Year 19X2 (000 omitted)

A. Sales	140,570	
Retained Earnings		140,570
B. Retained Earnings	133,510	
Cost of Goods Sold		111,910
Selling and Advertising Expense		7,480
General and Administrative Expense		7,340
Federal Income Tax Expense		6,780
C. Retained Earnings	240	
Loss on Sale of Equipment		240
D. Retained Earnings	1,710	
Dividends		1,710

Illustration 12-18

Talcott Tube Co.
Ledger, For the Year 19X2, (000 omitted)

Cash

√	2,940	(9)	2,030	
(6)	350	(11)	980	
(21)	152,180	(19)	1,710	
		(20)	147,410	
		√	3,340	
	155,470		155,470	
√	3,340			

Accounts Receivable

√	21,360	(21)	138,680
(1)	140,570	√	23,250
	161,930		161,930
√	23,250		

Finished Goods

√	6,990	(17)	111,910
(16)	112,130	√	7,210
	119,120		119,120
√	7,210		

Work in Process

√	9,300	(16)	112,130
(15)	114,030	√	11,200
	123,330		123,330
√	11,200		

Direct Materials

(3)	64,670	(15)	64,670

Raw Materials and Supplies

√	17,610	(3)	68,010
(2)	66,330	√	15,930
	83,940		83,940
√	15,930		

Factory Overhead

(3)	2,960	(15)	23,040
(4)	6,490		
(7)	4,550		
(8)	4,250		
(9)	2,030		
(10)	1,070		
(12)	720		
(14)	970		
	23,040		23,040

Direct Labor

(4)	26,320	(15)	26,320

Prepayments

√	1,180	(12)	950
(11)	980	√	1,210
	3,160		2,160
√	1,210		

Land

√	1,660		
(5)	440	√	2,100
	2,100		2,100
√	2,100		

Buildings

√	8,230		
(5)	870	√	9,100
	9,100		9,100
√	9,100		

Equipment

√	31,060	(6)	2,900
(5)	7,400	√	35,560
	38,460		38,460
√	35,560		

Accumulated Depreciation

(6)	2,310	√	20,020
√	22,870	(7)	5,160
	25,180		25,180
		√	22,870

Notes Payable to Bank

(20)	14,390	√	14,390
√	13,500	(21)	13,500
	27,890		27,890
		√	13,500

Accounts Payable

(20)	74,600	√	13,530
		(2)	66,330
√	13,970	(5)	8,710
	88,570		88,570
		√	13,970

Other Liabilities

(20)	52,900	√	7,060
		(4)	41,280
		(8)	4,430
		(10)	1,380
		(13)	4,090
√	6,860	(14)	1,520
	59,760		59,760
		√	6,860

Federal Income Taxes Payable

(20)	5,520	√	4,030
√	5,290	(18)	6,780
	10,810		10,810
		√	5,290

6% Notes Payable

		√	6,100

Capital Stock

		√	2,700

Retained Earnings

B.	133,510	√	32,500
C.	240	A.	140,570
D.	1,710		
√	37,610		
	173,070		173,070
		√	37,610

Sales

A.	140,570	(1)	140,570

Cost of Goods Sold

(17)	111,910	B.	111,910

Selling and Advertising Expense

(3)	110	B.	7,480
(4)	3,780		
(7)	290		
(8)	50		
(12)	60		
(13)	2,870		
(14)	320		
	7,480		7,480

General and Administrative Expense

(3)	270	B.	7,340
(4)	4,690		
(7)	320		
(8)	130		
(10)	310		
(12)	170		
(13)	1,220		
(14)	230		
	7,340		7,340

Federal Income Tax Expense

(18)	6,780	B.	6,780

Loss on Sale of Equipment

(6)	240	C.	240

Dividends

(19)	1,710	D.	1,710

Illustration 12-19

Talcott Tube Co.
Balance Sheet
December 31, 19X2
(000 omitted)

Assets

Current Assets:			
Cash		$ 3,340	
Accounts Receivable		23,250	
Inventories:			
Finished Goods	$ 7,210		
Work in Process	11,200		
Raw Materials and Supplies	15,930	34,340	
Prepayments		1,210	$62,140
Noncurrent Assets:			
Land	$ 2,100		
Buildings	9,100		
Equipment	35,560	$46,760	
Less: Accumulated Depreciation		22,870	23,890
Total Assets			$86,030

Equities

Current Liabilities:		
Notes Payable to Bank	$13,500	
Accounts Payable	13,970	
Other Liabilities (payroll, taxes, and others)	6,860	
Federal Income Taxes Payable	5,290	$39,620
Noncurrent Liabilities:		
6% Notes Payable—due 9/1/X4		6,100
Total Liabilities		$45,720
Stockholders' Equity:		
Capital Stock	$ 2,700	
Retained Earnings	37,610	40,310
Total Equities		$86,030

Illustration 12-20

Talcott Tube Co.
Statement of Income and Retained Earnings
For the Year 19X2
(000 omitted)

Revenues:		
Sales		$140,570
Expenses:		
Cost of Goods Sold	$111,910	
Selling and Advertising Expense	7,480	
General and Administrative Expense	7,340	
Federal Income Tax Expense	6,780	133,510

Net Income from Operations	$ 7,060
Loss on Sale of Equipment	240
Net Income	$ 6,820
Dividends	1,710
Increase in Retained Earnings	$ 5,110
Retained Earnings—12/31/X1	32,500
Retained Earnings—12/31/X2	$ 37,610

Illustration 12-21

Talcott Tube Co.
Cost of Goods Manufactured and Sold
For the Year 19X2
(000 omitted)

Direct Materials		$ 64,670
Direct Labor		26,320
Factory Overhead:		
Indirect Labor	$6,490	
Indirect Materials	2,960	
Depreciation	4,550	
Utilities	4,250	
Repairs and Maintenance	2,030	
Taxes	1,070	
Prepayments Expired	720	
Miscellaneous	970	23,040
Total Manufacturing Cost		$114,030
Work in Process Inventory—12/31/X1		9,300
Total		$123,330
Work in Process Inventory—12/31/X2		11,200
Cost of Goods Manufactured		$112,130
Finished Goods Inventory—12/31/X1		6,990
Total		$119,120
Finished Goods Inventory—12/31/X2		7,210
Cost of Goods Sold		$111,910

Solution 12-3:

The answer is $594.

The following solution is quite detailed, for the sake of providing maximum help to students who are having difficulties; if you don't need this much help, feel free to skim some of these details.

A. Purchases of merchandise totalled $2,206:

Merchandise Inventory—12/31/X2	$ 930
Cost of Goods Sold	2,288
	$3,218
Merchandise Inventory—12/31/X1	1,012
Merchandise purchases = (A)	$2,206

B. Payments of accounts payable totalled $3,122:

Accounts payable—12/31/X1	$1,330
Merchandise purchased (A)	2,206
	$3,536
Accounts Payable—12/31/X2	414
Payments on account—19X2 = (B)	$3,122

We know that:

C. The company paid $1,160 of selling and administrative expenses.
D. The company paid $230 of 19X1 taxes.
Here, then, is what we know about the company's cash account:

Cash

√	819	(B)	3,122
	?	(C)	1,160
		(D)	230
		√	1,735
	6,247		6,247

But cash and merchandise inventory are the company's *only* current assets:

	12/31/X1	*12/31/X2*
Cash	$ 819	$1,735
Merchandise Inventory	1,012	930
Total current assets	$1,831	$2,665

Therefore, there were no accounts receivable: all sales were for cash or all accounts receivable were collected. Accordingly, the missing $5,428 in the cash account ($6,247 − $819 = $5,428) must represent cash sales, resulting in the following:

Sales		$5,428
Cost of goods sold	$2,288	
Selling and administrative expenses	1,160	3,448
Net income before taxes		$1,980
Tax rate		30%
19X2 taxes expense		$ 594

This works because the problem specifies that no information needed to solve this problem has been omitted.

Assignment Problems

Problem 12-A:

As part of your training in accounting, you must become able to distinguish relevant from irrelevant information. Some of the data given in this and other problems, accordingly, is deliberately irrelevant. Part of your job is to determine which information is pertinent and which is not.

The following problem is self-contained, but is based on the material in Problems 4-C, 4-D, 4-E, 6-E, and 7-G. Given below are all of the 19X5 summary balance sheet changes affecting the 19X5 income statement of Putnam Pharmaceutical Corporation. Do not concern yourself with the remaining changes; you may assume that they have been (or will be) correctly recorded. All changes described pertain to 19X5 only, unless stated otherwise. The last three zeros have been omitted from all figures; you should do likewise. The company prepares a compressed income statement, employing two revenue accounts ("sales," and "interest, royalties and other income") and five expense accounts ("cost of goods sold," "marketing, administrative and general expenses," "depreciation and amortization," "interest expense," and "provision for United States and foreign income taxes"). Prepare Putnam Pharmaceutical Corporation's 19X5 income statement. Any nonoperating losses should be reported as "general expenses" unless they exceed 10% of net income.

1. The company's sales are made entirely on account. Sales totalled $502,524; collections on account totalled $512,580.

2. The company earned $1,382 of interest on time deposits (temporary savings bank deposits).

3. The company's royalties and miscellaneous revenues totalled $4,870.

4. The company declared $21,682 of dividends, but actually paid only $20,156 of dividends.

5. Interest on the company's debt totalled $2,923; depreciation and amortization expense totalled $10,602.

6. The company's cost of goods sold, and marketing, administrative and general expense are accumulated as follows:

	Cost of Goods Sold	Marketing, Administrative and General Expense
Inventories—12/31/X4	$ 93,559	$ –0–
Cost of inventories manufactured during the year	215,901	–0–
Inventories used in marketing and general efforts (samples for physicians, etc.)	(16,034)	16,034
Inventories—12/31/X5	(93,762)	–0–
Exhaustion of prepayments and other current assets	–0–	8,603
Costs incurred on account (administrative and sales salaries, advertising, etc.)	–0–	188,324
Total	$199,664	$212,961

7. The company's liability for U.S. and foreign income taxes was $19,685 on 12/31/X4, and $26,516 on 12/31/X5; the company paid $32,332 of such taxes in 19X5; its estimated U.S. and foreign income tax charges for 19X5 totalled $39,163.

8. During the year, the company sold land and buildings with a book value of $5,523 for $5,120, and old machinery and equipment with a book value of $3,985 for $3,243.

9. The firm's retained earnings at 12/31/X4 totalled $137,892.

Problem 12-B:

Problem 6-I (pages 331–335) gives the 12/31/X1 and 12/31/X0 comparative balance sheets of Perpetual Paper Products, together with the company's 19X1 cash statement and some of its 19X1 summary journal entries. The company prepares a compressed income statement, employing the following general form, which differs in some ways from the forms discussed in the text. "Product costs" is the company's name for cost of goods sold.

Perpetual Paper Products
Operations and Reinvested Earnings
(thousands of dollars)
Period

Sales		$XXX
Costs and expenses		
Product costs	$XXX	
Marketing and distribution	XXX	
Research, administration and general	XXX	
Depreciation	XXX	
Interest	XXX	XXX
Income from operations before taxes		$XXX
Taxes on income		
State and foreign	$XXX	
Federal	XXX	XXX
Net income from operations		$XXX
Dividends received and miscellaneous income		XXX
Net income		$XXX
Dividends		XXX
Earnings reinvested in the business		$XXX
Reinvested earnings—beginning of year		XXX
Reinvested earnings—end of year		$XXX

Prepare Perpetual Paper Products' 19X1 income statement. You may assume that no unusual balance sheet changes occurred during the year; instead, all changes were of the normal kinds discussed in this and previous chapters, and in the notes to the balance sheet of this firm.

(One possible line of attack in solving this problem would be to prepare the general outline of an income statement, leaving considerable space between captions, then fill in the details of this statement as you learn them from the problem data, using T-account analysis only where essential. If you emerge with an income statement entirely consistent with the problem data, do not be concerned with possible balance sheet changes about which you have not been told.)

Other data: Depreciation totalled $25,875; federal taxes on income were estimated to total $26,456; dividends totalling $23,913 were declared; sales totalled $476,383. Marketing and distribution expense, research, administration and general expense, and product costs are accumulated from a number of different costs, as follows:

	Marketing and Distribution Expense	Research, Administration and General Expense	Total	Product Costs
Costs incurred on account	$64,821	$15,125	$79,946	$270,705
Costs incurred by direct cash payment .	1,038	–0–	1,038	63
Exhaustion of prepaid items . . .	609	223	832	2,177
Exhaustion of other materials and supplies	5,881	6,014	11,895	13,205
Amortization of timber resources . .	–0–	–0–	–0–	1,498
Forest products inventories used in research	–0–	389	389	(389)
Forest products inventories—12/31/X0.	–0–	–0–	–0–	46,945
Forest products inventories—12/31/X1.	–0–	–0–	–0–	(48,748)
Total	$72,349	$21,751	$94,100	$285,456

Problem 12-C:

The following data summarize the manufacturing activities of Billy Fuqua Products, Inc. for the month of October, 19X7. Two zeros have been omitted from each of these figures; you should do likewise in your answers. The company prepares monthly financial statements, closing its books at the end of each month. The company's 9/30/X7 trial balance included the following accounts:

	Debit	Credit
Raw Materials Inventory	$ 32,580	
Work in Process Inventory	6,560	
Finished Goods Inventory.	38,920	
Factory Supplies Inventory	8,780	
Land	16,930	
Factory Buildings	93,610	
Machinery and Equipment	195,770	
Allowance for Depreciation, Factory Buildings		$ 42,530
Allowance for Depreciation, Machinery and Equipment		95,110
Accounts Payable		64,230
Payroll		6,770
Accrued Taxes		2,800

The following events occurred during October, 19X7:

1. Purchases of raw materials on account	$ 39,610
2. Purchases of factory supplies on account	19,470
3. Raw materials used in production	44,980
4. Factory supplies used in production	17,550

continued on page 690

5. Cost of indirect labor 2,720
6. Cost of direct labor 36,430
7. Payment of factory wages 42,650
8. Accounts payable paid 64,870

The following adjustments are necessary at the end of the month:
(a) Depreciation of factory buildings . . . . $ 400
(b) Depreciation of factory equipment 1,630
(c) Estimated property taxes 650
(d) Cost of goods finished during month 97,520
(e) Cost of goods sold 110,690

Record the company's October balance sheet changes in journal entries, using appropriate inventory nominal accounts. Close the inventory nominal accounts to work in process inventory.

Problem 12-D:

Refer to the data in Problem 12-C. Prepare a statement of cost of goods manufactured and sold for Billy Fuqua Products, Inc., for the month of October, 19X7.

Problem 12-E:

Pages 663–672 of your text discuss the 19X2 manufacturing activities of San Jose Home Art Co., its 19X2 statement of cost of goods manufactured and sold, and its 19X2 income statement. What follows summarizes the company's related activity for 19X3. Prepare appropriate journal entries, including closing entries.

1. A total of $252,200 of raw materials and supplies were consumed during 19X3. Of these, $216,800 were direct materials used in manufacturing, $29,500 were indirect factory materials and supplies, $3,400 were supplies used in the company's administrative offices, and $2,500 were supplies used in the company's selling activities.

2. 19X3 wages and salaries totalled $406,100. These consisted of $242,900 of direct labor, $53,000 of indirect labor, $46,600 of administrative salaries, and $63,600 of sales salaries.

3. Power, water, and other utilities were purchased on account at a total cost of $21,400. Of this, $16,300 pertained to the factory, $3,000 to the administration of the company, and $2,100 to selling activities.

4. Depreciation of buildings totalled the same as in 19X2: $24,200. Of this, $15,100 pertained to the factory, $5,200 to the company's administrative offices, and $3,900 to its sales offices.

5. Equipment depreciation totalled $34,000. Of this, $27,700 pertained to factory equipment, $4,900 to equipment used in the company's administrative offices, and $1,400 to sales equipment.

6. Property taxes were as follows: on the factory, $17,600; on the company's administrative offices, $1,900; on the company's sales offices, $800.

7. Repairs and maintenance to factory equipment totalling $3,700 were paid in cash.

8. Advertising costs totalled $3,300, cash.

9. All other costs were paid in cash and totalled $23,200, made up as follows: $11,100 of factory costs, $7,500 of administrative costs, and $4,600 of selling costs.

10. Raw materials and supplies costing $249,600 were purchased on account.

11. At various times during the year, inventory nominal accounts were closed to Work in Process Inventory.

12. During 19X3, inventories costing a total of $646,500 were completed.

13. 19X3 sales totalled $850,800, all on account. The goods that were sold had cost the company $637,300 to manufacture.

14. As of 12/31/X3, revenues and expenses were closed to Retained Earnings.

Other data: on 12/31/X2, the company's inventories included finished goods costing $54,700, work in process costing $19,600, and raw materials and supplies costing $33,400.

Problem 12-F:

Refer to the data in Problem 12-E. Post all journal entries to inventory accounts, and to inventory and retained earnings nominal accounts. To save time, do not bother with other ledger accounts.

Problem 12-G:

Refer to the data in Problem 12-E. Prepare San Jose Home Art Co.'s 19X3 statement of cost of goods manufactured and sold, and its 19X3 income statement.

Problem 12-H:

Gainesville Tool Corporation makes adjusting entries at the end of each month, but only makes closing entries once a year, every December 31st. The following is the company's 11/30/X8 trial balance, followed by details underlying some of the figures. Three zeros have been omitted from all figures; you should do likewise in your answers. Figures for the inventory and retained earnings accounts are 12/31/X7 balances. The company determines its inventory balances once a year, every December 31st. All purchases of raw materials and office supplies are recorded in the purchases account (another inventory nominal account). Freight-in is the cost of freight paid on purchases of raw materials inventories; freight-out is the cost of freight paid on shipments to customers. The company does not employ a direct materials account.

Cash	$ 10,528	
Accounts Receivable	18,199	
Raw Materials Inventory	13,629	
Work in Process Inventory	10,240	
Finished Goods Inventory.	4,532	
Office Supplies Inventory	526	
Prepaid Insurance	402	
Land	7,275	
Buildings—Cost	13,228	
—Accumulated Depreciation		$ 5,227
Machinery and Equipment—Cost	59,224	
—Accumulated Depreciation		17,734
Accounts and Other Current Payables		9,728
Notes Payable—due 2/15/X9		6,600
Capital Stock		90,000
Retained Earnings		22,790
Purchases	91,854	
Freight-In	13,133	
Direct Labor	54,416	
Factory Overhead	47,295	

continued on page 692

General and Administrative Expenses	21,126
Selling Expenses	25,246
Interest Expense	719
Sales	239,493

$391,572	$391,572

The amounts shown for factory overhead, general and administrative expenses, and selling expenses are composed as follows:

	Factory Overhead	General and Administrative Expenses	Selling Expenses
Wages, salaries, and commissions	$31,297	$15,058	$ 5,873
Depreciation	3,302	88	33
Insurance	1,120	29	10
Property taxes	1,178	168	41
Power	3,486	12	11
Miscellaneous	3,743	5,771	346
Maintenance and repairs	3,169	–0–	–0–
Advertising	–0–	–0–	2,942
Travel	–0–	–0–	1,996
Packing and freight-out	–0–	–0–	13,994
Total	$47,295	$21,126	$25,246

The following is a summary of the company's December, 19X8 economic activity:

1. Purchases of raw materials and supplies on account totalled $8,259; sales on account totalled $25,850.

2. Accounts receivable totalling $24,773 were collected; accounts payable totalling $9,364 were paid.

3. Cash payments were made for the following:

	Factory Overhead	General and Administrative Expenses	Selling Expenses
Wages, salaries, and commissions	$2,933	$1,461	$ 572
Power	316	2	2
Miscellaneous	401	529	30
Maintenance and repairs	333	–0–	–0–
Advertising	–0–	–0–	282
Travel	–0–	–0–	196
Packing and freight-out	–0–	–0–	1,511
Total	$3,983	$1,992	$2,593

4. Additional cash payments were made for freight-in, $1,181; and direct labor, $5,198.

5. Adjusting entries must be made as of 12/31/X8 for the following:

	Factory Overhead	General and Administrative Expenses	Selling Expenses
Depreciation (building $75; machinery and equipment $236)	$300	$ 8	$3
Prepaid insurance expired	101	3	1
Property taxes	106	15	4
Total	$507	$26	$8

6. Interest charges of $66 accrued during the month.

7. Of the company's 19X8 purchases, $662 were of office supplies, and the remainder of raw materials. The company had the following inventory balances at 12/31/X8.

Raw materials inventory	$12,727
Work in process inventory	14,013
Finished goods inventory	8,755
Office supplies inventory	387

Prepare ledger accounts for all inventory accounts, including inventory nominal accounts. Post 11/30/X8 balances, then record all December, 19X8 economic activity affecting inventories (including year-end closings) directly in the ledger accounts. Do not make any journal entries, and do not prepare ledger accounts for non-inventory accounts.

Problem 12-I:

Refer to the data in Problem 12-H. Prepare journal entries for all of the company's December, 19X8, economic activity (not just that activity which affected inventories) —including closing entries.

Problem 12-J:

Refer to the data in Problem 12-H. Prepare Gainesville Tool Corporation's 19X8 statement of cost of goods manufactured and sold.

Problem 12-K:

Professor Frank E. Aspinall, an American citizen, has unusually wide feet. After years of minor discomfort, he finally had the good fortune to discover a local shoe outlet (in Pulp, Vermont) which sold shoes that fitted him comfortably.

Early in 19X9, Professor Aspinall accepted a two-year teaching appointment at a Canadian university, to begin in September, 19X9. Broadly speaking, under Canadian customs regulations it is possible for an individual in Professor Aspinall's position to bring with him all of his personal possessions, free of customs duties, so long as they are owned by him and in his use at the time he enters Canada. In June, 19X9, Professor Aspinall noticed that the shoes he then owned were becoming shabby. Accordingly, he drove to the shoe store, intending to buy one pair of black and one pair of brown shoes. He estimates that a trip to downtown Pulp cost about 40¢ for gasoline and wear and tear on his car, plus 10¢ for the parking meter.

The store had a pair of black shoes in the proper size and style, but no brown. He bought the black shoes and ordered the brown, paying the retailer $25.96 apiece, for a total of $51.92. Several weeks later the retailer telephoned that the brown shoes had arrived. Professor Aspinall drove downtown and picked them up. That evening his wife remarked, "You know, it may just be the light, but these shoes look black to me." They were black. The next day, Professor Aspinall drove downtown and returned the shoes. The manufacturer had made an error. It was particularly frustrating that neither he nor the retailer had noticed anything amiss when he tried on the second pair of shoes in the store.

Several weeks later the retailer telephoned that the brown shoes had arrived. This was fortunate, since Professor Aspinall was to move the next day. He drove downtown. The shoes were the right color, style, and width. But they were seven sizes too small. He arranged with the retailer that the manufacturer would mail the correct shoes to his new address in Arnoldton, Ontario.

Several weeks after his arrival in Ontario, Professor Aspinall received a card from the Canadian postal customs authorities stating that his shoes had arrived and would be mailed to him once he had paid duty of $10.68. Being unfamiliar with the related customs regulations, Professor Aspinall visited the customs authorities in downtown Arnoldton. He estimates that this trip cost him 40¢ each way for gasoline and wear and tear on his car, plus 15¢ for parking. He learned from the customs authorities that had the shoes been in his possession when he arrived in Canada, no duty would have been charged; but if he wanted the shoes now there was no way to escape paying $10.68. He paid, after first inspecting and trying on both shoes.

The manufacturer had paid $1.60 postage to have the shoes shipped to Arnoldton, but never billed Professor Aspinall for this. He estimates that he spent a total of five hours in buying these shoes. When he works as a consultant, he charges a minimum of $100 for an eight-hour day. As far as he can tell, a pair of shoes of comparable quality would cost $27.50 in Canada, but he is not at all sure that he could find a pair that would really fit comfortably.

Professor Aspinall keeps detailed personal accounting records. At what amount should he record the purchase price of the brown shoes? Defend your answer. For purposes of this problem, do not concern yourself about exchange rates between Canadian and American dollars; instead assume that they are equivalent.

Problem 12-L:

As part of your training in accounting, you must become able to extend what you have learned into new situations. This problem provides an opportunity to increase your flexibility and broaden your understanding. The text provides all background information needed to solve this problem, but the circumstances described will be unfamiliar. Apply what you already have learned to this new situation.

Assume in what follows that, because of local laws relating to the flow of ground water, you have no legal recourse against your neighbor.

You buy a house that is built on a hillside lot. Before buying the property, you notice that the ground on the uphill side of the lot is moister than the rest of the yard. However, you become satisfied that there has not in the past been any serious problem of ground water drainage. The appraiser you hired to examine the property before its purchase confirms this. A month after you move in, your uphill neighbor begins to landscape his lot, using a small tractor-bulldozer. He alters the contour of his land considerably.

After the next rain, you notice that now when you walk across the uphill side of your lot, your shoes get soaked; besides, a small brook seems to be flowing into the drain beneath your cellar. Worried about what will happen to your house when the heavy fall rains begin, you hire a local handyman to dig a dry well and trench, and to lay a field of drain tile across the uphill side of your property. During the digging it became evident that the hillside has a top layer of two to four inches of topsoil, beneath which is a foot-thick layer of gray clay, then a deep layer of yellow clay. Water can flow through the gray clay, though very slowly. The underlying yellow clay is almost impermeable. Accordingly, any water on the hillside tends to flow on or near the ground. The handyman builds the trench and dry well, then charges you $275 for the job.

You have established the following three asset accounts to record the costs of this property (and you do not wish to open more accounts): Land, Buildings, and Land Improvements (the last account is used for fences, sidewalks, and the like). What is the best accounting treatment for this expenditure? Justify your answer.

Problem 12-M:

As part of your training in accounting, you must become able to extend what you have learned into new situations. This problem provides an opportunity to increase your flexibility and broaden your understanding. The text provides all background information needed to solve this problem, but the circumstances described will be unfamiliar. Apply what you already have learned to this new situation.

For several years, Mrs. Viola Gibbons has held a credit card from a major oil company. Early in 19X1 she received an offer from this company that allowed her to use her card to buy a new kitchen appliance. This machine opened cans and jars, crushed ice, ground meat and vegetables, and featured a clock, a timer, and a thermometer —as well as coming in a choice of two-tone colors. It cost only $69.95, plus postage and handling charges of $1.75. The purchase order was an agreement to pay for the machine in twelve equal monthly installments of $7.00 apiece. These included interest charges, at a rate equal to approximately $2\frac{1}{2}\%$ per month, that totalled $12.30 [($7.00 × 12) − ($69.95 + $1.75) = $12.30]. Apparently the only way one was permitted to pay for the machine was by making the twelve payments. No identical machines were available locally, though a similar machine (without the two-tone color, but with a self-winding cord) was obtainable through a nearby Happy Day Trading Stamp Redemption Center for 28 books of Happy Day trading stamps.

Mrs. Gibbons bought the machine from the oil company, choosing Avocado and Twilight Haze for colors. She suggested to her husband that they write the company a check for $69.95 + $1.75 = $71.70 in full payment—he replied, "You've got to be kidding, honey. You do that, and you'll throw their computer out of whack. We'd be getting bills for the next three years!"

The machine arrived eight weeks later, in satisfactory condition except for being smaller than Mrs. Gibbons had expected. She paid the twelve monthly installments, but has since come to believe that she would have been just as satisfied with the trading-stamp machine. This troubles her because, as she eventually remarked to a friend, "If I'd used the stamps, I could have got the thing free."

How much did the machine cost Mrs. Gibbons? What, if anything, else do you need to know before answering this? Defend your answers.

Problem 12-N:

As part of your training in accounting, you must become able to extend what you have learned into new situations. This problem provides an opportunity to increase your flexibility and broaden your understanding. The text provides all background information needed to solve this problem, but the circumstances described will be unfamiliar. Apply what you already have learned to this new situation.

You are the chief accountant of Vallejo Manufacturing Company. After lengthy negotiations, your company has just acquired the land, buildings, and equipment of Brasco Industries for a total price of $17,000,000, paying cash. Your problem is to divide this total purchase price among the three different kinds of assets acquired.

In both of the following cases you should be able to specify a fairly logical way of recording the transaction. Justify your answers. The two cases are independent of each other.

Case 1: During the negotiations, Vallejo Manufacturing Company had the Brasco Industries properties appraised by a reputable firm of independent appraisers, whose report valued the assets involved as follows:

Land	$ 2,000,000
Buildings	10,000,000
Equipment	8,000,000
Total	$20,000,000

You may assume that these assets have not depreciated since the appraisal date, and that the figures in the appraisal report are all equally reliable.

At the same time, the Brasco Industries records gave the following book values for these properties:

Land	$ 500,000
Buildings	6,000,000
Equipment	14,500,000
Total	$21,000,000

The assessed values of these assets for local property tax purposes were:

Land	$1,000,000
Buildings	3,000,000
Equipment	4,000,000
Total	$8,000,000

Case 2: During the negotiations, Vallejo Manufacturing Company had the Brasco Industries properties appraised by a reputable firm of independent appraisers, whose report valued the assets as follows:

Land	$ 2,000,000
Buildings	10,000,000
Equipment	8,000,000
Total	$20,000,000

You may assume that these assets have not depreciated since the appraisal date. In conversation with the appraisers, it became evident that they attached a high degree of reliability to the value estimated for the land (local prices for industrial land had been quite stable recently). The values estimated for buildings and equipment are subject to a wider range of possible error.

Problem 12-O:

As part of your training in accounting, you must become able to extend what you have learned into new situations. This problem provides an opportunity to increase your flexibility and broaden your understanding. The text provides all background information needed to solve this problem, but the circumstances described will be unfamiliar. Apply what you already have learned to this new situation.

George Edwards founded Edwards Outdoor Equipment, Inc. and managed the company until his death in 19X8. The company operated stores in Berkeley and Davis, California. Shortly before his death, Mr. Edwards had a third store constructed in San Mateo on land that the company had purchased a number of years earlier.

Upon the death of Mr. Edwards, his son-in-law, Donald Miller, assumed the presidency of the company. Mr. Miller felt that it would be unwise to try to operate a third store until he had a fuller understanding of the business. Besides, Mr. Edwards had been in failing health for the last year or so and had been unable to give the stores his full attention; a number of problems had developed that demanded immediate action, and any expansion seemed inappropriate for the present.

Fortunately, Mr. Miller was able to interest an older cousin of his, Arthur McLaughlin, in the San Mateo land and store building. Mr. McLaughlin was president of Younger-McLaughlin Surplus Sales. The following arrangement was worked out on March 10, 19X9: Younger-McLaughlin Surplus Sales acquired the San Mateo land and building for $100,000 and 2,100 shares of Younger-McLaughlin Surplus Sales capital stock. Because a continuing relationship between the two companies was envisioned, Mr. Miller became a member of the Board of Directors of Younger-McLaughlin Surplus Sales, and Mr. McLaughlin became a member of the Board of Directors of Edwards Outdoor Equipment, Inc.

The San Mateo land had cost Edwards Outdoor Equipment, Inc. $23,000; the San Mateo building had cost $285,300 to construct, had been completed on 10/12/X8, and had never been used. Mr. McLaughlin felt that it could be adapted to the needs of his company with little modification beyond changing the signs and enclosing an outdoor area that was originally intended for a permanent display of tents.

Just before it acquired the San Mateo properties, Younger-McLaughlin Surplus Sales had 6,100 shares of capital stock outstanding. The stockholders' equity section of its balance sheet appeared as follows:

Stockholders' Equity:
Capital Stock	$305,000	
Retained Earnings	366,000	671,000

You are the accountant for Younger-McLaughlin Surplus Sales. Naturally, you asked Mr. McLaughlin for any guidance that he might be able to provide in recording this transaction. He replied, "Beats me what figures we should use. Don let the property go easier than I expected. But now I've got to be teacher and show him how to run the old man's business; maybe I *deserve* a break on the price!"

What problems are there in recording this transaction? How would you go about resolving these problems? Be as specific as possible (but you need *not* decide what the appropriate figures are).

Thirteen

Nonmonetary
Assets: Cost Amortization

The Financial Accounting Dilemma

The financial accountant's amortization of nonmonetary assets has its intellectual basis in a matching theory requiring that revenues be compared (on the income statement) with the costs incurred to generate them. Unfortunately, this theory cannot be applied with precision to actual circumstances. As a result, a variety of different, and mutually conflicting, amortization practices have emerged.[1]

We saw on pages 91–92 and 225–226 that accountants restrict their interest in nonmonetary assets to the economic benefits that these assets offer to the company. The assets have numerous other characteristics, of course, but the accountant regards nonmonetary assets as nothing more than collections of future services to be received by the company. For example, Chapter Two pointed out that this "services" interpretation of nonmonetary assets provides the rationale for recording depreciation. The accountant could write off depreciable assets entirely in the year of purchase or entirely in the year of retirement. Yet he believes that this would be misleading: the depreciable assets offer services to all the years they are owned, so all years should bear a share of their costs. Accordingly, the accountant allocates some of the cost of the asset to each service year by means of an annual depreciation charge; he estimates the total services that the asset will provide over its life and those it will provide during each year, then allocates a portion of the asset's cost as an asset outflow for each year,

---

[1] Be warned that some of the theoretical discussion in this chapter is controversial; many would disagree that the problems facing accountants are as severe as depicted here. Technical arguments attempting to support the positions taken in this chapter will be found in *The Allocation Problem in Financial Accounting Theory* (Evanston, Illinois: American Accounting Association, 1969) and "Useful Arbitrary Allocations (With a Comment on the Neutrality of Financial Accounting Reports)," *The Accounting Review* XLVI (July, 1971), pages 472–479.

However, the description given here of accounting practice, though simplified, is conventional. *What* accountants do is relatively easy to describe; controversy arises when you try to explain *why* they do it.

based on the relationship between each year's services and total services. Notice again that two kinds of "matching" are involved here. First, estimated economic benefits are matched with assets; then, as a result, the costs of these assets are matched with the revenues to be earned in successive years. By the same kind of matching procedures, the purchase price of any nonmonetary good is allocated (assigned) to the activities or periods of time benefitted by this good: for example, fire insurance policies are amortized over the period of protection, and inventory lots are amortized as the individual inventory units are used.

"Services" must relate either to cash or to income

If the accountant's amortization pattern is to avoid being arbitrary, the nonmonetary asset's "services" (which form an element in his amortization calculations) must be translatable into effects on the firm's cash (or into related effects on the firm's income). Two reasons for this were given in Chapter Nine.

1. The amount amortized during each year must be incorporated on an income statement (as an expense) and used in the calculation of income. This is true even when the amortization charge first is allocated to the costs of some other asset (such as an inventory), and only later is charged to expense (as when the inventory costs, with their amortization components, are charged to cost of goods sold).

2. As was indicated in the final section of Chapter Four, all amounts reported in financial accounting are constructed out of a set of simple primary measurements of cash, counts of quantities of monetary assets and liabilities shown at figures corresponding to equivalent amounts of cash, and counts of quantities of nonmonetary assets and liabilities shown at figures corresponding to cash-equivalent market prices (or portions thereof).

Two additional, related, reasons are:

3. Many nonmonetary assets provide a great *variety* of services—for example, many different activities are sheltered by a building. If one is to talk of the totality of the services provided by such an asset, some common denominator is needed. Cash (or related concepts of income) provides this. Indeed, the main economic function of cash *is* to provide such a common denominator whereby different services may be expressed in common terms.

4. The accountant cannot fully defend his amortization allocation unless he translates the asset's services into their consequences on cash (or income). For example, suppose he expects a machine that makes a single product to operate for ten years, and wishes to write off one tenth of its cost each year (assume a zero scrap value). One might ask why he wishes to write off an equal amount each year since, as we shall see in this chapter, there are various other possibilities. His answer might be that he expects the machine to produce an equal number of units of product in each year. But this is not sufficient—why should each *unit of product* in effect carry the same depreciation charge? The accountant might answer this by saying "Because I expect that each unit of product will make the same contribution to cash (or to income)." But if the accountant *cannot* say something like this, then it is entirely possible that the units of product will make different contributions to cash (or revenue), in which case depreciation allocated to each unit of product would be arbitrary. Many novelty products, for instance, sell at higher prices during the early years of their popularity

than during their later years. If the aim is to allocate depreciation in terms of the services yielded to the firm, equal depreciation for all units of product would violate that goal. In general, since the economic concerns of profit-making firms ultimately relate to cash and income, the "services" provided by an asset must be translatable into cash or income effects.

An ideal example

A far-fetched example illustrates how the accountant's approach might work under ideal circumstances. Suppose that a company owns a totally automatic machine for extracting minerals from sea water. Operating without a crew, the machine propels itself into open ocean, extracts minerals until it is full, then returns to port, where it empties its contents into waiting railway cars. The machine runs on solar power, so that no additional nonmonetary assets such as fuel are needed. This machine cost $1,000,000, has an estimated five-year service life with zero scrap value upon retirement, and is expected to gather $220,000 worth of minerals each year.

Because this imaginary machine provides identical services during each year of its life, it is plausible to allocate equal portions of the machine's purchase price to each year of service life, that is, to charge straight-line depreciation of $200,000 per year.[2]

Suppose instead that the machine becomes progressively less efficient with age, and that its expected service pattern is as follows:

Year	Value of Minerals Gathered
1	$400,000
2	280,000
3	210,000
4	140,000
5	70,000

---

[2] Plausible, but not completely logical, as the following table indicates:

Year	(A) Beginning of Year Book Value	(B) Depreciation = (Purchases Price)/5	(C) End-of-Year Book Value = (A)−(B)	(D) Average Book Value = (A+C)/2	(E) Revenue	(F) Net Income = (E)−(B)	Rate of Return on Average Investment =(F)/(D)
1	$1,000,000	$200,000	$800,000	$900,000	$220,000	$20,000	2.2%
2	800,000	200,000	600,000	700,000	220,000	20,000	2.9%
3	600,000	200,000	400,000	500,000	220,000	20,000	4.0%
4	400,000	200,000	200,000	300,000	220,000	20,000	6.7%
5	200,000	200,000	-0-	100,000	220,000	20,000	20.0%

With equal annual depreciation charges, the rate of return on the average investment in the machine increases over the asset's life for no meaningful reason. If this seems troublesome, depreciation can be adjusted so that a bit less than $200,000 is charged in the early years, with the difference made up in the later years. This approach parallels that of the constant rate method of interest allocation, and employs similar compound interest calculations. Although it has received considerable theoretical support, it rarely (if ever) is employed in practice. The analysis in the next subsection can be used to demonstrate that this approach is just as arbitrary as any other depreciation method, since its use would require unambiguous measurements of the asset's contributions to cash or income. Accordingly, this complication will not be discussed in the remainder of this book.

In this case, each year would receive less than the year before. This would make it plausible to charge more depreciation in the early years, which receive the most benefit. Such a depreciation pattern is called a *decreasing-charge* method, to contrast it with the constant annual depreciation charge provided by straight-line depreciation. (Were the machine to increase in efficiency, an increasing charge pattern would be appropriate—at least in theory.) Here is one way in which a decreasing-charge pattern might be calculated:

Year	Value of Minerals Gathered	(A) Percent of Total Services To Be Received from Machine	Depreciation Charge for Year = Purchase Price × (A)
1	$ 400,000	36%	$ 360,000
2	280,000	26	260,000
3	210,000	19	190,000
4	140,000	13	130,000
5	70,000	6	60,000
	$1,100,000	100%	$1,000,000

Amortizations and arbitrariness

Unfortunately, there are two practical realities that limit the significance of the services approach to depreciation. As you can see, this approach requires the accountant to estimate the services that the machine will offer in each year of its life. The business world is so uncertain that such estimates are usually very unreliable.

More importantly, this approach requires the accountant to identify *which* assets provide *which* services. In the ideal example given, this creates no problem, for there is only one asset. But the typical business uses hundreds, even thousands, of nonmonetary assets. As we saw on pages 319–322 and 432–435, these assets *interact* with each other (and with other inputs); that is to say, the services provided by the assets in combination are usually greater in total than the services that would have been provided by the assets acting independently. A machine that is protected from the elements by a building will produce a more usable product than would an unprotected machine; a building with machines in it will produce more products than would an empty building. The total product will be greater than the sum of products produced by the parts.

In most businesses, there is great interaction among the firm's different inputs. This interaction makes it impossible to determine the effects upon cash or income of any individual input—just as you can't determine how much of a watch's total services are caused by any one gear. The concept of "an asset's contribution to cash or income" turns out to be something that cannot be measured, except in an arbitrary way. As was emphasized on pages 473–474, this has serious consequences for the accountant's allocations. Accountants wish to amortize nonmonetary assets as follows (assuming zero scrap values):

$$\frac{\text{Amortization}}{\text{for period}} = \frac{\text{Historical}}{\text{acquisition price}} \times \frac{\text{Services yielded}}{\text{during the period}} \div \frac{\text{Total services}}{\text{to be provided}} \atop \text{by the asset}$$

We just saw that if the amortization is not to be arbitrary, the asset's "services" must be interpreted as its effects on cash or income. But since these effects cannot be calculated, except in an arbitrary way, the accountant's amortization calculation reduces to:

$$\frac{\text{Amortization}}{\text{for period}} = \frac{\text{Historical}}{\text{acquisition price}} \times \frac{\textit{Arbitrary}}{\textit{figure}} \div \frac{\textit{Arbitrary}}{\textit{figure}}$$

The effort to avoid arbitrariness by interpreting an asset's "services" as its effects on cash or income *itself* leads to arbitrariness! There is no way the accountant's amortization of nonmonetary assets can avoid being arbitrary. One consequence is that, at least in theory, an unlimited number of amortization patterns might be followed for any nonmonetary asset, each of which is just as defensible (or indefensible) as any other. In practice, one usually finds only a few different kinds of amortization patterns for each kind of nonmonetary asset, and the patterns most easily calculated are most often used.

Another consequence of the arbitrariness of the accountant's amortizations of nonmonetary assets is that the related expense figures are also arbitrary. When we couple this conclusion with the ones reached in Chapter Eight, the following limitations of financial statements become evident:

> *Balance sheet.* It cannot be conclusively decided how to amortize nonmonetary assets; even if this problem were to be settled, it still could not be conclusively decided whether these assets should be reported at historical costs or at current market values. The retained earnings figure suffers from consequent limitations.
>
> *Income statement.* There is no conclusive way to decide what revenues should be recognized; there is no conclusive way to decide what expenses should be recognized (insofar as expenses involve amortization); there is no conclusive way to decide how much net income should be recognized.

From the standpoint of accounting *theory,* this is a terrible dilemma. Until it is solved, I see little chance of accounting theory significantly changing accounting practice, even though many theorists are deeply critical of accounting practice.[3]

From the standpoint of accounting *practice,* these conclusions serve to confirm what many practitioners have suspected all along: that one should follow accepted accounting customs and not worry too much about theory.

The arbitrariness of financial accounting's asset, revenue, expense, and income figures hinders resource-allocation uses of financial statements, but does not directly affect practical institutional uses. As long as the accountant follows generally accepted accounting practices (the conventional rules discussed in this text for calculating asset, revenue, expense, and income magnitudes), he will produce results that will satisfy most of his readers. However, eventually the practitioners may have to face up to the theorists' dilemma, too. If the figures they now report are as arbitrary as

---

[3] The reader who is interested in learning more about contemporary financial accounting theory is directed to the bibliography on pages 744–745.

they seem to be, it is unlikely that their readers will remain satisfied indefinitely. The phenomenon of bootleg calculations of "cash-flow income" (see pages 471–474) suggests that some readers are already dissatisfied.

Actual Depreciation Practices

The practical accountant usually does his amortizing in a rough, simplified manner. The allocation techniques discussed in this section, though arbitrary, satisfy all of the practical institutional constraints placed upon the accountant. I will discuss these techniques in a manner consistent with the ways in which the practitioner perceives and justifies them; this involves deliberately ignoring much of the previous section. To understand what the accountant is doing, we must also understand his reasoning, even if the theoretical foundations of that reasoning seem dubious.

Different kinds of depreciable assets provide different kinds of services. Two characteristics of these services are influential (in combination) in determining the particular depreciation method used.

1. Some assets offer a single kind of service; the amount of services received is easily measurable, and reliable advance estimates can be made of the total amount of this service that the asset will provide. Truck tires are often a good example of a single-service asset. Many companies that operate their own fleets of trucks have discovered that it saves money to replace tires before there is any significant chance of tire failure; blowouts are just too expensive in terms of failure to meet schedules and accident potential. Assume that a company has a policy of replacing all tires after, say, 20,000 miles. For this company, a set of tires offers a single kind of service (related to transportation), receipts of this service are easily measured (by the truck's mileage indicator), and the total amount of service is known in advance (because of company policy). Call such assets *known-service assets*.

Most assets lack one or more of the three characteristics of known-service assets. Buildings, for example, usually offer *multiple* services. A desk calculator in a company's administrative offices provides services that are both awkward to measure and difficult to estimate in total.

2. Some assets provide roughly the same amount of service in each year of their service lives. Call these *constant-service assets*. Other assets provide more of their services in their early years than in their later years. Call these *declining-service assets*. ("Increasing-service assets" are possible in theory, but they're so rare in practice that we will ignore them here.)

A chain-mesh guard fence is a good example of a constant-service asset; so is a wooden pallet on which goods are stored and moved by forklift trucks. In both cases, the services provided by the assets remain much the same until the assets are finally retired and replaced. In contrast, any machine that becomes increasingly inefficient with age is an example of a declining-service asset (if the inefficiency is significant). A private automobile is a good example of a declining-service asset for two reasons:

1. One of the services provided by a private automobile is related to its stylishness and appearance, both of which deteriorate with age. A new car offers more prestige and self-satisfaction than an old car.

2. The older car is not likely to perform as well as a new one. It may spend less time on the road and more time undergoing repairs.

The three main depreciation methods

Three main depreciation methods presently employed in financial accounting will be discussed in this book:[4]

1. Production depreciation.

If the asset is a known-service asset, the accountant may allocate an equal portion of the asset's acquisition price (less any estimated scrap value upon retirement) to each unit of service. This method usually is called *production depreciation*.

Example. A set of eight truck tires costs $440 and has an estimated scrap value on replacement of $40. The company makes a policy of replacing all tires after 25,000 miles. A set of these tires were mounted on a single truck trailer and driven as follows:

Year	Miles
19X1	18,000
19X2	7,000

The tires were replaced during 19X2. Under the production method, the tires would be depreciated at a rate of:

$$\frac{\$440 - \$40}{25,000} = 1.6\cancel{c} \text{ per mile}$$

19X1 depreciation would be $18,000 \times 1.6\cancel{c} = \$288$; 19X2 depreciation would be $7,000 \times 1.6\cancel{c} = \$112$. ($288 + $112 + $40 = $440).

Depreciation as a product or period cost

To use a distinction that was mentioned in Chapter Eight (page 392), the choice between production depreciation and the other kinds of depreciation depends largely upon whether the accountant has enough information to be able to treat the expiration of the depreciable asset's services as a product cost—i.e., to associate it with some specific physical output. With known-service assets he has this information; with all other depreciable assets he must treat depreciation as a cost of particular periods of time—as a period cost.

2. Straight-line depreciation

If an asset is not a known-service asset, but it will offer roughly equal services in each year of its service life, the familiar straight-line depreciation method (the only

---

[4] There are several other methods besides the three discussed here. The most common of these is called "group depreciation"—a constant-service method by which the accountant depreciates a group of similar assets in much the same way that a life insurance actuary prepares mortality tables for a group of people who are all of the same age and share other characteristics. The remaining methods are only rarely used.

one used so far in this book) may be used. Because of its simplicity, this method may also be used with known-service assets if little variation in service is expected from year to year.

3. Declining-charge depreciation

If an asset is not a known-service asset, and it is estimated that its services will be greater in its early years than in its later years, some form of declining-charge depreciation may be employed. *No attempt is made to tailor the declining-charge method to the particular pattern of services estimated for the asset.* As shown earlier, the accountant does his matching in a rough manner. With a declining-service asset that is not a known-service asset, the accountant will use any declining-charge depreciation method that is easy to calculate.

This point should be emphasized, for it often confuses students. If the accountant decides that neither the production nor the straight-line method is appropriate, he will use a declining-charge method. Because of the difficulties of matching, he doesn't try to be precise. If declining-charge depreciation seems appropriate, he will use any depreciation method that easily generates a declining pattern of annual depreciation charges (subject to one constraint to be discussed later). At present, two such declining-charge methods are widely employed. Both may seem strange until you recognize *that their sole purpose is to generate an easy-to-calculate declining-charge pattern of depreciation.* There is no mysterious significance to either of these methods; they are merely tools for obtaining a rough approximation to a declining-service pattern.[5]

(a) *Sum-of-the-years'-digits depreciation.* One way to obtain a declining depreciation pattern is to divide the total amount to be depreciated into equal parts, charge several parts to depreciation in the first year, then charge one less part to depreciation in each subsequent year. For example, a declining-service machine cost $95,000, has an estimated service life of four years, and an estimated scrap value upon retirement of $5,000. The total amount to be depreciated is $90,000 ($95,000 − $5,000 = $90,000). You might divide this $90,000 into ten equal parts of $9,000, and charge four parts to the first year, three parts to the second year, two parts to the third year, and one part to the fourth year. This would result in the depreciation pattern shown below:

Year	Amount of One Part	Number of Parts	Depreciation Charge
1	$9,000	4	$36,000
2	9,000	3	27,000
3	9,000	2	18,000
4	9,000	1	9,000
Total	10	10	$90,000

---

[5] I noticed a parallel to this in my own home, a few years ago. We have three children, then aged seven, five, and two. When nonessential foods (such as crackers) were to be passed out, my wife believed that older children should get more than young ones; rightly or wrongly, the children agreed that this was fair, but there were so many complicating factors in the situation that it was hopeless to seek a precise allocation. If there were 15 crackers to divide, my wife would give 7 to the oldest, 5 to the middle child, and 3 to the youngest (actually, the

Why was the amount to be depreciated divided into exactly ten parts? Because doing so resulted in charging one part to the last year, and one additional part to each successive previous year, and this is a satisfying, systematic pattern. Similarly, if the estimated service life had been 5 years, you would have divided the amount to be depreciated into $5 + 4 + 3 + 2 + 1 = 15$ parts of $6,000 apiece (90,000/15 = $6,000). You would then have charged depreciation as shown below.

Year	Amount of One Part	Number of Parts	Depreciation Charge
1	$6,000	5	$30,000
2	6,000	4	24,000
3	6,000	3	18,000
4	6,000	2	12,000
5	6,000	1	6,000
Total 15		15	$90,000

This method is called *sum-of-the-years'-digits* depreciation because it involves assigning consecutive digits to each service year, and setting the number of parts into which the amount to be depreciated is divided equal to the total of these digits. In general, to calculate a sum-of-the-years'-digits declining depreciation pattern, follow these steps:

(1) Determine the total amount to be depreciated. This will equal the asset's acquisition price, less its estimated scrap value upon retirement. In the previous example, the total amount to be depreciated was $90,000 ($95,000 − $5,000 = $90,000).

(2) Assign consecutive numbers to the years of the asset's estimated service life. Add these numbers together to obtain a total, which will be represented by the letter T. In the immediately previous example, the estimated service life was five years, and $T = 1 + 2 + 3 + 4 + 5 = 15$.

(3) Divide the total amount to be depreciated by the total (T) of the digits. This will give you T equal parts. In the immediately previous example, the fifteen equal parts are $6,000 apiece ($90,000/15 = $6,000).

(4) The depreciation charge in the first year should be the amount of one part times the number of years of the asset's estimated service life. One less part should be charged to depreciation in each subsequent year. In the previous example, five parts were charged in the first year ($6,000 × 5 = $30,000), four in the second ($6,000 × 4 = $24,000), three in the third ($6,000 × 3 = $18,000), two in the fourth ($6,000 × 2 = $12,000), and one in the fifth ($6,000 × 1 = $6,000), resulting in a total depreciation of $90,000.

Another example of sum-of-the-years'-digits depreciation: A declining-service machine cost $32,000 and has an estimated service life of five years, with an estimated

---

youngest should have gotten only two, since he was only two years old; but she rounded upward for him to avoid too great a disparity). There was no mystery to my wife's action; it was just a rough way to obtain a cracker allocation pattern that declined with age. Yet the method corresponds well to the sum-of-the-years'-digits depreciation method, soon to be discussed.

scrap value of $2,000 upon retirement. The sum of the digits is once again fifteen: $1 + 2 + 3 + 4 + 5 = 15$. The depreciation charge for each year is calculated in Illustration 13-1 (you will recall that an asset's "book value" is its acquisition price, less accumulated depreciation):

Illustration 13-1

Sum-of-the-Years'-Digits Depreciation

Year	(A) *Acquisition Price* *Less Estimated* *Scrap Value*	(B) *Multiplier*	*Depreciation* *Charge* (A) × (B)	*End-of-Year* *Book Value*	
1	$30,000	5/15	$10,000	$22,000	($32,000 − $10,000)
2	30,000	4/15	8,000	14,000	($22,000 − $ 8,000)
3	30,000	3/15	6,000	8,000	etc.
4	30,000	2/15	4,000	4,000	
5	30,000	1/15	2,000	2,000	
Total		15/15	$30,000		

The depreciation charge is smaller each year; by the end of the fifth year, the $32,000 acquisition price has been reduced to exactly the $2,000 estimated scrap value. If that estimate is correct, there will be neither a gain nor a loss on the asset's retirement. To repeat, there is no reason to expect that sum-of-the-years'-digits depreciation will *exactly* parallel the particular declining pattern of the asset's services, but it does give a declining-charge pattern that serves as a rough approximation to the asset's estimated declining service pattern.

When an asset has a long service life, it is a nuisance to add up the sum of the digits. The correct total can be calculated by the following formula, where N represents the total estimated service life, in years:

$$T = \frac{(N)(N + 1)}{2}$$

For instance, in the previous example:

$$T = \frac{(5)(6)}{2} = 15.$$

(b) *Twice-straight-line-on-the-declining-balance depreciation.* The other popular declining-charge method requires that you determine what the straight-line rate would be, double that rate, then apply it to the *book value* of the asset at the beginning of each year. Since that book value decreases from year to year, so does the annual depreciation charge. In the previous example, the asset had a five-year estimated service life; the straight-line depreciation rate would be $1/5 = 20$ percent. Twice this is 40 percent. Illustration 13-2 shows how depreciation would be calculated under this method were it followed consistently throughout the asset's life. This method is often called by the alternate name *double declining balance depreciation*; we will use this shorter nomenclature in the rest of this book.

Illustration 13-2

Consistent Double Declining Balance Depreciation

Year	(A) Beginning- of-Year Book Value	(B) Multiplier	(C) Depreciation Charge (A) × (B)	End-of- Year Book Value (A) − (C)
1	$32,000	40%	$12,800	$19,200
2	19,200	40%	7,680	11,520
3	11,520	40%	4,608	6,912
4	6,912	40%	2,765	4,147
5	4,147	40%	1,659	2,488

Three things should be pointed out concerning this method:

(1) It amortizes the purchase price a bit faster than does sum-of-the-years'-digits depreciation—at least in the early years.

(2) It is applied to the beginning-of-year book value of the asset, instead of to its purchase price less estimated scrap value (unlike the sum-of-the-years'-digits method).

(3) Instead of a scrap value, this method automatically generates a positive residual amount at the end of the expected service life—in this case $2,488 (as compared with the $2,000 estimated scrap value). If the difference is small, it may be ignored (or the depreciation expense in the year of retirement may be adjusted). If large, a more extensive adjustment of the depreciation pattern may be necessary (one similar to adjustments used for correcting *mistaken* depreciation estimates, discussed later in this chapter). The following summary example is artificially constructed so that this problem does not arise. You may wish to try to solve it before looking at the answers. On the other hand, if you had no difficulty in understanding the foregoing discussion, feel free to move on to page 711 after familiarizing yourself with this example (its data are referred to later).

A summary example

Ojai Company purchased a machine for $30,618. The machine had an estimated service life of six years, and an estimated scrap value upon retirement of $2,688. The company expected to run this machine for a total of 10,000 hours during its service life. Actual hours used were:

Year	Hours Used
1	2,011
2	2,865
3	358
4	2,506
5	1,432
6	828
Total	10,000

Here are the depreciation patterns for this machine under straight-line depreciation, sum-of-the-years'-digits depreciation, double declining balance depreciation, and production depreciation.

Straight-line depreciation: The acquisition price, less estimated scrap value upon retirement, is $27,930 ($30,618 − $2,688 = $27,930). The depreciation charge will be $4,655 ($27,930/6 = $4,655) in each of the six years.

Sum-of-the-years'-digits depreciation: The sum of the digits one through six is $(6 \times 7)/2 = 21$.

Illustration 13-3

Ojai Company
Sum-of-the-Years'-Digits Depreciation

Year	*(A)* *Acquisition Price Less Estimated Scrap Value*	*(B)* *Multiplier*	*Depreciation Charge* *(A) × (B)*	*End-of-Year* *Book Value*
1	$27,930	6/21	$ 7,980	$22,638
2	27,930	5/21	6,650	15,988
3	27,930	4/21	5,320	10,668
4	27,930	3/21	3,990	6,678
5	27,930	2/21	2,660	4,018
6	27,930	1/21	1,330	2,688
Total			$27,930	

Double declining balance depreciation: Twice the straight-line rate is $1/6 \times 2 = 1/3$.

Illustration 13-4

Ojai Company
Double Declining Balance Depreciation

Year	*(A)* *Beginning-of-Year Book Value*	*(B)* *Multiplier*	*(C)* *Depreciation Charge =* *(A) × (B)*	*End-of-Year Book Value =* *(A) − (C)*
1	$30,618	1/3	$10,206	$20,412
2	20,412	1/3	6,804	13,608
3	13,608	1/3	4,536	9,072
4	9,072	1/3	3,024	6,048
5	6,048	1/3	2,016	4,032
6	4,032	1/3	1,344	2,688
Total			$27,930	

Production depreciation: Under the production approach, the company will depreciate the machine for each hour of service at a rate of:

$$\frac{\$30,618 - \$2,688}{10,000} = \$2.793$$

Illustration 13-5

Ojai Company
Production Depreciation

Year	Hours Used	Multiplier	Depreciation Charge
1	2,011	$2.793	$ 5,617
2	2,865	2.793	8,002
3	358	2.793	1,000
4	2,506	2.793	6,999
5	1,432	2.793	3,999
6	828	2.793	2,313
Total			$27,930

Comparison of depreciation methods

The four depreciation methods are compared graphically in Illustration 13-6. Several comments should be made about this illustration, especially about the graph of end-of-year book values:

1. The actual pattern of receipts of service from the machine (as reflected in production depreciation) was deliberately chosen to represent an ambiguous case, in which neither straight-line depreciation nor the declining-charge methods really fits the service pattern. Such cases are fairly common in practice.

2. Double declining balance depreciation gives a more rapid amortization of the purchase price (higher depreciation charges in early years) than does sum-of-the-years'-digits depreciation. This will be true in almost all realistic circumstances.

3. One reason for straight-line depreciation's name should be self-evident—the method yields a straight line on both the Annual Depreciation Charges and the End-of-Year Book Values graphs. Notice that sum-of-the-years'-digits depreciation yields a straight line only on the Annual Depreciation Charges graph.

Illustration 13-6

Ojai Company
Comparison of Depreciation Methods

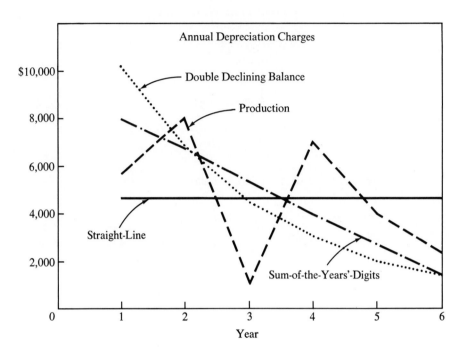

Annual Depreciation Charges

Double Declining Balance

Production

Straight-Line

Sum-of-the-Years'-Digits

Year

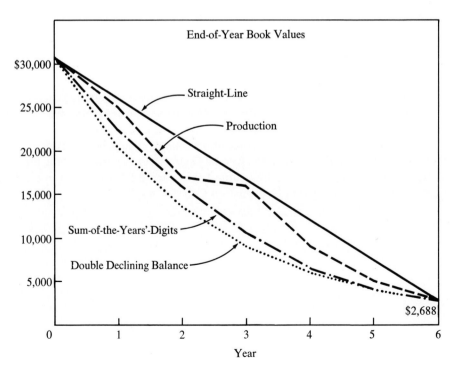

End-of-Year Book Values

Straight-Line

Production

Sum-of-the-Years'-Digits

Double Declining Balance

$2,688

Year

The amounts upon which these graphs are based are as follows:

Annual Depreciation Charges

Year	Straight-Line	Sum-of-the-Years'-Digits	Double Declining Balance	Production
1	$4,655	$7,980	$10,206	$5,617
2	4,655	6,650	6,804	8,002
3	4,655	5,320	4,536	1,000
4	4,655	3,990	3,024	6,999
5	4,655	2,660	2,016	3,999
6	4,655	1,330	1,344	2,313

End-of-Year Book Values

Year	Straight-Line	Sum-of-the-Years'-Digits	Double Declining Balance	Production
1	$25,963	$22,638	$20,412	$25,001
2	21,308	15,988	13,608	16,999
3	16,653	10,668	9,072	15,999
4	11,998	6,678	6,048	9,000
5	7,343	4,018	4,032	5,001
6	2,688	2,688	2,688	2,688

Problems for Study and Self-Examination

Problem 13-1:

Baldwin Mfg. Co. has purchased a machine that will be used in producing one of its products. This machine cost $12,500, has an estimated service life of five years, and an estimated scrap value upon retirement of $1,100. The particular product involved is a novelty item whose sales appeal will probably decline sharply after the first two or three years of production. The company's accountant has made several estimates, based on different sets of assumptions, of the numbers of units of this product that will be produced and sold. The average of these estimates, broken down by years, is shown below. While the accountant admits that his estimates are inexact, he believes that some significant decline in production and sales can be anticipated.

Year	Estimated Number of Units To Be Produced
1	18,000
2	16,000
3	4,000
4	4,000
5	3,600
Total	45,600

The accountant must use his present estimates to determine which depreciation method will be the most appropriate for this machine. He is curious about the different patterns of depreciation charges and book values that would result from using straight-line, production, sum-of-the-years'-digits, and double declining balance depreciation, assuming that his estimates are correct.

1. Prepare a tabular comparison of the annual depreciation charges and end-of-year book values resulting from employing each of these four depreciation methods over the asset's five-year service life.

2. Using graph paper, prepare a graphic comparison of these annual depreciation charges and end-of-year book values. Model your answer after Illustration 13-6.

3. In determining the most appropriate method for depreciating this machine, what questions must the accountant try to answer? How would he go about obtaining his answers? (Use your imagination here; this question raises issues not thoroughly discussed in the text.)

Problem 13-2 (*Brain-teaser*):

As part of your training in accounting, you must become able to extend what you have learned into new situations. This problem provides an opportunity to increase your flexibility and broaden your understanding. The text provides all background information needed to solve this problem, but the circumstances described will be unfamiliar. Apply what you have already learned to this new situation.

Several years ago a student came up after class with a personal accounting problem. His mother owned a motel in Idaho. She prepared monthly financial statements, charging such expenses as cleaning, heat, electricity, and repairs to the months in which the related expenditures of funds were made, charging depreciation on a straight-line basis, and allocating one-twelfth of her annual property taxes to each month.

Although she stayed open year-round, the tourist business in that part of Idaho was at its height during the summer; relatively few guests stayed at her motel during the winter, though she always kept a few units open and ran the furnace to keep the pipes from freezing. According to the student, his mother was distressed about the losses that she suffered each winter, as reflected on her monthly income statements. When I asked him how she was doing over the year as a whole, he replied that she was doing quite well.

What accounting advice should I have given to the student to convey to his mother?

Solution 13-1:

1.

Illustration 13-7

Baldwin Mfg. Co.
Tabular Comparison of Different Depreciation Methods

Year	Straight-Line Depreciation Charge	Straight-Line End-of-Year Book Value	Production Depreciation Charge	Production End-of-Year Book Value	Sum-of-the-Years'-Digits Depreciation Charge	Sum-of-the-Years'-Digits End-of-Year Book Value	Double-Declining Balance Depreciation Charge	Double-Declining Balance End-of-Year Book Value
0		$12,500		$12,500		$12,500		$12,500
1	$ 2,280	10,220	$ 4,500	8,000	$ 3,800	8,700	$ 5,000	7,500
2	2,280	7,940	4,000	4,000	3,040	5,660	3,000	4,500
3	2,280	5,660	1,000	3,000	2,280	3,380	1,800	2,700
4	2,280	3,380	1,000	2,000	1,520	1,860	1,080	1,620
5	2,280	1,100	900	1,100	760	1,100	648	972
Total	$11,400		$11,400		$11,400		$11,528	

If the initial prediction of scrap value ($1,100) is correct, Year 5 depreciation under the twice-straight-line-on-the-declining-balance method will be $128 less than shown above ($1,100 − $972 = $128).

Calculations:

Straight-line. The annual depreciation charge will be one-fifth of the total amount to be amortized: ($12,500 − $1,100)/5 = $11,400/5 = $2,280.

Production. If the $11,400 amount to be amortized is to be allocated to the 45,600 estimated units of product, the depreciation rate will be 25¢ per unit ($11,400/45,600 = 25¢). Alternatively, the depreciation charges may be calculated as follows:

Year	Estimated Amount to be Amortized	×	Estimated Production for Year	÷	Estimated Total Production	=	Depreciation Charge
1	$11,400	×	18,000	÷	45,600	=	$4,500
2	11,400	×	16,000	÷	45,600	=	4,000
3	11,400	×	4,000	÷	45,600	=	1,000
4	11,400	×	4,000	÷	45,600	=	1,000
5	11,400	×	3,600	÷	45,600	=	900

Sum-of-the-years'-digits. The sum of the integers 1 through 5 is 15; therefore, depreciation for Year 1 will be five-fifteenths the $11,400 amount to be amortized, and so forth:

Year	Amount to be Amortized	Multiplier	Depreciation Charge
1	$11,400	5/15	$3,800
2	11,400	4/15	3,040
3	11,400	3/15	2,280
4	11,400	2/15	1,520
5	11,400	1/15	760

Double declining balance. The straight-line depreciation rate is one-fifth of the total amount to be amortized. Therefore, the double declining balance rate will be two-fifths of the beginning-of-year book value:

Year	Beginning-of-Year Book Value	Multiplier	Depreciation Charge	End-of-Year Book Value
1	$12,500	2/5	$5,000	$7,500
2	7,500	2/5	3,000	4,500
3	4,500	2/5	1,800	2,700
4	2,700	2/5	1,080	1,620
5	1,620	2/5	648	972

2.

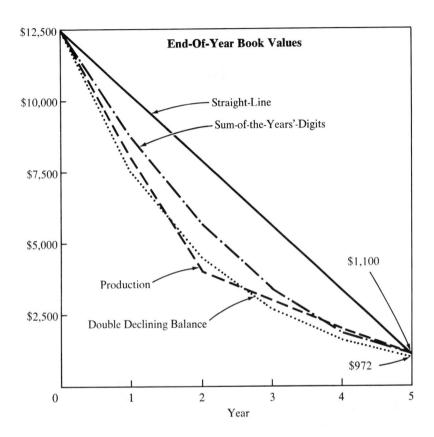

Illustration 13-8

Baldwin Mfg. Co.
Comparison of Depreciation Methods

End-Of-Year Book Values

Straight-Line

Sum-of-the-Years'-Digits

$1,100

Production

Double Declining Balance

$972

Year

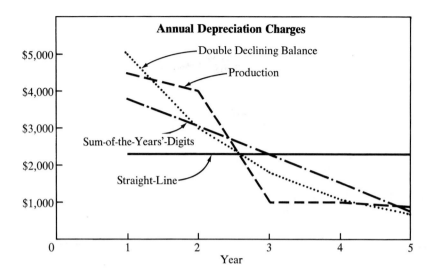

3. The accountant might first wish to know whether this machine could be used to manufacture some product other than the novelty product. If such additional use seems likely, the machine might offer approximately the same amount of services in each of the five years. In that case, straight-line depreciation would seem the most appropriate, but some further questions should first be answered. Will the machine be more expensive to run in later years? (Will it spoil work, require higher maintenance expenditures or more skilled labor?) If so, the net services that the machine provides may decline to such an extent that straight-line depreciation would not be so appropriate as a declining-charge method.

If the machine is so specialized that it can produce only the novelty product, are the accountant's production estimates reliable enough to justify using production depreciation, or can the accountant really say nothing more than that he expects the services offered by the machine to decline? In the latter case, one of the declining-charge methods may be the most appropriate. If a declining-charge method *is* to be used, should it be the one that gives the most rapid amortization?

These questions are intended to be suggestive of the problems facing the accountant, not an exhaustive list of all problems facing him. Five-year estimates of output are risky for *any* product, and for something as unpredictable as a novelty product, they may be of little significance. Hence, the production method seems inappropriate here. The choice between a straight-line and a declining-charge method would depend heavily on the prospects of an alternate use for the machine. Notice that the accountant's decision will be based on a number of subjective considerations—what *he* predicts as the outcome of the situation, how reliable *he* believes the various estimates are, and so forth.

Solution 13-2 (*Brain-teaser*):

The student's mother was allocating one-twelfth of annual property taxes and depreciation to each month. Since monthly revenues were very low in the winter, the result was that she was comparing normal-sized expenses with subnormal revenues—operations at a loss—for about one-third of the year. (Cleaning expenses were less than normal during the winter, but this was offset by higher-than-normal heating and lighting bills and, possibly, by higher-than-normal repair bills if repairs tended to be done when business was slack.)

The obvious first suggestion was that she stop preparing monthly financial statements, since they didn't mean much in her circumstances. She was required to prepare them, however, as part of a loan agreement. That being so, her problem was that she was allocating to the winter months costs that really were incurred for benefits to be obtained in the summer months—a poor way to match revenues with expenses.

It would have been less confusing had she allocated most of such costs as charges against related summer revenues. For instance, she might better have allocated the annual depreciation charge to the individual months in the following manner:

$$\text{Depreciation charge for month} = \text{Annual depreciation charge} \times \frac{\text{Revenue for same month last year}}{\text{Total revenue for last year}}$$

A similar allocation would be made of property taxes and other annual charges. (According to her son, she eventually adopted some such allocation method.)

Variety allowed in accounting practice

Earlier in this chapter it was stressed that accountants are unable to make defensible depreciation calculations and have had to settle for rough, arbitrary estimates. This has had a confusing side effect.

Financial statements are reports *by management* about what has happened to the company during the year and about the company's current status. As mentioned in Chapter One, the job of the auditor is to review management's report to make sure that it meets minimum standards of propriety:

> Financial accounting reports are prepared by the company's own financial accountants from the company's own records. The auditor examines these financial reports and the underlying records to make sure that the required information is complete, that it is supported by evidence, *and that it is prepared according to good accounting practice.*

When matters of objective fact (such as the primary measurements of cash balance at year end) are under consideration, the auditor is in a strong position to insist that one particular amount be reported. If management decides to follow one depreciation method, however, and the auditor prefers another, there are serious limits on what the auditor can do (assuming that management has chosen one of the standard methods). *The auditor has no way of conclusively demonstrating to management that his depreciation method is correct and that management's is wrong!* For, as we have seen, any depreciation method is as defensible (or indefensible) as any of an unlimited number of others. And this problem is not confined to depreciation, but pertains to the amortization of *any* nonmonetary asset (and, for that matter, to secondary measurements in general).

To be sure, any auditor worth his salt will argue with the company's management when he believes that a mistaken judgment has been made. The auditor also can insist upon the following:

1. The depreciation method selected by the company must be one from a limited set of "standard" accounting practices—a set that is acceptable for institutional purposes, and that reflects the varying practices of other companies in similar circumstances. For example, the company may have the option of amortizing a depreciable asset according to any one of several different depreciation methods. It also may be able to choose from a range of possible estimated service lives and estimated scrap values, for these are matters of estimate and subjective judgment. The auditor may have to accept all of these decisions, but he still can insist that the company refrain from writing off the entire expenditure in the year of purchase or in the year of retirement. This is what the auditor means when he says in his formal opinion that the financial statements were prepared "in conformity with generally accepted accounting principles."[6]

2. The alternatives employed must be followed consistently. Once a company has decided to depreciate a particular asset by the straight-line method, it ordinarily may not change its mind a few years later and depreciate the same asset according to sum-of-the-years'-digits depreciation. This is what the auditor means when he says in his formal opinion that the company's accounting practices have been "applied on a basis consistent with that of the preceding year." It is hoped that this requirement, together with insistence upon use of a "generally accepted" method, will prevent deliberate manipulation of the profit figures by management. However, the requirement of consistency does *not* mean that the company cannot use sum-of-the-years'-digits depreciation with the next depreciable asset it purchases, even though it is depreciating the latest asset straight-line. The company can do whatever it likes (limited only by the "standard" alternatives) the next time, so long as the surrounding circumstances differ enough that management's subjective evaluation of the situation can also differ.[7]

---

[6] The auditor's opinion was illustrated in Chapter One. Here again is the usual language employed in it. Take special note of the last phrase, beginning with "in conformity. . . ."

We have examined the balance sheet of NAME OF COMPANY as of DATE and the related statements of income and sources and uses of net working capital for the year then ended. Our examination was made in accordance with generally accepted auditing standards, and accordingly included such tests of the accounting records and such other auditing procedures as we considered necessary in the circumstances.

In our opinion, the accompanying financial statements present fairly the financial position of NAME OF COMPANY at DATE and the results of its operations for the year ended, in conformity with generally accepted accounting principles applied on a basis consistent with that of the preceding year.

[7] Some accountants would argue that the requirement of consistency restricts management more than I have stated. I agree that management *should* be consistent from one decision to the next, but, from what I've seen in practice, companies may employ quite different depreciation methods with assets purchased in successive years, even when the assets seem similar. This will be acceptable under present APB opinions as long as factors determining the choice of method are perceived to have changed, and footnote information concerning the effects of the change in method is provided to readers.

As long as management chooses its alternatives from among "generally accepted accounting principles"—chooses one of the four depreciation methods mentioned and one of the many possible service-life and scrap-value estimates—most auditors believe that there is little that they can do to challenge the results, even if they disagree with the subjective evaluations involved. *This means that in matters requiring subjective judgment, management is free within the limits set by law, regulation, custom, and the policy of other companies, to specify whatever accounting practices it wishes.* These limits allow management great latitude in the depreciation pattern selected. Accordingly, companies in similar situations may report quite different figures on their financial statements, which hinders comparability of one company with another. Investors wish to use financial statements in making such comparisons; thus the problems discussed here place a major restriction on the usefulness of the accountant's reports.

This discussion has been simplified: other factors have influenced the variety of amortization methods allowed to management (one of these, taxation, is discussed toward the end of this chapter), and differences in amortization methods tend to cancel out (on the income statement, but *not* on the balance sheet) if they are applied consistently for a number of years to various assets of different ages. Still the comparability problem remains one of the more serious problems affecting financial accounting today.

Correction of errors in depreciation estimates

Considering all of the estimates and rough approximations required in depreciation accounting, it should be evident that errors are bound to occur. How are these errors handled?

If the error in depreciation estimates is minor, it will be dealt with by reporting a gain or a loss on the ultimate retirement of the asset; such a gain or loss would never have happened had all estimates been precise. Even though such gains and losses appear on the income statement of a particular year, they really apply to the activities of all previous years since the asset was acquired, and are largely a correction of past years' reported incomes.

If detected in time, serious errors should be corrected *during* the service life of the depreciable asset. There are two possible ways to do this:

1. In theory, you should determine what the depreciation charges of prior years should have been, make a correction, and thereafter show "correct" depreciation figures, consistent with the revised estimates.

2. In practice, the accountant usually changes only the remaining depreciation on the asset to make it consistent with the revised estimates of service life and/or scrap value. This is partly an expedient decision, but can be defended on the grounds that depreciation estimates are rough at best. The effect of this approach is to offset past errors with future errors in the opposite direction.

Example of correcting depreciation estimates

An example will clarify the alternatives involved here. Presuppose the same facts as in the previous example for Ojai Company. In the situation described here, Ojai Company elects to use straight-line depreciation. The journal entries for the first three years (assuming that the machine is factory equipment and was purchased on account) would be:

Beginning	Equipment	30,618	
of Year 1	Accounts Payable		30,618
End of Years	Factory Overhead	4,655	
1, 2, and 3	Equipment—Accumulated Depreciation		4,655

At the end of Year 3, accumulated depreciation on this equipment is $13,965 ($4,655 × 3 = $13,965); the machine's book value is $16,653 ($30,618 − $13,965 = $16,653).

Suppose that, during Year 4, new estimates are prepared, and it is decided that the machine will have a total service life of only five years, with a scrap value upon retirement of only $618. This means that depreciation for the last three years has been insufficient. Nothing can be done *directly* to change past depreciation figures, for the books have been closed on these years, and the related financial statements have been published and distributed. In theory, however, you could correct the error on Year 4's income statement. In the correction that follows, it is assumed that all finished goods manufactured in Year 3 have been sold, so that no prior-year depreciation remains as part of the acquisition price of the company's inventories.

Accumulated depreciation is $13,965. It *should be* $18,000 [($30,618 − $618) × 3/5 = $18,000]. Accumulated depreciation therefore has been underestimated by $4,035 ($18,000 − $13,965 = $4,035). The following entry could be made to correct this error:

During	Correction of Prior Years' Earnings for		
Year 4	Underestimation of Depreciation	4,035	
	Equipment—Accumulated Depreciation		4,035

What is the nature of the account Correction of Prior Years' Earnings for Underestimation of Depreciation? From a standpoint of strict logic, it could be argued that the firm's retained earnings is the place where errors of prior years are reflected; therefore this account represents what should be a direct correction of retained earnings, having nothing whatever to do with the current years' income statement or statement of cost of goods manufactured and sold.

In recent years, however, the accountant has been required to reflect almost all such corrections on the income statement. The logic behind this requirement is that such corrections are generally unfavorable, and that if these corrections were not reflected on the income statement there would, over a period of years, be an upward bias to reported net income. Since the error was *made* on past income statements, it should be corrected on an income statement, too.

As we saw on pages 405–406, if this correction is large enough in comparison to net income, it will be reported at the bottom of the income statement as an extraordinary item. Otherwise (and more often) it simply would be added to the year's total depreciation charge (thus it would be reflected immediately on the statement of cost of goods manufactured and sold, and as the goods of that year were sold, it would appear on the income statement as additional cost of goods sold). In any event, in Years 4 and 5, depreciation would be charged at the "correct" rate of $6,000 per year [($30,618 − $618)/5 = $6,000].

End of Years	Factory Overhead	6,000	
4 and 5	Equipment—Accumulated Depreciation		6,000

In Illustration 13-9, the line ABE represents the original straight-line depreciation pattern whereby the acquisition price of $30,618 was to be amortized to an estimated scrap value of $2,618. The line ACD represents the depreciation pattern appropriate to the revised estimates. The segment BC represents the $4,035 correction. Using this approach, the overall depreciation pattern will follow the line ABCD.

Illustration 13-9

Ojai Company
Two Ways of Correcting Errors in Depreciation

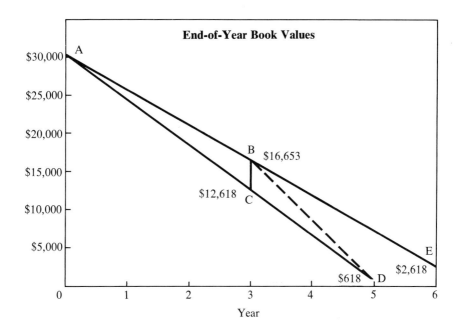

Usually, though, the accountant will avoid making any correction of prior years' earnings, and will merely compensate for his previous underdepreciation by over-depreciating in Years 4 and 5. At the end of Year 3, the machine had a book value of $16,653. It is now estimated that, after two more years of life, it will have a scrap value of $618. Amortization from $16,653 to $618 can be accomplished by charging depreciation of $8,017.50 [($16,653 − $618)/2 = $8,017.50] per year during Years 4 and 5:

End of Years	Factory Overhead	8,017.50	
4 and 5	Equipment—Accumulated Depreciation		8,017.50

In Illustration 13-9, this tactic is represented by line segment BD.

Of course, if the amount involved is not material (not significant), the accountant might make no correction or change in depreciation rates. Instead, he might wait until the asset was retired at the end of Year 5, and record a loss on retirement of $6,725 [$30,618 − (5 × $4,655) − $618 = $6,725]:

End of Years	Factory Overhead	4,655	
1 through 5	Equipment—Accumulated Depreciation		4,655
End of	Cash	618	
Year 5	Equipment—Accumulated Depreciation	23,275	
	Loss on Retirement of Equipment	6,725	
	Equipment		30,618

Although this example involved a case of underdepreciation, the same alternatives would arise had depreciation been excessive. The one exception would occur in the case where an asset had been depreciated below its true scrap value on retirement. Here, either recognition of a gain on retirement or a correction of prior years' earnings would be the only alternatives (since what had been the third alternative with underdepreciation would here require *ap*preciating the asset over its remaining life, something the accountant ordinarily refuses to do).

Misconceptions about depreciation

One final point might be made about depreciation before we turn to other matters. At present the public holds several misconceptions concerning depreciation. Two of these were discussed in connection with funds statements on pages 471–472: that depreciation is a source of funds, and that depreciation is not a bona-fide expense. There are at least two more popular misconceptions:

1. That depreciation reflects declines in market values. As we have seen throughout this book, depreciable assets are recorded at their historical costs instead of at their current market values. Therefore, except by coincidence there is no correspondence between a depreciation charge and the decline in market value of the depreciable asset during a particular period. Indeed, an asset may properly be depreciated during a period in which its market value is *rising*; the two phenomena are simply unrelated.

2. That depreciation is being charged to provide for replacement of assets. This misconception may be related to the misconception that depreciation is a source of funds. Depreciation charges do reduce reported net income, and this reduction may result in lower dividend payments; depreciation for tax purposes results in lower taxable income and, therefore, lower tax payments. But otherwise depreciation has no connection whatever with the firm's monetary position, and therefore has no direct relationship to the availability of funds for purchases of replacement assets. Instead, as we saw in Chapter Seven, these funds come from operations, from incidental sales of used non-

monetary assets, and from issue of long-term equities. Finally, it might be noted that many industries are experiencing technological change so rapid that assets now being depreciated will never be replaced at all.

The main point that unifies most of these misconceptions is that many members of the general public are unaware of the very strict interpretation accountants give to depreciation: as nothing more than an allocation of historical cost. Unfortunately, the discussion in this chapter suggests that even when depreciation figures are understood in the sense intended by the accountant, still another misconception may remain: depreciation figures may be much less reliable than many individuals have supposed.

Problem for Study and Self-Examination

Problem 13-3:

On January 1, 19X1, McFall Chrome Products Co. purchased plating equipment for $295,000. It was expected that this equipment would have a service life of 14 years, and a scrap value upon retirement of $15,000. The equipment was depreciated straight-line, at a rate of $20,000 per year [($295,000 − $15,000)/14 = $20,000]. The company prepares financial statements once a year, every December 31. By December 31, 19X6, six years' depreciation had accumulated on this equipment, a total of $120,000 ($20,000 × 6 = $120,000); the equipment's book value was $175,000 ($295,000 − $120,000 = $175,000).

During 19X7, it became evident that the equipment was becoming increasingly obsolete when compared with competing machinery, and that it would have to be retired and replaced when only 10 years old. (It was estimated, however, that it would still have a $15,000 scrap value upon retirement.) The error is regarded as being of material significance.

Discuss in detail the alternatives open to the accountant.

Solution

Solution 13-3:

Since the error is considered material, there are two alternatives open to the accountant:

1. The equipment's present book value is $175,000. In four years, it will be worth $160,000 less ($175,000 − $15,000 = $160,000). The accountant *could* depreciate the machine at a rate of $40,000 per year during its remaining four-year service life ($160,000/4 = $40,000).

2. Alternately, the accountant could argue that this machine has been depreciated too slowly—that instead of being depreciated at a rate of $20,000 per year, it should have been depreciated at a rate of $28,000 per year [($295,000 − $15,000)/10 = $28,000]. Using this reasoning, the accountant would correct the accumulated depreciation for six years of insufficient depreciation, a total error of $48,000 [($28,000 − $20,000) × 6 = $48,000], then charge depreciation at the "correct" $28,000 rate for the four remaining years.

Illustration 13-10 is a graphic comparison of these two possibilities.

Inventories

Up to now we have assumed that all units of any individual inventory item were purchased at the same price. As long as this is the case, the accountant finds it simple to allocate inventory costs: he simply counts the units used and multiplies the result by the common price, using the procedures illustrated on pages 103–104.

Things become more complicated when, as is more often the case, the firm buys several lots of a particular inventory item at different prices. Earlier in this chapter you learned that if a nonmonetary asset is a known-service asset (performing a single type of service, and for which individual receipts and total amounts are easily and reliably estimated), the accountant will use a production approach in its amortization. An inventory lot (defined on page 103) is a nonmonetary asset that meets this test. The kind of service provided depends upon how the inventory is used—that is, whether units are sold to outsiders or employed in manufacturing; however, inventory service is usually clear-cut. Amounts of service received and available are conventionally reflected in numbers of individual units of inventory; if the total lot contained 10,000 units and 2,000 have subsequently been employed in manufacturing, it is easily argued that the lot should now be 20 percent amortized.

Accordingly, inventory lots are always amortized by the production method; yet another problem arises with inventories—one that leads to as diverse a set of alternative accounting techniques as those employed for depreciation. The discussion of depreciable assets did not become concerned over the *order* in which assets are employed, for they are all used simultaneously. With inventory lots, the order of use is not this clear.

Illustration 13-10

McFall Chrome Products Co.
Alternate Ways of Correcting Depreciation Error

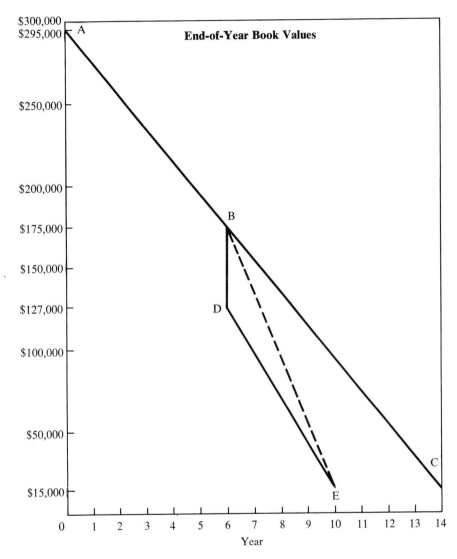

Legend:

Line ABC is the equipment's original depreciation pattern, based on the original service-life
   estimate.
Line ABE is the depreciation pattern if no correction is made and the remaining depreciable
   base is charged over the remaining life.
Line ABDE is the depreciation pattern if a correction is made and correct depreciation is
   charged over the remaining life.

Here is an example: Martinez Company is a retailer. During 19X1, the company began dealing in a new product, for which the acquisition price was somewhat variable. The company sold 7,500 units of this product, at $9.98 per unit:

Cash	74,850	
Sales		74,850

Purchases were as follows:

Lot Number	Number of Units	Unit Price	Total Price
1	2,000	$6.00	$12,000
2	3,000	5.80	17,400
3	3,000	6.10	18,300
4	2,000	6.30	12,600
Total	10,000		$60,300

The problem is to determine the total cost of goods sold, and the amount to associate with the 2,500 units in the ending inventory (10,000 − 7,500 = 2,500).

Specific identification method

One plausible-sounding way to do this would be to keep separate track of each lot, and see exactly which units of which lot were sold. For example, it might be determined that all of Lots 1 and 2 had been sold, and that 1,250 units each remained from Lots 3 and 4. In that case, the cost of the 2,500-unit ending inventory would be:

Lot 3	1,250 @ $6.10 =	$ 7,625
Lot 4	1,250 @ $6.30 =	7,875
Total	2,500	$15,500

The cost of goods sold would then be $44,800 ($60,300 − $15,500 = $44,800). There are three main drawbacks to such specific identification of inventory units with the lots from which they came:

1. First, from a theoretical standpoint the method seems inappropriate. The specific identification method matches costs with revenues on the basis of actual physical phenomena (goods physically sold versus goods not physically sold). Yet the accounting model is designed to reflect economic, not physical relationships— and, of course, the economic significance of the various units of the inventory item is the same. Accordingly, the specific identification approach is based on an irrelevant consideration. This argument should not be pressed very hard, though, since the cost flows assumed by the inventory methods discussed below have implicit physical flows, too. The difference is that the physical flow is crucial to the specific identification method, whereas it is of only peripheral significance to the other inventory methods (indeed, at least one of these is used *despite* its implied physical flow).

2. It is costly to keep units of identical items distinct from each other. The specific identification approach to inventory costing usually involves excessive ac-

counting effort unless the individual units are fairly expensive (the method *is* often employed with automobiles and fine jewelry).

3. Use of the specific identification method offers obvious opportunities for unintentional or intentional manipulation of profits by management. This will be illustrated by an extreme example. Suppose that the inventory of a securities dealer includes 200 shares of the common stock of a manufacturing company: 100 of these shares were purchased in 1933 at $5 per share, the other 100 in 1968 at $200 per share. The securities dealer sells 100 shares at $180 per share. If specific identification is employed (and it *is* used with securities inventories), management may report anywhere from a $17,500 profit to a $2,000 loss depending upon which shares it elects to sell [100 × ($180 − $5) = $17,500; 100 × ($200 − $180) = $2,000]. While the extent of potential manipulation is rarely this extreme, its possibility has given the method a bad name.[8]

Cost-flow assumptions

If the accountant does not specifically identify the lots from which individual inventory units come, he must make some assumption, usually called a *cost-flow assumption,* about the pattern of lot utilization. Just as it is common for depreciation methods to correspond only roughly with the estimated pattern of the depreciable asset's service, so *it is common for accountants to employ lot-utilization assumptions that fail to correspond closely with the actual pattern of lot utilization.* In fact, and this also parallels the depreciation situation, management is free to choose any of several such assumptions. There are three widely accepted inventory cost-flow assumptions:

1. Simultaneous utilization of all lots at the same proportionate rate.
2. Utilization of lots in sequence, oldest lots first.
3. Utilization of lots in sequence, newest lots first.

Simultaneous utilization of all lots

One very natural approach would be to treat inventory lots in the same way that the accountant treats depreciable assets, and assume that all lots that are on hand during a given period of time are utilized proportionately. In the Martinez Company example, 4 lots containing a total of 10,000 units were available during the year, at a total cost of $60,300. Proportionate utilization would involve 75 percent (7,500/ 10,000 = 75%) of each lot being sold. The cost of goods sold would be:

Lot 1	2,000 × $6.00 × 75% =	$ 9,000
Lot 2	3,000 × $5.80 × 75% =	13,050
Lot 3	3,000 × $6.10 × 75% =	13,725
Lot 4	2,000 × $6.30 × 75% =	9,450
Total		$45,225

---

[8] You may already have concluded that equally serious dangers of manipulation are present with depreciable assets, but none of the individual depreciation methods provides as clear-cut and obvious a danger as does specific identification of inventories.

Of course, this is an inefficient way to calculate the cost of goods sold. A quicker way to get the same result is:

$60,300 × 7,500/10,000 = $45,225,
    where 7,500/10,000 is again the proportion of the total units sold.

The ending inventory would then be reported as $15,075:

$$\begin{array}{ccc} & \text{Cost of} & \text{Ending} \\ \text{Total cost} - & \text{goods sold} = & \text{inventory} \\ \$60,300 \quad - & \$45,225 \quad = & \$15,075 \end{array}$$

or, alternately,

$$\begin{array}{ccc} & \text{Proportion of total} & \text{Ending} \\ \text{Total cost} \times & \text{units that were not sold} = & \text{inventory} \\ \$60,300 \quad \times & 2,500/10,000 & = \$15,075[9] \end{array}$$

The inventory method involved here is usually called (naturally enough) the *average approach,* for, as the second cost of goods sold calculation reveals, the 7,500 units sold are simply being recorded at the average cost of all inventories on hand during the year.

Utilization in sequence, oldest lots first

If you do not assume simultaneous utilization of all lots, you must assume that they are used in some kind of sequence, or order. It should be emphasized again that once you reject the specific identification method, the *actual* sequence of utilization becomes irrelevant. But it is natural enough to use the sequence in which, ordinarily, inventory lots *should* be utilized.

Typically, it is good business practice to use oldest lots first, before they have time to deteriorate. Antiques and whiskey are exceptions. Ordinarily, good inventory management resembles a thrifty housewife who serves the leftovers before preparing a new roast. Following this oldest-lot-is-used-first assumption, the cost of goods sold would be:

Lot 1	2,000 @ $6.00 =	$12,000
Lot 2	3,000 @ $5.80 =	17,400
Lot 3	2,500 @ $6.10 =	15,250
Lot 4	–0– @ $6.30 =	–0–
Total	7,500	$44,650

---

[9] You may have noticed that there is an implicit assumption here that the "given period of time" during which all inventory lots are pictured as being used proportionately is *one year*. This one-year assumption will be used throughout this discussion, but obviously it need not be made: there are simultaneous utilization approaches in which the period is as short as one day, leading to somewhat different cost of goods sold and ending inventory figures.

The ending inventory would be $15,650 ($60,300 − $44,650 = $15,650):

Lot 3	500 @ $6.10 =	$ 3,050
Lot 4	2,000 @ $6.30 =	12,600
Total	2,500	$15,650

This inventory method is called the *first-in-first-out method,* abbreviated as *FIFO.* The FIFO abbreviation, pronounced to rhyme with "pie dough," is used more often than the full name.

Utilization in sequence, newest lots first

The FIFO method represents one possible extreme. Since the accountant is not paying attention to the actual sequence of lot utilization, he could just as well go to the opposite extreme, and assume that the lots most recently acquired were used first. In most cases this would be a dreadful way to manage the physical units, but it is entirely possible as a *cost-flow assumption.* Following this newest-lot-is-used-first assumption, the cost of goods sold would be:

Lot 1	–0– @ $6.00 = $	–0–
Lot 2	2,500 @ $5.80 =	14,500
Lot 3	3,000 @ $6.10 =	18,300
Lot 4	2,000 @ $6.30 =	12,600
Total	7,500	$45,400

The ending inventory would be $14,900 ($60,300 − $45,400 = $14,900):

Lot 1	2,000 @ $6.00 =	$12,000
Lot 2	500 @ $5.80 =	2,900
Total	2,500	$14,900

This inventory method is usually called the *last-in-first-out,* or LIFO method. Once again, the LIFO abbreviation, which also rhymes with "pie dough," is used more often than the full name.

The inventory methods compared

Illustration 13-11 compares the results of the three cost-flow assumptions. LIFO gives the highest cost of goods sold in this case, as it usually does in a period of rising prices, simply because it composes the cost of goods sold out of the most recent (highest) prices. The figures for average cost fall between those for LIFO and FIFO, but not symmetrically because there have not been equal-sized lots and uniform price increases. Even though it is common for the average figures to fall between the FIFO and LIFO figures, this need not occur under certain kinds of price fluctuations, as demonstrated in the subsection immediately below.

Illustration 13-11

Martinez Company
Inventory Cost-Flow Assumptions
19X1

	Cost of Goods Sold	Ending Inventory
FIFO	$44,650	$15,650
Average	45,225	15,075
LIFO	45,400	14,900

The different inventory methods yield different cost of goods sold figures. Ignoring taxes for the time being, no other expense is affected by the choice of an inventory method, nor is the amount of sales. Therefore, the different inventory methods also affect reported net income for the period in question. In the previous example, FIFO leads to reporting the lowest cost of goods sold and, therefore, to reporting the highest net income. Similarly, in the previous example, the next highest net income will be reported under the average method, and the lowest will be yielded by LIFO. However just as the relative sizes of cost of goods sold under the three methods will vary under different circumstances, it is perfectly possible for, say, LIFO to yield the highest net income under other circumstances.

The previous example involved the merchandise inventory of a retailer. But similar examples could have been prepared for a manufacturer's inventories of raw materials or finished goods. An average or a FIFO cost flow usually is assumed for work in process inventories.

Extending the example. As a further illustration, the previous example of Martinez Company will be extended into a second year. You may wish to make the calculations for yourself before looking at the results.

During 19X2, Martinez Company purchased the following lots:

Lot Number	Number of Units	Unit Price	Total Price
5	3,500	$6.15	$21,525
6	2,000	6.35	12,700
7	4,000	6.10	24,400
Total	9,500		$58,625

A total of 9,000 units was sold. Determine the cost of goods sold and the ending inventory under the average, FIFO, and LIFO cost-flow assumptions.

Average. Unlike the 19X1 example, there now is a beginning inventory to be taken into consideration. The following units were available during 19X2:

	Number of Units	Amount
Beginning inventory	2,500	$15,075
Purchased during year	9,500	58,625
Total	12,000	$73,700

The cost of goods sold will be $55,275 [(9,000/12,000) × $73,700 = $55,275]. The ending inventory will be $18,425 [($73,700 − $55,275 = $18,425) or (3,000/12,000 × $73,700 = $18,425)].

FIFO. The beginning inventory was 500 units from Lot 3 and 2,000 units from Lot 4. The cost of goods sold will be:

Lot 3	500 @ $6.10 =	$ 3,050
Lot 4	2,000 @ $6.30 =	12,600
Lot 5	3,500 @ $6.15 =	21,525
Lot 6	2,000 @ $6.35 =	12,700
Lot 7	1,000 @ $6.10 =	6,100
Total	9,000	$55,975

The ending inventory will be $18,300 ($15,650 + $58,625 − $55,975 = $18,300):

Lot 7	3,000 @ $6.10 =	$18,300

LIFO. The beginning inventory was 2,000 units from Lot 1 and 500 units from Lot 2. The cost of goods sold will be:

Lot 1	–0– @ $6.00 =	$ –0–
Lot 2	–0– @ $5.80 =	–0–
Lot 5	3,000 @ $6.15 =	18,450
Lot 6	2,000 @ $6.35 =	12,700
Lot 7	4,000 @ $6.10 =	24,400
Total	9,000	$55,550

The ending inventory will be $17,975 ($14,900 + $58,625 − $55,550 = $17,975):

Lot 1	2,000 @ $6.00 =	$12,000
Lot 2	500 @ $5.80 =	2,900
Lot 5	500 @ $6.15 =	3,075
Total	3,000	$17,975

The three methods are compared in Illustration 13-12.

Illustration 13-12

Martinez Company
Inventory Cost-Flow Assumptions
19X2

	Cost of Goods Sold	*Ending Inventory*	*Net Income*
Average	$55,275	$18,425	Highest
LIFO	55,550	17,975	Middle
FIFO	55,975	18,300	Lowest

The result of the somewhat erratic price fluctuations in 19X2 is that the *average* method gives the lowest cost of goods sold, the highest net income, and the highest ending inventory. Generally speaking, in periods of fluctuating prices it is hard to guess in advance what the effect of any particular cost-flow assumption will be. All you are entitled to say is that if prices are rising, LIFO *tends* to give the highest cost of goods sold, lowest net income, and lowest ending inventory figures, whereas if prices are falling, the reverse tends to be true.

Strict versus modified LIFO

In the previous example, the number of inventory units purchased in 19X2 exceeded the number that was sold. Had the reverse been true, there would have been two ways in which 19X2 LIFO cost of goods sold and ending inventory could be calculated. This can be demonstrated by modifying the Martinez Company example. As before, Martinez Company's 19X2 beginning inventory and purchases were:

Lot 1	2,000 @ $6.00 =	$12,000
Lot 2	500 @ $5.80 =	2,900
Beginning inventory	2,500	$14,900
Lot 5	3,500 @ $6.15 =	21,525
Lot 6	2,000 @ $6.35 =	12,700
Lot 7	4,000 @ $6.10 =	24,400
Total	12,000	$73,525

Suppose now that in 19X2 the firm sold 10,000 units. Under any LIFO method 19X2 cost of goods sold will include costs of Lots 5, 6, and 7. But how shall the costs of the beginning inventory be handled? Under what may be called the *strict LIFO* approach, one would systematically continue to work backward through the lots, and calculate 19X2 cost of goods sold as follows:

Lot 1	–0– @ $6.00 = $	–0–
Lot 2	500 @ $5.80 =	2,900
Lot 5	3,500 @ $6.15 =	21,525
Lot 6	2,000 @ $6.35 =	12,700
Lot 7	4,000 @ $6.10 =	24,400
	10,000	$61,525

The 12/31/X2 ending inventory then would be reported at the cost of Lot 1, or $12,000.

The main difficulty with the strict LIFO method is a clerical one: it requires keeping records of the detailed composition of beginning inventories. This composition may become quite complicated if, over a number of years, purchases have slightly exceeded sales (as they are apt to in a growing business). The beginning inventory of each inventory item may be composed of numerous fractional lots.

As a practical alternative, the beginning inventory often is treated as a single lot—in this case 2,500 units at an average unit cost of $14,900 ÷ 2,500 = $5.96. In that event, 19X2 cost of goods sold would be calculated as follows:

Beginning inventory	500 @ $5.96 =	$ 2,980
Lot 5	3,500 @ $6.15 =	21,525
Lot 6	2,000 @ $6.35 =	12,700
Lot 7	4,000 @ $6.10 =	24,400
	10,000	$61,605

and the 12/31/X2 ending inventory would be 2,000 × $5.96 = $11,920. This clerically simpler form of LIFO may be called the *modified LIFO* method. The "modification," of course, is to apply the average method to the firm's beginning inventory.

Consistency

We saw earlier in this chapter that, although a firm had several different depreciation methods from which to choose, once a particular method had been selected for a particular asset, that method must be adhered to consistently. There is a similar consistency requirement for inventories: once an inventory method has been chosen for a particular inventory item, the firm must use the same method for that item in subsequent years. But, as was also true of depreciable assets, there is no requirement that the same inventory method be used with all kinds of inventories. Instead, the firm could use FIFO with one kind of inventory, LIFO with another, and average with a third without being regarded as inconsistent, as long as the underlying circumstances were perceived to differ and the firm continued to use the different methods in subsequent years.

Similar problems with other nonmonetary assets

Allocation problems similar to those of inventories can emerge whenever a firm owning two or more identical nonmonetary assets that were purchased at different prices wishes to sell part of its holdings. In most such cases the specific identification method is used. Once again, the results will be arbitrary.

Problems for Study and Self-Examination

Problem 13-4:

Manteca Industries prepares financial statements once a year, every December 31. The following data refer to a valve purchased by the company and used in manufacturing one of its products.

19X1	Number of Units	Unit Cost	Amount
Beginning inventory	–0–		
Purchases*	500	$4.00	$2,000
	300	$4.10	1,230
	300	$4.23	1,269
Total	1,100		
Used in manufacturing	700		
Ending inventory	400		
19X2			
Beginning inventory	400		
Purchases*	200	$4.27	$ 854
	400	$4.30	1,720
Total	1,000		
Used in manufacturing	800		
Ending inventory	200		

* *Listed in order of purchase.*

Determine the company's cost of valves used in manufacturing and its ending valve inventory for 19X1 and 19X2. Use the average, FIFO, and both strict and modified LIFO cost-flow assumptions.

Problem 13-5:

Champaign-Shipley Inc. uses the periodic inventory method. It records purchases of merchandise correctly, but its procedures for determining the amounts of its year-end merchandise inventories are imperfect and lead to minor errors that are never detected by the firm. The following mistakes were made by the firm during the period 12/31/X0 through 12/31/X6:

> 12/31/X0: No errors
> 12/31/X1: Ending inventories were overstated by $2,130
> 12/31/X2: No errors
> 12/31/X3: Ending inventories were understated by $1,170
> 12/31/X4: Ending inventories were overstated by $920
> 12/31/X5: Ending inventories were overstated by $1,360
> 12/31/X6: No errors

What were the effects of these errors on the firm's income statements and year-end balance sheets for 19X1 through 19X6? You may assume that all inventories on hand at year-end are sold during the subsequent year and that the firm uses FIFO.

Solutions

Solution 13-4:

	Average	FIFO	LIFO
19X1 cost of valves used in manufacturing	$2,863	$2,820	$2,899
19X1 cost of ending valve inventory	1,636	1,679	1,600
19X2 cost of valves used in manufacturing	$3,368	$3,393	$3,374
19X2 cost of ending valve inventory	842	860	800

Calculations:

Average: In 19X1, 1,100 units were available at a total cost of $4,499 ($2,000 + $1,230 + $1,269 = $4,499).

The cost of valves used was 7/11 × $4,499	$2,863	
The ending inventory was 4/11 × $4,499	1,636	$4,499

In 19X2, 1,000 units were available at a total cost of $4,210 ($1,636 + $854 + $1,720 = $4,210).

The cost of valves used was 8/10 × $4,210	$3,368	
The ending inventory was 2/10 × $4,210	842	$4,210

FIFO:

19X1 cost of valves used:	500 @ $4.00	$2,000	
	200 @ $4.10	820	$2,820
19X1 ending inventory:	100 @ $4.10	410	
	300 @ $4.23	1,269	1,679
Total amount available			$4,499
19X2 cost of valves used:	100 @ $4.10	$ 410	
	300 @ $4.23	1,269	
	200 @ $4.27	854	
	200 @ $4.30	860	$3,393
19X2 ending inventory:	200 @ $4.30		860
Proof: 19X2 beginning inventory		$1,679	
19X2 purchases ($854 + $1,720)		2,574	$4,253

LIFO:

19X1 cost of valves used:	300 @ $4.23	$1,269	
	300 @ $4.10	1,230	
	100 @ $4.00	400	$2,899
19X1 ending inventory:	400 @ $4.00		1,600
Total amount available			$4,499

Since the 12/31/X1 ending LIFO inventory reflects the cost of only one lot, strict LIFO and modified LIFO give the same results in 19X2.

19X2 cost of valves used: 400 @ $4.30 . . . . $1,720
200 @ $4.27   854
200 @ $4.00 . . . .   800 $3,374

19X2 ending inventory: 200 @ $4.00   800

Proof: 19X2 beginning inventory $1,600
19X2 purchases ($854 + $1,720) 2,574 $4,174

Solution 13-5:

The following solution is quite detailed, for the sake of providing maximum help to students who are having difficulties; if you don't need this much help, feel free to skim some of these details.

At the end of each year the inventory balances will be overstated or understated by the amount of that year's error (if any), and there will be a corresponding overstatement or understatement of retained earnings. The effect on the income statement can be slightly more complicated, since cost of goods sold is affected by errors in both beginning and ending inventory balances. Any understatement of cost of goods sold will result in an overstatement of net income, and vice-versa. The effects of errors on cost of goods sold are indicated below. The following abbreviations are used:

$$BI = \text{Beginning inventory}$$
$$P = \text{Purchases}$$
$$CGS = \text{Cost of goods sold}$$
$$EI = \text{Ending inventory}$$
$$+ = \text{Overstated}$$
$$- = \text{Understated}$$
$$0 = \text{Neither overstated nor understated}$$

Of course, each year's ending inventory becomes next year's beginning inventory; accordingly, in each case the understatement or overstatement of cost of goods sold is the net effect of any errors in beginning and ending inventory figures.

Merchandise Inventory

BI—1/1/X1	0	CGS—19X1	−2,130
P—19X1	0	EI—12/31/X1	+2,130
	0		0
BI—1/1/X2	+2,130	CGS—19X2	+2,130
P—19X2	0	EI—12/31/X2	0
	+2,130		+2,130
BI—1/1/X3	0	CGS—19X3	+1,170
P—19X3	0	EI—12/31/X3	−1,170
	0		0
BI—1/1/X4	−1,170	CGS—19X4	−2,090
P—19X4	0	EI—12/31/X4	+ 920
	−1,170		−1,170
BI—1/1/X5	+ 920	CGS—19X5	− 440
P—19X5	0	EI—12/31/X5	+1,360
	+ 920		+ 920
BI—1/1/X6	+1,360	CGS—19X6	+1,360
P—19X6	0	EI—12/31/X6	0
	+1,360		+1,360

In each case, the effect of these errors on cost of goods sold is "plugged" by adding beginning inventory and purchases figures then subtracting those for ending inventory.

Accordingly, the effects of the firm's errors on its financial statements were as follows:

Year	Year-End Merchandise Inventory	Year-End Retained Earnings	Cost of Goods Sold	Net Income
19X1	+2,130	+2,130	−2,130	+2,130
19X2	0	0	+2,130	−2,130
19X3	−1,170	−1,170	+1,170	−1,170
19X4	+ 920	+ 920	−2,090	+2,090
19X5	+1,360	+1,360	− 440	+ 440
19X6	0	0	+1,360	−1,360

Notice that the effect on year-end retained earnings can also be calculated from the effect on the previous year-end retained earnings and the error in the current year's net income. For example, at 12/31/X3, retained earnings was understated by $1,170; the $2,090 19X4 overstatement of net income results in 12/31/X4 retained earnings being overstated by $2,090 − $1,170 = $920, and so forth.

Some Tax Matters

Tax influences on amortization

Chapter One (pages 28–29) stated that tax accounting is ordinarily irrelevant to financial accounting. An important exception occurs with the amortization of non-monetary assets. Prior to 1954, it was rare to see declining-charge depreciation used in published financial statements. After 1954, declining-charge depreciation became generally allowable for federal income tax purposes. In a period of rising prices, such as have been experienced in America since World War II, the declining-charge depreciation method gives a larger amortization and a higher expense during the years in which it is first used than does the straight-line method. This means a lower taxable income and, thereby, a lower tax than would otherwise be owed. To be sure, some of this is only temporary: rapid depreciation in early years means correspondingly small depreciation charges (and higher taxes) in later years. But if the company is constantly replacing old assets with new ones, it is constantly able to offset these later-year disadvantages with early-year advantages. In effect anyway, there may be a permanent tax saving from the use of declining-charge depreciation, and some companies have elected to use declining-charge depreciation for tax purposes.

Occasionally, this may affect financial accounting. Certain companies wish to use the same figures on both their tax returns and their financial statements. It's a nuisance (and moderately expensive) to maintain two different sets of depreciable asset records and, besides, there may be concern over appearing deceitful by keeping a different set of books for the government than for the stockholders—even though no deceit is involved (since tax accounting is different from financial accounting). Indications are, though, that the majority of firms are not influenced in this way.[10]

However, this tax influence does explain something that often puzzles students: "Why *twice*-straight-line-on-the-declining-balance instead of one-and-a-half-times-, or three-times-straight-line-on-the-declining-balance? The answer is simply that *twice* straight-line is the maximum allowed for tax purposes, and that any firm seeking to minimize its tax liability uses the method to its maximum permitted rate.

Much the same thing happened with the LIFO inventory method. It was not at all widely used in published financial statements until companies began using it for income tax purposes. (This was accentuated by a unique tax law: LIFO may not be used for income tax purposes unless it is also used for financial statement purposes.) Study of successive editions of *Accounting Trends and Techniques* indicates that at one time LIFO may have been the most popular inventory method. Since then, it has declined to third place (behind first-place FIFO and the average method).

Deferred income taxes

One further matter related to taxation should be mentioned briefly, just so you will not be puzzled by something frequently found in published financial statements.

---

[10] The American Institute of Certified Public Accountants publishes surveys of actual accounting practices under the title *Accounting Trends and Techniques*. The surveys indicated that by 1969, only about one-third of all firms studied used declining-charge depreciation on their own records; about 70% of all firms studied were willing to use different depreciation methods for financial accounting and tax purposes.

Suppose that a firm uses straight-line depreciation for financial accounting purposes, but uses a declining-charge method for its federal income-tax return, and that its taxable income is lower than its financial accounting net income. The firm would be required by the Accounting Principles Board to report a tax expense on its income statement equal in effect to what its tax expense would have been had it calculated taxable income in the same way it calculated financial accounting net income. To balance this increased expense on the income statement (an additional debit), the firm must credit some balance sheet account such as "deferred federal income taxes." For example, if the firm's actual tax bill for the year is $300,000 and this bill would have been $325,000 had the firm used straight-line depreciation (instead of declining-charge depreciation) for both tax and financial accounting purposes, the firm would be required to make the entry:

Taxes Expense	325,000	
Taxes Payable		300,000
Deferred Federal Income Taxes		25,000

Of course, only $300,000 of the $325,000 taxes expense pertains to taxes that are currently payable.

The reasoning behind this requirement is complicated and controversial, as are certain possible alternatives to making this particular entry.[11] None of this will be discussed here. Instead, it will suffice to point out that if the firm does use declining-charge depreciation for tax purposes, in later years the depreciation allowable for tax purposes on the related assets will be less than that allowable under straight-line depreciation, and that taxable income may then *exceed* financial accounting net income (with correspondingly higher income tax bills). Therefore, the account deferred federal income taxes might be interpreted as representing an anticipated increase in the firm's future income taxes resulting from its present tax savings. Deferred federal income taxes usually is listed among a firm's noncurrent liabilities. Although a depreciation example has been used here, deferred taxes can arise from many other situations in which the net income reported on a firm's financial statements exceeds its taxable income.

Other nonmonetary assets

A few concluding remarks will suffice for the amortization of other kinds of nonmonetary assets. Supplies are similar enough to other kinds of inventories that they are amortized according to any of the inventory methods described above. As for remaining nonmonetary assets, although the amortization method varies from one asset to another, there is little variety within any one kind of asset. For example, even though plausible cases could be made for other amortization patterns, to my knowledge patents and leases always are amortized straight-line, as are prepayments. The reason for this may be little more than custom—but straight-line amortization of these assets does satisfy the criteria for amortization discussed in the next section.

---

[11] An allocation of the firm's total lifetime tax bill is involved here; this allocation seems to suffer from the same ambiguities as the other allocations discussed in this book.

The same can be said of other nonmonetary assets: the methods used to amortize them are customary but satisfy the criteria discussed below. Assets subject to depletion (such as mines) are amortized on a production basis. Investments in the capital stock of other companies are amortized by specific identification when the related shares are sold (except that a "conservative" writedown may be employed prior to sale in cases where the market values of shares seem to have suffered permanent impairment); a similar treatment is given to land.[12]

Tentative Suggestions for Nonmonetary Asset Amortization[13]

In the first section of this chapter I argued that amortizations of nonmonetary assets were bound to be arbitrary. Yet such amortizations are required for many of the institutional purposes served by accounting. Statutes, the courts, and many regulatory bodies require them; most importantly, they are *expected* by most users of financial statements. We have seen that a substantial variety of amortization methods are allowed in practice. Must choice among these be chaotic, or can guidance be given in the selection of specific arbitrary allocation methods for institutional purposes?

At present, only very general answers can be given, and these fail to provide direction in many instances. But some guidance can be given:

1. There are cases where only one of the various allocation methods is actually used in practice. The treatment of prepaid insurance is an excellent example of this: the universal practice seems to be to amortize prepaid insurance straight-line. In such cases, the accountant need only comply with prevailing practice. Similarly, a particular allocation method may be specified by statute—examples of this are occasionally found in regulated industries; however, such situations go beyond the scope of this text. Once again, the accountant need only comply with the appropriate statute or regulation.

2. In theory, there could be cases in which a limited number of alternative allocation methods were allowed to the accountant, and in which it clearly was to the advantage of the accounting entity that one of these allocation methods be chosen. (Cases of this kind are rare in financial accounting, but common in tax accounting; for instance, it often is to a firm's financial advantage to claim the maximum depreciation allowable for tax purposes.) In such cases, the accountant should choose the most advantageous approach.

3. In other cases allowing a limited number of alternative allocation methods to

---

[12] The same specific identification treatment is given to the remaining book values of depreciable or depletable assets and patents when these assets are retired; gain or loss on the retirement is figured on the book value of the specific asset that is retired.

[13] Parts of this section are based upon "Report of the Committee on Foundations of Accounting Measurement," *The Accounting Review,* Supplement to Vol. XLVI (1971), pages 1–48.

the accountant, it may not be clear which of the alternatives is the most advantageous. In fact, all allocation methods may appear to be equally advantageous.

In such cases, presumably the allocation method that requires the least clerical costs should be used. Often, this will be the method the firm uses for tax purposes, since use of any other method would require additional calculations. In other cases, the least expensive allocation method will usually be the simplest one: total writeoff at some point in time (if this is one of the allowed alternatives), or straight-line amortization over the shortest allowable period.

4. The difficult cases arise where more than one allocation method is allowed, and different parties to the financial statements are affected unequally by the different methods. As an example, the interests of those who presently own stock in a firm are in conflict with the interests of those who are potential owners: the present owners would like the market price per share to be as high as possible, while the potential owner would prefer it to be low until he has bought his shares (after which, of course, his interests become those of a present owner). Suppose it could be demonstrated that the market price per share is depressed by large depreciation charges, and that the firm had just made a large purchase of new plant (buying more land, buildings, and equipment in the current year than during the previous five years combined). Then, other things being equal, it will be to the advantage of present stockholders if the firm uses straight-line depreciation, and to the advantage of potential stockholders if it uses accelerated depreciation on this new plant.

In general, there is a serious conflict of interest in financial accounting whenever present stockholders benefit from allocations resulting in high net income figures, prospective stockholders have opposed interests, and the accountant is responsible to both groups. (Various authors have pointed out that the accountant's penchant for "conservatism" leads him to favor the interests of prospective stockholders over those of present stockholders.)

Accountants have developed solutions to certain of these situations. But no general solutions exist, nor do any appear to be immediately forthcoming. The best that the accountant can do is to accept the choice of the dominant party among the contending interests, or, as is often the case, accept the choice of management. This is not very satisfactory, but it seems to be all that is available to the accountant at present.

The future

In the long run, it is hoped that accountants will be able to develop non-arbitrary systems for amortizing nonmonetary assets that harmonize with the resource-allocation needs of users of financial statements. If this cannot be done, accountants should be trying to devise ways to satisfy present institutional requirements without using allocations. One such method was mentioned in Chapter Nine: substituting the funds statement for the income statement as the principal financial report.

At present this suggestion is considered disreputable. The form it has taken has been the calculation of so-called "cash-flow income"—which, as Chapter Nine indicated, is a bastard concept, since it measures neither cash-flow nor income. Yet when it is not compressed into a single figure, the funds-from-operations portion of a funds statement provides a substantial portion of the information now reported on the income statement. If the net-quick-assets variety of funds statement (see pages 477–479) is employed, *its information is free of nonmonetary asset amortizations*. For example, purchases of depreciable assets are reported, but not their amortizations; purchases of inventories are reported, but not the cost of goods sold.

Similarly, the net-quick-assets funds statement reports receipts instead of revenues, and the effects of the firm's operating activities on funds instead of their effects on income. Accordingly, such a funds statement avoids all of the arbitrary allocations that presently characterize the income statement—though at the price of ceasing to measure income and measuring funds from operations instead. Eventually, institutional users of financial accounting reports may become persuaded that income calculations are sufficiently arbitrary that they serve no useful purpose. In that event, some respectable descendant of the present "cash-flow income" calculation, based upon a net-quick-assets funds statement, may become the dominant financial accounting report. This is one of the several reasons this book has emphasized funds statements.

A Short Accounting Theory Bibliography

Students who are interested in reading more about revenue recognition, allocation, or accounting theory in general might wish to begin with the following works:

Eldon S. Hendriksen, *Accounting Theory,* Revised Edition (Homewood, Illinois: Richard D. Irwin, Inc., 1970) summarizes much of the recent theoretical literature of financial accounting from a balanced, middle-of-the-road perspective. It probably is the first book to which you should turn, especially for its excellent bibliographies and broad overviews of accounting controversies.

The following are committee reports rather than works of individual authors. As such, they are good reflections of the kinds of compromise positions on accounting theory that many academic authors would be willing to accept. All of the following reports appeared in *The Accounting Review*: "Accounting for Land, Buildings, and Equipment," Vol. XXXIX (July, 1964) pages 693–699; "A Discussion of Various Approaches to Inventory Measurement," Vol. XXXIX (July, 1964) pages 700–714; "The Realization Concept," Vol. XL (April, 1965) pages 312–322; "The Matching Concept," Vol. XL (April, 1965) pages 368–372; "An Evaluation of External Reporting Practices," supplement to Vol. XLIV (1969) pages 79–123; and "Report of the Committee on Foundations of Accounting Measurement," Supplement to Vol. XLVI (1971) pages 1–48.

In contrast, the following are individualistic, controversial works: Raymond J. Chambers, *Accounting, Evaluation and Economic Behavior* (Englewood Cliffs, New Jersey: Prentice-Hall, Inc., 1966); and Robert R. Sterling, *Theory of the Measurement of Enterprise Income* (Lawrence, Kansas: The University Press of Kansas, 1970). A relatively brief introduction to Chambers' thinking may be found in the article "Towards a General Theory of Accounting," in R. J. Chambers, *Accounting, Finance and Management* (Chicago, Illinois: Arthur Andersen & Co., 1969), pages 477–517.

The classic theoretical defense of what practicing accountants do is William A. Paton and A. C. Littleton, *An Introduction to Corporate Accounting Standards* (Columbus, Ohio: American Accounting Association, 1940). The single best reflection of current APB thinking on accounting theory is *Basic Concepts and Accounting Principles Underlying Financial Statements of Business Enterprises,* Statement of the Accounting Principles Board No. 4 (American Institute of Certified Public Accountants, Inc., October, 1970). This may be supplemented by *APB Accounting Principles* (New York: Commerce Clearing House, August 1, 1969, and subsequent editions as these become available). More recent pronouncements of the APB will be found in *The Journal of Accountancy*; discussions in this book have relied heavily upon APB Opinions in the June, October, and November 1971 issues on the equity approach to reporting investments (Opinion No. 18), funds statements (Opinion No. 19), reporting changes in accounting methods and estimates (Opinion No. 20), and interest on receivables and payables (Opinion No. 20). Finally, three periodicals are especially important outlets for new thinking on accounting theory: *The Accounting Review, Journal of Accounting Research,* and *Abacus.*

Concluding comment

At the beginning of this book I described financial accounting as a system whereby economic information about business firms is gathered and made available to investors. I also emphasized that financial accounting provides a simplified model of a firm's economic position and activity, and that all models are unavoidably limited. This text has devoted much space to acquainting you with the limitations of the financial accounting model. But the significance of these limitations should not be overstated.

The accountant has developed reports that are fully satisfactory for most institutional purposes. Financial accounting is also satisfactory for resource-allocation purposes whenever the accountant is able to meet investor requests for information by making primary measurements. Financial accounting's difficulties arise with secondary measurements—especially with allocations. Yet even here, accountants often have developed approaches that, even if ultimately arbitrary, are satisfactory to many investors.

The history of financial accounting has been one of change—sometimes active, sometimes beneath the surface. At present there is great intellectual ferment in financial accounting circles, and much of it centers on the theoretical issues discussed in this book. Generally accepted accounting rules have remained quite stable since the late 1930s. It seems likely that this period of stability is drawing to a close, and that the last quarter of this century will witness substantial changes in accounting rules.

But the basic functions of financial accounting and the kinds of investor questions that financial accounting tries to answer may be expected to remain the same. And financial accounting should continue, as it is today, to be the single most important public source of economic information about individual business enterprises.

Appendix

The Lower of Cost or Market Rule

On several occasions, I have mentioned the accountant's "conservatism" rule, whereby nonmonetary assets being held for resale or retirement are reported at their amortized historical costs or their current market values, whichever are the lower (see in particular page 148). I also have noted that the "current market value" of an asset can mean more than one thing. When conservatism is applied to merchandise or finished goods inventories, it turns out that two different meanings of "current market value" are used, and that *which* is used depends upon the particular circumstances of the case. These two meanings are:

> *Replacement cost:* the price the firm would have to pay in order to acquire more of the same kind of inventory. In calculating this price, it is assumed that the firm will acquire the inventory from its customary source of supply and in its usual lot sizes.
>
> *Net realizable value:* the *net* amount the firm expects to receive from selling the inventory. This will equal its estimated selling price less any costs to complete, package, and market the inventory (for brevity, I will call these latter costs *completion costs*).

Notice that replacement cost is a current market value of the inventory when it is regarded as an *input,* whereas net realizable value is a current market value of the inventory when it is regarded as an *output.*

We will need one additional concept in order to discuss how conservatism is applied to merchandise and finished goods inventories: a firm's "normal profit margin." Precise definition of this concept requires raising theoretical issues that are best reserved for an advanced course. For our purposes it will suffice to define the *normal profit margin* of a firm as the average gross margin (sales less cost of goods sold) on all inventories of the same general kind as the inventory in question.

Market

The accountant's rule for determining the amount at which inventories of merchandise or finished goods should be reported is called the "lower of cost or market" rule or, alternatively, "cost or market, whichever is lower." "Cost" is calculated in the usual ways described in Chapter Twelve, but "market" is given the following relatively complicated definition, which depends upon the replacement cost of the particular inventory item involved:

> *Case I:* replacement cost is greater than or equal to net realizable value; in this case *market* = net realizable value.
>
> *Case II:* replacement cost is less than net realizable value, but greater than the amount obtained when net realizable value is reduced by a normal profit margin (hereafter called "net realizable value less a normal profit margin"); in this case *market* = replacement cost.
>
> *Case III:* replacement cost is less than or equal to net realizable value less a normal profit margin; in this case, *market* = net realizable value less a normal profit margin.

An example

The following example illustrates this rule. Olney Aquarium Products owns an inventory of garishly colored plastic three-dimensional backdrops for 15-gallon aquariums. These backdrops, which feature generously endowed mermaids, have not been selling very well. The firm estimates that if it spent $5,000 on additional marketing efforts, it could sell these backdrops for a total of $28,000. Normally, this firm earns a profit margin of 25% on its sales.

$$\text{Net realizable value} = \$28,000 - \$5,000 = \$23,000;$$

$$\text{Net realizable value less a normal profit margin} = \$23,000 - (25\% \times \$28,000)$$
$$= \$16,000.$$

"Market" for this inventory is arrived at as indicated in Illustration 13-13:

Illustration 13-13

"Market" for a Particular Inventory Item

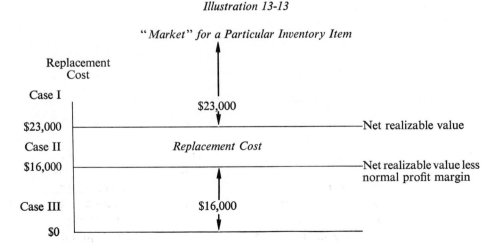

Case I: If replacement cost exceeds the $23,000 net realizable value, market = $23,000 no matter how high replacement cost actually is.

Case II: If replacement cost is between $16,000 and $23,000, market equals replacement cost.

Case III: If replacement cost is less than the $16,000 net realizable value less a normal profit margin, market = $16,000, no matter how low replacement cost is.

Finally, once you have calculated market, you then compare it with the historical cost of the good in question; the amount reported for the inventory is the lower of the two.

Why this rule is used

A complete discussion of why this slightly complicated rule is used is also best reserved for an advanced course. But a fairly plausible brief explanation may be given:

1. The accountant wishes to report inventories at input prices—after all, this is what he does with historical costs. Accordingly, if he uses a current market value he prefers that this be an input price, too. Therefore, his primary rule is that a current market value should be a replacement (input) cost.

2. Yet, as we have repeatedly seen, the significance of an asset to a firm is its future economic benefits. For a good that is held for sale, these will equal its net realizable value. Accordingly, the accountant will not recognize replacement costs that are greater than net realizable values.

3. If a replacement cost lower than net realizable value less a normal profit margin were recognized and the firm's estimates turned out to be correct, then next year's profit margin would be abnormally high. (This is simply a consequence of something that we just saw in Problem 13-5: other things being equal, the lower an ending inventory figure is, the higher will be next year's profits.) The accountant wishes to avoid this result, so he will not recognize replacement costs if they are lower than net realizable value less a normal profit margin.

A flowchart for the lower-of-cost-or-market rule

The lower-of-cost-or-market rule is best summarized by a flowchart. Notice that, as in the previous discussion, this flowchart first shows how market is calculated, then shows how the lower of cost or market is calculated. It is assumed that net realizable value, the normal profit margin, replacement cost, and historical cost all are known in advance. For compactness, the following notation will be used:

RC = Replacement cost   HC = Historical cost
NRV = Net realizable value $\geq$ = Greater than or equal to
NPM = Normal profit margin $\leq$ = Less than or equal to

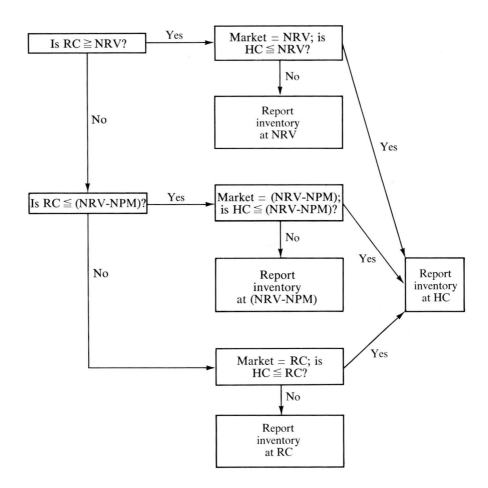

Degree of aggregation of rule

The lower-of-cost-or-market rule may be separately applied to each individual kind of inventory, or to groups of similar inventories. The greater the detail employed in applying the rule, the more conservative the amount reported for inventories is apt to be. This is illustrated by the following example. Suppose that a firm owns two similar kinds of inventories:

Kind of Inventory	Cost	Market
A	$2,000	$2,500
B	1,750	1,500
Total	$3,750	$4,000

If the accountant applies the lower-of-cost-or-market rule to the combined inventories, cost ($3,750) is less than market ($4,000), and the combined inventories would be reported at $3,750. But if he applies this rule to the individual inventory items, we get:

Kind of Inventory	Cost	Market	Lower of Cost or Market
A	$2,000	$2,500	$2,000
B	1,750	1,500	1,500
Amount reported			$3,500

This will always be true as long as cost is higher than market on some items and lower on others.

Applicability of this rule

The lower-of-cost-or-market rule is used with the FIFO and average inventory methods; its use with LIFO is inappropriate since in a period of generally rising prices (such as have characterized our economy), LIFO reports conservative amounts for inventory, anyway. Finally, a version of the lower-of-cost-or-market rule is also used with raw materials—but with these the net realizable value calculations are so obviously arbitrary that *market* usually is simply regarded as equal to replacement cost.

Problem for Study and Self-Examination

Problem 13-6:

Among other products, East St. Louis Novelty Co. makes plastic caricature statuettes of prominent celebrities. Some celebrities are in demand over long periods of time; the popularity of others fades. *Hunchback* was a musical group that became very popular after the release of its second and third LP's, but that has since dissolved because of the hubris of its members. East St. Louis Novelty Co. had manufactured statuettes of all six members of *Hunchback*: Brian, Ian, Leon, Sean, Dean, and Dianna. Fortunately, most of these have been sold, but the following statuettes remain in the firm's 12/31/X5 ending inventory:

Ian: 2,000, at an historical cost of 45¢ apiece	$ 900
Dianna: 2,500, at an historical cost of 48¢ apiece	1,200
Total	$2,100

The firm could make virtually unlimited numbers of these statuettes from its present molds, therefore additional statuettes could be made at a lower cost: 35¢ apiece for either. Marketing costs for the 4,500 statuettes on hand now are expected to be about 10¢ apiece. The firm's normal profit margin on sales is 60%.

A. At what amount should the firm report its inventory of Ians if it can sell Ian statuettes for:

(a) $1.50 apiece?
(b) $1.00 apiece?
(c) $0.40 apiece?

B. Suppose that Ians sell for $1.00 apiece but Diannas sell for $2.00 apiece. At what two amounts could this firm report its statuette inventory?

Solution

Solution 13-6:

	(a)	Case (b)	(c)
(1) Unit selling price of Ians	$ 1.50	$ 1.00	$ 0.40
(2) Net realizable value [= (1) − 10¢]	1.40	0.90	0.30
Replacement cost	0.35	0.35	0.35
Net realizable value less normal profit margin [= (2) − [(1) × 60%]]	0.50	0.30	0.06
Market	$ 0.50	$ 0.35	$ 0.30
Historical cost	0.45	0.45	0.45
Lower of cost or market	$ 0.45	$ 0.35	$ 0.30
Number of units	2,000	2,000	2,000
Amount to be reported	$ 900	$ 700	$ 600

B. The Diannas cost $1,200. Their market value would be calculated as follows:

Net realizable value ($2.00 − 10¢)	$ 1.90
Replacement cost	0.35
Net realizable value less normal profit margin [$1.90 − (60% × $2.00)]	0.70
Market	$ 0.70
Number of units	2,500
Total market value	$1,750

Therefore, the following will be true:

	Cost	Market
Ian	$ 900	$ 700
Dianna	1,200	1,750
Total	$2,100	$2,450

Grouped together, the cost of these statuettes is less than their market value, and they would be reported at $2,100. If the lower-of-cost-or-market rule is applied to the individual kinds of statuette, however, the inventory will be reported at a total of only $1,900:

	Cost	Market	Lower of Cost or Market
Ian	$ 900	$ 700	$ 700
Dianna	1,200	1,750	1,200
Amount reported			$1,900

Assignment Problems

Problem 13-A:

Winter Park Manufacturing Company constructed complex facilities for the production of a single product, at a total cost of $7,378,945.28. The company estimated that these facilities would have a 7-year service life and a scrap value upon retirement of $700,000.00. It further estimated that these facilities would produce a total of 5,600,000 units of product over their service life. Actual product output was as follows:

Year	# Units
1	1,400,000
2	1,350,000
3	800,000
4	1,000,000
5	300,000
6	600,000
7	150,000
	5,600,000

Calculate depreciation expenses for Years 1 through 7 under each of the four depreciation methods discussed in the text. If you need to round, do so to the nearest penny.

Problem 13-B:

The woolly bear is a brown-and-black-banded caterpillar sometimes used to predict the severity of winters. Under one theory, the longer the fur of the woolly bear, and the wider the central black band, the colder the winter will be.

On January 1, 19X6, Woolly Bear Labs, Inc., bought a fur-measuring machine. This machine was expected to wear out in 4 years, or after 100,000 caterpillar applications. The machine had an acquisition price of $12,000. The company estimated that the machine's scrap value when it was retired would be $2,000, and that selling and removal costs would total $800 at that time. The company paid for the machine on March 1, 19X6. Total caterpillar applications were as follows:

19X6	15,000
19X7	37,000

On December 31, 19X7 the company sold the machine for $5,700, cash (in order to purchase a more accurate machine).

What was the gain or loss on this sale, assuming that the company uses:

1. Straight-line depreciation?
2. Double declining balance depreciation?
3. Sum-of-the-years'-digits depreciation?
4. Production-basis depreciation?

Ignore tax considerations.

Problem 13-C:

Gary Home Products, Inc., sells kitchen and cleaning products to retailers. It manufactures some of these products itself and purchases others from smaller manufacturers who do not have Gary's nation-wide marketing facilities. On December 31, 19X6, the firm had a large inventory of Valley Forge Colonial Vegetable Choppers, which it had purchased from Schmidhauser Sanitary Kitchen Corp.

In theory, these choppers are ingeniously designed, but in practice they wear out rapidly. They come in two sizes: large and super. The firm has been selling them to retailers for $5.00 and $7.00 respectively but, because of increasing dealer resistance, has decided to reduce their price. Schmidhauser has already informed Gary that it is willing to manufacture future orders at a price to Gary of $3.00 for large and $4.50 for super choppers. Here are the details of Gary's 12/31/X6 chopper inventory:

	Large	Super
Unit cost	$ 3.20	$ 4.80
Quantity	8,000	3,000
Total cost	$25,600	$14,400

Gary estimates that a large chopper costs approximately 30¢ to market, and a super chopper approximately 40¢. The firm's normal profit margin is 20% of sales.

Shown below are three possible price combinations at which Gary might sell choppers. In each case, indicate the amount at which Gary should report its 12/31/X6 inventory of 11,000 choppers. There may be more than one possible answer in some cases, if so, indicate all of the possibilities.

	Gary's New Selling Price	
Case	Large	Super
A	$4.50	$6.00
B	4.00	6.75
C	3.75	6.00

Problem 13-D:

Cramer Corporation bought a machine for $7,290. This machine had a 6-year estimated service life and an estimated scrap value upon retirement of $570.

Prepare a tabular comparison of the depreciation charges and end-of-year book values that would be reported for this machine under straight-line, sum-of-the-years'-digits, and double declining balance depreciation.

Problem 13-E:

Refer to the data in Problem 13-D. Prepare a graphic comparison of the depreciation charges and end-of-year book values that would be reported for this machine under straight-line, sum-of-the-years'-digits, and double declining balance depreciation.

Problem 13-F:

Refer to the data in Problem 13-D. Estimates of service lives and scrap values upon retirement are usually only approximate. Other, equally well-trained, individuals might take the same basic situation and arrive at quite different estimates. Suppose that the 6-year, $570-scrap-value estimate in Problem 13-D was an *average* of a 4- to 8-year possible life, with related scrap values of from $1,050 to $90. To keep things simple, suppose that it already had been decided that sum-of-the-years'-digits depreciation was the most appropriate for this asset. Determine the range of possible patterns of depreciation charges and end-of-year book values for this asset. Make your comparisons in both tabular and graphic form.

Problem 13-G:

Hagan Stores prepares financial statements once a year, every December 31st. The following information pertains to a particular kind of dark-colored dress shirt stocked by the company.

	# Units	@	Total
Balance—12/31/X7	120	$6.00	$ 720.00
Purchases: 2/26/X8	48	6.20	297.60
4/15/X8	144	6.25	900.00
5/25/X8	144	6.25	900.00
8/28/X8	144	6.10	878.40
9/23/X8	288	6.20	1,785.60
11/2/X8	144	6.25	900.00
11/29/X8	72	6.30	453.60
	1,104		$6,835.20

During 19X8 the company sold 950 shirts. Determine the related cost of goods sold and ending inventory figures under the FIFO, LIFO, and average cost-flow assumptions. If you need to round, do so to five significant digits.

Problem 13-H:

Refer to the data in Problem 13-G. 19X9 purchases of these dark-colored shirts were as follows:

	# Units	@	Total
4/10/X9	288	$6.40	$1,843.20
5/27/X9	144	6.50	936.00
8/16/X9	288	6.25	1,800.00
9/20/X9	288	6.10	1,756.80
11/15/X9	144	6.05	871.20
	1,152		$7,207.20

During 19X9 the company sold 1,240 shirts. Determine the related cost of goods sold and ending inventory figures under the FIFO, strict LIFO, modified LIFO, and average cost-flow assumptions. If you need to round, do so to five significant digits (modified LIFO does not happen to come out even).

Problem 13-I:

Refer to the data in Problem 13-G, but ignore what is said in Problem 13-H. Assume that at the end of 19X8 this particular kind of dark-colored dress shirt was going out of style and that the firm could acquire any additional quantities it might want for $6.20 apiece. The firm estimates that selling costs for these shirts total about 10¢ apiece; its normal profit margin on sales is 40%.

At what amount should the firm report its ending inventory of shirts if it believes that it can sell them for:

(a) $11.00 apiece?
(b) $ 7.00 apiece?
(c) $ 6.00 apiece?

Calculate your answers according to two different assumptions about the inventory method used by the company: (1) the company uses FIFO, and (2) the company uses the average approach. Notice that this problem requires six different answers:

	(a)	(b)	(c)
(1) FIFO	X	X	X
(2) Average	X	X	X

Problem 13-J:

As part of your training in accounting, you must become able to extend what you have learned into new situations. This problem provides an opportunity to increase your flexibility and broaden your understanding. The text provides all background information needed to solve this problem, but the circumstances described will be unfamiliar. Apply what you have already learned to this new situation.

Refer to the data in Problem 13-G. Mr. William C. Hagan, President of Hagan Stores, is not particularly fond of accountants. Shortly after December 31, 19X8, he makes the following statement:

"FIFO, LIFO, Average, Flub-Flub . . . I don't care. All these inventory methods are arbitrary, right? OK; let's us be one company that at least is *honest* about it. Let's use an inventory method that's *obviously* arbitrary. So nobody could ever be confused into thinking we did something that we could back up. Hold on—I've got some figures here. Yeah. I've just invented a new arbitrary inventory method: Earliest Day First. We'll assume that anything purchased on the first day of any month is used first, that anything bought on the second day of any month is used next, and so on. Heck, do what you like if we buy on the same day in two different months—run the months in alphabetical order! We'll treat the beginning inventory as being on day zero. Here: this is how it would work with the #3071 shirts."

Mr. Hagan had prepared the following schedule:

Cost of Goods Sold:

Begin	120 @	$6.00	=	$ 720.00
11/12	144 @	6.25	=	900.00
4/15	144 @	6.25	=	900.00
9/23	288 @	6.20	=	1,785.00
5/25	144 @	6.25	=	900.00
2/26	48 @	6.20	=	297.60
8/28	62 @	6.10	=	378.20
	950			$5,880.80

"OK, now let's face it. My $5,880.80 cost of goods sold is just as logical—or illogical—a figure as the one you'd get under any other method, while it has the advantage of being obviously silly. As far as I'm concerned, from now on this company uses the Earliest Day First inventory method, and if the auditors don't like it they can go FIFO themselves."

You are the auditor for Hagan Stores. What will your response be to Mr. Hagan's decision? Defend your answer.

Problem 13-K:

On 7/1/X1, Holloway Enterprises completed construction of a motel next to a major East-West national highway. The building cost $3,500,000 and the company estimated that it would have a 20-year service life with a scrap value of $400,000 upon retirement. The company prepares financial statements every June 30th, and uses straight-line depreciation.

During the first half of 19X9, the company learned that a new throughway would be constructed some thirty miles to the south. This throughway, to be completed within five years, will attract most of the interstate traffic presently going past the company's motel. Accordingly, the company now intends to sell the building about four years from 6/30/X9 to a firm that operates a chain of combination trailer courts and small residential apartments. It expects to receive about $500,000 for the building at that date.

Discuss the accounting treatments that might result from this change in the company's estimates. Ignore tax considerations.

Problem 13-L:

As part of your training in accounting, you must become able to extend what you have learned into new situations. This problem provides an opportunity to increase your flexibility and broaden your understanding. The text provides all background information needed to solve this problem, but the circumstances described will be unfamiliar. Apply what you already have learned to this new situation.

On August 1, 19X3, Gilroy Mining Company purchased a tract of land containing a surface ore deposit for $800,000, issuing a 6% note payable, principal and interest of which were both due on 2/1/X5. The company estimated that this deposit contained approximately 200,000 tons of ore, and that after the ore had been exhausted, the land could be resold for $30,000 (this is a net price that allows for certain costs of restoring the appearance of the tract).

The company used two kinds of equipment and structures at the mine site:

1. Mobile excavation equipment. This equipment had an original cost of $320,000 when it was purchased in 19X1, and had been depreciated at a rate of $30,000 per year, straight-line. It was expected that all mobile excavation equipment would be moved to another site when the present ore deposit was exhausted.

2. Other fixed assets: roads, shacks, and certain other equipment, all of which would be abandoned at the site when the deposit was exhausted. These assets cost a total of $60,000; they were purchased or constructed during the fall of 19X3. It was estimated that none of these other fixed assets would need to be replaced during the time required to exhaust the deposit.

Before any ore could be mined, it was necessary to use the mobile excavation equipment to remove "overburden"—surface brush, dirt, and rock covering the deposit. This was done during the fall of 19X3 and cost $10,000 in employee wages, two months' services of the mobile excavation equipment, and $5,000 in other costs (which required cash expenditure). The company prepares financial statements every December 31st.

During 19X4, 450,000 tons of ore were mined. This cost $95,000 in mining wages and $32,500 in other items involving cash expenditure. Besides the costs of mining ore, the company incurred various administrative costs totalling $19,300, also paid in cash. 380,000 tons of ore were sold, at $1.10 per ton. Delivery and other selling expenses totalled $16,700, cash. 19X4 taxes (to be paid in 19X5) totalled $18,500.

Prepare appropriate journal entries for 19X3 and 19X4.

Problem 13-M:

Refer to the data in Problem 13-L. Prepare a statement of cost of ore mined and sold and an income statement for Gilroy Mining Company for 19X4. In preparing the latter you may assume that at 12/31/X3 the firm had a deficit of $33,000.

Problem 13-N:

At the beginning of Year 1, St. Petersburg Manufacturing Co. completed a machine installation costing $823,543. It was estimated that this installation would have a 7-year service life, and a scrap value of $95,543 upon retirement. Shown below are two graphic comparisons of four different depreciation methods that might be employed with this installation, followed by the related tabular comparisons of these four methods.

Identify each of these depreciation methods.

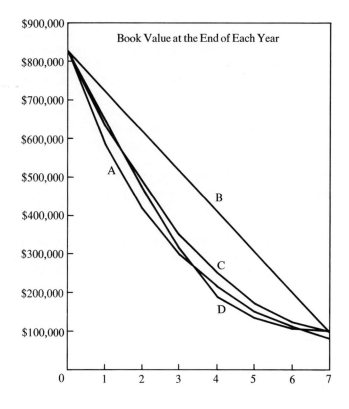

Book Value at the End of Each Year

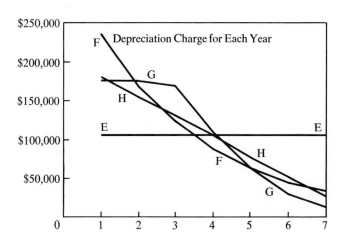

Depreciation Charge for Each Year

End of Year Book Value
Method

Year	A	B	C	D
1	$588,245	$719,543	$641,543	$648,440
2	420,175	615,543	485,543	474,040
3	300,125	511,543	355,543	304,000
4	214,375	407,543	251,543	195,543
5	153,125	303,543	173,543	135,543
6	109,375	199,543	121,543	105,543
7	78,125	95,543	95,543	95,000

Depreciation Charge
Method

Year	E	F	G	H
1	$104,000	$235,298	$175,103	$182,000
2	104,000	168,070	174,400	156,000
3	104,000	120,050	170,040	130,000
4	104,000	85,750	108,457	104,000
5	104,000	61,250	60,000	78,000
6	104,000	43,750	30,000	52,000
7	104,000	31,250	10,000	26,000

Problem 13-O:

As part of your training in accounting, you must become able to extend the concepts and techniques you have learned into situations that require different methods of analysis. This problem provides an opportunity to increase your flexibility and broaden your understanding. The background needed to solve this problem has been provided by the text, but the particular method of analysis required may at first seem unusual. Apply what you already have learned to this new situation.

Each of the following questions requires an *algebraic* solution. Numerical solutions are not acceptable.

A machine has an acquisition price of C, an estimated scrap value upon retirement of S, and an estimated service life of N years. This machine can physically produce U units of output. Assume that Year K falls somewhere between Year 1 and Year N, and that the machine was bought on the first day of Year 1.

Part O is solved below as an example.

O. Give the formula for depreciation expense in Year K under the straight-line approach.

$$\text{Answer:} \frac{C - S}{N}$$

1. Give the formula for depreciation expense in Year K, under the sum-of-the-years'-digits approach.

2. Give the formula for depreciation expense in Year 3, under the double declining balance method. (Assume here that N is greater than 5.)

3. Give the formula for depreciation expense in Year K under the production method; you may assume that P units were actually produced in Year K.

4. Assume that the company has been using straight-line depreciation and that it wishes to continue to do so. However, at the end of Year K (but before depreciation expense is recorded) the company revises its depreciation estimates. It now believes that the machine will last a total of Y years (Y is larger than N) and will have a scrap value of zero upon retirement. Give the appropriate journal entries at the end of Year K, assuming that the company decides to:

    (a) write off the remaining book value over the newly-estimated remaining life.

    (b) correct the present book value, then write the remaining book value off over the newly-estimated remaining life.

Problem 13-P:

Fort Wayne Institute of Commerce and Applied Technology is a privately owned, profit-making college (whose emblem is a flying cat saying "Take Your Pick and Learn it Quick—at FWICAT!"). Three different kinds of depreciable assets owned by this firm are described below. In each case, indicate the method of depreciation that would seem most appropriate for this asset under the reasoning ordinarily employed by accountants in such matters. Explain your reasoning.

1. New blackboards purchased for one of the college's classrooms. This classroom is being used to full capacity now, and this rate of use is expected to continue for the foreseeable future. The blackboards have an expected total service life of ten years.

2. New furniture for the office of the college's president, and principal stockholder, Dr. Leon I. Saxon. Dr. Saxon believes that it is vital to the college's public image that its executive offices appear modern. Accordingly, his office furniture is replaced every two years on the average. The old furniture is first used in senior faculty offices then, as it becomes increasingly marred and decrepit, is entrusted to progressively less-important uses. The total service life of such furniture averages about twenty years.

3. New duplicating equipment with an estimated service life of ten years. The college's enrollment is expected to increase at a steady rate of about six percent per year. This equipment will be adequate for all demands to be placed upon it over its expected service life. Since these demands are also expected to increase at an average rate of six percent per year, this equipment will initially be used at less than its full capacity.

Problem 13-Q:

Refer to Problem 13-1 and its solution (pages 713–714, 715–718). This problem, like most of the other illustrations in the text, considers just one depreciable asset at a time. But of course firms buy many assets at many different times; and at any one time, a company will own assets of differing ages. What follows modifies Problem 13-1 to reflect this (though still in a simplified way).

Suppose that Baldwin Mfg. Company buys a new machine *each year*. Each machine costs $12,500, has an estimated service life of five years, and an estimated scrap value upon retirement of $1,100. Prepare a comparison of total straight-line, sum-of-the-years'-digits, and double declining balance depreciation charges for Years 1 through 7. Prepare a similar comparison of end-of-year book values under these three methods. Discuss the general implications of your answers for financial accounting. For simplicity, you may assume that each machine's scrap value upon retirement actually *is* $1,100, and that under the double declining balance approach, the depreciation charge in each machine's fifth year is set to equal the amount necessary to reduce its book value to this $1,100 scrap value; ignore tax considerations.

Problem 13-R:

As part of your training in accounting, you must become able to extend what you have learned into new situations. This problem provides an opportunity to increase your flexibility and broaden your understanding. The text provides all background information needed to solve this problem, but the circumstances described will be unfamiliar. Apply what you have already learned to this new situation.

Ever since it was founded, 20 years ago, Bell Specialty Supply Corporation has made a policy of using LIFO and of keeping on hand at all times a two-months' supply of inventories. During this 20 years, both company activities and the quantity of inventory it carries quadrupled, while inventory prices doubled.

The company's 19X3 sales and cost of goods sold were $5,000,000 and $3,000,000, respectively; cost of goods sold has been 60% of sales consistently for the past five years. The company's 12/31/X3 ending inventory was $300,000, at LIFO cost; these goods would have cost the firm between $525,000 and $550,000 if it had bought them at 12/31/X3 prices.

During 19X4, company sales totalled $5,400,000, but its cost of goods sold was only $3,040,000, or approximately 56% of sales. Mr. Daniel J. Voormis, president of the company, was asked why this change had occurred; he replied:

"That's a very good question. For years we've been following a rule of keeping a 60-day supply of all inventories on hand. But this is a kind of costly thing to do, so last December we experimented by just not reordering until the inventories got down to about a sixth of their normal sizes. This was a good time to experiment, anyway— payment on that Annunzio damage suit was due next month, and we were going to be a bit strapped for cash otherwise.

"I wouldn't say that the experiment actually failed; but things got pretty close, and we had to special-order a number of items. I wouldn't try running inventories that low again."

The adverse judgment for damages mentioned by Mr. Voormis was for $200,000, had unexpectedly been awarded by the courts in 19X4, and was reported as a $200,000 loss on the firm's 19X4 income statement. The suit had been in litigation for several years. The firm's 19X4 net income was reported as being $537,000, up approximately 8% from 19X3 net income.

Comment. Defend your comments.

Problem 13-S:

Mr. Sam M. Gurney has invented what he calls a *TV Liquarium*. Basically, this is an elaborate kind of TV light: a sealed tank filled with plastic goldfish and a chemical

similar to that used in bubbling Christmas-tree lights, the whole thing gently illumin-
ated from below. A Liquarium is placed on one's TV set; when the TV is running the
set gives off heat, the liquid in the tank boils, and the fish move around.

Mr. Gurney has found that his Liquariums are selling much faster than he can
make them by hand. Accordingly, at considerable expense he has built a specialized
machine that manufactures them automatically. What would be an appropriate
depreciation method for Mr. Gurney to use with this machine? Why?

Problem 13-T:

Illinois-Tarzania Oil Company operates oil production and refining facilities in
the Republic of Tarzania. The Tarzanian oil field itself is located deep in the interior
of the country, but economic considerations require the company's refinery to be
located on the coast, at Port Jane. Oil is pumped from the well to the refinery by
pipeline.

During the disturbances preceding the establishment of Tarzania's present pro-
Western military government, two of the five pumping stations serving the pipeline
were demolished, thereby depriving the refinery of crude oil and forcing it to be shut
down until new pumping stations could be built. This reconstruction has now been
completed, at a substantial cost.

The company believes that its Tarzanian field will be worth continued operation
for another fifteen years. Although the company believes that eventually it will have
to share a greater portion of its profits with the Tarzanian government than it does
at present, it also expects that world oil prices will rise, and that the two effects will
cancel each other. The company tries to follow a policy of depreciating plant and
equipment in a manner consistent with the expected patterns of their contributions
to profits over their service lives.

What difficulties will there be in applying company depreciation policies to the
new pumping stations? Be as specific as possible.

Problem 13-U:

The 19X4–19X5 activities of Campus Store have been the subject of numerous
discussions in this book, beginning with the one on pages 358–361. You will recall
that in April, 19X4, the company began construction of a new store building because
it was outgrowing its present location. This building was completed on 7/2/X7, at
the beginning of the firm's 19X7–19X8 fiscal year; it cost a total of $1,000,000 and is
expected to have a service life of 20 years with a zero scrap value. The firm's recent
net incomes have been as follows:

19X4–19X5	$75,800
19X5–19X6	86,100
19X6–19X7	91,700

The company expects that its profits (exclusive of unusual gains or losses and
the effects of changes in depreciation charges) will be 50% to 60% higher in the new
building than the old, because it will be able to stock a much greater variety of
merchandise.

Besides the building, during the early summer of 19X7 the firm purchased new furniture and fixtures costing a total of $200,000. These assets had an average estimated service life of ten years, with a zero scrap value upon retirement.

On 8/1/X7, the company sold its old building at a price that was $57,000 higher than the depreciated amount at which it was carried on Campus Store's books. Depreciation on this old building had been at a straight-line rate of $7,500 per year since it was purchased on 7/1/X0. No old furniture and fixtures are to be retired— they all are being used in the new building.

Upon inquiry, the firm's auditors, Littrell, Rostenkowski & Co., indicate that either straight-line or double declining balance depreciation would be acceptable for the new building and new furniture and fixtures.

Ignore tax considerations and July, 19X7 depreciation on the old building. If present profits trends continue into the future and company estimates are correct, approximately what will the company's reported net incomes be under the two different depreciation alternatives in 19X7–19X8 and 19X8–19X9? Comment on your answer; defend your comments.

Recreational Problem:

Contradiction Corp. bought a new plant, at a total cost of $30,000,000; this installation is expected to have a total service life of 30 years, and a scrap value of zero. Assume that both the straight-line and double declining balance depreciation methods give the true depreciation charge for the plant's first year of operation.

It is possible from the foregoing for you to prove that you are the President of the United States. Do so.

Glossary

No attempt is made in what follows to provide the depth of definition that would be found in a dictionary. Instead, this glossary indicates the sense in which these terms are employed in the text. Whenever more than one definition is provided for a particular term, the *italicized* definition is the one most often used in this book.

Account. (1) *Any asset, equity, revenue, expense, gain, or loss for which a separate record is maintained in a ledger.* (2) An amount owed by one entity to another.

Account, purchases or sales on. Purchases or sales made on credit.

Accounting cycle. A firm's accounting activities over an entire period at the end of which financial statements are prepared.

Accounting Principles Board. An agency of the American Institute of Certified Public Accountants that has the responsibility of studying and publishing opinions upon disputed matters of financial accounting practice.

Accounting theory. An intellectual discipline concerned with why accountants choose a particular model of economic activity in reporting on firms, the kinds of information their reports can provide, the limitations of these reports, and the rules to be followed in constructing these reports.

Account payable. A non-interest-bearing informal obligation to pay for goods or services purchased on ordinary credit terms.

Account receivable. An informal, usually non-interest-bearing, debt owed to a firm as a result of an ordinary sale of goods or services by that firm.

Accrual. (1) *An incomplete transaction that is given partial recognition:* (a) The proration of a contractual fee to the periods during which it is earned, even though this fee is not yet legally due. (b) Recognition of a receivable or a liability prior to the date upon which it is a legal liability of the debtor.
(2) Any kind of regular systematic increase or adding on.

Accrual accounting. That system of accounting in which the calculation of income is based upon changes in all assets and liabilities, instead of in changes in cash.

Accrued asset. A receivable for a contractual fee that has been recognized proportionately to goods and services provided under the contract prior to the date that it is legally owed to the firm.

Accrued liability. A liability for a contractual fee that has been recognized proportionately to goods or services provided under the contract prior to the date that it is legally owed to its creditor.

Adjusting entry. An entry made at the end of an accounting period to record a correction, accrual, or internal change.

Advances from customers. A liability that reflects the firm's obligations to its customers to provide them with products or services for which the customers have already paid.

Advances to employees. A receivable resulting from prepayment of salaries, advance reimbursement of employee travel or entertainment expenses, etc.

Advances to suppliers. Deposits made on orders of goods or services; therefore rights to obtain goods or services.

Airline deposits. Noncurrent receivables from airlines reflecting amounts given them by the firm to guarantee payment for extending credit to the firm's employees for travel charges.

Allocation. (1) *The assignment of costs, revenues, income, cash flows, or funds flows to individual inputs or groups of inputs to the firm,* including assignment to individual periods of time, divisions of the firm, etc. (2) The division of any total into parts. (3) The assignment of costs to revenues, called *matching*.

Amortization. (1) *The writing down of any nonmonetary asset.* (2) The writing down of an intangible nonmonetary asset, such as a patent, lease, or insurance prepayment. (3) The gradual retirement of a debt, discount, or debt premium.

Amortized historical cost. The purchase price of a nonmonetary asset, proportionately reduced to the extent that some of the services originally offered by the asset have since been received and no longer are available to the firm.

Annual report. A document prepared once a year by the firm for distribution to its stockholders and often to the public, containing the firm's financial statements and other information deemed to be of interest to investors.

Annuity. A series of equal payments evenly spaced in time.

APB. Abbreviation of Accounting Principles Board.

Asset. An *economic good* reported by the financial accountant, offering future economic benefits to the firm, and either (a) cash or a legally enforceable right to receive a specific amount of cash at a specific date, or (b) a *good* for which each of the following can be determined: the historical purchase price incurred by the firm to acquire the good; the benefits provided to the firm by the good; the total of such benefits that the good will provide the firm and the total received to date. (It must be possible to make any estimates required in a manner the accountant considers sufficiently reliable.)

Auditing. Investigation and critical review to determine or substantiate the quality of accounting records or financial statements, usually including the preparation of a formal report of findings.

Auditor. Unless the term is qualified, a *certified public accountant* who is *auditing* a firm.

Balance, of an account. The net total of all inputs to and outputs from the *account* as of a particular point in time; the amount used to represent the account as of that point in time.

Balance sheet. A financial statement that summarizes the assets and equities of an entity and their associated dollar magnitudes as of a particular point in time.

Board of directors. The *directors* of a corporation, considered as a group.

Bonds payable. A highly formal, long-lived, interest-bearing debt owed by the firm, usually to numerous investors who are often afforded special protection for their investment.

Bonds receivable. Highly formal, long-lived, interest-bearing debts owed to the firm by another firm. Bonds often offer special protection to creditors and are usually issued to more than one creditor.

Bookkeeping. The detailed preparation and maintenance of a firm's accounting records.

Books. Colloquial language for the accounting records maintained by a firm.

Book value, of a depreciable asset. The asset's original cost, less all depreciation to date.

Book value per share, of common stock. Assuming that only one class of stock has been issued by the firm, total stockholders' equity divided by the number of shares of stock outstanding.

Budgeting. The firm's estimation of future resource needs, and its planning activities to ensure that these needs will be met.

Building. The term is used in its lay sense, as any kind of habitable structure.

Burden. Same as *Overhead*.

Capitalize. To treat a cost as resulting in a nonmonetary asset, or to include a cost in the total cost of a nonmonetary asset. (The alternative would be to treat the cost as resulting in an expense or loss.)

Capital stock. (1) *A title for all or part of what stockholders intend as their permanent investment in the corporation.* (2) The shares of stock that reflect these ownership rights.

Certified Public Accountant. An accountant who has received a license to practice public accounting and to call himself a "certified public accountant" from a state, territory, possession, or the District of Columbia.

Closing entry. An entry made at the end of an accounting period to transfer information from a *nominal account* to its *parent account*.

Commissions payable. A liability for amounts owed to salesmen who are paid, at least in part, on the basis of the volume of their sales.

Common stock. Same as *Capital stock*.

Compound change. A balance sheet change that affects three or more accounts.

Compound interest. Interest calculated on the principal plus accumulated unpaid interest of an amount borrowed or invested.

Comptroller. Same as *Controller*.

Conservatism. The rule (to which exceptions are often made in practice for goods that the firm does not intend to sell) that the amount reported for nonmonetary assets should be either the *current market value* or the *amortized historical cost,* whichever is lower.

Consolidated financial statements. Combined statements of two or more firms, treated as though they were a single entity.

Constant rate amortization of a premium or discount. Writeoff of premium or discount by a *compound interest* approach that yields an interest charge each period that bears a constant percentage relationship to the principal plus accumulated interest of the related debt as of the beginning of each period.

Controller. The chief accounting officer of a firm.

Corporation. A legal entity (distinct from its owners and management) that has been created by a grant of authority from a state, territory, possession, or the federal government, whose capital is represented by transferable shares, and which has *limited liability*.

Cost, of a nonmonetary asset. The total market value of all that the entity gave up to obtain the benefits of that asset. *Cost* may also refer to this amount less accumulated *amortization*.

Cost accounting. A branch of *managerial accounting* especially concerned with cost behavior and identification of waste.

CPA. Abbreviation of *Certified Public Accountant*.

Credit. To record something to appear on the right-hand side of a *ledger account*; therefore, a decrease in an asset or an increase in an equity, revenue, or gain.

Creditors. Firms, individuals, and other entities to which the firm owes money, goods, or services.

Current asset. An asset that is expected to be used up and replenished within one year or the length of the firm's *operating cycle*, whichever is longer. (Assume one year unless indicated otherwise.)

Current liability. A liability that is expected to be paid within one year or the length of the firm's *operating cycle*, whichever is longer. (Assume one year unless indicated otherwise.)

Current market value. An estimated figure representing the price that the firm might get if it sold an asset, or the price that it might have to pay if it bought the asset now, or at the time the asset's service will be received.

Current maturation of long-term debt. The process whereby a long-term debt changes from a noncurrent to a current liability one year from its due date.

Current operations. Same as *Operating-cycle activity*.

Current ratio. Total *current assets* divided by total *current liabilities*, used as a very rough test of a firm's ability to pay its current debts as they mature.

Customer deposits on uncompleted goods. See *Advances from Customers*.

Debenture. A bond secured only by the general debt-paying ability of the firm, rather than by a claim upon specific company assets.

Debit. To record something to appear on the left side of a ledger account; therefore, a decrease in an equity or an increase in an asset, expense, or loss.

Declaration of a dividend. A promise by a *board of directors* to pay a dividend to the corporation's stockholders at some future date, thereby creating a liability for that dividend.

Deficit. *Retained earnings*, when its balance is negative.

Depletion. The *writing down* of the historical cost of a natural resource asset, such as a mine or a stand of timber, to reflect exhaustion of the quantity of resources originally available to the firm.

Depreciable assets. Buildings and equipment: structures, machinery, vehicles, tools, fixtures, and other long-lived nonmonetary assets that were created by construction or manufacture.

Depreciation. The decreasing or *writing down* of the historical cost of a long-lived nonmonetary asset that was created by construction or manufacture, to reflect its yielding up part of the services that it originally offered to the firm.

Depreciation expense. The total cost of those services of *depreciable assets* that are deemed to have expired in earning the revenues of a particular period of time, without having resulted in the creation of any new assets.

Direct labor. The wages and salaries of all individuals directly involved in making or assembling a manufactured product and its components.

Direct materials. Raw materials, purchased components, and any other materials that end up in the finished product of a manufacturer.

Directors. Individuals elected by a corporation's stockholders to supervise the firm's activities and thereby represent the stockholders' interests. These directors appoint the corporation's *management*.

Discount, on debt. (1) *The amount by which the proceeds received when a debt is issued are exceeded by the principal amount (exclusive of interest charges) that will be owed at maturity.* (2) An amount that a purchaser on credit is entitled to deduct from his payment in settlement of the debt, from the price that appears on the related bill.

Discounting. (1) *Reducing a future sum to its present value.* (2) Selling a note received from another entity to some third party before the note's maturity date.

Dividend. A distribution of corporate assets to its stockholders, most often reflecting profits earned by the firm.

Dividends payable. A liability for dividends owed by a corporation to its stockholders.

Earned surplus. An alternate, somewhat misleading, name for *retained earnings*.

Economic goods. Goods that are bought and sold in a market.

Effective rate of interest. The ratio, during a set period, between the income that an investor recognizes on an investment and the total amount of that investment (including unpaid interest). Assuming a constant rate of interest, the effective rate of interest is equal to the rate at which the total *present value* of the payments to be received by the lender equals the amount lent.

Enter. To record information in a journal.

Entity. Any individual, group, organization, or other center of economic activity for which separate, self-contained accounting records are maintained.

Entity rule. A rule specifying that the accounting records and reports of different entities are to be kept separate from and independent of the records and reports of all other entities.

Equipment. (1) In a broad sense, *any machinery, furniture, fixtures, bins, shelves, tools, and the like.* (2) Depreciable assets ancillary to buildings and other structures, such as elevators or air conditioners. (3) Portable depreciable assets.

Equity. (1) *An obligation to an investor; the investor's corresponding claim against the firm.* (2) An ownership interest in a firm: *stockholders' equity*.

Exchange. A complete transaction; a purchase or sale that takes place in a market.

Expense. A cost of obtaining revenues; one of the costs of the assets expired or liabilities incurred (without acquiring any new assets) in the course of selling the products or services in which the firm ordinarily deals.

Extraordinary item. A nonoperating gain or loss that the accountant believes should be reported separately from the calculation of net income from operations.

Financial accounting. A system for gathering objective information about the economic conditions and histories of individual profit seeking enterprises, and for summarizing and reporting that information to investors.

Financial change.   Same as *Nonoperating change*: any balance sheet change that is not an *operating change.*

Financial statements.   Formal reports by a firm of its economic position and history. These reports usually consist of balance sheets, funds statements, and statements of income and retained earnings. They may also include supplementary schedules.

Fixed asset.   (1) In a narrow sense, *land, buildings, and equipment.* (2) In a broader sense, any noncurrent nonmonetary asset.

Fixtures.   Shelves, lighting installations, and other more or less permanent installations to buildings.

Funds from operations.   On a statement of sources and uses of net working capital, the net effect of the firm's operating activities upon its net working capital.

Funds statement.   A report in which all of a firm's major financial changes are summarized; usually a statement of sources and uses of net working capital, though the term also is applicable to a statement of sources and uses of net current monetary assets and liabilities. The term is sometimes (misleadingly) applied to statements of sources and uses of cash.

Going-concern assumption.   The assumption that a firm will continue its present operations far enough into the future for its present assets to be used up (or otherwise disposed of) in an orderly way.

Going-concern rule.   A rule specifying that if a firm is expected to go out of business soon, all nonmonetary assets should be reported at their *current market values;* otherwise, only goods held for sale should be so treated, while all other nonmonetary assets should be recorded at their *amortized historical costs.*

Good.   (1) *Anything wanted or desired by some entity or capable of satisfying some entity's wants.* (2) An item of inventory.

Goodwill.   An asset that results from a firm paying more to purchase another firm than the total market value of the separately identifiable assets purchased (less the total value of any liabilities assumed), the difference being payment for the superior earning power or other economic advantage associated with the purchased firm.

Gross margin.   Sales less cost of goods sold.

Historical cost.   Either the purchase price of a nonmonetary asset or that price less accumulated *amortization.*

Historical cost rule.   A rule specifying that nonmonetary assets are to be reported at their *amortized historical costs.*

Income statement.   A firm's profits report for a period; a summary of its revenues, expenses, gains, losses, net income, and dividends.

Indirect labor.   All factory wages and salaries other than those for *direct labor,* e.g., those of the plant superintendent, maintenance men, and quality control inspectors.

Institutional uses of accounting.   The use of accounting to comply with record keeping and reporting requirements imposed by the law and other social institutions.

Interaction.   When the output of a combination of two or more inputs differs from the output that would be obtained from using these inputs separately.

Interaction effect.   The result when two or more inputs jointly generate a total output; the difference between that total output and what the inputs would have generated were they operating in isolation from each other.

Interest method of amortizing premium or discount.   Same as *constant rate amortization.*

Interest payable. The unpaid portion of a fee, either billed by a creditor or accrued, for borrowing money.

Interest receivable. The unpaid portion of a fee, either billed by the firm or accrued, for lending money.

Internal change. Any balance sheet change that is not a transaction, and that therefore involves only the entity and its owners (in their role as residual equity holders).

Inventory. (1) In a broad sense, *any collection of goods.* (2) Of a retailer, merchandise held for resale. (3) Of a manufacturer, raw materials and parts to be used in manufacturing, incomplete goods that are being manufactured, and finished goods held for sale. (4) Of supplies, such things as paper clips, machine oil, and lightbulbs that are not to be sold to the firm's customers.

Invoice. A bill written by a seller to a buyer indicating the amount that the buyer owes for goods or services supplied him.

Issue of an equity. Obtaining cash or other assets in exchange for debt or capital stock.

Journal. A record book providing an event-by-event record of the firm's *transactions* and *internal changes.*

Land. Either *site land* and improvements thereto or what is meant by *land* in ordinary English.

Ledger. A collection of *ledger accounts.*

Ledger account. A device by which the accountant records all of the changes in any given asset, equity, expense, revenue, loss or gain in a single place.

Liability. (1) *A debt, or other obligation, owed to a creditor.* (2) In practice (loosely), any obligation to an investor.

Limited liability. The restriction upon creditors of a corporation whereby they are not ordinarily allowed to collect the debts of the corporation from its owners if the corporation fails to satisfy these debts.

Liquidity. A firm's command over cash and near-cash resources; its capacity to quickly raise the financial wherewithal to seize unexpected opportunities or respond to emergencies.

Long columns. Right-hand columns in a multi-column schedule or statement.

Long-lived. Another name for *Noncurrent.*

Long-term. Another name for *Noncurrent.*

Long-term creditor. A creditor whose rights against the firm need not be completely satisfied for more than one year from the date under consideration, or for more than one full *operating cycle,* if the firm's operating cycle exceeds one year.

Loss. (1) *The cost of an asset expired or liability incurred without acquiring a revenue, gain, or any new asset.* (2) In the lay sense, a negative profit.

Lot. A set or batch of inventory.

Maintenance. See *Repairs and maintenance.*

Management. The top officers of a firm responsible for the detailed conduct of its everyday activities.

Managerial accounting. A system for gathering, summarizing, and reporting that economic information about the firm which is of particular interest to management.

Marketable securities. Various investments that can be converted easily into cash. Usually the term is restricted to investments that either mature within one year, or that the firm intends to sell within one year.

Market price per share, of stock. The price per share that investors are willing to pay for the firm's capital stock at a particular moment in time.

Matching rule. A rule stipulating that whenever it is proper to assume a *going concern,* the historical purchase prices of nonmonetary assets should be allocated to the activities or periods of time benefitted by these assets, and that once revenues have been recognized, all expenses of earning them should also be recognized.

Materiality. The relative importance of data; therefore, a characteristic of data whenever reporting them would be likely to affect a decision made by a trained, intelligent reader of the related financial statements.

Materiality rule. A rule stipulating that minor items are to be treated in convenient, expedient ways.

Maturity date of a loan. The due date of the loan, at which time the principal and any unpaid interest charges must be paid by the borrower.

Monetary asset. Cash or a legally enforceable right to receive a specific amount of cash on a specific date.

Negotiating a receivable. Selling one's rights reflected in the receivable to receive cash (or other assets) to another entity.

Net current monetary accounts. Current monetary assets less current monetary liabilities.

Net income. The difference (which may be negative) between the total of revenues and gains and the total of expenses and losses for a period—a concept that corresponds to the lay notion of *profit.*

Net income from operations. Same as *Operating income*: total revenues less total expenses for a period.

Net quick assets. Same as *Net current monetary accounts.*

Net working capital. Total current assets less total current liabilities; an index of the firm's general *liquidity.*

Net worth. Ownership equity. For a corporation, *net worth* is equivalent to *stockholders' equity*; for an individual, the term signifies his assets less his liabilities.

Nominal account. A "special name" account used to record a particular type of change in some other account (the *parent account*) during a period, and whose balance is closed to the parent account at the end of the period.

Nominal rate of interest. The "official" rate written or printed on whatever document is the contract or evidence for a debt.

Noncurrent asset. Any asset that is not *current.*

Noncurrent liability. Any liability that is not *current.*

Non-interest-bearing note. A note in which no explicit charge is made for interest, yet the borrower receives less when the note is issued than the amount that must be paid at maturity.

Nonmonetary asset. An asset that is not monetary: an object or right offering future economic benefits to the firm, purchased by the firm for a known price; the dollar amount of this price, which is used to represent the asset, can be reduced in some accepted way as parts of the economic benefits are determined to have been yielded.

Nonoperating change. Any balance sheet change that is not an *operating change.*

Nonoperating gains and losses. The reflections in retained earnings of activities that affect profits but that do not directly relate to selling the products or services in which the firm ordinarily deals.

Note payable. A formal (often interest-bearing) debt owed by the firm, usually arising from the firm's purchasing goods or services, or borrowing from a single creditor, and usually having a total life of less than three years.

Note receivable. A formal, often interest-bearing, debt owed to the firm, usually arising from a customer's purchasing goods or services from the firm, and usually having a total life of less than three years.

On account, purchases or sales. Purchases or sales made on credit.

Operating activity. Either an *operating-cycle activity* or a writedown of a noncurrent non-monetary asset to reflect its provision of services to current-period operations.

Operating change. Same as *Operating activity.*

Operating cycle. The average period of time required to convert cash to inventory or services to customers, to accounts receivable, then back to cash again.

Operating-cycle activities. Changes in a firm's current assets or current liabilities resulting from *operations.*

Operating income. Total revenues less total expenses for a period.

Operations. A firm's activities directly related to providing and selling those products and services that it is in business to provide and sell.

Opportunity cost. The cost of not having done something that one might have done, or the cost of pursuing some alternative that, in fact, was not actually followed through.

Ordinary entry. An entry made during the accounting period; one that is neither an adjusting nor a closing entry.

Overhead. All manufacturing costs other than *direct materials* and *direct labor.*

Parent account. A balance sheet account for which there are either nominal accounts or one or more valuation accounts.

Parent company. A firm that has acquired a substantial portion of the voting capital stock of another firm and exercises control over that other firm. This term is often restricted to cases of 50% or greater ownership.

Partitioning, of a balance sheet. Division of the balance sheet accounts into two subsets as a way of obtaining a selection rule for those balance sheet changes that will be summarized on a particular financial statement.

Partnership. An unincorporated business owned jointly by two or more individuals who share its profits and losses.

Patent. A right granted to an entity by the government entitling that entity to be the sole manufacturer of a product or the sole user of a process; a nonmonetary right to receive protection for a period of years against the entity's competitors making the product or using the process.

Period expense. An expense that cannot be associated with, or traced to, a particular sale, except arbitrarily, but that can be seen to help cause the revenues of a year as a whole.

Periodic inventory method. The recording of inventory outflows only at the end of the accounting period.

Perpetual inventory method. The recording of inventory outflows at the time of their occurrence.

Post. To record information in a ledger.

Premium, on debt. The amount by which the proceeds received, when a debt is issued, exceed the principal amount (exclusive of interest charges) that will be owed at maturity.

Present value, of a future sum.   The amount that would have to be invested now, at a specified interest rate and system of compounding, to accumulate to that sum at a future date; thus, what the right to receive that future sum is worth now (given the interest rate and system of compounding).

Present worth, of a future sum.   Same as *Present value.*

President.   The chief executive officer who assumes general responsibility for the firm as a whole.

Primary measurement.   Any direct, straightforward measurement, such as a count of a quantity or an observation of a market price.

Principal of a loan.   The amount borrowed, exclusive of interest charges.

Product expense.   An expense that is easily associated with, or traceable to, a particular revenue.

Profit.   A lay term; the difference between the amount for which a firm sells its goods and services and the costs of providing these goods and services.

Quarterly report.   A document prepared at three-month intervals by the firm for distribution to its stockholders and often to the public, containing the firm's financial statements and other information deemed to be of interest to investors.

Quick ratio.   Current monetary assets divided by current liabilities; used as a rough index of the firm's abilities to pay its current liabilities as they mature.

Realization.   Having satisfied all criteria necessary for *recognition*.

Realization rule.   Revenues, gains, and income are not to be recognized on nonmonetary assets owned or services provided by the firm until the time of their sale or retirement.

Recognition.   Being reported in a financial statement. Accordingly, an asset is recognized when an economic good is reported as an asset on a balance sheet, and a revenue is recognized when an inflow of assets is reported as a revenue on an income statement.

Repairs and maintenance.   Replacement or correction of defects in components of nonmonetary assets—defects that have developed during the period the asset has been providing its services to the firm.

Resource-allocation uses of accounting.   The use of accounting to determine how the entity's cash and other assets should be employed, usually with the goal of maximizing the entity's profits.

Retained earnings.   The cumulative increase in the owners' equity in a firm, resulting from profits less an amount equalling total dividends paid to date.

Retirement of an equity.   Repayment of the entity's own debt or reacquisition of its own capital stock.

Revenue.   An inflow of new assets, or an extinction of an advance from a customer, resulting from the company's selling the products or services in which it ordinarily deals; equivalently, the reflection of that inflow in retained earnings.

Ruling.   A method of obtaining the end-of-period balance of a ledger account by inserting in it a figure just large enough to make the left and right sides equal.

Scrap value.   Any actual or prospective residual value possessed by an asset after it has yielded the services for which it was primarily purchased.

Secondary measurement.   A measurement that is not a primary measurement; an indirect measurement derived by performing a transformation (such as an allocation) upon a primary measurement or another indirect measurement.

Separate effect.   The effect on output that an individual input operating in isolation would have.

Service life. The period of time during which the services yielded to the firm by an asset are great enough to outweigh the costs of using that asset, and during which it is uneconomical to acquire the same services from some competing source.

Short columns. The left-hand column or columns in a multi-column schedule or statement.

Short-term. Another name for *current*; ordinarily, one year or less from the date under consideration.

Short-term creditor. A creditor whose rights against the firm must be satisfied within one year from the date under consideration, or within one operating cycle, if this is longer than a year.

Simple change. A balance sheet change that affects only two accounts.

Simple interest. Interest calculated on the *principal* of a loan only.

Single proprietorship. A one-man business operated by its owner and his immediate family.

Site land. Land that is used to support factories, warehouses, stores, etc.

Source. Something that increases the balance of an account or group of accounts.

Statements of cost of goods manufactured and sold. A detailed statement of a firm's manufacturing costs for a period, ending with a calculation of the cost of goods sold for that period.

Statement of income and retained earnings. See *Income statement.*

Statement of sources and uses of net working capital. A summary of the firm's financial activities, such as its purchases and sales of noncurrent assets, and its issues and retirements of noncurrent liabilities. Simultaneously, this statement reports changes in the firm's net working capital.

Stockholder. A part-owner of a corporation; the legal owner of one or more shares of the corporation's capital stock.

Stockholders' equity. The obligations of a corporation to its owners; the owners' total investment in the corporation, including both their permanent investment and retained earnings; the residual equity in all assets not claimed by creditors.

Straight-line amortization of premium or discount. Writeoff of an equal amount of premium or discount during each period.

Subsidiary company. A firm that has had a substantial portion of its voting capital stock purchased by another firm, and which is controlled by that other firm.

Supplies. See fourth definition under *Inventory.*

T-account. A simplified *ledger account.*

Taxes payable. A liability for taxes owed to city, state, and federal taxing authorities.

Transaction. (1) *Any change in an entity's assets or equities that is accompanied by a related change in the assets or equities of some other entity.* (2) More broadly, any balance sheet change.

Treasurer. The officer responsible for making sure that the firm has the financial resources necessary to conduct its activities.

Trial balance. A labeled list of ledger account balances as of a particular point in time, usually divided into debit and credit columns.

Unamortized historical cost. See *Amortized historical cost.*

Use. Something that decreases the balance of an account or group of accounts.

Valuation account. A "special name" account used to adjust or correct the reported balance of another balance sheet account, and which appears on the balance sheet at the end of the period.

Wages payable.   A liability for amounts owed to employees for their services.

Wholesaler.   A middleman that purchases goods in large lots from manufacturers and sells them in smaller lots to its customers.

Working capital.   Another name for *current assets,* sometimes used to signify *net working capital.*

Work in process inventory.   Incompletely manufactured inventory in which either the individual items are incomplete, or the batch is incomplete, or both.

Writing down.   Decreasing the amount at which an account is reported.

Writing up.   Increasing the amount at which an account is reported.

Yield rate, of interest.   Same as *effective rate.*

Index